T0332160

HANDBOOK OF PRACTICAL LOGIC
AND AUTOMATED REASONING

John Harrison

The sheer complexity of computer systems has meant that automated reasoning, i.e. the use of computers to perform logical inference, has become a vital component of program construction and of programming language design. This book meets the demand for a self-contained and broad-based account of the concepts, the machinery and the use of automated reasoning. The mathematical logic foundations are described in conjunction with their practical application, all with the minimum of prerequisites.

The approach is constructive, concrete and algorithmic: a key feature is that methods are described with reference to actual implementations (for which code is supplied) that readers can use, modify and experiment with.

This book is ideally suited for those seeking a one-stop source for the general area of automated reasoning. It can be used as a reference, or as a place to learn the fundamentals, either in conjunction with advanced courses or for self study.

JOHN HARRISON is a Principal Engineer at Intel Corporation in Portland, Oregon. He specialises in formal verification, automated theorem proving, floating-point arithmetic and mathematical algorithms.

HANDBOOK OF PRACTICAL LOGIC AND AUTOMATED REASONING

JOHN HARRISON

CAMBRIDGE
UNIVERSITY PRESS

CAMBRIDGE
UNIVERSITY PRESS

University Printing House, Cambridge CB2 8BS, United Kingdom

Cambridge University Press is part of the University of Cambridge.

It furthers the University's mission by disseminating knowledge in the pursuit of
education, learning and research at the highest international levels of excellence.

www.cambridge.org
Information on this title: www.cambridge.org/9780521899574

© J. Harrison 2009

First published 2009
Reprinted 2011

A catalogue record for this publication is available from the British Library

ISBN 978-0-521-89957-4 Hardback

To Porosusha

When a man *Reasoneth*, hee does nothing else but conceive a summe totall, from *Addition* of parcels.

For as Arithmeticians teach to adde and substract in *numbers*; so the Geometricians teach the same in *lines, figures* (solid and superficiall,) *angles, proportions, times*, degrees of *swiftnesse, force, power*, and the like; The Logicians teach the same in *Consequences of words*; adding together *two Names*, to make an *Affirmation*; and *two Affirmations*, to make a *Syllogisme*; and many *Syllogismes* to make a *Demonstration*; and from the *summe*, or *Conclusion* of a *Syllogisme*, they substract one *Proposition*, to finde the other.

For REASON, in this sense, is nothing but *Reckoning* (that is, Adding and Substracting) of the Consequences of generall names agreed upon, for the *marking* and *signifying* of our thoughts.

And as in Arithmetique, unpractised men must, and Professors themselves may often erre, and cast up false; so also in any other subject of Reasoning, the ablest, most attentive, and most practised men, may deceive themselves and inferre false Conclusions; Not but that Reason it selfe is always Right Reason, as well as Arithmetique is a certain and infallible Art: But no one mans Reason, nor the Reason of any one number of men, makes the certaintie; no more than an account is therefore well cast up, because a great many men have unanimously approved it.

Thomas Hobbes (1588–1697), '*Leviathan, or The Matter, Forme, & Power of a Common-Wealth Ecclesiasticall and Civill*'. Printed for ANDREW CROOKE, at the Green Dragon in St. *Pauls* Church-yard, 1651.

Contents

Preface

This book is about computer programs that can perform *automated reasoning*. I interpret 'reasoning' quite narrowly: the emphasis is on formal deductive inference rather than, for example, poker playing or medical diagnosis. On the other hand I interpret 'automated' broadly, to include interactive arrangements where a human being and machine reason together, and I'm always conscious of the applications of deductive reasoning to real-world problems. Indeed, as well as being inherently fascinating, the subject is deriving increasing importance from its industrial applications.

This book is intended as a first introduction to the field, and also to logical reasoning itself. No previous knowledge of mathematical logic is assumed, although readers will inevitably find some prior experience of mathematics and of computer programming (especially in a functional language like OCaml, F#, Standard ML, Haskell or LISP) invaluable. In contrast to the many specialist texts on the subject, this book aims at a broad and balanced general introduction, and has two special characteristics.

- Pure logic and automated theorem proving are explained in a closely intertwined manner. Results in logic are developed with an eye to their role in automated theorem proving, and wherever possible are developed in an explicitly computational way.
- Automated theorem proving methods are explained with reference to actual concrete implementations, which readers can experiment with if they have convenient access to a computer. All code is written in the high-level functional language OCaml.

Although this organization is open to question, I adopted it after careful consideration, and extensive experimentation with alternatives. A more detailed self-justification follows, but most readers will want to skip straight to the main content, starting with 'How to read this book' on page xvi.

Ideological orientation

This section explains in more detail the philosophy behind the present text, and attempts to justify it. I also describe the focus of this book and major topics that I do not include. To fully appreciate some points made in the discussion, knowledge of the subject matter is needed. Readers may prefer to skip or skim this material.

My primary aim has been to present a broad and balanced discussion of many of the principal results in automated theorem proving. Moreover, readers mainly interested in pure mathematical logic should find that this book covers most of the traditional results found in mainstream elementary texts on mathematical logic: compactness, Löwenheim–Skolem, completeness of proof systems, interpolation, Gödel's theorems etc. But I consistently strive, even when it is not directly necessary as part of the code of an automated prover, to present results in a concrete, explicit and algorithmic fashion, usually involving real code that can actually be experimented with and used, at least in principle. For example:

- the proof of the interpolation theorem in Section 5.13 contains an algorithm for constructing interpolants, utilizing earlier theorem proving code;
- decidability based on the finite model property is demonstrated in Section 5.5 by explicitly interleaving proving and refuting code rather than a general appeal to Theorem 7.13.

I hope that many readers will share my liking for this concrete hands-on style. Formal logic usually involves a considerable degree of care over tedious syntactic details. This can be quite painful for the beginner, so teachers and authors often have to make the unpalatable choice between (i) spelling everything out in excruciating detail and (ii) waving their hands profusely to cover over sloppy explanations. While teachers rightly tend to recoil from (i), my experience of teaching has shown me that many students nevertheless resent the feeling of never being told the whole story. By implementing things on a computer, I think we get the best of both worlds: the details are there in precise formal detail, but we can mostly let the computer worry about their unpleasant consequences.

It is true that mathematics in the last 150 years has become more abstractly set-theoretic and less constructive. This is particularly so in contemporary model theory, where traditional topics that lie at the historical root of the subject are being de-emphasized. But I'm not alone in swimming against this tide, for the rise of the computer is helping to restore the place of explicit algorithmic methods in several areas of mathematics. This is particularly notable in algebraic geometry and related areas (Cox, Little and O'Shea 1992; Schenk 2003) where computer algebra and specifically Gröbner bases (see Section 5.11) have made considerable impact. But similar ideas are being explored in other areas, even in category theory (Rydeheard and Burstall 1988), often seen as the quintessence of abstract nonconstructive mathematics. I can do no better than quote Knuth (1974) on the merits of a concretely algorithmic point of view in mathematics generally:

For three years I taught a sophomore course in abstract algebra for mathematics majors at Caltech, and the most difficult topic was always the study of "Jordan canonical forms" for matrices. The third year I tried a new approach, by looking at the subject algorithmically, and suddenly it became quite clear. The same thing happened with the discussion of finite groups defined by generators and relations, and in another course with the reduction theory of binary quadratic forms. By presenting the subject in terms of algorithms, the purpose and meaning of the mathematical theorems became transparent.

Later, while writing a book on computer arithmetic [Knuth (1969)], I found that virtually every theorem in elementary number theory arises in a natural, motivated way in connection with the problem of making computers do high-speed numerical calculations. Therefore I believe that the traditional courses in number theory might well be changed to adopt this point of view, adding a practical motivation to the already beautiful theory.

In the case of logic, this approach seems especially natural. From the very earliest days, the development of logic was motivated by the desire to reduce reasoning to calculation: the word *logos*, the root of 'logic', can mean not just logical thought but also computation or 'reckoning'. More recently, it was decidability questions in logic that led Turing and others to define precisely the notion of a 'computable function' and set up the abstract models that delimit the range of algorithmic methods. This relationship between logic and computation, which dates from before the Middle Ages, has continued to the present day. For example, problems in the design and verification of computer systems are stimulating more research in logic, while logical principles are playing an increasingly important role in the design of programming languages. Thus, logical reasoning can be seen not only as one of the many beneficiaries of the modern computer age, but as its most important intellectual wellspring.

Another feature of the present text that some readers may find surprising is its systematically model-theoretic emphasis; by contrast many other texts such as Goubault-Larrecq and Mackie (1997) place proof theory at the centre. I introduce traditional proof systems late (Chapter 6), and I hardly mention, and never exploit, structural properties of natural deduction or sequent calculus proofs. While these topics are fascinating, I believe that all the traditional computer-based proof methods for classical logic can be presented perfectly well without them. Indeed the special refutation-complete calculi for automated theorem proving (binary resolution, hyperresolution, etc.) also provide strong results on canonical forms for proofs. In some situations these are even more convenient for theoretical results than results from Gentzen-style proof theory (Matiyasevich 1975), as with our proof of the Nullstellensatz in Section 5.10 à la Lifschitz (1980). In any case, the details of particular proof systems can be much less significant for automated reasoning than the way in which the corresponding search space is examined. Note, for example, how different tableaux and the inverse method are, even though they can both be understood as search for cut-free sequent proofs.

I wanted to give full, carefully explained code for all the methods described. (In my experience it's easy to underestimate the difficulty in passing from a straightforward-looking algorithm to a concrete implementation.) In order to present real executable code that's almost as readable as the kind of pseudocode often used to describe algorithms, it seemed necessary to use a very high-level language where concrete issues of data representation and memory allocation can be ignored. I selected the functional programming language Objective CAML (OCaml) for this purpose. OCaml is a descendant of Edinburgh ML, a programming language specifically designed for writing theorem provers, and several major systems are written in it.

A drawback of using OCaml (rather than say, C or Java) is that it will be unfamiliar to many readers. However, I only use a simple subset, which is briefly explained in Appendix 2; the code is functional in style with no assignments or sequencing (except for producing diagnostic output). In a few cases (e.g. threading the state through code for binary decision diagrams), imperative code might have been simpler, but it seemed worthwhile to stick to the simplest subset possible. Purely functional programming is particularly convenient for the kind of tinkering that I hope to encourage, since one doesn't have to worry about accidental side-effects of one computation on others.

I will close with a quotation from McCarthy (1963) that nicely encapsulates the philosophy underlying this text, implying as it does the potential new role of logic as a truly *applied* science.

It is reasonable to hope that the relationship between computation and mathematical logic will be as fruitful in the next century as that between analysis and physics in the last.

What's not in this book

Although I aim to cover a broad range of topics, selectivity was essential to prevent the book from becoming unmanageably huge. I focus on theories in classical one-sorted first-order logic, since in this coherent setting many of the central methods of automated reasoning can be displayed. Not without regret, I have therefore excluded from serious discussion major areas such as model checking, inductive theorem proving, many-sorted logic, modal logic, description logics, intuitionistic logic, lambda calculus, higher-order logic and type theory. I believe, however, that this book will prepare the reader quite well to proceed with any of those areas, many of which are best understood precisely in terms of their contrast with classical first-order logic.

Another guiding principle has been to present topics only when I felt competent to do so at a fairly elementary level, without undue technicalities or difficult theory. This has meant the neglect of, for example, ordered paramodulation, cylindrical algebraic decomposition and Gödel's second incompleteness theorem. However, in such cases I have tried to give ample references so that interested readers can go further on their own.

Acknowledgements

This book has taken many years to evolve in haphazard fashion into its current form. During this period, I worked in the University of Cambridge Computer Laboratory, Åbo Akademi University/TUCS and Intel Corporation, as well as spending shorter periods visiting other institutions; I'm grateful above all to Tania and Yestin, for accompanying me on these journeys and tolerating the inordinate time I spent working on this project. It would be impossible to fairly describe here the extent to which my thinking has been shaped by the friends and colleagues that I have encountered over the years. But I owe particular thanks to Mike Gordon, who first gave me the opportunity to get involved in this fascinating field.

I wrote this book partly because I knew of no existing text that presents the range of topics in logic and automated reasoning that I wanted to cover. So the general style and approach is my own, and no existing text can be blamed for its malign influence. But on the purely logical side, I have mostly followed the presentation of basic metatheorems given by Kreisel and Krivine (1971). Their elegant development suits my purposes precisely, being purely model-theoretic and using the workaday tools of automated theorem proving such as Skolemization and the (so-called) Herbrand theorem. For example, the appealingly algorithmic proof of the interpolation theorem given in Section 5.13 is essentially theirs.

Though I have now been a researcher in automated reasoning for almost 20 years, I'm still routinely finding old results in the literature of which I was previously unaware, or learning of them through personal contact with colleagues. In this connection, I'm grateful to Grigori Mints for pointing me at Lifschitz's proof of the Nullstellensatz (Section 5.10) using resolution proofs, to Loïc Pottier for telling me about Hörmander's algorithm for real quantifier elimination (Section 5.9), and to Lars Hörmander himself for answering my questions on the genesis of this procedure.

I've been very lucky to have numerous friends and colleagues comment on drafts of this book, offer welcome encouragement, take up and modify the associated code, and even teach from it. Their influence has often clarified my thinking and sometimes saved me from serious errors, but needless to say, they are not responsible for any remaining faults in the text. Heartfelt thanks to Rob Arthan, Jeremy Avigad, Clark Barrett, Robert Bauer, Bruno Buchberger, Amine Chaieb, Michael Champigny, Ed Clarke, Byron Cook, Nancy Day, Torkel Franzén (who, alas, did not live to see the finished book), Dan Friedman, Mike Gordon, Alexey Gotsman, Jim Grundy, Tom Hales, Tony Hoare, Peter Homeier, Joe Hurd, Robert Jones, Shuvendu Lahiri, Arthur van Leeuwen, Sean McLaughlin, Wojtek Moczydlowski, Magnus Myreen, Tobias Nipkow, Michael Norrish, John O'Leary, Cagdas Ozgenc, Heath Putnam, Tom Ridge, Konrad Slind, Jørgen Villadsen, Norbert Voelker, Ed Westbrook, Freek Wiedijk, Carl Witty, Burkhart Wolff, and no doubt many other correspondents whose contributions I have thoughtlessly forgotten about over the course of time, for their invaluable help.

Even in the age of the Web, access to good libraries has been vital. I want to thank the staff of the Cambridge University Library, the Computer Laboratory and DPMMS libraries, the mathematics and computer science libraries of Åbo Akademi, and more recently Portland State University Library and Intel Library, who have often helped me track down obscure references. I also want to acknowledge the peerless Powell's Bookstore (`www.powells.com`), which has proved to be a goldmine of classic logic and computer science texts.

Finally, let me thank Frances Nex for her extraordinarily painstaking copyediting, as well as Catherine Appleton, Charlotte Broom, Clare Dennison and David Tranah at Cambridge University Press, who have shepherded this book through to publication despite my delays, and have provided invaluable advice, backed up by the helpful comments of the Press's anonymous reviewers.

How to read this book

The text is designed to be read sequentially from beginning to end. However, after a study of Chapter 1 and a good part of each of Chapters 2 and 3, the reader may be in a position to dip into other parts according to taste.

To support this, I've tried to make some important cross-references explicit, and to avoid over-elaborate or non-standard notation where possible.

Each chapter ends with a number of exercises. These are almost never intended to be routine, and some are very difficult. This reflects my belief that it's more enjoyable and instructive to solve one really challenging problem than to plod through a large number of trivial drill exercises. The reader shouldn't be discouraged if most of them seem too hard. They are all optional, i.e. the text can be understood without doing any of them.

The mathematics used in this book

Mathematics plays a double role in this book: the subject matter itself is treated mathematically, and automated reasoning is also applied to some problems *in* mathematics. But for the most part, the mathematical knowledge needed is not all that advanced: basic algebra, sets and functions, induction, and perhaps most fundamentally, an understanding of the notion of a proof. In a few places, more sophisticated analysis and algebra are used, though I have tried to explain most things as I go along. Appendix 1 is a summary of relevant mathematical background that the reader might refer to as needed, or even skim through at the outset.

The software in this book

An important part of this book is the associated software, which includes simple implementations, in the OCaml programming language, of the various theorem-proving techniques described. Although the book can generally be understood without detailed study of the code, explanations are often organized around it, and code is used as a proxy for what would otherwise be a lengthy and formalistic description of a syntactic process. (For example, the completeness proof for first-order logic in Sections 6.4–6.8 and the proof of Σ_1-completeness of Robinson arithmetic in Section 7.6 are essentially detailed informal arguments that some specific OCaml functions always work.) So without at least a weak impressionistic idea of how the code works, you will probably find some parts of the book heavy going.

Since I expect that many readers will have little or no experience of programming, at least in a functional language like OCaml, I have summarized some of the key ideas in Appendix 2. I don't delude myself into believing that reading this short appendix will turn a novice into an accomplished functional programmer, but I hope it will at least provide some orientation, and it does include references that the reader can pursue if necessary. In fact, the whole book can be considered an extended case study in functional programming, illustrating many important ideas such as structured data types, recursion, higher-order functions, continuations and abstract data types.

I hope that many readers will not only look at the code, but actually run it, apply it to new problems, and even try modifying or extending it. To do any of these, though, you will need an OCaml interpreter (see Appendix 2 again). The theorem-proving code itself is almost entirely listed in piecemeal fashion within the text. Since the reader will presumably profit little from actually typing it in, all the code can be downloaded from the website for this book (www.cambridge.org/9780521899574) and then just loaded into the OCaml interpreter with a few keystrokes or cut-and-pasted one phrase at a time.

In the future, I hope to make updates to the code and perhaps ports to other languages available at the same URL. More details can be found there about how to run the code, and hence follow along the explanations given in the book while trying out the code in parallel, but I'll just mention a couple of important points here. Probably the easiest way to proceed is to load the entire code associated with this book, e.g. by starting the OCaml interpreter `ocaml` in the directory (folder) containing the code and typing:

```
#use "init.ml";;
```

The default environment is set up to automatically parse anything in French-style ≪quotations≫ as a first-order formula. To use some code in Chapter 1 you will need to change this to parse arithmetic expressions:

```
let default_parser = make_parser parse_expression;;
```

and to use some code in Chapter 2 on propositional logic, you will need to change it to parse propositional formulas:

```
let default_parser = parse_prop_formula;;
```

Otherwise, you can more or less dip into any parts of the code that interest you. In a very few cases, a basic version of a function is defined first as part of the expository flow but later replaced by a more elaborate or efficient version with the same name. The default environment in such cases will always give you the latest one, and if you want to follow the exposition conscientiously you may want to cut-and-paste the earlier version from its source file.

The code is mainly intended to serve a pedagogical purpose, and I have always given clarity and/or brevity priority over efficiency. Still, it sometimes might be genuinely useful for applications. In any case, before using it, please pay careful attention to the (minimal) legal restrictions listed on the website. Note also that Stålmarck's algorithm (Section 2.10) is patented, so the code in the file `stal.ml` should not be used for commercial applications.

1

Introduction

In this chapter we introduce logical reasoning and the idea of mechanizing it, touching briefly on important historical developments. We lay the ground-work for what follows by discussing some of the most fundamental ideas in logic as well as illustrating how symbolic methods can be implemented on a computer.

1.1 What is logical reasoning?

There are many reasons for believing that something is true. It may seem obvious or at least immediately plausible, we may have been told it by our parents, or it may be strikingly consistent with the outcome of relevant scientific experiments. Though often reliable, such methods of judgement are not infallible, having been used, respectively, to persuade people that the Earth is flat, that Santa Claus exists, and that atoms cannot be subdivided into smaller particles.

What distinguishes *logical* reasoning is that it attempts to avoid any unjus-tified assumptions and confine itself to inferences that are infallible and beyond reasonable dispute. To avoid making any unwarranted assumptions, logical reasoning cannot rely on any special properties of the objects or con-cepts being reasoned about. This means that logical reasoning must abstract away from all such special features and be equally valid when applied in other domains. Arguments are accepted as logical based on their conformance to a general *form* rather than because of the specific *content* they treat. For instance, compare this traditional example:

All men are mortal
Socrates is a man
Therefore Socrates is mortal

with the following reasoning drawn from mathematics:

All positive integers are the sum of four integer squares
15 is a positive integer
Therefore 15 is the sum of four integer squares

These two arguments are both correct, and both share a common pattern:

All X are Y
a is X
Therefore a is Y

This pattern of inference is logically valid, since its validity does not depend on the content: the meanings of 'positive integer', 'mortal' etc. are irrelevant. We can substitute anything we like for these X, Y and a, provided we respect grammatical categories, and the statement is still valid. By contrast, consider the following reasoning:

All Athenians are Greek
Socrates is an Athenian
Therefore Socrates is mortal

Even though the conclusion is perfectly true, this is not logically valid, because it does depend on the content of the terms involved. Other arguments with the same superficial form may well be false, e.g.

All Athenians are Greek
Socrates is an Athenian
Therefore Socrates is beardless

The first argument can, however, be turned into a logically valid one by making explicit a hidden assumption 'all Greeks are mortal'. Now the argument is an instance of the general logically valid form:

All G are M
All A are G
s is A
Therefore s is M

At first sight, this forensic analysis of reasoning may not seem very impressive. Logically valid reasoning never tells us anything fundamentally new about the world – as Wittgenstein (1922) says, 'I know nothing about the weather when I know that it is either raining or not raining'. In other words, if we *do* learn something new about the world from a chain of reasoning, it must contain a step that is *not* purely logical. Russell, quoted in Schilpp (1944) says:

Hegel, who deduced from pure logic the whole nature of the world, including the non-existence of asteroids, was only enabled to do so by his logical incompetence.[†]

But logical analysis can bring out clearly the necessary relationships *between* facts about the real world and show just where possibly unwarranted assumptions enter into them. For example, from 'if it has just rained, the ground is wet' it follows logically that 'if the ground is not wet, it has not just rained'. This is an instance of a general principle called *contraposition*: from 'if P then Q' it follows that 'if not Q then not P'. However, passing from 'if P then Q' to 'if Q then P' is *not* valid in general, and we see in this case that we cannot deduce 'if the ground is wet, it has just rained', because it might have become wet through a burst pipe or device for irrigation.

Such examples may be, as Locke (1689) put it, 'trifling', but elementary logical fallacies of this kind are often encountered. More substantially, deductions in mathematics are very far from trifling, but have preoccupied and often defeated some of the greatest intellects in human history. Enormously lengthy and complex chains of logical deduction can lead from simple and apparently indubitable assumptions to sophisticated and unintuitive theorems, as Hobbes memorably discovered (Aubrey 1898):

Being in a Gentleman's Library, Euclid's Elements lay open, and 'twas the 47 *El. libri* 1 [Pythagoras's Theorem]. He read the proposition. *By G—*, sayd he (he would now and then sweare an emphaticall Oath by way of emphasis) *this is impossible!* So he reads the Demonstration of it, which referred him back to such a Proposition; which proposition he read. That referred him back to another, which he also read. *Et sic deinceps* [and so on] that at last he was demonstratively convinced of that trueth. This made him in love with Geometry.

Indeed, Euclid's seminal work *Elements of Geometry* established a particular style of reasoning that, further refined, forms the backbone of present-day mathematics. This style consists in asserting a small number of *axioms*, presumably with mathematical content, and deducing consequences from them using *purely logical reasoning*.[‡] Euclid himself didn't quite achieve a complete separation of logical and non-logical, but his work was finally perfected by Hilbert (1899) and Tarski (1959), who made explicit some assumptions such as 'Pasch's axiom'.

[†] To be fair to Hegel, the word *logic* was often used in a broader sense until quite recently, and what we consider logic would have been called specifically *deductive logic*, as distinct from *inductive logic*, the drawing of conclusions from observed data as in the physical sciences.

[‡] Arguably this approach is foreshadowed in the Socratic method, as reported by Plato. Socrates would win arguments by leading his hapless interlocutors from their views through chains of apparently inevitable consequences. When absurd consequences were derived, the initial position was rendered untenable. For this method to have its uncanny force, there must be no doubt at all over the steps, and no hidden assumptions must be sneaked in.

1.2 Calculemus!

'Reasoning is reckoning'. In the epigraph of this book we quoted Hobbes on the similarity between logical reasoning and numerical calculation. While Hobbes deserves credit for making this better known, the idea wasn't new even in 1651.[†] Indeed the Greek word *logos*, used by Plato and Aristotle to mean reason or logical thought, can also in other contexts mean computation or reckoning. When the works of the ancient Greek philosophers became well known in medieval Europe, *logos* was usually translated into *ratio*, the Latin word for reckoning (hence the English words rational, ratiocination, etc.). Even in current English, one sometimes hears 'I reckon that ... ', where 'reckon' refers to some kind of reasoning rather than literally to computation.

However, the connection between reasoning and reckoning remained little more than a suggestive slogan until the work of Gottfried Wilhelm von Leibniz (1646–1716). Leibniz believed that a system for reasoning by calculation must contain two essential components:

- a universal language (*characteristica universalis*) in which anything can be expressed;
- a calculus of reasoning (*calculus ratiocinator*) for deciding the truth of assertions expressed in the *characteristica*.

Leibniz dreamed of a time when disputants unable to agree would not waste much time in futile argument, but would instead translate their disagreement into the *characteristica* and say to each other '*calculemus*' (let us calculate). He may even have entertained the idea of having a machine do the calculations. By this time various mechanical calculating devices had been designed and constructed, and Leibniz himself in 1671 designed a machine capable of multiplying, remarking:

It is unworthy of excellent men to lose hours like slaves in the labour of calculations which could safely be relegated to anyone else if machines were used.

So Leibniz foresaw the essential components that make automated reasoning possible: a language for expressing ideas precisely, rules of calculation for manipulating ideas in the language, and the mechanization of such calculation. Leibniz's concrete accomplishments in bringing these ideas to fruition were limited, and remained little-known until recently. But though his work had limited direct influence on technical developments, his dream still resonates today.

[†] The Epicurean philosopher Philodemus, writing in the first century B.C., introduced the term *logisticos* (λογιστικός) to describe logic as the science of calculation.

1.3 Symbolism

Leibniz was right to draw attention to the essential first step of developing an appropriate language. But he was far too ambitious in wanting to express all aspects of human thought. Eventual progress came rather by extending the scope of the symbolic notations already used in mathematics. As an example of this notation, we would nowadays write '$x^2 \leq y + z$' rather than 'x multiplied by itself is less than or equal to the sum of y and z'. Over time, more and more of mathematics has come to be expressed in formal symbolic notation, replacing natural language renderings. Several sound reasons can be identified.

First, a well-chosen symbolic form is usually shorter, less cluttered with irrelevancies, and helps to express ideas more briefly and intuitively (at least to cognoscenti). For example Leibniz's own notation for differentiation, dy/dx, nicely captures the idea of a ratio of small differences, and makes theorems like the chain rule $dy/dx = dy/du \cdot du/dx$ look plausible based on the analogy with ordinary algebra.

Second, using a more stylized form of expression can avoid some of the ambiguities of everyday language, and hence communicate meaning with more precision. Doubts over the exact meanings of words are common in many areas, particularly law.[†] Mathematics is not immune from similar basic disagreements over exactly what a theorem says or what its conditions of validity are, and the consensus on such points can change over time (Lakatos 1976; Lakatos 1980).

Finally, and perhaps most importantly, a well-chosen symbolic notation can contribute to making mathematical reasoning itself easier. A simple but outstanding example is the 'positional' representation of numbers, where a number is represented by a sequence of numerals each implicitly multiplied by a certain power of a 'base'. In decimal the base is 10 and we understand the string of digits '179' to mean:

$$179 = 1 \times 10^2 + 7 \times 10^1 + 9 \times 10^0.$$

In binary (currently used by most digital computers) the base is 2 and the same number is represented by the string 10110011:

$$10110011 = 1 \times 2^7 + 0 \times 2^6 + 1 \times 2^5 + 1 \times 2^4 + 0 \times 2^3 + 0 \times 2^2 + 1 \times 2^1 + 1 \times 2^0.$$

[†] For example 'Since the object of ss 423 and 425 of the Insolvency Act 1986 was to remedy the avoidance of debts, the word 'and' between paragraphs (a) and (b) of s 423(2) must be read conjunctively and not disjunctively.' (Case Summaries, *Independent* newspaper, 27th December 1993.)

These positional systems make it very easy to perform important operations on numbers like comparing, adding and multiplying; by contrast, the system of Roman numerals requires more involved algorithms, though there is evidence that many Romans were adept at such calculations (Maher and Makowski 2001). For example, we are normally taught in school to add decimal numbers digit-by-digit from the right, propagating a carry leftwards by adding one in the next column. Once it becomes second nature to follow the rules, we can, and often do, forget about the underlying meaning of these sequences of numerals. Similarly, we might transform an equation $x - 3 = 5 - x$ into $x = 3 + 5 - x$ and then to $2x = 5 + 3$ without pausing each time to think about *why* these rules about moving things from one side of the equation to the other are valid. As Whitehead (1919) says, symbolism and formal rules of manipulation:

[...] have invariably been introduced to make things easy. [...] by the aid of symbolism, we can make transitions in reasoning almost mechanically by the eye, which otherwise would call into play the higher faculties of the brain. [...] Civilisation advances by extending the number of important operations which can be performed without thinking about them.

Indeed, such formal rules can be followed reliably by people who do *not* understand the underlying justification, or by computers. After all, computers are expressly designed to follow formal rules (programs) quickly and reliably. They do so without regard to the underlying justification, and will faithfully follow even erroneous sets of rules (programs with 'bugs').

1.4 Boole's algebra of logic

The word *algebra* is derived from the Arabic 'al-jabr', and was first used in the ninth century by Mohammed al-Khwarizmi (ca. 780–850), whose name lies at the root of the word 'algorithm'. The term 'al-jabr' literally means 'reunion', but al-Khwarizmi used it to describe in particular his method of solving equations by collecting together ('reuniting') like terms, e.g. passing from $x + 4 = 6 - x$ to $2x = 6 - 4$ and so to the solution $x = 1$.[†] Over the following centuries, through the European renaissance, algebra continued to mean, essentially, rules of manipulation for solving equations.

During the nineteenth century, algebra in the traditional sense reached its limits. One of the central preoccupations had been the solving of equations of higher and higher degree, but Niels Henrik Abel (1802–1829) proved in

---

[†] The first use of the phrase in Europe was nothing to do with mathematics, but rather the appellation 'algebristas' for Spanish barbers, who also set ('reunited') broken bones as a sideline to their main business.

1824 that there is no general way of solving polynomial equations of degree 5 and above using the 'radical' expressions that had worked for lower degrees. Yet at the same time the scope of algebra expanded and it became generalized. Traditionally, variables had stood for real numbers, usually unknown numbers to be determined. However, it soon became standard practice to apply all the usual rules of algebraic manipulation to the 'imaginary' quantity i assuming the formal property $i^2 = -1$. Though this procedure went for a long time without any rigorous justification, it was effective.

Algebraic methods were even applied to objects that were not numbers in the usual sense, such as matrices and Hamilton's 'quaternions', even at the cost of abandoning the usual 'commutative law' of multiplication $xy = yx$. Gradually, it was understood that the underlying interpretation of the symbols could be ignored, provided it was established once and for all that the rules of manipulation used are all valid under that interpretation. The state of affairs was described clear-sightedly by George Boole (1815–1864).

They who are acquainted with the present state of the theory of Symbolic Algebra, are aware, that the validity of the processes of analysis does not depend upon the interpretation of the symbols which are employed, but solely on their laws of combination. Every system of interpretation which does not affect the truth of the relations supposed, is equally admissible, and it is true that the same process may, under one scheme of interpretation, represent the solution of a question on the properties of numbers, under another, that of a geometrical problem, and under a third, that of a problem of dynamics or optics. (Boole 1847)

Boole went on to observe that nevertheless, by historical or cultural accident, all algebra at the time involved objects that were in some sense quantitative. He introduced instead an algebra whose objects were to be interpreted as 'truth-values' of true or false, and where variables represent *propositions*.[†] By a proposition, we mean an assertion that makes a declaration of fact and so may meaningfully be considered either true or false. For example, '1 < 2', 'all men are mortal', 'the moon is made of cheese' and 'there are infinitely many prime numbers p such that $p + 2$ is also prime' are all propositions, and according to our present state of knowledge, the first two are true, the third false and the truth-value of the fourth is unknown (this is the 'twin primes conjecture', a famous open problem in mathematics).

We are familiar with applying to numbers various arithmetic operations like unary 'minus' (negation) and binary 'times' (multiplication) and 'plus' (addition). In an exactly analogous way, we can combine truth-values using

---

[†] Actually Boole gave two different but related interpretations: an 'algebra of classes' and an 'algebra of propositions'; we'll focus on the latter.

so-called *logical connectives*, such as unary 'not' (logical negation or complement) and binary 'and' (conjunction) and 'or' (disjunction).[†] And we can use letters to stand for arbitrary *propositions* instead of *numbers* when we write down expressions. Boole emphasized the connection with ordinary arithmetic in the precise formulation of his system and in the use of the familiar algebraic notation for many logical constants and connectives:

0	false
1	true
pq	p and q
$p + q$	p or q

On this interpretation, many of the familiar algebraic laws still hold. For example, 'p and q' always has the same truth-value as 'q and p', so we can assume the commutative law $pq = qp$. Similarly, since 0 is false, '0 and p' is false whatever p may be, i.e. $0p = 0$. But the Boolean algebra of propositions satisfies additional laws that have no counterpart in arithmetic, notably the law $p^2 = p$, where p^2 abbreviates pp.

In everyday English, the word 'or' is ambiguous. The complex proposition 'p or q' may be interpreted either inclusively (p or q or both) or exclusively (p or q but not both).[‡] In everyday usage it is often implicit that the two cases are mutually exclusive (e.g. 'I'll do it tomorrow or the day after'). Boole's original system restricted the algebra so that $p + q$ only made sense if $pq = 0$, rather as in ordinary algebra x/y only makes sense if $y \neq 0$. However, following Boole's successor William Stanley Jevons (1835–1882), it became customary to allow use of 'or' without restriction, and interpret it in the inclusive sense. We will always understand 'or' in this now-standard sense, 'p or q' meaning 'p or q *or both*'.

Mechanization

Even before Boole, machines for logical deduction had been developed, notably the 'Stanhope demonstrator' invented by Charles, third Earl of Stanhope (1753–1816). Inspired by this, Jevons (1870) subsequently designed and built his 'logic machine', a piano-like device that could perform certain calculations in Boole's algebra of classes. However, the limits of mechanical

---

[†] Arguably *disjunction* is something of a misnomer, since the two truth-values need not be disjoint, so some like Quine (1950) prefer *alternation*. And the word 'connective' is a misnomer in the case of unary operations like 'not', since it does not connect two propositions, but merely negates a single one. However, both usages are well-established.

[‡] Latin, on the other hand, has separate phrases 'p vel q' and 'aut p aut q' for the inclusive and exclusive readings, respectively.

engineering and the slow development of logic itself meant that the mechanization of reasoning really started to develop somewhat later, at the start of the modern computer age. We will cover more of the history later in the book in parallel with technical developments. Jevons's original machine can be seen in the Oxford Museum for the History of Science.[†]

Logical form

In Section 1.1 we talked about arguments 'having the same form', but did not define this precisely. Indeed, it's hard to do so for arguments expressed in English and other natural languages, which often fail to make the logical structure of sentences apparent: superficial similarities can disguise fundamental structural differences, and vice versa. For example, the English word 'is' can mean 'has the property of being' ('4 is even'), or it can mean 'is the same as' ('2 + 2 is 4'). This example and others like it have often generated philosophical confusion.

Once we have a precise symbolism for logical concepts (such as Boole's algebra of logic) we can simply say that two arguments have the same form if they are both instances of the same formal expression, consistently replacing variables by other propositions. And we can use the formal language to make a mathematically precise definition of logically valid arguments. This is not to imply that the definition of logical form and of purely logical argument is a philosophically trivial question; quite the contrary. But we are content not to solve this problem but to finesse it by adopting a precise mathematical definition, rather as Hertz (1894) evaded the question of what 'force' means in mechanics. After enough concrete experience we will briefly consider (Section 7.8) how our demarcation of the logical arguments corresponds to some traditional philosophical distinctions.

1.5 Syntax and semantics

An unusual feature of logic is the careful separation of symbolic expressions and what they stand for. This point bears emphasizing, because in everyday mathematics we often pass unconsciously to the mathematical objects denoted by the symbols. For example when we read and write '12' we think of it as a number, a member of the set $\mathbb{N}$, not as a sequence of two numeral symbols used to represent that number. However, when we want to make precise our formal manipulations, whether these be adding decimal numbers

---

[†] See `www.mhs.ox.ac.uk/database/index.htm?fname=brief&invno=18230` for some small pictures.

digit-by-digit or using algebraic laws to rearrange symbolic expressions, we need to maintain the distinction. After all, when deriving equations like $x + y = y + x$, the whole point is that the mathematical objects denoted are the same; we cannot directly talk about such manipulations if we only consider the underlying meaning.

Typically then, we are concerned with (i) some particular set of allowable formal expressions, and (ii) their corresponding meanings. The two are sharply distinguished, but are connected by an *interpretation*, which maps expressions to their meanings:

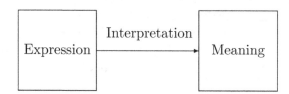

The distinction between formal expressions and their meanings is also important in linguistics, and we'll take over some of the jargon from that subject. Two traditional subfields of linguistics are *syntax*, which is concerned with the grammatical formation of sentences, and *semantics*, which is concerned with their meanings. Similarly in logic we often refer to methods as 'syntactic' if 'like algebraic manipulations' they are considered in isolation from meanings, and 'semantic' or 'semantical' if meanings play an important role. The words 'syntax' and 'semantics' are also used in linguistics with more concrete meanings, and these too are adopted in logic.

- The *syntax* of a language is a system of grammar laying out rules about how to produce or recognize grammatical phrases and sentences. For example, we might consider 'I went to the shop' grammatical English but not 'I shop to the went' because the noun and verb are swapped. In logical systems too, we will often have rules telling us how to generate or recognize well-formed expressions, perhaps for example allowing '$x + 1$' but not '$+1\times$'.
- The *semantics* of a particular word, symbol, sign or phrase is simply its meaning. More broadly, the semantics of a language is a systematic way of ascribing such meanings to all the (grammatical) expressions in the language. Translated into linguistic jargon, choosing an interpretation amounts exactly to giving a semantics to the language.

Object language and metalanguage

It may be confusing that we will be describing formal rules for performing logical reasoning, and yet will reason *about* those rules using ... logic! In this connection, it's useful to keep in mind the distinction between the (formal) logic we are talking about and the (everyday intuitive) logic we are using to reason about it. In order to emphasize the contrast we will sometimes deploy the following linguistic jargon. A *metalanguage* is a language used to talk *about* another distinct *object language*, and likewise a *metalogic* is used to reason about an *object logic*. Thus, we often call the theorems we derive about formal logic and automated reasoning systems *metatheorems* rather than merely *theorems*. This is not (only) to sound more grandiose, but to emphasize the distinction from 'theorems' expressed *inside* those formal systems. Likewise, metalogical reasoning applied to formalized mathematical proofs is often called *metamathematics* (see Section 7.1). By the way, our chosen programming language OCaml is derived from Edinburgh ML, which was expressly designed for writing theorem proving programs (Gordon, Milner and Wadsworth 1979) and whose name stands for Meta Language. This object–meta distinction (Tarski 1936; Carnap 1937) isn't limited to logical languages. For instance, in a Russian language lesson given in English, we can consider Russian to be the object language and English the metalanguage.

Abstract and concrete syntax

Fine details of syntax are of no fundamental importance. Some mathematics is typed, some is handwritten, and people make various essentially arbitrary choices that do not change anything about the structural way symbols are used together. When mechanizing logic on the computer, we will, for simplicity, restrict ourselves to the usual stock of ASCII characters,[†] which includes unaccented Latin letters, numbers and some common punctuation signs and spaces. For the fancy letters and special symbols that many logicians use, we will use other letters or words, e.g. 'forall' instead of '$\forall$'. We will, however, continue to employ the usual symbols in theoretical discussions. This continual translation may even be helpful to the reader who hasn't seen or understood the symbols before.

Regardless of how the symbolic expressions are read or written, it's more convenient to manipulate them in a form better reflecting their structure. Consider the expression '$x + y \times z - w$' in ordinary algebra. This linear form

---

[†] See en.wikipedia.org/wiki/ASCII.

obscures the meaningful structure. To understand which operators have been applied to which subexpressions, or even what constitutes a subexpression, we need to know rules of precedence and associativity, e.g. that '×' 'binds tighter' than '+'. For instance, despite their apparent similarity in the linear form, '$y \times z$' is a subexpression while '$x + y$' is not. Even if we make the structure explicit by fully bracketing it as '$(x + (y \times z)) - w$', basic useful operations on expressions like finding subexpressions, or evaluating the expression for particular values of the variables, become tiresome to describe precisely; one needs to shuffle back and forth over the formula matching up brackets.

A 'tree' structure is much better: just as a family tree makes relations among family members clearly apparent, a tree representation of an expression displays its structure and makes most important manipulations straightforward. As in genealogy, it's customary to draw trees growing downwards on the printed page, so the same expression might be represented as follows:

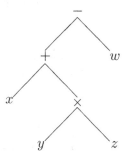

Generally we refer to the (mainly linear) format used by people as the *concrete syntax*, and the structural (typically tree-like) form used for manipulations as the *abstract syntax*. Trees like the above are often called *abstract syntax trees* (ASTs) and are widely used as the internal representation of formal languages in all kinds of symbolic programs, including the compilers that translate high-level programming languages into machine instructions.

Despite their making the structure of an expression clearer, most people prefer not to think or communicate using trees, but to use the less structured concrete syntax.[†] Hence in our theorem-proving programs we will need to translate input from concrete syntax to abstract syntax, and translate output back from abstract syntax to concrete syntax. These two tasks, known to computer scientists as *parsing* and *prettyprinting*, are now well understood

---

[†] This is not to say that concrete syntax is necessarily a linear sequence of symbols. Mathematicians often use semi-graphical symbolism (matrix notation, commutative diagrams), and the pioneering logical notation introduced by Frege (1879) was tree-like.

and fairly routine. The small overhead of writing parsers and prettyprint-ers is amply repaid by the greater convenience of the tree form for internal manipulation. There are enthusiastic advocates of systems of concrete syntax such as 'Polish notation', 'reverse Polish notation (RPN)' and LISP 'S-expressions', where our expression would be denoted, respectively, by

```
- + x × y z w
x y z × + w -
(- (+ x (× y z)) w)
```

but we will use more traditional notation, with infix operators like '+' and rules of precedence and bracketing.[†]

1.6 Symbolic computation and OCaml

In the early days of modern computing it was commonly believed that computers were essentially devices for numeric calculation (Ceruzzi 1983). Their input and output devices were certainly biased in that direction: when Samuels wrote the first checkers (draughts) program at IBM in 1948, he had to encode the output as a number because that was all that could be printed.[‡] However, it had already been recognized, long before Turing's theoretical construction of a universal machine (see Section 7.5), that the potential applicability of computers was much wider. For example, Ada Lovelace observed in 1842 (Huskey and Huskey 1980):[§]

Many persons who are not conversant with mathematical studies, imagine that because the business of [Babbage's analytical] engine is to give its results in numerical notation, the nature of its processes must consequently be arithmetical and numerical, rather than algebraical and analytical. This is an error. The engine can arrange and combine its numerical quantities exactly as if they were letters or any other general symbols; and in fact it might bring out its results in algebraical notation, were provisions made accordingly.

There are now many programs that perform symbolic computation, including various quite successful 'computer algebra systems' (CASs). Theorem proving programs bear a strong family resemblance to CASs, and even overlap in some of the problems they can solve (see Section 5.11, for example).

[†] Originally the spartan syntax of LISP 'S-expressions' was to be supplemented by a richer and more conventional syntax of 'M-expressions' (meta-expressions), and this is anticipated in some of the early publications like the LISP 1.5 manual (McCarthy 1962). However, such was the popularity of S-expressions that M-expressions were seldom implemented and never caught on.
[‡] Related in his speech to the 1985 International Joint Conference on Artificial Intelligence.
[§] See www.fourmilab.to/babbage/sketch.html.

The preoccupations of those doing symbolic computation have influenced their favoured programming languages. Whereas many system programmers favour C, numerical analysts FORTRAN and so on, symbolic programmers usually prefer higher-level languages that make typical symbolic operations more convenient, freeing the programmer from explicit details of memory representation etc. We've chosen to use Objective CAML (OCaml) as the vehicle for the programming examples in this book. Our code does not use any of OCaml's more exotic features, and should be easy to port to related functional languages such as F♯, Standard ML or Haskell.

Our insistence on using explicit OCaml code may be disquieting for those with no experience of computer programming, or for those who only know imperative and relatively low-level languages like C or Java. However, we hope that with the help of Appendix 2 and additional study of some standard texts recommended at the end of this chapter, the determined reader will pick up enough OCaml to follow the discussion and play with the code. As a gentle introduction to symbolic computation in OCaml, we will now implement some simple manipulations in ordinary algebra, a domain that will be familiar to many readers.

The first task is to define a datatype to represent the abstract syntax of algebraic expressions. We will allow expressions to be built from numeric constants like 0, 1 and 33 and named variables like x and y using the operations of addition ('+') and multiplication ('*'). Here is the corresponding recursive datatype declaration:

```
type expression =
   Var of string
 | Const of int
 | Add of expression * expression
 | Mul of expression * expression;;
```

That is, an expression is either a variable identified by a string, a constant identified by its integer value, or an addition or multiplication operator applied to two subexpressions. (A '*' indicates that the domain of a type constructor is a Cartesian product, so it can take two expressions as arguments. It is nothing to do with the multiplication being defined!) We can use the syntax constructors introduced by this type definition to create the symbolic representation for any particular expression, such as $2 \times x + y$:

```
# Add(Mul(Const 2,Var "x"),Var "y");;
- : expression = Add (Mul (Const 2, Var "x"), Var "y")
```

A simple but representative example of symbolic computation is applying specified transformation rules like $0 + x \longrightarrow x$ and $3 + 5 \longrightarrow 8$ to 'simplify' an expression. Each rule is expressed in OCaml by a starting and finishing *pattern*, e.g. `Add(Const(0),x) -> x` for a transformation $0 + x \longrightarrow x$. (The special pattern '_' matches anything, so the last line ensures that if none of the other patterns match, `expr` is returned unchanged.) When the function is applied, OCaml will run through the rules in order and apply the first one whose starting pattern matches the input expression `expr`, replacing variables like `x` by the relevant subexpression.

```
let simplify1 expr =
  match expr with
    Add(Const(m),Const(n)) -> Const(m + n)
  | Mul(Const(m),Const(n)) -> Const(m * n)
  | Add(Const(0),x) -> x
  | Add(x,Const(0)) -> x
  | Mul(Const(0),x) -> Const(0)
  | Mul(x,Const(0)) -> Const(0)
  | Mul(Const(1),x) -> x
  | Mul(x,Const(1)) -> x
  | _ -> expr;;
```

However, simplifying just once is not necessarily adequate; we would like instead to simplify repeatedly until no further progress is possible. To do this, let us apply the above function in a bottom-up sweep through an expression tree, which will simplify in a cascaded manner. In traditional OCaml recursive style, we first simplify any immediate subexpressions as much as possible, then apply `simplify1` to the result:[†]

```
let rec simplify expr =
  match expr with
    Add(e1,e2) -> simplify1(Add(simplify e1,simplify e2))
  | Mul(e1,e2) -> simplify1(Mul(simplify e1,simplify e2))
  | _ -> simplify1 expr;;
```

Rather than a simple bottom-up sweep, a more sophisticated approach would be to mix top-down and bottom-up simplification. For example, if E is very large it would seem more efficient to simplify $0 \times E$ immediately to 0 without any examination of E. However, this needs to be implemented with care to ensure that all simplifiable subterms are simplified without the danger of looping indefinitely. Anyway, here is our simplification function in action on the expression $(0 \times x + 1) * 3 + 12$:

[†] We could leave `simplify1` out of the last line, since no simplification will be applicable to any expression reaching this case, but it seems more thematic to include it.

```
# let e = Add(Mul(Add(Mul(Const(0),Var "x"),Const(1)),Const(3)),
              Const(12));;
val e : expression =
  Add (Mul (Add (Mul (Const 0, Var "x"), Const 1), Const 3), Const 12)
# simplify e;;
- : expression = Const 15
```

Getting this far is straightforward using standard OCaml functional programming techniques: recursive datatypes to represent tree structures and the definition of functions via pattern-matching and recursion. We hope the reader who has not used similar languages before can begin to see why OCaml is appealing for symbolic computing. But of course, those who are fond of other programming languages are more than welcome to translate our code into them.

As planned, we will implement a parser and prettyprinter to translate between abstract syntax trees and concrete strings ('x + 0'), setting them up to be invoked automatically by OCaml for input and output of expressions. We model our concrete syntax on ordinary algebraic notation, except that in a couple of respects we will follow the example of computer languages rather than traditional mathematics. We allow arbitrarily long 'words' as variables, whereas mathematicians traditionally use mostly single letters with superscripts and subscripts; this is especially important given the limited stock of ASCII characters. And we insist that multiplication is written with an explicit infix symbol ('x * y'), rather than simple juxtaposition ('x y'), which later on we will use for function application. In everyday mathematics we usually rely on informal cues like variable names and background knowledge to see at once that $f(x+1)$ denotes function application whereas $y(x+1)$ denotes multiplication, but this kind of context-dependent parsing is a bit more complicated to implement.

1.7 Parsing

Translating concrete into abstract syntax is a well-understood topic because of its central importance to programming language compilers, interpreters and translators. It is now conventional to separate the transformation into two separate stages:

- lexical analysis (scanning) decomposes the sequences of input characters into 'tokens' (roughly speaking, words);
- parsing converts the linear sequences of tokens into an abstract syntax tree.

For example, lexical analysis might split the input 'v10 + v11' into three tokens 'v10', '+' and 'v11', coalescing adjacent alphanumeric characters into words and throwing away any number of spaces (and perhaps even line breaks) between these tokens. Parsing then only has to deal with sequences of tokens and can ignore lower-level details.

Lexing

We start by classifying characters into broad groups: spaces, punctuation, symbolic, alphanumeric, etc. We treat the underscore and prime characters as alphanumeric, in deference to the usual conventions in computing ('x_1') and mathematics ('f'''). The following OCaml predicates tell us whether a character (actually, one-character string) belongs to a certain class:[†]

```
let matches s = let chars = explode s in fun c -> mem c chars;;

let space = matches " \t\n\r"
and punctuation = matches "()[]{},"
and symbolic = matches "~`!@#$%^&*-+=|\\:;<>.?/"
and numeric = matches "0123456789"
and alphanumeric = matches
  "abcdefghijklmnopqrstuvwxyz_'ABCDEFGHIJKLMNOPQRSTUVWXYZ0123456789";;
```

A token will be either a sequence of adjacent alphanumeric characters (like 'x' or 'size1'), a sequence of adjacent symbolic characters ('+', '<='), or a single punctuation character ('(').[‡] Lexical analysis, scanning left-to-right, will assume that a token is the longest possible, for instance that 'x1' is a single token, not two. We treat punctuation characters differently from other symbols just to avoid some counterintuitive effects of the 'longest possible token' rule, such as the detection of a token '((' in the string '((x + y) + z)'.

Next we will define an auxiliary function `lexwhile` that takes a property `prop` of characters, such as one of the classifying predicates above, and a list of input characters, separating off as a string the longest initial sequence of that list of characters satisfying `prop`:

```
let rec lexwhile prop inp =
  match inp with
    c::cs when prop c -> let tok,rest = lexwhile prop cs in c^tok,rest
  | _ -> "",inp;;
```

[†] Of course, this is a very inefficient procedure. However, we care even less than usual about efficiency in these routines since parsing is not usually a critical component in overall runtime.

[‡] In the present example, the only meaningful symbolic tokens consist of a single character, like '+'. However, by allowing longer symbolic tokens we will be able to re-use this lexical analyzer unchanged in later work.

The lexical analyzer itself maps a list of input characters into a list of token strings. First any initial spaces are separated and thrown away, using `lexwhile space`. If the resulting list of characters is nonempty, we classify the first character and use `lexwhile` to separate the longest string of characters of the same class; for punctuation (or other unexpected) characters we give `lexwhile` an always-false property so it stops at once. Then we add the first character back on to the token and recursively analyze the rest of the input.

```
let rec lex inp =
  match snd(lexwhile space inp) with
    [] -> []
  | c::cs -> let prop = if alphanumeric(c) then alphanumeric
                        else if symbolic(c) then symbolic
                        else fun c -> false in
             let toktl,rest = lexwhile prop cs in
             (c^toktl)::lex rest;;
```

We can try the lexer on a typical input string, and another example reminiscent of C syntax to illustrate longer symbolic tokens.

```
# lex(explode "2*((var_1 + x') + 11)");;
- : string list =
["2"; "*"; "("; "("; "var_1"; "+"; "x'"; ")"; "+"; "11"; ")"]
# lex(explode "if (*p1-- == *p2++) then f() else g()");;
- : string list =
["if"; "("; "*"; "p1"; "--"; "=="; "*"; "p2"; "++"; ")"; "then"; "f";
 "("; ")"; "else"; "g"; "("; ")"]
```

Parsing

Now we want to transform a sequence of tokens into an abstract syntax tree. We can reflect the higher precedence of multiplication over addition by considering an expression like $2 * w + 3 * (x + y) + z$ to be a sequence of 'product expressions' (here '$2 * w$', '$3 * (x + y)$' and 'z') separated by '+'. In turn each product expression, say $2 * w$, is a sequence of 'atomic expressions' (here '2' and 'w') separated by '*'. Finally, an atomic expression is either a constant, a variable, or an arbitrary expression enclosed in brackets; note that we require *parentheses* (round brackets), though we could if we chose allow square brackets and/or braces as well. We can invent names for these three categories, say 'expression', 'product' and 'atom', and illustrate how each is built up from the others by a series of rules often called a 'BNF[†]

[†] BNF stands for 'Backus–Naur form', honouring two computer scientists who used this technique to describe the syntax of the programming language ALGOL. Similar grammars are used in formal language theory.

grammar'; read '$\longrightarrow$' as 'may be of the form' and '$|$' as 'or'.

$$
\begin{aligned}
\text{expression} &\longrightarrow \text{product} + \cdots + \text{product} \\
\text{product} &\longrightarrow \text{atom} * \cdots * \text{atom} \\
\text{atom} &\longrightarrow (\text{expression}) \\
&| \quad \text{constant} \\
&| \quad \text{variable}
\end{aligned}
$$

Since the grammar is already recursive ('expression' is defined in terms of itself, via the intermediate categories), we might as well use recursion to replace the repetitions:

$$
\begin{aligned}
\text{expression} &\longrightarrow \text{product} \\
&| \quad \text{product} + \text{expression} \\
\text{product} &\longrightarrow \text{atom} \\
&| \quad \text{atom} * \text{product} \\
\text{atom} &\longrightarrow (\text{expression}) \\
&| \quad \text{constant} \\
&| \quad \text{variable}
\end{aligned}
$$

This gives rise to a very direct way of parsing the input using three mutually recursive functions for the three different categories of expression, an approach known as *recursive descent parsing*. Each parsing function is given a list of tokens and returns a pair consisting of the parsed expression tree together with any unparsed input. Note that the pattern of recursion exactly matches the above grammar and simply examines tokens when necessary to decide which of several alternatives to take. For example, to parse an expression, we first parse a product, and then test whether the first unparsed character is '+'; if it is, then we make a recursive call to parse the rest and compose the results accordingly.

```
let rec parse_expression i =
  match parse_product i with
    e1,"+"::i1 -> let e2,i2 = parse_expression i1 in Add(e1,e2),i2
  | e1,i1 -> e1,i1
```

A product works similarly in terms of a parser for atoms:

```
and parse_product i =
  match parse_atom i with
    e1,"*"::i1 -> let e2,i2 = parse_product i1 in Mul(e1,e2),i2
  | e1,i1 -> e1,i1
```

and an atom parser handles the most basic expressions, including an arbitrary expression in brackets:

```
and parse_atom i =
  match i with
     [] -> failwith "Expected an expression at end of input"
   | "("::i1 -> (match parse_expression i1 with
                  e2,")"::i2 -> e2,i2
                | _ -> failwith "Expected closing bracket")
   | tok::i1 -> if forall numeric (explode tok)
                then Const(int_of_string tok),i1
                else Var(tok),i1;;
```

The 'right-recursive' formulation of the grammar means that we interpret repeated operations that lack disambiguating brackets as right-associative, e.g. $x+y+z$ as $x+(y+z)$. Had we instead defined a 'left-recursive' grammar:

$$expression \longrightarrow product$$
$$| \quad expression + product$$

then $x + y + z$ would have been interpreted as $(x + y) + z$. For an associative operation like '+' it doesn't matter that much, since at least the meanings are the same, but for '−' this latter policy is clearly more appropriate.[†]

Finally, we define the overall parser via a wrapper function that explodes the input string, lexically analyzes it, parses the sequence of tokens and then finally checks that no input remains unparsed. We define a generic function for this, applicable to any core parser `pfn`, since it will be useful again later:

```
let make_parser pfn s =
  let expr,rest = pfn (lex(explode s)) in
  if rest = [] then expr else failwith "Unparsed input";;
```

We call our parser `default_parser`, and test it on a simple example:

```
# let default_parser = make_parser parse_expression;;
val default_parser : string -> expression = <fun>
# default_parser "x + 1";;
- : expression = Add (Var "x", Const 1)
```

But we don't even need to invoke the parser explicitly. Our setup exploits OCaml's quotation facility so that any French-style ≪quotation≫ will automatically have its body passed as a string to the function `default_parser`:[‡]

[†] Translating such a left-recursive grammar naively into recursive parsing functions would cause an infinite loop since `parse_expression` would just call itself directly right at the beginning and never get started on useful work. However, a small modification copes with this difficulty – see the definition of `parse_left_infix` in Appendix 3.

[‡] OCaml's treatment of quotations is programmable; our action of feeding the string to `default_parser` is set up in the file `Quotexpander.ml`.

```
# <<(x1 + x2 + x3) * (1 + 2 + 3 * x + y)>>;;
- : expression =
Mul (Add (Var "x1", Add (Var "x2", Var "x3")),
  Add (Const 1, Add (Const 2, Add (Mul (Const 3, Var "x"), Var "y"))))
```

The process by which parsing functions were constructed from the grammar is almost mechanical, and indeed there are tools to produce parsers automatically from slightly augmented grammars. However, we thought it worthwhile to be explicit about this programming task, which is not really so difficult and provides a good example of programming with recursive functions.

1.8 Prettyprinting

For presentation to the user we need the reverse transformation, from abstract to concrete syntax. A crude but adequate solution is the following:

```
let rec string_of_exp e =
  match e with
    Var s -> s
  | Const n -> string_of_int n
  | Add(e1,e2) -> "("^(string_of_exp e1)^" + "^(string_of_exp e2)^")"
  | Mul(e1,e2) -> "("^(string_of_exp e1)^" * "^(string_of_exp e2)^")";;
```

Brackets are necessary in general to reflect the groupings in the abstract syntax, otherwise we could mistakenly print, say '$6 \times (x+y)$' as '$6 \times x+y$'. Our function puts brackets uniformly round each instance of a binary operator, which is perfectly correct but sometimes looks cumbersome to a human:

```
# string_of_exp <<x + 3 * y>>;;
- : string = "(x + (3 * y))"
```

We would (probably) prefer to omit the outermost brackets, and others that are implicit in rules for precedence or associativity. So let's give `string_of_exp` an additional argument for the 'precedence level' of the operator of which the expression is an immediate subexpression. Now, brackets are only needed if the current expression has a top-level operator with lower precedence than this 'outer precedence' argument.

We arbitrarily allocate precedence 2 to addition, 4 to multiplication, and use 0 at the outermost level. Moreover, we treat the operators asymmetrically to reflect right-associativity, so the left-hand recursive subcall is given a slightly higher outer precedence to force brackets if iterated instances of the same operation are left-associated.

```
let rec string_of_exp pr e =
  match e with
    Var s -> s
  | Const n -> string_of_int n
  | Add(e1,e2) ->
        let s = (string_of_exp 3 e1)^" + "^(string_of_exp 2 e2) in
        if 2 < pr then "("^s^")" else s
  | Mul(e1,e2) ->
        let s = (string_of_exp 5 e1)^" * "^(string_of_exp 4 e2) in
        if 4 < pr then "("^s^")" else s;;
```

Our overall printing function will print with starting precedence level 0 and surround the result with the kind of quotation marks we use for input:

```
let print_exp e = Format.print_string ("<<"^string_of_exp 0 e^">>");;
```

As with the parser, we can set up the printer to be invoked automatically on any result of the appropriate type, using the following magic incantation (the hash is part of the directive that is entered, not the OCaml prompt):

```
#install_printer print_exp;;
```

Now we get output quite close to the concrete syntax we would naturally type in:

```
# <<x + 3 * y>>;;
- : expression = <<x + 3 * y>>
# <<(x + 3) * y>>;;
- : expression = <<(x + 3) * y>>
# <<1 + 2 + 3>>;;
- : expression = <<1 + 2 + 3>>
# <<((1 + 2) + 3) + 4>>;;
- : expression = <<((1 + 2) + 3) + 4>>
```

The main rough edge remaining is that expressions too large to fit on one line are not split up in an intelligent way to reflect the structure via the line breaks, as in the following example. The printers we use later (see Appendix 3) make a somewhat better job of this by employing a special OCaml library `Format`.

```
# <<(x1 + x2 + x3 + x4 + x5 + x6 + x7 + x8 + x9 + x10) *
    (y1 + y2 + y3 + y4 + y5 + y6 + y7 + y8 + y9 + y10)>>;;
- : expression =
<<(x1 + x2 + x3 + x4 + x5 + x6 + x7 + x8 + x9 + x10) * (y1 + y2 + y3 +
y4 + y5 + y6 + y7 + y8 + y9 + y10)>>
```

Having demonstrated the basic programming needed to support symbolic computation, we will end this chapter and move on to the serious study of logic and automated reasoning.

Further reading

We confine ourselves here to general references and those for topics that we won't cover ourselves in more depth later. More specific and technical references will be presented at the end of each later chapter.

Davis (2000) and Devlin (1997) are general accounts of the development of logic and its mechanization, as well as related topics in computer science and linguistics. There are many elementary textbooks on logic such as Hodges (1977), Mates (1972) and Tarski (1941). Two logic books that, like this one, are accompanied by computer programs are Keisler (1996) and Barwise and Etchemendy (1991). There are also several books discussing carefully the role of logical reasoning in mathematics, e.g. Garnier and Taylor (1996).

Bocheński (1961), Dumitriu (1977) and Kneale and Kneale (1962) are detailed and scholarly accounts of the history of logic. Kneebone (1963) is a survey of mathematical logic which also contains a lot of historical information, while Marciszewski and Murawski (1995) shares our emphasis on mechanization. For a readable account of Jevons's logical piano and other early 'reasoning machines', starting with the Spanish mystic Ramon Lull in the thirteenth century, see Gardner (1958). MacKenzie (2001) is a historical overview of the development of automated theorem proving and its applications.

There are numerous introductions to philosophical logic that discuss issues like the notion of logical consequence in more depth; e.g. Engel (1991), Grayling (1990) and Haack (1978). Philosophically inclined readers may enjoy considering the claims of Mill (1865) and Mauthner (1901) that logical consequence is merely a psychological accident, and the polemical replies by Frege (1879) and Husserl (1900).

For further OCaml and functional programming references, see Appendix 2. The basic parsing techniques we have described are explained in detail in virtually every book ever written on compiler technology. The 'dragon book' by Aho, Sethi and Ullman (1986) has long been considered a classic, though its treatment of parsing is probably too extensive for those whose primary interest is elsewhere. A detailed theoretical analysis of what kind of parsing tasks are and aren't decidable leads naturally into the theory of computation. Davis, Sigal and Weyuker (1994) not only covers this material thoroughly, but is also a textbook on logic. For more on prettyprinting, see Oppen (1980b) and Hughes (1995).

Other discussions of theorem proving in the same implementation-oriented style as ours are given by Huet (1986), Newborn (2001) and Paulson (1992), while Gordon (1988) also describes, in similar style, the use of theorem provers within a program verification environment. Other general textbooks on automated theorem proving are Chang and Lee (1973), Duffy (1991) and Fitting (1990), as well as some more specialized texts we will mention later.

Exercises

1.1   Modify the parser and printer to support a concrete syntax where juxtaposition is an acceptable (or the only) way of denoting multiplication.

1.2   Add an infix exponentiation operation '^' to the parser, printer and simplification functions. You can make it right-associative so that 'x^y^z' is interpreted as 'x^(y^z)'.

1.3   Add a subtraction operation to the parser, printer and simplification functions. Be careful to make subtraction associate to the left, so that $x - y - z$ is understood as $(x - y) - z$ not $x - (y - z)$. If you get stuck, you can see how similar things are done in Appendix 3.

1.4   After adding subtraction as in the previous exercise, add a unary negation operator using the same '$-$' symbol. Take care that you can parse an expression such as $x - - - x$, correctly distinguishing instances of subtraction and negation, and simplify it to 0.

1.5   Write a simplifier that uses a more intelligent traversal strategy to avoid wasteful evaluation of subterms such as E in $0 \cdot E$ or $E - E$. Write a function to generate huge expressions in order to test how much more efficient it is.

1.6   Write a more sophisticated simplifier that will put terms in a canonical polynomial form, e.g. transform $(x+1)^3 - 3 \cdot (x+1)^2 + 3 \cdot (2 \cdot x - x)$ into $x^3 - 2$. We will eventually develop similar functions in Chapter 5.

1.7   Many concrete strings with slightly different bracketing or spacing correspond to the same abstract syntax tree, so we can't expect print(parse(s)) = s in general. But how about parse(print(e)) = e? If not, how could you change the code to make sure it does hold? (There is a probably apocryphal story of testing an English/Russian translation program by translating the English expression 'the spirit is willing, but the flesh is weak' into Russian and back to English, resulting in 'the vodka is good and the meat is tender'. Another version has 'out of sight, out of mind' returned as 'invisible idiot'.)

2
Propositional logic

We study propositional logic in detail, defining its formal syntax in OCaml together with parsing and printing support. We discuss some of the key propositional algorithms and prove the compactness theorem, as well as indicating the surprisingly rich applications of propositional theorem proving.

2.1 The syntax of propositional logic

Propositional logic is a modern version of Boole's algebra of propositions as presented in Section 1.4.[†] It involves expressions called *formulas*[‡] that are intended to represent propositions, i.e. assertions that may be considered true or false. These formulas can be built from constants 'true' and 'false' and some basic *atomic propositions* (*atoms*) using various logical connectives ('not', 'and', 'or', etc.). The atomic propositions are like variables in ordinary algebra, and we sometimes refer to them as *propositional variables* or *Boolean variables*. As the word 'atomic' suggests, we do not analyze their internal structure; that will be considered when we treat first-order logic in the next chapter.

Representation in OCaml

We represent propositional formulas using an OCaml datatype by analogy with the type of expressions in Section 1.6. We allow the 'constant' propositions `False` and `True` and atomic formulas `Atom p`, and can build up formulas from them using the unary operator `Not` and the binary connectives

---

[†] Indeed, propositional logic is sometimes called 'Boolean algebra'. But this is apt to be confusing because mathematicians refer to any algebraic structure satisfying certain axioms, roughly the usual laws of algebra together with $x^2 = x$, as a Boolean algebra (Halmos 1963).

[‡] When consulting the literature, the reader may find the phrase *well-formed formula* (wff for short) used instead of just 'formula'. This is to emphasize that in the concrete syntax, we are only interested in strings with a syntactically valid form, not arbitrary strings of symbols.

And, Or, Imp ('implies') and Iff ('if and only if'). We defer a discussion of the exact meanings of these connectives, and deal first with immediate practicalities.

The underlying set of atomic propositions is largely arbitrary, although for some purposes it's important that it be infinite, to avoid a limit on the complexity of formulas we can consider. In abstract treatments it's common just to index the primitive propositions by number. We make the underlying type 'a of atomic propositions a parameter of the definition of the type of formulas, so that many basic functions work equally well whatever it may be. This apparently specious generality will be useful to avoid repeated work later when we consider the extension to first-order logic. For the same reason we include two additional formula type constructors Forall and Exists. These will largely be ignored in the present chapter but their role will become clear later on.

```
type ('a)formula = False
               | True
               | Atom of 'a
               | Not of ('a)formula
               | And of ('a)formula * ('a)formula
               | Or of ('a)formula * ('a)formula
               | Imp of ('a)formula * ('a)formula
               | Iff of ('a)formula * ('a)formula
               | Forall of string * ('a)formula
               | Exists of string * ('a)formula;;
```

Concrete syntax

As we've seen, Boole used traditional algebraic signs like '+' for the logical connectives. This makes many logical truths look beguilingly familiar, e.g.

$$p(q + r) = pq + pr$$

But some logical truths then look quite alien, such as the following, resulting from systematically exchanging 'and' and 'or' in the first formula:

$$p + qr = (p + q)(p + r)$$

In its logical guise this says that if either p holds or both q and r hold, then either p or q holds, and also either p or r holds, and vice versa. A little thought should convince the reader that this is indeed always the case; recall that 'p or q' is inclusive, meaning p or q or both.

To avoid confusion or misleading analogies with ordinary algebra, we will use special symbols for the connectives that are nowadays fairly standard.

In each row of the following table we give the English reading of each construct, followed by the standard symbolism we will adopt in discussions, then the ASCII approximations that we will support in our programs, the corresponding abstract syntax construct, and finally some other symbolisms in use. (This last column can be ignored for the purposes of this book, but may be useful when consulting the literature.)

English	Symbolic	ASCII	OCaml	Other symbols
false	$\bot$	`false`	`False`	0, F
true	$\top$	`true`	`True`	1, T
not p	$\neg p$	`~p`	`Not p`	$\bar{p}$, $-p$, $\sim p$
p and q	$p \wedge q$	`p /\ q`	`And(p,q)`	pq, $p\&q$, $p \cdot q$
p or q	$p \vee q$	`p \/ q`	`Or(p,q)`	$p+q$, $p \mid q$, p or q
p implies q	$p \Rightarrow q$	`p ==> q`	`Imp(p,q)`	$p \rightarrow q$, $p \supset q$
p iff q	$p \Leftrightarrow q$	`p <=> q`	`Iff(p,q)`	$p \leftrightarrow q$, $p \equiv q$, $p \sim q$

The symbol '$\vee$' is derived from the first letter of 'vel', the Latin word for inclusive or, $\top$ looks like the first letter of 'true', while $\bot$ and $\wedge$ are just mirror-images of $\top$ and $\vee$, reflecting a principle of *duality* to be explained in Section 2.4.[†] The sign for negation is close enough to the sign for arithmetical negation to be easy to remember. Some readers may have seen the symbols for implication and 'if and only if' in informal mathematics.

As with ordinary algebra, we establish rules of precedence for the connectives, overriding it by bracketing if necessary. The (quite standard) precedence order we adopt is indicated in the ordering of the table above, with '$\neg$' the highest and '$\Leftrightarrow$' the lowest. For example $p \Rightarrow q \wedge \neg r \vee s$ means $p \Rightarrow ((q \wedge (\neg r)) \vee s)$. Perhaps it would be more appropriate to give $\wedge$ and $\vee$ equal precedence, but only a few authors do that (Dijkstra and Scholten 1990) and we will follow the herd by giving $\wedge$ higher precedence.

All our binary connectives are parsed in a right-associated fashion, so $p \wedge q \wedge r$ means $p \wedge (q \wedge r)$, and so on. In informal practice, iterated implications of the form $p \Rightarrow q \Rightarrow r$ are often used as a shorthand for '$p \Rightarrow q$ and $q \Rightarrow r$', just as $x \leq y \leq z$ is for '$x \leq y$ and $y \leq z$'. For us, however, $p \Rightarrow q \Rightarrow r$ just means $p \Rightarrow (q \Rightarrow r)$, which is not the same thing.[‡]

In informal discussions, we will not make the `Atom` constructor explicit, but will try to use variable names like p, q and r for general formulas and

---

[†] The symbols for 'and' and 'or' are also just more angular versions of the standard symbols for set intersection and union. This is no coincidence: $x \in S \cap T$ iff $x \in S \wedge x \in T$ and $x \in S \cup T$ iff $x \in S \vee x \in T$.

[‡] It is logically equivalent to $p \wedge q \Rightarrow r$, as the reader will be able to confirm when we have defined the term precisely.

x, y and z for general atoms. For example, when we talk about a formula $x \Leftrightarrow p$, we usually mean a formula of the form `Iff(Atom(x),p)`.

Generic parsing and printing

We set up automated parsing and printing support for formulas, just as we did for ordinary algebraic expressions in Sections 1.7–1.8. Since the details are not important for present purposes, a detailed description of the code is deferred to Appendix 3. We do want to emphasize, however, that since the type of formulas is parametrized by a type of atomic propositions, the parsing and printing functions are similarly parametrized. The function `parse_formula` has type:

```
# parse_formula;;
- : (string list -> string list -> 'a formula * string list) *
    (string list -> string list -> 'a formula * string list) ->
    string list -> string list -> 'a formula * string list
= <fun>
```

This takes as additional arguments a pair of parsers for atoms and a list of strings. For present purposes the first atom parser in the pair and the list of strings can essentially be ignored; they will be used when we extend parsing to first-order formulas in the next chapter, the former to handle special infix atomic formulas like $x < y$ and the latter to retain a context of non-propositional variables. Similarly, `print_qformula` (print a formula with quotation marks) has type:

```
# print_qformula;;
- : (int -> 'a -> unit) -> 'a formula -> unit = <fun>
```

expecting a basic 'primitive proposition printer' (which as well as the proposition gets supplied with the current precedence level) and producing a printer for the overall type of formulas.

Primitive propositions

Although many functions will be generic, it makes experimentation with some of the operations easier if we fix on a definite type of primitive propositions. Accordingly we define the following type of primitive propositions indexed by names (i.e. strings):

```
type prop = P of string;;
```

We define the following to get the name of a proposition:

```
let pname(P s) = s;;
```

Now we just need to provide a parser for atomic propositions, which is quite straightforward. For reasons explained in Appendix 3 we need to check that the first input character is not a left bracket, but otherwise we just take the first token in the input stream as the name of a primitive proposition:

```
let parse_propvar vs inp =
  match inp with
    p::oinp when p <> "(" -> Atom(P(p)),oinp
  | _ -> failwith "parse_propvar";;
```

Now we feed this to the generic formula parser, with an always-failing function for the presently unused infix atom parser and an empty list for the context of non-propositional variables:

```
let parse_prop_formula = make_parser
  (parse_formula ((fun _ _ -> failwith ""),parse_propvar) []);;
```

and we can set it to automatically apply to anything typed in quotations by:

```
let default_parser = parse_prop_formula;;
```

Now we turn to printing, constructing a (trivial) function to print propositional variables, ignoring the additional precedence argument:

```
let print_propvar prec p = print_string(pname p);;
```

and then setting up and installing the overall printer:

```
let print_prop_formula = print_qformula print_propvar;;

#install_printer print_prop_formula;;
```

We are now in an environment where propositional formulas will be automatically parsed and printed, e.g.:

```
# <<p \/ q ==> r>>;;
- : prop formula = <<p \/ q ==> r>>
# let fm = <<p ==> q <=> r /\ s \/ (t <=> ~ ~u /\ v)>>;;
val fm : prop formula = <<p ==> q <=> r /\ s \/ (t <=> ~(~u) /\ v)>>
```

(Note that the space between the two negation symbols is necessary or it would be interpreted as a single token, resulting in a parse error.)

The printer is designed to split large formulas across lines in a reasonable fashion:

```
# And(fm,fm);;
- : prop formula =
<<((p ==> q <=> r /\ s \/ (t <=> ~(~u) /\ v)) /\
   (p ==> q <=> r /\ s \/ (t <=> ~(~u) /\ v))>>
# And(Or(fm,fm),fm);;
- : prop formula =
<<(((p ==> q <=> r /\ s \/ (t <=> ~(~u) /\ v)) \/
    (p ==> q <=> r /\ s \/ (t <=> ~(~u) /\ v))) /\
   (p ==> q <=> r /\ s \/ (t <=> ~(~u) /\ v))>>
```

Syntax operations

It's convenient to have syntax operations corresponding to the formula constructors usable as ordinary OCaml functions:

```
let mk_and p q = And(p,q) and mk_or p q = Or(p,q)
and mk_imp p q = Imp(p,q) and mk_iff p q = Iff(p,q)
and mk_forall x p = Forall(x,p) and mk_exists x p = Exists(x,p);;
```

Dually, it's often convenient to be able to break formulas apart without explicit pattern-matching. This function breaks apart an *equivalence* (or *bi-implication* or *biconditional*), i.e. a formula of the form $p \Leftrightarrow q$, into the pair (p, q):

```
let dest_iff fm =
  match fm with Iff(p,q) -> (p,q) | _ -> failwith "dest_iff";;
```

Similarly this function breaks apart a formula $p \wedge q$, called a *conjunction*, into its two *conjuncts* p and q:

```
let dest_and fm =
  match fm with And(p,q) -> (p,q) | _ -> failwith "dest_and";;
```

while the following recursively breaks down a conjunction into a list of conjuncts:

```
let rec conjuncts fm =
  match fm with And(p,q) -> conjuncts p @ conjuncts q | _ -> [fm];;
```

The following similar functions break down a formula $p \vee q$, called a *disjunction*, into its *disjuncts* p and q, one at the top level, one recursively:

```
let dest_or fm =
  match fm with Or(p,q) -> (p,q) | _ -> failwith "dest_or";;

let rec disjuncts fm =
  match fm with Or(p,q) -> disjuncts p @ disjuncts q | _ -> [fm];;
```

This is a top-level destructor for implications:

```
let dest_imp fm =
  match fm with Imp(p,q) -> (p,q) | _ -> failwith "dest_imp";;
```

The formulas p and q in an implication $p \Rightarrow q$ are referred to as its *antecedent* and *consequent* respectively, and we define corresponding functions:

```
let antecedent fm = fst(dest_imp fm);;
let consequent fm = snd(dest_imp fm);;
```

We'll often want to define functions by recursion over formulas, just as we did with simplification in Section 1.6. Two patterns of recursion seem sufficiently common that it makes sense to define generic functions. The following applies a function to all the atoms in a formula, but otherwise leaves the structure unchanged. It can be used, for example, to perform systematic replacement of one particular atomic proposition by another formula:

```
let rec onatoms f fm =
  match fm with
    Atom a -> f a
  | Not(p) -> Not(onatoms f p)
  | And(p,q) -> And(onatoms f p,onatoms f q)
  | Or(p,q) -> Or(onatoms f p,onatoms f q)
  | Imp(p,q) -> Imp(onatoms f p,onatoms f q)
  | Iff(p,q) -> Iff(onatoms f p,onatoms f q)
  | Forall(x,p) -> Forall(x,onatoms f p)
  | Exists(x,p) -> Exists(x,onatoms f p)
  | _ -> fm;;
```

The following is an analogue of the list iterator `itlist` for formulas, iterating a binary function over all the atoms of a formula.

```
let rec overatoms f fm b =
  match fm with
    Atom(a) -> f a b
  | Not(p) -> overatoms f p b
  | And(p,q) | Or(p,q) | Imp(p,q) | Iff(p,q) ->
        overatoms f p (overatoms f q b)
  | Forall(x,p) | Exists(x,p) -> overatoms f p b
  | _ -> b;;
```

A particularly common application is to collect together some set of attributes associated with the atoms; in the simplest case just returning the set of all atoms. We can do this by iterating a function f together with an 'append' over all the atoms, and finally converting the result to a set to remove duplicates. (We could use `union` to remove duplicates as we proceed, but the present implementation can be more efficient where the sets involved are large.)

```
let atom_union f fm = setify (overatoms (fun h t -> f(h)@t) fm []);;
```

We will soon see some illustrations of how these very general functions can be used in practice.

2.2 The semantics of propositional logic

Since propositional formulas are intended to represent assertions that may be true or false, the ultimate meaning of a formula is just one of the two *truth-values* 'true' and 'false'. However, just as an algebraic expression like $x + y + 1$ only has a definite meaning when we know what the variables x and y stand for, the meaning of a propositional formula depends on the truth-values assigned to its atomic formulas. This assignment is encoded in a *valuation*, which is a function from the set of atoms to the set of truth-values {false, true}. Given a formula p and a valuation v we then evaluate the overall truth-value by the following recursively defined function:

```
let rec eval fm v =
  match fm with
    False -> false
  | True -> true
  | Atom(x) -> v(x)
  | Not(p) -> not(eval p v)
  | And(p,q) -> (eval p v) & (eval q v)
  | Or(p,q) -> (eval p v) or (eval q v)
  | Imp(p,q) -> not(eval p v) or (eval q v)
  | Iff(p,q) -> (eval p v) = (eval q v);;
```

This is our mathematical *definition* of the semantics of propositional logic,[†] intended to be a natural formalization of our intuitions. (The semantics of implication is unobvious, and we discuss this at length below.) Each logical connective is interpreted by a corresponding operator on OCaml's inbuilt type `bool`. To be quite explicit about what these operators mean, we

---

[†] We may choose to regard the partially evaluated `eval p`, a function from valuations to values, as the semantics of the formula p, rather than make the valuation an additional argument. This is mainly a question of terminology.

can enumerate all possible combinations of inputs and see the corresponding output, for example for the & operator:

```
# false & false;;
- : bool = false
# false & true;;
- : bool = false
# true & false;;
- : bool = false
# true & true;;
- : bool = true
```

We can lay out this information in a *truth-table* showing how the truth-value assigned to a formula is determined by those of its immediate subformulas:[†]

p	q	$p \wedge q$	$p \vee q$	$p \Rightarrow q$	$p \Leftrightarrow q$
false	false	false	false	true	true
false	true	false	true	true	false
true	false	false	true	false	false
true	true	true	true	true	true

Of course, for the sake of completeness we should also include a truth-table for the unary negation:

p	$\neg p$
false	true
true	false

Let's try evaluating a formula $p \wedge q \Rightarrow q \wedge r$ in a valuation where p, q and r are set to 'true', 'false' and 'true' respectively. (We don't bother to define the value on atoms not involved in the formula, and OCaml issues a warning that we have not done so.)

```
# eval <<p /\ q ==> q /\ r>>
      (function P"p" -> true | P"q" -> false | P"r" -> true);;
...
- : bool = true
```

In another valuation, however, the formula evaluates to 'false'; readers may find it instructive to check these results by hand:

```
eval <<p /\ q ==> q /\ r>>
      (function P"p" -> true | P"q" -> true | P"r" -> false);;
```

[†] Truth-tables were popularized by Post (1921) and Wittgenstein (1922), though they had been used earlier by Peirce in unpublished work.

Truth-tables mechanized

We would expect the evaluation of a formula to be independent of how the valuation assigns atoms not occurring in that formula. Let us make this precise by defining a function to extract the set of atomic propositions occurring in a formula. In abstract mathematical terms, we would define atoms as follows by recursion on formulas:

$$
\begin{aligned}
\mathtt{atoms}(\bot) &= \emptyset \\
\mathtt{atoms}(\top) &= \emptyset \\
\mathtt{atoms}(x) &= \{x\} \\
\mathtt{atoms}(\neg p) &= \mathtt{atoms}(p) \\
\mathtt{atoms}(p \wedge q) &= \mathtt{atoms}(p) \cup \mathtt{atoms}(q) \\
\mathtt{atoms}(p \vee q) &= \mathtt{atoms}(p) \cup \mathtt{atoms}(q) \\
\mathtt{atoms}(p \Rightarrow q) &= \mathtt{atoms}(p) \cup \mathtt{atoms}(q) \\
\mathtt{atoms}(p \Leftrightarrow q) &= \mathtt{atoms}(p) \cup \mathtt{atoms}(q)
\end{aligned}
$$

As a simple example of proof by structural induction (see appendices 1 and 2) on formulas, will show that $\mathtt{atoms}(p)$ is always finite, and hence we do not distort it by interpreting it in terms of ML lists. (Of course, we need to remember that list equality and set equality are not in general the same.)

Theorem 2.1 *For any propositional formula p, the set $\mathtt{atoms}(p)$ is finite.*

Proof By induction on the structure of the formula.

If p is $\bot$ or $\top$, then $\mathtt{atoms}(p)$ is the empty set, and if p is an atom, $\mathtt{atoms}(p)$ is a singleton set. In all cases, these are finite.

If p is of the form $\neg q$, then by the induction hypothesis, $\mathtt{atoms}(q)$ is finite and by definition $\mathtt{atoms}(\neg q) = \mathtt{atoms}(q)$.

If p is of the form $q \wedge r$, $q \vee r$, $q \Rightarrow r$ or $q \Leftrightarrow r$, then $\mathtt{atoms}(p) = \mathtt{atoms}(q) \cup \mathtt{atoms}(r)$. By the inductive hypothesis, both $\mathtt{atoms}(q)$ and $\mathtt{atoms}(r)$ are finite, and the union of two finite sets is finite. □

Similarly, we can justify formally the intuitively obvious fact mentioned above.

Theorem 2.2 *For any propositional formula p, if two valuations v and v' agree on the set $\mathtt{atoms}(p)$ (i.e. $v(x) = v'(x)$ for all x in $\mathtt{atoms}(p)$), then $\mathtt{eval}\ p\ v = \mathtt{eval}\ p\ v'$.*

Proof By induction on the structure of p.

If p is of the form $\bot$ or $\top$, then it is interpreted as true or false independent of the valuation.

If p is an atom x, then $\texttt{atoms}(x) = \{x\}$ and by assumption $v(x) = v'(x)$. Hence $\texttt{eval } p \; v = v(x) = v'(x) = \texttt{eval } p \; v'$.

If p is of the form $q \wedge r$, $q \vee r$, $q \Rightarrow r$ or $q \Leftrightarrow r$, then $\texttt{atoms}(p) = \texttt{atoms}(q) \cup \texttt{atoms}(r)$. Since the valuations agree on the union of the two sets, they agree, a fortiori, on each of $\texttt{atoms}(q)$ and $\texttt{atoms}(r)$. We can therefore apply the inductive hypothesis to conclude that $\texttt{eval } q \; v = \texttt{eval } q \; v'$ and that $\texttt{eval } r \; v = \texttt{eval } r \; v'$. Since the evaluation of p is a function of these subevaluations, $\texttt{eval } p \; v = \texttt{eval } p \; v'$. $\qquad\square$

The definition of $\texttt{atoms}$ above can be translated directly into an OCaml function, for example using $\texttt{union}$ for '$\cup$' and $\texttt{[x]}$ for '$\{x\}$'. However, we prefer to define it in terms of the existing iterator $\texttt{atom\_union}$:

```
let atoms fm = atom_union (fun a -> [a]) fm;;
```

For example:

```
# atoms <<p /\ q \/ s ==> ~p \/ (r <=> s)>>;;
- : prop list = [P "p"; P "q"; P "r"; P "s"]
```

Because the interpretation of a propositional formula p depends only on the valuation's action on the finite (say n-element) set $\texttt{atoms}(p)$, and it can only make two choices for each, the final truth-value is completely determined by all 2^n choices for those atoms. Hence we can naturally extend the enumeration in truth-table form from the basic operations to arbitrary formulas. To implement this in OCaml, we start by defining a function that tests whether a function $\texttt{subfn}$ returns $\texttt{true}$ on all possible valuations of the atoms $\texttt{ats}$, using an existing valuation $\texttt{v}$ for all other atoms. The space of all valuations is explored by successively modifying $\texttt{v}$ to consider setting each atom $\texttt{p}$ to 'true' and 'false' and calling recursively:

```
let rec onallvaluations subfn v ats =
  match ats with
    [] -> subfn v
  | p::ps -> let v' t q = if q = p then t else v(q) in
             onallvaluations subfn (v' false) ps &
             onallvaluations subfn (v' true) ps;;
```

We can apply this to a function that draws one row of the truth table and then returns 'true'. (The return value is important, because '&' will only evaluate its second argument if the first argument is `true`.) This can then be used to draw the whole truth table for a formula:

```
let print_truthtable fm =
  let ats = atoms fm in
  let width = itlist (max ** String.length ** pname) ats 5 + 1 in
  let fixw s = s^String.make(width - String.length s) ' ' in
  let truthstring p = fixw (if p then "true" else "false") in
  let mk_row v =
      let lis = map (fun x -> truthstring(v x)) ats
      and ans = truthstring(eval fm v) in
      print_string(itlist (^) lis ("| "^ans)); print_newline(); true in
  let separator = String.make (width * length ats + 9) '-' in
  print_string(itlist (fun s t -> fixw(pname s) ^ t) ats "| formula");
  print_newline(); print_string separator; print_newline();
  let _ = onallvaluations mk_row (fun x -> false) ats in
  print_string separator; print_newline();;
```

Note that we print in columns of width `width` that are wide enough to hold the names of all the atoms together with `true` and `false`, plus a final space. Then all the items in the table line up nicely. For example:

```
# print_truthtable <<p /\ q ==> q /\ r>>;;
p     q     r    | formula
---------------------------
false false false | true
false false true  | true
false true  false | true
false true  true  | true
true  false false | true
true  false true  | true
true  true  false | false
true  true  true  | true
---------------------------
- : unit = ()
```

Formal and natural language

Propositional logic gives us a formal way to express some of the complex propositions that can be stated in English or other natural languages. It can be instructive to practice the formalization (translation into formal logic) of compound propositions in English. As with translation between pairs of natural languages, one can't always expect a word-for-word correspondence. But with some awareness of the structure of an informal proposition, a quite direct formalization is often possible.

In propositional logic, apart from the rules of precedence given above, we can group propositions together using the standard mathematical technique of bracketing, distinguishing for example between '$p \wedge (q \vee r)$' and '$(p \wedge q) \vee r$'.

Brackets are used quite differently in English and most other languages (to make asides like this one). Indicating the precedence in English is a more ad hoc and awkward affair and is usually done by inserting additional punctuation and 'noise words' to bracket phrases and hence disambiguate. For example we might distinguish the above two examples as 'p, and also either q or r' and 'either both p and q, or else r'. This gets unwieldy for complicated propositions, and indeed this is part of the reason for having a formal language.

Generally speaking, constructs like 'and', 'or' and 'not' can be translated quite directly from English to the corresponding logical connectives. The connective 'not' can also be implicit in English prefixes such as 'dis-' and 'un-', so we might translate 'You are either honest and kind, or dishonest, or unkind' into '$H \wedge K \vee \neg H \vee \neg K$'. However, sometimes English phrases suggest nuances beyond the merely truth-functional. For example 'and' often indicates a causal connection ('he dropped the plate and it broke') or a temporal ordering ('she climbed into bed and turned out the light'). The word 'but' arguably has the same truth-functional interpretation as 'and', yet it expresses the idea that the component propositions connect in a surprising or unfortunate way. Similarly, 'unless' can reasonably be translated by 'or', but the consequent symmetry between 'p unless q' and 'q unless p' seems surprising.

More problematical is the relationship between the implication or *conditional* $p \Rightarrow q$ and the intended English reading 'p implies q' or 'if p then q'. An apparent dissonance on this point disturbs many newcomers to formal logic, and put at least one off the subject permanently (Waugh 1991). Indeed, debates about the meaning of implication go back over 2000 years to the Megarian-Stoic logicians (Bocheński 1961). According to Sextus Empiricus, the librarian Callimachus at Alexandria said in the second century BC that 'even the crows on the rooftops are cawing about which conditionals are true'.

First of all, let's be clear that if we adopt *any* truth-functional semantics of $p \Rightarrow q$, i.e. define the truth-value of $p \Rightarrow q$ in terms of the truth-values of p and q, then the semantics we have chosen is the only reasonable one. The most fundamental principle of implication as intuitively understood is that if p and $p \Rightarrow q$ are true, then so is q; consequently if p is true and q is false, then $p \Rightarrow q$ must be false. Moreover it is also plausible that $p \wedge q \Rightarrow p$ is always true, and only the chosen semantics makes this true whatever the truth-values of p and q.

But how do we justify giving implication a truth-functional semantics at all? In everyday life, when we say 'p implies q' or 'if p then q' we usually have in mind a causal connection between p and q. It doesn't seem reasonable to assert 'p implies q' just because it happens not to be the case that p is true while q is false. This definition commits us to accepting 'p implies q' as true whenever q is true, regardless of whether p is true or not, let alone whether it has any relation to q. Perhaps even more surprising, we also have to accept that 'p implies q' is true whenever p is *false*, regardless of q. For example, we would have to accept 'if Paris is the capital of France then $2 + 2 = 4$' and 'if the moon is made of cheese then $2 + 2 = 5$' as both true.

However, further reflection reveals that these peculiar cases do have their parallel in everyday phrases like 'if Smith wins the election then I'll eat my hat'. In mathematician's jargon we may think of such implications as being true 'trivially', with the consequent irrelevant. Similarly, if a friend plans definitely to leave town tomorrow, it seems hard to argue that his assertion 'I will leave town tomorrow or the day after' is not *true*, merely that it is a peculiar and misleading way to express himself. Again, if James is 40 years old and 2 metres tall, a remark by his mother that 'he is tall for his age' might be accepted as literally true while provoking giggles.

One can argue, roughly as the Megarian-Stoic logician Diodorus did, that the intuitive meaning of 'if p, then q' is not simply that we *do not* have $p \wedge \neg q$, but more strongly that we *cannot* under any circumstances have $p \wedge \neg q$. Rather than 'under any circumstances', Diodorus said 'at all times', being mainly concerned with propositions denoting states of affairs in the world. In mathematical assertions, the equivalent might be 'whatever the value(s) taken by the component variables'. Indeed, in everyday speech we may tend to interpret implication in a 'universalized' sense, just as we understand equations like $e^{x+y} = e^x e^y$ as implicitly valid for all values of the variables.[†] However, in formal logic we need to be much more precise about which variables are universal, and in the next chapter we will introduce *quantifiers* that allow us to say 'for all x ...' and so make the universal status of variables quite explicit. Once we have this ability, our truth-functional implication can be used to build up other notions of implication with the aid of explicit quantifiers, and by then we hope the reader's qualms will have eased somewhat in any case.

Readers who are still uncomfortable may choose to regard our *material* or *truth-functional* conditional '$p \Rightarrow q$' as something distinct from the various everyday notions. The use of the same terminology may seem unfortunate,

---

[†] Quine (1950) refers to $p \Rightarrow q$ as a *conditional* statement and always reads it as 'if p then q', reserving the reading 'p implies q' for the universal validity of that conditional. Thus, implication for Quine not only contains an implicit universal quantification but is also a meta-level statement *about* propositional formulas.

but it's often the case that superficially equivalent terminologies in everyday speech and in a precise science differ. It is unlikely, for example, that words like 'energy', 'power', 'force' and 'momentum' as used in everyday speech correspond to the formal definitions of a physicist, nor 'glass' and 'metal' to those of a chemist.

In ordinary usage and our formal definitions, 'if and only if' naturally corresponds to implication in both directions: 'p if and only if q' is the same as 'p implies q and q implies p'. We've already noted that the connective is frequently called *bi-implication*, and indeed we often prove mathematical theorems of the form 'p if and only if q' by separately proving 'if p then q' and 'if q then p', just as one might prove $x = y$ by separately proving $x \leq y$ and $y \leq x$. So if the semantics of implication is accepted, that for bi-implication should be acceptable too.

2.3 Validity, satisfiability and tautology

We say that a valuation v *satisfies* a formula p if `eval` $p\ v =$ true. A formula is said to be:

- a *tautology* or *logically valid* if is satisfied by *all* valuations, or equivalently, if its truth-table value is 'true' in *all* rows;
- *satisfiable* if it is satisfied by *some* valuation(s) i.e. if its truth-table value is 'true' in *at least one* row;
- *unsatisfiable* or a *contradiction* if *no* valuation satisfies it, i.e. if its truth-table value is 'false' in all rows.

Note that a tautology is also satisfiable, and as the names suggest, a formula is unsatisfiable precisely if it is not satisfiable. Moreover, in any valuation `eval` $(\neg p)\ v$ is false iff `eval` $p\ v$ is true, so p is a tautology if and only if $\neg p$ is unsatisfiable.

The simplest tautology is just '$\top$'; a slightly more interesting example is $p \wedge q \Rightarrow p \vee q$ ('if both p and q are true then at least one of p and q is true'), while one that many people find surprising at first sight is 'Peirce's Law' $((p \Rightarrow q) \Rightarrow p) \Rightarrow p$:

```
# print_truthtable <<((p ==> q) ==> p) ==> p>>;;
p       q      | formula
---------------------
false false | true
false true  | true
true   false | true
true   true  | true
---------------------
```

The formula $p \wedge q \Rightarrow q \wedge r$ whose truth-table we first produced in OCaml is satisfiable, since its truth table has a 'true' in the last column, but it's not a tautology because it also has one 'false'. The simplest contradiction is just '$\bot$', and another simple one is $p \wedge \neg p$ ('p is both true and false'):

```
# print_truthtable <<p /\ ~p>>;;
p     | formula
---------------
false | false
true  | false
---------------
```

Intuitively speaking, tautologies are 'always true', satisfiable formulas are 'sometimes (but possibly not always) true' and contradictions are 'always false'. Indeed, the notion of a tautology is intended to capture formally, insofar as we can in propositional logic, the idea of a logical truth that we discussed in a non-technical way in the introductory chapter. A tautology is exactly analogous to an algebraic equation like $x^2 - y^2 = (x+y)(x-y)$ that is universally true whatever the values of the constituent variables. A satisfiable formula is analogous to an equation that has at least one solution but may not be universally valid, e.g. $x^2 + 2 = 3x$. A contradiction is analogous to an unsolvable equation like $0 \cdot x = 1$.

It's useful to extend the idea of (un)satisfiability from a single formula to a set of formulas: a set Γ of formulas is said to be satisfiable if there is a valuation v that *simultaneously* satisfies them all. Note the 'simultaneously': $\{p \wedge \neg q, \neg p \wedge q\}$ is unsatisfiable even though each formula by itself is satisfiable. When the set concerned is finite, $\Gamma = \{p_1, \ldots, p_n\}$, satisfiability of Γ is equivalent to that of the single formula $p_1 \wedge \cdots \wedge p_n$, as the reader will see from the definitions. However, in our later work it will be essential to consider satisfiability of infinite sets of formulas, where it cannot so directly be reduced to satisfiability of a single formula. We also use the notation $\Gamma \models q$ to mean 'for all valuations in which all $p \in \Gamma$ are true, q is true'. Note that in the case of finite $\Gamma = \{p_1, \ldots, p_n\}$, this is equivalent to the assertion that $p_1 \wedge \cdots \wedge p_n \Rightarrow q$ is a tautology. In the case $\Gamma = \emptyset$ it's common just to write $\models p$ rather than $\emptyset \models p$, both meaning that p is a tautology.

Tautology and satisfiability checking

Although we can decide the status of formulas by examining their truth tables, it's simpler to let the computer do all the work. The following function tests whether a formula is a tautology by checking that it evaluates to 'true' for all valuations.

```
let tautology fm =
  onallvaluations (eval fm) (fun s -> false) (atoms fm);;
```

Note that as soon as any evaluation to 'false' is encountered this will, by the way `onallvaluations` was written, terminate with 'false' at once, rather than plough on through all possible valuations.

```
# tautology <<p \/ ~p>>;;
- : bool = true
# tautology <<p \/ q ==> p>>;;
- : bool = false
# tautology <<p \/ q ==> q \/ (p <=> q)>>;;
- : bool = false
# tautology <<(p \/ q) /\ ~(p /\ q) ==> (~p <=> q)>>;;
- : bool = true
```

Using the interrelationships noticed above, we can define satisfiability and unsatisfiability in terms of tautology:

```
let unsatisfiable fm = tautology(Not fm);;

let satisfiable fm = not(unsatisfiable fm);;
```

Substitution

As with algebraic identities, we expect to be able to substitute other formulas consistently for the atomic propositions in a tautology, and still get a tautology. We can define such substitution of formulas for atoms as follows, where `subfn` is a finite partial function (see Appendix 2):

```
let psubst subfn = onatoms (fun p -> tryapplyd subfn p (Atom p));;
```

For example, using the substitution function $p \mapsto p \wedge q$, which maps p to $p \wedge q$ but is otherwise undefined, we get:

```
# psubst (P"p" |=> <<p /\ q>>) <<p /\ q /\ p /\ q>>;;
- : prop formula = <<(p /\ q) /\ q /\ (p /\ q) /\ q>>
```

We will prove that substituting in tautologies yields a tautology, via a more general result that can be proved directly by structural induction on formulas:

Theorem 2.3 *For any atomic proposition x and arbitrary formulas p and q, and any valuation v, we have*[†]

$$\text{eval (psubst } (x \Mapsto q)\ p)\ v = \text{eval } p\ ((x \mapsto \text{eval } q\ v)\ v).$$

Proof By induction on the structure of p. If p is $\bot$ or $\top$ then the valuation plays no role and the equation clearly holds. If p is an atom y, we distinguish two possibilities. If $y = x$ then using the definitions of substitution and evaluation we find:

$$
\begin{aligned}
\text{eval (psubst } (x \Mapsto q)\ x)\ v \ &=\ \text{eval } q\ v \\
&=\ \text{eval } x\ ((x \mapsto \text{eval } q\ v)\ v).
\end{aligned}
$$

If, on the other hand, $y \neq x$ then:

$$
\begin{aligned}
\text{eval (psubst } (x \Mapsto q)\ y)\ v \ &=\ \text{eval } y\ v \\
&=\ \text{eval } y\ ((x \mapsto \text{eval } q\ v)\ v).
\end{aligned}
$$

For other kinds of formula, evaluation and substitution follow the structure of the formula so the result follows easily by the inductive hypothesis. For example, if p is of the form $\neg r$ then by definition and using the inductive hypothesis for r:

$$
\begin{aligned}
\text{eval (psubst } (x \Mapsto q)\ (\neg r))\ v \ &=\ \text{eval } (\neg(\text{psubst } (x \Mapsto q)\ r))\ v \\
&=\ \text{not}(\text{eval (psubst } (x \Mapsto q)\ r)\ v) \\
&=\ \text{not}(\text{eval } r\ ((x \mapsto \text{eval } q\ v)\ v)) \\
&=\ \text{eval } (\neg r)\ ((x \mapsto \text{eval } q\ v)\ v).
\end{aligned}
$$

The binary connectives all follow the same essential pattern but with two distinct formulas r and s instead of just r.   □

Corollary 2.4 *If p is a tautology, x is any atom and q any other formula, then* $\text{psubst } (x \Mapsto q)\ p$ *is also a tautology.*

[†] The notation $(x \mapsto a)v$ means the function v' that maps $v'(x) = a$ and $v'(y) = v(y)$ for $y \neq x$, and $x \Mapsto a$ is the function that maps x to a and is undefined elsewhere (see Appendix 1). In our OCaml implementation there are corresponding operators '|->' and '|=>' for finite partial functions; see Appendix 2.

Proof By the previous theorem we have for any valuation v:

$$\texttt{eval (psubst } (x \mapsto\!\!\!| q)\ p)\ v = \texttt{eval } p\ ((x \mapsto \texttt{eval } q\ v)\ v)$$

But since p is a tautology it evaluates to 'true' in all valuations, including the one on the right of this equation. Hence $\texttt{eval (psubst } (x \mapsto\!\!\!| q)\ p)\ v =$ true, and since v is arbitrary, this means the formula is a tautology. $\qquad\square$

Note that this result only applies to substituting for atoms, not arbitrary propositions. For example, $p \wedge q \Rightarrow q \wedge p$ is a tautology, but if we substitute $p \vee q$ for $p \wedge q$ it ceases to be so. This again is just as in ordinary algebra, and the fact that our substitution function is a function from names of atoms helps to enforce such a restriction. The main results are however easily generalized to substitution for multiple atoms simultaneously. These can always be done using individual substitutions repeatedly, but one might have to use additional substitutions to change variables and avoid spurious effects of later substitutions on earlier ones. For example, we would expect to be able to simultaneously substitute x for y and y for x in $x \wedge y$ to get $y \wedge x$. Yet if we perform the substitutions sequentially we get:

$$\begin{aligned}
&\texttt{psubst } (x \mapsto\!\!\!| y)\ (\texttt{psubst } (y \mapsto\!\!\!| x)\ (x \wedge y)) \\
=\ &\texttt{psubst } (x \mapsto\!\!\!| y)\ (x \wedge x) \\
=\ &y \wedge y.
\end{aligned}$$

However, by renaming variables appropriately using other substitutions such problems can always be avoided. For example:

$$\begin{aligned}
&\texttt{psubst } (z \mapsto\!\!\!| y)\ (\texttt{psubst } (y \mapsto\!\!\!| x)\ (\texttt{psubst } (x \mapsto\!\!\!| z)\ (x \wedge y)) \\
=\ &\texttt{psubst } (z \mapsto\!\!\!| y)\ (\texttt{psubst } (y \mapsto\!\!\!| x)\ (z \wedge y)) \\
=\ &\texttt{psubst } (z \mapsto\!\!\!| y)\ (z \wedge x) \\
=\ &y \wedge x.
\end{aligned}$$

It's useful to get a feel for propositional logic by listing some common tautologies. Some are simple and plausible such as the *law of the excluded middle* '$p \vee \neg p$' stating that every proposition is either true or false. A more surprising tautology, no doubt because of the poor accord between '$\Rightarrow$' and the intuitive notion of implication, is:

```
# tautology <<(p ==> q) \/ (q ==> p)>>;;
- : bool = true
```

If $p \Rightarrow q$ is a tautology, i.e. any valuation that satisfies p also satisfies q, we say that q is a *logical consequence* of p. If $p \Leftrightarrow q$ is a tautology, i.e.

a valuation satisfies p if and only if it satisfies q, we say that p and q are *logically equivalent.* Many important tautologies naturally take this latter form, and trivially if p is a tautology then so is $p \Leftrightarrow \top$, as the reader can confirm. In algebra, given a valid equation such as $2x = x+x$, we can replace $2x$ by $x+x$ in any other expression without changing its value. Similarly, if a valuation satisfies $p \Leftrightarrow q$, then we can substitute q for p or vice versa in another formula r (even if p is not just an atom) without affecting whether the valuation satisfies r. Since we haven't formally defined substitution for non-atoms, we imagine identifying the places to substitute using some other atom x in a 'pattern' term.

Theorem 2.5 *Given any valuation v and formulas p and q such that* eval p $v =$ eval q v, *for any atom x and formula r we have*

$$\text{eval } (\text{psubst } (x \Mapsto p)\ r)\ v = \text{eval } (\text{psubst } (x \Mapsto q)\ r)\ v.$$

Proof We have eval $(\text{psubst } (x \Mapsto p)\ r)\ v = $ eval $r\ ((x \mapsto \text{eval } p\ v)\ v)$ and eval $(\text{psubst } (x \Mapsto q)\ r)\ v = $ eval $r\ ((x \mapsto \text{eval } q\ v)\ v)$ by Theorem 2.3. But since by hypothesis eval $p\ v = $ eval $q\ v$ these are the same. $\square$

Corollary 2.6 *If p and q are logically equivalent, then*

$$\text{eval } (\text{psubst } (x \Mapsto p)\ r)\ v = \text{eval } (\text{psubst } (x \Mapsto q)\ r)\ v.$$

In particular psubst $(x \Mapsto p)\ r$ *is a tautology iff* psubst $(x \Mapsto q)\ r$ *is.*

Proof Since p and q are logically equivalent, we have eval $p\ v = $ eval $q\ v$ for any valuation v, and the result follows from the previous theorem. $\square$

Some important tautologies

Without further ado, here's a list of tautologies. Many of these correspond to ordinary algebraic laws if rewritten in the Boolean symbolism, e.g. $p \wedge \bot \Leftrightarrow \bot$ to $p \cdot 0 = 0$.

$$\neg \top \Leftrightarrow \bot$$
$$\neg \bot \Leftrightarrow \top$$
$$\neg \neg p \Leftrightarrow p$$
$$p \wedge \bot \Leftrightarrow \bot$$
$$p \wedge \top \Leftrightarrow p$$
$$p \wedge p \Leftrightarrow p$$

$$p \wedge \neg p \Leftrightarrow \bot$$
$$p \wedge q \Leftrightarrow q \wedge p$$
$$p \wedge (q \wedge r) \Leftrightarrow (p \wedge q) \wedge r$$
$$p \vee \bot \Leftrightarrow p$$
$$p \vee \top \Leftrightarrow \top$$
$$p \vee p \Leftrightarrow p$$
$$p \vee \neg p \Leftrightarrow \top$$
$$p \vee q \Leftrightarrow q \vee p$$
$$p \vee (q \vee r) \Leftrightarrow (p \vee q) \vee r$$
$$p \wedge (q \vee r) \Leftrightarrow (p \wedge q) \vee (p \wedge r)$$
$$p \vee (q \wedge r) \Leftrightarrow (p \vee q) \wedge (p \vee r)$$
$$\bot \Rightarrow p \Leftrightarrow \top$$
$$p \Rightarrow \top \Leftrightarrow \top$$
$$p \Rightarrow \bot \Leftrightarrow \neg p$$
$$p \Rightarrow p \Leftrightarrow \top$$
$$p \Rightarrow q \Leftrightarrow \neg q \Rightarrow \neg p$$
$$p \Rightarrow q \Leftrightarrow (p \Leftrightarrow p \wedge q)$$
$$p \Rightarrow q \Leftrightarrow (q \Leftrightarrow q \vee p)$$
$$p \Leftrightarrow q \Leftrightarrow q \Leftrightarrow p$$
$$p \Leftrightarrow (q \Leftrightarrow r) \Leftrightarrow (p \Leftrightarrow q) \Leftrightarrow r$$

The last couple are perhaps particularly surprising, since we are not accustomed to 'equations within equations' from everyday mathematics. Effectively, they show that '$\Leftrightarrow$' is a symmetric and associative operator (like '+' in arithmetic), in that the order and association of iterated equivalences makes no logical difference. Some other tautologies involving equivalence are given by Dijkstra and Scholten (1990) and can be checked in OCaml; they refer to the second of these tautologies as the 'Golden Rule'.

```
# tautology <<p \/ (q <=> r) <=> (p \/ q <=> p \/ r)>>;;
- : bool = true
# tautology <<p /\ q <=> ((p <=> q) <=> p \/ q)>>;;
- : bool = true
```

Another tautology in our list corresponds to the principle of *contraposition*, the equivalence of $p \Rightarrow q$ and its *contrapositive* $\neg q \Rightarrow \neg p$, or of $p \Rightarrow \neg q$ and $q \Rightarrow \neg p$. (For example 'those who mind don't matter' and 'those who matter don't mind' are logically equivalent.) By contrast, we can confirm that $p \Rightarrow q$ and $q \Rightarrow p$ are *not* equivalent, refuting a common fallacy:

```
# tautology <<(p ==> q) <=> (~q ==> ~p)>>;;
- : bool = true
# tautology <<(p ==> ~q) <=> (q ==> ~p)>>;;
- : bool = true
# tautology <<(p ==> q) <=> (q ==> p)>>;;
- : bool = false
```

2.4 The De Morgan laws, adequacy and duality

The following important tautologies are called *De Morgan's laws*, after Augustus De Morgan, a near-contemporary of Boole who made important contributions to the field of logic.[†]

$$\neg(p \vee q) \quad \Leftrightarrow \quad \neg p \wedge \neg q$$
$$\neg(p \wedge q) \quad \Leftrightarrow \quad \neg p \vee \neg q$$

An everyday example of the first is that 'I can not speak either Finnish or Swedish' means that same as 'I can not speak Finnish and I can not speak Swedish'. An example of the second is that 'I am not a wife and mother' is the same as 'either I am not a wife or I am not a mother (or both)'. Variants of the De Morgan laws, also easily seen to be tautologies, are:

$$p \vee q \quad \Leftrightarrow \quad \neg(\neg p \wedge \neg q)$$
$$p \wedge q \quad \Leftrightarrow \quad \neg(\neg p \vee \neg q)$$

These are interesting because they show how to express either connective $\wedge$ and $\vee$ in terms of the other. By virtue of the above theorems on substitution, this means for example that we can 'rewrite' any formula to a logically equivalent formula not involving '$\vee$', simply by systematically replacing each subformula of the form $q \vee r$ with $\neg(\neg q \wedge \neg r)$. There are many other options for expressing some logical connectives in terms of others. For instance, using the following equivalences, one can find an equivalent for any formula using only atomic formulas, $\wedge$ and $\neg$. In the jargon, $\{\wedge, \neg\}$ is said to be an *adequate set* of connectives.

$$\bot \quad \Leftrightarrow \quad p \wedge \neg p$$
$$\top \quad \Leftrightarrow \quad \neg(p \wedge \neg p)$$
$$p \vee q \quad \Leftrightarrow \quad \neg(\neg p \wedge \neg q)$$

[†] These were given quite explicitly by John Duns the Scot (1266-1308) in his *Universam Logicam Quaestiones*. However, De Morgan was the first to put them in algebraic form.

$$p \Rightarrow q \iff \neg(p \wedge \neg q)$$
$$p \iff q \iff \neg(p \wedge \neg q) \wedge \neg(\neg p \wedge q)$$

Similarly the following equivalences, which we check in OCaml, show that $\{\Rightarrow, \bot\}$ is also adequate:

```
forall tautology
 [<<true <=> false ==> false>>;
  <<~p <=> p ==> false>>;
  <<p /\ q <=> (p ==> q ==> false) ==> false>>;
  <<p \/ q <=> (p ==> false) ==> q>>;
  <<(p <=> q) <=> ((p ==> q) ==> (q ==> p) ==> false) ==> false>>];;
- : bool = true
```

Is any single connective alone enough to express all the others? For the connectives we have introduced, the answer is no. We need one of the binary connectives, otherwise we could never introduce formulas that involve, and hence depend on the valuation of, more than one variable. And in fact not even the whole set $\{\top, \wedge, \vee, \Rightarrow, \iff\}$, without negation or falsity, forms an adequate set, so a fortiori, neither does any one binary connective individually. To see this, note that all these binary connectives with entirely 'true' arguments yield the result 'true'. (In other words, the last row of each of their truth tables contains 'true' in the final column.) Hence any formula built up from these components must evaluate to 'true' in the valuation that maps all atoms to 'true', so negation is not representable.

However, there are $2^{2^2} = 16$ possible truth-tables for a binary truth-function (there are $2^2 = 4$ rows in the truth table and each can be given one of two truth-values) and the conventional binary connectives only cover four of them. Perhaps a connective with one of the other 12 functions for its truth-table would be adequate? As argued above, any single adequate connective must have 'false' in the last row of its truth table, so that it can express negation. By a similar argument, we can also see that the first row of its truth-table must be 'true'. This only leaves us freedom of choice for the middle two rows, for which there are four choices. Two of them are trivial in that they are just the negation of one of the arguments, and hence cannot be used to build expressions whose evaluation depends on the value of more than a single atom. However, either of the other two is adequate alone: the 'not and' operation p NAND $q = \neg(p \wedge q)$, or the 'not or' operation p NOR $q = \neg(p \vee q)$, both of whose truth tables are written out below:

p	q	p NAND q	p NOR q
false	false	true	true
false	true	true	false
true	false	true	false
true	true	false	false

For example, we can express negation by $\neg p = p$ NAND p and then get $p \wedge q = \neg(p$ NAND $q)$, and we already know that $\{\wedge, \neg\}$ is adequate; NOR works similarly. In fact, once we have an adequate set of connectives, we can find formulas whose semantics corresponds to any of the other 12 truth-functions as well, as will become clear when we discuss disjunctive normal form in Section 2.6.

The adequacy of either one of the connectives NAND and NOR is well-known to electronics designers: corresponding gates are often the basic building blocks of digital circuits (see Section 2.7). Among pure logicians it's customary to denote one or the other of these connectives by $p \mid q$ and refer to '$\mid$' as the 'Sheffer stroke' (Sheffer 1913).[†]

Duality

In Section 1.4 we noted the choice to be made between the 'inclusive' and 'exclusive' readings of 'or'. No doubt a pleasing symmetry between 'and' and 'inclusive or' was a strong motivation for what might seem an arbitrary choice of the inclusive reading. Suppose we have a formula involving only the connectives $\bot$, $\top$, $\wedge$ and $\vee$. By its *dual* we mean the result of systematically exchanging '$\wedge$'s and '$\vee$'s and also '$\top$'s and '$\bot$'s, thus:

```
let rec dual fm =
  match fm with
    False -> True
  | True -> False
  | Atom(p) -> fm
  | Not(p) -> Not(dual p)
  | And(p,q) -> Or(dual p,dual q)
  | Or(p,q) -> And(dual p,dual q)
  | _ -> failwith "Formula involves connectives ==> or <=>";;
```

[†] Nowadays people usually interpret the stroke as NAND, but Sheffer originally used his stroke for NOR, and it was used in a parsimonious presentation of propositional logic by Nicod (1917). The idea had been well known to Peirce 30 years earlier. Schönfinkel (1924) elaborated it into a 'quantifier stroke', where $\phi(x) \mid_x \psi(x)$ means $\neg\exists x.\ \phi(x) \wedge \psi(x)$, and this led on to an interest in performing the same paring-down for more general mathematical expressions, and hence to his development of combinators.

for example:

```
# dual <<p \/ ~p>>;;
- : prop formula = <<p /\ ~p>>
```

A little thought shows that `dual(dual(p)) = p`. The key semantic property of duality is:

Theorem 2.7 `eval (dual p) v` $= not($`eval p` $(not \circ v))$ *for any valuation* v.

Proof This can be proved by a formal structural induction on formulas (see Exercise 2.5), but it's perhaps easier to see using more direct reasoning based on the De Morgan laws. Let p^* be the result of negating all the atoms in a formula and replacing $\bot$ by $\neg\top$, $\top$ by $\neg\bot$. We then have `eval p` $(not \circ v) =$ `eval` p^* v. Now using the De Morgan laws we can repeatedly pull the newly introduced negations up from the atoms in p^* giving a logically equivalent form:

$$\neg p \wedge \neg q \;\;\Leftrightarrow\;\; \neg(p \vee q)$$
$$\neg p \vee \neg q \;\;\Leftrightarrow\;\; \neg(p \wedge q).$$

By doing so, we exchange '$\wedge$'s and '$\vee$'s, and bubble the newly introduced negation signs upwards, until we just have one additional negation sign at the top, resulting in exactly $\neg($`dual` $p)$. The result follows. $\square$

Corollary 2.8 *If p and q are logically equivalent, so are* `dual` p *and* `dual` q. *If p is a tautology then so is* $\neg($`dual` $p)$.

Proof `eval (dual p) v` $= not($`eval p` $(not \circ v)) = not($`eval q` $(not \circ v)) =$ `eval (dual q) v`. If p is a tautology, then p and $\top$ are logically equivalent, so `dual` p and `dual` $\top = \bot$ are logically equivalent and the result follows. $\square$

For example, since $p \wedge (q \vee r)$ and $(p \wedge q) \vee (p \wedge r)$ are equivalent, so are $p \vee (q \wedge r)$ and $(p \vee q) \wedge (p \vee r)$, and since $p \vee \neg p$ is a tautology, so is $\neg(p \wedge \neg p)$.

2.5 Simplification and negation normal form

In ordinary algebra it's common to systematically transform an expression into an equivalent standard or *normal* form. One approach involves expanding and cancelling, e.g. obtaining from $(x+y)(y-x)+y+x^2$ the normal form $y^2 + y$. By putting expressions in normal form, we can sometimes see that superficially different expressions are equivalent. Moreover, if the normal form is chosen appropriately, it can yield valuable information. For example, looking at $y^2 + y$ we can see that the value of x is irrelevant, whereas this isn't at all obvious from the initial form. In logic, normal forms for formulas are of great importance, and just as in algebra the normal form can often yield important information.

Before proceeding to create the normal forms proper, it's convenient to apply routine simplifications to the formula to eliminate the basic propositional constants '$\bot$' and '$\top$', precisely by analogy with the algebraic example in Section 1.6. Whenever '$\bot$' and '$\top$' occur in combination, there is always a tautology justifying the equivalence with a simpler formula, e.g. $\bot \wedge p \Leftrightarrow \bot$, $\bot \vee p \Leftrightarrow p$, $p \Rightarrow \bot \Leftrightarrow \neg p$. For good measure, we also eliminate double negation $\neg\neg p$. The code just uses pattern-matching to consider the possibilities case-by-case:[†]

```
let psimplify1 fm =
  match fm with
    Not False -> True
  | Not True -> False
  | Not(Not p) -> p
  | And(p,False) | And(False,p) -> False
  | And(p,True) | And(True,p) -> p
  | Or(p,False) | Or(False,p) -> p
  | Or(p,True) | Or(True,p) -> True
  | Imp(False,p) | Imp(p,True) -> True
  | Imp(True,p) -> p
  | Imp(p,False) -> Not p
  | Iff(p,True) | Iff(True,p) -> p
  | Iff(p,False) | Iff(False,p) -> Not p
  | _ -> fm;;
```

and we then apply the simplification in a recursive bottom-up sweep:

```
let rec psimplify fm =
  match fm with
  | Not p -> psimplify1 (Not(psimplify p))
  | And(p,q) -> psimplify1 (And(psimplify p,psimplify q))
  | Or(p,q) -> psimplify1 (Or(psimplify p,psimplify q))
  | Imp(p,q) -> psimplify1 (Imp(psimplify p,psimplify q))
  | Iff(p,q) -> psimplify1 (Iff(psimplify p,psimplify q))
  | _ -> fm;;
```

For example:

```
# psimplify <<(true ==> (x <=> false)) ==> ~(y \/ false /\ z)>>;;
- : prop formula = <<~x ==> ~y>>
```

[†] Note that the clauses resulting in $\neg p$ given $p \Rightarrow \bot$, $p \Leftrightarrow \bot$ and $\bot \Leftrightarrow p$ are placed at the end of their group so that, for example, $\bot \Rightarrow \bot$ gets simplified to $\top$ rather than $\neg\bot$, which would then need further simplification at the same level.

If we start by applying this simplification function, we can almost ignore the propositional constants, which makes things more convenient. However, we need to remember two trivial exceptions: though in the simplified formula '⊥' and '⊤', cannot occur in combination, the entire formula may simply be one of them, e.g.:

```
# psimplify <<((x ==> y) ==> true) \/ ~false>>;;
- : prop formula = <<true>>
```

A *literal* is either an atomic formula or the negation of one. We say that a literal is *negative* if it is of the form $\neg p$ and *positive* otherwise. This is tested by the following OCaml functions, both of which assume they are indeed applied to a literal:

```
let negative = function (Not p) -> true | _ -> false;;

let positive lit = not(negative lit);;
```

When we speak later of *negating* a literal l, written $-l$, we mean applying negation if the literal is positive, and *removing* a negation if it is negative (not double-negating it, since then it would no longer be a literal). Two literals are said to be *complementary* if one is the negation of the other:

```
let negate = function (Not p) -> p | p -> Not p;;
```

A formula is in *negation normal form* (NNF) if it is constructed from literals using only the binary connectives '∧' and '∨', or else is one of the degenerate cases '⊥' or '⊤'. In other words it does not involve the other binary connectives '⇒' and '⇔', and '¬' is applied only to atomic formulas. Examples of formulas in NNF include $\bot$, p, $p \wedge \neg q$ and $p \vee (q \wedge (\neg r) \vee s)$, while formulas not in NNF include $p \Rightarrow p$ (involves other binary connectives) as well as $\neg \neg p$ and $p \wedge \neg(q \vee r)$ (involve negation of non-atomic formulas).

We can transform any formula into a logically equivalent NNF one. As in the last section, we can eliminate '⇒' and '⇔' in favour of the other connectives, and then we can repeatedly apply the De Morgan laws and the law of double negation:

$$\neg(p \wedge q) \quad \Leftrightarrow \quad \neg p \vee \neg q$$
$$\neg(p \vee q) \quad \Leftrightarrow \quad \neg p \wedge \neg q$$
$$\neg \neg p \quad \Leftrightarrow \quad p$$

to push the negations down to the atomic formulas, exactly the reverse of the transformation considered in the proof of Theorem 2.7. (The present transformation is analogous to the following procedure in ordinary algebra: replace subtraction by its definition $x - y = x + -y$ and then systematically push negations down using $-(x + y) = -x + -y$, $-(xy) = (-x)y$, $-(-x) = x$.) This is rather straightforward to program in OCaml, and in fact we can eliminate '$\Rightarrow$' and '$\Leftrightarrow$' as we recursively push down negations rather than in a separate phase.

```
let rec nnf fm =
  match fm with
  | And(p,q) -> And(nnf p,nnf q)
  | Or(p,q) -> Or(nnf p,nnf q)
  | Imp(p,q) -> Or(nnf(Not p),nnf q)
  | Iff(p,q) -> Or(And(nnf p,nnf q),And(nnf(Not p),nnf(Not q)))
  | Not(Not p) -> nnf p
  | Not(And(p,q)) -> Or(nnf(Not p),nnf(Not q))
  | Not(Or(p,q)) -> And(nnf(Not p),nnf(Not q))
  | Not(Imp(p,q)) -> And(nnf p,nnf(Not q))
  | Not(Iff(p,q)) -> Or(And(nnf p,nnf(Not q)),And(nnf(Not p),nnf q))
  | _ -> fm;;
```

The elimination by this code of '$\Rightarrow$' and '$\Leftrightarrow$', unnegated and negated respectively, is justified by the following tautologies:

$$
\begin{aligned}
p \Rightarrow q &\Leftrightarrow \neg p \vee q \\
\neg(p \Rightarrow q) &\Leftrightarrow p \wedge \neg q \\
p \Leftrightarrow q &\Leftrightarrow p \wedge q \vee \neg p \wedge \neg q \\
\neg(p \Leftrightarrow q) &\Leftrightarrow p \wedge \neg q \vee \neg p \wedge q.
\end{aligned}
$$

although for some purposes we might have preferred other variants, e.g.

$$
\begin{aligned}
p \Leftrightarrow q &\Leftrightarrow (p \vee \neg q) \wedge (\neg p \vee q) \\
\neg(p \Leftrightarrow q) &\Leftrightarrow (p \vee q) \wedge (\neg p \vee \neg q).
\end{aligned}
$$

To finish, we redefine nnf to include initial simplification, then call the main function just defined. (This is *not* a recursive definition, but rather a redefinition of nnf using the former one, since there is no rec keyword.)

```
let nnf fm = nnf(psimplify fm);;
```

Let's try this function on an example, and confirm that the resulting formula is logically equivalent to the original.

```
# let fm = <<(p <=> q) <=> ~(r ==> s)>>;;
val fm : prop formula = <<(p <=> q) <=> ~(r ==> s)>>
# let fm' = nnf fm;;
val fm' : prop formula =
  <<(p /\ q \/ ~p /\ ~q) /\ r /\ ~s \/
    (p /\ ~q \/ ~p /\ q) /\ (~r \/ s)>>
# tautology(Iff(fm,fm'));;
- : bool = true
```

The NNF formula is significantly larger than the original. Indeed, because each time a formula '$p \Leftrightarrow q$' is expanded the formulas p and q both get duplicated, in the worst case a formula with n connectives can expand to an NNF with more than 2^n connectives — see Exercise 2.6 below. This sort of exponential blowup seems unavoidable while preserving logical equivalence, but we can at least avoid doing an exponential amount of *computation* by rewriting the **nnf** function in a more efficient way (Exercise 2.7). If the objective were simply to push negations down to the level of atoms, we could keep '$\Leftrightarrow$' and avoid the potentially exponential blowup, using a tautology such as $\neg(p \Leftrightarrow q) \Leftrightarrow (\neg p \Leftrightarrow q)$:

```
let rec nenf fm =
  match fm with
    Not(Not p) -> nenf p
  | Not(And(p,q)) -> Or(nenf(Not p),nenf(Not q))
  | Not(Or(p,q)) -> And(nenf(Not p),nenf(Not q))
  | Not(Imp(p,q)) -> And(nenf p,nenf(Not q))
  | Not(Iff(p,q)) -> Iff(nenf p,nenf(Not q))
  | And(p,q) -> And(nenf p,nenf q)
  | Or(p,q) -> Or(nenf p,nenf q)
  | Imp(p,q) -> Or(nenf(Not p),nenf q)
  | Iff(p,q) -> Iff(nenf p,nenf q)
  | _ -> fm;;
```

with simplification once again rolled in:

```
let nenf fm = nenf(psimplify fm);;
```

This function will have its uses. However, the special appeal of NNF is that we can distinguish 'positive' and 'negative' occurrences of the atomic formulas. The connectives '$\wedge$' and '$\vee$', unlike '$\neg$', '$\Rightarrow$' and '$\Leftrightarrow$', are *monotonic*, meaning that their truth-functions f have the property $p \leq p' \wedge q \leq q' \Rightarrow f(p,q) \leq f(p',q')$, where '$\leq$' is the truth-function for implication. Another way of putting this is that the following are tautologies:

```
# tautology <<(p ==> p') /\ (q ==> q') ==> (p /\ q ==> p' /\ q')>>;;
- : bool = true
# tautology <<(p ==> p') /\ (q ==> q') ==> (p \/ q ==> p' \/ q')>>;;
- : bool = true
```

Consequently, if an atom x in a NNF formula p occurs only unnegated, we can deduce a corresponding monotonicity property for the whole formula:

$$(x \Rightarrow x') \Rightarrow (p \Rightarrow \texttt{psubst}\ (x \mapsto x')\ p),$$

while if it occurs only negated, we have an anti-monotonicity, since $(p \Rightarrow p') \Rightarrow (\neg p' \Rightarrow \neg p)$ is a tautology:

$$(x \Rightarrow x') \Rightarrow (\texttt{psubst}\ (x \mapsto x')\ p \Rightarrow p).$$

2.6 Disjunctive and conjunctive normal forms

A formula is said to be in *disjunctive normal form* (DNF) when it is of the form:

$$D_1 \vee D_2 \vee \cdots \vee D_n$$

with each disjunct D_i of the form:

$$l_{i1} \wedge l_{i2} \wedge \cdots \wedge l_{im_i}$$

and each l_{ij} a literal. Thus a formula in DNF is also in NNF but has the additional restriction that it is a 'disjunction of conjunctions' rather than having '∧' and '∨' intermixed arbitrarily. It is exactly analogous to a fully expanded 'sum of products' expression like $x^3 + x^2 y + xy + z$ in algebra.

Dually, a formula is said to be in *conjunctive normal form* (CNF) when it is of the form:

$$C_1 \wedge C_2 \wedge \cdots \wedge C_n$$

with each conjunct C_i in turn of the form:

$$l_{i1} \vee l_{i2} \vee \cdots \vee l_{im_i}$$

and each l_{ij} a literal. Thus a formula in CNF is also in NNF but has the additional restriction that it is a 'conjunction of disjunctions'. It is exactly analogous to a fully factorized 'product of sums' form in ordinary algebra like $(x + 1)(y + 2)(z + 3)$. In ordinary algebra we can always expand into a sum of products equivalent, but not in general a product of sums (consider $x^2 + y^2 - 1$ for example). This asymmetry does not exist in logic, as one might expect from the duality of ∧ and ∨. We will first show how to transform a formula into a DNF equivalent, and then it will be easy to adapt it to produce a CNF equivalent.

DNF via truth tables

If a formula involves the atoms $\{p_1, \ldots, p_n\}$, each row of the truth table identifies a particular assignment of truth-values to $\{p_1, \ldots, p_n\}$, and thus a class of valuations that make the same assignments to that set (we don't care how they assign other atoms). Now given any valuation v, consider the formula:

$$l_1 \wedge \cdots \wedge l_n$$

where

$$l_i = \begin{cases} p_i & \text{if } v(p_i) = \text{true} \\ \neg p_i & \text{if } v(p_i) = \text{false}. \end{cases}$$

By construction, a valuation w satisfies $l_1 \wedge \cdots \wedge l_n$ if and only if v and w agree on all the $p_1, \ldots, p_n$. Now, the rows of the truth table for the original formula having 'true' in the last column identify precisely those classes of valuations that satisfy the formula. Accordingly, for each of the k 'true' rows, we can select a corresponding valuation v_i (for definiteness, we can map all variables except $\{p_1, \ldots, p_n\}$ to 'false'), and construct the formula as above:

$$D_i = l_{i1} \wedge \cdots \wedge l_{in}.$$

Now the disjunction $D_1 \vee \cdots \vee D_k$ is satisfied by exactly the same valuations as the original formula, and therefore is logically equivalent to it; moreover, by the way it was constructed, it must be in DNF.

To implement this procedure in OCaml, we start with functions `list_conj` and `list_disj` to map a list of formulas $[p_1; \ldots; p_n]$ into, respectively, an iterated conjunction $p_1 \wedge \cdots \wedge p_n$ and an iterated disjunction $p_1 \vee \cdots \vee p_n$. In the special case where the list is empty we return $\top$ and $\bot$ respectively. These choices avoid some special case distinctions later, and in any case are natural if one thinks of the formulas as saying 'all of the $p_1, \ldots, p_n$ are true' (which is vacuously true if there aren't any p_i) and 'some of the $p_1, \ldots, p_n$ are true' (which must be false if there aren't any p_i).

```
let list_conj l = if l = [] then True else end_itlist mk_and l;;

let list_disj l = if l = [] then False else end_itlist mk_or l;;
```

Next we have a function `mk_lits`, which, given a list of formulas `pvs`, makes a conjunction of these formulas and their negations according to whether each is satisfied by the valuation `v`.

```
let mk_lits pvs v =
  list_conj (map (fun p -> if eval p v then p else Not p) pvs);;
```

We now define `allsatvaluations`, a close analogue of `onallvaluations` that now collects the valuations for which `subfn` holds into a list:

```
let rec allsatvaluations subfn v pvs =
  match pvs with
    [] -> if subfn v then [v] else []
  | p::ps -> let v' t q = if q = p then t else v(q) in
             allsatvaluations subfn (v' false) ps @
             allsatvaluations subfn (v' true) ps;;
```

Using this, we select the list of valuations satisfying the formula, map `mk_lits` over it and collect the results into an iterated disjunction. Note that in the degenerate cases when the formula contains no variables or is unsatisfiable, the procedure returns $\bot$ or $\top$ as appropriate.

```
let dnf fm =
  let pvs = atoms fm in
  let satvals = allsatvaluations (eval fm) (fun s -> false) pvs in
  list_disj (map (mk_lits (map (fun p -> Atom p) pvs)) satvals);;
```

For example:

```
# let fm = <<(p \/ q /\ r) /\ (~p \/ ~r)>>;;
val fm : prop formula = <<(p \/ q /\ r) /\ (~p \/ ~r)>>
# dnf fm;;
- : prop formula = <<~p /\ q /\ r \/ p /\ ~q /\ ~r \/ p /\ q /\ ~r>>
```

As expected, the disjuncts of the formula naturally correspond to the three classes of valuations yielding the 'true' rows of the truth table:

```
# print_truthtable fm;;
p     q     r     | formula
---------------------------
false false false | false
false false true  | false
false true  false | false
false true  true  | true
true  false false | true
true  false true  | false
true  true  false | true
true  true  true  | false
---------------------------
```

This approach requires no initial simplification or pre-normalization, and emphasizes the relationship between DNF and truth tables. We can now confirm the claim made in Section 2.4: given any n-ary truth function, we can consider it as a truth table with n atoms and 2^n rows, and directly construct a formula (in DNF) that has that truth-function as its interpretation. On the other hand, the fact that we need to consider all 2^n valuations is rather unattractive when n, the number of atoms in the original formula, is large. For example, the following formula, that is already in a nice simple DNF, gets blown up into a much more complicated variant:

```
# dnf <<p /\ q /\ r /\ s /\ t /\ u \/ u /\ v>>;;
...
```

DNF via transformation

An alternative approach to creating a DNF equivalent is by analogy with ordinary algebra. There, in order to arrive at a fully-expanded form, we can just repeatedly apply the distributive laws $x(y + z) = xy + xz$ and $(x + y)z = xz + yz$. Similarly, starting with a propositional formula in NNF, we can put it into DNF by repeatedly rewriting it based on the tautologies:

$$p \wedge (q \vee r) \quad \Leftrightarrow \quad p \wedge q \vee p \wedge r$$
$$(p \vee q) \wedge r \quad \Leftrightarrow \quad p \wedge r \vee q \wedge r.$$

To encode this as an efficient OCaml function that doesn't run over the formula tree too many times requires a little care. We start with a function to repeatedly apply the distributive laws, assuming that the immediate subformulas are already in DNF:

```
let rec distrib fm =
  match fm with
    And(p,(Or(q,r))) -> Or(distrib(And(p,q)),distrib(And(p,r)))
  | And(Or(p,q),r) -> Or(distrib(And(p,r)),distrib(And(q,r)))
  | _ -> fm;;
```

Now, when the input formula is a conjunction or disjunction, we first recursively transform the immediate subformulas into DNF, then if necessary 'distribute' using the previous function:

```
let rec rawdnf fm =
  match fm with
    And(p,q) -> distrib(And(rawdnf p,rawdnf q))
  | Or(p,q) -> Or(rawdnf p,rawdnf q)
  | _ -> fm;;
```

For example:

```
# rawdnf <<(p \/ q /\ r) /\ (~p \/ ~r)>>;;
- : prop formula =
<<(p /\ ~p \/ (q /\ r) /\ ~p) \/ p /\ ~r \/ (q /\ r) /\ ~r>>
```

Although this is in DNF, it's quite hard to read because of the mixed associations in iterated conjunctions and disjunctions. Moreover, some disjuncts are completely redundant: both $p \wedge \neg p$ and $(q \wedge r) \wedge \neg r$ are logically equivalent to $\bot$, and so could be omitted without destroying logical equivalence.

Set-based representation

To render the association question moot, and make simplification easier using standard list operations, it's convenient to represent the DNF formula as a set of sets of literals, e.g. rather than $p \wedge q \vee \neg p \wedge r$ using $\{\{p, q\}, \{\neg p, r\}\}$. Since the logical structure is always a disjunction of conjunctions, and (the semantics of) both disjunction and conjunction are associative, commutative and idempotent, nothing essential is lost in such a translation, and it's easy to map back to a formula. We can now write the DNF function like this, using OCaml lists for sets but taking care to avoid duplicates in the way they are constructed:

```
let distrib s1 s2 = setify(allpairs union s1 s2);;

let rec purednf fm =
  match fm with
    And(p,q) -> distrib (purednf p) (purednf q)
  | Or(p,q) -> union (purednf p) (purednf q)
  | _ -> [[fm]];;
```

The essential structure is the same; this time `distrib` simply takes two sets of sets and returns the union of all possible pairs of sets taken from them. If we apply it to the same example, we get the same result, modulo the new representation:

```
# purednf <<(p \/ q /\ r) /\ (~p \/ ~r)>>;;
- : prop formula list list =
[[<<p>>; <<~p>>]; [<<p>>; <<~r>>]; [<<q>>; <<r>>; <<~p>>];
 [<<q>>; <<r>>; <<~r>>]]
```

But thanks to the list representation, it's now rather easy to simplify the resulting formula. First we define a function `trivial` to check if there are *complementary* literals of the form p and $\neg p$ in the same list. We do this by partitioning the literals into positive and negative ones, and then seeing if the set of positive ones has any common members with the negations of the negated ones:

```
let trivial lits =
  let pos,neg = partition positive lits in
  intersect pos (image negate neg) <> [];;
```

We can now filter to leave only noncontradictory disjuncts, e.g.

```
# filter (non trivial) (purednf <<(p \/ q /\ r) /\ (~p \/ ~r)>>);;
- : prop formula list list = [[<<p>>; <<~r>>]; [<<q>>; <<r>>; <<~p>>]]
```

This already gives a smaller DNF. Another refinement worth applying in many situations is based on *subsumption*. Note that if $\{l'_1, \ldots, l'_m\} \subseteq \{l_1, \ldots, l_n\}$ every valuation satisfying $D = l_1 \wedge \cdots \wedge l_n$ also satisfies $D' = l'_1 \wedge \cdots \wedge l'_m$. Therefore the disjunction $D \vee D'$ is logically equivalent to just D'. In such a case we say that D' *subsumes* D, or that D is *subsumed by* D'. Here is our overall function to produce a set-of-sets DNF equivalent for a formula already in NNF, obtaining the initial unsimplified DNF then filtering out contradictory and subsumed disjuncts:

```
let simpdnf fm =
  if fm = False then [] else if fm = True then [[]] else
  let djs = filter (non trivial) (purednf(nnf fm)) in
  filter (fun d -> not(exists (fun d' -> psubset d' d) djs)) djs;;
```

Note that we deal specially with '⊥' and '⊤', returning the empty list and the singleton list with an empty conjunction respectively. Moreover, in the main code, stripping out the contradictory disjuncts may also result in the empty list. If indeed all disjuncts are contradictory, the formula must be logically equivalent to '⊥', and that is consistent with the stated interpretation of the empty list as implemented by the `list_disj` function we defined earlier. To turn everything back into a formula we just do:

```
let dnf fm = list_disj(map list_conj (simpdnf fm));;
```

We can check that we have indeed, despite the rather complicated construction, returned a logical equivalent:

```
# let fm = <<(p \/ q /\ r) /\ (~p \/ ~r)>>;;
val fm : prop formula = <<(p \/ q /\ r) /\ (~p \/ ~r)>>
# dnf fm;;
- : prop formula = <<p /\ ~r \/ q /\ r /\ ~p>>
# tautology(Iff(fm,dnf fm));;
- : bool = true
```

Note that a DNF formula is satisfiable precisely if one of the disjuncts is, just by the semantics of disjunction. In turn, any of these disjuncts, itself a conjunction of literals, is satisfiable precisely when it does not contain two complementary literals (and when it does not, we can find a satisfying valuation as when finding DNFs using truth-tables). Thus, having transformed a formula into a DNF equivalent we can recognize quickly and efficiently whether it is satisfiable. (Indeed, our latest DNF function eliminated any such contradictory disjuncts, so a formula is satisfiable iff the *simplified* DNF contains any disjuncts at all.) This approach is not necessarily superior to truth-tables, however, since the DNF equivalent can be exponentially large.

CNF

For CNF, we will similarly use a list-based representation, but this time the implicit interpretation will be as a conjunction of disjunctions. Note that by the De Morgan laws, if:

$$\neg p \Leftrightarrow \bigvee_{i=1}^{m} \bigwedge_{j=1}^{n} p_{ij}$$

then

$$p \Leftrightarrow \bigwedge_{i=1}^{m} \bigvee_{j=1}^{n} -p_{ij}.$$

In list terms, therefore, we can produce a CNF equivalent by negating the starting formula (putting it back in NNF), producing its DNF and negating all the literals in that:[†]

```
let purecnf fm = image (image negate) (purednf(nnf(Not fm)));;
```

In terms of formal list manipulations, the code for eliminating superfluous and subsumed conjuncts is the same, even though the interpretation is different. For example, trivial conjuncts now represent disjunctions containing some literal and its negation and are hence equivalent to $\top$; since $\top \wedge C \Leftrightarrow C$ we are equally justified in leaving them out of the final conjunction. Only the two degenerate cases need to be treated differently:

[†] Recall that the nnf function expands $p \Leftrightarrow q$ into $p \wedge q \vee \neg p \wedge \neg q$. This is not so well suited to CNF since the expanded formula will suffer a further expansion that may complicate the resulting expression unless the intermediate result is simplified. However, applying nnf to the negation of the formula, as here, not only saves code but makes this expansion appropriate since the roles of '$\wedge$' and '$\vee$' will subsequently change.

```
let simpcnf fm =
  if fm = False then [[]] else if fm = True then [] else
  let cjs = filter (non trivial) (purecnf fm) in
  filter (fun c -> not(exists (fun c' -> psubset c' c) cjs)) cjs;;
```

We now just need to map back to the correct interpretation as a formula:

```
let cnf fm = list_conj(map list_disj (simpcnf fm));;
```

for example:

```
# let fm = <<(p \/ q /\ r) /\ (~p \/ ~r)>>;;
val fm : prop formula = <<(p \/ q /\ r) /\ (~p \/ ~r)>>
# cnf fm;;
- : prop formula = <<(p \/ q) /\ (p \/ r) /\ (~p \/ ~r)>>
# tautology(Iff(fm,cnf fm));;
- : bool = true
```

Just as we can quickly test a DNF formula for satisfiability, we can quickly test a CNF formula for validity. Indeed, a conjunction $C_1 \wedge \cdots \wedge C_n$ is valid precisely if each C_i is valid. And since each C_i is a disjunction of literals, it is valid precisely if it contains the disjunction of a literal and its negation; if not, we could produce a valuation not satisfying it. Once again, using our simplifying CNF, things are even easier: a formula is valid precisely if its simplified CNF is just $\top$. And once again, this is not necessarily a good practical algorithm because of the possible exponential blowup when converting to CNF.

2.7 Applications of propositional logic

We have completed the basic study of propositional logic, identifying the main concepts to be used later and mechanizing various operations including the recognition of tautologies. From a certain point of view, we are finished. But these methods for identifying tautologies are impractical for many more complex formulas, and in subsequent sections we will present more efficient algorithms. It's quite hard to test such algorithms, or even justify their necessity, without a stock of non-trivial propositional formulas. There are various propositional problems available in collections such as Pelletier (1986), but we will develop some ways of generating whole classes of interesting propositional problems from concise descriptions.

Ramsey's theorem

We start by considering some special cases of Ramsey's combinatorial theorem (Ramsey 1930; Graham, Rothschild and Spencer 1980).[†] A simple
Ramsey-type result is that in any party of six people, there must either be a
group of three people *all* of whom know each other, or a group of three people
none of whom know each other. It's customary to think of such problems in
terms of a *graph*, i.e. a collection V of *vertices* with certain pairs connected
by *edges* taken from a set E. A generalization of the 'party of six' result,
still much less general than Ramsey's theorem, is:

Theorem 2.9 *For each $s, t \in \mathbb{N}$ there is some $n \in \mathbb{N}$ such that any graph
with n vertices either has a completely connected subgraph of size s or a
completely disconnected subgraph of size t. Moreover if the 'Ramsey number'
$R(s, t)$ denotes the minimal such n for a given s and t we have:*

$$R(s, t) \leq R(s - 1, t) + R(s, t - 1).$$

Proof By complete induction on $s + t$. We can assume by the inductive
hypothesis that the result holds for any s' and t' with $s' + t' < s + t$, and we
need to prove it for s and t.

Consider any graph of size $n = R(s - 1, t) + R(s, t - 1)$. Pick an arbitrary
vertex v. Either there are at least $R(s - 1, t)$ vertices connected to v, or there
are at least $R(s, t - 1)$ vertices *not* connected to v, for otherwise the total size
of the graph would be at most $(R(s - 1, t) - 1) + (R(s, t - 1) - 1) + 1 = n - 1$,
contrary to hypothesis. Suppose the former, the argument being symmetrical
in the latter case.

Consider the subgraph based on set of a vertices attached to v, which
has size at least $R(s - 1, t)$. By the inductive hypotheses, this either has a
completely connected subgraph of size $s - 1$ or a completely disconnected
subgraph of size t. If the former, including v gives a completely connected
subgraph of the main graph of size s, so we are finished. If the latter, then
we already have a disconnected subgraph of size t as required. Consequently
any graph of size n has a completely connected subgraph of size s or a
completely disconnected subgraph of size t, so $R(s, t) \leq n$.   □

For any specific positive integers s, t and n, we can formulate a propositional formula that is a tautology precisely if $R(s, t) \leq n$. We index the
vertices using integers 1 to n, calculate all s-element and t-element subsets,

---

[†] See Section 5.5 for the logical problem Ramsey was attacking when he introduced his theorem.
Another connection with logic is that the first 'natural' statement independent of first-order
Peano Arithmetic (Paris and Harrington 1991) is essentially a numerical encoding of a Ramsey-
type result.

and then for each of these s or t-element subsets in turn, all possible 2-element subsets of them. We want to express the fact that for one of the s-element sets, each pair of elements is connected, or for one of the t-element sets, each pair of elements is disconnected. The local definition `e[m;n]` produces an atomic formula `p_m_n` that we think of as 'm is connected to n' (or 'm knows n', etc.):

```
let ramsey s t n =
  let vertices = 1 -- n in
  let yesgrps = map (allsets 2) (allsets s vertices)
  and nogrps = map (allsets 2) (allsets t vertices) in
  let e[m;n] = Atom(P("p_"^(string_of_int m)^"_"^(string_of_int n))) in
  Or(list_disj (map (list_conj ** map e) yesgrps),
     list_disj (map (list_conj ** map (fun p -> Not(e p))) nogrps));;
```

For example:

```
# ramsey 3 3 4;;
- : prop formula =
<<(p_1_2 /\ p_1_3 /\ p_2_3 \/
   p_1_2 /\ p_1_4 /\ p_2_4 \/
   p_1_3 /\ p_1_4 /\ p_3_4 \/ p_2_3 /\ p_2_4 /\ p_3_4) \/
   ~p_1_2 /\ ~p_1_3 /\ ~p_2_3 \/
   ~p_1_2 /\ ~p_1_4 /\ ~p_2_4 \/
   ~p_1_3 /\ ~p_1_4 /\ ~p_3_4 \/ ~p_2_3 /\ ~p_2_4 /\ ~p_3_4>>
```

We can confirm that the number 6 in the initial party example is the best possible, i.e. that $R(3,3) = 6$:

```
# tautology(ramsey 3 3 5);;
- : bool = false
# tautology(ramsey 3 3 6);;
- : bool = true
```

However, the latter example already takes an appreciable time, and even slightly larger input parameters can create propositional problems way beyond those that can be solved in a reasonable time by the methods we've described so far. In fact, relatively few Ramsey numbers are known exactly, with even $R(5,5)$ only known to lie between 43 and 49 at time of writing.

Digital circuits

Digital computers operate with electrical signals that may only occupy one of a finite number of voltage levels. (By contrast, in an *analogue* computer, levels can vary continuously.) Almost all modern computers are binary, i.e. use just two levels, conventionally called 0 ('low') and 1 ('high'). At any particular time, we can regard each internal or external wire in a binary digital computer as having a Boolean value, 'false' for 0 and 'true' for 1, and think of each circuit element as a Boolean function, operating on the values on its input wire(s) to produce a value at its output wire. (Of course, in taking such a view we are abstracting away many important physical aspects, but our interest here is only in the logical structure.)

The key building-blocks of digital circuits, *logic gates*, correspond closely to the usual logical connectives. For example an 'AND gate' is a circuit element corresponding to the 'and' ($\wedge$) connective: it has two inputs and one output, and the output wire is high (true) precisely if both the input wires are high. Similarly a 'NOT gate', or *inverter*, has one input wire and one output wire, and the output is high when the input is low and low when the input is high, thus corresponding to the 'not' connective ($\neg$). So there is a close correspondence between digital circuits and formulas, which can be crudely summarized as follows:

Digital design	Propositional logic
circuit	formula
logic gate	propositional connective
input wire	atom
internal wire	subexpression
voltage level	truth value

For example, the following logic circuit corresponds to the propositional formula $\neg s \wedge x \vee s \wedge y$. A compound circuit element with this behaviour is known as a *multiplexer*, since the output is either the input x or y, selected by whether s is low or high respectively.[†]

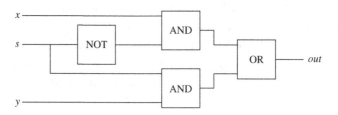

One notable difference is that in the circuit we duplicate the input s simply by splitting the wire into two, whereas in the expression, we need to write s twice. This becomes more significant for a large subexpression: in

---

[†] We draw gates simply as boxes with a word inside indicating their kinds. Circuit designers often use special symbols for gates.

the formula we may need to write it several times, whereas in the circuit we can simply run multiple wires from the corresponding circuit element. In Section 2.8 we will develop an analogous technique for formulas.

Addition

Given their two-level circuits, it's natural that the primary representation of numbers in computers is the binary positional representation, rather than decimal or some other scheme. A binary digit or *bit* can be represented by the value on a single wire. Larger numbers with n binary digits can be represented by an ordered sequence of n bits, and implemented as an array of n wires. (Special names are used for arrays of a particular size, e.g. *bytes* or *octets* for sequences of eight bits.) The usual algorithms for arithmetic on many-digit numbers that we learn in school can be straightforwardly modified for the binary notation; in fact they often become simpler.

Suppose we want to add two binary numbers, each represented by a group of n bits. This means that each number is in the range $0 \ldots 2^n - 1$, and so the sum will be in the range $0 \ldots 2^{n+1} - 2$, possibly requiring $n + 1$ bits for its storage. We simply add the digits from right to left, as in decimal. When the sum in one position is ≥ 2, we reduce it by 2 and generate a 'carry' of 1 into the next bit position. Here is an example, corresponding to the decimal $179 + 101 = 280$:

$$
\begin{array}{ccccccccccc}
 & & 1 & 0 & 1 & 1 & 0 & 0 & 1 & 1 \\
+ & & 0 & 1 & 1 & 0 & 0 & 1 & 0 & 1 \\
\hline
= & 1 & 0 & 0 & 0 & 1 & 1 & 0 & 0 & 0 \\
\end{array}
$$

In order to implement addition of n-bit numbers as circuits or propositional formulas, the simplest approach is to exploit the regularity of the algorithm, and produce an adder by replicating a 1-bit adder n times, propagating the carry between each adjacent pair of elements. The first task is to produce a 1-bit adder, which isn't very difficult. We can regard the 'sum' (s) and 'carry' (c) produced by adding two digits as separate Boolean functions with the following truth-tables, which we draw using 0 and 1 rather than 'false' and 'true' to emphasize the arithmetical link:

x	y	c	s
0	0	0	0
0	1	0	1
1	0	0	1
1	1	1	0

The truth-table for carry might look familiar: it's just an 'and' operation $x \wedge y$. As for the sum, it is an exclusive version of 'or', which we can represent by $\neg(x \Leftrightarrow y)$ or $x \Leftrightarrow \neg y$ and abbreviate XOR. We can implement functions in OCaml corresponding to these operations as follows:

```
let halfsum x y = Iff(x,Not y);;

let halfcarry x y = And(x,y);;
```

and now we can assert the appropriate relation between the input and output wires of a *half-adder* as follows:

```
let ha x y s c = And(Iff(s,halfsum x y),Iff(c,halfcarry x y));;
```

The use of 'half' emphasizes that this is only part of what we need. Except for the rightmost digit position, we need to add three bits, not just two, because of the incoming carry. A *full-adder* adds three bits, which since the answer is ≤ 3 can still be returned as just one sum and one carry bit. The truth table is:

x	y	z	c	s
0	0	0	0	0
0	0	1	0	1
0	1	0	0	1
0	1	1	1	0
1	0	0	0	1
1	0	1	1	0
1	1	0	1	0
1	1	1	1	1

and one possible implementation as gates is the following:

```
let carry x y z = Or(And(x,y),And(Or(x,y),z));;

let sum x y z = halfsum (halfsum x y) z;;

let fa x y z s c = And(Iff(s,sum x y z),Iff(c,carry x y z));;
```

It is now straightforward to put multiple full-adders together into an n-bit adder, which moreover allows a carry propagation in at the low end and propagates out bit $n + 1$ at the high end. The corresponding OCaml function expects the user to supply functions x, y, out and c that, when given an index, generate an appropriate new variable. The values x and y return variables for the various bits of the inputs, out does the same for the desired output and c is a set of variables to be used internally for carry, and to carry in c(0) and carry out c(n).

```
let conjoin f l = list_conj (map f l);;

let ripplecarry x y c out n =
  conjoin (fun i -> fa (x i) (y i) (c i) (out i) (c(i + 1)))
          (0 -- (n - 1));;
```

For example, using indexed extensions of stylized names for the inputs and generating a 3-bit adder:

```
let mk_index x i = Atom(P(x^"_"^(string_of_int i)))
and mk_index2 x i j =
  Atom(P(x^"_"^(string_of_int i)^"_"^(string_of_int j)));;
val mk_index : string -> int -> prop formula = <fun>
val mk_index2 : string -> int -> int -> prop formula = <fun>
# let [x; y; out; c] = map mk_index ["X"; "Y"; "OUT"; "C"];;
...
```

we get:

```
# ripplecarry x y c out 2;;
- : prop formula =
<<((OUT_0 <=> (X_0 <=> ~Y_0) <=> ~C_0) /\
   (C_1 <=> X_0 /\ Y_0 \/ (X_0 \/ Y_0) /\ C_0)) /\
  (OUT_1 <=> (X_1 <=> ~Y_1) <=> ~C_1) /\
  (C_2 <=> X_1 /\ Y_1 \/ (X_1 \/ Y_1) /\ C_1)>>
```

If we are not interested in a carry in at the low end, we can modify the structure to use only a half-adder in that bit position. A simpler, if crude, alternative, is simply to feed in **False** (i.e. 0) and simplify the resulting formula:

```
let ripplecarry0 x y c out n =
  psimplify
    (ripplecarry x y (fun i -> if i = 0 then False else c i) out n);;
```

The term 'ripple-carry' adder is used because the carry flows through the full-adders from right to left. In practical circuits, there is a *propagation delay* between changes in inputs to a gate and the corresponding change in output. In extreme cases (e.g. $11111\ldots111+1$), the final output bits are only available after the carry has propagated through n stages, taking about $2n$ gate delays. When n is quite large, say 64, this delay can be unacceptable, and a different design needs to be used. For example, in a *carry-select* adder[†] the n-bit inputs are split into several blocks of k, and corresponding k-bit blocks are added *twice*, once assuming a carry-in of 0 and once assuming a carry-in of 1. The correct answer can then be decided by multiplexing using the actual carry-in from the previous stage as the selector. Then the carries only need to be propagated through n/k blocks with a few gate delays in each.[‡] To implement such an adder, we need another element to supplement `ripplecarry0`, this time forcing a carry-in of 1:

```
let ripplecarry1 x y c out n =
  psimplify
    (ripplecarry x y (fun i -> if i = 0 then True else c i) out n);;
```

and we will be selecting between the two alternatives when we do carry propagation using a multiplexer:

```
let mux sel in0 in1 = Or(And(Not sel,in0),And(sel,in1));;
```

Now the overall function can be implemented recursively, using an auxiliary function to offset the indices in an array of bits:

```
let offset n x i = x(n + i);;
```

Suppose we are dealing with bits $0,\ldots,k-1$ of an overall n bits. We separately add the block of k bits assuming 0 and 1 carry-in, giving outputs `c0,s0` and `c1,s1` respectively. The final output and carry-out bits are selected by a multiplexer with selector `c(0)`. The remaining $n-k$ bits can be dealt with by a recursive call, but all the bit-vectors need to be offset by k since we start at 0 each time. The only additional point to note is that n might not be an exact multiple of k, so we actually use k' each time, which is either k or the total number of bits n, whichever is smaller:

[†] This is perhaps the oldest technique for speeding up carry propagation, since it was used in Babbage's design for the Analytical Engine.

[‡] For very large n the process of subdivision into blocks can be continued recursively giving $O(\log(n))$ delay.

```
let rec carryselect x y c0 c1 s0 s1 c s n k =
  let k' = min n k in
  let fm =
    And(And(ripplecarry0 x y c0 s0 k',ripplecarry1 x y c1 s1 k'),
        And(Iff(c k',mux (c 0) (c0 k') (c1 k')),
            conjoin (fun i -> Iff(s i,mux (c 0) (s0 i) (s1 i)))
                    (0 -- (k' - 1)))) in
  if k' < k then fm else
  And(fm,carryselect
              (offset k x) (offset k y) (offset k c0) (offset k c1)
              (offset k s0) (offset k s1) (offset k c) (offset k s)
              (n - k) k);;
```

One of the problems of circuit design is to verify that some efficiency optimization like this has not made any logical change to the function computed. Thus, if the optimization in moving from a ripple-carry to a carry-select structure is sound, the following should always generate tautologies. It states that if the same input vectors x and y are added by the two different methods (using different internal variables) then the all sum outputs and the carry-out bit should be the same in each case.

```
let mk_adder_test n k =
  let [x; y; c; s; c0; s0; c1; s1; c2; s2] = map mk_index
      ["x"; "y"; "c"; "s"; "c0"; "s0"; "c1"; "s1"; "c2"; "s2"] in
  Imp(And(And(carryselect x y c0 c1 s0 s1 c s n k,Not(c 0)),
          ripplecarry0 x y c2 s2 n),
      And(Iff(c n,c2 n),
          conjoin (fun i -> Iff(s i,s2 i)) (0 -- (n - 1))));;
```

This is a useful generator of arbitrarily large tautologies. It also shows how practical questions in computer design can be tackled by propositional methods.

Multiplication

Now that we can add n-bit numbers, we can multiply them using repeated addition. Once again, the traditional algorithm can be applied. Consider multiplying two 4-bit numbers A and B. We will use the notation A_i, B_i for the ith bit of A or B, with the least significant bit (LSB) numbered zero so that bit i is implicitly multiplied by 2^i. Just as we do by hand in decimal arithmetic, we can lay out the numbers as follows with the product terms $A_i B_j$ with the same $i + j$ in the same column, then add them all up:

	P_7	P_6	P_5	P_4	P_3	P_2	P_1	P_0
					A_0B_3	A_0B_2	A_0B_1	A_0B_0
$+$				A_1B_3	A_1B_2	A_1B_1	A_1B_0	
$+$			A_2B_3	A_2B_2	A_2B_1	A_2B_0		
$+$		A_3B_3	A_3B_2	A_3B_1	A_3B_0			
$=$	P_7	P_6	P_5	P_4	P_3	P_2	P_1	P_0

In future we will write X_{ij} for the product term A_iB_j; each such product term can be obtained from the input bits by a single AND gate. The calculation of the overall result can be organized by adding the rows together from the top. Note that by starting at the top, each time we add a row, we get the rightmost bit fixed since there is nothing else to add in that row. In fact, we just need to repeatedly add two n-bit numbers, then at each stage separate the result into the lowest bit and the other n bits (for in general the sum has $n+1$ bits). The operation we iterate is thus:

	U_{n-1}	U_{n-1}	$\cdots$	U_2	U_1	U_0
$+$	V_{n-1}	V_{n-1}	$\cdots$	V_2	V_1	V_0
$=$	W_{n-1}	W_{n-2}	$\cdots$ $\cdots$		W_1	W_0
$+$						Z

The following adaptation of `ripplecarry0` does just that:

```
let rippleshift u v c z w n =
  ripplecarry0 u v (fun i -> if i = n then w(n - 1) else c(i + 1))
               (fun i -> if i = 0 then z else w(i - 1)) n;;
```

Now the multiplier can be implemented by repeating this operation. We assume the input is an n-by-n array of input bits representing the product terms, and use the other array u to hold the intermediate sums and v to hold the carries at each stage. (By 'array', we mean a function of two arguments.)

```
let multiplier x u v out n =
  if n = 1 then And(Iff(out 0,x 0 0),Not(out 1)) else
  psimplify
   (And(Iff(out 0,x 0 0),
        And(rippleshift
               (fun i -> if i = n - 1 then False else x 0 (i + 1))
               (x 1) (v 2) (out 1) (u 2) n,
            if n = 2 then And(Iff(out 2,u 2 0),Iff(out 3,u 2 1)) else
            conjoin (fun k -> rippleshift (u k) (x k) (v(k + 1)) (out k)
                                (if k = n - 1 then fun i -> out(n + i)
                                 else u(k + 1)) n) (2 -- (n - 1)))));;
```

A few special cases need to be checked because the general pattern breaks down for $n \leq 2$. Otherwise, the lowest product term `x 0 0` is fed to the lowest bit of the output, and then `rippleshift` is used repeatedly. The first stage is separated because the topmost bit of one argument is guaranteed to be zero (note the blank space above $A_1 B_3$ in the first diagram). At each stage `k` of the iterated operation, the addition takes a partial sum in `u k`, a new row of input `x k` and the carry within the current row, `v(k + 1)`, and produces one bit of output in `out k` and the rest in the next partial sum `u(k + 1)`, except that in the last stage, when `k = n - 1` is true, it is fed directly to the output.

Primality and factorization

Using these formulas representing arithmetic operations, we can encode some arithmetical assertions as tautology/satisfiability questions. For example, consider the question of whether a specific integer $p > 1$ is prime, i.e. has no factors besides itself and 1. First, we define functions to tell us how many bits are needed for p in binary notation, and to extract the nth bit of a nonnegative integer x:

```
let rec bitlength x = if x = 0 then 0 else 1 + bitlength (x / 2);;

let rec bit n x = if n = 0 then x mod 2 = 1 else bit (n - 1) (x / 2);;
```

We can now produce a formula asserting that the atoms `x(i)` encode the bits of a value `m`, at least modulo 2^n. We simply form a conjunction of these variables or their negations depending on whether the corresponding bits are 1 or 0 respectively:

```
let congruent_to x m n =
  conjoin (fun i -> if bit i m then x i else Not(x i))
          (0 -- (n - 1));;
```

Now, if a number p is composite and requires at most n bits to store, it must have a factorization with both factors at least 2, hence both $\leq p/2$ and so storable in $n - 1$ bits. To assert that p is prime, then, we need to state that for any two $(n - 1)$-element sequences of bits, their product does not correspond to the value p. Note that without further restrictions, the product could take as many as $2n - 2$ bits. While we only need to consider those products less than p, it's easier not to bother with encoding this property in propositional terms. Thus the following function applied to a positive integer `p` should give a tautology precisely if `p` is prime.

```
let prime p =
  let [x; y; out] = map mk_index ["x"; "y"; "out"] in
  let m i j = And(x i,y j)
  and [u; v] = map mk_index2 ["u"; "v"] in
  let n = bitlength p in
  Not(And(multiplier m u v out (n - 1),
      congruent_to out p (max n (2 * n - 2))));;
```

For example:

```
# tautology(prime 7);;
- : bool = true
# tautology(prime 9);;
- : bool = false
# tautology(prime 11);;
- : bool = true
```

The power of propositional logic

This section has given just a taste of how certain problems can be reduced to 'SAT', satisfiability checking of propositional formulas. Cook (1971) famously showed that a wide class of combinatorial problems, including SAT itself, are in a precise sense exactly as difficult as each other. (Roughly, an algorithm for solving any one of them gives rise to an algorithm for solving any of the others with at most a polynomial increase in runtime.) This class of *NP-complete* problems is now known to contain many apparently very difficult problems of great practical interest (Garey and Johnson 1979).

Our `tautology` or `satisfiable` functions can in the worst case take a time exponential in the size of the input formula, since they may need to evaluate the formula on all 2^n valuations of its n atomic propositions. The algorithms we will develop later are much more effective in practice, but nevertheless also have exponential worst-case complexity. A polynomial-time algorithm for SAT or any other NP-complete problem would give rise to a polynomial-time algorithm for *all* NP-complete problems. Since none has been found to date, there is a widespread belief that it is impossible, but at time of writing this has not been proved. This is the famous P=NP problem, perhaps the outstanding open question in discrete mathematics and computer science.[†] Baker, Gill and Solovay (1975) give some reasons why many plausible attacks on the problem are unlikely to work.

Still, the reducibility of many other problems to SAT has positive implications too. Considerable effort has been devoted to algorithms for SAT and

---

[†] A \$1000000 prize is offered by the Clay Institute for settling it either way. See www.claymath. org/millennium/ for more information.

their efficient implementation. It often turns out that a careful reduction of
a problem to SAT followed by the use of one of these tools works better than
all but the finest specialized algorithms.[‡]

2.8 Definitional CNF

We have observed that tautology checking for a formula in CNF is easy, as is
satisfiability checking for a formula in DNF (Section 2.6). Unfortunately, the
simple matter of transforming a formula into a logical equivalent in either
of these normal forms can make it blow up exponentially. This is not simply
a defect of our particular implementation but is unavoidable in principle
(Reckhow 1976).

However, if we require a weaker property than logical equivalence, we
can do much better. We will show how any formula p can be transformed
to a CNF formula p' that is at worst a few times as large as p and is
equisatisfiable, i.e. p' is satisfiable if and only if p is, even though they are
not in general logically equivalent. We can as usual dualize the procedure
to give a DNF formula that is *equivalid* with the original, i.e. is a tautology
iff the original formula is. Neither of these then immediately yields a trivial
tautology or satisfiability test, since the CNF and DNF are the wrong way
round. However, at least they make a useful simplified starting point for
more advanced algorithms.

The basic idea, originally due to Tseitin (1968) and subsequently refined
in many ways (Wilson 1990), is to introduce new atoms as abbreviations or
'definitions' for subformulas, hence the name 'definitional CNF'. The method
is probably best understood by looking at a simple paradigmatic example.
Suppose we want to transform the following formula to CNF:

$$(p \lor (q \land \neg r)) \land s.$$

We introduce a new atom p_1, not used elsewhere in the formula, to abbreviate $q \land \neg r$, conjoining the abbreviated formula with the 'definition' of p_1:

$$(p_1 \Leftrightarrow q \land \neg r) \land$$
$$(p \lor p_1) \land s.$$

[‡] This is *not* the case for primality or factorization as far as we know. There is a polynomial-time
algorithm known for testing primality (Agrawal, Kayal and Saxena 2004), and probabilistic
algorithms are often even faster in practice. However, there is (at the time of writing) no
known polynomial-time algorithm for factoring a composite number.

We now proceed through additional steps of the same kind, introducing another variable p_2 abbreviating $p \lor p_1$:

$$(p_1 \Leftrightarrow q \land \neg r) \land$$
$$(p_2 \Leftrightarrow p \lor p_1) \land$$
$$p_2 \land s$$

and then p_3 as an abbreviation for $p_2 \land s$:

$$(p_1 \Leftrightarrow q \land \neg r) \land$$
$$(p_2 \Leftrightarrow p \lor p_1) \land$$
$$(p_3 \Leftrightarrow p_2 \land s) \land$$
$$p_3.$$

Finally, we just put each of the conjuncts into CNF using traditional methods:

$$(\neg p_1 \lor q) \land (\neg p_1 \lor \neg r) \land (p_1 \lor \neg q \lor r) \land$$
$$(\neg p_2 \lor p \lor p_1) \land (p_2 \lor \neg p) \land (p_2 \lor \neg p_1) \land$$
$$(\neg p_3 \lor p_2) \land (\neg p_3 \lor s) \land (p_3 \lor \neg p_2 \lor \neg s) \land$$
$$p_3.$$

We can see that the resulting formula can only be a modest constant factor larger than the original. The number of definitional conjuncts introduced is bounded by the number of connectives in the original formula. And the final expansion of each conjunct into CNF only causes a modest expansion because of their simple form. Even the worst case, $p \Leftrightarrow (q \Leftrightarrow r)$, only has 11 binary connectives in its CNF equivalent:

```
# cnf <<p <=> (q <=> r)>>;;
- : prop formula =
<<(p \/ q \/ r) /\
  (p \/ ~q \/ ~r) /\ (q \/ ~p \/ ~r) /\ (r \/ ~p \/ ~q)>>
```

So our claim about the size of the formula is justified. For the equisatisfiability, we just need to show that each definitional step is satisfiability-preserving, for the overall transformation is just a sequence of such steps followed by a transformation to a logical equivalent.

Theorem 2.10 *If x does not occur in q, the formulas* psubst $(x \mapsto q)$ p *and* $(x \Leftrightarrow q) \land p$ *are equisatisfiable.*

Proof If psubst $(x \mapsto q)$ p is satisfiable, say by a valuation v, then by Theorem 2.3 the modified valuation $v' = (x \mapsto$ eval q $v)$ v satisfies p. It also satisfies $x \Leftrightarrow q$ because by construction $v'(x) =$ eval q v and since x

does not occur in q, this is the same as `eval` $q\ v'$ (Theorem 2.2). Therefore v' satisfies $(x \Leftrightarrow q) \wedge p$ and so that formula is satisfiable.

Conversely, suppose a valuation v satisfies $(x \Leftrightarrow q) \wedge p$. Since it satisfies the first conjunct, $v(x) = $ `eval` $q\ v$ and therefore $(x \mapsto $ `eval` $q\ v)\ v$ is just v. By Theorem 2.3, v therefore satisfies `psubst` $(x \mapsto\!\!\!| \ q)\ p$. $\qquad\qquad\square$

The second part of this proof actually shows that the right-to-left implication $(x \Leftrightarrow q) \wedge p \Rightarrow$ `psubst` $(x \mapsto\!\!\!| \ q)\ p$ is a tautology. However, the implication in the other direction is *not*, and hence we do not have logical equivalence. For if a valuation v satisfies `psubst` $(x \mapsto\!\!\!| \ q)\ p$, then since x does not occur in that formula, so does $v' = (x \mapsto \text{not}(v(x)))\ v$. But one or other of these must fail to satisfy $x \Leftrightarrow q$.

Implementation of definitional CNF

For the new propositional variables we will use stylized names of the form `p_n`. The following function returns such an atom as well as the incremented index ready for next time.

```
let mkprop n = Atom(P("p_"^(string_of_num n))),n +/ Int 1;;
```

For simplicity, suppose that the starting formulas has been pre-simplified by `nenf`, so that negation is only applied to atoms, and implication has been eliminated. The main recursive function `maincnf` takes a triple consisting of the formula to be transformed, a finite partial function giving the 'definitions' made so far, and the current variable index counter value. It returns a similar triple with the transformed formula, the augmented definitions and a new counter moving past variables used in these definitions. All it does is decompose the top-level binary connective into the type constructor and the immediate subformulas, then pass them as arguments `op` and `(p,q)` to a general function `defstep` that does the main work. (The two functions `maincnf` and `defstep` are mutually recursive and so we enter them in one phrase: note that there is no double-semicolon after the code in the next box.)

```
let rec maincnf (fm,defs,n as trip) =
  match fm with
    And(p,q) -> defstep mk_and (p,q) trip
  | Or(p,q) -> defstep mk_or (p,q) trip
  | Iff(p,q) -> defstep mk_iff (p,q) trip
  | _ -> trip
```

Inside **defstep**, a recursive call to **maincnf** transforms the left-hand subformula p, returning the transformed formula **fm1**, an augmented list of definitions **defs1** and a counter **n1**. The right-hand subformula q together with the new list of definitions and counter are used in another recursive call, giving a transformed formula **fm2** and further modified definitions **defs2** and counter **n2**. We then construct the appropriate composite formula **fm'** by applying the constructor **op** passed in. Next, we check if there is already a definition corresponding to this formula, and if so, return the defining variable. Otherwise we create a new variable and insert a new definition, afterwards returning this variable as the simplified formula, and of course the new counter after the call to **mkprop**.

```
and defstep op (p,q) (fm,defs,n) =
  let fm1,defs1,n1 = maincnf (p,defs,n) in
  let fm2,defs2,n2 = maincnf (q,defs1,n1) in
  let fm' = op fm1 fm2 in
  try (fst(apply defs2 fm'),defs2,n2) with Failure _ ->
  let v,n3 = mkprop n2 in (v,(fm'|->(v,Iff(v,fm'))) defs2,n3);;
```

We need to make sure that none of our newly introduced atoms already occur in the starting formula. This tedious business will crop up a few times in the future, so we implement a more general solution now. The **max_varindex** function returns whichever is larger of the argument n and all possible m such that the string argument s is **pfx** followed by the string corresponding to m, if any:

```
let max_varindex pfx =
  let m = String.length pfx in
  fun s n ->
    let l = String.length s in
    if l <= m or String.sub s 0 m <> pfx then n else
    let s' = String.sub s m (l - m) in
    if forall numeric (explode s') then max_num n (num_of_string s')
    else n;;
```

Now we can implement the overall function. First the formula is simplified and negations are pushed down, giving **fm'**, and we use this formula to choose an appropriate starting variable index, adding 1 to the largest n for which there is an existing variable 'p_n'. We then call the main function, kept as a parameter **fn** to allow future modification, starting with no definitions and with the variable-name counter set to the starting index. We then return the resulting CNF in the set-of-sets representation:

```
let mk_defcnf fn fm =
  let fm' = nenf fm in
  let n = Int 1 +/ overatoms (max_varindex "p_" ** pname) fm' (Int 0) in
  let (fm'',defs,_) = fn (fm',undefined,n) in
  let deflist = map (snd ** snd) (graph defs) in
  unions(simpcnf fm'' :: map simpcnf deflist);;
```

Our first definitional CNF function just applies this to `maincnf` and converts the result back to a formula:

```
let defcnf fm = list_conj(map list_disj(mk_defcnf maincnf fm));;
```

Trying it out on the example formula gives the expected result, coinciding with the result obtained by hand above, except for ordering of conjuncts and literals within them:

```
# defcnf <<(p \/ (q /\ ~r)) /\ s>>;;
- : prop formula =
<<(p \/ p_1 \/ ~p_2) /\
  (p_1 \/ r \/ ~q) /\
  (p_2 \/ ~p) /\
  (p_2 \/ ~p_1) /\
  (p_2 \/ ~p_3) /\
  p_3 /\
  (p_3 \/ ~p_2 \/ ~s) /\ (q \/ ~p_1) /\ (s \/ ~p_3) /\ (~p_1 \/ ~r)>>
```

Instead of transforming each definition into CNF in isolation, we could have formed the final conjunction first and called the old CNF function once. This would be slightly simpler to program, and would eliminate more subsumed conjuncts, such as $\neg p_2 \vee \neg s \vee p_3$ in that example, which is subsumed by p_3. However, for very large formulas the subsumption testing becomes extremely slow since (in our simple-minded implementation) it performs about n^2 operations for a formula of size n.

Optimizations

We can optimize the procedure by avoiding some obviously redundant definitions. First, when dealing with an iterated conjunction in the initial formula, we can just put the conjuncts into CNF separately and conjoin them.[†] And if any of those conjuncts in their turn contain disjunctions, we can ignore atomic formulas within them and only introduce definitions for other subformulas.

[†] Note that the initial `nenf` is beneficial here, since it can expose existing CNF structure that was formerly hidden by nested negations. For example, after this transformation the formula $\neg(p \vee q \wedge r)$ is already in CNF.

The coding is fairly simple: we first descend through arbitrarily many nested conjunctions, and then through arbitrarily many nested disjunctions, before we begin the definitional work. However, we still need to link the definitional transformations in the different parts of the formula, so we maintain the same overall structure with three arguments. The function `subcnf` has the same structure as `defstep` except that it handles the linkage housekeeping without introducing new definitions, and has the function called recursively as an additional parameter `sfn`:

```
let subcnf sfn op (p,q) (fm,defs,n) =
  let fm1,defs1,n1 = sfn(p,defs,n) in
  let fm2,defs2,n2 = sfn(q,defs1,n1) in (op fm1 fm2,defs2,n2);;
```

This is used first to define a function that recursively descends through disjunctions performing the definitional transformation of the disjuncts:

```
let rec orcnf (fm,defs,n as trip) =
  match fm with
    Or(p,q) -> subcnf orcnf mk_or (p,q) trip
  | _ -> maincnf trip;;
```

and in turn a function that recursively descends through conjunctions calling `orcnf` on the conjuncts:

```
let rec andcnf (fm,defs,n as trip) =
  match fm with
    And(p,q) -> subcnf andcnf mk_and (p,q) trip
  | _ -> orcnf trip;;
```

Now the overall function is the same except that `andcnf` is used in place of `maincnf`. We separate the actual reconstruction of a formula from the set of sets into a different function, since it will be useful later to intercept the intermediate result.

```
let defcnfs fm = mk_defcnf andcnf fm;;

let defcnf fm = list_conj (map list_disj (defcnfs fm));;
```

This does indeed give a significantly simpler result on our running example:

```
# defcnf <<(p \/ (q /\ ~r)) /\ s>>;;
- : prop formula =
<<(p \/ p_1) /\ (p_1 \/ r \/ ~q) /\ (q \/ ~p_1) /\ s /\ (~p_1 \/ ~r)>>
```

With a little more care one can design a definitional CNF procedure so that it will always at least equal a naive algorithm in the size of the output (Boy de la Tour 1990). However, the function `defcnf` that we have now arrived at is not bad and will be quite adequate for our purposes. For one possible optimization, see Exercise 2.11.

3-CNF

Note that after the unoptimized definitional CNF conversion, the resulting formula is in '3-CNF', meaning that each conjunct contains a disjunction of *at most three* literals. The reader can verify this by confirming that at most three literals result for each conjunct in the CNF translation of every definition $p \Leftrightarrow q \otimes r$ for all connectives '$\otimes$'. However, the final optimization of leaving alone conjuncts that are already a disjunction of literals spoils this property. If 3-CNF is considered important, it can be reinstated while still treating individual conjuncts separately. A crude but adequate method is simply to omit the intermediate function `orcnf`:

```
let rec andcnf3 pos (fm,defs,n as trip) =
  match fm with
    And(p,q) -> subcnf (andcnf3 pos) (fun (p,q) -> And(p,q)) (p,q) trip
  | _ -> maincnf pos trip;;

let defcnf3 fm = list_conj (map list_disj(mk_defcnf andcnf3 fm));;
```

The results of this section show that we can reduce SAT, testing satisfiability of an arbitrary formula, to testing satisfiability of a formula in CNF that is only a few times as large. Indeed, by the above we only need to be able to test '3-SAT', satisfiability of formulas in 3-CNF. For this reason, many practical algorithms assume a CNF input, and theoretical results often consider just CNF or 3-CNF formulas.

2.9 The Davis–Putnam procedure

The Davis–Putnam procedure is a method for deciding satisfiability of a propositional formula in conjunctive normal form.[†] There are actually two significantly different algorithms commonly called 'Davis–Putnam', but we'll consider them separately and try to maintain a terminological distinction. The original algorithm presented by Davis and Putnam (1960) will be referred to simply as 'Davis–Putnam' (DP), while the later and now more popular variant developed by Davis, Logemann and Loveland (1962) will be called 'Davis–Putnam–Loveland–Logemann' (DPLL). Following the historical line, we consider DP first.

[†] As we shall see in section 3.8, the Davis–Putnam procedure for propositional logic was originally presented as a component of a first-order search procedure. Since this was based on refuting ever-larger conjunctions of substitution instances, the use of CNF was particularly attractive.

We found a 'set of sets' representation useful in transforming a formula *into* CNF, and we'll use it in the DP and DPLL procedures themselves. An implicit 'set of sets' representation of a CNF formula is often referred to as *clausal* form, and each conjunct is called a *clause*. The earlier auxiliary function `simpcnf` already puts a formula in clausal form, and `defcnfs` does likewise using definitional CNF. We will just use the latter, avoiding the final reconstruction of a formula from the set-of-sets representation. In our discussions, we will write clauses with the implicit logical connectives, but with the understanding that we are really performing set operations.

The degenerate cases of clausal form should be kept in mind: a list including the empty clause corresponds to the formula '$\perp$', while an empty list of clauses corresponds to the formula '$\top$'; this interpretation is often used in what follows. The DP procedure successively transforms a formula in clausal form through a succession of others, maintaining clausal form and equisatisfiability with the original formula. It terminates when the clausal form either contains an empty clause, in which case the original formula must be unsatisfiable, or is itself empty, in which case the original formula must be satisfiable. There are three basic satisfiability-preserving transformations used in the DP procedure:

I   the 1-literal rule,
II the affirmative-negative rule,
III the rule for eliminating atomic formulas.

Rules I and II always make the formula simpler, reducing the total number of literals. Hence they are always applied as much as possible, and the third rule, which may greatly increase the size of the formula, is used only when neither of the first two is applicable. However, from a logical point of view we can regard I as a special case of III, so we will re-use the argument that III preserves satisfiability to show that I does too.

The 1-literal rule

This rule can be applied whenever one of the clauses is a *unit clause*, i.e. simply a single literal rather than the disjunction of more than one. If p is such a unit clause, we can get a new formula by:

- removing any instances of $-p$ from the other clauses,
- removing any clauses containing p, including the unit clause itself.

We will show later that this transformation preserves satisfiability. The 1-literal rule is also called *unit propagation* since it propagates the information that p is true into the the other clauses. To implement it in the list-of-lists representation, we search for a unit clause, i.e. a list of length 1, and let u be the sole literal in it and u' its negation. Then we first remove all clauses containing u and then remove u' from the remaining clauses.[†]

```
let one_literal_rule clauses =
  let u = hd (find (fun cl -> length cl = 1) clauses) in
  let u' = negate u in
  let clauses1 = filter (fun cl -> not (mem u cl)) clauses in
  image (fun cl -> subtract cl [u']) clauses1;;
```

If there is no unit clause, the application of `find` will raise an exception. This makes it easy to apply `one_literal_rule` repeatedly to get rid of multiple unit clauses, until failure indicates there are no more left. Note that even if there is only one unit clause in the initial formula, an application of the rule may itself create more unit clauses by deleting other literals.

The affirmative–negative rule

This rule, also sometimes called the *pure literal* rule, exploits the fact that if any literal occurs either *only positively* or *only negatively*, then we can delete all clauses containing that literal while preserving satisfiability. For the implementation, we start by collecting all the literals together and partitioning them into positive (`pos`) and negative (`neg'`). From these we obtain the literals `pure` that occur either only positively or only negatively, then eliminate all clauses that contain any of them. We make it fail if there are no pure literals, since it then fits more easily into the overall procedure.

```
let affirmative_negative_rule clauses =
  let neg',pos = partition negative (unions clauses) in
  let neg = image negate neg' in
  let pos_only = subtract pos neg and neg_only = subtract neg pos in
  let pure = union pos_only (image negate neg_only) in
  if pure = [] then failwith "affirmative_negative_rule" else
  filter (fun cl -> intersect cl pure = []) clauses;;
```

If any valuation satisfies the original set of clauses, then it must also satisfy the new set, which is a subset of it. Conversely, if a valuation v satisfies the new set, we can modify it to set $v'(p) = $ true for all positive-only literals p in the original and $v'(n) = $ false for all negative-only literals $\neg n$, setting $v'(a) = v(a)$ for all other atoms. By construction this satisfies the deleted

---

[†] We use a setifying map `image` rather than just `map` because we may otherwise get duplicates, e.g. removing $\neg u$ from $\neg u \lor p \lor q$ when there is already a clause $p \lor q$. This is not essential, but it seems prudent not to have more clauses than necessary.

clauses, and since it does not change the assignment to any atom occurring in the final clauses, satisfies them too and hence the original set of clauses.

Rule for eliminating atomic formulas

This rule is the only one that can make the formula increase in size, and in the worst case the increase can be substantial. However, it completely eliminates some particular atom from consideration, without any special requirements on the clauses that contain it. The rule is parametrized by a literal p that occurs positively in at least one clause and negatively in at least one clause. (If the pure literal rule has already been applied, any remaining literal has this property. Indeed, if we've also filtered out trivial, i.e. tautologous, clauses, no literal will occur both positively and negatively in the *same* clause, but we won't rely on that when stating and proving the next theorem.)

Theorem 2.11 *Given a literal p, separate a set of clauses S into those clauses containing p only positively, those containing it only negatively, and those for which neither is true:*

$$S = \{p \vee C_i \mid 1 \leq i \leq m\} \cup \{-p \vee D_j \mid 1 \leq j \leq n\} \cup S_0,$$

where none of the C_i or D_j include the literal p or its negation, and if either p or $-p$ occurs in any clause in S_0 then they both do. Then S is satisfiable iff S' is, where:

$$S' = \{C_i \vee D_j \mid 1 \leq i \leq m, 1 \leq j \leq n\} \cup S_0.$$

Proof We can assume without loss of generality that p is positive, i.e. an atomic formula, since otherwise the same reasoning applies to $-p$.

If a valuation v satisfies S, there are two possibilities. If $v(p) = $ false, then since each $p \vee C_i$ is satisfied but p is not, each C_i is satisfied and a fortiori each $C_i \vee D_j$. If $v(p) = $ true, then since each $-p \vee D_j$ is satisfied but $-p$ is not, each D_j is satisfied and hence so is each $C_i \vee D_j$. The formulas in S_0 were already in the original clauses S and hence are still satisfied by v.

Conversely, suppose a valuation v satisfies S'. We claim that v either satisfies all the C_i or else satisfies all the D_j. Indeed, if it doesn't satisfy some particular C_k, the fact that it does nevertheless satisfy all the $C_k \vee D_j$ for $1 \leq j \leq n$ shows at once that it satisfies all D_j; similarly if it fails to satisfy some D_l then it must satisfy all C_i. Now, if v satisfies all C_i, modify it by setting $v'(p) = $ false and setting $v'(a) = v(a)$ for all other atoms. All the $p \vee C_i$ are satisfied by v' because all the C_i are, and all the $-p \vee D_j$

are because $-p$ is. Since the formulas in S_0 either do not involve p or are tautologies, they are still satisfied by v'. The other case is symmetrical: if v satisfies all D_j, modify it by setting $v(p) = $ true and reason similarly. $\qquad\square$

Rule III is also commonly called the *resolution* rule, and we will study it in more detail in Chapter 3. Correspondingly, the clause $C_i \vee D_j$ is said to be a *resolvent* of the clauses $p \vee C_i$ and $-p \vee D_j$, and to have been obtained *by resolution*, or more specifically *by resolution on p*. In the implementation, we also filter out trivial (tautologous) clauses at the end:

```
let resolve_on p clauses =
  let p' = negate p and pos,notpos = partition (mem p) clauses in
  let neg,other = partition (mem p') notpos in
  let pos' = image (filter (fun l -> l <> p)) pos
  and neg' = image (filter (fun l -> l <> p')) neg in
  let res0 = allpairs union pos' neg' in
  union other (filter (non trivial) res0);;
```

Theoretically, we can regard the 1-literal rule applied to a unit clause p as subsumption followed by resolution on p, and hence deduce as promised:

Corollary 2.12 *The 1-literal rule preserves satisfiability.*

Proof If the original set S contains the unit clause $\{p\}$, then, by subsumption, the set of all other formulas involving p positively can be removed without affecting satisfiability, giving S', say. Now by the above theorem the new set resulting from resolution on p is also equisatisfiable, and this precisely removes the unit clause itself and all instances of $-p$. $\qquad\square$

In practice, we will only apply the resolution rule after the 1-literal and affirmative–negative rules have already been applied. In this case we can assume that *any* literal present occurs both positively and negatively, and are faced with a choice of which literal to resolve on. Given a literal l, we can predict the change in the number of clauses resulting from resolution on l:

```
let resolution_blowup cls l =
  let m = length(filter (mem l) cls)
  and n = length(filter (mem (negate l)) cls) in
  m * n - m - n;;
```

We will pick the literal that minimizes this blowup. (While this looks plausible, it is simplistic; much more sophisticated heuristics are possible and perhaps desirable.)

```
let resolution_rule clauses =
  let pvs = filter positive (unions clauses) in
  let p = minimize (resolution_blowup clauses) pvs in
  resolve_on p clauses;;
```

The DP procedure

The main DP procedure is defined recursively. It terminates if the set of clauses is empty (returning **true** since that set is trivially satisfiable) or contains the empty clause (returning **false** for unsatisfiability). Otherwise, it applies the first of the rules I, II and III to succeed and then continues recursively on the new set of clauses.[†] This recursion must terminate, for each rule either decreases the number of distinct atoms (in the case of III, assuming that tautologies are always removed first) or else leaves the number of atoms unchanged but reduces the total size of the clauses.

```
let rec dp clauses =
  if clauses = [] then true else if mem [] clauses then false else
  try dp (one_literal_rule clauses) with Failure _ ->
  try dp (affirmative_negative_rule clauses) with Failure _ ->
  dp(resolution_rule clauses);;
```

The code can be used for satisfiability and tautology checking functions:

```
let dpsat fm = dp(defcnfs fm);;

let dptaut fm = not(dpsat(Not fm));;
```

Encouragingly, **dptaut** proves the formula **prime 11** much more quickly than the **tautology** function:

```
# tautology(prime 11);;
- : bool = true
# dptaut(prime 11);;
- : bool = true
```

The DPLL procedure

For more challenging problems, the number and size of the clauses generated in the DP procedure can grow enormously, and may exhaust available memory before a decision is reached. This effect was even more pronounced on the early computers available when the DP algorithm was developed, and

---

[†] The overall procedure will never fail, so any **Failure** exceptions must be from the rule.

it motivated Davis, Logemann and Loveland (1962) to replace the resolution rule III with a *splitting rule*. If neither of the rules I and II is applicable, then some literal p is chosen and the satisfiability of a clause set Δ is reduced to the satisfiability of $\Delta \cup \{-p\}$ and of $\Delta \cup \{p\}$, which are tested separately. Note that this preserves satisfiability: Δ is satisfiable if and only if one of $\Delta \cup \{-p\}$ and $\Delta \cup \{p\}$ is, since any valuation must satisfy either $-p$ or p. The new unit clauses will then immediately be used by the 1-literal rule to simplify the clause set. Since this step reduces the number of atoms, the termination of the procedure is guaranteed.

A reasonable choice of splitting literal seems to be the one that occurs most often (either positively or negatively), since the subsequent unit propagation will then cause the most substantial simplification.[†] Accordingly we define the analogue of the DP procedure's `resolution_blowup`:

```
let posneg_count cls l =
  let m = length(filter (mem l) cls)
  and n = length(filter (mem (negate l)) cls) in
  m + n;;
```

Now the basic algorithm is as before except that the resolution rule is replaced by a case-split:

```
let rec dpll clauses =
  if clauses = [] then true else if mem [] clauses then false else
  try dpll(one_literal_rule clauses) with Failure _ ->
  try dpll(affirmative_negative_rule clauses) with Failure _ ->
  let pvs = filter positive (unions clauses) in
  let p = maximize (posneg_count clauses) pvs in
  dpll (insert [p] clauses) or dpll (insert [negate p] clauses);;
```

Once again, it can be applied to give tautology and satisfiability testing functions:

```
let dpllsat fm = dpll(defcnfs fm);;

let dplltaut fm = not(dpllsat(Not fm));;
```

and the time for the same example is even better than for DP:

```
# dplltaut(prime 11);;
- : bool = true
```

[†] It is in fact, in a precise sense, harder to make the optimal choice of split variable than to solve the satisfiability question itself (Liberatore 2000).

Iterative DPLL

For really large problems, the DPLL procedure in the simple recursive form that we have presented can require an impractical amount of memory, because of the storage of intermediate states when case-splits are nested. Most modern implementations are based instead on a tail-recursive (iterative) control structure, using an explicit *trail* to store information about the recursive case-splits. We will implement this trail as just a list of pairs, the first member of each pair being a literal we are assuming, the second a flag indicating whether it was just assumed as one half of a case-split (**Guessed**) or deduced by unit propagation from literals assumed earlier (**Deduced**). The trail is stored in reverse order, so that the head of the list is the literal most recently assumed or deduced, and the flags are taken from this enumerated type:

```
type trailmix = Guessed | Deduced;;
```

In general, we no longer modify the clauses of the input problem as we explore case-splits, but retain the original formula, recording our further (and in general temporary) assumptions only in the trail. All literals in the trail are assumed to hold at the current stage of exploration. In order to find potential atomic formulas to case-split over, we use the following to indicate which atomic formulas in the problem have no assignment either way in the trail, whether that literal was guessed or deduced:

```
let unassigned =
  let litabs p = match p with Not q -> q | _ -> p in
  fun cls trail -> subtract (unions(image (image litabs) cls))
                            (image (litabs ** fst) trail);;
```

To perform unit propagation, it is convenient *internally* to modify the problem clauses `cls`, and also to process the trail `trail` into a finite partial function `fn` for more efficient lookup. This is all implemented inside the following subfunction, which performs unit propagation until either no further progress is possible or the empty clause is derived:

```
let rec unit_subpropagate (cls,fn,trail) =
  let cls' = map (filter ((not) ** defined fn ** negate)) cls in
  let uu = function [c] when not(defined fn c) -> [c] | _ -> failwith "" in
  let newunits = unions(mapfilter uu cls') in
  if newunits = [] then (cls',fn,trail) else
  let trail' = itlist (fun p t -> (p,Deduced)::t) newunits trail
  and fn' = itlist (fun u -> (u |-> ())) newunits fn in
  unit_subpropagate (cls',fn',trail');;
```

This is then used in the overall function, returning both the modified clauses and the trail, though the former is only used for convenience and will not be retained around the main loop:

```
let unit_propagate (cls,trail) =
  let fn = itlist (fun (x,_) -> (x |-> ())) trail undefined in
  let cls',fn',trail' = unit_subpropagate (cls,fn,trail) in cls',trail';;
```

When we reach a contradiction or *conflict,* we need to backtrack to try the other branch of the most recent case-split. This is where the distinction between the *decision literals* (those flagged with `Guessed`) and the others is used: we remove items from the trail until we reach the most recent decision literal or there are no items left at all.

```
let rec backtrack trail =
  match trail with
    (p,Deduced)::tt -> backtrack tt
  | _ -> trail;;
```

Now we will express the classic DPLL algorithm using this iterative reformulation. The arguments to `dpli` are the clauses `cls` of the original problem, which is unchanged over recursive calls, and the current `trail`. First of all we perform exhaustive unit propagation to obtain a new set of clauses `cls'` and trail `trail'`. (We do not bother with the affirmative–negative rule, though it could be added without difficulty.) If we have deduced the empty clause, then we backtrack to the most recent decision literal. If there are none left then we are done: the formula is unsatisfiable. Otherwise we take the most recent one and put its negation back in the trail, now flagged as `Deduced` to indicate that it follows from the previously assumed literals in the trail. (Operationally, this means that on the next conflict we will not negate it again and go into a loop.) If there is no conflict, then as in the recursive formulation we pick an unassigned literal `p` and initiate a case-split, while if there *are* no unassigned literals the formula is satisfiable.

```
let rec dpli cls trail =
  let cls',trail' = unit_propagate (cls,trail) in
  if mem [] cls' then
    match backtrack trail with
      (p,Guessed)::tt -> dpli cls ((negate p,Deduced)::tt)
    | _ -> false
  else
      match unassigned cls trail' with
        [] -> true
      | ps -> let p = maximize (posneg_count cls') ps in
              dpli cls ((p,Guessed)::trail');;
```

As usual we can turn this into satisfiability and tautology tests for an arbitrary formula:

```
let dplisat fm = dpli (defcnfs fm) [];;

let dplitaut fm = not(dplisat(Not fm));;
```

It works just as well as the recursive implementation, though it is often somewhat slower because our naive data structures don't support efficient lookup and unit propagation. But the iterative structure really comes into its own when we consider some further optimizations.

Backjumping and learning

For an unsatisfiable set of clauses, after recursively case-splitting enough times, we always get the empty clause showing that some particular combination of literal assignments is inconsistent. However, it may be that not all of the assignments made in a particular case-split are really necessary to get the empty clause. For example, suppose we perform nested case-splits over the atoms $p_1, \ldots, p_{10}$ in that order, first assuming them all to be true. If we have clauses $\neg p_1 \vee \neg p_{10} \vee p_{11}$ and $\neg p_1 \vee \neg p_{10} \vee \neg p_{11}$, we will then be able to reach a conflict and initiate backtracking. The next combination to be tried will be $p_1, \ldots, p_9, \neg p_{10}$. Since the clauses were assumed to be unsatisfiable, we will eventually, perhaps after further nested case-splits, reach a contradiction and backtrack again. Unfortunately, for each subsequent assignment of the atoms $p_2, \ldots, p_9$, we will waste time once again exploring the case where p_{10} holds.

How can we avoid this? When first backtracking, we could instead have observed that assumptions about $p_2, \ldots, p_9$ make no difference to the clauses from which the conflict was derived. Thus we could have chosen to backtrack more than one level, going back to just p_1 in the trail and adding $\neg p_{10}$ as a *deduced* clause. This is known as (non-chronological) *backjumping*. A simple version, just going back through the trail as far as possible while ensuring that the most recent decision p still leads to a conflict, can be implemented as follows:

```
let rec backjump cls p trail =
  match backtrack trail with
    (q,Guessed)::tt ->
        let cls',trail' = unit_propagate (cls,(p,Guessed)::tt) in
        if mem [] cls' then backjump cls p tt else trail
  | _ -> trail;;
```

In the example above, a conflict arose via unit propagation from assuming just p_1 and p_{10} even though there isn't simply a clause $\neg p_1 \lor \neg p_{10}$ in the initial clauses. Still, the fact that the simple combination of p_1 and p_{10} leads to a conflict is useful information that could be retained in case it shortcuts later deductions. We can do this by adding a corresponding *conflict clause* $\neg p_1 \lor \neg p_{10}$, negating the conjunction of the decision literals in the trail. Adding such clauses to our problem is known as *learning*. For example, in the following version we perform backjumping and use the backjump trail to construct a conflict clause that is added to the problem.

```
let rec dplb cls trail =
  let cls',trail' = unit_propagate (cls,trail) in
  if mem [] cls' then
    match backtrack trail with
      (p,Guessed)::tt ->
        let trail' = backjump cls p tt in
        let declits = filter (fun (_,d) -> d = Guessed) trail' in
        let conflict = insert (negate p) (image (negate ** fst) declits) in
        dplb (conflict::cls) ((negate p,Deduced)::trail')
    | _ -> false
  else
    match unassigned cls trail' with
      [] -> true
    | ps -> let p = maximize (posneg_count cls') ps in
            dplb cls ((p,Guessed)::trail');;
```

Note that modifying `cls` in this way doesn't break the essentially iterative structure of the code, since the conflict clause is a consequence of the input problem regardless of the temporary assignments and we will not need to reverse the modification. We can turn `dplb` into satisfiability and tautology tests as before:

```
let dplbsat fm = dplb (defcnfs fm) [];;

let dplbtaut fm = not(dplbsat(Not fm));;
```

For example, on this problem the use of backjumping and learning leads to about a 4X improvement:

```
# dplitaut(prime 101);;
# dplbtaut(prime 101);;
```

Of course, all our implementations were designed for clarity, and by using more efficient data structures to represent clauses, as well as careful low-level programming, they can be made substantially more efficient. It is also probably worth performing at least some selective subsumption to reduce the number of redundant clauses; more efficient data structures can make this practical. Our implementation of backjumping was rather trivial, just skipping over a contiguous series of guesses in the trail. This can be further improved using a more sophisticated *conflict analysis*, working backwards from the conflict clause and 'explaining' how the conflict arose. Some SAT solvers even perform periodic *restarts* where the learned clauses are retained but the current branching abandoned, which can often be surprisingly beneficial. Finally, the heuristics for picking literals in both DP and DPLL can be modified in various ways, and sometimes the particular choice can spectacularly affect efficiency. For example, in DPLL, rather than pick the literal occurring most often, one can select one that occurs in the shortest clause, to maximize the chance of getting an additional unit clause out of the 1-literal rule and causing a cascade of simplifications without a further case-split.

It is sometimes desirable that a SAT algorithm like DPLL should return not just a yes/no answer but some additional information. For example, if a formula is satisfiable, we might like to know a satisfying assignment, e.g. to support its use within an SMT system (Section 5.13), and it is reasonably straightforward to modify any of our DPLL implementations to do so (Exercise 2.12). In the case of an *unsatisfiable* formula, we might want a complete 'proof' in some sense of that unsatisfiability, either to verify it more rigorously in case of a program bug, or to support other applications (McMillan 2003). A more modest requirement is for the system to return an *unsat core*, a 'minimal' subset of the initial clauses that are unsatisfiable. Some current SAT solvers can do all this, producing an unsat core and also a proof, as a sequence of resolution steps, of the empty clause starting from those clauses (see Exercise 2.13).

2.10 Stålmarck's method

The DPLL procedure and the naive `tautology` code both perform nested case-splits to explore the space of all valuations, although DPLL's simplification rules I and II often terminate paths without going through all possible combinations. By contrast, Stålmarck's method (Stålmarck and Säflund 1990)[†] tries to minimize the number of nested case-splits using a *dilemma rule*, which applies a case-split and garners common conclusions from the two branches.

Suppose we have some basic 'simple' deduction rules R that generate certain logical consequences of a set of formulas. (We'll specify these rules

---

[†] **Note that Stålmarck's method is patented for commercial use** (Stålmarck 1994b).

later, but most of the present general discussion is independent of the exact choice.) The dilemma rule based on R performs a case-split over some literal p, considering the new sets of formulas $\Delta \cup \{-p\}$ and $\Delta \cup \{p\}$. To each of these it applies the simple rules R to yield sets of formulas Δ_0 and Δ_1 in the respective branches (we at least have $-p \in \Delta_0$ and $p \in \Delta_1$). If these have any common elements, then since they are consequences of both $\Delta \cup \{-p\}$ and $\Delta \cup \{p\}$, they must be consequences of Δ alone, so we are justified in augmenting the original set of formulas with $\Delta_0 \cap \Delta_1$:

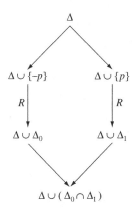

The process of applying the simple rules until no further progress is possible is referred to as *0-saturation* and will be written S_0. Repeatedly applying the dilemma rule with simple rules S_0 until no further progress is possible is *1-saturation* and written S_1. Similarly, $(n + 1)$-saturation, S_{n+1}, is the process of applying the dilemma rule with simple rules S_n. Roughly speaking, a formula's satisfiability is decidable by n-saturation if it is decidable by the primitive rules and at most n-deep nesting of case-splits. (Note that the dilemma rule may still be applied many times *sequentially*, but not necessarily in a deeply nested fashion.) A formula decidable by n-saturation is said to be *n-easy*, and if it is decidable by n-saturation but not $(n-1)$-saturation, it is said to be *n-hard*. Many practically significant classes of problems turn out to be n-easy for quite moderate n, often just $n = 1$. This is quite appealing because (Stålmarck 1994a) an n-easy formula with p connectives can be tested for satisfiability in time proportional to $O|p|^{2n+1}$.

Triplets

We'll present Stålmarck's method in its original setting, although the basic dilemma rule can also be incorporated into the same clausal framework as DPLL, as considered in Exercise 2.15 below. The formula to be tested for satisfiability is first reduced to a conjunction of 'triplets' $l_i \Leftrightarrow l_j \otimes l_k$ with the literals l_i representing subformulas of the original formula. We derive this as in the 3-CNF procedure from Section 2.8, introducing abbreviations for all nontrivial subformulas but omitting the final CNF transformation of the triplets:

```
let triplicate fm =
  let fm' = nenf fm in
  let n = Int 1 +/ overatoms (max_varindex "p_" ** pname) fm' (Int 0) in
  let (p,defs,_) = main (fm',undefined,n) in
  p,map (snd ** snd) (graph defs);;
```

Simple rules

Rather than deriving *clauses*, the rules in Stålmarck's method derive *equivalences* $p \Leftrightarrow q$ where p and q are either literals or the formulas $\top$ or $\bot$.[†] The underlying 'simple rules' in Stålmarck's method enumerate the new equivalences that can be deduced from a triplet given some existing equivalences. For example, if we assume a triplet $p \Leftrightarrow q \wedge r$ then:

- if we know $r \Leftrightarrow \top$ we can deduce $p \Leftrightarrow q$,
- if we know $p \Leftrightarrow \top$ we can deduce $q \Leftrightarrow \top$ and $r \Leftrightarrow \top$,
- if we know $q \Leftrightarrow \bot$ we can deduce $p \Leftrightarrow \bot$,
- if we know $q \Leftrightarrow r$ we can deduce $p \Leftrightarrow q$ and $p \Leftrightarrow r$,
- if we know $p \Leftrightarrow \neg q$ we can deduce $p \Leftrightarrow \bot$, $q \Leftrightarrow \top$ and $r \Leftrightarrow \bot$.

We'll try to avoid deducing redundant sets of equivalences. To identify equivalences that are essentially the same (e.g. $p \Leftrightarrow \neg q$, $\neg q \Leftrightarrow p$ and $q \Leftrightarrow \neg p$) we force alignment of each $p \Leftrightarrow q$ such that the atom on the right is no bigger than the one on the left, and the one on the left is never negated:

```
let atom lit = if negative lit then negate lit else lit;;

let rec align (p,q) =
  if atom p < atom q then align (q,p) else
  if negative p then (negate p,negate q) else (p,q);;
```

Our representation of equivalence classes rests on the union-find data structure from Appendix 2. The `equate` function described there merges two equivalence classes, but we will ensure that whenever p and q are to be identified, we also identify $-p$ and $-q$:

[†] An older variant (Stålmarck and Säflund 1990) just accumulates unit clauses, but the use of equivalences is more powerful.

```
let equate2 (p,q) eqv = equate (negate p,negate q) (equate (p,q) eqv);;
```

We'll also ignore redundant equivalences, i.e. those that already follow from the existing equivalence, including the immediately trivial $p \Leftrightarrow p$:

```
let rec irredundant rel eqs =
  match eqs with
    [] -> []
  | (p,q)::oth ->
      if canonize rel p = canonize rel q then irredundant rel oth
      else insert (p,q) (irredundant (equate2 (p,q) rel) oth);;
```

It would be tedious and error-prone to enumerate by hand all the ways in which equivalences follow from each other in the presence of a triplet, so we will deduce this information automatically. The following takes an assumed equivalence **peq** and triplet **fm**, together with a list of putative equivalences **eqs**. It returns an irredundant set of those equivalences from **eqs** that follow from **peq** and **fm** together:

```
let consequences (p,q as peq) fm eqs =
  let follows(r,s) = tautology(Imp(And(Iff(p,q),fm),Iff(r,s))) in
  irredundant (equate2 peq unequal) (filter follows eqs);;
```

To generate the entire list of 'triggers' generated by a triplet, i.e. a list of equivalences with their consequences, we just need to apply this function to each canonical equivalence:

```
let triggers fm =
  let poslits = insert True (map (fun p -> Atom p) (atoms fm)) in
  let lits = union poslits (map negate poslits) in
  let pairs = allpairs (fun p q -> p,q) lits lits in
  let npairs = filter (fun (p,q) -> atom p <> atom q) pairs in
  let eqs = setify(map align npairs) in
  let raw = map (fun p -> p,consequences p fm eqs) eqs in
  filter (fun (p,c) -> c <> []) raw;;
```

For instance, we can confirm and extend the examples noted above:

```
# triggers <<p <=> (q /\ r)>>;;
- : ((prop formula * prop formula) * (prop formula * prop formula) list)
    list
=
[(((<<p>>, <<true>>), [(<<q>>, <<true>>); (<<r>>, <<true>>)]);
 ((<<q>>, <<true>>), [(<<r>>, <<p>>)]);
 ((<<q>>, <<~true>>), [(<<p>>, <<~true>>)]);
 ((<<q>>, <<~p>>), [(<<p>>, <<~true>>); (<<r>>, <<p>>)]);
 ((<<r>>, <<true>>), [(<<q>>, <<p>>)]);
 ((<<r>>, <<q>>), [(<<q>>, <<p>>)]);
 ((<<r>>, <<~true>>), [(<<p>>, <<~true>>)]);
 ((<<r>>, <<~p>>), [(<<p>>, <<~true>>); (<<q>>, <<p>>)]);
 ((<<r>>, <<~q>>), [(<<p>>, <<~true>>)])]
```

We could apply this to the actual triplets in the formula (indeed, it is applicable to *any* formula fm), but it's more efficient to precompute it for the possible forms $p \Leftrightarrow q \wedge r$, $p \Leftrightarrow q \vee r$, $p \Leftrightarrow q \Rightarrow r$ and $p \Leftrightarrow (q \Leftrightarrow r)$ and then instantiate the results for each instance in question. However, after instantiation, we may need to realign, and also eliminate double negations if some of p, q and r are replaced by negative literals.

```
let trigger =
  let [trig_and; trig_or; trig_imp; trig_iff] = map triggers
      [<<p <=> q /\ r>>; <<p <=> q \/ r>>;
       <<p <=> (q ==> r)>>; <<p <=> (q <=> r)>>]
  and ddnegate fm = match fm with Not(Not p) -> p | _ -> fm in
  let inst_fn [x;y;z] =
    let subfn = fpf [P"p"; P"q"; P"r"] [x; y; z] in
    ddnegate ** psubst subfn in
  let inst2_fn i (p,q) = align(inst_fn i p,inst_fn i q) in
  let instn_fn i (a,c) = inst2_fn i a,map (inst2_fn i) c in
  let inst_trigger = map ** instn_fn in
  function (Iff(x,And(y,z))) -> inst_trigger [x;y;z] trig_and
         | (Iff(x,Or(y,z))) -> inst_trigger [x;y;z] trig_or
         | (Iff(x,Imp(y,z))) -> inst_trigger [x;y;z] trig_imp
         | (Iff(x,Iff(y,z))) -> inst_trigger [x;y;z] trig_iff;;
```

0-saturation

The core of Stålmarck's method is 0-saturation, i.e. the exhaustive application of the simple rules to derive new equivalences from existing ones. Given an equivalence, only triggers sharing some atoms with it could yield new information from it, so we set up a function mapping literals to *relevant* triggers:

```
let relevance trigs =
  let insert_relevant p trg f = (p |-> insert trg (tryapplyl f p)) f in
  let insert_relevant2 ((p,q),_ as trg) f =
    insert_relevant p trg (insert_relevant q trg f) in
  itlist insert_relevant2 trigs undefined;;
```

The principal 0-saturation function, `equatecons`, defined below, derives new information from an equation p0 = q0, and in general modifies both the equivalence relation `eqv` between literals and the 'relevance' function `rfn`.

We maintain the invariant that the relevance function maps a literal l that is a canonical equivalence class representative to the set of triggers where the triggering equation contains some l' equivalent to l under the equivalence relation. Initially, there are no non-trivial equations, so this collapses to the special case $l' = l$, corresponding to the action of the `relevance` function.

First of all, we get canonical representatives p and q for the two literals. If these are already the same then the equation p0 = q0 yields no new information and we return the original equivalence and relevance. Otherwise, we similarly canonize the negations of p0 and q0 to get p' and q', which we also need to identify.

The equivalence relation is updated just by using `equate2`, but updating the relevance function is a bit more complicated. We get the set of triggers where the triggering equation involves something (originally) equivalent to p (sp_pos) and p' (sp_neg), and similarly for q and q'. Now, the new equations we have effectively introduced by identifying p and q are all those with something equivalent to p on one side *and* something equivalent to q on the other side, or equivalent to p' and q'. These are collected as the set `news`.

As for the new relevance function, we just collect the triggers componentwise from the two equivalence classes. This has to be indexed by the *canonical* representatives of the merged equivalence classes corresponding to p and p', and we have to re-canonize these as we can't a priori predict which of the two representatives that were formerly canonical will actually get chosen.

```
let equatecons (p0,q0) (eqv,rfn as erf) =
  let p = canonize eqv p0 and q = canonize eqv q0 in
  if p = q then [],erf else
  let p' = canonize eqv (negate p0) and q' = canonize eqv (negate q0) in
  let eqv' = equate2(p,q) eqv
  and sp_pos = tryapplyl rfn p and sp_neg = tryapplyl rfn p'
  and sq_pos = tryapplyl rfn q and sq_neg = tryapplyl rfn q' in
  let rfn' =
      (canonize eqv' p |-> union sp_pos sq_pos)
      ((canonize eqv' p' |-> union sp_neg sq_neg) rfn) in
  let nw = union (intersect sp_pos sq_pos) (intersect sp_neg sq_neg) in
  itlist (union ** snd) nw [],(eqv',rfn');;
```

Though this function was a bit involved, it's now easy to perform 0-saturation, taking an existing equivalence-relevance pair and updating it with new equations `assigs` and all the consequences:

```
let rec zero_saturate erf assigs =
  match assigs with
    [] -> erf
  | (p,q)::ts -> let news,erf' = equatecons (p,q) erf in
                 zero_saturate erf' (union ts news);;
```

At some point, we would like to check whether a contradiction has been reached, i.e. some literal has become identified with its negation. The following function performs 0-saturation, then if a contradiction has been reached equates 'true' and 'false':

```
let zero_saturate_and_check erf trigs =
  let (eqv',rfn' as erf') = zero_saturate erf trigs in
  let vars = filter positive (equated eqv') in
  if exists (fun x -> canonize eqv' x = canonize eqv' (Not x)) vars
  then snd(equatecons (True,Not True) erf') else erf';;
```

to allow a simple test later on when needed:

```
let truefalse pfn = canonize pfn (Not True) = canonize pfn True;;
```

Higher saturation levels

To implement higher levels of saturation, we need to be able to take the intersection of equivalence classes derived in two branches. We start with an auxiliary function to equate a whole set of elements:

```
let rec equateset s0 eqfn =
  match s0 with
    a::(b::s2 as s1) -> equateset s1 (snd(equatecons (a,b) eqfn))
  | _ -> eqfn;;
```

Now to intersect two equivalence classes `eqv1` and `eqv2`, we repeatedly pick some literal `x`, find its equivalence classes `s1` and `s2` w.r.t. each equivalence relation, intersect them to give `s`, and then identify that set of literals in the 'output' equivalence relation using `equateset`. Here `rev1` and `rev2` are reverse mappings from a canonical representative back to the equivalence class, and `erf` is an equivalence relation to be augmented with the new equalities resulting.

```
let rec inter els (eq1,_ as erf1) (eq2,_ as erf2) rev1 rev2 erf =
  match els with
    [] -> erf
  | x::xs ->
      let b1 = canonize eq1 x and b2 = canonize eq2 x in
      let s1 = apply rev1 b1 and s2 = apply rev2 b2 in
      let s = intersect s1 s2 in
      inter (subtract xs s) erf1 erf2 rev1 rev2 (equateset s erf);;
```

We can obtain reversed equivalence class mappings thus:

```
let reverseq domain eqv =
  let al = map (fun x -> x,canonize eqv x) domain in
  itlist (fun (y,x) f -> (x |-> insert y (tryapplyl f x)) f)
         al undefined;;
```

The overall intersection function can exploit the fact that if contradiction is detected in one branch, the other branch can be taken over in its entirety.

```
let stal_intersect (eq1,_ as erf1) (eq2,_ as erf2) erf =
  if truefalse eq1 then erf2 else if truefalse eq2 then erf1 else
  let dom1 = equated eq1 and dom2 = equated eq2 in
  let comdom = intersect dom1 dom2 in
  let rev1 = reverseq dom1 eq1 and rev2 = reverseq dom2 eq2 in
  inter comdom erf1 erf2 rev1 rev2 erf;;
```

In n-saturation, we run through the variables, case-splitting over each in turn, $(n-1)$-saturating the subequivalences and intersecting them. This is repeated until a contradiction is reached, when we can terminate, or no more information is derived, in which case the formula is not n-easy and a higher saturation level must be tried. The implementation uses two mutually recursive function: `saturate` takes new assignments, 0-saturates to derive new information from them, and repeatedly calls `splits`:

```
let rec saturate n erf assigs allvars =
  let (eqv',_ as erf') = zero_saturate_and_check erf assigs in
  if n = 0 or truefalse eqv' then erf' else
  let (eqv'',_ as erf'') = splits n erf' allvars allvars in
  if eqv'' = eqv' then erf'' else saturate n erf'' [] allvars
```

which in turn runs splits over each variable in turn, performing $(n - 1)$-saturations and intersecting the results:

```
and splits n (eqv,_ as erf) allvars vars =
  match vars with
    [] -> erf
  | p::ovars ->
          if canonize eqv p <> p then splits n erf allvars ovars else
          let erf0 = saturate (n - 1) erf [p,Not True] allvars
          and erf1 = saturate (n - 1) erf [p,True] allvars in
          let (eqv',_ as erf') = stal_intersect erf0 erf1 erf in
          if truefalse eqv' then erf' else splits n erf' allvars ovars;;
```

Top-level function

We are now ready to implement a tautology prover based on Stålmarck's method. The main loop saturates up to a limit, with progress indications:

```
let rec saturate_upto vars n m trigs assigs =
  if n > m then failwith("Not "^(string_of_int m)^"-easy") else
    (print_string("*** Starting "^(string_of_int n)^"-saturation");
    print_newline();
    let (eqv,_) = saturate n (unequal,relevance trigs) assigs vars in
    truefalse eqv or saturate_upto vars (n + 1) m trigs assigs);;
```

The top-level function transforms the negated input formula into triplets, sets the entire formula equal to `True` and saturates. The triggers are collected together initially in a triggering function, which is then converted to a set:

```
let stalmarck fm =
  let include_trig (e,cqs) f = (e |-> union cqs (tryapplyl f e)) f in
  let fm' = psimplify(Not fm) in
  if fm' = False then true else if fm' = True then false else
  let p,triplets = triplicate fm' in
  let trigfn = itlist (itlist include_trig ** trigger)
                      triplets undefined
  and vars = map (fun p -> Atom p) (unions(map atoms triplets)) in
  saturate_upto vars 0 2 (graph trigfn) [p,True];;
```

The procedure is quite effective in many cases; in particular for instances of `mk_adder_test` it degrades much more gracefully with size than `dplltaut`

```
# stalmarck (mk_adder_test 6 3);;
*** Starting 0-saturation
*** Starting 1-saturation
*** Starting 2-saturation
- : bool = true
```

Since we only saturate up to a limit of 2, we can't conclude from the failure of `stalmarck` that a formula is *not* a tautology (this is why we make it fail rather than returning `false`). It's not hard to see that a formula with n atoms is n-easy, so it could easily be made complete. However, for non-tautologies, DPLL seems more effective, so some kind of combined algorithm may be appropriate, using saturation as well as DPLL-style splitting.

2.11 Binary decision diagrams

Consider the 2^n valuations of atoms $p_1, \ldots, p_n$ as paths through a binary tree labelled with atomic formulas. Starting at the root, we take the left (solid) path from a node labelled with p if $v(p) = \text{true}$ and the right (dotted) path if $v(p) = \text{false}$, and proceed similarly for the other atoms. For a given formula, we can label the leaves of the tree with 'T' if the formula holds in that valuation and 'F' otherwise, giving another presentation of its truth table, or the trace of the calls of `onallvaluations` hidden inside `tautology`. For the formula $p \land q \Rightarrow q \land r$ we might get:

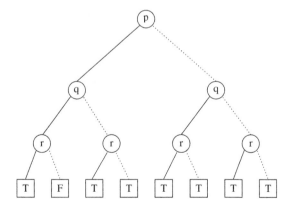

We can simplify such a *binary decision tree* in two ways:

- replace any nodes with the same subtree to the left and right by that subtree;

- share any common subtrees, creating a directed acyclic graph.

Such a reduced graph representation of a Boolean function is called a *binary decision diagram* (Lee 1959; Akers 1978), or if a fixed order of the atoms is used in all subtrees, a *reduced ordered binary decision diagram* (Bryant 1986). The reduced ordered binary decision diagram arising from the formula $p \wedge q \Rightarrow q \wedge r$, using alphabetical ordering of variables, can be represented as follows, using dotted lines to indicate a 'false' branch whether we show it to the left or right:

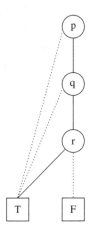

The use of a fixed variable ordering is now usual, and when people talk about binary decision diagrams (BDDs), they normally mean the reduced ordered kind. A fixed ordering tends to maximize sharing, and it turns out that many important Boolean functions, such as those corresponding to adders and other digital hardware components, have fairly compact ordered BDD representations. Another appealing feature not shared by unordered BDDs (even if they are reduced) is that, given a particular variable ordering, there is a unique BDD representation for any function. This means that testing equivalence of two Boolean expressions represented as BDDs (with the same variable order) simply amounts to checking graph isomorphism. In particular, a formula is a tautology iff its BDD representation is the single node 'T'.

Complement edges

Since Bryant's introduction of the BDD representation, the basic idea has been refined and extended in many ways. The use of *complement edges* (Madre and Billon 1988; Brace, Rudell and Bryant 1990) seems worth incorporating into our implementation, since the basic operations can be made more efficient and in many ways simpler. The idea is to allow each edge of the BDD graph to carry a tag, usually denoted by a small black circle in pictures, indicating the complementation (logical negation) of the subgraph it points to. With this representation, negating a BDD now takes constant time: one simply needs to flip its top tag. Furthermore, greater sharing is achieved because a graph and its complement can be shared; only the edges pointing into it need differ. In particular we only need one terminal node, which we choose (arbitrarily) to be 'true', with 'false' represented by a complement edge into it.

Complement edges do create one small problem: without some extra constraints, canonicality is lost. This is illustrated below: each of the four BDDs at the top is equivalent to the one below it. This ambiguity is (arbitrarily) resolved by ensuring that whenever we construct a BDD node, we transform between such equivalent pairs to ensure that the 'true' branch is uncomplemented, i.e. always replace any node listed on the top row by its corresponding node on the bottom row.

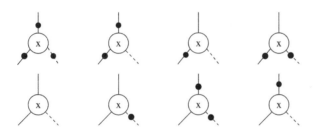

Implementation

Our OCaml representation of a BDD graph works by associating an integer index with each node.[†] Complementation is indicated by negating the node index, and since $-0 = 0$ we don't use 0 as an index. Index 1 is reserved for the 'true' node, and hence -1 for 'false'; other nodes are allocated indices n with $|n| \geq 2$. A BDD node itself is then just a propositional variable together with the 'left' and 'right' node indices:

```
type bddnode = prop * int * int;;
```

[†] All the code in this book is written in a purely functional subset of OCaml. It's tempting to implement BDDs imperatively: sharing could be implemented more directly using references as pointers, and we wouldn't need the messy threading of global tables through various functions. However, the purely functional style is more convenient for experimentation so we will stick with it.

The BDD graph is essentially just the association between BDD nodes and their integer indices, implemented as a finite partial function in each direction. But the data structure also stores the smallest (positive) unused node index and the ordering on atoms used in the graph:

```
type bdd = Bdd of ((bddnode,int)func * (int,bddnode)func * int) *
                   (prop->prop->bool);;
```

We don't print the internal structure of a BDD, just a size indication:

```
let print_bdd (Bdd((unique,uback,n),ord)) =
  print_string ("<BDD with "^(string_of_int n)^" nodes>");;

#install_printer print_bdd;;
```

To pass from an index to the corresponding node, we just apply the 'expansion' function in the data structure, negating appropriately to deal with complementation. For indices without an expansion, e.g. the terminal nodes 1 and −1, a trivial atom and two equivalent children are returned, since this makes some later code more regular.

```
let expand_node (Bdd((_,expand,_),_)) n =
  if n >= 0 then tryapplyd expand n (P"",1,1)
  else let (p,l,r) = tryapplyd expand (-n) (P"",1,1) in (p,-l,-r);;
```

Before any new node is added to the BDD, we check whether there is already such a node present, by looking it up using the function from nodes to indices. (Because its role is to ensure a single occurrence of each node in the graph, that function is traditionally called the *unique table*.) Otherwise a new node is added; in either case the (possibly modified) BDD and the final node index are returned:

```
let lookup_unique (Bdd((unique,expand,n),ord) as bdd) node =
  try bdd,apply unique node with Failure _ ->
  Bdd(((node|->n) unique,(n|->node) expand,n+1),ord),n;;
```

The core 'make a new BDD node' function first checks whether the two subnodes are identical, and if so returns one them together with an unchanged BDD. Otherwise it inserts a new node in the table, taking care to maintain an unnegated left subnode for canonicality.

```
let mk_node bdd (s,l,r) =
  if l = r then bdd,l
  else if l >= 0 then lookup_unique bdd (s,l,r)
  else let bdd',n = lookup_unique bdd (s,-l,-r) in bdd',-n;;
```

To get started, we want to be able to create a trivial BDD structure, with a user-specified ordering of the propositional variables:

```
let mk_bdd ord = Bdd((undefined,undefined,2),ord);;
```

The following function extracts the ordering from a BDD, treating the trivial variable as special so we can sometimes treat terminal nodes uniformly:

```
let order (Bdd(_,ord)) p1 p2 = (p2 = P"" & p1 <> P"") or ord p1 p2;;
```

The BDD representation of a formula is constructed bottom-up. For example, to create a BDD for a formula $p \wedge q$, we first create BDDs for p and q and then combine them appropriately by a function `bdd_and`. In order to avoid repeating work, we maintain a second function called the 'computed table' that stores previously computed results from `bdd_and`.[†] For updating the various tables, the following is convenient: it's similar to `g(f1 x2,f2 x2)` but with all the functions `f1`, `f2` and `g` also taking and returning some 'state' that we want to successively update through the evaluation:

```
let thread s g (f1,x1) (f2,x2) =
  let s',y1 = f1 s x1 in let s'',y2 = f2 s' x2 in g s'' (y1,y2);;
```

To implement conjunction of BDDs, we first consider the trivial cases where one of the BDDs is 'false' or 'true', in which case we return 'false' and the other BDD respectively. We also check whether the result has already been computed; since conjunction is commutative, we can equally well accept an entry with the arguments either way round. Otherwise, both BDDs are branches. In general, however, they may not branch on the same variable – although the *order* of variables is the same, many choices may be (and we hope are) omitted because of sharing. If the variables are the same, then we recursively deal with the left and right pairs, then create a new node. Otherwise, we pick the variable that comes first in the ordering and consider its two sides, but the other side is, at this level, not broken down. Note that at the end, we update the computed table with the new information.

[†] The unique table is essential for canonicality, but the computed table is purely an efficiency optimization, and we could do without it, at a sometimes considerable performance cost.

```
let rec bdd_and (bdd,comp as bddcomp) (m1,m2) =
  if m1 = -1 or m2 = -1 then bddcomp,-1
  else if m1 = 1 then bddcomp,m2 else if m2 = 1 then bddcomp,m1 else
  try bddcomp,apply comp (m1,m2) with Failure _ ->
  try  bddcomp,apply comp (m2,m1) with Failure _ ->
  let (p1,l1,r1) = expand_node bdd m1
  and (p2,l2,r2) = expand_node bdd m2 in
  let (p,lpair,rpair) =
      if p1 = p2 then p1,(l1,l2),(r1,r2)
      else if order bdd p1 p2 then p1,(l1,m2),(r1,m2)
      else p2,(m1,l2),(m1,r2) in
  let (bdd',comp'),(lnew,rnew) =
    thread bddcomp (fun s z -> s,z) (bdd_and,lpair) (bdd_and,rpair) in
  let bdd'',n = mk_node bdd' (p,lnew,rnew) in
  (bdd'',((m1,m2) |-> n) comp'),n;;
```

We can use this to implement all the other binary connectives on BDDs:

```
let bdd_or bdc (m1,m2) = let bdc1,n = bdd_and bdc (-m1,-m2) in bdc1,-n;;

let bdd_imp bdc (m1,m2) = bdd_or bdc (-m1,m2);;

let bdd_iff bdc (m1,m2) =
  thread bdc bdd_or (bdd_and,(m1,m2)) (bdd_and,(-m1,-m2));;
```

Now to construct a BDD for an arbitrary formula, we recurse over its structure; for the binary connectives we produce BDDs for the two subformulas then combine them appropriately:

```
let rec mkbdd (bdd,comp as bddcomp) fm =
  match fm with
    False -> bddcomp,-1
  | True -> bddcomp,1
  | Atom(s) -> let bdd',n = mk_node bdd (s,1,-1) in (bdd',comp),n
  | Not(p) -> let bddcomp',n = mkbdd bddcomp p in bddcomp',-n
  | And(p,q) -> thread bddcomp bdd_and (mkbdd,p) (mkbdd,q)
  | Or(p,q) -> thread bddcomp bdd_or (mkbdd,p) (mkbdd,q)
  | Imp(p,q) -> thread bddcomp bdd_imp (mkbdd,p) (mkbdd,q)
  | Iff(p,q) -> thread bddcomp bdd_iff (mkbdd,p) (mkbdd,q);;
```

This can now be made into a tautology-checker simply by creating a BDD for a formula and comparing the overall node index against the index for 'true'. We just use the default OCaml ordering '<' on variables:

```
let bddtaut fm = snd(mkbdd (mk_bdd (<),undefined) fm) = 1;;
```

Exploiting definitions

The tautology checker **bddtaut** performs quite well on some examples; for example it works markedly faster than **dplltaut** here:

```
# bddtaut (mk_adder_test 4 2);;
- : bool = true
```

However, it's relatively inefficient on larger formulas of the same kind, such as **mk_adder_test 9 5**. These formulas, as a result of the way they were created, use 'definitions' of the form $x_i \Leftrightarrow E_i$ occurring positively in the antecedent of an implication, or the body of a negated formula. We can break down the overall formula uniformly, regarding $\neg p$ as $p \Rightarrow \bot$:

```
let dest_nimp fm = match fm with Not(p) -> p,False | _ -> dest_imp fm;;
```

The 'defined' variables are used to express sharing of common subexpressions within a propositional formula via equivalences $x \Leftrightarrow E$, just as they were in the construction of definitional CNF. However, since a BDD structure already shares common subexpressions, we'd rather exclude the variable x and replace it by the BDD for E wherever it appears elsewhere. The following breaks down a definition:

```
let rec dest_iffdef fm =
  match fm with
    Iff(Atom(x),r) | Iff(r,Atom(x)) -> x,r
  | _ -> failwith "not a defining equivalence";;
```

However, we can't treat any conjunction of suitable formulas as a sequence of definitions, because they might be cyclic, e.g. $(x \Leftrightarrow y \wedge r) \wedge (y \Leftrightarrow x \vee s)$. In order to change our mind and put a definition $x \Leftrightarrow e$ back as an antecedent to the formula, we use:

```
let restore_iffdef (x,e) fm = Imp(Iff(Atom(x),e),fm);;
```

We then try to organize the definitions into an acyclic dependency order by repeatedly picking out one $x \Leftrightarrow e$ that is *suitable*, meaning that no other atom potentially 'defined' later occurs in e:

```
let suitable_iffdef defs (x,q) =
  let fvs = atoms q in not (exists (fun (x',_) -> mem x' fvs) defs);;
```

The main code for sorting definitions is recursive. The list **acc** holds the definitions already processed into a suitable order, **defs** is the unprocessed definitions and **fm** is the main formula. The code looks for a definition $x \Leftrightarrow e$

that is suitable, adds it to `acc` and moves any other definitions $x \Leftrightarrow e'$
from `defs` back into the formula. Should no suitable definition be found, all
remaining definitions are put back into the formula and the processed list is
reversed so that the earliest items in the dependency order occur first:

```
let rec sort_defs acc defs fm =
  try let (x,e) = find (suitable_iffdef defs) defs in
      let ps,nonps = partition (fun (x',_) -> x' = x) defs in
      let ps' = subtract ps [x,e] in
      sort_defs ((x,e)::acc) nonps (itlist restore_iffdef ps' fm)
  with Failure _ -> rev acc,itlist restore_iffdef defs fm;;
```

The BDD for a formula will be constructed as before, but each atom will
first be looked up using a 'subfunction' `sfn` to see if it is already considered
just a shorthand for another BDD:

```
let rec mkbdde sfn (bdd,comp as bddcomp) fm =
  match fm with
    False -> bddcomp,-1
  | True -> bddcomp,1
  | Atom(s) -> (try bddcomp,apply sfn s with Failure _ ->
                  let bdd',n = mk_node bdd (s,1,-1) in (bdd',comp),n)
  | Not(p) -> let bddcomp',n = mkbdde sfn bddcomp p in bddcomp',-n
  | And(p,q) -> thread bddcomp bdd_and (mkbdde sfn,p) (mkbdde sfn,q)
  | Or(p,q) -> thread bddcomp bdd_or (mkbdde sfn,p) (mkbdde sfn,q)
  | Imp(p,q) -> thread bddcomp bdd_imp (mkbdde sfn,p) (mkbdde sfn,q)
  | Iff(p,q) -> thread bddcomp bdd_iff (mkbdde sfn,p) (mkbdde sfn,q);;
```

We now create the BDD for a series of definitions and final formula by
successively forming BDDs for the definitions, including those into the subfunction `sfn` and recursing, forming the BDD for the formula when all definitions have been used:

```
let rec mkbdds sfn bdd defs fm =
  match defs with
    [] -> mkbdde sfn bdd fm
  | (p,e)::odefs -> let bdd',b = mkbdde sfn bdd e in
                    mkbdds ((p |-> b) sfn) bdd' odefs fm;;
```

For the overall tautology checker, we break the formula into definitions
and a main formula, sort the definitions into dependency order, and then
call `mkbdds` before testing at the end:

```
let ebddtaut fm =
  let l,r = try dest_nimp fm with Failure _ -> True,fm in
  let eqs,noneqs = partition (can dest_iffdef) (conjuncts l) in
  let defs,fm' = sort_defs [] (map dest_iffdef eqs)
                          (itlist mk_imp noneqs r) in
  snd(mkbdds undefined (mk_bdd (<),undefined) defs fm') = 1;;
```

This is substantially more efficient on many of the examples that were
barely feasible before:

```
# ebddtaut (prime 101);;
- : bool = true
# ebddtaut (mk_adder_test 9 5);;
- : bool = true
```

However, there are many other optimizations worthy of note. In particular, our naive choice of the default alphabetical variable order has little to
recommend it. For circuit examples, variable orders reflecting the topology
are often effective (Malik, Wang, Brayton and Sangiovanni-Vincentelli 1988).
However, there is no feasible algorithm for arriving at the best variable ordering, and in fact many available BDD packages automatically try reordering
variables partway through the BDD construction. Indeed, for certain classes
of formulas, the BDD representation has exponential size whatever variable
ordering is used, e.g. those involving multipliers (Bryant 1986) or the 'hidden
weighted bit' function (Bryant 1991).

We should emphasize that BDDs are not simply a path to tautology or
satisfiability checking, but an alternative *representation* for propositional
formulas. This gives them a useful role in various methods for formal verification such as symbolic simulation (Bryant 1985), symbolic trajectory evaluation (Seger and Bryant 1995) and temporal logic model checking (Burch,
Clarke, McMillan, Dill and Hwang 1992), where their canonical nature is
particularly appropriate.

2.12 Compactness

We now establish a key theoretical property of propositional logic, used
essentially in the next chapter, concerning the satisfiability of an *infinite*
set of formulas. Recall that a set Γ of propositional formulas is said to be
satisfiable if there is a valuation that simultaneously satisfies them all. The
compactness theorem[†] states:

[†] The name comes from a link with point-set topology (Engelking 1989; Kelley 1975). Give the
set of all valuations $\mathbb{B}^{\mathbb{N}}$, where $\mathbb{B} = \{\text{false}, \text{true}\}$, the product topology based on the discrete
topology for $\mathbb{B}$. (This is sometimes called Cantor space.) For any formula p, the set V_p of
valuations satisfying it is closed (in fact open too) in this topology because each formula only
involves finitely many propositional variables. Since $\mathbb{B}$ is compact, so is $\mathbb{B}^{\mathbb{N}}$ by Tychonoff's
theorem. By hypothesis, all finite intersections from the set $\{V_p \mid p \in \Gamma\}$ are nonempty, and so
by definition of compactness, the intersection of all of them is nonempty, as required. Assuming
the Axiom of Choice, Tychonoff's theorem holds if $\mathbb{N}$ is replaced by any set of atoms, giving a
proof of the compactness theorem in the general case.

Theorem 2.13 *For any set Γ of propositional formulas, if each finite subset $\Delta \subseteq \Gamma$ is satisfiable, then Γ itself is satisfiable.*

Proof We will assume that the set of atoms is countable, and enumerate them in some way $p_1, p_2, \ldots$ This is sufficient for all the applications to automated reasoning, and requires less mathematical machinery. The method of proof is to produce a valuation v that satisfies Γ by considering the atoms in sequence and choosing appropriate $v(p_1)$, $v(p_2)$, $\ldots$ one at a time.

First we will show that *if* there are truth values t_1, t_2, $\ldots$, t_n such that every finite $\Delta \subseteq \Gamma$ is satisfiable by a valuation v with $v(p_1) = t_1$, $\ldots$, $v(p_n) = t_n$ *then* there is a truth-value t_{n+1} such that every finite $\Delta \subseteq \Gamma$ is satisfiable by a valuation v with $v(p_1) = t_1$, $\ldots$, $v(p_{n+1}) = t_{n+1}$. For suppose not. Then setting $t_{n+1} =$ false doesn't work, so there's some finite $\Delta_0 \subseteq \Gamma$ not satisfiable by any valuation v with $v(p_1) = t_1$, $\ldots$, $v(p_n) = t_n$, $v(p_{n+1}) =$ false. Similarly, setting $t_{n+1} =$ true doesn't work so there's some finite $\Delta_1 \subseteq \Gamma$ not satisfiable by any valuation v with $v(p_1) = t_1$, $\ldots$, $v(p_n) = t_n$, $v(p_{n+1}) =$ true. Therefore the set $\Delta_0 \cup \Delta_1$ is not satisfiable by any valuation v with $v(p_1) = t_1$, $\ldots$, $v(p_n) = t_n$ since any such valuation must either set $v(p_{n+1}) =$ false, in which case it fails to satisfy Δ_0, or $v(p_{n+1}) =$ true in which case it fails to satisfy Δ_1. However since $\Delta_0 \cup \Delta_1$ is the union of two finite sets, it is also finite, contradicting the assumption.

Therefore we can define an infinite sequence of truth values (t_i) by recursion with the property that for any $n \in \mathbb{N}$, any finite $\Delta \subseteq \Gamma$ is satisfiable by a valuation v with $v(p_1) = t_1$, $\ldots$, $v(p_n) = t_n$, and this defines a valuation by $v(p_n) = t_n$. We claim v satisfies Γ, i.e. satisfies every formula $p \in \Gamma$. For any such p, since the number of atoms in p is finite, we can find some N so that each p_n occurring in p has $n \leq N$. But by construction all finite subsets of Γ, in particular $\{p\}$, are satisfiable by a valuation w where $w(p_n) = t_n = v(p_n)$ for $n \leq N$. Since assignments to variables not in p are irrelevant, this shows that p is indeed satisfied by v as required. $\square$

Corollary 2.14 *If an arbitrary set Γ of propositional formulas is unsatisfiable, then some finite subset $\Delta \subseteq \Gamma$ is unsatisfiable.*

Proof Suppose instead that every finite subset $\Delta \subseteq \Gamma$ were satisfiable. By the compactness theorem, Γ is satisfiable, contradicting the hypothesis. $\square$

Corollary 2.15 *If a set Γ of formulas is such that for any valuation v there is some $p \in \Gamma$ that is satisfied by v, then there is a finite disjunction of $p_i \in \Gamma$, say $p_1 \vee \cdots \vee p_n$, that is a tautology.*

Proof Let $\overline{\Gamma} = \{\neg p \mid p \in \Gamma\}$. Since every valuation satisfies some $p \in \Gamma$ it must fail to satisfy the corresponding $\neg p \in \overline{\Gamma}$. Hence $\overline{\Gamma}$ is unsatisfiable. By the previous corollary, some finite subset $\{\neg p_1, \ldots, \neg p_n\}$ is unsatisfiable. However by definition, a valuation satisfies this set precisely if it satisfies the conjunction $\neg p_1 \wedge \cdots \wedge \neg p_n$, and so this formula is unsatisfiable. Hence its negation $\neg(\neg p_1 \wedge \cdots \wedge \neg p_n)$ is a tautology, and by the De Morgan laws this is logically equivalent to $p_1 \vee \cdots \vee p_n$. $\square$

In the next chapter, we will apply the Compactness Theorem to automated theorem proving. However, perhaps it's interesting to see a direct mathematical application. Readers may skip the remainder of this section without impairing their understanding of the rest of the book.

Colouring infinite graphs

How many different colours are needed to colour the regions on a map so that no two regions sharing a border have the same colour? (These 'regions' might be countries, states, counties, etc. depending on the map.) The following map needs at least four:

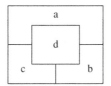

Remarkably, four colours are enough for *any* map. (We assume no region is split into two disconnected pieces, and ignore common borders consisting of just a point.) This was first conjectured by the map-maker Francis Guthrie who had been colouring the counties on a map of England. De Morgan (of the De Morgan laws) communicated the problem to other leading mathematicians. The first 'proof' was published by Kempe (1879), but rather later Heawood (1890) showed that it was flawed, and only proves that five colours suffice. The conjecture remained open for almost a century until it was proved by Appel and Haken (1976) using a refinement of Kempe's original argument supported by extensive computer checking of particular configurations. The fact that important parts of the proof were delegated to a computer has caused controversy ever since (Lam 1990), though recent work by Gonthier (2005) on a thoroughgoing formalization may have helped to dispel some worries.

First, let us formulate the result in a more mathematical way, ignoring inessential details like the shapes of regions and making clear that we are considering maps drawn on a plane rather than, say, the surface of a torus (where as many as seven colours may be needed). We consider the map as a graph where the regions are represented by vertices V and those sharing a common border are connected by an edge. We will consider the edges as binary relations, with $E(a, b)$ meaning 'there is an edge between a and b'. E is irreflexive, i.e. it is never the case that $E(a, a)$, and symmetric, i.e. $E(a, b)$ iff $E(b, a)$. A graph is said to be *planar* if there is a mapping $f :$ $V \to \mathbb{R}^2$ of vertices to points in the Euclidean plane so that paths can be drawn between each pair $(f(a), f(b))$ where $E(a, b)$ such that no two distinct paths touch except at the vertices, i.e. it can be drawn on a plane without edges crossing. By a *k-colouring* of a graph, we mean a mapping $C : V \to \{1, \ldots, k\}$ assigning to each vertex one of k distinct 'colours'. We say that a graph is *k-colourable* if an assignment C of k colours can be made such that whenever $E(x, y)$ then $C(x) \neq C(y)$, i.e. no connected vertices have the same colour. In this guise, the 4-colour theorem can be stated as follows:

Theorem 2.16 *Every planar graph with a finite number of vertices is 4-colourable.*

Proof Too complex to be given. See Appel and Haken (1976) for a brief account of the original proof, and Robertson, Sanders, Seymour and Thomas (1996) for a simpler proof. ☐

Given any particular graph, we can formulate 4-colourability as a propositional satisfiability problem on a set of atoms $\{p_v^i \mid v \in V \wedge i \in \{1, 2, 3, 4\}\}$ representing the assignment of colour i to vertex v. To encode the assertion that the assignment of colours is indeed a valid colouring, we need three things.

- Every vertex has some colour. This can be represented by the formulas $\{p_v^1 \vee p_v^2 \vee p_v^3 \vee p_v^4 \mid v \in V\}$.
- No vertex has more than one colour. This can be represented by the formulas $\{\neg(p_v^1 \wedge p_v^2) \wedge \neg(p_v^1 \wedge p_v^3) \wedge \neg(p_v^1 \wedge p_v^4) \wedge \neg(p_v^2 \wedge p_v^3) \wedge \neg(p_v^2 \wedge p_v^4) \wedge \neg(p_v^3 \wedge p_v^4) \mid v \in V\}$.
- Two vertices connected by an edge do not have the same colour. This can be represented by the formulas $\{\neg(p_a^1 \wedge p_b^1) \wedge \neg(p_a^2 \wedge p_b^2) \wedge \neg(p_a^3 \wedge p_b^3) \wedge \neg(p_a^4 \wedge p_b^4) \mid E(a, b)\}$.

We claim that the graph is 4-colourable precisely if the set of all these formulas together, say Γ, is satisfiable. In fact, given a colouring $C : V \to \{1, \ldots, 4\}$, create a corresponding valuation v where $v(p_v^i) =$ true precisely when $C(v) = i$. Note that C is a valid colouring precisely when the set of formulas is satisfied by v.

We can now apply the compactness theorem to deduce that the 4-colour theorem remains true even for infinite graphs. Consider any finite subset Δ of Γ. This finite collection of formulas can only involve finitely many propositional variables p_v^i and hence only finitely many v, say some finite subset $V' \subseteq V$. Consider the subgraph based on the vertex set V', i.e. restrict the edges to $E'(x, y)$ meaning $E(x, y)$ and $x \in V'$, $y \in V'$. Create the corresponding finite set of formulas Γ'. By the 4-colour theorem this is satisfiable, and clearly includes Δ. Therefore by the compactness theorem, the whole set Γ is satisfiable and so the entire graph, even if infinite, is 4-colourable.

Thanks to the formulation of colourability in terms of propositional satisfiability, the proof based on compactness was relatively simple. It easily generalizes to prove that if every finite subset of a graph is k-colourable, so is the whole graph, as was originally proved by de Bruijn (1951) using a more direct argument. Dually, by formulating certain properties as propositional tautologies, we can sometimes deduce a finite version of a theorem from an infinite one – see Exercise 2.22.

Further reading

For the general theory of Boolean algebra, which includes propositional, set-theoretic and other interpretations of Boole's original system, see for example Abian (1976), Davey and Priestley (1990) and Halmos (1963). There are discussions of Boolean algebras in many logic textbooks such as Bell and Slomson (1969), some of which we will recommend later for other technical topics. Finally, Halmos and Givant (1998) treats logic in the modern way but adopts a more explicitly algebraic style.

Propositional logic is covered in many standard logic texts, e.g. Church (1956), van Dalen (1994), Enderton (1972), Goodstein (1971), Hilbert and Ackermann (1950), Hodges (1977), Johnstone (1987), Kreisel and Krivine (1971), Mates (1972), Quine (1950) and Tarski (1941); many of these also prove the compactness theorem. Most books on automated theorem proving also discuss propositional logic and classical decision methods such as Davis–Putnam, though often spend little time on propositional logic before moving on to first-order logic (our next chapter). Davis, Sigal and Weyuker (1994) is a combination of theoretical logic with automated theorem proving, as well as being a textbook on computability and complexity. More focused on automated theorem proving are Bibel (1987), Chang and Lee (1973), Duffy (1991), Fitting (1990), Loveland (1978), Newborn (2001) and Wos, Overbeek, Lusk and Boyle (1992).

Backjumping and learning were first used in DPLL in the SAT solvers GRASP (Marques-Silva and Sakallah 1996) and rel_sat (Bayardo and Schrag 1997). Some more recent DPLL-based systems, in approximately chronological order of development, are SATO (Zhang 1997), Chaff (Moskewicz, Madigan, Zhao, Zhang and Malik 2001), BerkMin (Goldberg and Novikov 2002) and MiniSat (Een and Sörensson 2003). The papers describing these systems are a valuable source of information about both the fundamental DPLL algorithm versions and the clever implementation tricks. Nieuwenhuis, Oliveras and Tinelli (2006) and Krstić and Goel (2007) describe iterative DPLL by a nondeterministic sequence of abstract rules, so that particular implementations can be seen as ways of deploying these rules. Kroening and Strichman (2008) also discuss the architectures of 'industrial-strength' SAT solvers, as well as discussing numerous extensions of propositional logic and how they are used in applications. Some of these topics will be discussed later in this book, but some will not, notably *quantified Boolean formulas* (QBF), where formulas may be quantified over the atoms. (This is different from first-order logic described in the next chapter where quantification is over elements of the domain, not propositions.)

Some of the topics we have discussed are not (yet) widely covered in general textbooks and the reader must consult more specialist monographs or research papers. This is notably the case for Stålmarck's algorithm, though a survey of the theory and its successful practical applications is given by Sheeran and Stålmarck (2000). The idea of *recursive learning* (Kunz and Pradhan 1994) shares important ideas with Stålmarck's method.

The survey article by Bryant (1992) and the textbook by Kropf (1999) discuss BDDs and their role in automated methods for formal hardware verification. Most strikingly, temporal logic model checking (Clarke and Emerson 1981; Queille and Sifakis 1982) underwent a minor revolution when McMillan and others (Coudert, Berthet and Madre 1989; Burch, Clarke, McMillan, Dill and Hwang 1992; Pixley 1990) married them with a BDD representation.[†] For a detailed introduction to model checking, see Clarke, Grumberg

---

[†] However, there has recently been interest in approaches using other, non-canonical, representations (Bjesse 1999; Abdulla, Bjesse and Eén 2000) as well as pure SAT solving (Biere, Cimatti, Clarke and Zhu 1999; McMillan 2003).

and Peled (1999), as well as some books on logic in computer science like Huth and Ryan (1999).

Propositional satisfiability can be reduced to linear integer arithmetic, interpreting 0 as false and 1 as true and mapping each propositional atom p to a variable v_p with a constraint $0 \leq v_p \leq 1$. Now, for example, $p \lor \neg q \lor r$ holds if $v_p + (1 - v_q) + v_r \geq 1$. Thus we can convert satisfiability for a propositional formula in clausal form into an integer arithmetic problem consisting of a conjunction of such inequalities. See Hooker (1988) for more on this kind of technique, which is radically different from those algorithms we have considered.

Exercises

2.1 Implement a function to generate all propositional formulas with a given number of symbols (measuring either the number of nodes in the abstract syntax tree or some standard linear form). Plot the proportion of such formulas that are tautologies or contradictions against the size. Can you generate results for large enough lengths to see a trend? Is the trend as expected?

2.2 Prove the following nice result in equivalential logic due to Leśniewski (1929). We remarked that features of logical equivalence '$\Leftrightarrow$' such as associativity often seem peculiar because we are not accustomed to thinking of propositional functions. Show in fact that a propositional formula involving only atoms, '$\top$' and '$\Leftrightarrow$' is a tautology iff each atom occurs an even number of times. Show that if '$\neg$' is also allowed, a formula is a tautology iff each atom occurs an even number of times *and* the negation operator appears an even number of times.

2.3 Prove this elegant result from Post (1941); see Goodstein (1971) for an easier proof and further generalizations. We showed earlier that all truth-functions can be generated from the binary operations 'NAND' and 'NOR', i.e. either variant of the 'Sheffer stroke'. More generally, call an n-ary truth-function $f : \{0,1\}^n \to \{0,1\}$ a *Sheffer function* if all truth-functions can be generated from it alone. Show that f is a Sheffer function iff (i) for all p we have $f(p, p, \ldots, p) = \neg p$ and (ii) for some $p_1, \ldots, p_n$ we have $f(\neg p_1, \ldots, \neg p_n) \neq \neg f(p_1, \ldots, p_n)$.

2.4 Implement an algorithm to generate all n-ary Sheffer functions for a given n. Implement another algorithm that takes a basic propositional function, perhaps specified by a formula, and a second formula p, and expresses p in terms of the basic function if possible, or fails if not.

2.5   Prove the key duality result `eval (dual p) v = not(eval p (not ∘ v))`
       by a formal induction on formulas.

2.6   Show that applying our `nnf` function to a right-associated chain of
       equivalences $p_1 \Leftrightarrow p_2 \Leftrightarrow \cdots \Leftrightarrow p_n$ results in a formula with A_n
       atoms (and therefore $A_n - 1$ binary connectives) where $A_1 = 1$ and
       for $n \geq 1$ we have $A_{n+1} = 2(A_n + 1)$. Show that this is the worst
       possible result for any starting formula with n atoms.

2.7   We can avoid the potentially exponential duplication of work when
       transforming a formula to NNF by the trick of returning for a formula
       p *two* NNF formulas, one equivalent to p and the other equivalent
       to $\neg p$. Write a direct recursive OCaml implementation of such a
       function, `nnfp`, whose runtime is linear in the size of the formula.
       For example, the clause for an equivalence `Iff(p,q)` might be:

```
let p',p'' = nnfp p and q',q'' = nnfp q in
Or(And(p',q'),And(p'',q'')),Or(And(p',q''),And(p'',q'))
```

       Test the function on heavily nested instances of '⇔'. Note that
       the resulting formulas will still be exponentially large when printed
       out, but internally will share common subexpressions. Thus, when
       testing the efficiency you will want to avoid looking at the result,
       e.g. by

```
let fm' = time nnfp (simplify fm) in ();;
```

2.8   Look at some alternative digital circuits for multiplication, e.g. Wal-
       lace trees, in standard computer arithmetic texts such as Koren
       (1992). Realize them as propositional formulas and verify equiva-
       lence to the implementations we have given by tautology checking.

2.9   Show how to construct a digital circuit with three inputs a, b and c
       and three outputs that are the respective negations $\neg a$, $\neg b$ and $\neg c$,
       using an arbitrary number of 'AND' and 'OR' gates but *at most two*
       'NOT' gates (inverters). This surprisingly difficult puzzle in logic
       circuit design (Wos 1998) was suggested by E. Snow from Intel.
       Can you prove a more general result about how many wires can be
       inverted using any number of 'AND' and 'OR' gates together with n
       inverters?

2.10   Show that if an atomic proposition x occurs only *positively* in a
       formula p, then `psubst` $(x \mapsto q)$ p is satisfiable precisely if $(x \Rightarrow q) \wedge p$
       is (Plaisted and Greenbaum 1986). Use this to create an variant of
       `defcnf` using implication rather than equivalence for the definitions

wherever possible. How does this affect subsequent performance of algorithms like DPLL, on both satisfiable and unsatisfiable formulas?

2.11   The comparison between `tautology` and `dplltaut` is rather unfair in that we don't test the particular CNF form and Davis–Putnam rules against other ways of simplifying the formula. Implement a version of `tautology` that simplifies the formula (perhaps using `psimplify`) between case-splits and uses similar variable-picking heuristics to `dplltaut`. How does this compare?

2.12   Modify one of our DPLL implementations so that when a formula is satisfiable, it returns a satisfying assignment in some form (e.g. a finite partial function into booleans, or the set of atoms to be assigned 'true').

2.13   Modify one of our DPLL implementations so that when given an unsatisfiable set of clauses, it provides a *proof* of that unsatisfiability as a sequence of resolution steps. Can you make this work both when doing backjumping/learning *and* when doing purely the traditional DPLL splitting?

2.14   In an early presentation (Stålmarck and Säflund 1990) of Stålmarck's method, negations were eliminated by pulling them *up* the formula, leaving just implication and conjunction. Define a function `nunf` to do this. Show that if the final formula is unnegated, the whole formula is automatically satisfiable.

2.15   Implement a variant of Stålmarck's method based on 3-CNF along the lines described by Groote (2000), accumulating unit and 2-clauses (which can be considered as implications). How does performance compare with the usual version? Suppose that instead of splitting over variables, one uses the clauses themselves and splits over the various disjuncts (in general a three-way split). How does that compare? Does it help if when splitting over $p \vee q \vee r$ one assumes separately p, $\neg p \wedge q$, and $\neg p \wedge \neg q \wedge r$?

2.16   'Urquhart formulas' are tautologies of the form $p_1 \Leftrightarrow p_2 \Leftrightarrow \cdots \Leftrightarrow p_n \Leftrightarrow p_1 \Leftrightarrow p_2 \Leftrightarrow \cdots \Leftrightarrow p_n$ for some n. Show that they are all 2-easy for Stålmarck's method. Implement an OCaml function to return an Urquhart formula for a given parameter `n`, and compare the performance of our implementations of DPLL and Stålmarck on them.

2.17   Try modifying the BDD construction functions to choose variable orderings reflecting the characteristics of the problem, perhaps derived from the sequence of 'definitions' in `ebddtaut`. Can you find some simple approaches that work well on a wide class of examples?

2.18   Implement a function to generate (pseudo-)random formulas in 3-CNF, based on input parameters giving the desired number of clauses (C) and the number of distinct atoms (V). A naive statistical analysis would suggest that, since each clause excludes $\left(\frac{1}{2}\right)^3 = \frac{1}{8}$ of the possible valuations, the number of satisfying valuations would be of the order of $2^V \left(\frac{7}{8}\right)^C$. Regardless of the method used, satisfiability of problems where $2^V \left(\frac{7}{8}\right)^C \approx 1$, i.e. $C \approx 5.2V$, might be expected to be the most difficult to resolve, since they are on the borderline between satisfiability and unsatisfiability. Empirical studies of algorithms such as DPLL often suggest a difficulty peak closer to $C \approx 4.3V$ (Kirkpatrick and Selman 1994; Crawford and Auton 1996). But the difficulty peak, and the onset of other qualitative changes, is quite subtle and apparently algorithm-dependent (Coarfa, Demopoulos, Alfonso, Subramanian and Vardi 2000). Experiment with the performance of various tautology-checking or satisfiability-checking methods on your random formulas as the C/V ratio is varied. Are your results in line with theoretical expectations? Can you refine the analysis, e.g. using techniques presented by Kirousis, Kranakis, Krizanc and Stamatiou (1998), so that they are? How does the difficulty peak vary if one considers 4-CNF, 5-CNF etc.? Is this again in line with expectations?

2.19   A set of formulas Γ is said to be *independent* if whenever $\phi \in \Gamma$, $\Gamma - \{\phi\} \not\models \phi$, i.e. no formula in Γ follows from all the others. Two sets Γ and Δ are said to be *equivalent* if for any formula ϕ, $\Gamma \models \phi$ iff $\Delta \models \phi$. Prove that:

- any finite set Γ has an equivalent independent subset;
- not every countable set of formulas has an equivalent independent subset;
- every countable set of formulas does have an equivalent independent *set*, not necessarily a subset of the original set.

Does the last result extend to uncountable sets?

2.20   Let B be an infinite set of boys, each of whom has at most a finite number of girlfriends. If for each integer k, any k of the boys have between them at least k girlfriends, prove that it is possible for each boy to marry one of his girlfriends without any of them committing bigamy (Bell and Slomson 1969).

2.21   Gardner (1975) gave a planar map which he claimed (as an April Fool's joke) not to be 4-colourable. Construct the corresponding propositional formula and refute the claim by proving it satisfiable.

2.22   An infinite variant of Ramsey's Theorem 2.9 states that any graph
        on vertices $\mathbb{N}$ has either an infinite connected subgraph or an infinite
        completely disconnected subgraph. (You might want to try and prove
        that.) Use the compactness theorem to deduce our finite Ramsey
        Theorem 2.9 from that infinite variant.

2.23   Prove the following combinatorial theorems taken from Bonet, Buss
        and Pitassi (1995). (i) If a town has n citizens and there is a set of
        clubs such that each club has an odd number of citizens and any
        two distinct clubs have an even number of citizens in common, then
        there are at most n clubs. (ii) If $F_1, \ldots, F_m$ is a system of distinct
        nonempty subsets of $\{1, \ldots, n\}$ such that for each $i \neq j$, $|F_i \cap F_j| = k$,
        for some fixed k, then $m \leq n$. Write programs to encode particular
        instances of these assertions as propositional satisfiability problems
        and test some of the methods we have covered in this chapter.

2.24   A group (not necessarily abelian) is said to be *ordered* by $\leq$ iff $\leq$ is a
        total order such that $a \leq b \Rightarrow ac \leq bc \wedge ca \leq cb$. Show that a group
        can be ordered iff each *finitely generated* subgroup can be ordered.
        Deduce that an abelian group can be ordered iff it is torsion-free, i.e.
        there is no $n \geq 1$ such that $x^n = 1$ for $x \neq 1$ (Kreisel and Krivine
        1971).

2.25   Although no polynomial-time algorithm for SAT is known at the time
        of writing, show that you could implement a function `polysat` that
        accepts propositional formulas and always correctly tests them for
        satisfiability, and is such that *if* $P = NP$ then there is a polynomial
        $p(n)$ so that the runtime of `polysat` on *satisfiable* formulas of size
        n is $\leq p(n)$. (The author learned of this result from Carl Witty,
        and Martin Hofmann pointed out that it is a special case of Levin's
        search theorem in recursion theory.)

3

First-order logic

We now move from propositional logic to richer first-order logic, where propositions can involve non-propositional variables that may be universally or existentially quantified. We show how proof in first-order logic can be mechanized naively via Herbrand's theorem. We then introduce various refinements, notably unification, that help make automated proof more efficient.

3.1 First-order logic and its implementation

Propositional logic only allows us to build formulas from primitive propositions that may independently be true or false. However, this is too restrictive to capture patterns of reasoning where the truth or falsity of propositions depends on the values of *non-propositional* variables. For example, a typical proposition about numbers is '$m < n$', and its truth depends on the values of m and n. If we simply introduce a distinct propositional variable for each such proposition, we lose the ability to interrelate different instances according to the variables they contain, e.g. to assert that $\neg(m < n \wedge n < m)$. *First-order (predicate) logic* extends propositional logic in two ways to accommodate this need:

- the atomic propositions can be built up from non-propositional variables and constants using functions and predicates;
- the non-propositional variables can be *bound* with *quantifiers*.

We make a syntactic distinction between *formulas*, which are intuitively intended to be true or false, and *terms*, which are intended to denote 'objects' in the domain being reasoned about (numbers, people, sets or whatever). Terms are built up from (object-denoting) variables using functions. In discussions we use $f(s, t, u)$ for a term built from subterms s, t and u using

118

the function f, or sometimes infix notation like $s + t$ rather than $+(s,t)$ where it seems more natural or familiar. All of these are merely understood as presentations of the underlying abstract syntax of terms where a term is either a variable or a function applied to any number of other 'argument' terms:

```
type term = Var of string
          | Fn of string * term list;;
```

Functions can have any number of arguments, this number being known as the *arity* of the function (from a pun on the words unary, binary, ternary, quaternary, etc.) In particular we can accommodate constants like 1 or π as *nullary* functions, i.e. functions with zero arguments. Most mathematical expressions can be quite directly formalized as terms, e.g. $\sqrt{1 - \cos^2(x + y)}$ as:

```
Fn("sqrt",[Fn("-",[Fn("1",[]);
                Fn("cos",[Fn("power",[Fn("+",[Var "x"; Var "y"]);
                                Fn("2",[])])])])]);;
```

All the logical connectives of propositional logic carry over into first-order logic. However, each atomic proposition is now analyzed into a named *predicate* or *relation* applied to any finite number of terms. Once again we write $P(s,t)$ for a predicate P applied to arguments s and t, but use infix notation like $s < t$ where it seems natural instead of $< (s,t)$. We create a new type `fol` of first-order atomic propositions, so we get a natural `fol formula` type for the type of first-order formulas:

```
type fol = R of string * term list;;
```

For example, $x + y < z$ can be formalized as the atomic formula:

```
Atom(R("<",[Fn("+",[Var "x"; Var "y"]); Var "z"]))
```

A predicate may have zero arguments, corresponding to a simple propositional variable. We call functions and predicates with one argument *unary* or *monadic*, those with two arguments *binary* or *dyadic*, and those with n arguments n-ary.

In certain contexts, we will consider terms and/or formulas in a restricted *language*. Formally, we define a *signature* as a pair of sets, one a list of functions and one a list of predicates, both as name–arity pairs, and the corresponding *language* as the sets of terms and formulas that can be built using only functions and predicates appearing in that signature (but any variables). For example the *language of arithmetic* that we use in Chapter 7 has the following signature:

$$(\{(\texttt{"0"}, 0), (\texttt{"S"}, 1), (\texttt{"+"}, 2), (\texttt{"*"}, 2)\}, \{(\texttt{"="}, 2), (\texttt{"<"}, 2), (\texttt{"<="}, 2)\}),$$

so terms like $x + S(0)$ and formulas like $S(S(0)) < x + y$ are in the language but $1 + x$ and $P(0, x)$ are not. The exact formal definitions of 'language' and 'signature' are unimportant (these vary in the literature, and some authors identify the two), provided the concept of a term or formula being in a restricted language is clear.

Quantifiers

Now we come to the other main change compared with propositional logic: the introduction of quantifiers.

- The formula $\forall x.\, p$, or `Forall("x",p)` in our OCaml formulation, where x is a variable and p any formula, means intuitively 'for *all* values of x, p is true'. For this reason $\forall$ is referred to as the *universal quantifier*; the symbol is derived from the first letter of 'all'.
- The analogous formula $\exists x.\, p$, or `Exists("x",p)` in OCaml, means intuitively 'there exists an x such that p is true', i.e. 'p is true for *some* value(s) of x'. For this reason $\exists$ is referred to as the *existential quantifier*; the symbol is derived from the first letter of 'exists'.

In the formulas $\forall x.\, P[x]$ and $\exists x.\, P[x]$, the subformula $P[x]$ is referred to as the *scope* of the corresponding quantifier. (In informal discussions we often write expressions like $P[x]$ for 'some arbitrary formula possibly involving x'.) The quantifier is said to *bind* instances of x within its scope, and these variables are said to be *bound*. Instances of variables not within the scope of a quantifier are called *free*. Note that the same variable can occur both free and bound in the same formula, e.g. in $R(x, a) \wedge \forall x.\, R(y, x)$, where the variable x has one free occurrence and one bound occurrence.

Intuitively speaking, a bound variable is just a placeholder referring back to the corresponding binding operation, rather than an independent variable in the usual sense. Bound variables can be compared with English pronouns referring back to some particular noun established at the start: 'Although the money was missing, John denied that he stole it'. Binding operations are quite common in mathematical notation, e.g. the variable n in $\sum_{n=1}^{\infty} 1/n^2$, the variable x in $\int_{-\infty}^{\infty} e^{-x^2}\, dx$ and the variable k in $\{k^2 \mid k \in \mathbb{N}\}$. They also occur in programming languages, e.g. for OCaml the x in the definition `let f(x) = 2 * x` and the a in the expression `let a = 2 in a * a * a`.

As in logic, variables in mathematics sometimes occur both free and bound in the same expression, e.g. in $\int_0^x 2x\,\mathrm{d}x$, where the variable x has both a free occurrence (as the upper limit of the integral) and a bound occurrence (inside the body of the integral). Similarly, x really occurs both free and bound in $\mathrm{d}(x^2)/\mathrm{d}x$, though the conventional notation obscures the fact. We can analyze it as the derivative of $x \mapsto x^2$ (in which x is bound) evaluated at point x (where x is a free variable).

In our concrete syntax, the scope of a quantifier extends as far to the right as possible, e.g. $\forall x.P(x) \Rightarrow Q(x)$ means $\forall x.(P(x) \Rightarrow Q(x))$ not $(\forall x.P(x)) \Rightarrow Q(x)$. (Many, especially older, texts use exactly the opposite convention, making quantifiers bind tighter than propositional connectives. The reader should keep this in mind when consulting the literature.) If we apply the universal or existential quantifier to several variables in succession, then we usually only write one quantifier symbol, e.g. $\forall x\ y\ z.\,x+(y+z) = (x+y)+z$ rather than $\forall x.\forall y.\forall z.x+(y+z) = (x+y)+z$. Moreover, it is sometimes useful to assert that there exists *exactly one* x such that p is true. We write this $\exists!x.\,p$ and consider $\exists!x.\,P[x]$ as a shorthand for $\exists x.\,P[x] \wedge \forall y.\,P[y] \Rightarrow y = x$.

Intuitively, the ordering of a sequence of quantifiers of the same kind (all universal or all existential) shouldn't matter: 'for all x, for all y, ...' means the same as 'for all y, for all x, ...', and so on. When we define logical equivalence precisely below, the reader will be able to confirm this intuition. However, where quantifiers of different kinds are nested inside each other, or where the derived quantifier $\exists!$ is involved (see Exercise 3.1), the order is often important. For example, if we think of loves(x, y) as 'x loves y', the formula $\forall x.\,\exists y.\,$loves(x, y) asserts that everybody loves somebody, whereas $\exists y.\,\forall x.\,$loves(x, y) asserts that somebody is loved by everybody. For a more mathematical example, consider the $\epsilon - \delta$ definitions of continuity and uniform continuity of a function $f : \mathbb{R} \to \mathbb{R}$. Continuity asserts that given $\epsilon > 0$, for each x there is a $\delta > 0$ such that whenever $|x' - x| < \delta$, we also have $|f(x') - f(x)| < \varepsilon$:

$$\forall \epsilon.\, \epsilon > 0 \Rightarrow \forall x.\, \exists \delta.\, \delta > 0 \wedge \forall x'.\, |x' - x| < \delta \Rightarrow |f(x') - f(x)| < \varepsilon.$$

Uniform continuity, on the other hand asserts that given $\epsilon > 0$ there is a $\delta > 0$ *independent of x* such that for any x and x', whenever $|x' - x| < \delta$, we also have $|f(x') - f(x)| < \varepsilon$:

$$\forall \epsilon.\, \epsilon > 0 \Rightarrow \exists \delta.\, \delta > 0 \wedge \forall x.\, \forall x'.\, |x' - x| < \delta \Rightarrow |f(x') - f(x)| < \varepsilon.$$

Note how the changed order of quantification radically changes the asserted property. (For example, $f(x) = x^2$ is continuous on the real line, but not uniformly continuous there.) The notion of uniform continuity was only articulated relatively late in the arithmetization of analysis, and several early 'proofs' supposedly requiring only continuity in fact require uniform continuity. Perhaps the use of a formal language would have cleared up many conceptual difficulties sooner.[†]

The name 'first-order logic' arises because quantifiers can be applied only to object-denoting variables, not to functions or predicates. Logics where quantification over functions and predicates is permitted (e.g. $\exists f. \forall x. P[x, f(x)]$) are said to be *second-order* or *higher-order*. But we restrict ourselves to first-order quantifiers: the parser defined next will treat such a string as if the first f were just an ordinary object variable and the second a unary function that just happens to have the same name.

3.2 Parsing and printing

Parsing and printing of terms and formulas in concrete syntax is implemented using a mostly familiar pattern, described in detail in Appendix 3. Any quotation `<<...>>` is automatically passed to the formula parser `parse`, except that surrounding bars `<<|...|>>` force parsing as a term using the term parser `parset`. Printers for terms and formulas are installed in the toplevel so no explicit invocation is needed.

As well as the general concrete syntax `f(x)`, `g(x,y)` etc. for terms, we allow infix use of the customary binary function symbols '+', '-', '*', '/' and '^' (exponentiation), all with conventional precedences, as well as an infix list constructor `::` with the lowest precedence. Unary negation may be written with or without the brackets required by the general unary function notation, as `-(x)` or `-x`. Remember in the latter case that all unary functions have higher precedence than binary ones, so `-x^2` is interpreted as `(-x)^2`, not `-(x^2)` as one might expect.

Users can always force a name `c` to be recognized as a constant by explicitly writing a nullary function application `c()`. However, this is apt to look a bit peculiar, so we adopt some additional conventions. All alphanumeric identifiers apparently within the scope of a quantifier over a variable with the same name will be treated as variables; otherwise they will be treated as constants if and only if the OCaml predicate `is_const_name` returns `true` when applied to them. We have set this up to recognizes only strings of digits

---

[†] Even with a formal language, it is often hard to grasp the meaning of repeated alternations of '∀' and '∃' quantifiers. As we will see in Chapter 7, the number of quantifier alternations is a significant metric of the 'mathematical complexity' of a formula. It has even been suggested that the whole array of mathematical concepts and structures like complex numbers and topological spaces are mainly a means of hiding larger numbers of quantifier alternations and so making them more accessible to our intuition.

and the special name `nil` (the empty list) as constants, but the reader can change this behaviour. For example, one might borrow the conventions from the Prolog programming language (see Section 3.14), where names beginning with uppercase letters (like '`X`' or '`First`') are taken to be variables and those beginning with lowercase letters or numbers (like '`12`' or '`const_A`') are taken to be constants.

Our concrete syntax for '$\forall x. P[x]$' is '`forall x. P[x]`', and for '$\exists x. P[x]$' we use '`exists x. P[x]`'. There seemed no single symbols sufficiently like the backward letters to be recognizable, though the HOL theorem prover (Gordon and Melham 1993) uses '`!x. P[x]`' and '`?x. P[x]`'. For example:

```
# <<forall x y. exists z. x < z /\ y < z>>;;
- : fol formula = <<forall x y. exists z. x < z /\ y < z>>
# <<~(forall x. P(x)) <=> exists y. ~P(y)>>;;
- : fol formula = <<~(forall x. P(x)) <=> (exists y. ~P(y))>>
```

Note that the printer includes brackets around quantified statements even though they can sometimes be omitted without ambiguity based on the fact that both we humans and the OCaml parser read expressions from left to right.

3.3 The semantics of first-order logic

As with a propositional formula, the meaning of a first-order formula is defined recursively and depends on the basic meanings given to the components. In propositional logic the only components are propositional variables, but in first-order logic the variables, function symbols and predicate symbols all need to be interpreted. It's customary to separate these concerns, and define the meaning of a term or formula with respect to both an *interpretation*, which specifies the interpretation of the function and predicate symbols, and a *valuation* which specifies the meanings of variables. Mathematically, an interpretation M consists of three parts.

- A nonempty set D called the *domain* of the interpretation. The intention is that all terms have values in D.[†]
- A mapping of each n-ary function symbol f to a function $f_M : D^n \to D$.
- A mapping of each n-ary predicate symbol P to a Boolean function $P_M : D^n \to \{\text{false}, \text{true}\}$. Equivalently we can think of the interpretation as a subset $P_M \subseteq D^n$.

[†] Some authors such as Johnstone (1987) allow empty domains, giving *free* or *inclusive* logic. This seems quite natural since one does sometimes consider empty structures (partial orders, graphs etc.) in mathematics. However, several results such as the validity of $(\forall x. P[x]) \Rightarrow P[x]$ and the existence of prenex normal forms (see Section 3.5) fail when empty domains are allowed.

We define the value of a term in a particular interpretation M and valuation v by recursion, simply taking note of how all variables are interpreted by v and function symbols by M:

$$\text{termval } M \ v \ x \ = \ v(x),$$

$$\text{termval } M \ v \ (f(t_1, \ldots, t_n)) \ = \ f_M(\text{termval } M \ v \ t_1, \ldots, \text{termval } M \ v \ t_n).$$

Whether a formula holds (i.e. has value 'true') in a particular interpretation M and valuation v is similarly defined by recursion (Tarski 1936) and mostly follows the pattern established for propositional logic. The main added complexity is specifying the meaning of the quantifiers. We intend that $\forall x. \ P[x]$ should hold in a particular interpretation M and valuation v precisely if the body $P[x]$ is true for *any* interpretation of the variable x, in other words, if we modify the effect of the valuation v on x in any way at all.

$$
\begin{aligned}
\text{holds } M \ v \ \bot \ &= \ \text{false} \\
\text{holds } M \ v \ \top \ &= \ \text{true} \\
\text{holds } M \ v \ (R(t_1, \ldots, t_n)) \ &= \ R_M(\text{termval } M \ v \ t_1, \ldots, \text{termval } M \ v \ t_n) \\
\text{holds } M \ v \ (\neg p) \ &= \ \text{not}(\text{holds } M \ v \ p) \\
\text{holds } M \ v \ (p \wedge q) \ &= \ (\text{holds } M \ v \ p) \text{ and } (\text{holds } M \ v \ q) \\
\text{holds } M \ v \ (p \vee q) \ &= \ (\text{holds } M \ v \ p) \text{ or } (\text{holds } M \ v \ q) \\
\text{holds } M \ v \ (p \Rightarrow q) \ &= \ \text{not}(\text{holds } M \ v \ p) \text{ or } (\text{holds } M \ v \ q) \\
\text{holds } M \ v \ (p \Leftrightarrow q) \ &= \ (\text{holds } M \ v \ p = \text{holds } M \ v \ q) \\
\text{holds } M \ v \ (\forall x. \ p) \ &= \ \text{for all } a \in D, \text{ holds } M \ ((x \mapsto a)v) \ p \\
\text{holds } M \ v \ (\exists x. \ p) \ &= \ \text{for some } a \in D, \text{ holds } M \ ((x \mapsto a)v) \ p
\end{aligned}
$$

The domain D in an interpretation is assumed nonempty, but otherwise may have arbitrary finite or infinite cardinality (e.g. the set $\{0, 1\}$ or the set of real numbers $\mathbb{R}$), and the functions and predicates may be interpreted by arbitrary (possibly uncomputable) mathematical functions. For infinite D we cannot directly realize the **holds** function in OCaml, since interpreting a quantifier involves running a test on all elements of D. However, we will implement a cut-down version that works for a finite domain.

An interpretation is represented by a triple of the domain, the interpretation of functions, and the interpretation of predicates. (To be a meaningful interpretation, the domain D should be nonempty, and each n-ary function f should be interpreted by an f_M that maps n-tuples of elements of D back into D. The OCaml functions below just assume that the argument m *is* meaningful in this sense.) The valuation is represented as a finite partial function (see Appendix 2). Then the semantics of terms can be defined following very closely the abstract description we gave above:

```
let rec termval (domain,func,pred as m) v tm =
  match tm with
    Var(x) -> apply v x
  | Fn(f,args) -> func f (map (termval m v) args);;
```

and the semantics of a formula as:

```
let rec holds (domain,func,pred as m) v fm =
  match fm with
    False -> false
  | True -> true
  | Atom(R(r,args)) -> pred r (map (termval m v) args)
  | Not(p) -> not(holds m v p)
  | And(p,q) -> (holds m v p) & (holds m v q)
  | Or(p,q) -> (holds m v p) or (holds m v q)
  | Imp(p,q) -> not(holds m v p) or (holds m v q)
  | Iff(p,q) -> (holds m v p = holds m v q)
  | Forall(x,p) -> forall (fun a -> holds m ((x |-> a) v) p) domain
  | Exists(x,p) -> exists (fun a -> holds m ((x |-> a) v) p) domain;;
```

To clarify the concepts, let's try a few examples of interpreting formulas involving the nullary function symbols '0', '1', the binary function symbols '+' and '·' and the binary predicate symbol '='. We can consider an interpretation à la Boole, with '+' as exclusive 'or':

```
let bool_interp =
  let func f args =
    match (f,args) with
      ("0",[]) -> false
    | ("1",[]) -> true
    | ("+",[x;y]) -> not(x = y)
    | ("*",[x;y]) -> x & y
    | _ -> failwith "uninterpreted function"
  and pred p args =
    match (p,args) with
      ("=",[x;y]) -> x = y
    | _ -> failwith "uninterpreted predicate" in
  ([false; true],func,pred);;
```

An alternative interpretation is as arithmetic modulo n for some arbitrary positive integer n:

```
let mod_interp n =
  let func f args =
    match (f,args) with
      ("0",[]) -> 0
    | ("1",[]) -> 1 mod n
    | ("+",[x;y]) -> (x + y) mod n
    | ("*",[x;y]) -> (x * y) mod n
    | _ -> failwith "uninterpreted function"
  and pred p args =
    match (p,args) with
      ("=",[x;y]) -> x = y
    | _ -> failwith "uninterpreted predicate" in
  (0--(n-1),func,pred);;
```

If all variables are bound by quantifiers, the valuation plays no role in whether a formula holds or not. (We will state and prove this more precisely shortly.) In such cases, we can just use **undefined** to experiment. For example, $\forall x.\ x = 0 \lor x = 1$ holds in bool_interp and mod_interp 2, but not in mod_interp 3:

```
# holds bool_interp undefined <<forall x. (x = 0) \/ (x = 1)>>;;
- : bool = true
# holds (mod_interp 2) undefined <<forall x. (x = 0) \/ (x = 1)>>;;
- : bool = true
# holds (mod_interp 3) undefined <<forall x. (x = 0) \/ (x = 1)>>;;
- : bool = false
```

Consider now the assertion that every nonzero object of the domain has a multiplicative inverse.

```
# let fm = <<forall x. ~(x = 0) ==> exists y. x * y = 1>>;;
```

As the reader who knows some number theory may be able to anticipate, this holds in mod_interp n precisely when n is prime, or trivially 1:

```
# filter (fun n -> holds (mod_interp n) undefined fm) (1--45);;
- : int list = [1; 2; 3; 5; 7; 11; 13; 17; 19; 23; 29; 31; 37; 41; 43]
```

This formula holds in bool_interp too, as the reader can confirm. (In fact, even though they are based on different domains, mod_interp 2 and bool_interp are *isomorphic*, i.e. essentially the same, a concept explained in Section 4.2.)

The set of free variables

We write FVT(t) for the set of all the variables involved in a term t, e.g. FVT($f(x + y, y + z)) = \{x, y, z\}$, implemented recursively in OCaml as follows:

```
let rec fvt tm =
  match tm with
    Var x -> [x]
  | Fn(f,args) -> unions (map fvt args);;
```

A term t is said to be *ground* when it contains no variables, i.e. FVT(t) = $\emptyset$. As might be expected, the semantics of a term depends only on the action of the valuation on variables that actually occur in it, so in particular, the valuation is irrelevant for a ground term.

Theorem 3.1 *If two valuations v and v' agree on all variables in a term t, i.e. for all $x \in FVT(t)$ we have $v(x) = v'(x)$, then* `termval` M v t = `termval` M v' t.

Proof By induction on the structure of t. If t is just a variable x then FVT(t) = $\{x\}$ so `termval` M v x = $v(x) = v'(x)$ = `termval` M v' x by hypothesis.

If t is of the form $f(t_1, \ldots, t_n)$ then by hypothesis v and v' agree on the set FVT($f(t_1, \ldots, t_n)$) and hence on each FVT(t_i). By the inductive hypothesis, `termval` M v t_i = `termval` M v' t_i for each t_i, so as required we have `termval` M v $(f(t_1, \ldots, t_n))$ = `termval` M v' $(f(t_1, \ldots, t_n))$. $\square$

The following function returns the set of all variables occurring in a formula.

```
let rec var fm =
  match fm with
    False | True -> []
  | Atom(R(p,args)) -> unions (map fvt args)
  | Not(p) -> var p
  | And(p,q) | Or(p,q) | Imp(p,q) | Iff(p,q) -> union (var p) (var q)
  | Forall(x,p) | Exists(x,p) -> insert x (var p);;
```

As with terms, a formula p is said to be *ground* when it contains no variables, i.e `var` p = $\emptyset$. However, we're usually more interested in the set of *free* variables FV(p) in a formula, ignoring those that only occur bound. In this case, when passing through a quantifier we need to subtract the quantified variable from the free variables of its body rather than add it:

```
let rec fv fm =
  match fm with
    False | True -> []
  | Atom(R(p,args)) -> unions (map fvt args)
  | Not(p) -> fv p
  | And(p,q) | Or(p,q) | Imp(p,q) | Iff(p,q) -> union (fv p) (fv q)
  | Forall(x,p) | Exists(x,p) -> subtract (fv p) [x];;
```

Indeed, it is the set of free variables that is significant in extending the above theorem from terms to formulas:

Theorem 3.2 *If two valuations v and v' agree on all free variables in a formula p, i.e. for all $x \in FV(p)$ we have $v(x) = v'(x)$, then* holds M v $p =$ holds M v' p.

Proof By induction on the structure of p. If p is $\perp$ or $\top$ the theorem is trivially true. If p is of the form $R(t_1, \ldots, t_n)$ then since v and v' agree on $FV(R(t_1, \ldots, t_n))$ and hence on each $FVT(t_i)$, Theorem 3.1 shows that for each t_i we have termval M v t_i = termval M v' t_i, and therefore holds M v $(R(t_1, \ldots, t_n))$ = holds M v' $(R(t_1, \ldots, t_n))$.

If p is of the form $\neg q$ then since by definition $FV(p) = FV(q)$ the inductive hypothesis gives holds M v p = not(holds M v p) = not(holds M v' q) = holds M v' p. Similarly, if p is of the form $q \wedge r$ then since $FV(q \wedge r) = FV(q) \cup FV(r)$ the inductive hypothesis ensures that holds M v q = holds M v' q and holds M v r = holds M v' r and so holds M v $(q \wedge r)$ = holds M v' $(q \wedge r)$. The other binary connectives are almost the same.

If p is of the form $\forall x. q$ then by hypothesis $v(y) = v'(y)$ for all $y \in FV(p)$, which since $FV(\forall x. q) = FV(q) - \{x\}$, means that $v(y) = v'(y)$ for all $y \in FV(q)$ except possibly $y = x$. But this ensures that for any a in the domain of M we have $((x \mapsto a)v)(y) = ((x \mapsto a)v')(y)$ for *all* $y \in FV(q)$. So, by the inductive hypothesis, for all such a we have holds M $((x \mapsto a)v)$ q = holds M $((x \mapsto a)v')$ q. By definition this means holds M v p = holds M v' p. The case of the existential quantifier is similar. $\square$

A formula p is said to be a *sentence* if it has no free variables, i.e. $FV(p) = \emptyset$. A ground formula is also a sentence, but a sentence may contain variables so long as all instances are bound, e.g. $\forall x. \exists y. P(x, y)$.

Corollary 3.3 *If p is a sentence, i.e. $FV(p) = \emptyset$, then for any interpretation M and any valuations v and v' we have* holds M v p = holds M v' p.

Proof If $\mathrm{FV}(p) = \emptyset$ then whatever the valuations are they agree on $\mathrm{FV}(p)$. □

Validity and satisfiability

By analogy with propositional logic, a first-order formula is said to be *logically valid* if it holds in all interpretations *and* all valuations. And again, if $p \Leftrightarrow q$ is logically valid we say that p and q are *logically equivalent*. Valid formulas are the first-order analogues of propositional tautologies, and the word 'tautology' is sometimes used for the first-order case too. Indeed, all propositional tautologies give rise to corresponding valid first-order formulas (see Corollary 3.13 below). A valid formula involving quantifiers is $(\forall x. P[x]) \Rightarrow P[a]$, which asserts that if P is true for all x, then it is true for any particular constant a. The presence and scope of the quantifier are crucial, though; neither $P[x] \Rightarrow P[a]$ nor $\forall x. P[x] \Rightarrow P[a]$ is valid. For instance, the latter holds in some interpretations but fails in others:

```
# holds (mod_interp 3) undefined <<(forall x. x = 0) ==> 1 = 0>>;;
- : bool = true
# holds (mod_interp 3) undefined <<forall x. x = 0 ==> 1 = 0>>;;
- : bool = false
```

A rather more surprising logically valid formula is $\exists x. \forall y. P(x) \Rightarrow P(y)$. Intuitively speaking, either P is true of everything, in which case the consequent $P(y)$ is always true, or there is some x so that the antecedent $P(x)$ is false. Either way, the whole implication is true. (This is often called 'the drinker's principle' since it can be thought of as asserting the existence of someone x such that if x drinks, everybody does.)

We say that an interpretation M *satisfies* a first-order formula p, or simply that p holds in M, if *for all valuations v* we have `holds M v p` = true. Similarly, we say that M satisfies a *set* of formulas, or that S holds in M, if it satisfies each formula in the set. We say that a first-order formula or set of first-order formulas is *satisfiable* if there is *some* interpretation that satisfies it. Note the asymmetry between the interpretation and valuation in the definition of satisfiability: there is *some* interpretation M such that for *all* valuations v we have `holds M v p`; this looks surprising but makes later material technically easier.[†] In any case, the asymmetry disappears when we consider sentences, since then the valuation plays no role. It is easily seen

---

[†] Indeed, many logic texts use a definition with 'some valuation', while others carefully avoid defining the notion of satisfiability for formulas with free variables. When consulting other sources, the reader should keep this lack of unanimity in mind. Our definition is particularly convenient for considering satisfiability of quantifier-free formulas after Skolemization. With another definition, we would repeatedly need to keep in mind implicit universal quantification.

that a sentence p is valid iff $\neg p$ is unsatisfiable, just as in the propositional case. For formulas with free variables, however, this is no longer true. For example, $P(x) \vee \neg P(y)$ is not valid, yet the negated form $\neg P(x) \wedge P(y)$ is unsatisfiable because it would have to be satisfied by *all* valuations, including those assigning the same object to x and y.

An interpretation that satisfies a set of formulas Γ is said to be a *model* of Γ. The notation $\Gamma \models p$ means 'p holds in all models of Γ', and we usually just $\models p$ instead of $\emptyset \models p$. In particular, Γ is unsatisfiable iff $\Gamma \models \bot$ (since $\bot$ never holds, there must be no models of Γ). However, in contrast to propositional logic, even when $\Gamma = \{p_1, \ldots, p_n\}$ is finite, it is *not* necessarily the case that $\{p_1, \ldots, p_n\} \models p$ is equivalent to $\models p_1 \wedge \cdots \wedge p_n \Rightarrow p$. The reason is that the quantification over valuations is happening at a different place. For example $\{P(x)\} \models P(y)$ is true, but $\models P(x) \Rightarrow P(y)$ is not. However, if each p_i is a *sentence* (no free variables) then the two are equivalent. We occasionally use $\Gamma \models_M p$ to indicate that p holds in a *specific* model M whenever all the Γ do, so $\models_M p$ just means that M satisfies p.

As we have noted, we cannot possibly implement a test for validity or satisfiability based directly on the semantics. We have no way at all of evaluating whether a formula holds in an interpretation with an infinite domain. And while we *can* test whether it holds in a finite interpretation, we can't test whether it holds in all such interpretations, because there are infinitely many. Note the contrast with propositional logic, where the propositional variables range over a finite (2-element) set which can therefore be enumerated exhaustively, and there is no separate notion of interpretations.

This, however, does not a priori destroy all hope of testing first-order validity in subtler ways. Indeed, we will attack the problem of validity testing more indirectly, first transforming a first-order formula into a set of propositional formulas that are satisfiable if and only if the original formula is. Thus, we will first consider how to transform a formula to put the quantifiers at the outside, and then eliminate them altogether. However, before we set about the task, we need to deal precisely with some rather tedious syntactic issues.

3.4 Syntax operations

We often want to take a first-order formula and universally quantify it over all its free variables, e.g. pass from $\exists y.\ x < y + z$ to $\forall x.\ \exists y.\ x < y + z$. Note that this 'generalization' or 'universal closure' is valid iff the original formula is, since either way we demand that the core formula holds under arbitrary assignments of domain elements to that variable. (More formally,

use Theorem 3.2 to show that for all valuations v and $a \in D$ we have
holds M $((x \mapsto a)v)$ p iff simply for all v we have **holds** M v p.) And it's
often more convenient to work with sentences; for example if all formulas
involved are sentences, $\{p_1, \ldots, p_n\} \models q$ iff $\models p_1 \wedge \cdots \wedge p_n \Rightarrow q$, and validity
of p is the same as unsatisfiability of $\neg p$, both as in propositional logic. Here
is an OCaml implementation of universal generalization:

```
let generalize fm = itlist mk_forall (fv fm) fm;;
```

Substitution in terms

The other key operation we need to define is substitution of terms for variables in another term or formula, e.g. substituting 1 for the variable x in
$x < 2 \Rightarrow x \le y$ to obtain $1 < 2 \Rightarrow 1 \le y$. We will specify the desired variable
assignment or *instantiation* as a finite partial function from variable names
to terms, which can either be undefined or simply map x to `Var(x)` for variables we don't want changed. Given such an assignment `sfn`, substitution
on terms can be defined by recursion:

```
let rec tsubst sfn tm =
  match tm with
    Var x -> tryapplyd sfn x tm
  | Fn(f,args) -> Fn(f,map (tsubst sfn) args);;
```

We will observe some important properties of this notion. First of all, the
variables in a substituted term are as expected:

Lemma 3.4 *For any term t and instantiation i, the free variables in the
substituted term are precisely those free in the terms substituted for the free
variables of t, i.e.*

$$FVT(\texttt{tsubst } i \ t) = \bigcup_{y \in FVT(t)} FVT(i(y)).$$

Proof By induction on the structure of the term. If t is a variable z, then
$\text{FVT}(\texttt{tsubst } i \ t) = \text{FVT}(i(z)) = \bigcup_{y \in \{z\}} \text{FVT}(i(y))$ and since $\text{FVT}(z) = \{z\}$
the result follows.

If t is of the form $f(t_1, \ldots, t_n)$ then by the inductive hypothesis we have
for each $k = 1, \ldots, n$:

$$\text{FVT}(\texttt{tsubst } i \ t_k) = \bigcup_{y \in \text{FVT}(t_k)} \text{FVT}(i(y)).$$

Consequently:

$$\text{FVT}(\text{tsubst } i \ (f(t_1, \ldots, t_n)))$$
$$= \ \text{FVT}(f(\text{tsubst } i \ t_1, \ldots, \text{tsubst } i \ t_n)$$
$$= \ \bigcup_{k=1}^{n} \text{FVT}(\text{tsubst } i \ t_k)$$
$$= \ \bigcup_{k=1}^{n} \bigcup_{y \in \text{FVT}(t_k)} \text{FVT}(i(y))$$
$$= \ \bigcup_{y \in \bigcup_{k=1}^{n} \text{FVT}(t_k)} \text{FVT}(i(y))$$
$$= \ \bigcup_{y \in \text{FVT}(f(t_1, \ldots, t_n))} \text{FVT}(i(y)).$$

$\square$

The following result gives a simple property, which on reflection would be expected, for the interpretation of a substituted term.

Lemma 3.5 *For any term t and instantiation i, then in any interpretation M and valuation v, the substituted term has the same value as the original formula in the modified valuation* termval $M \ v \circ i$, *i.e.*

$$\text{termval } M \ v \ (\text{tsubst } i \ t) = \text{termval } M \ (\text{termval } M \ v \circ i) \ t.$$

Proof If t is a variable x then

$$\text{termval } M \ v \ (\text{tsubst } i \ x) = \text{termval } M \ v \ (i(x)) = (\text{termval } M \ v \circ i)(x)$$

as required. If t is of the form $f(t_1, \ldots, t_n)$ then by the inductive hypothesis we have for each $k = 1, \ldots, n$:

$$\text{termval } M \ v \ (\text{tsubst } i \ t_k) = \text{termval } M \ (\text{termval } M \ v \circ i) \ t_k$$

and so:

$$\text{termval } M \ v \ (\text{tsubst } i \ (f(t_1, \ldots, t_n)))$$
$$= \ \text{termval } M \ v \ (f(\text{tsubst } i \ t_1, \ldots, \text{tsubst } i \ t_n))$$
$$= \ f_M(\text{termval } M \ v \ (\text{tsubst } i \ t_1), \ldots, \text{termval } M \ v \ (\text{tsubst } i \ t_n))$$
$$= \ f_M(\ \text{termval } M \ (\text{termval } M \ v \circ i) \ t_1, \ldots,$$
$$\text{termval } M \ (\text{termval } M \ v \circ i) \ t_n)$$
$$= \ \text{termval } M \ (\text{termval } M \ v \circ i) \ (f(t_1, \ldots, t_n)).$$

$\square$

Substitution in formulas

It might seem at first sight that we could define substitution in formulas by a similar structural recursion. However, the presence of bound variables makes matters considerably more complicated.

We have already observed that bound variables are just placeholders indicating a correspondence between bound variables and the binding instance, and for this reason they should not be substituted for. For example, substitutions for x should have no effect on the formula $\forall x.\, x = x$ because each instance of x is bound by the quantifier. Moreover, even avoiding substitution of the bound variables themselves, we still run the risk of having free variables in the substituted terms 'captured' by an outer variable-binding operation. For example if we straightforwardly replace y by x in the formula $\exists x.\, x + 1 = y$, the resulting formula $\exists x.\, x + 1 = x$ is not what we want, since the substituted variable x has become bound. What we'd like to do is *alpha-convert*,[†] i.e. rename the bound variable, e.g. to z. We can then safely substitute to get $\exists z.\, z + 1 = x$, replacing the free variable as required while maintaining the correct binding correspondence. To implement this, we start with a function to invent a 'variant' of a variable name by adding prime characters to it until it is distinct from some given list of variables to avoid; this will be used to rename bound variables when necessary:

```
let rec variant x vars =
  if mem x vars then variant (x^"'") vars else x;;
```

For example:

```
# variant "x" ["y"; "z"];;
- : string = "x"
# variant "x" ["x"; "y"];;
- : string = "x'"
# variant "x" ["x"; "x'"];;
- : string = "x''"
```

Now, the definition of substitution starts with a series of straightforward structural recursions. However, the two tricky cases of quantified formulas $\forall x.\, p$ and $\exists x.\, p$ are handled by a mutually recursive function **substq**:

[†] The terminology originates with lambda-calculus (Church 1941; Barendregt 1984).

```
let rec subst subfn fm =
  match fm with
    False -> False
  | True -> True
  | Atom(R(p,args)) -> Atom(R(p,map (tsubst subfn) args))
  | Not(p) -> Not(subst subfn p)
  | And(p,q) -> And(subst subfn p,subst subfn q)
  | Or(p,q) -> Or(subst subfn p,subst subfn q)
  | Imp(p,q) -> Imp(subst subfn p,subst subfn q)
  | Iff(p,q) -> Iff(subst subfn p,subst subfn q)
  | Forall(x,p) -> substq subfn mk_forall x p
  | Exists(x,p) -> substq subfn mk_exists x p
```

This `substq` function checks whether there would be variable capture if the bound variable x is not renamed. It does this by testing if there is a $y \neq x$ in $FV(p)$ such that applying the substitution to y gives a term with x free. If so, it picks a new bound variable x' that will not clash with any of the results of substituting in p; otherwise, it just sets $x' = x$. The overall result is then deduced by applying substitution to the body p with an additional mapping $x \mapsto x'$. Note that in the case where no renaming is needed, this still inhibits the (non-trivial) replacement of x, as required.

```
and substq subfn quant x p =
  let x' = if exists (fun y -> mem x (fvt(tryapplyd subfn y (Var y))))
                     (subtract (fv p) [x])
           then variant x (fv(subst (undefine x subfn) p)) else x in
  quant x' (subst ((x |-> Var x') subfn) p);;
```

For example:

```
# subst ("y" |=> Var "x") <<forall x. x = y>>;;
- : fol formula = <<forall x'. x' = x>>
# subst ("y" |=> Var "x") <<forall x x'. x = y ==> x = x'>>;;
- : fol formula = <<forall x' x''. x' = x ==> x' = x''>>
```

We hope that this renaming trickery looks at least vaguely plausible. But the ultimate vindication of our definition is really that `subst` satisfies analogous properties to Lemmas 3.4 and 3.5 for `tsubst`, though we have to work much harder to establish them.

Lemma 3.6 *For any formula p and instantiation i, the free variables in the substituted formula are precisely those free in the terms substituted for the free variables of p, i.e.*

$$FV(\text{subst } i \ p) = \bigcup_{y \in FV(p)} FVT(i(y)).$$

Proof We will prove by induction on the structure of p that *for all i* the above holds. This allows us to use the inductive hypothesis even when renaming occurs and we have to consider a different instantiation for a subformula.

If p is $\bot$ or $\top$ the theorem holds trivially. If p is an atomic formula $R(t_1, \ldots, t_n)$ then, by Lemma 3.4, for each $k = 1, \ldots, n$:

$$\text{FVT}(\texttt{tsubst } i\ t_k) = \bigcup_{y \in \text{FVT}(t_k)} \text{FVT}(i(y)).$$

Consequently:

$$\text{FV}(\texttt{subst } i\ (R(t_1, \ldots, t_n))$$
$$= \text{FV}(R(\texttt{tsubst } i\ t_1, \ldots, \texttt{tsubst } i\ t_n)$$
$$= \bigcup_{k=1}^{n} \text{FVT}(\texttt{tsubst } i\ t_k)$$
$$= \bigcup_{k=1}^{n} \bigcup_{y \in \text{FVT}(t_k)} \text{FVT}(i(y))$$
$$= \bigcup_{y \in \bigcup_{k=1}^{n} \text{FVT}(t_k)} \text{FVT}(i(y))$$
$$= \bigcup_{y \in \text{FV}(R(t_1, \ldots, t_n))} \text{FVT}(i(y)).$$

If p is of the form $\neg q$ then by the inductive hypothesis $\text{FV}(\texttt{subst } i\ q) = \bigcup_{y \in \text{FV}(q)} \text{FVT}(i(y))$ and so

$$\text{FV}(\texttt{subst } i\ (\neg q)$$
$$= \text{FV}(\neg(\texttt{subst } i\ q))$$
$$= \text{FV}(\texttt{subst } i\ q)$$
$$= \bigcup_{y \in \text{FV}(q)} \text{FVT}(i(y))$$
$$= \bigcup_{y \in \text{FV}(\neg q)} \text{FVT}(i(y)).$$

If p is of the form $q \wedge r$ then by the inductive hypothesis $\text{FV}(\texttt{subst } i\ q) = \bigcup_{y \in \text{FV}(q)} \text{FVT}(i(y))$ and $\text{FV}(\texttt{subst } i\ r) = \bigcup_{y \in \text{FV}(r)} \text{FVT}(i(y))$ and so:

$$\text{FV}(\texttt{subst } i\ (q \wedge r))$$
$$= \text{FV}((\texttt{subst } i\ q) \wedge (\texttt{subst } i\ r))$$
$$= \text{FV}(\texttt{subst } i\ q) \cup \text{FV}(\texttt{subst } i\ r)$$

$$= \bigcup_{y \in \mathrm{FV}(q)} \mathrm{FVT}(i(y)) \cup \bigcup_{y \in \mathrm{FV}(r)} \mathrm{FVT}(i(y))$$

$$= \bigcup_{y \in \mathrm{FV}(q) \cup \mathrm{FV}(r)} \mathrm{FVT}(i(y))$$

$$= \bigcup_{y \in \mathrm{FV}(q \wedge r)} \mathrm{FVT}(i(y)).$$

The other binary connectives are similar. Now suppose p is of the form $\forall x. q$. With the possibly-renamed variable x' from the definition of substitution, we have:

$$\mathrm{FV}(\mathsf{subst}\ i\ (\forall x. q))$$

$$= \mathrm{FV}(\forall x'. (\mathsf{subst}\ ((x \mapsto x')i)\ q)$$

$$= \mathrm{FV}(\mathsf{subst}\ ((x \mapsto x')i)\ q) - \{x'\}$$

$$= \bigcup_{y \in \mathrm{FV}(q)} \mathrm{FVT}(((x \mapsto x')i)(y)) - \{x'\}.$$

We can remove the case $y = x$ from the union, because in that case we have $\mathrm{FVT}(((x \mapsto x')i)(y)) = \mathrm{FVT}(((x \mapsto x')i)(x)) = \mathrm{FVT}(x') = \{x'\}$, and this set is removed again on the outside. Hence this is equal to:

$$\bigcup_{y \in \mathrm{FV}(q) - \{x\}} \mathrm{FVT}(((x \mapsto x')i)(y)) - \{x'\}$$

$$= \bigcup_{y \in \mathrm{FV}(q) - \{x\}} \mathrm{FVT}(i(y)) - \{x'\}.$$

Now we distinguish two cases according to the test in the substq function.

- If $x \notin \bigcup_{y \in \mathrm{FV}(q) - \{x\}} \mathrm{FVT}(i(y))$ then $x' = x$.
- If $x \in \bigcup_{y \in \mathrm{FV}(q) - \{x\}} \mathrm{FVT}(i(y))$ then $x' \notin \mathrm{FV}(\mathsf{subst}\ ((x \mapsto x)i)\ q)$ by construction. That set is equal to $\bigcup_{y \in \mathrm{FV}(q)} \mathrm{FVT}(((x \mapsto x)i)(y))$ by the inductive hypothesis, and so it includes the set

$$\bigcup_{y \in \mathrm{FV}(q) - \{x\}} \mathrm{FVT}(((x \mapsto x)i)(y)) = \bigcup_{y \in \mathrm{FV}(q) - \{x\}} \mathrm{FVT}(i(y)).$$

In either case, $x' \notin \bigcup_{y \in \mathrm{FV}(q) - \{x\}} \mathrm{FVT}(i(y))$ and so we always have

$$\bigcup_{y \in \mathrm{FV}(q) - \{x\}} \mathrm{FVT}(i(y)) - \{x'\} = \bigcup_{y \in \mathrm{FV}(q) - \{x\}} \mathrm{FVT}(i(y)),$$

which is exactly $\bigcup_{y \in \mathrm{FV}(\forall x. q)} \mathrm{FVT}(i(y))$ as required. The case of the existential quantifier is exactly analogous. $\qquad\square$

Theorem 3.7 *For any formula p, instantiation i, interpretation M and valuation v, we have* `holds` M v `(subst` i p`)` = `holds` M `(termval` M $v \circ i$`)` p.

Proof We will fix M at the outset, but as with the previous theorem, will prove by induction on the structure of p that for all valuations v and instantiations i the result holds. This will allow us to deploy the inductive hypothesis with modified valuation and/or substitution.

If p is $\bot$ or $\top$ the result holds trivially. If p is an atomic formula $R(t_1, \ldots, t_n)$ then by Lemma 3.5 for each $k = 1, \ldots, n$:

$$\texttt{termval } M\ v\ (\texttt{tsubst } i\ t_k) = \texttt{termval } M\ (\texttt{termval } M\ v \circ i)\ t_k$$

and so:

$$
\begin{aligned}
&\texttt{holds } M\ v\ (\texttt{subst } i\ (R(t_1, \ldots, t_n)))\\
=\ &\texttt{holds } M\ v\ (R(\texttt{tsubst } i\ t_1, \ldots, \texttt{tsubst } i\ t_n))\\
=\ &R_M(\texttt{termval } M\ v\ (\texttt{tsubst } i\ t_1), \ldots, \texttt{termval } M\ v\ (\texttt{tsubst } i\ t_n))\\
=\ &R_M(\ \texttt{termval } M\ (\texttt{termval } M\ v \circ i)\ t_1, \ldots,\\
&\qquad \texttt{termval } M\ (\texttt{termval } M\ v \circ i)\ t_n)\\
=\ &\texttt{holds } M\ (\texttt{termval } M\ v \circ i)\ (R(t_1, \ldots, t_n)).
\end{aligned}
$$

If p is of the form $\neg q$, then using the inductive hypothesis we know that `holds` M v `(subst` i q`)` = `holds` M `(termval` M $v \circ i$`)` q and so:

$$
\begin{aligned}
&\texttt{holds } M\ v\ (\texttt{subst } i\ (\neg q))\\
=\ &\texttt{holds } M\ v\ (\neg(\texttt{subst } i\ q))\\
=\ &\texttt{not}(\texttt{holds } M\ v\ (\texttt{subst } i\ q))\\
=\ &\texttt{not}(\texttt{holds } M\ (\texttt{termval } M\ v \circ i)\ q)\\
=\ &\texttt{holds } M\ (\texttt{termval } M\ v \circ i)\ (\neg q).
\end{aligned}
$$

Similarly, if p is of the form $q \wedge r$ then by the inductive hypothesis we have `holds` M v `(subst` i q`)` = `holds` M `(termval` M $v \circ i$`)` q and also `holds` M v `(subst` i r`)` = `holds` M `(termval` M $v \circ i$`)` r, so:

$$
\begin{aligned}
&\texttt{holds } M\ v\ (\texttt{subst } i\ (q \wedge r))\\
=\ &\texttt{holds } M\ v\ ((\texttt{subst } i\ q) \wedge (\texttt{subst } i\ r))\\
=\ &(\texttt{holds } M\ v\ (\texttt{subst } i\ q))\ \texttt{and}\ (\texttt{holds } M\ v\ (\texttt{subst } i\ r))\\
=\ &(\texttt{holds } M\ (\texttt{termval } M\ v \circ i)\ q)\ \texttt{and}\ (\texttt{holds } M\ (\texttt{termval } M\ v \circ i)\ r)\\
=\ &\texttt{holds } M\ (\texttt{termval } M\ v \circ i)\ (q \wedge r).
\end{aligned}
$$

The other binary connectives follow the same pattern. For the case where p is of the form $\forall x.\, q$, we again need a bit more care because of variable renaming. Using the inductive hypothesis we have, with x' the possibly-renamed variable:

$$\texttt{holds } M\ v\ (\texttt{subst } i\ (\forall x.\, q))$$
$$= \quad \texttt{holds } M\ v\ (\forall x'.\, (\texttt{subst } ((x \mapsto x')i)\ q))$$
$$= \quad \text{for all } a \in D,\ \texttt{holds } M\ ((x' \mapsto a)v)\ (\texttt{subst } ((x \mapsto x')i)\ q)$$
$$= \quad \text{for all } a \in D,\ \texttt{holds } M\ (\texttt{termval } M\ ((x' \mapsto a)v) \circ ((x \mapsto x')i))q.$$

We want to show that this is equivalent to

$$\texttt{holds } M\ (\texttt{termval } M\ v \circ i)\ (\forall x.\, q)$$
$$= \quad \text{for all } a \in D,\ \texttt{holds } M\ ((x \mapsto a)(\texttt{termval } M\ v \circ i))\ q.$$

By Theorem 3.2, it's enough to show that for arbitrary $a \in D$, the valuations $\texttt{termval } M\ ((x' \mapsto a)v) \circ ((x \mapsto x')i)$ and $(x \mapsto a)(\texttt{termval } M\ v \circ i)$ agree on each variable $z \in \text{FV}(q)$. There are two cases to distinguish. If $z = x$ then

$$(\texttt{termval } M\ ((x' \mapsto a)v) \circ ((x \mapsto x')i))(x)$$
$$= \quad \texttt{termval } M\ ((x' \mapsto a)v)\ (((x \mapsto x')i)(x))$$
$$= \quad \texttt{termval } M\ ((x' \mapsto a)v)\ (x')$$
$$= \quad ((x' \mapsto a)v)(x')$$
$$= \quad a$$
$$= \quad ((x \mapsto a)(\texttt{termval } M\ v \circ i))(x)$$

as required, and if $z \neq x$ then:

$$(\texttt{termval } M\ ((x' \mapsto a)v) \circ ((x \mapsto x')i))(z)$$
$$= \quad \texttt{termval } M\ ((x' \mapsto a)v)\ (((x \mapsto x')i)(z))$$
$$= \quad \texttt{termval } M\ ((x' \mapsto a)v)\ (i(z)).$$

By hypothesis, $z \in \text{FV}(q)$, and since $z \neq x$ we have $z \in \text{FV}(q) - \{x\}$. However, as noted in the proof of Theorem 3.6, $x' \notin \bigcup_{y \in \text{FV}(q)-\{x\}} \text{FVT}(i(y))$ and so in particular $x' \notin \text{FV}(i(z))$. Thus we can continue the chain of equivalences:

$$= \quad \texttt{termval } M\ v\ (i(z))$$
$$= \quad (\texttt{termval } M\ v \circ i)(z)$$
$$= \quad ((x \mapsto a)(\texttt{termval } M\ v \circ i))(z)$$

as required. $\square$

One straightforward consequence, unsurprising if we think of free variables as implicitly universally quantified, is the following:

Corollary 3.8 *If a formula is valid, so is any substitution instance.*

Proof Let p be a logically valid formula. For any instantiation i we have holds M v (subst i p) = holds M (termval M $v \circ i$) p = true, since holds M v p = true for *any* valuation v, in particular termval M $v \circ i$. □

The definition of substitution and the proofs of its key properties were rather tedious. An alternative is to separate free and bound variables into different syntactic categories so that capture is impossible. A particularly popular scheme, using numerical indices indicating nesting degree for bound variables, is given by de Bruijn (1972). However, this has some drawbacks of its own.

3.5 Prenex normal form

A first-order formula is said to be in *prenex normal form* (PNF) if all quantifiers occur on the outside with a body (or 'matrix') where only propositional connectives are used. For example, $\forall x. \exists y. \forall z. P(x) \wedge P(y) \Rightarrow P(z)$ is in PNF but $(\exists x. P(x)) \Rightarrow \exists y. P(y) \wedge \forall z. P(z)$ is not, because quantified subformulas are combined using propositional connectives. We will show in this section how to transform an arbitrary first-order formula into a logically equivalent one in PNF.

When implementing DNF in propositional logic (Section 2.6) we considered two approaches, one based on truth tables and the other repeatedly applying tautological transformations like $p \wedge (q \vee r) \longrightarrow (p \wedge q) \vee (p \wedge r)$. In first-order logic there is no analogue of truth tables, but we can similarly transform a formula to PNF by repeatedly transforming subformulas into logical equivalents that move the quantifiers further out. There is no convenient way of pulling quantifiers out of logical equivalences, so it's useful to eliminate them as we did in propositional NNF. In fact, it simplifies matters if we follow a similar pattern to the earlier DNF transformation:

- simplify away **False**, **True**, vacuous quantification, etc.;
- eliminate implication and equivalence, push down negations;
- pull out quantifiers.

The simplification stage proceeds as before for eliminating **False** and **True** from formulas. But we also eliminate *vacuous quantifiers*, where the quantified variable does not occur free in the body.

Theorem 3.9 *If $x \notin FV(p)$ then $\forall x.\, p$ is logically equivalent to p.*

Proof The formula $\forall x.\, p$ holds in a model M and valuation v if and only if for each a in the domain of M, p holds in M under valuation $(x \mapsto a)v$. However, since x is not free in p, this is the case precisely if p holds in M and v, given that the domain is nonempty. $\qquad\square$

Similarly, if $x \notin \mathrm{FV}(p)$ then $\exists x.\, p$ is logically equivalent to p. Thus we can see that the following simplification function always returns a logical equivalent:

```
let simplify1 fm =
  match fm with
    Forall(x,p) -> if mem x (fv p) then fm else p
  | Exists(x,p) -> if mem x (fv p) then fm else p
  | _ -> psimplify1 fm;;
```

and hence we can apply it repeatedly at depth:

```
let rec simplify fm =
  match fm with
    Not p -> simplify1 (Not(simplify p))
  | And(p,q) -> simplify1 (And(simplify p,simplify q))
  | Or(p,q) -> simplify1 (Or(simplify p,simplify q))
  | Imp(p,q) -> simplify1 (Imp(simplify p,simplify q))
  | Iff(p,q) -> simplify1 (Iff(simplify p,simplify q))
  | Forall(x,p) -> simplify1(Forall(x,simplify p))
  | Exists(x,p) -> simplify1(Exists(x,simplify p))
  | _ -> fm;;
```

For example:

```
# simplify <<true ==> (p <=> (p <=> false))>>;;
- : fol formula = <<p <=> ~p>>
# simplify <<exists x y z. P(x) ==> Q(z) ==> false>>;;
- : fol formula = <<exists x z. P(x) ==> ~Q(z)>>
# simplify <<(forall x y. P(x) \/ (P(y) /\ false)) ==> exists z. Q>>;;
- : fol formula = <<(forall x. P(x)) ==> Q>>
```

Next, we transform into NNF by eliminating implication and equivalence and pushing down negations. Recall the De Morgan laws, which can be used repeatedly to obtain the equivalences:

$$\neg(p_1 \wedge p_2 \wedge \cdots \wedge p_n) \quad \Leftrightarrow \quad \neg p_1 \vee \neg p_2 \vee \cdots \vee \neg p_n,$$

$$\neg(p_1 \vee p_2 \vee \cdots \vee p_n) \quad \Leftrightarrow \quad \neg p_1 \wedge \neg p_2 \wedge \cdots \wedge \neg p_n.$$

By analogy, we have the following 'infinite De Morgan laws' for quantifiers. The logical equivalence should be similarly clear; for example if it is not the case that $P(x)$ holds for all x, there must exist some x for which $P(x)$ does not hold, and vice versa:

$$\neg(\forall x.\, p) \;\;\Leftrightarrow\;\; \exists x.\, \neg p,$$
$$\neg(\exists x.\, p) \;\;\Leftrightarrow\;\; \forall x.\, \neg p.$$

These justify additional transformations to push negation down through quantifiers, to supplement the transformations already used in the propositional case. Thus we define:

```
let rec nnf fm =
  match fm with
    And(p,q) -> And(nnf p,nnf q)
  | Or(p,q) -> Or(nnf p,nnf q)
  | Imp(p,q) -> Or(nnf(Not p),nnf q)
  | Iff(p,q) -> Or(And(nnf p,nnf q),And(nnf(Not p),nnf(Not q)))
  | Not(Not p) -> nnf p
  | Not(And(p,q)) -> Or(nnf(Not p),nnf(Not q))
  | Not(Or(p,q)) -> And(nnf(Not p),nnf(Not q))
  | Not(Imp(p,q)) -> And(nnf p,nnf(Not q))
  | Not(Iff(p,q)) -> Or(And(nnf p,nnf(Not q)),And(nnf(Not p),nnf q))
  | Forall(x,p) -> Forall(x,nnf p)
  | Exists(x,p) -> Exists(x,nnf p)
  | Not(Forall(x,p)) -> Exists(x,nnf(Not p))
  | Not(Exists(x,p)) -> Forall(x,nnf(Not p))
  | _ -> fm;;
```

For example:

```
# nnf <<(forall x. P(x))
        ==> ((exists y. Q(y)) <=> exists z. P(z) /\ Q(z))>>;;
- : fol formula =
<<(exists x. ~P(x)) \/
  (exists y. Q(y)) /\ (exists z. P(z) /\ Q(z)) \/
  (forall y. ~Q(y)) /\ (forall z. ~P(z) \/ ~Q(z))>>
```

Now we come to the really distinctive part of PNF, pulling out the quantifiers. By the time we have simplified and made the NNF transformation, any quantifiers not already at the outside must be connected by '$\wedge$' or '$\vee$', since negations have been pushed down past them to the atomic formulas while other propositional connectives have been eliminated. Thus, the crux is to pull quantifiers upward in formulas like $p \wedge (\exists x.\, q)$. Once again by infinite analogy with the DNF distribution rule:

$$p \wedge (q_1 \vee \cdots \vee q_n) \Leftrightarrow p \wedge q_1 \vee \cdots \vee p \wedge q_n$$

it would seem that the following should be logically valid:

$$p \wedge (\exists x.\, q) \Leftrightarrow \exists x.\, p \wedge q.$$

This is almost true, but we have to watch out for variable capture if x is free in p. For example, the following isn't logically valid:

$$P(x) \wedge (\exists x.\, Q(x)) \Leftrightarrow \exists x.\, P(x) \wedge Q(x).$$

We can always avoid such problems by renaming the bound variable, if necessary, to some y that is not free in either p or q:

$$p \wedge (\exists x.\, q) \Leftrightarrow \exists y.\, p \wedge (\texttt{subst}\ (x \mapsto y)\ q).$$

This equivalence can be justified rigorously using the theorems from the previous section. By definition, in a model M (with domain D) and valuation v, the formula $p \wedge (\exists x.\, q)$ holds if $\texttt{holds}\ M\ v\ p$ and there exists some $a \in D$ such that $\texttt{holds}\ M\ ((x \mapsto a)v)\ q$. The formula $\exists y.\, p \wedge (\texttt{subst}\ (x \mapsto y)\ q)$ holds if there is an $a \in D$ such that both $\texttt{holds}\ M\ ((y \mapsto a)v)\ p$ and $\texttt{holds}\ M\ ((y \mapsto a)v)\ (\texttt{subst}\ (x \mapsto y)\ q)$. However, since by construction y is not free in the whole formula and hence not free in p, Theorem 3.2 shows that $\texttt{holds}\ M\ ((y \mapsto a)v)\ p$ is equivalent to $\texttt{holds}\ M\ v\ p$. As for $\texttt{holds}\ M\ ((y \mapsto a)v)\ (\texttt{subst}\ (x \mapsto y)\ q)$, this is by Theorem 3.7 equivalent to $\texttt{holds}\ M\ (\texttt{termval}\ M\ ((y \mapsto a)v) \circ \texttt{subst}\ (x \mapsto y))\ q$ and hence to $\texttt{holds}\ M\ ((x \mapsto a)v)\ q$ as required. Exactly analogous results allow us to pull either universal or existential quantifiers past conjunction or disjunction. If any of them seem doubtful, they can be rigorously justified in a similar way:

$$
\begin{aligned}
(\forall x.\, p) \wedge q &\Leftrightarrow \forall y.\, (\texttt{subst}\ (x \mapsto y)\ p) \wedge q \\
p \wedge (\forall x.\, q) &\Leftrightarrow \forall y.\, p \wedge (\texttt{subst}\ (x \mapsto y)\ q) \\
(\forall x.\, p) \vee q &\Leftrightarrow \forall y.\, (\texttt{subst}\ (x \mapsto y)\ p) \vee q \\
p \vee (\forall x.\, q) &\Leftrightarrow \forall y.\, p \vee (\texttt{subst}\ (x \mapsto y)\ q) \\
(\exists x.\, p) \wedge q &\Leftrightarrow \exists y.\, (\texttt{subst}\ (x \mapsto y)\ p) \wedge q \\
p \wedge (\exists x.\, q) &\Leftrightarrow \exists y.\, p \wedge (\texttt{subst}\ (x \mapsto y)\ q) \\
(\exists x.\, p) \vee q &\Leftrightarrow \exists y.\, (\texttt{subst}\ (x \mapsto y)\ p) \vee q \\
p \vee (\exists x.\, q) &\Leftrightarrow \exists y.\, p \vee (\texttt{subst}\ (x \mapsto y)\ q)
\end{aligned}
$$

In the special cases that both immediate subformulas are quantified, we can sometimes produce a result with fewer quantifiers using these equivalences, where z is chosen not to be free in the original formula.

$$
\begin{aligned}
(\forall x.\, p) \wedge (\forall y.\, q) &\Leftrightarrow \forall z.\, (\texttt{subst}\ (x \mapsto z)\ p) \wedge (\texttt{subst}\ (y \mapsto z)\ q), \\
(\exists x.\, p) \vee (\exists y.\, q) &\Leftrightarrow \exists z.\, (\texttt{subst}\ (x \mapsto z)\ p) \vee (\texttt{subst}\ (y \mapsto z)\ q).
\end{aligned}
$$

However, the following are *not* logically valid:

$$(\forall x.\, p) \vee (\forall y.\, q) \quad \not\Leftrightarrow \quad \forall z.\, (\text{subst } (x \mapsto z)\, p) \vee (\text{subst } (y \mapsto z)\, q),$$
$$(\exists x.\, p) \wedge (\exists y.\, q) \quad \not\Leftrightarrow \quad \exists z.\, (\text{subst } (x \mapsto z)\, p) \wedge (\text{subst } (y \mapsto z)\, q).$$

For example, the first implies that $(\forall n.\, \text{Even}(n)) \vee (\forall n.\, \text{Odd}(n)))$ is equivalent to $\forall n.\, \text{Even}(n) \vee \text{Odd}(n)$, yet the former is false in the obvious interpretation in terms of evenness and oddity of integers, while the latter is true. Similarly, the second implies that $(\exists n.\, \text{Even}(n)) \wedge (\exists n.\, \text{Odd}(n))$ is equivalent to $\exists n.\, \text{Even}(n) \wedge \text{Odd}(n)$, yet in the obvious interpretation the former is true and the latter false.

Now, to pull out all quantifiers that occur as immediate subformulas of either conjunction or disjunction, we implement these transformations in OCaml:

```
let rec pullquants fm =
  match fm with
    And(Forall(x,p),Forall(y,q)) ->
                         pullq(true,true) fm mk_forall mk_and x y p q
  | Or(Exists(x,p),Exists(y,q)) ->
                         pullq(true,true) fm mk_exists mk_or x y p q
  | And(Forall(x,p),q) -> pullq(true,false) fm mk_forall mk_and x x p q
  | And(p,Forall(y,q)) -> pullq(false,true) fm mk_forall mk_and y y p q
  | Or(Forall(x,p),q) ->  pullq(true,false) fm mk_forall mk_or x x p q
  | Or(p,Forall(y,q)) ->  pullq(false,true) fm mk_forall mk_or y y p q
  | And(Exists(x,p),q) -> pullq(true,false) fm mk_exists mk_and x x p q
  | And(p,Exists(y,q)) -> pullq(false,true) fm mk_exists mk_and y y p q
  | Or(Exists(x,p),q) ->  pullq(true,false) fm mk_exists mk_or x x p q
  | Or(p,Exists(y,q)) ->  pullq(false,true) fm mk_exists mk_or y y p q
  | _ -> fm
```

where for economy various similar subcases are dealt with by the mutually recursive function `pullq`, which calls the main `pullquants` functions again on the body to pull up further quantifiers:

```
and pullq(l,r) fm quant op x y p q =
  let z = variant x (fv fm) in
  let p' = if l then subst (x |=> Var z) p else p
  and q' = if r then subst (y |=> Var z) q else q in
  quant z (pullquants(op p' q'));;
```

The overall prenexing function leaves quantified formulas alone, and for conjunctions and disjunctions recursively prenexes the immediate subformulas and then uses `pullquants`:

```
let rec prenex fm =
  match fm with
    Forall(x,p) -> Forall(x,prenex p)
  | Exists(x,p) -> Exists(x,prenex p)
  | And(p,q) -> pullquants(And(prenex p,prenex q))
  | Or(p,q) -> pullquants(Or(prenex p,prenex q))
  | _ -> fm;;
```

Combining this with the NNF and simplification stages we get:

```
let pnf fm = prenex(nnf(simplify fm));;
```

for example:

```
# pnf <<(forall x. P(x) \/ R(y))
        ==> exists y z. Q(y) \/ ~(exists z. P(z) /\ Q(z))>>;;
- : fol formula =
<<exists x. forall z. ~P(x) /\ ~R(y) \/ Q(x) \/ ~P(z) \/ ~Q(z)>>
```

3.6 Skolemization

Prenex normal form separates out the quantifiers from the propositional part or 'matrix', but the quantifier prefix may still contain an arbitrarily complicated nesting of universal and existential quantifiers. We can go further, eliminating existential quantifiers and leaving only universal ones using a technique called *Skolemization* after Thoraf Skolem (1928). Note that the following are generally considered to be mathematically equivalent:

(1) for all $x \in D$, there exists a $y \in D$ such that $P[x, y]$;
(2) there exists an $f : D \to D$ such that for all $x \in D$, $P[x, f(x)]$.

One direction is relatively easy: if (2) holds then by taking $y = f(x)$ we see that (1) does too. The other direction is subtler: even if for each x there is at least one y such that $P[x, y]$, there might be many such, and to get a function f we need to restrict ourselves to one specific y for each x. In general, the assertion that there always exists such a selection of exactly one y per x, even if we can't write down a recipe for choosing it, is the famous Axiom of Choice, AC (Moore 1982; Jech 1973). In accordance with usual mathematical practice, we will simply assume this axiom, though this is only a convenience and we could avoid it if necessary.[†]

[†] The Axiom of Choice is unproblematically derivable when the domain D is wellordered, in particular countable, because we can define $f(x)$ as the *least* y such that $P[x, y]$. It is a consequence of the downward Löwenheim–Skolem Theorem 3.49 that for our countable languages we may essentially restrict our attention to countable models. Although our proof of that result uses

Even accepting the equivalence of (1) and (2), the latter doesn't correspond to the semantics of a first-order formula. If we were allowed to existentially quantify the function symbols, extending the notion of semantics in an intuitively plausible way, this equivalence means that the following should be logically valid:

$$(\forall x.\, \exists y.\, P[x, y]) \Leftrightarrow (\exists f.\, \forall x.\, P[x, f(x)]),$$

and more generally:

$$(\forall x_1, \ldots, x_n.\, \exists y.\, P[x_1, \ldots, x_n, y]) \Leftrightarrow$$
$$(\exists f.\, \forall x_1, \ldots, x_n.\, P[x_1, \ldots, x_n, f(x_1, \ldots, x_n)]).$$

In a suitable system of *second-order logic*, these are indeed logical equivalences, and we can use them to transform the quantifier prefix of a prenex formula so that all the existential quantifiers come before all the universal ones, e.g.

$$(\forall x.\, \exists y.\, \forall u.\, \exists v.\, P[u, v, x, y])$$
$$\Leftrightarrow (\exists f.\, \forall x\ u.\, \exists v.\, P[u, v, x, f(x)])$$
$$\Leftrightarrow (\exists f\ g.\, \forall x\ u.\, P[u, g(x, u), x, f(x)]).$$

As noted, neither the transforming equivalences nor even the eventual results are expressible as first-order formulas, so we can't follow this procedure exactly. However, we can get roughly the same effect if we accept a transformed formula that is not logically equivalent but merely *equisatisfiable* (see Section 2.8). The point is that an existential quantification over functions is already implicit in an assertion of satisfiability: a formula is satisfiable if there *exists* some domain and interpretation of the function and predicate symbols that satisfies it. Thus we are justified in simply *Skolemizing*, i.e. making the same transformation without the explicit quantification over functions, e.g. transforming the formula

$$\forall x.\, \exists y.\, \forall u.\, \exists v.\, P[u, v, x, y]$$

to:

$$\forall x\ u.\, P[u, g(x, u), x, f(x)],$$

where f and g are distinct function symbols not present in the original formula. Indeed, since universal quantification over free variables is implicit in the definition of satisfaction, we can equally well pass to

Skolemization, a more elaborate method due to Henkin (1949) avoids this, instead expanding the language with new constants in a countable set of stages. Several texts such as Enderton (1972) prove completeness in this way.

$$P[u, g(x, u), x, f(x)].$$

Although no two of these formulas are logically equivalent, they *are* all equisatisfiable. Hence, if we want to decide if the first formula is satisfiable, we need only consider the last one, which has no explicit quantifiers at all. We will see in the next section that the satisfiability problem for such *quantifier-free* formulas can be tackled using techniques from propositional logic. But let us first give a more careful and rigorous justification of the main Skolemizing transformation, defining as we go some of the auxiliary notions used in the actual implementation.

It is necessary to introduce new function symbols called *Skolem functions* (or *Skolem constants* in the nullary case), and these must not occur in the original formula. So, first of all, we define a procedure to get the functions already present in a term and in a formula, so that we can avoid clashes with them. This is straightforward to implement; note that we identify functions by name–arity pairs since functions of the same name but different arities are treated as distinct.

```
let rec funcs tm =
  match tm with
    Var x -> []
  | Fn(f,args) -> itlist (union ** funcs) args [f,length args];;

let functions fm =
  atom_union (fun (R(p,a)) -> itlist (union ** funcs) a []) fm;;
```

Just as `holds M v p` only depends on the values of $v(x)$ for $x \in \mathrm{FV}(p)$ (Theorem 3.2), it only depends on the interpretation M gives to functions that actually appear in p. (The proof of Theorem 3.2 is routinely adapted; indeed things are somewhat simpler since binding of variables plays no role.) When we say from now on 'p does not involve the n-ary function symbol f', we mean formally that $(f, n) \notin$ `functions` p.

Theorem 3.10 *If p is a formula not involving the n-ary function symbol f, with $FV(\exists y.\, p) = \{x_1, \ldots, x_n\}$ (distinct x_i in an arbitrary order), then given any interpretation M there is another interpretation M' that differs from M only in the interpretation of f, such that in all valuations v:*

$$\textsf{holds } M\, v\, (\exists y.\, p) = \textsf{holds } M'\, v\, (\textsf{subst } (y \mapsto f(x_1, \ldots, x_n))\, p).$$

and also holds $M\, v\, (\exists y.\, p) =$ holds $M'\, v\, (\exists y.\, p)$ *as p does not involve f.*

Proof We define M' to be M with the interpretation $f_{M'}$ of f changed as follows. Given $a_1, \ldots, a_n \in D$, if there is some $b \in D$ such that

$$\texttt{holds } M \ (x_1 \Mapsto a_1, \ \ldots, x_n \Mapsto a_n, \ y \Mapsto b) \ p$$

then $f_{M'}(a_1, \ldots, a_n)$ is some such b, otherwise it is any arbitrary b. The point of this definition is that for an arbitrary assignment v the assertions

$$\texttt{holds } M' \ ((y \mapsto f_{M'}(v(x_1), \ldots, v(x_n))) \ v) \ p$$

and

$$\text{for some } b \in D, \texttt{holds } M \ ((y \mapsto b) \ v) \ p$$

are equivalent, since if there is such a b, $f_{M'}$ will pick one. Using Theorem 3.7 and that equivalence we deduce

$$
\begin{aligned}
& \texttt{holds } M' \ v \ (\texttt{subst } (y \Mapsto f(x_1, \ldots, x_n)) \ p) \\
=\ & \texttt{holds } M' \ (\texttt{termval } M' \ v \circ (y \Mapsto f(x_1, \ldots, x_n))) \ p \\
=\ & \texttt{holds } M' \ ((y \mapsto \texttt{termval } M' \ v \ (f(x_1, \ldots, x_n))) \ v) \ p \\
=\ & \texttt{holds } M' \ ((y \mapsto f_{M'}(v(x_1), \ldots, v(x_n))) \ v) \ p \\
=\ & \text{for some } b \in D, \texttt{holds } M \ ((y \mapsto b) \ v) \ p \\
=\ & \texttt{holds } M \ v \ (\exists y.\ p)
\end{aligned}
$$

as required. □

Since this equivalence holds for all valuations, it propagates up through a formula when a subformula is replaced, since in the recursive definitions of $\texttt{termval}$ and $\texttt{holds}$ only the valuation changes. Thus the theorem establishes the following: if we take some arbitrary interpretation M and a formula p with some subformula $\exists y.\ q$, then provided f does not occur in the whole formula p, we can Skolemize the subformula with f and get a new formula p', and a new model M' differing from M only in the interpretation of f, such that for all valuations v:

$$\texttt{holds } M \ v \ p = \texttt{holds } M' \ v \ p'.$$

This can then be done repeatedly, replacing all existentially quantified subformulas, at each stage choosing some function not present in the formula as processed so far. Starting with the initial formula p and some interpretation M, we get a sequence of formulas $p_1, \ldots, p_m$ and interpretations $M_1, \ldots, M_m$ such that each M_{k+1} modifies M_k's interpretation of a new Skolem function only, and

$$\texttt{holds } M_k \ v \ p_k = \texttt{holds } M_{k+1} \ v \ p_{k+1}.$$

By induction, we have for all valuations v and all M:

$$\texttt{holds } M \; v \; p = \texttt{holds } M_m \; v \; p_m,$$

where p_m contains no existential quantifiers. Thus, if the original formula p is satisfiable, by some model M, then the Skolemized formula p_m is satisfied by M_m.

None of this depends on any kind of initial normal form transformation; we are free to apply Skolemization to any existentially quantified subformula, and if the original formula is satisfiable, so is its Skolemization. Conversely, the Skolemized form of an existential formula implies the original, so *provided* all Skolemized subformulas occur positively (in the sense of Section 2.5), the overall Skolemized formula logically implies the original, so is equisatisfiable. Without this condition, we cannot expect it; for example if we Skolemize the second existential subformula in the unsatisfiable formula $(\exists y.\ P(y)) \wedge \neg(\exists x.\ P(x))$ we get the satisfiable $(\exists y.\ P(y)) \wedge \neg P(c)$.

Thus, it makes sense to first transform the formula into NNF so we can identify positive and negative subformulas, and then Skolemize away the existential quantifiers, which all occur positively. We could go further and put the formula into PNF, but it's often advantageous to apply Skolemization first, since the PNF transformation can introduce more free variables into the scope of an existential quantifier, necessitating more arguments on the Skolem functions. For example $\forall x\ z.\ x = z \vee \exists y.\ x \cdot y = 1$ can be Skolemized directly to give $\forall x\ z.\ x = z \vee x \cdot f(x) = 1$, whereas if we first prenex to $\forall x\ z.\ \exists y.\ x = z \vee x \cdot y = 1$, subsequent Skolemization gives $\forall x\ z.x = z \vee x \cdot f(x, z) = 1$. For the same reason, it seems sensible to Skolemize outer quantifiers before inner ones, since this also reduces the number of free variables, e.g.

$$\exists x\ y.\ x \cdot y = 1 \longrightarrow \exists y.\ c \cdot y = 1 \longrightarrow c \cdot d = 1$$

rather than

$$\exists x\ y.\ x \cdot y = 1 \longrightarrow \exists x.\ x \cdot f(x) = 1 \longrightarrow c \cdot f(c) = 1.$$

So, for the overall Skolemization function, we simply recursively descend the formula, Skolemizing any existential formulas and then proceeding to subformulas. We retain a list of the functions $\texttt{fns}$ already in the formula, so we can avoid using them as Skolem functions. (We conservatively avoid even functions with the same name and different arity, which is not logically necessary but may sometimes give less confusing results. A refinement in the other direction would be to re-use the same Skolem function for identical

Skolem formulas; a little reflection on the main Skolemization theorem shows that this is permissible.)

```
let rec skolem fm fns =
  match fm with
    Exists(y,p) ->
        let xs = fv(fm) in
        let f = variant (if xs = [] then "c_"^y else "f_"^y) fns in
        let fx = Fn(f,map (fun x -> Var x) xs) in
        skolem (subst (y |=> fx) p) (f::fns)
  | Forall(x,p) -> let p',fns' = skolem p fns in Forall(x,p'),fns'
  | And(p,q) -> skolem2 (fun (p,q) -> And(p,q)) (p,q) fns
  | Or(p,q) -> skolem2 (fun (p,q) -> Or(p,q)) (p,q) fns
  | _ -> fm,fns
```

When dealing with binary connectives, the set of functions to avoid needs to be updated with new Skolem functions introduced into one formula before tackling the other, hence the auxiliary function `skolem2`:

```
and skolem2 cons (p,q) fns =
  let p',fns' = skolem p fns in
  let q',fns'' = skolem q fns' in
  cons(p',q'),fns'';;
```

The `skolem` function is specifically intended to be applied after NNF transformation, and hence returns unchanged any formulas involving negation, implication or equivalence, as well as simply atomic formulas. For the overall Skolemization function we simplify, transform into NNF then apply `skolem` with an appropriate initial set of function symbols to avoid:

```
let askolemize fm =
  fst(skolem (nnf(simplify fm)) (map fst (functions fm)));;
```

Frequently we just want to transform the result into PNF and omit the universal quantifiers, giving an equisatisfiable formula with no explicit quantifiers. The last step needs a new function, albeit a fairly simple one:

```
let rec specialize fm =
  match fm with
    Forall(x,p) -> specialize p
  | _ -> fm;;
```

and then we just put all the pieces together:

```
let skolemize fm = specialize(pnf(askolemize fm));;
```

For example:

```
# skolemize <<exists y. x < y ==> forall u. exists v. x * u < y * v>>;;
- : fol formula = <<~x < f_y(x) \/ x * u < f_y(x) * f_v(u,x)>>
# skolemize
 <<forall x. P(x)
           ==> (exists y z. Q(y) \/ ~(exists z. P(z) /\ Q(z)))>>;;
    - : fol formula = <<~P(x) \/ Q(c_y) \/ ~P(z) \/ ~Q(z)>>
```

Although in practice we will usually be interested in Skolemizing away *all* existential quantifiers in a formula or set of formulas, it's worth pointing out that we don't need to do so. If we Skolemize a formula p to get p^*, not only are the two formulas equisatisfiable, but provided none of the new Skolem functions appear in some other formula q, so are $p \wedge q$ and $p^* \wedge q$, just applying the same reasoning to $p \wedge q$ but leaving existential quantifiers in q alone. This further implies that for sentences p and q, we have $\models p \Rightarrow q$ iff $\models p^* \Rightarrow q$ provided q does not involve any of the Skolem functions, since $\models p \Rightarrow q$ iff $p \wedge \neg q$ is unsatisfiable. We express this by saying that Skolemization is *conservative*: if q follows from a Skolemized formula, it must follow from the un-Skolemized one, provided q does not itself involve any of the Skolem functions.

In a different direction we can immediately deduce the following theorem, though the direct proof is not hard either:

Theorem 3.11 *A formula p is valid iff p' is, where p' is the result of replacing all free variables in p with distinct constants not present in p.*

Proof Generalize over all free variables, negate, and apply Skolemization to those outer quantified variables.   □

Skolem functions may seem purely an artifact of formal logic, but the use of functions instead of quantifier nesting to indicate dependencies is common in mathematics, even if it is sometimes unconscious and only semi-formal. For example, analysis textbooks like Burkill and Burkill (1970) sometimes write for a typical $\epsilon - \delta$ logical assertion of the form '$\forall \epsilon. \epsilon > 0 \Rightarrow \exists \delta. \ldots$' something like 'for all $\epsilon > 0$ there is a $\delta(\epsilon) > 0$ such that $\ldots$', emphasizing the (possible) dependence of δ on ϵ by the notation '$\delta(\epsilon)$'. As the discussions in this section show, such functional notation can be taken at face value by regarding δ as a Skolem function arising from Skolemizing $\forall \epsilon. \exists \delta. P[\epsilon, \delta]$ into $\exists \delta. \forall \epsilon. P[\epsilon, \delta(\epsilon)]$. In fact, Skolem functions can express more refined dependencies than first-order quantifiers can, suggesting the study of more general 'branching' quantifiers (Hintikka 1996).

3.7 Canonical models

A quantifier-free formula can be considered as a formula of propositional logic. Instead of `prop` as the primitive set of propositional variables, we have relations applied to terms, corresponding to our OCaml type `fol`, but this makes no essential difference, since the theoretical results depended very little on the nature of the underlying set. In particular, a given first-order formula can only involve finitely many variables, functions and predicates, so the set of atomic propositions is countable, and our proof of propositionally compactness (Theorem 2.13) can be carried over. We will use a slight variant of the notion of propositional evaluation `eval` where for convenience a propositional valuation `d` maps atomic formulas themselves to truth values. The function `pholds` determines whether a formula holds in the sense of propositional logic for this notion of valuation. (This function will fail if applied to a formula containing quantifiers.)

```
let pholds d fm = eval fm (fun p -> d(Atom p));;
```

The modified notion of valuation is purely cosmetic, to avoid the repeated appearance of the `Atom` mapping in our theorems, but composition with `Atom` defines a natural bijection with the original notion of propositional valuation, so a quantifier-free formula `p` is valid (respectively satisfiable) in the sense of propositional logic iff `pholds d p` for all (resp. some) valuations `d`. We now prove also that a quantifier-free formula is valid in the first-order sense if and only if it is valid in the propositional sense, by setting up a correspondence between first-order interpretations and valuations and corresponding propositional valuations. One direction is fairly straightforward. Every interpretation M and valuation v defines a corresponding propositional valuation of the atomic formulas in a natural way, namely `holds M v`. We then have:

Theorem 3.12 *If p is a quantifier-free formula, then for all interpretations M and valuations v we have* `pholds (holds M v) p = holds M v p`.

Proof A straightforward structural induction on the structure of p, since for quantifier-free formulas the definitions of `holds` and `pholds` have the same recursive pattern, while for atomic formulas the result holds by definition. □

Corollary 3.13 *If a quantifier-free first-order formula is a propositional tautology, it is also first-order valid.*

Proof In any interpretation M and valuation v, we have shown in the previous theorem that holds M v p = pholds (holds M v) p. However, if p is a propositional tautology, the right-hand side is just 'true'. □

Now we turn to the opposite direction: given a propositional valuation d on the atomic formulas, constructing an interpretation M and valuation v such that holds M v p = pholds d p. Again, it's enough to make sure this is true for atomic formulas, since as noted in the proof of Theorem 3.12 the recursions of holds and pholds are exactly the same for quantifier-free formulas. All atomic formulas are of the form $R(t_1, \ldots, t_n)$, and by definition

$$\text{holds } M \text{ } v \text{ } (R(t_1, \ldots, t_n)) = R_M(\text{termval } M \text{ } v \text{ } t_1, \ldots, \text{termval } M \text{ } v \text{ } t_n).$$

We want to concoct an interpretation M and valuation v such that this is the same as pholds d $(R(t_1, \ldots, t_n))$. It suffices to construct the interpretation of functions and the valuation such that distinct tuples of terms $(t_1, \ldots, t_n)$ map to distinct tuples $(\text{termval } M \text{ } v \text{ } t_1, \ldots, \text{termval } M \text{ } v \text{ } t_n)$ of domain elements, for then we can choose the interpretations of predicate symbols R_M as required to match the propositional valuation d. (This would not be possible if $d(R(s_1, \ldots, s_n)) \neq d(R(t_1, \ldots, t_n))$ yet the tuples of terms had the same interpretation.)

This condition can be achieved in various ways, but perhaps the most straightforward is to take for the domain of the model some subset of the set of terms itself. A *canonical interpretation* for a formula p is one whose domain is some subset of the set of terms and in which each n-ary function f occurring in p is interpreted in the natural way as a syntax constructor, i.e. $f_M(t_1, \ldots, t_n) = f(t_1, \ldots, t_n)$, or properly speaking in terms of our OCaml implementation, Fn$(f, [t_1; \cdots; t_n])$. Since interpretations of function symbols need to map $D^n \to D$, we require that the domain is closed under application of functions occurring in p, i.e. if $t_1, \ldots, t_n \in D$ then $f(t_1, \ldots, t_n) \in D$, and in particular $c \in D$ for each constant (nullary function) in p; one possibility is just to take for D the set of *all* terms. Now, given a propositional valuation d, we can construct a corresponding canonical interpretation M_d by interpreting the functions as we must:

$$f_{M_d}(t_1, \ldots, t_n) = f(t_1, \ldots, t_n)$$

and predicates as follows:

$$R_{M_d}(t_1, \ldots, t_n) = d(R(t_1, \ldots, t_n)).$$

Now we have the required correspondence, at least for the identity valuation $\mathtt{Var}$ that maps a variable 'to itself'. This has the unsurprising property that $\mathtt{termval}\ M_d\ \mathtt{Var}$ is the identity:

Lemma 3.14 *For all terms t, $\mathtt{termval}\ M_d\ \mathtt{Var}\ t = t$.*

Proof By induction on the structure of t. If t is a variable $\mathtt{Var}(x)$ then $\mathtt{termval}\ M_d\ \mathtt{Var}\ (\mathtt{Var}(x)) = \mathtt{Var}(x)$ by definition. Otherwise, if t is of the form $f(t_1, \ldots, t_n)$, we have $\mathtt{termval}\ M_d\ \mathtt{Var}\ t_k = t_k$ for each $k = 1, \ldots, n$ by the inductive hypothesis, and so

$$
\begin{aligned}
&\mathtt{termval}\ M_d\ \mathtt{Var}\ (f(t_1, \ldots, t_n)) \\
={}&f_{M_d}(\mathtt{termval}\ M_d\ \mathtt{Var}\ t_1, \ldots, \mathtt{termval}\ M_d\ \mathtt{Var}\ t_n) \\
={}&f_{M_d}(t_1, \ldots, t_n) \\
={}&f(t_1, \ldots, t_n) \\
={}&t
\end{aligned}
$$

as required.   □

Theorem 3.15 *If d is a propositional valuation of atomic formulas, then for any quantifier-free formula p we have:*

$$\mathtt{holds}\ M_d\ \mathtt{Var}\ p = \mathtt{pholds}\ d\ p.$$

Proof By induction on the structure of p. For atomic formulas:

$$
\begin{aligned}
&\mathtt{holds}\ M_d\ \mathtt{Var}\ (R(t_1, \ldots, t_n)) \\
={}&R_{M_d}(\mathtt{termval}\ M_d\ \mathtt{Var}\ t_1, \ldots, \mathtt{termval}\ M_d\ \mathtt{Var}\ t_n) \\
={}&R_{M_d}(t_1, \ldots, t_n) \\
={}&d(R(t_1, \ldots, t_n)) \\
={}&\mathtt{pholds}\ d\ (R(t_1, \ldots, t_n)).
\end{aligned}
$$

The other cases are straightforward since for quantifier-free formulas the definitions of $\mathtt{holds}$ and $\mathtt{pholds}$ have the same recursive pattern.   □

This allows us to prove that first-order and propositional validity coincide.

Corollary 3.16 *A quantifier-free first-order formula is a propositional tautology if and only if it is first-order valid.*

Proof The left-to-right direction was proved in Corollary 3.13. Conversely, suppose p is first-order valid. Then for any propositional valuation d we have by the above theorem $\texttt{pholds}\; d\; p = \texttt{holds}\; M_d\; \texttt{Var}\; p$. However, since p is first-order valid, it holds in all interpretations and valuations so the right-hand side is 'true'.   □

This is an interesting result, but for our overall project we're more interested in analogous results for satisfiability, since Skolemization (our means of reaching a quantifier-free formula) is satisfiability-preserving but not validity-preserving. For *ground* formulas, everything is easy:

Corollary 3.17 *A ground formula is propositionally valid iff it is first-order valid, and propositionally satisfiable iff it is first-order satisfiable.*

Proof The first part is a special case of Corollary 3.16, and the second part follows because validity of p is the same as unsatisfiability of $\neg p$ for propositional logic and for ground formulas in first-order logic.   □

Thus we are justified in switching freely between propositional and first-order validity or satisfiability for ground formulas. What about quantifier-free formulas in general? Again, one way is straightforward:

Corollary 3.18 *If a quantifier-free first-order formula is first-order satisfiable, it is also (propositionally) satisfiable.*

Proof If p were not propositionally satisfiable, then $\neg p$ would be propositionally valid and hence, by Corollary 3.16, first-order valid, so p cannot also be first-order satisfiable.   □

However, a little reflection shows that the converse relationship is not so simple. For example, $P(x) \wedge \neg P(y)$ is satisfiable as a propositional formula, since the atomic subformulas $P(x)$ and $P(y)$ are distinct and can be interpreted as 'true' and 'false' respectively. However, it is not satisfiable as a first-order formula, since a model for it would have to be found where it holds in *all valuations*, in particular those that assign x and y the same domain value.

We proceed by first generalizing Theorem 3.15. Note that a valuation in a canonical model is a mapping from variable names to terms, and so can be considered as an instantiation.

Lemma 3.19 *If M is any canonical interpretation and v any valuation then for any term t we have $\texttt{termval}\; M\; v\; t = \texttt{tsubst}\; v\; t$.*

Proof The definitions of `termval` M and `tsubst` are the same in any canonical model because each f_M is just f as a syntax constructor. ◻

We first note a simple consequence, though it is also relatively easy to prove directly.

Corollary 3.20 *If i and j are two instantiations and t any term, then*

$$\texttt{tsubst } i \text{ (tsubst } j \ t) = \texttt{tsubst (tsubst } i \circ j) \ t.$$

Proof Pick an arbitrary canonical interpretation M (e.g. interpret all relations as identically false). By Lemma 3.19 the claim is the same as

$$\texttt{termval } M \ i \text{ (tsubst } j \ t) = \texttt{termval } M \text{ (termval } M \ i \circ j) \ t,$$

which is exactly Theorem 3.5. ◻

Our main goal, however, is the following.

Theorem 3.21 *If p is a quantifier-free formula, d is a propositional valuation of atomic formulas and M is some canonical interpretation for p with $R_M(t_1, \ldots, t_n) = d(R(t_1, \ldots, t_n))$, then for any valuation v we have:*

$$\texttt{holds } M \ v \ p = \texttt{pholds } d \text{ (subst } v \ p).$$

Proof By induction on the structure of p. For atomic formulas:

$$
\begin{aligned}
&\texttt{holds } M \ v \ (R(t_1, \ldots, t_n)) \\
=\ & R_M(\texttt{termval } M \ v \ t_1, \ldots, \texttt{termval } M \ v \ t_n) \\
=\ & R_M(\texttt{tsubst } v \ t_1, \ldots, \texttt{tsubst } v \ t_n) \\
=\ & d(R(\texttt{tsubst } v \ t_1, \ldots, \texttt{tsubst } v \ t_n) \\
=\ & d(\texttt{subst } v \ (R(t_1, \ldots, t_n))) \\
=\ & \texttt{pholds } d \text{ (subst } v \ (R(t_1, \ldots, t_n))),
\end{aligned}
$$

while for the other classes of formulas, the recursions match up as before. ◻

For practical purposes, it can be convenient to make the domain of a canonical model as small as possible. The *Herbrand universe* or *Herbrand domain* for a particular first-order language is the set of all *ground* terms of that language, i.e. all terms that can be built from constants and function symbols of the language without using variables, except that if the language has no constants, a constant c is added to make the Herbrand universe nonempty. Usually in what follows we are interested in the language of a single formula p, and we will refer simply to the Herbrand universe for p, meaning for the language of p. We can get the set of the functions in a term, separated into nullary and non-nullary and including the tweak for the case where we want to add a constant to the language, as follows:

```
let herbfuns fm =
  let cns,fns = partition (fun (_,ar) -> ar = 0) (functions fm) in
  if cns = [] then ["c",0],fns else cns,fns;;
```

Note that the Herbrand universe for p is infinite precisely if p involves a non-nullary function; for example, with just a constant c and a unary function f, the Herbrand universe is $\{c, f(c), f(f(c)), f(f(f(c))), \ldots\}$. A *Herbrand interpretation* is a canonical interpretation whose domain is the Herbrand universe for some suitable language (usually the symbols occurring in the formula(s) of interest) and a *Herbrand model* of a set of formulas is a model of those formulas that is a Herbrand interpretation. We will refer to some `subst i p` where i maps into the Herbrand universe as a *ground instance* of p.

Theorem 3.22 *A Herbrand interpretation H satisfies a quantifier-free formula p iff it satisfies the set of all ground instances* `subst i p`.

Proof If H satisfies p, it also satisfies all ground instances, since by Theorem 3.7, `holds H v (subst i p)` = `holds H (termval H v ∘ i) p` = `true`. Conversely, suppose H satisfies all ground instances. Any valuation v for H is a mapping into ground terms, so using Lemma 3.19 we have `termval H v ∘ v = tsubst v ∘ v = v`. But then by Theorem 3.7 we have `holds H v p = holds H (termval H v ∘ v) p = holds H v (tsubst v p)` = `true`. □

Indeed, the same kind of result holds not just for satisfaction in a particular Herbrand model, but for satisfiability as a whole.

Theorem 3.23 *A quantifier-free formula p is first-order satisfiable iff the set of all its ground instances is (propositionally) satisfiable.*

Proof If p is satisfiable, then it holds in some model M under all valuations. Let i be any ground instantiation, i.e. mapping from the variables to members of the Herbrand universe. Using Theorem 3.7 and Theorem 3.12 we deduce that, for any valuation v:

$$\text{pholds (holds } M \ v) \ (\text{subst } i \ p)$$
$$= \ \text{holds } M \ v \ (\text{subst } i \ p)$$

$$= \text{holds } M \text{ (termval } M \ v \circ i) \ p$$

$$= \text{true},$$

so the propositional valuation **holds** M v simultaneously satisfies all ground instances of p.

Conversely, if some propositional valuation d satisfies all ground instances, define a Herbrand interpretation H by $R_H(t_1, \ldots, t_n) = d(R(t_1, \ldots, t_n))$. By Theorem 3.21 we have for any valuation/ground instantiation i that

$$\text{holds } H \ i \ p = \text{pholds } d \ (\text{subst } i \ p) = \text{true}$$

and so H satisfies p. ∎

This crucial result is usually known as *Herbrand's theorem*, though this is a misnomer.[†] By essentially the same proof, we can also deduce the following important equivalence, bypassing the propositional step.

Theorem 3.24 *A quantifier-free formula has a model (i.e. is satisfiable) iff it has a Herbrand model.*

Proof The right-to-left direction is immediate since a Herbrand model is indeed a model. In the other direction, we just re-use both parts of the proof of Theorem 3.23, noting that the model constructed is indeed a Herbrand model. That is, if p has a model, then all its ground instances are propositionally satisfiable, and therefore it has a Herbrand model. ∎

Note that this reasoning only covers quantifier-free or universal formulas. For example, $P(c) \wedge \exists x. \ \neg P(x)$ is satisfiable (e.g. set P to 'is even' and c to zero on the natural numbers), but has no Herbrand model, since the Herbrand universe is just $\{c\}$ and the formula fails in a 1-element model. For the same reason, analogous results to Theorems 3.23 and 3.24 fail for validity: $P(c) \Rightarrow P(x)$ is not logically valid, but its only ground instance $P(c) \Rightarrow P(c)$ is a propositional tautology and the formula holds in the Herbrand model with domain $\{c\}$. On the other hand, by similarly re-examining the proof of Theorem 3.16, one can deduce that a quantifier-free formula is valid iff it holds in all canonical models (not just those whose domain is the Herbrand universe).

[†] The theorem here was present with varying degrees of explicitness in earlier work of Skolem and Gödel and so is sometimes referred to as the Skolem–Gödel–Herbrand theorem. The theorem given by Herbrand (1930) has a similar flavour but talks about proof rather than semantic validity, and in fact Herbrand's original demonstration was not entirely correct (Andrews 2003).

3.8 Mechanizing Herbrand's theorem

After a lot of work, we have finally succeeded in reducing first-order satisfiability to propositional satisfiability. But our triumph is marred by the
fact that we need to test propositional satisfiability of the set of *all* ground
instances, of which there are usually infinitely many. However, the compactness Theorem 2.13 for propositional logic comes to our rescue.

Theorem 3.25 *A quantifier-free formula is first-order satisfiable iff all finite
sets of ground instances are (propositionally) satisfiable.*

Proof Immediate from Herbrand's Theorem 3.23 and compactness for propositional logic (Theorem 2.13).   □

Corollary 3.26 *A quantifier-free formula p is first-order unsatisfiable iff
some finite set of ground instances is (propositionally) unsatisfiable.*

Proof The contraposition of the previous theorem.   □

This gives rise to a procedure whereby we can verify that a formula p is
unsatisfiable. We simply enumerate larger and larger sets of ground instances
and test them for propositional satisfiability. Provided that every ground
instance appears eventually in the enumeration, we are sure that if p is
unsatisfiable we will eventually reach a finite unsatisfiable set of propositional formulas. If p is in fact satisfiable, this process may never terminate,
so this is only a semi-decision procedure, but, as we'll see in Section 7.6, this
is the best we can hope for in general.

In the late 1950s, perhaps inspired by a suggestion from A. Robinson
(1957) at the 1954 Summer Institute for Symbolic Logic at Cornell University, there were several implementations of theorem-proving systems along
these lines, one of the earliest being due to Gilmore (1960). Gilmore enumerated larger and larger sets of ground instances, at each stage checking
for contradiction by putting them into disjunctive normal form and checking
each disjunct for complementary literals. Let's follow this approach to get
an idea of how well it works.

We need to set up an appropriate enumeration of the ground instances,
or more precisely, of m-tuples of ground terms where m is the number of
free variables in the formula. If we want to ensure that every unsatisfiable
formula will eventually be proved unsatisfiable, then the enumeration must
eventually include every possible ground instance. One reasonable approach
is to first generate all m-tuples involving no functions (i.e. just combinations

of constant terms), then all those involving one function, then two, three, etc. Every tuple will appear eventually, and the 'simpler' possibilities will be tried first. We can set up this enumeration via two mutually recursive functions, both taking among their arguments the set of constant terms cntms and the set of functions with their arities, funcs.

The function groundterms enumerates all ground terms involving n functions. If n = 0 the constant terms are returned. Otherwise all possible functions are tried, and since we then need to fill the argument places of each m-ary function with terms involving in total n − 1 functions, one already having been used, we recursively call groundtuples:

```
let rec groundterms cntms funcs n =
  if n = 0 then cntms else
  itlist (fun (f,m) l -> map (fun args -> Fn(f,args))
                             (groundtuples cntms funcs (n - 1) m) @ l)
         funcs []
```

while the mutually recursive function groundtuples generates all m-tuples of ground terms involving (in total) n functions.[†] For all k up to n, this in turn tries all ways of occupying the first argument place with a k-function term and then recursively produces all (m − 1)-tuples involving all the remaining n − k functions.

```
and groundtuples cntms funcs n m =
  if m = 0 then if n = 0 then [[]] else [] else
  itlist (fun k l -> allpairs (fun h t -> h::t)
                    (groundterms cntms funcs k)
                    (groundtuples cntms funcs (n - k) (m - 1)) @ l)
         (0 -- n) [];;
```

Gilmore's method can be considered just one member of a family of 'Herbrand procedures' that somehow test larger and larger conjunctions of ground instances until unsatisfiability is verified. We can generalize over the way the satisfiability test is done (tfn) and the modification function (mfn) that augments the ground instances with a new instance, whatever form they may be stored in. This generalization, which not only saves code but emphasizes that the key ideas are independent of the particular propositional satisfiability test at the core, is carried through in the following loop:

[†] Note that this can involve repeated recomputation of the same instances; a more efficient approach would be to compute lower levels once and recall them when needed. But in our simple experiments this won't be the time-critical aspect.

```
let rec herbloop mfn tfn fl0 cntms funcs fvs n fl tried tuples =
  print_string(string_of_int(length tried)^" ground instances tried; "^
            string_of_int(length fl)^" items in list");
  print_newline();
  match tuples with
    [] -> let newtups = groundtuples cntms funcs n (length fvs) in
            herbloop mfn tfn fl0 cntms funcs fvs (n + 1) fl tried newtups
  | tup::tups ->
          let fl' = mfn fl0 (subst(fpf fvs tup)) fl in
          if not(tfn fl') then tup::tried else
          herbloop mfn tfn fl0 cntms funcs fvs n fl' (tup::tried) tups;;
```

Several parameters are carried around unchanged: the modification and testing function parameters, the initial formula in some transformed list representation (fl0), then constant terms cntms and functions funcs and the free variables fvs of the formula. The other arguments are n, the next level of the enumeration to generate, fl, the set of ground instances so far, tried, the instances tried, and tuples, the remaining ground instances in the current level. When tuples is empty, we simply generate the next level and step n up to n + 1. In the other case, we use the modification function to update fl with another instance. If this is unsatisfiable, then we return the successful set of instances tried; otherwise, we continue. In the particular case of the Gilmore procedure, formulas are maintained in fl0 and fl in a DNF representation, and the modification function applies the instantiation to the starting formula fl0 and combines the DNFs by distribution:

```
let gilmore_loop =
  let mfn djs0 ifn djs =
    filter (non trivial) (distrib (image (image ifn) djs0) djs) in
  herbloop mfn (fun djs -> djs <> []);;
```

We're more usually interested in proving validity rather than unsatisfiability. For this, we generalize, negate and Skolemize the initial formula and set up the appropriate sets of free variables, functions and constants. Then we simply start the main loop, and report if it terminates how many ground instances were tried:

```
let gilmore fm =
  let sfm = skolemize(Not(generalize fm)) in
  let fvs = fv sfm and consts,funcs = herbfuns sfm in
  let cntms = image (fun (c,_) -> Fn(c,[])) consts in
  length(gilmore_loop (simpdnf sfm) cntms funcs fvs 0 [[]] [] []);;
```

Let's try out our new first-order prover on some examples. We'll start small:

```
# gilmore <<exists x. forall y. P(x) ==> P(y)>>;;
...
1 ground instances tried; 1 items in list
- : int = 2
```

So far, so good. This should be an easy problem. However, to clarify what's going on inside, it's worth tracing through this example. The negated formula, after Skolemization, is:

```
# let sfm = skolemize(Not <<exists x. forall y. P(x) ==> P(y)>>);;
val sfm : fol formula = <<P(x) /\ ~P(f_y(x))>>
```

The reader can confirm by running through the other steps inside `gilmore` that the set of constant terms consists purely of one 'invented' constant c[†] and there is a single unary Skolem function `f_y`. The first ground instance to be generated is

```
P(c) /\ ~P(f_y(c))
```

Since this is still propositionally satisfiable, a second instance is generated:

```
P(f_y(c)) /\ ~P(f_y(f_y(c)))
```

Since the conjunction of these two instances is propositionally unsatisfiable (the conjunction includes both `P(f_y(c))` and its negation), the procedure terminates, indicating that two ground instances were used and that the formula is valid as claimed. The reader may find it very instructive to step through more of the examples that follow in a similar way. In this chapter, we will take many of our examples from a suite given by Pelletier (1986), in an attempt to get some idea of the merits of different approaches. Some are very easily handled by the present program:

```
# let p24 = gilmore
   <<~(exists x. U(x) /\ Q(x)) /\
     (forall x. P(x) ==> Q(x) \/ R(x)) /\
     ~(exists x. P(x) ==> (exists x. Q(x))) /\
     (forall x. Q(x) /\ R(x) ==> U(x))
     ==> (exists x. P(x) /\ R(x))>>;;
0 ground instances tried; 1 items in list
0 ground instances tried; 1 items in list
val p24 : int = 1
```

[†] That this case is called for shows that if we were to allow interpretations with an empty domain, the formula would in fact be invalid.

Some take a little more time and require quite a few ground instances to be tried, like:

```
# let p45 = gilmore
 <<(forall x. P(x) /\ (forall y. G(y) /\ H(x,y) ==> J(x,y))
              ==> (forall y. G(y) /\ H(x,y) ==> R(y))) /\
   ~(exists y. L(y) /\ R(y)) /\
   (exists x. P(x) /\ (forall y. H(x,y) ==> L(y)) /\
                     (forall y. G(y) /\ H(x,y) ==> J(x,y)))
   ==> (exists x. P(x) /\ ~(exists y. G(y) /\ H(x,y)))>>;;
4 ground instances tried; 2511 items in list
val p45 : int = 5
```

Still others appear quite intractable, running for a long time and eventually causing the machine to run out of memory, so large is the number of disjuncts generated.

```
let p20 = gilmore
 <<(forall x y. exists z. forall w. P(x) /\ Q(y) ==> R(z) /\ U(w))
   ==> (exists x y. P(x) /\ Q(y)) ==> (exists z. R(z))>>;;
```

All in all, although the Gilmore procedure is a promising start to first-order theorem proving, there is plenty of room for improvement. Since the main limitation seems to be the explosion in the number of disjuncts in the DNF, a natural approach is to maintain the same kind of enumeration procedure but check the propositional satisfiability of the conjunction of ground instances generated so far by a more efficient propositional algorithm.

In fact, it was for exactly this purpose that Davis and Putnam (1960) developed their procedure for propositional satisfiability testing (see Section 2.9). In this context, clausal form has the particular advantage that there is no analogue of the multiplicative explosion of disjuncts. One simply puts the (negated, Skolemized) formula into clausal form, with say k conjuncts, and each new ground instance generated just adds another k clauses to the accumulated pile. Against this, of course, one needs a real satisfiability test algorithm to be run, whereas in the Gilmore procedure this is simply a matter of looking for complementary literals. Slightly anachronistically, we will use the DPLL rather than the DP procedure, since our earlier experiments suggested it is usually better, and it certainly has better space behaviour. The structure of the Davis–Putnam program is very similar to the Gilmore one. This time the stored formulas are all in CNF rather than DNF, and

each time we incorporate a new instance, we check for unsatisfiability using
`dpll`:

```
let dp_mfn cjs0 ifn cjs = union (image (image ifn) cjs0) cjs;;

let dp_loop = herbloop dp_mfn dpll;;
```

The outer wrapper is unchanged except that the formula is put into CNF
rather than DNF:

```
let davisputnam fm =
  let sfm = skolemize(Not(generalize fm)) in
  let fvs = fv sfm and consts,funcs = herbfuns sfm in
  let cntms = image (fun (c,_) -> Fn(c,[])) consts in
  length(dp_loop (simpcnf sfm) cntms funcs fvs 0 [] [] []);;
```

This code turns out to be much more effective in most cases. For example,
the formerly problematic `p20` is solved rapidly, using 19 ground instances:

```
# let p20 = davisputnam
   <<(forall x y. exists z. forall w. P(x) /\ Q(y) ==> R(z) /\ U(w))
     ==> (exists x y. P(x) /\ Q(y)) ==> (exists z. R(z))>>;;
0 ground instances tried; 0 items in list
...
18 ground instances tried; 37 items in list
val p20 : int = 19
```

Although the Davis–Putnam procedure avoids the catastrophic explosion
in memory usage that was the bane of the Gilmore procedure, it still often
generates a very large number of ground instances and becomes quite slow
at each propositional step. Typically, most of these instances make no contribution to the final refutation, and a much smaller set would be adequate.
The overall runtime (and ultimately feasibility) depends on how quickly an
adequate set turns up in the enumeration, which is quite unpredictable.
Suppose we define a function that runs through the list of possibly-needed
instances (**dunno**), putting them onto the list of needed ones **need** only if
the other instances are satisfiable:

```
let rec dp_refine cjs0 fvs dunno need =
  match dunno with
    [] -> need
  | cl::dknow ->
      let mfn = dp_mfn cjs0 ** subst ** fpf fvs in
      let need' =
        if dpll(itlist mfn (need @ dknow) []) then cl::need else need in
      dp_refine cjs0 fvs dknow need';;
```

We can use this refinement process after the main loop has succeeded:

```
let dp_refine_loop cjs0 cntms funcs fvs n cjs tried tuples =
  let tups = dp_loop cjs0 cntms funcs fvs n cjs tried tuples in
  dp_refine cjs0 fvs tups [];;
```

As the reader can confirm, replacing `dp_loop` by `dp_refine_loop` in the Davis–Putnam procedure massively reduces the number of final instances, e.g. from 40 to just 3 in the case of p36, and from 181 to 5 for p29. However, while cutting down the number like this may be beneficial if we want to use the set of ground instances for something (as we will in Section 5.13), it doesn't help to improve the efficiency of the procedure itself, which still needs to examine the whole set of instances so far at each iteration. As Davis (1983) admits in retrospect:

... effectively eliminating the truth-functional satisfiability obstacle only uncovered the deeper problem of the combinatorial explosion inherent in unstructured search through the Herbrand universe ...

The next major step forward in theorem proving was a more intelligent means of choosing instances, to pick out the small set of relevant ones instead of blindly trying all possibilities.

3.9 Unification

The `gilmore` and `davisputnam` procedures follow essentially the same pattern. Decision methods for propositional logic, respectively disjunctive normal forms and the Davis–Putnam method, are used together with a systematic enumeration of ground instances. A more sophisticated idea, first used by Prawitz, Prawitz and Voghera (1960), is to perform propositional operations on the *uninstantiated* formulas, or at least instantiate them intelligently just as much as is necessary to make progress with propositional reasoning. Prawitz's work was extended by J. A. Robinson (1965b), who gave an effective syntactic procedure called *unification* for deciding on appropriate instantiations to make terms match up correctly. Suppose for example that we have the following uninstantiated clauses in the Davis–Putnam method:

$$P(x, f(y)) \vee Q(x, y),$$
$$\neg P(g(u), v).$$

Instead of enumerating blindly, we can choose instantiations for the variables in the two clauses so that $P(x, f(y))$ and $\neg P(g(u), v)$ become complementary, e.g. setting $x = g(u)$ and $v = f(y)$. After instantiation, we have the clauses:

$$P(g(u), f(y)) \vee Q(g(u), y),$$
$$\neg P(g(u), f(y)).$$

and so we are able to derive a new clause using the resolution rule:

$$Q(g(u), y).$$

By contrast, in the enumeration-based approach, we would have to wait until instances allowing the same kind of resolution step were generated, by which time we may have become overwhelmed by other (often irrelevant) instances.

Definition 3.27 *Given a set of pairs of terms*

$$S = \{(s_1, t_1), \ldots, (s_n, t_n)\},$$

a unifier *of the set S is an instantiation σ such that*

$$\texttt{tsubst } \sigma \ s_i = \texttt{tsubst } \sigma \ t_i$$

for each $i = 1, \ldots, n$. In the special case of a single pair of terms, we often talk about a 'unifier of s and t', meaning a unifier of $\{(s, t)\}$.

Unifying a set of pairs of terms is analogous to solving a system of simultaneous equations such as $2x + y = 3$ and $x - y = 6$ in ordinary algebra, and we will emphasize this parallel in the following discussion. Just as a set of equations may be unsolvable, so may a unification problem. First of all, there is no unifier of $f(x)$ and $g(y)$ where f and g are different function symbols, for whatever terms replace the variables x and y, the instantiated terms will have different functions at the top level. Slightly more subtly, there is no unifier of x and $f(x)$, or more generally of x and any term involving x as a proper subterm, for whatever the instantiation of x, one term will remain a proper subterm of the other, and hence unequal. This is exactly analogous to trying to solve $x = x + 1$ in ordinary algebra. A more complicated example of this kind of circularity is the unification problem $\{(x, f(y)), (y, g(x))\}$, analogous to the unsolvable simultaneous equations $x = y + 1$ and $y = x + 2$.

On the other hand, if a unification problem has a solution, it always has infinitely many, because if σ is a unifier of the s_i and t_i, then so is tsubst $\tau \circ \sigma$ for any other instantiation τ, using Corollary 3.20:

$$
\begin{aligned}
& \text{tsubst } (\text{tsubst } \tau \circ \sigma) \; s_i \\
= \; & \text{tsubst } \tau \; (\text{tsubst } \sigma \; s_i) \\
= \; & \text{tsubst } \tau \; (\text{tsubst } \sigma \; t_i) \\
= \; & \text{tsubst } (\text{tsubst } \tau \circ \sigma) \; t_i.
\end{aligned}
$$

For example, instead of unifying $P(x, f(y))$ and $P(g(u), v)$ by setting $x = g(u)$ and $v = f(y)$, we could have used other variables or even arbitrarily complicated terms like $x = g(f(g(y)))$, $u = f(g(y))$ and $v = f(y)$. But it will turn out that we can always find a 'most general' unifier that keeps the instantiating terms as 'simple' as possible.

We say that an instantiation σ is *more general* than another one τ, and write $\sigma \leq \tau$, if there is some instantiation δ such that

$$
\text{tsubst } \tau = \text{tsubst } \delta \circ \text{tsubst } \sigma.
$$

We say σ is a *most general unifier* (MGU) of S if (i) it is a unifier of S, and (ii) for every other unifier τ of S, we have $\sigma \leq \tau$. Most general unifiers are not necessarily unique. For example, the set $\{(x, y)\}$ has two different MGUs, one that maps $x \mapsto y$ and one that maps $y \mapsto x$. However, one can quite easily show that two MGUs of a given set S can, like these two, differ only up to a permutation of variable names. (Assuming that we restrict unifiers to instantiations that affect a finite number of variables.)

A unification algorithm

Let us now turn to a general method for solving a unification problem or deciding that it has no solution. Our main function unify is recursive, with two arguments: env, which is a finite partial function from variables to terms, and eqs, which is a list of term–term pairs to be unified. The unification function essentially applies some transformations to eqs and incorporates the resulting variable–term mappings into env. This env is not quite the final unifying mapping itself, because it may map a variable to a term containing variables that are themselves assigned, e.g. $x \mapsto y$ and $y \mapsto z$ instead of just $x \mapsto z$ directly. But we will require env to be free of *cycles*. Write $x \longrightarrow y$ to indicate that there is an assignment $x \mapsto t$ in env with $y \in \text{FVT}(t)$. By a cycle, we mean a nonempty finite sequence leading back to the starting point:

$$x_0 \longrightarrow x_1 \longrightarrow \cdots \longrightarrow x_p \longrightarrow x_0.$$

Our main unification algorithm will only incorporate new entries $x \mapsto t$ into **env** that preserve the property of being cycle-free. It is sufficient to ensure the following:

(1) there is no existing assignment $x \mapsto s$ in **env**;
(2) there is no variable $y \in \mathrm{FVT}(t)$ such that $y \longrightarrow^* x$, i.e. there is a sequence of zero or more $\longrightarrow$-steps leading from y to x; in particular $x \notin \mathrm{FVT}(t)$.

To see that if **env** is cycle-free and these properties hold then $(x \mapsto t)$**env** is also cycle-free, note that if there were now a cycle for the new relation $\longrightarrow'$:

$$z \longrightarrow' x_1 \longrightarrow' \cdots \longrightarrow' x_p \longrightarrow' z$$

then there must be one of the following form:

$$z \longrightarrow x_1 \longrightarrow x \longrightarrow' y \longrightarrow \cdots \longrightarrow x_p \longrightarrow z$$

for some $y \in \mathrm{FVT}(t)$. For there must be at least one case where the new assignment $x \mapsto t$ plays a role, since **env** was originally cycle-free, while if there is more than one instance of x, we can cut out any intermediate steps between the first and the last. However, a cycle of the above form also gives us the following, contradicting assumption (2):

$$y \longrightarrow \cdots \longrightarrow x_p \longrightarrow z \longrightarrow x_1 \longrightarrow x.$$

The following function will return 'false' if condition (2) above holds for a new assignment $x \mapsto t$. If condition (2) does not hold then it fails, except in the case $t = x$ when it returns 'true', indicating that the assignment is 'trivial'.

```
let rec istriv env x t =
  match t with
    Var y -> y = x or defined env y & istriv env x (apply env y)
  | Fn(f,args) -> exists (istriv env x) args & failwith "cyclic";;
```

This is effectively calculating a reflexive-transitive closure of $\longrightarrow$, which could be done much more efficiently. However, this simple recursive implementation is usually fast enough, and is certainly guaranteed to terminate, precisely because the existing **env** is cycle-free.

Now we come to the main unification function. This just transforms the list of pairs eqs from the front using various transformations until the front pair is of the form (x, t). If there is already a definition $x \mapsto s$ in env, then the pair is expanded into (s, t) and the recursion proceeds. Otherwise we know that condition (1) holds, so $x \mapsto t$ is a candidate for incorporation into env. If there is a benign cycle istriv env x t is true and env is unchanged. Any other kind of cycle will cause failure, which will propagate out. Otherwise condition (2) holds, and $x \mapsto t$ is incorporated into env for the next recursive call.

```
let rec unify env eqs =
  match eqs with
    [] -> env
  | (Fn(f,fargs),Fn(g,gargs))::oth ->
        if f = g & length fargs = length gargs
        then unify env (zip fargs gargs @ oth)
        else failwith "impossible unification"
  | (Var x,t)::oth ->
        if defined env x then unify env ((apply env x,t)::oth)
        else unify (if istriv env x t then env else (x|->t) env) oth
  | (t,Var x)::oth -> unify env ((Var x,t)::oth);;
```

Let us regard the assignments $x_i \mapsto t_i$ in env and the pairs (s_j, s'_j) in eqs as a collective set of pairs $S = \{\ldots, (x_i, t_i), \ldots, (s_j, s'_j), \ldots\}$. The unify function is tail-recursive and the key observation is that the successive recursive calls have arguments env and eqs satisfying two properties:

- the finite partial function env is cycle-free;
- the set S combining env and eqs has *exactly the same* set of unifiers as the original problem.

The first claim follows because a new assignment $x \mapsto t$ is only added to the environment when there is no existing assignment $x \mapsto s$, hence confirming condition (1), and when defined env x returns false, hence confirming condition (2). To verify the other claim, we consider the clauses that can lead to recursive calls. The second clause will lead to a recursive call only when the front pair in eqs is of the form $(f(s_1, \ldots, s_n), f(t_1, \ldots, t_n))$, and the claim then follows since

$$\{(f(s_1, \ldots, s_n), f(t_1, \ldots, t_n))\} \cup E$$

has exactly the same unifiers as

$$\{(s_1, t_1), \ldots, (s_n, t_n)\} \cup E$$

because any instantiation unifies $f(s_1, \ldots, s_n)$ and $f(t_1, \ldots, t_n)$ iff it unifies each corresponding pair s_i and t_i. When the front pair is (x, t) and there is already an assignment $x \mapsto s$, we get a recursive call with (x, t) replaced by (s, t), which also preserves the claimed property since $\{(x, t), (x, s)\} \cup E$ has exactly the same unifiers as $\{(s, t), (x, s)\} \cup E$. The final clause just reverses the front pair, and this order is immaterial to the unifiers. Thus the claim is verified.

Any failure indicates that one of the intermediate problems is unsolvable, because it involves either incompatible toplevel functions like a pair $(f(s), g(t))$, or a circularity where a unifier would unify (x, t) where $x \in$ FVT(t) and $x \neq t$. Since this intermediate problem has exactly the same set of unifiers as the original problem, failure therefore indicates the unsolvability of the original problem.

We will next show that successful termination of **unify** indicates that there *is* a unifier of the initial set of pairs, and in fact that a most general unifier can be obtained from the resulting **env** by applying the following function to reach a 'fully solved' form:

```
let rec solve env =
  let env' = mapf (tsubst env) env in
  if env' = env then env else solve env';;
```

Once again, this transforms **env** in a way that preserves the set of unifiers of the corresponding pairs across recursive calls, because the set

$$\{(x_1, t_1), \ldots, (x_n, t_n)\}$$

has exactly the same set of unifiers as

$$\{(x_1, \mathtt{tsubst}\ (x_1 \mapsto t_1)\ t_1), \ldots, (x_n, \mathtt{tsubst}\ (x_1 \mapsto t_1)\ t_n)\}.$$

Moreover, because the initial **env** was free of cycles, the function terminates and the result is an instantiation σ whose assignments $x_i \mapsto t_i$ satisfy $x_i \notin$ FVT(t_j) for all i and j. It is immediate that σ unifies each pair (x_i, t_i) in its own assignment, since x_i is instantiated to t_i by this very assignment while t_i is unchanged as it contains none of the variables x_j. In fact, σ is

actually a *most general* unifier of the set of pairs (x_i, t_i), because for any
other unifier τ of these pairs we have:

$$\mathsf{tsubst}\ \tau\ x_i$$
$$=\quad \mathsf{tsubst}\ \tau\ t_i$$
$$=\quad \mathsf{tsubst}\ \tau\ (\mathsf{tsubst}\ \sigma\ x_i)$$
$$=\quad (\mathsf{tsubst}\ \tau\ \circ\ \mathsf{tsubst}\ \sigma)\ x_i$$

for each variable x_i involved in σ. For all other variables x, we have $\mathsf{tsubst}\ \sigma$
$x = \mathsf{tsubst}\ \tau\ x = \mathsf{Var}(x)$ so the same is trivially true. Hence

$$\mathsf{tsubst}\ \tau = \mathsf{tsubst}\ \tau\ \circ\ \mathsf{tsubst}\ \sigma$$

and so $\sigma \leq \tau$ by definition. (And even stronger, the δ we need to exist
for this to hold can be taken to be τ itself.) Moreover, since by the basic
preservation property the set of pairs (x_i, t_i) has exactly the same unifiers as
the original problem, we conclude that if `unify undefined eqs` terminates
successfully with result `env`, then $\sigma = \mathsf{solve}\ \mathsf{env}$ is an MGU of the original
pairs `eqs`.

Finally, we will prove that `unify env eqs` does always terminate if `env` is
cycle-free, in particular for the starting value `undefined`. Let n be the 'size'
of `eqs`, which we define as the total number of `Var` and `Fn` constructors in the
instantiated terms $t' = \mathsf{tsubst}\ (\mathsf{solve}\ \mathsf{env})\ t$ for all t on either side of a pair
in `eqs`. Now note that across recursive calls, either the number of variables
in `eqs` that have no assignment in `env` decreases (when a new assignment
is added to `env`), or else this count stays the same and n decreases (when a
function is split apart or a trivial pair (x, x) is discarded), or both those stay
the same but the front pair is either reversed (which cannot happen twice in
a row) or has one member instantiated using `env` (which can only happen
finitely often since `env` is cycle-free). Thus termination is guaranteed.

In summary, we have proved that (i) failure indicates unsolvability, (ii)
successful termination results in an MGU, and (iii) termination, either with
success or failure, is guaranteed. Therefore the function terminates with
success if and only if the unification problem is solvable, and in such cases
returns an MGU.

We can now finally package up everything as a function that solves the
unification problem completely and creates an instantiation.

```
let fullunify eqs = solve (unify undefined eqs);;
```

For example, we can use this to find a unifier for a pair of terms, then
apply it, to check that the terms are indeed unified:

```
# let unify_and_apply eqs =
    let i = fullunify eqs in
    let apply (t1,t2) = tsubst i t1,tsubst i t2 in
    map apply eqs;;
val unify_and_apply : (term * term) list -> (term * term) list = <fun>
# unify_and_apply [<<|f(x,g(y))|>>,<<|f(f(z),w)|>>];;
- : (term * term) list = [(<<|f(f(z),g(y))|>>, <<|f(f(z),g(y))|>>)]
# unify_and_apply [<<|f(x,y)|>>,<<|f(f(x)|>>];;
- : (term * term) list = [(<<|f(y,y)|>>, <<|f(y,y)|>>)]
# unify_and_apply [<<|f(x,g(y))|>>,<<|f(y,x)|>>];;
Exception: Failure "cyclic".
```

Note that unification problems can generate exponentially large unifiers, e.g.

```
# unify_and_apply [<<|x_0|>>,<<|f(x_1,x_1)|>>;
                   <<|x_1|>>,<<|f(x_2,x_2)|>>;
                   <<|x_2|>>,<<|f(x_3,x_3)|>>];;
- : (term * term) list =
[(<<|f(f(f(x_3,x_3),f(x_3,x_3)),f(f(x_3,x_3),f(x_3,x_3)))|>>,
  <<|f(f(f(x_3,x_3),f(x_3,x_3)),f(f(x_3,x_3),f(x_3,x_3)))|>>);
 (<<|f(f(x_3,x_3),f(x_3,x_3))|>>, <<|f(f(x_3,x_3),f(x_3,x_3))|>>);
 (<<|f(x_3,x_3)|>>, <<|f(x_3,x_3)|>>)]
```

The core function **unify** avoids creating these large unifiers, but can still take exponential time because of its descent through the list of assignments, which can cause exponential branching in cases like the one above. It is possible to implement more efficient unification algorithms like those given by Martelli and Montanari (1982), but we will not usually find the time or space usage of unification a serious problem in our applications. For a good discussion of several unification algorithms, see Baader and Nipkow (1998).

Using unification

We will explore several ways of incorporating unification into first-order theorem proving, combining it with different methods for propositional logic. Before getting involved in the details, however, we want to emphasize a useful distinction.

In the Davis–Putnam example at the beginning of this section we started with some clauses, which are implicitly conjoined and universally quantified over all their variables. Consequently, the variables in the new clause $Q(g(u), y)$ derived can be regarded as universal and may freely be instantiated differently each time it is used later. Suppose, on the other hand, we had decided to use the DPLL procedure, and used the first clause as the basis for a case-split, assuming separately $P(x, f(y))$ and $Q(x, y)$ and trying to derive a contradiction separately from each of these together with the other clauses. In this case, if the variables x and y later need to be instantiated, they must be instantiated in the *same* way. We can only assume

$$\forall x\, y.\ P(x, f(y)) \vee Q(x, y),$$

which does *not* imply

$$(\forall x\, y.\ P(x, f(y))) \vee (\forall x, y.\ Q(x, y)).$$

Consequently, when we perform operations like case-splitting, we need to maintain a correlation between certain variables, and make sure they are instantiated consistently.

Methods like the first, where no case-splits are performed and all variables may be treated as universally quantified and independently instantiated, are called *local*, because the variable instantiations in the immediate steps do not affect other parts of the overall proof; they are also referred to as *bottom-up* because they can build up independent lemmas without regard to the overall problem. Unification-based methods that do involve case-splits, on the other hand, are called *global* or *top-down* because certain variable instantiations need to be propagated throughout the proof, and often the instantiations end up being driven by the overall problem.

There are characteristic differences between local and global methods that correlate strongly with the kinds of problems where they perform well or badly. In local methods, all intermediate results are absolute, independent of context, and can be re-used at will with different variable instantiations later in the proof. They can be used just like lemmas in ordinary mathematical proofs, which are often used several times in different contexts. By contrast, using lemmas in global methods is more difficult, because they depend on the ambient environment of variable assignments and may, at one extreme, have to be proved separately each time they are used. Nevertheless, the tendency of global methods to use variable instantiations relevant to the overall result can be a strength, giving a measure of goal-direction.

The best-known local method is *resolution*, and it was in the context of resolution that J. A. Robinson (1965b) introduced unification in its full generality to automated theorem proving. Another important local method quite close to resolution and developed independently at about the same time is the inverse method (Maslov 1964; Lifschitz 1986). As for global methods, two of the best-known are tableaux, which were implicitly used in an implementation by Prawitz, Prawitz and Voghera (1960), and model elimination (Loveland 1968; Loveland 1978). Crudely speaking:

- tableaux = Gilmore procedure + unification;
- resolution = Davis–Putnam procedure (DP, not DPLL) + unification.

We will consider these important techniques in the next sections. Note that resolution is a unification-based extension of the original DP procedure, not DPLL. Adding unification to DPLL naturally yields a global rather than a local method, since literals used in case-splits must be instantiated consistently in both branches; one such approach is *model evolution* (Baumgartner and Tinelli 2003). An interesting intermediate case is the first-order extension (Björk 2005) of Stålmarck's method from Section 2.10. Here the variables in the two branches of the dilemma rule need to be correlated, but the common results in merged branches can have those variables promoted to universal status so they can later be instantiated freely.

3.10 Tableaux

By Herbrand and compactness, if a first-order formula $P[x_1, \ldots, x_n]$ is unsatisfiable, there are finitely many ground instances (say k of them) such that the following conjunction is propositionally unsatisfiable:

$$P[t_1^1, \ldots, t_n^1] \wedge \cdots \wedge P[t_1^k, \ldots, t_n^k].$$

In Gilmore's method, this propositional unsatisfiability is verified by expanding the conjunction into DNF and checking that each disjunct contains a conjoined pair of complementary literals. Suppose that instead of creating ground instances, we replace the variables $x_1, \ldots, x_n$ with tuples of distinct variables:

$$P[z_1^1, \ldots, z_n^1] \wedge \cdots \wedge P[z_1^k, \ldots, z_n^k].$$

This formula can similarly be expanded out into DNF. If we now apply the instantiation θ that maps each new variable z_i^j to the corresponding ground term t_i^j, we obtain a DNF equivalent of the original conjunction of substitution instances. (This is not necessarily exactly the same as the one that would have been obtained by instantiating first and then making the DNF transformation, because the instantiation might have caused distinct terms to become identified, but that doesn't matter.) Since this conjunction of ground instances is unsatisfiable, and ground, it is itself propositionally unsatisfiable, and hence when the instantiation θ is applied, each disjunct in the DNF must have (at least) two complementary literals. This means that each disjunct in the uninstantiated DNF must contain two literals:

$$\cdots \wedge R(s_1, \ldots, s_m) \wedge \cdots \wedge \neg R(s_1', \ldots, s_m') \wedge \cdots$$

such that θ unifies the set of terms $S = \{(s_i, s'_i) \mid i = 1, \ldots, m\}$. However, since S has some unifier, it also has a most general unifier σ, which we can find using the algorithm of the previous section. By the MGU property, we have $\sigma \leq \theta$, and so θ can be obtained by applying σ first and then some other instantiation. Now, applying σ to the original DNF makes one (or maybe more) of the disjuncts contradictory, and the original instantiation θ can still be obtained by further instantiation.

Thus, we can now proceed to the next disjunct, and so on, until all possibilities are exhausted. In this way, we never have to generate the ground terms, but rather let the necessary instantiations emerge gradually by need. In the terminology of the last section, this is a global, free-variable method, because the same variable instantiation needs to be applied (or further specialized) when performing the same kind of matching up in other disjuncts. We will maintain the environment of variable assignments globally, represented as a cycle-free finite partial function just as in `unify` itself. To unify atomic formulas, we treat the predicates as if they were functions, then use the existing unification code, and we also deal with negation by recursion, and handle the degenerate case of $\perp$ since we will use this later:

```
let rec unify_literals env tmp =
  match tmp with
    Atom(R(p1,a1)),Atom(R(p2,a2)) -> unify env [Fn(p1,a1),Fn(p2,a2)]
  | Not(p),Not(q) -> unify_literals env (p,q)
  | False,False -> env
  | _ -> failwith "Can't unify literals";;
```

To unify complementary literals, we just first negate one of them:

```
let unify_complements env (p,q) = unify_literals env (p,negate q);;
```

Next we define a function that iteratively runs down a list (representing a disjunction), trying all possible complementary pairs in each member, unifying them and trying to finish the remaining items with the instantiation so derived. Each disjunct d is itself an implicitly conjoined list, so we separate it into positive and negative literals, and for each possible positive–negative pair, attempt to unify them as complementary literals and solve the remaining problem with the resulting instantiation.

```
let rec unify_refute djs env =
  match djs with
    [] -> env
  | d::odjs -> let pos,neg = partition positive d in
               tryfind (unify_refute odjs ** unify_complements env)
                 (allpairs (fun p q -> (p,q)) pos neg);;
```

Now, for the main loop, we maintain the original DNF of the uninstantiated formula `djs0`, the set `fvs` of its free variables, and a counter `n` used to generate the fresh variable names as needed. The main loop creates a new substitution instance using fresh variables `newvars`, and incorporates this into the previous DNF `djs` to give `djs1`. The refutation of this DNF is attempted, and if it succeeds, the final instantiation is returned together with the number of instances tried (the counter divided by the number of free variables). Otherwise, the counter is increased and a larger conjunction tried. Because this approach is quite close to the pioneering work by Prawitz, Prawitz and Voghera (1960), we name the procedure accordingly.

```
let rec prawitz_loop djs0 fvs djs n =
  let l = length fvs in
  let newvars = map (fun k -> "_"^string_of_int (n * l + k)) (1--l) in
  let inst = fpf fvs (map (fun x -> Var x) newvars) in
  let djs1 = distrib (image (image (subst inst)) djs0) djs in
  try unify_refute djs1 undefined,(n + 1)
  with Failure _ -> prawitz_loop djs0 fvs djs1 (n + 1);;
```

Now, for the overall proof procedure, we just need to start by negating and Skolemizing the formula to be proved. We throw away the instantiation information and just return the number of instances tried, though it might sometimes be interesting to reconstruct the set of ground instances from the instantiation, and the reader may care to try a few examples.

```
let prawitz fm =
  let fm0 = skolemize(Not(generalize fm)) in
  snd(prawitz_loop (simpdnf fm0) (fv fm0) [[]] 0);;
```

Generally speaking, this is a substantial improvement on the Gilmore procedure. For example, one problem that previously seemed infeasible is solved almost instantly:

```
# let p20 = prawitz
   <<(forall x y. exists z. forall w. P(x) /\ Q(y) ==> R(z) /\ U(w))
     ==> (exists x y. P(x) /\ Q(y)) ==> (exists z. R(z))>>;;
val p20 : int = 2
```

Although the original Davis–Putnam procedure also solved this problem quickly, it only did so after trying 19 ground instances, whereas here we only needed two. In some cases, unification saves us from searching through a much larger number of substitution instances. On the other hand, there are a few cases where the original enumeration-based Gilmore procedure is actually faster, including Pelletier (1986) problem 45.

Tableaux

Although the `prawitz` procedure is usually far more efficient than `gilmore`, some further improvements are worthwhile. In `prawitz` we prenexed the formula and replaced formerly universally quantified variables with fresh ones at once, then expanded the DNF completely. Instead, we can do all these things incrementally. Suppose we have a set of assumptions to refute. If it contains two complementary literals p and $-p$, we are already done. Otherwise we pick a non-atomic assumption and deal with it as follows:

- for $p \wedge q$, separately assume p and q;
- for $p \vee q$, perform two refutations, one assuming p and one assuming q;
- for $\forall x.\ P[x]$, introduce a new variable y and assume $P[y]$, but also keep the original $\forall x.\ P[x]$ in case multiple instances are needed.

This is essentially the method of *analytic tableaux*. (Analytic because the new formulas assumed are subformulas of the current formula, and tableaux because they systematically lay out the assumptions and case distinctions to be considered.) When used on paper, it's traditional to write the current assumptions along a branch of a tree, extending the branch with the new assumptions and splitting it into two sub-branches when handling disjunctions. In our implementation, we maintain a 'current' disjunct, which we separate into its literals (`lits`) and other conjuncts not yet broken down to literals (`fms`), together with the remaining disjuncts that we need to refute. Rather than maintain an explicit list for the last item, we use a *continuation* (`cont`). A continuation (Reynolds 1993) merely encapsulates the remaining computation as a function, in this case one that is intended to try and refute all remaining disjuncts under the given instantiation. Initially this continuation is just the identity function, and as we proceed, it is augmented to 'remember' what more remains to be done.

Rather than bounding the number of instances, we bound the number of universal variables that have been replaced with fresh variables by a limit `n`. The other variable `k` is a counter used to invent new variables when eliminating a universal quantifier. This must be passed together with the current environment to the continuation, since it must avoid re-using the same variable in later refutations.

```
let rec tableau (fms,lits,n) cont (env,k) =
  if n < 0 then failwith "no proof at this level" else
  match fms with
    [] -> failwith "tableau: no proof"
  | And(p,q)::unexp ->
      tableau (p::q::unexp,lits,n) cont (env,k)
  | Or(p,q)::unexp ->
      tableau (p::unexp,lits,n) (tableau (q::unexp,lits,n) cont) (env,k)
  | Forall(x,p)::unexp ->
      let y = Var("_" ^ string_of_int k) in
      let p' = subst (x |=> y) p in
      tableau (p'::unexp@[Forall(x,p)],lits,n-1) cont (env,k+1)
  | fm::unexp ->
      try tryfind (fun l -> cont(unify_complements env (fm,l),k)) lits
      with Failure _ -> tableau (unexp,fm::lits,n) cont (env,k);;
```

For the overall procedure, we simply recursively increase the 'depth' (bound on the number of fresh variables) until the core function succeeds. Since we'll be using such *iterative deepening* with other proof procedures, it's worth defining a generic function to handle this, which also outputs information to the user to give an idea what's happening:[†]

```
let rec deepen f n =
  try print_string "Searching with depth limit ";
      print_int n; print_newline(); f n
  with Failure _ -> deepen f (n + 1);;
```

Now everything can be packaged up as a refutation procedure for a list of formulas:

```
let tabrefute fms =
  deepen (fun n -> tableau (fms,[],n) (fun x -> x) (undefined,0); n) 0;;
```

The top-level function to verify a formula uses `askolemize` rather than `skolemize` to retain the universal quantifiers explicitly. We also handle the degenerate case of refuting ⊥ specially so the main logic doesn't have to deal with it:

```
let tab fm =
  let sfm = askolemize(Not(generalize fm)) in
  if sfm = False then 0 else tabrefute [sfm];;
```

This turns out to be generally much more effective than our earlier procedures, any of which would find the following problem difficult:

---

† A more detailed discussion of the merits of iterative deepening is deferred until our discussion of Prolog in Section 3.14.

```
# let p38 = tab
  <<(forall x.
      P(a) /\ (P(x) ==> (exists y. P(y) /\ R(x,y))) ==>
      (exists z w. P(z) /\ R(x,w) /\ R(w,z))) <=>
    (forall x.
      (~P(a) \/ P(x) \/ (exists z w. P(z) /\ R(x,w) /\ R(w,z))) /\
      (~P(a) \/ ~(exists y. P(y) /\ R(x,y)) \/
      (exists z w. P(z) /\ R(x,w) /\ R(w,z))))>>;;
Searching with depth limit 0
Searching with depth limit 1
Searching with depth limit 2
Searching with depth limit 3
Searching with depth limit 4
val p38 : int = 4
```

In fact, most of the Pelletier problems dealing with pure first-order logic, are solved quite easily with `tab`. We can add a further tweak that helps with problems like **p46**, and particularly **p34** ('Andrews's challenge') which involves many instances of logical equivalence. After the initial normalization, we can try transforming the formula into DNF, and deal with each of the disjuncts separately. Of course, we can only split up a disjunction if it contains no free variables, but this is quite often the case. The existing DNF function treats quantified formulas as atomic, so provided the initial formula is closed, any disjunctions created at the top level are also closed. Now, applying the tableau procedure to each one independently is often beneficial, since variables are not instantiated together when they cannot possibly affect each other, and so the necessary variable limit is kept low, cutting down the search space.

```
let splittab fm =
  map tabrefute (simpdnf(askolemize(Not(generalize fm))));;
```

With this, we can solve all the pure first-order logic Pelletier problems in a reasonable time, except **p47**, 'Schubert's Steamroller' (Stickel 1986). Note that Andrews's challenge **p34** splits into no fewer than 32 independent subproblems:

```
# let p34 = splittab
  <<((exists x. forall y. P(x) <=> P(y)) <=>
    ((exists x. Q(x)) <=> (forall y. Q(y)))) <=>
    ((exists x. forall y. Q(x) <=> Q(y)) <=>
    ((exists x. P(x)) <=> (forall y. P(y))))>>;;
  ...
val p34 : int list =
  [5; 4; 5; 3; 3; 3; 2; 4; 6; 2; 3; 3; 4; 3; 3; 3; 3; 2; 2; 3; 6; 3; 2;
   4; 3; 3; 3; 3; 3; 4; 4; 4]
```

Thus, at least measured by the somewhat arbitrary metric of success on the Pelletier problems, the successive refinement from `gilmore` to `splittab` represents continuous progress. We can now easily solve some quite interesting problems that were barely feasible before, e.g. the following, attributed by Dijkstra (1989) to Hoare:

```
# let ewd1062 = splittab
   <<(forall x. x <= x) /\
     (forall x y z. x <= y /\ y <= z ==> x <= z) /\
     (forall x y. f(x) <= y <=> x <= g(y))
     ==> (forall x y. x <= y ==> f(x) <= f(y)) /\
         (forall x y. x <= y ==> g(x) <= g(y))>>;;
...
val ewd1062 : int list = [9; 9]
```

Tableaux were developed and named by logicians (Beth 1955; Hintikka 1955) some time before computer implementations. Nevertheless, Beth (1958) at least clearly had mechanization in mind. Indeed, tableaux are very appealing from this point of view, because the decision as to what to do next is largely driven by the structure of the formula. The later addition of unification, apparently first done by Cohen, Trilling and Wegner (1974) to show off the facilities of ALGOL 68, further improves their structure-directedness. The particularly straightforward code we have presented is very similar to leanT^AP (Beckert and Posegga 1995). Although quite powerful, it is still fairly simplistic. For example, the formulas are broken down left-to-right and universal formulas instantiated in an undirected round-robin fashion. One can often improve performance by a more intelligent and directed approach, and in Section 3.15 we will see a more goal-directed variation on the tableau theme.

3.11 Resolution

The centrepiece of the propositional Davis–Putnam procedure is the *resolution* rule, deducing from the two clauses $p \vee C_1$ and $-p \vee C_2$ the conclusion $C_1 \vee C_2$. In fact, given a set of propositional clauses, if we form all resolvents on any literal p and then discard all formulas involving p or $-p$, the resulting set is equisatisfiable with the original: this follows from Theorem 2.11 and the fact that discarding tautologies makes no difference to satisfiability of a set. Moreover, assuming p does occur in the initial clauses, the result involves fewer distinct propositional variables since p has been eliminated. Thus, just exhaustively applying the resolution rule to an unsatisfiable set of clauses, resolving on each literal in turn, one can derive the empty clause. Of course, preferential use of the 1-literal rule and affirmative–negative rule are useful for efficiency, but not logically essential.

Just as the Prawitz procedure improved on the Gilmore procedure by working with the most general instances possible, the first-order resolution principle (J. A. Robinson 1965b) employs unification so that the most general forms of the clauses possible are resolved directly. By Herbrand's theorem, if a set of clauses is unsatisfiable, then a finite conjunction of propositional instances of them is propositionally unsatisfiable. As we noted, this propositional unsatisfiability can be detected by repeatedly applying the propositional resolution rule. Suppose that two clauses $C[x_1, \ldots, x_n]$ and $D[y_1, \ldots, y_m]$ have instances to which propositional resolution is applicable, say:

$$C[x_1, \ldots, x_n] = \cdots \vee P(s_1, \ldots, s_m) \vee \cdots$$

and

$$D[y_1, \ldots, y_n] = \cdots \vee \neg P(s'_1, \ldots, s'_m) \vee \cdots$$

such that when the appropriate ground instantiation θ is applied, it unifies the set $S = \{(s_i, s'_i) \mid i = 1, \ldots, m\}$ and allows us to apply resolution. Suppose now that we use an MGU of S instead of θ. (We will first rename variables to ensure the two clauses have no variables in common.) Are we guaranteed that if we now perform resolution on the instantiated clauses, the original result can be obtained by a further instantiation? At first sight the answer seems to be 'yes'. For example, if we have the two input clauses

$$\{\neg P(x) \vee P(f(x)), \quad \neg P(f(f(y))) \vee Q(y)\}$$

we may decide first to instantiate them to

$$\{\neg P(f(g(c))) \vee P(f(f(g(c)))), \quad \neg P(f(f(g(c)))) \vee Q(g(c))\},$$

then perform a resolution step to get $\neg P(f(g(c))) \vee Q(g(c))$, but we could just as well use an MGU $x = f(y)$ and get the clause $\neg P(f(y)) \vee Q(y)$, of which $\neg P(f(g(c))) \vee Q(g(c))$ is just an instance. Yet things aren't always so simple. The MGU may be *too* general to cause certain literals in one of the input clauses to become identified, and this identification may be essential for the propostional proof, where clauses were *sets*. This phenomenon is illustrated by the following example, a variant of Russell's paradox proving that in a given village, there cannot be a barber who shaves exactly those people who do not shave themselves. The formula to be proved is:

```
let barb = <<~(exists b. forall x. shaves(b,x) <=> ~shaves(x,x))>>;;
```

The reader can confirm by trying any of the earlier proof procedures that it is valid. But if we simply negate the formula and reduce it to clausal form:

```
# simpcnf(skolemize(Not barb));;
- : fol formula list list =
[[<<~shaves(x,x)>>; <<~shaves(c_b,x)>>];
 [<<shaves(x,x)>>; <<shaves(c_b,x)>>]]
```

it turns out that we cannot refute this using naive resolution based on most general unifiers. There are four possible pairs of potentially complementary literals, but, as the reader can confirm, whichever pair we choose to unify, we just get a tautology that is of no further help in proof search.

So as well as merely unifying complementary literals, we need to consider unifying some subset of the literals in the same clause to allow the possibility that the notional ground instance may identify them. If we start by doing this, we get the simpler clauses `shaves(c_b,c_b)` and `~shaves(c_b,c_b)`, trivially contradictory. The following result, often called the 'lifting lemma', states the key result precisely. Given a set C of literals, we write C^- as a shorthand for $\{-p \mid p \in C\}$, and we will often write `subst` θ C for the application of an instantiation θ to a set C, where we should more properly write `image` (`subst` θ) C.

Lemma 3.28 *Suppose A and B are first-order clauses with no variables in common, and A' and B' are instances (not necessarily ground) of A and B respectively, such that A' and B' have a propositional resolvent C'. Then there are nonempty subsets $A_1 \subseteq A$ and $B_1 \subseteq B$ such that $S = A_1 \cup B_1^-$ is unifiable, and for any σ that is an MGU of S, C' is an instance of* `subst` σ $((A - A_1) \cup (B - B_1))$.

Proof Since A and B have no variables in common, there is a single instantiation θ such that $A' = $ `subst` θ A and $B' = $ `subst` θ B. Since C' is a resolvent of A' and B', there must be some literal p such that $p \in A'$, $-p \in B'$ and $C' = (A' - \{p\}) \cup (B' - \{-p\})$. Let $A_1 = \{q \in A \mid$ `subst` θ $q = p\}$ and $B_1 = \{q \in B \mid$ `subst` θ $q = -p\}$, and abbreviate $S = A_1 \cup B_1^-$. By definition of A_1 and A_2, θ is a unifier of S. Let σ be any MGU of S. Then we have `subst` $\theta = $ `subst` τ $\circ$ `subst` σ for some τ. So:

$$C' = (A' - \{p\}) \cup (B' - \{-p\})$$
$$= (\text{subst } \theta \ (A - A_1)) \cup (\text{subst } \theta \ (B - B_1))$$

$$= \ \textsf{subst } \theta \ ((A - A_1) \cup (B - B_1))$$
$$= \ (\textsf{subst } \tau \ \circ \textsf{subst } \sigma \ )((A - A_1) \cup (B - B_1))$$
$$= \ \textsf{subst } \tau \ (\textsf{subst } \sigma \ ((A - A_1) \cup (B - B_1)))$$

showing that C' is an instance of $\textsf{subst } \sigma \ ((A - A_1) \cup (B - B_1)))$ as claimed.

□

Accordingly, given some fixed scheme for producing renamed versions of clauses and for arriving at MGUs, we define a (first-order) *resolvent* of two clauses A and B to be $\textsf{subst } \sigma \ ((A_0 - A_1) \cup (B_0 - B_1))$, where A_0 and B_0 are renamed versions of A and B with no variables in common, and A_1 and B_1 are arbitrary nonempty subsets of A_0 and B_0 respectively with σ the selected MGU of $A_1 \cup B_1^-$. A clause is said to be derivable by resolution from an initial set S if it can be obtained by repeatedly deriving resolvents of clauses from S and other resolvents.

Consequently, we can deduce the fundamental result that *resolution is refutation complete*, i.e. if a set of clauses is unsatisfiable, resolution can, by deriving the empty clause, verify that unsatisfiability. Resolution is in fact *not* complete in the stronger sense that if a clause C is a logical consequence of a set of clauses Γ then C can be derived from Γ by resolution. For example, from the singleton clause set $\{P\}$ there is no resolution derivation of the logical consequence $P \vee Q$, or indeed of anything else. But since we typically start by transforming the initial problem into an equivalent refutation, the distinction is not too important here and we sometimes loosely talk about just 'completeness' of proof procedures when we really mean refutation completeness.

Corollary 3.29 *If a set S of first-order clauses is unsatisfiable, the empty clause is derivable using resolution.*

Proof By Herbrand's theorem and compactness, some finite set of ground instances of clauses in S is unsatisfiable, and so by the refutation completeness of propositional resolution there is a resolution derivation of the empty clause. By induction on the structure or size of this proof, we can apply the lifting Lemma 3.28 to show that for each subproof of a clause C' there is a corresponding proof by first-order resolution of a clause C of which C' is an instance. In particular, for the final empty clause conclusion, the empty clause must be derivable by first-order resolution, since the empty clause cannot be an instance of a nonempty one.   □

The reader should bear in mind when consulting the literature that, despite the important role of resolution in automated reasoning, there are several subtle differences between the notions of resolution presented in different texts (Leitsch 1997). In particular, while we have followed the original treatment of resolution (J. A. Robinson 1965b) in common with some other standard texts (Chang and Lee 1973), it is quite common to restrict the notion of resolvent to insist that A_1 and B_1 have exactly one member, and separately define a *factor* of a clause A to be `subst` σ A for σ an MGU of some subset $A_1 \subseteq A$ (Loveland 1978). The corresponding completeness result is that repeatedly applying the resolution rule and the separate factoring rule is a refutation-complete proof method. Indeed, if a clause can be obtained by (our) resolution, it can separately be obtained by possible factorings of the two input clauses followed by a restricted resolution, since an MGU of $S_1 \cup S_2$ can always be decomposed though an MGU of S_1.

From a practical point of view, combining resolution and factoring in a single rule is simpler to implement and restricts the formation of factors to those necessary to 'lift' a particular propositional resolution step. On the other hand, generating all factors separately often avoids recomputation of factors for numerous different resolutions. The reader might like to experiment with separate resolution and factoring rules, but we will stick to a single combined rule in what follows. Exercise 3.19 describes a simple further refinement of this combined rule with factoring only applied to one of the input clauses.

Implementation

In contrast with the top-down method of tableaux, all variable assignments are local, so we actually want to translate the results of unification into an instantiation for immediate application. Moreover, it's convenient to directly unify a set of literals rather than a list of equations between them:

```
let rec mgu l env =
  match l with
    a::b::rest -> mgu (b::rest) (unify_literals env (a,b))
  | _ -> solve env;;
```

On the other hand, we'll also use a simple test for unifiability, and there's no point here in fully expanding the unifier:

```
let unifiable p q = can (unify_literals undefined) (p,q);;
```

We'll need to apply renaming to the hypothesis clauses. This is done via the following function, which adds a prefix to each variable name in a clause:

```
let rename pfx cls =
  let fvs = fv(list_disj cls) in
  let vvs = map (fun s -> Var(pfx^s)) fvs  in
  map (subst(fpf fvs vvs)) cls;;
```

We find all resolvents of two clauses `cl1` and `cl2` via an auxiliary function
that takes a particular literal p in `cl1` and an accumulator `acc` of results
so far. First, all literals `ps2` in `cl2` that could possibly be unified with `-p`
are selected, and if there are none no resolvents are added. Otherwise we
filter out the literals `ps1` in `cl1` that are unifiable with p, other than p itself.
Then we form all possible pairs of nonempty subsets of `ps1` and `ps2`, always
including p in the former. We then pick those pairs where `ps1 ∪ ps2⁻` are
unifiable (just because each member of this set is in itself unifiable with p
doesn't mean the whole set is). For each such pair we form the resolvent and
add it into the accumulator:

```
let resolvents cl1 cl2 p acc =
  let ps2 = filter (unifiable(negate p)) cl2 in
  if ps2 = [] then acc else
  let ps1 = filter (fun q -> q <> p & unifiable p q) cl1 in
  let pairs = allpairs (fun s1 s2 -> s1,s2)
                       (map (fun pl -> p::pl) (allsubsets ps1))
                       (allnonemptysubsets ps2) in
  itlist (fun (s1,s2) sof ->
              try image (subst (mgu (s1 @ map negate s2) undefined))
                        (union (subtract cl1 s1) (subtract cl2 s2)) :: sof
              with Failure _ -> sof) pairs acc;;
```

The overall function to generate all possible resolvents of a set of clauses
now proceeds by renaming the input clauses and mapping the previous function over all literals in the first clause:

```
let resolve_clauses cls1 cls2 =
  let cls1' = rename "x" cls1 and cls2' = rename "y" cls2 in
  itlist (resolvents cls1' cls2') cls1' [];;
```

For the main loop of the resolution procedure, we simply keep generating resolvents of existing clauses until the empty clause is derived. To avoid
repeating work, we split the clauses into two lists, **used** and **unused**. The
main loop consists of taking one *given clause* cls from **unused**, moving it
to **used** and generating all possible resolvents of the new clause with clauses
from **used** (including itself), appending the new clauses to the end of **unused**.
The idea is that, provided **used** is initially empty, every pair of clauses is

tried once: if clause 1 comes before clause 2 in unused, then clause 1 will be moved to used and later clause 2 will be the given clause and have the opportunity to participate in an inference. On the other hand, once they have participated, both clauses are moved to used and will never be used together again. (This organization, used in various resolution implementations at the Argonne National Lab, is often referred to as the *given clause algorithm*.)

```
let rec resloop (used,unused) =
  match unused with
    [] -> failwith "No proof found"
  | cl::ros ->
      print_string(string_of_int(length used) ^ " used; "^
                   string_of_int(length unused) ^ " unused.");
      print_newline();
      let used' = insert cl used in
      let news = itlist(@) (mapfilter (resolve_clauses cl) used') [] in
      if mem [] news then true else resloop (used',ros@news);;
```

Overall, we split up the formula, put it into clausal form and start the main loop.

```
let pure_resolution fm = resloop([],simpcnf(specialize(pnf fm)));;

let resolution fm =
  let fm1 = askolemize(Not(generalize fm)) in
  map (pure_resolution ** list_conj) (simpdnf fm1);;
```

This procedure can solve many simple problems in a reasonable time, e.g. this from Davis and Putnam (1960):

```
# let davis_putnam_example = resolution
   <<exists x. exists y. forall z.
       (F(x,y) ==> (F(y,z) /\ F(z,z))) /\
       ((F(x,y) /\ G(x,y)) ==> (G(x,z) /\ G(z,z)))>>;;
...
val davis_putnam_example : bool list = [true]
```

3.12 Subsumption and replacement

Some problems solved easily by tableaux, such as Pelletier's (1986) p26, are very difficult for our basic resolution procedure, and result in the generation of tens of thousands of clauses without leading to a solution. Often, many apparently pointless clauses such as tautologous ones

$$\ldots \vee P \vee \ldots \vee \neg P \vee \ldots$$

get generated, particularly through factoring; for example, a clause $\neg R(x, y) \vee \neg R(y, z) \vee R(x, z)$ asserting that a binary relation is transitive gives rise to the tautologous factor $\neg R(x, x) \vee R(x, x)$. We might expect tautologies to make no useful contribution to the search for a refutation. Logically, after all, a set of formulas Δ is satisfiable if the set of its non-tautological members Δ' is. This doesn't however immediately justify deleting tautologies at arbitrary intermediate steps of the resolution process, and we defer a rigorous proof till after we have considered the related question of *subsumption*.

In the propositional case, we said that a clause C subsumes a clause D if C logically implies D, which is equivalent to the syntactic condition that C is a subset of D. In the first-order case, validity of implication between clauses is actually undecidable in general (Schmidt-Schauss 1988). We adopt a more manageable definition: a first-order clause C subsumes another D, written $C \leq_{ss} D$, if there is some instantiation θ such that $\mathsf{subst}\ \theta\ C$ (a set operation collapsing identical literals) is a subset of D. If this is the case, then C does logically imply D, but the converse does not hold, as can be seen by noting that the clause $\neg P(x) \vee P(f(x))$ logically implies $\neg P(x) \vee P(f(f(x)))$, remembering that the variables in each clause are implicitly universally quantified, yet does not subsume it.[†]

In order to implement a subsumption test, we first want a procedure for *matching*, which is a cut-down version of unification allowing instantiation of variables in only the first of each pair of terms. Note that in contrast to unification we treat the variables in the two terms of a pair as distinct even if their names coincide, and maintain the left–right distinction in recursive calls. This means that we won't need to rename variables first, and won't need to check for cycles. On the other hand, we must remember that apparently 'trivial' mappings $x \mapsto x$ are in general necessary, so if x does not have a mapping already and we need to match it to t, we always add $x \mapsto t$ to the function even if $t = x$. But, stylistically, the definition is very close to that of `unify`.

[†] Many resolution refinements are justified at the first-order level by 'lifting' from the propositional level. When doing this, the standard notion of subsumption has the merit that it interacts well with lifting: if D' is a ground instance of D and $C \leq_{ss} D$ then there is a ground instance C' of C that subsumes D' propositionally. So even if logical entailment were decidable, it might be undesirable to use it as a subsumption test.

```
let rec term_match env eqs =
  match eqs with
    [] -> env
  | (Fn(f,fa),Fn(g,ga))::oth when f = g & length fa = length ga ->
        term_match env (zip fa ga @ oth)
  | (Var x,t)::oth ->
        if not (defined env x) then term_match ((x |-> t) env) oth
        else if apply env x = t then term_match env oth
        else failwith "term_match"
  | _ -> failwith "term_match";;
```

We can straightforwardly modify this to attempt to match a pair of literals instead of a list of pairs of terms:

```
let rec match_literals env tmp =
  match tmp with
    Atom(R(p,a1)),Atom(R(q,a2)) | Not(Atom(R(p,a1))),Not(Atom(R(q,a2))) ->
        term_match env [Fn(p,a1),Fn(q,a2)]
  | _ -> failwith "match_literals";;
```

Now our subsumption test proceeds along the first clause `cls1`, systematically considering all ways of instantiating the first literal to match one in the second clause `cls2`, then, given the necessary instantiations, trying to do likewise for the others.

```
let subsumes_clause cls1 cls2 =
  let rec subsume env cls =
    match cls with
      [] -> env
    | l1::clt ->
        tryfind (fun l2 -> subsume (match_literals env (l1,l2)) clt)
                cls2 in
  can (subsume undefined) cls1;;
```

Note that when we successfully instantiate a literal in the first clause to match one in the second, we do not then eliminate that literal in the second, because it may be matchable by another literal in the first clause. This has the rather counterintuitive consequence that, for example, $P(1, x) \vee P(y, 2)$ subsumes $P(1, 2)$, even though it is longer. Logically, this is irreproachable since the latter is indeed a logical consequence of the former and not vice versa, but it can be pragmatically unappealing since unit clauses tend to be more useful.

Note that subsumption is reflexive ($C \leq_{ss} C$), by considering the identity instantiation. It is also transitive: if $C \leq_{ss} D$ and $D \leq_{ss} E$ then $C \leq_{ss} E$, since if subst θ_C $C \subseteq D$ and subst θ_D $D \subseteq E$ we also have (subst θ_D $\circ$ subst θ_C) $C \subseteq E$. But why is discarding subsumed clauses permissible without destroying refutation completeness? The key property is that subsumption is 'preserved' by resolution:

Theorem 3.30 *If $C \leq_{ss} C'$, then any resolvent of C' and D is subsumed either by a resolvent of C and D or by C itself.*

Proof Suppose $E' = \text{subst } \sigma ((C' - C_1) \cup (D - D_1))$ is a resolvent of C' and D, σ being an MGU of the nonempty set $C_1 \cup D_1^-$, where $C_1 \subseteq C'$ and $D_1 \subseteq D$.

Since $C \leq_{ss} C'$ we have $\text{subst } \theta C \subseteq C'$ for some θ. Because of the renaming of D that occurs in resolution, we can assume without loss of generality that θ has no effect on D. There are now two cases to consider. If $C_1 \cap \text{subst } \theta C = \emptyset$ then $\text{subst } \theta C \subseteq (C' - C_1) \cup (D - D_1)$, so we have $(\text{subst } \sigma \circ \text{subst } \theta)C \subseteq E'$ and therefore $C \leq_{ss} E'$. The more interesting case is where $C_1 \cap \text{subst } \theta C \neq \emptyset$, i.e. the set $C_0 = \{p \in C \mid \text{subst } \theta p \in C_1\}$ is nonempty. We will derive a resolvent E of C and D that subsumes E'.

Since $\text{subst } \theta C_0 \subseteq C_1$ and we assumed that θ does not affect D, we have $\text{subst } \theta (C_0 \cup D_1^-) \subseteq C_1 \cup D_1^-$ and so the set $C_0 \cup D_1^-$ is unified by $\text{subst } \sigma \circ \text{subst } \theta$. Thus it also has an MGU τ where $\text{subst } \sigma \circ \text{subst } \theta = \text{subst } \delta \circ \text{subst } \tau$ for some δ. Let

$$E = \text{subst } \tau ((C - C_0) \cup (D - D_1)).$$

Then, remembering that $C_0 = \{p \in C \mid \text{subst } \theta p \in C_1\}$ and that θ does not affect D, we have:

$$
\begin{aligned}
\text{subst } \delta E &= (\text{subst } \delta \circ \text{subst } \tau)((C - C_0) \cup (D - D_1)) \\
&= (\text{subst } \sigma \circ \text{subst } \theta)((C - C_0) \cup (D - D_1)) \\
&= \text{subst } \sigma (\text{subst } \theta ((C - C_0) \cup (D - D_1))) \\
&= \text{subst } \sigma (\text{subst } \theta (C - C_0) \cup \text{subst } \theta (D - D_1)) \\
&= \text{subst } \sigma (\text{subst } \theta (C - C_0) \cup (D - D_1)) \\
&= \text{subst } \sigma ((\text{subst } \theta C - C_1) \cup (D - D_1)) \\
&\subseteq \text{subst } \sigma ((C' - C_1) \cup (D - D_1)) \\
&= E'
\end{aligned}
$$

and so $E \leq_{ss} E'$ as required. $\qquad\qquad\square$

Corollary 3.31 *If $D \leq_{ss} D'$, then any resolvent of C and D' is subsumed either by a resolvent of C and D or by D itself.*

Proof One can routinely adapt the previous proof. Alternatively, note that although it is not strictly true to say that the result of resolving C and D on literal set S is the same as the result of resolving D and C on literals S^-, it is nevertheless the case that each subsumes the other, so resolution is 'essentially' symmetrical. So one can deduce this directly as a corollary of the previous theorem. □

Corollary 3.32 *If $C \leq_{ss} C'$ and $D \leq_{ss} D'$, then any resolvent of C' and D' is subsumed either by a resolvent of C and D or by C or D itself.*

Proof By Theorem 3.30, any resolvent of C' and D' is subsumed either by a resolvent of C and D' or by C itself. In the latter case we are done. In the former case, use Corollary 3.31 and observe that a resolvent of C and D' is subsumed either by a resolvent of C and D or by D itself. By transitivity of subsumption, the result follows. □

Using this result, we can at least show that we can restrict ourselves, without losing refutation completeness, to derivations where no clause C is subsumed by any of its ancestors, i.e. the clauses C is derived from, including the initial clauses and intermediate results in C's derivation.

Corollary 3.33 *If C is derivable by resolution from hypotheses S, then there is a resolution derivation of some C' with $C' \leq_{ss} C$ from S in which no clause is subsumed by any of its ancestors.*

Proof By induction on the structure of the proof. If $C \in S$ then the result holds trivially with $C' = C$, $S' = S$. Otherwise, suppose C is derived by resolving on C_1 and C_2. By the inductive hypothesis, there are $C_1' \leq_{ss} C_1$ and $C_2' \leq_{ss} C_2$ derivable without subsumption by an ancestor. By the lemma, C is subsumed by either C_1', or C_2', or a resolvent of C_1' and C_2'. In the case of a resolvent, unless the result C' is subsumed by an ancestor of C_1' or C_2' we are finished. And if it is, simply take the subproof of that ancestor. □

In particular, if the empty clause is derivable, it is derivable without ever deriving an intermediate clause subsumed by one of its ancestors. Moreover:

Lemma 3.34 *If a resolution proof of a non-tautologous conclusion involves a tautology, it also involves subsumption by an (immediate) ancestor.*

Proof Suppose a proof of a non-tautology involves a tautology. Since the conclusion is not tautologous, there must be at least one 'maximal' tautology, where a clause C contains complementary literals p and $-p$ and is resolved with another clause D to give a non-tautologous resolvent. This must be of the form

$$E = \mathtt{subst}\ \sigma\ ((C - C_1) \cup (D - D_1))$$

for nonempty $C_1 \subseteq C$ and $D_1 \subseteq D$ with σ an MGU of $C_1 \cup D_1^-$. We must have either $p \in C_1$ or $-p \in C_1$, otherwise $\mathtt{subst}\ \sigma\ p \in E$ and $-(\mathtt{subst}\ \sigma\ p) \in E$, making it tautologous. Clearly, however, we cannot have both, or C_1 would not have a unifier. So, without loss of generality, we can suppose $p \in C_1$ and $-p \in C - C_1$. But now, since $\mathtt{subst}\ \sigma\ C_1 = \{\mathtt{subst}\ \sigma\ p\}$ and $\mathtt{subst}\ \sigma\ D_1 = \{\mathtt{subst}\ \sigma\ (-p)\}$ we have:

$$
\begin{aligned}
&\mathtt{subst}\ \sigma\ D \\
\subseteq\ &\{\mathtt{subst}\ \sigma\ (-p)\} \cup \mathtt{subst}\ \sigma\ (D - D_1) \\
\subseteq\ &\mathtt{subst}\ \sigma\ (C - C_1) \cup \mathtt{subst}\ \sigma\ (D - D_1) \\
=\ &E
\end{aligned}
$$

so subsumption by an immediate ancestor occurs, as claimed.   □

This justifies our immediately discarding tautologies, since a proof can always be found without using them at all. As for discarding subsumed clauses, we still need to take care, because the relationship between the way in which clauses are generated and used in the proof search algorithm and the ancestral relation in any eventual proof is not trivial. We can envisage using subsumption as part of the search procedure in at least three different ways:

- forward deletion – if a newly generated clause is subsumed by one already present, discard the newly generated clause;
- backward deletion – if a newly generated clause subsumes one already present, discard the one already present;
- backward replacement – if a newly generated clause subsumes one already present, replace the one already present by the newly generated one.

Intuitively, forward deletion should be safe since anything one could generate from the newly generated clause will (earlier) be generated from existing clauses. However, if the subsuming clause is in **used**, this is not quite so clear, since the newly generated clause would be put on **unused** and so eventually have the opportunity to be resolved with another clause from **used**, whereas because of the way the enumeration is structured, two clauses from **used** are never resolved together. It looks plausible that this doesn't matter, since by the time they get to **used** clauses have already 'had their chance' to be resolved. However, the argument is a little more complicated, especially in conjunction with additional refinements considered in the next section. Accordingly, we will only discard newly generated clauses if they are subsumed by a clause in **unused**.

Backward deletion is also fraught with problems. If one too readily discards existing clauses when subsumed by a newly generated one, there are pathological situations where the desired clause recedes indefinitely: before it can reach the front of the **unused** list, it is discarded in favour of a subsuming clause further back in the list, and before that can reach the front it is subsumed by another, and so on. It's not too hard to concoct real examples of this phenomenon (Kowalski 1970b). But, provided the newly generated clause C' *properly* subsumes the original clause C, that is, $C' \leq_{ss} C$ but $C \not\leq_{ss} C'$, this cannot happen indefinitely, since the 'properly subsumes' relation is wellfounded (see Exercise 3.13). Proper subsumption will automatically be enforced if we check for forward subsumption *before* back subsumption. Nevertheless, even though recession can't continue indefinitely, it can happen enough times to substantially delay the drawing of important conclusions. Thus, it seems that the policy of *replacement*, where the subsumed clause is replaced by the subsuming one at the original point in the **unused** list, is probably better, and this is what we will do. The following **replace** function puts **cl** in place of the first clause in **lis** that it subsumes, or at the end if it doesn't subsume any of them.

```
let rec replace cl lis =
  match lis with
    [] -> [cl]
  | c::cls -> if subsumes_clause cl c then cl::cls
              else c::(replace cl cls);;
```

Now, the procedure for inserting a newly generated clause **cl**, generated from given clause **gcl**, into an **unused** list is as follows. First we check if **cl** is a tautology (using **trivial**) or subsumed by either **gcl** or something already in **unused**, and if so we discard it. Otherwise we perform the replacement, which if no back-subsumption is found will simply put the new clause at the back of the list.

```
let incorporate gcl cl unused =
  if trivial cl or
     exists (fun c -> subsumes_clause c cl) (gcl::unused)
  then unused else replace cl unused;;
```

With the subsumption handling buried inside this auxiliary function, the main loop is almost the same as before, with **incorporate** used iteratively

on all the newly generated clauses, rather than their simply being appended
at the end.

```
let rec resloop (used,unused) =
  match unused with
    [] -> failwith "No proof found"
  | cls::ros ->
        print_string(string_of_int(length used) ^ " used; "^
                     string_of_int(length unused) ^ " unused.");
        print_newline();
        let used' = insert cls used in
        let news =
           itlist (@) (mapfilter (resolve_clauses cls) used') [] in
        if mem [] news then true else
        resloop(used',itlist (incorporate cls) news ros);;
```

We then redefine `pure_resolution` and `resolution` exactly as before.
The addition of subsumption and tautology deletion already results in dramatic efficiency improvements. All the problems solved by tableaux, and
more besides, are now quickly solved by resolution. All those solved with
difficulty by the naive resolution procedure are solved very quickly and with
far fewer redundant clauses generated, e.g. for the Davis–Putnam example:

```
...
6 used; 3 unused.
7 used; 2 unused.
val davis_putnam_example : bool list = [true]
```

Before proceeding, we will prove more precisely that the given resolution procedure, with forward subsumption and back replacement, is refuta-
tion complete. To do this, it's helpful to denote by $\mathrm{Used}(n)$ and $\mathrm{Unused}(n)$
the state of the 'used' and 'unused' lists after n iterations of the inner
loop. (In our resolution variants so far, $\mathrm{Used}(0) = \emptyset$ and $\mathrm{Unused}(0)$ is the
set of input clauses, but we will later consider the 'set of support' restric-
tion where some input clauses go straight into **used**.) Because of replacement, the invariants satisfied by these sets are a bit involved, so it's also
convenient to introduce $\mathrm{Sub}(n)$ to denote the set of 'given clauses' processed so far. In order to state the invariants simply, we will also extend the
notion of subsumption from pairs of clauses to pairs of sets of clauses. We
abbreviate

$$S \leq_{\mathrm{SS}} S' =_{\mathrm{def}} \forall C' \in S'. \exists C \in S. \, C \leq_{\mathrm{ss}} C'.$$

It is easy to see that, like subsumption on pairs of clauses, this notion is
reflexive and transitive. Now, the first and simplest invariant of the algorithm

simply records the fact that after being resolved with, all the given clauses are simply inserted into the 'used' list:

$$\mathrm{Used}(n) = \mathrm{Used}(0) \cup \mathrm{Sub}(n).$$

Moreover, if $\mathrm{Res}(S, T)$ denotes all non-tautologous resolvents of pairs of clauses from S and T, we note that all resolvents generated are subsumed by clauses that are retained, at first in the **unused** list and later as subsequent given clauses:

$$\mathrm{Sub}(n) \cup \mathrm{Unused}(n) \leq_{SS} \mathrm{Res}(\mathrm{Sub}(n), \mathrm{Used}(n)).$$

This is trivially true at the beginning, since $\mathrm{Sub}(0)$ is empty and there are no resolvents. And to show that this invariant is preserved in passing from stage n to stage $n + 1$, note that if G is the next given clause then

$$\mathrm{Res}(\mathrm{Sub}(n + 1), \mathrm{Used}(n + 1)) = \mathrm{Res}(\mathrm{Sub}(n) \cup \{G\}, \mathrm{Used}(n) \cup \{G\})$$

and this is subsumed, using the symmetry of resolution up to subsumption and the fact that $\mathrm{Sub}(n) \subseteq \mathrm{Used}(n)$, by

$$\mathrm{Res}(\mathrm{Sub}(n), \mathrm{Used}(n)) \cup \mathrm{Res}(\{G\}, \mathrm{Used}(n) \cup \{G\}).$$

The first set in this union, by hypothesis, is already subsumed by $\mathrm{Sub}(n) \cup \mathrm{Unused}(n)$. The others are precisely the newly generated resolvents in our implementation, which are subsequently incorporated into $\mathrm{Unused}(n + 1)$ and hence subsumed by it. Finally, since clauses already in $\mathrm{Unused}(n)$ are either maintained, replaced by those subsuming them, or in the case of the given clause moved into $\mathrm{Sub}(n+1)$, we have $\mathrm{Sub}(n+1) \cup \mathrm{Unused}(n+1) \leq_{SS} \mathrm{Unused}(n)$. Hence the invariant is maintained.

Now note that, starting at stage n, if we make a further $|\mathrm{Unused}(n)|$ iteration, all clauses from $\mathrm{Unused}(n)$, or others subsuming them that are introduced later, are moved into $\mathrm{Sub}(n + |\mathrm{Unused}(n)|)$. This allows us to define a particular sequence of values of n where we get a stratification into levels. Define:

$$\begin{aligned} \mathrm{brk}(0) &= |\mathrm{Unused}(0)| \\ \mathrm{brk}(n + 1) &= \mathrm{brk}(n) + |\mathrm{Unused}(\mathrm{brk}(n))| \end{aligned}$$

and write $\mathrm{level}(n) = \mathrm{Sub}(\mathrm{brk}(n))$. Then we have $\mathrm{level}(0) \leq_{SS} \mathrm{Unused}(0)$ and our main invariant yields

$$\mathrm{level}(n + 1) \leq_{SS} \mathrm{level}(n) \cup \mathrm{Res}(\mathrm{level}(n), \mathrm{Used}(0) \cup \mathrm{level}(n)).$$

In our algorithms so far putting all input clauses in **unused**, all the input clauses are contained in Unused(0) and hence subsumed by level(0), while since Used(0) = ∅, level($n + 1$) subsumes level(n) and all non-tautologous resolvents of pairs of clauses taken from level(n). Consequently, if a resolution refutation of those clauses exists, the empty clause will be derived in some level. Moreover, assuming that the empty clause was not in Unused(0), it can only have got into a level by being one of the newly generated resolvents, and hence will be detected. That it does not occur in the initial input clauses is assured by the use of **simpdnf**, which filters out such trivially unsatisfiable disjuncts.

3.13 Refinements of resolution

Unfortunately, it often happens that resolution can arrive at the same intermediate clause in many different ways. For example, the two pictures below show two different ways in which the conclusion $X \vee Y \vee Z$ at the root of the tree can be derived by resolution steps from the input clauses at the leaves.

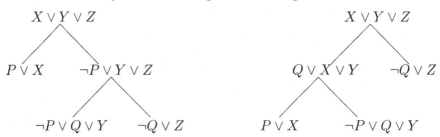

Although many duplicates are eventually removed by subsumption checking, there is still an unfortunate blowup in the search space being explored, for the duplication may occur over much longer ranges than in this simple example. It would be much better if we could cut down on this redundancy in the search space, for example by systematically preferring one kind of proof tree whenever there are many alternatives.

Linear resolution

In fact, we can regard the duplication above as indicating a possible proof transformation. Given a resolution proof where some right branch is itself a branch rather than one of the input clauses (for example $\neg P \vee Y \vee Z$ in the earlier figure), we can 'rotate' the proof tree to eliminate it. This transformation can apparently be applied repeatedly until the proof 'tree' is maximally lopsided, consisting of a single linear 'trunk' with input clauses suspended from it. Thus, we seem to be justified in searching only for such a *linear input* proof, avoiding a great deal of redundancy. Such a conclusion is too hasty, however, as the reader can see by attempting to linearize a resolution refutation of the clauses $\{P \vee Q, P \vee \neg Q, \neg P \vee Q, \neg P \vee \neg Q\}$. The problem with treating the first figure as a paradigm is that the clauses X, Y and Z might be, or might contain, P or Q or their negations. Considering this, it turns out that we *can* always apply such a rotation, but we may need an additional step where one of the earlier clauses on the trunk is re-used. With this extension, the above set of clauses can be refuted thus:

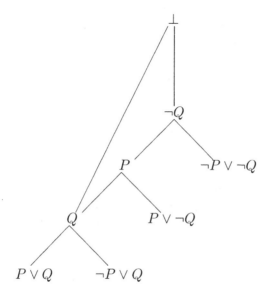

One can show that in this fashion, any resolution proof of a clause C can, by such 'rotations', be transformed into a linear one of some $C' \leq_{ss} C$, allowing at each stage resolution of the previously deduced clause either with an input clause or an earlier one in the linear sequence. In particular, if a set of clauses has a refutation, it has a linear refutation. The idea of searching just for linear refutations gives *linear resolution* (Loveland 1970; Luckham 1970; Zamov and Sharanov 1969). Although this greatly reduces redundancy, compatibility with subsumption and elimination of tautologies becomes more complicated. For example (Loveland 1970), the set of clauses $\{p \vee q, p, q, \neg p \vee \neg q\}$ has a linear resolution refutation with root $p \vee q$. However it is clear that such a proof must necessarily involve a tautology, since the only resolvents of other clauses with $p \vee q$ are $p \vee \neg p$ or $q \vee \neg q$; thus it is no longer the case if tautologies are forbidden that an arbitrary clause can be chosen as the 'root'. We will not go into more detail, since we will not actually implement linear resolution. However it is useful to understand the concept of linear resolution since it is related to material covered in the following two sections on Prolog and Model elimination.

Positive resolution

Another way of imposing restrictions on resolution proofs was introduced by Robinson (1965a) very soon after his original paper on resolution. He showed that refutation completeness is retained if each resolution operation is restricted so that one of the two hypothesis clauses is all-positive, i.e. contains no negative literals. This often cuts down the search space quite dramatically. Robinson referred to resolution subject to this restriction as P_1-*resolution*, though it is more often nowadays referred to simply as *positive resolution*.

We will now demonstrate the refutation completeness of this restriction, following Robinson. As usual, we need only establish the result for ground clauses at the propositional level and can then lift it to general clauses, since instantiation or factoring has no effect on the positivity of a clause. We start with the following.

Lemma 3.35 *If S is a finite unsatisfiable set of propositional clauses not containing the empty clause, then there is a positive resolution step with two clauses from S resulting in a clause not already in S.*

Proof Partition the set S into two disjoint sets, the all-positive clauses P and the clauses with at least one negative literal N. Thus $S = P \cup N$. Note that neither P nor N can be empty, otherwise S would be satisfiable in either the propositional valuation mapping all atomic propositions to 'false' or the one mapping them all to 'true'.

In fact, since P is satisfied by any valuation that maps the finitely many atoms A appearing in S to true, it follows that there is a 'minimal' valuation $v : A \to$ bool satisfying P, i.e. one such that there is no valuation satisfying P that assigns 'true' to fewer propositional variables.

Now, since S as a whole is unsatisfiable and v satisfies P, there must be at least one clause in N that is false under v. Let K be some clause from N that is false in v and has the minimal number of negative literals among such clauses; i.e. no other $K' \in N$ that is false in v has fewer negative literals.

K must contain at least one negative literal, say $\neg p$, since it belongs to N. Note that $v(p) = \top$, since otherwise K would hold in v, contrary to our assumption. Now the positive literal p must occur in some clause $J \in P$ such that $J - \{p\}$ is not satisfied by v, for otherwise the valuation v' setting

$v'(p) = \perp$ and treating other propositional variables in the same way as v would satisfy P, contrary to the minimality assumption on v. Now J is all-positive and so

$$R = (J - \{p\}) \cup (K - \{\neg p\})$$

is derivable by a positive resolution step. This contains fewer negative literals than K, since J is all-positive. Since K was false in v, all the literals in $K - \{\neg p\}$ must be false in v, and by hypothesis so are all the literals in $J - \{p\}$. Thus R has fewer negative literals than K and is false in v. This contradicts the minimality of K unless R is actually empty and therefore belongs to P. However by hypothesis the empty clause was not in S and so the result is proved. □

Theorem 3.36 *If S is a finite unsatisfiable set of propositional clauses then there is a positive resolution derivation of the empty clause from S.*

Proof Since S is finite there can only be a finite set of propositional variables involved in S and therefore the set of all resolvents (positive or not) derivable from S is finite. (Remember that we work at the propositional level and treat clauses as *sets* of literals, so repetitions of a literal do not give distinct clauses). By the above lemma, given any set S_n of resolvents of S, if S_n does not contain the empty clause we can find another positive resolvent C_n of clauses in S_n and set $S_{n+1} = S_n \cup \{C_n\}$. Starting with $S_0 = S$ we can repeat this procedure; since the number of possible resolvents is finite, we cannot do so indefinitely and therefore must eventually reach the empty clause. □

Corollary 3.37 *If S is an unsatisfiable set of first-order clauses there is a deduction by positive resolution of the empty clause.*

Proof The usual lifting argument. By compactness and Herbrand's theorem there is a finite set of ground instances of clauses in S that is unsatisfiable. By the previous theorem, there is a derivation of the empty clause by positive resolution. Now we simply repeatedly apply the lifting Lemma 3.28 and derive a proof by first-order positive resolution; note that instantiation does not affect positivity of clauses. □

It is easy to see using the same argument as above that positive resolution is compatible with our subsumption and replacement policies. The key property of resolution used to justify these refinements was Corollary 3.32, asserting that if $C \leq_{ss} C'$ and $D \leq_{ss} D'$, then any resolvent of C' and

D' is subsumed either by a resolvent of C and D or by C or D itself. This remains true if we change 'resolvent' to 'positive resolvent' since if $C_1 \leq_{ss} C_2$ and C_2 is positive, so is C_1. Thus we will modify the resolution prover with subsumption to perform positive resolution. The modification is simplicity itself: we restrict the core function `resolve_clauses` so that it returns the empty set unless one of the two input clauses is all-positive:

```
let presolve_clauses cls1 cls2 =
  if forall positive cls1 or forall positive cls2
  then resolve_clauses cls1 cls2 else [];;
```

Now we simply re-enter the definition of `resloop`, this time calling it `presloop` and replacing `resolve_clauses` with `presolve_clauses`, and then define the positive variant of `pure_resolution` in the same way:

```
let pure_presolution fm = presloop([],simpcnf(specialize(pnf fm)));;
```

followed by the same function with a different name:

```
let presolution fm =
  let fm1 = askolemize(Not(generalize fm)) in
  map (pure_presolution ** list_conj) (simpdnf fm1);;
```

It turns out, in fact, that positive resolution is often much more efficient than unrestricted resolution. For example, the following interesting first-order formula due to Łoś:[†]

```
# let los = time presolution
   <<(forall x y z. P(x,y) /\ P(y,z) ==> P(x,z)) /\
     (forall x y z. Q(x,y) /\ Q(y,z) ==> Q(x,z)) /\
     (forall x y. Q(x,y) ==> Q(y,x)) /\
     (forall x y. P(x,y) \/ Q(x,y))
     ==> (forall x y. P(x,y)) \/ (forall x y. Q(x,y))>>;;
...
val los : bool list = [true]
```

is solvable reasonably quickly, whereas it is hopelessly slow with either tableaux or unrestricted resolution.

Semantic resolution

The special role of positivity isn't essential; we could equally well have considered *negative* resolution where at least one of the input clauses must be all-negative, or more generally for each propositional variable given it a

---

[†] Most people find it less than obvious (Rudnicki 1987) and the reader may enjoy understanding it intuitively.

particular 'positive' or 'negative' status. Essentially the same argument can be used to establish refutation completeness in each case. All these can be seen as special cases of a more general technique of *semantic resolution* (Slagle 1967).

Theorem 3.38 *If S is an unsatisfiable set of propositional clauses and v an arbitrary propositional valuation, then there is a resolution derivation of S restricting resolution steps to those where at least one of the hypothesis clauses is not satisfied by v (i.e. all literals in that clause are false in v).*

Proof Essentially the same as the completeness proof for positive resolution, replacing 'positive' with 'does not hold in v' and 'negative' with 'holds in v'. □

Theorem 3.39 *If S is an unsatisfiable set of clauses and I an arbitrary interpretation of the symbols used in those clauses, there is a resolution derivation of S restricting resolution steps to those where at least one of the hypothesis clauses does not hold in I. (That is, for some valuation does not hold, because we regard the clauses as implicitly universally quantified.)*

Proof As usual, we will perform lifting. By compactness and Herbrand's theorem there is a finite set of ground instances of clauses in S that is unsatisfiable. Given the interpretation I, pick an arbitrary valuation w and hence define a propositional valuation on atoms by

$$v(P(a_1, \ldots, a_n)) = \texttt{holds}\ I\ w\ (P(a_1, \ldots, a_n)).$$

By the previous theorem, there is a refutation of the set of ground instances by resolution where at least one hypothesis is false in v. But in the lifting argument, we simply need to note that if a ground instance C' of C does not hold propositionally in v, then C cannot hold in I, since otherwise all instances would hold in all valuations, in particular w. □

Positive resolution, for example, is the special case where the interpretation sets $R_I(a_1, \ldots, a_n) = \bot$ for all predicate letters R and elements a_i in the domain of I.

The set of support strategy

The flexibility of semantic resolution is appealing, since we may be able to use semantic concerns to pick an appropriate interpretation. However, it might be easier if we did not need to spell out an appropriate interpretation, but only kept it implicitly at the background.

In the main resolution setup above, we started with the **used** list empty, ensuring that all pairs of clauses had the opportunity to be resolved. However, it may be that we would do better to forbid resolutions entirely among some particular subset of the initial clauses. The idea is that by this means, resolution can be focused away from deducing valid but irrelevant conclusions, and towards deducing those that contribute to the problem at hand. This is the basic principle of the *set of support* strategy (Wos, Robinson and Carson 1965).

We start by separating the set of input clauses into two disjoint subsets, the *set of support* S and the 'unsupported' clauses U. Now we simply impose the requirement on resolution refutations that no two clauses of U are resolved together. A linear refutation can be seen as one where the set of support is the singleton set $\{C_0\}$, where C_0 is the start clause. However, a set-of-support refutation from $\{C_0\}$ may have multiple separate branches that join higher up the proof tree, provided that each one starts from C_0, whereas in a linear refutation there is only one.

Theorem 3.40 *If a subset S of a set T of input clauses has the property that T is unsatisfiable, but $T - S$ is satisfiable, then there is a resolution refutation of T with set of support S.*

Proof Since by hypothesis, $T - S$ is satisfiable, there is an interpretation I that satisfies it. By the refutation completeness of semantic resolution, there is therefore a resolution refutation in which at least one of the clauses that is resolved does not hold in I. In particular, this implies that no two clauses of $T - S$ are resolved together. $\qquad\square$

The condition in the theorem that $T - S$ should be satisfiable cannot in general be relaxed. For example, the clauses:

$$\{\neg P \vee R, P, Q, \neg P \vee \neg Q\}$$

are clearly unsatisfiable. However, if we choose $\{\neg P \vee R\}$ as the set of support, then no refutation is possible; we can deduce the clause R but make no further progress.

To implement the set-of-support restriction, we need no major changes to the given clause algorithm: simply set the initial **used** to be the unsupported clauses rather than the empty set. This precisely ensures that two unsupported clauses are never resolved together. Recall that

$$\text{level}(n+1) \leq_{\text{SS}} \text{level}(n) \cup \text{Res}(\text{level}(n), \text{Used}(0) \cup \text{level}(n)),$$

so the successive levels enumerate precisely the desired sets of resolvents.

One satisfactory choice for the set of support is the collection of all-negative input clauses. This is because any set of clauses in which each clause contains a positive literal is satisfiable (just interpret all predicates as true everywhere), so the basic theoretical condition is satisfied. Thus we make the following modification:

```
let pure_resolution fm =
  resloop(partition (exists positive) (simpcnf(specialize(pnf fm))));;
```

and re-enter the definition of **resolution**. Although this may not be optimal, it often works quite well. The Łoś problem is solved much faster than with unrestricted resolution, though not as quickly as with positive resolution.

However, resolution experts usually like to make a particular choice of set of support themselves rather than using the simple syntactically-based default we have adopted. Suppose, for example, one is trying to use a standard set of mathematical axioms A together with special additional hypothesis B to prove a conclusion C. In a refutational framework, this amounts to deriving the empty clause from $A \wedge B \wedge \neg C$. Reasonable choices for the set of support are $B \wedge \neg C$ or just $\neg C$, since they will inhibit general exploration of axioms A.

Indeed, $\neg C$ will often be the choice of our default in such situations, because it may well be the only all-negative clause. Note that simply imposing negative resolution would be more restrictive than set-of-support proofs starting with all-negative clauses as the set of support, but in many cases the set-of-support restriction allows shorter proofs that compensate for the larger search space.

Hyperresolution

Robinson's introduction of positive resolution was just a prelude to an additional refinement called positive *hyperresolution*, which is based on the following observation. Every step in a positive resolution refutation involves one all-positive clause, and in order for resolution to be possible, there must be at least one negative literal in the other clause. Consider a clause participating in a positive resolution refutation that contains some number $n \geq 1$ of negative literals:

$$\neg L_1 \vee \neg L_2 \vee \cdots \vee \neg L_n \vee P.$$

Since it contains negative literals, the other hypothesis in any resolution where it is used must be all-positive, and hence must resolve with one of the literals $\neg L_i$; say L_1 for simplicity. If we ignore instantiation and the possibility of factoring, the result is of the form

$$\neg L_2 \vee \cdots \vee \neg L_n \vee P \vee Q$$

for all-positive P and Q. If $n \geq 2$ then any subsequent resolution step using that clause must in its turn be with another all-positive clause, and so on. In general, a clause containing n negative literals, if it participates in a positive resolution derivation, must be repeatedly resolved with positive clauses until all the negative literals have disappeared. (This might, because factoring merges some of the L_i together, take fewer than n resolution steps.) We can imagine combining all these successive resolutions into a single *hyperresolution* step. That is, although we might still implement it as a succession of resolution steps, we don't need to keep the intermediate results, since we know that if they participate at all in a refutation, it will be via more resolutions with all-positive clauses and give one of the results of the hyperresolution step.

By performing hyperresolution as a single step, we avoid repeatedly deriving the same result by resolving with the same clauses in a slightly different order, and hence cut down on redundancy. Of course, a single hyperresolution step still has to enumerate all the essentially different possibilities, which makes it in general a much more productive rule than binary resolution. However it is sometimes efficient for dealing with certain kinds of problems. We will not actually implement hyperresolution, but later (Section 4.9) we will exploit for theoretical purposes the restriction on the form of refutations implied by positive hyperresolution.

We have only scratched the surface of the huge literature on resolution refinements. For more detail on these and many other refinements, including some relatively modern methods using orderings and selection functions, the reader can refer, for example, to Loveland (1978), Leitsch (1997), Bachmair and Ganzinger (2001) and de Nivelle (1995).

3.14 Horn clauses and Prolog

With respect to any Herbrand interpretation H, a valuation v is a mapping into the set of ground terms of the language, and using Lemma 3.19 we see that for any atomic formula $P(t_1, \ldots, t_n)$:

$$\mathtt{holds}\ H\ v\ (P(t_1, \ldots, t_n)) = P_H(\mathtt{tsubst}\ v\ t_1, \ldots, \mathtt{tsubst}\ v\ t_n).$$

In the special case that all t_i are ground, this is simply $P_H(t_1, \ldots, t_n)$. The set of *all* atomic ground formulas in a language is often called the *Herbrand base*. Our observation sets up a natural bijection between Herbrand interpretations and subsets of the Herbrand base, viz. the set of elements of the Herbrand base that hold in the interpretation.

Let S be a set of clauses. We construct a Herbrand interpretation M interpreting each n-ary predicate P by

$$P_M(t_1, \ldots, t_n) = \text{true}$$

if and only if $P_H(t_1, \ldots, t_n) = \text{true}$ for *every* Herbrand model H of S. From the above remarks, it is clear that a ground atom holds in M iff it holds in every Herbrand model of H. In fact, since any Herbrand interpretation satisfies a quantifier-free formula iff it satisfies all its ground instances, it follows that *any* atomic formula is satisfied by M iff it is satisfied by all Herbrand models of S. Accordingly, *if M so constructed is in fact a model of S*, we say that it is the *least* or *minimal* Herbrand model of S. But under what circumstances *is* it indeed a model of S?

To see what can go wrong, consider $S = \{P(0) \vee Q(0)\}$. There are three different Herbrand models of S, one of which makes $P(0)$ true and $Q(0)$ false, one that makes $P(0)$ false and $Q(0)$ true, and one that makes both of them true. Since neither $P(0)$ nor $Q(0)$ holds in all Herbrand models, M makes neither of them hold, and so is not a model of S.

However, in a precise sense, a disjunction of more than one positive literal in S is the only case where things go wrong. We define a *Horn clause* to be a clause containing *at most one* positive literal, and a *definite clause* to be one containing *exactly one* positive literal. (Thus, a definite clause is also a Horn clause.) The significance of this classification becomes a little clearer if we write clauses in a slightly different style using implication instead of negation:

- $P_1 \wedge \cdots \wedge P_n \Rightarrow Q$ for the definite clause $\neg P_1 \vee \cdots \vee \neg P_n \vee Q$ with $n \geq 1$ negative literals, or just Q if there are no negative literals;
- $P_1 \wedge \cdots \wedge P_n \Rightarrow \bot$ for a non-definite Horn clause $\neg P_1 \vee \cdots \vee \neg P_n$;
- $P_1 \wedge \cdots \wedge P_n \Rightarrow Q_1 \vee \cdots \vee Q_m$ for a non-Horn clause $\neg P_1 \vee \cdots \vee \neg P_n \vee Q_1 \vee \cdots \vee Q_m$ containing $m \geq 2$ positive literals.

It is clear that any set of definite clauses is satisfiable by any model M that sets $P_M(a_1, \ldots, a_n) = \text{true}$ without restriction, since each clause contains a positive literal. More interestingly, the construction above does indeed yield a *least* model of it:[†]

[†] The reasoning justifying the existence of a least Herbrand model for a set of definite clauses is

Lemma 3.41 *Any set S of definite clauses has a least Herbrand model M, which satisifes an atomic formula p iff every Herbrand model of S satisfies p.*

Proof Consider a definite clause in S, perhaps meaning just $Q(s_1, \ldots, s_p)$ in the case $n = 0$:

$$P^1(t_1^1, \ldots, t_{m_1}^1) \wedge \cdots \wedge P^n(t_1^n, \ldots, t_{m_n}^n) \Rightarrow Q(s_1, \ldots, s_p).$$

We want to show that this holds in M for any valuation v. Consistently abbreviating $t' = \mathtt{tsubst}\ v\ t$, this amounts to showing that if for each $1 \leq k \leq n$ we have $P_M^k(t_1^{k'}, \ldots, t_{m_k}^{k\,'}) = \text{true}$, then also $Q_M(s_1', \ldots, s_p') = \text{true}$. But if each $P_M^k(t_1^{k'}, \ldots, t_{m_k}^{k\,'})$ is true, it means by definition that for *every* Herbrand model H of S, we have $P_H^k(t_1^{k'}, \ldots, t_{m_k}^{k\,'}) = \text{true}$. But since each such H is a model of S, it follows that $Q_H(s_1', \ldots, s_p') = \text{true}$. Thus $Q_M(s_1', \ldots, s_p') = \text{true}$ as required. $\qquad\square$

By contrast, a set of general Horn clauses may not be satisfiable at all, e.g. the set $S = \{P, \neg P\}$. But if it *is* satisfiable, we have the same least model property.

Theorem 3.42 *If a set S of Horn clauses is satisfiable, it has a least Herbrand model M, which satisifes an atomic formula p iff every Herbrand model of S satisfies p.*

Proof Separate $S = D \cup N$ into disjoint sets of definite clauses D and non-definite Horn clauses N. Let M be the least Herbrand model of D, whose existence is guaranteed by the previous lemma. We claim that it is in fact a model of N as well. For if a clause $P^1(t_1^1, \ldots, t_{m_1}^1) \wedge \cdots \wedge P^n(t_1^n, \ldots, t_{m_n}^n) \Rightarrow \bot$ in S fails to hold in M, there is some valuation v such that, consistently abbreviating $t' = \mathtt{tsubst}\ v\ t$, for each $1 \leq k \leq n$ we have $P_M^k(t_1^{k'}, \ldots, t_{m_k}^{k\,'}) = \text{true}$. But this means that each $P_H^k(t_1^{k'}, \ldots, t_{m_k}^{k\,'}) = \text{true}$ for *every* Herbrand model of D, implying that the clause holds in *no* Herbrand model of D. Thus $D \cup N$ has no Herbrand model and so by Theorem 3.24 no model at all, contradicting the assumption that S was satisfiable. $\qquad\square$

Several interesting consequences flow from the existence of least models, in particular the following *convexity* property.

---

strongly reminiscent of monotone inductive definitions (see Appendix 1), and in fact we could consider the subset of the Herbrand base corresponding to the least model as being defined inductively by treating the set of ground instances of clauses as rules.

Theorem 3.43 *If S is a set of Horn clauses and the A_i are atomic formulas, then $S \models A_1 \vee \cdots \vee A_n$ iff $S \models A_i$ for some $1 \leq i \leq n$.*

Proof The right-to-left definition is immediate, so we need only consider left-to-right. By expanding the language if necessary, we can assume that all the A_i are ground (cf. Theorem 3.11). If S is unsatisfiable, then the result follows trivially. Otherwise S has a least model M, and since $S \models A_1 \vee \cdots \vee A_n$ and all the A_i are ground, it follows that some A_i holds in M. It therefore, by definition, holds in all Herbrand models of S and therefore by Theorem 3.24 in all models of S, as required. $\square$

Although, as is traditional, we have mainly focused on refutation of an unsatisfiable formula as the core of our proof procedures, we could dualize and present it in terms of validity. In this case, a more natural version of Herbrand's theorem is the following (cf. also corollary 2.15):

Theorem 3.44 *If $P[x_1, \ldots, x_n]$ and all formulas in the set S are quantifier-free, then $S \models \exists x_1, \ldots, x_n. P[x_1, \ldots, x_n]$ iff there is a finite disjunction of ground instances such that $S \models P[t_1^1, \ldots, t_n^1] \vee \cdots \vee P[t_1^m, \ldots, t_n^m]$*

Proof The right-to-left direction is straightforward. Conversely if we have $S \models \exists x_1, \ldots, x_n. P[x_1, \ldots, x_n]$ then the set of formulas $S \cup \{\neg P[x_1, \ldots, x_n]\}$, where as usual the variables x_i are implicitly universally quantified, is unsatisfiable. By Theorem 3.25 there is a finite set of ground instances such that

$$S' \cup \{\neg P[t_1^1, \ldots, t_n^1], \ldots, \neg P[t_1^m, \ldots, t_n^m]\}$$

is unsatisfiable, so $S' \models P[t_1^1, \ldots, t_n^1] \vee \cdots \vee P[t_1^m, \ldots, t_n^m]$ and therefore $S \models P[t_1^1, \ldots, t_n^1] \vee \cdots \vee P[t_1^m, \ldots, t_n^m]$ as required. $\square$

In the case of Horn clauses, we can sharpen this to a kind of infinitary analogue of convexity.

Theorem 3.45 *If $P[x_1, \ldots, x_n]$ is quantifier-free and S is a set of Horn clauses, then $S \models \exists x_1, \ldots, x_n. P[x_1, \ldots, x_n]$ iff there is some ground instance such that $S \models P[t_1, \ldots, t_n]$.*

Proof Combine Theorems 3.43 and 3.44. $\square$

Given a set of definite clauses S, consider the set of finite trees T whose nodes are labelled by ground atoms and such that whenever a node Q has children $P_1, \ldots, P_n$, there is a ground instance $P_1 \wedge \cdots \wedge P_n \Rightarrow Q$ of a clause in S. We claim that the set B of ground atoms that can form the root of such a tree is exactly the subset of the Herbrand base corresponding to the least model. In one direction, the model corresponding to this set B satisfies all ground instances $P_1 \wedge \cdots \wedge P_n \Rightarrow Q$ of the clauses in S, because if each P_i forms the root of such a tree, we can construct a tree with root Q and children P_i forming the roots of corresponding subtrees. Conversely, it is clear that any model of the ground instances of the clauses in S must include B, since if each P_i holds in a model, so does Q. By Theorem 3.22, being a Herbrand model of S and being a Herbrand model of the set of its ground instances coincide, so the result follows.

This gives a nice goal-directed way of verifying that some atomic ground formula holds in all models of a set of definite clauses S. It does if there is a finite set of ground instances of formulas in S by which it can be deduced via a kind of tree search. Given an initial goal P, we know that if it holds in the least model there is some clause that when instantiated, say to $Q_1 \wedge \cdots \wedge Q_n \Rightarrow P$, has P as its conclusion. Thus it suffices to show that all the 'subgoals' Q_i hold in the least model, by further search of the same kind. As with tableaux, the appropriate instantiations can be discovered gradually by unification of the goal with the heads of clauses. Indeed, if we start with an initial goal containing variables that we regard as implicitly existentially quantified, Theorem 3.45 implies that there is a specific ground instance that is a consequence of the clauses, and the process of unification will not only prove the goal but even provide *witnesses*, i.e. specific terms that can replace the existentially quantified variables. We will exploit this feature when we consider Prolog below.

Satisfiability of a set of Horn clauses can be reduced to definite clause theorem proving, and hence tested in the same goal-directed way. To see this, take a set S of Horn clauses, and introduce a new nullary predicate symbol F that does not occur in S. Intuitively we think of F as standing for $\bot$, so we replace every all-negative clause in S of the form:

$$\neg P_1 \vee \cdots \vee \neg P_n$$

by

$$\neg P_1 \vee \cdots \vee \neg P_n \vee F,$$

hence turning the set S of Horn clauses into a set S' of definite clauses. Note that S is satisfiable if and only if $S' \cup \{\neg F\}$ is. Modulo propositional equivalence, we are replacing each clause $\neg C$ by $C \Rightarrow F$. Now any model of $S' \cup \{\neg F\}$ must be a model of S, since if both $C \Rightarrow F$ and $\neg F$ hold, so does $\neg C$. Conversely, we claim that any model of S can be extended to a model of $S' \cup \{\neg F\}$ by also interpreting F as false. This trivially satisfies $\neg F$, and it also still satisfies S since the interpretation within the language of S has not changed. But if a clause $\neg C$ in S holds then certainly the corresponding clause $C \Rightarrow F$ of S' does too.

Implementation

The implementation of this backchaining search with unification is quite similar to the tableau implementation from Section 3.10. Variable instantiations are kept globally, and backtracking is initiated when a given instantiation does not lead to a complete solution. Since the rules are considered universally quantified, we can introduce fresh variable names each time we use one, so that different instances of the same rule can be used without restriction. The following takes an integer k and a rule's assumptions `asm` and conclusion `c`, and renames the variables schematically starting with '`_k`', returning both the modified formula and a new index that can be used next time.

```
let renamerule k (asm,c) =
  let fvs = fv(list_conj(c::asm)) in
  let n = length fvs in
  let vvs = map (fun i -> "_" ^ string_of_int i) (k -- (k+n-1)) in
  let inst = subst(fpf fvs (map (fun x -> Var x) vvs)) in
  (map inst asm,inst c),k+n;;
```

The core function `backchain` organizes the backward chaining with unification and backtracking search. If the list of `goals` is empty, it simply succeeds and returns the current instantiation `env`, unpacked into a list of pairs for later manipulation, while if n, which is a limit on the maximum number of rule applications, is zero, it fails. Otherwise it searches through the rules for one whose consequent `c` can be unified with the current goal `g` and such that the new subgoals `a` together with the original subgoals `gs` can be solved under that instantiation.

```
let rec backchain rules n k env goals =
  match goals with
    [] -> env
  | g::gs ->
    if n = 0 then failwith "Too deep" else
    tryfind (fun rule ->
      let (a,c),k' = renamerule k rule in
      backchain rules (n - 1) k' (unify_literals env (c,g)) (a @ gs))
    rules;;
```

In order to apply this to validity checking, we need to convert a raw Horn clause into a rule. Note that we do not literally introduce a new symbol F to turn a Horn clause into a definite clause, but just use $\perp$ directly:

```
let hornify cls =
  let pos,neg = partition positive cls in
  if length pos > 1 then failwith "non-Horn clause"
  else (map negate neg,if pos = [] then False else hd pos);;
```

As with the tableau provers, we now simply need to iteratively increase the proof size bound n until a proof is found. As well as the instantiations, the necessary size bound is returned.

```
let hornprove fm =
  let rules = map hornify (simpcnf(skolemize(Not(generalize fm)))) in
  deepen (fun n -> backchain rules n 0 undefined [False],n) 0;;
```

Where it is applicable, it is quite effective, e.g.

```
# let p32 = hornprove
   <<(forall x. P(x) /\ (G(x) \/ H(x)) ==> Q(x)) /\
     (forall x. Q(x) /\ H(x) ==> J(x)) /\
     (forall x. R(x) ==> H(x))
     ==> (forall x. P(x) /\ R(x) ==> J(x))>>;;
...
val p32 : (string, term) func * int = (<func>, 8)
```

However, it is limited to problems that give rise to a set of Horn clauses, and so is inapplicable to some quite trivial problems, even on the propositional level:

```
# hornprove <<(p \/ q) /\ (~p \/ q) /\ (p \/ ~q) ==> ~(~q \/ ~q)>>;;
Exception: Failure "non-Horn clause".
```

In the next section we will see how to retain some of the attractive features of this backchaining style of proof search, while at the same time dealing with arbitrary first-order formulas. First, however, it is worth noting another interesting feature of the present setup. Even though it is limited as a theorem prover, it can actually be used as a programming language.

Prolog

To ensure completeness, we performed iterative deepening over the total number of rule applications. Other approaches are possible, e.g. bounding on the maximum depth of the 'proof tree', and we'll examine a more refined approach in more detail in the next section. We could also store the possible 'tree fringes' at a given limit, and then instead of recalculating them when the limit is increased, consider all ways of extending them with one more rule application. The drawback is that doing so requires a large amount of storage, whereas with the recalculation-based approach, storage requirements are not significant. Besides, as pointed out by Korf (1985), the additional load of recalculation is usually relatively small because the number of possibilities tends to expand exponentially with depth, making the latest level dominate the runtimes anyway.

A radical alternative is simply to abandon any kind of bound. The practical effect of this is that the goal tree will be expanded in a depth-first fashion, with the first possible rule applied to the current goal tree, backtracking only when no more unifications are possible.

At first sight, this looks a dubious idea, since looping can occur and completeness is lost. For example, if the two rules are $P(f(x)) \Rightarrow P(x)$ and $P(0)$, in that order, then attempting to solve the goal $P(0)$, the first rule will be applied ad infinitum, generating increasingly complicated subgoals $P(0)$, $P(f(0))$, $P(f(f(0)))$,.... Only by placing a limit on the number of rule applications did backtracking force **hornprove** to consider the second rule.

However, when it does succeed, the unlimited search is often quicker, because it avoids the wasteful duplication and excessive search space exploration that can result from iterative deepening. This style of search is the basis of the popular 'logic programming' language Prolog (Colmerauer, Kanoi, Roussel and Pasero 1973). Although it is not a complete proof procedure even for the Horn subset of first-order logic, it can be used as an effective programming language.

As noted by Kowalski (1974), a set of definite clauses can be given a *procedural* interpretation. It is customary in Prolog to write a definite clause $P_1 \wedge \cdots \wedge P_n \Rightarrow Q$ as Q :- P$_1$, $\cdots$, P$_n$ to emphasize this interpretation. We can think of this clause as defining a procedure Q in terms of other procedures P$_i$. Application of this rule amounts to calling Q which in its turn will call the sub-procedures P$_i$. Unification of variables handles the passing of parameters to and from procedures in a uniform way. This is perhaps best understood by implementing it and demonstrating a few simple examples. First, we will write a parser for rules in their Prolog syntax:[†]

[†] In actual Prolog syntax, all rules should be terminated by '.'. Moreover, upper-case identifiers are variables and lower-case identifiers are constants, and for conformance we use upper-case variable names below.

```
let parserule s =
  let c,rest = parse_formula parse_atom [] (lex(explode s)) in
  let asm,rest1 =
    if rest <> [] & hd rest = ":-"
    then parse_list "," (parse_formula parse_atom []) (tl rest)
    else [],rest in
  if rest1 = [] then (asm,c) else failwith "Extra material after rule";;
```

The core of our Prolog interpreter will be the `backchain` function without taking into account the bounding size **n**. We could modify the code to remove it, but the path of least resistance, albeit a slightly sleazy one, is simply to start it off with a negative number, since we test for its becoming exactly zero, and this will never happen (at least, not until integer wraparound occurs).

```
let simpleprolog rules gl =
  backchain (map parserule rules) (-1) 0 undefined [parse gl];;
```

To illustrate how it may be used, consider a zero-successor representation of numerals, with $1 = S(0)$, $2 = S(S(0))$ etc. We can define the '$\leq$' relation by a pair of definite clauses:

```
let lerules = ["0 <= X"; "S(X) <= S(Y) :- X <= Y"];;
```

for example:

```
# simpleprolog lerules "S(S(0)) <= S(S(S(0)))";;
- : (string, term) func = <func>
# simpleprolog lerules "S(S(0)) <= S(0)";;
Exception: Failure "tryfind".
```

At first sight, Prolog is more limited than a functional language like OCaml because we can only define predicates, not functions with non-Boolean values. However, because of unification, Prolog can actually return values by binding one of the variables in the goal.

Before demonstrating this idea, we'll set up code to output these variable bindings clearly. Although we can't predict whether a free variable in the goal clause will occur on the left or right of the lists returned, we know, because no variables are repeated on the left and no composite terms are there, that any interesting instantiations (i.e. other than temporary variables, which are equally general) will be derivable by reading the equations left-to-right. Thus we can modify the interpreter:

```
let prolog rules gl =
  let i = solve(simpleprolog rules gl) in
  mapfilter (fun x -> Atom(R("=",[Var x; apply i x]))) (fv(parse gl));;
```

Now we see at once that $S(S(0)) \leq X$ is true for any X of the form $S(S(Y))$:

```
# prolog lerules "S(S(0)) <= X";;
- : fol formula list = [<<X = S(S(_3))>>]
```

So where in OCaml we would define a function f of n arguments, in Prolog we can define a corresponding predicate P of $n + 1$ arguments, where $P(x_1, \ldots, x_n, y)$ is true precisely if $f(x_1, \ldots, x_n) = y$. In fact, this mechanism is very general, since it allows P to have multiple possible values, giving a natural vehicle for nondeterministic programming. Moreover, Prolog treats inputs and outputs more symmetrically. Consider the following Prolog analogue of the standard OCaml list append operation:

```
let appendrules =
  ["append(nil,L,L)"; "append(H::T,L,H::A) :- append(T,L,A)"];;
```

We can exploit this in the usual way:

```
# prolog appendrules "append(1::2::nil,3::4::nil,Z)";;
- : fol formula list = [<<Z = 1::2::3::4::nil>>]
```

but we can also use it backwards, to discover what list would give a certain result:

```
# prolog appendrules "append(1::2::nil,Y,1::2::3::4::nil)";;
- : fol formula list = [<<Y = 3::4::nil>>]
# prolog appendrules "append(X,3::4::nil,1::2::3::4::nil)";;
- : fol formula list = [<<X = 1::2::nil>>]
# prolog appendrules "append(X,Y,1::2::3::4::nil)";;
- : fol formula list = [<<X = nil>>; <<Y = 1::2::3::4::nil>>]
```

In the last case, we just get the first of many possible answers returned, and real Prolog implementations allow one to obtain multiple answers if desired. In such cases, Prolog seems to be showing an impressive degree of intelligence. However, under the surface it is just using a simple search strategy, and this can be thwarted. For example, the following loops indefinitely rather than failing:

```
prolog appendrules "append(X,3::4::nil,X)";;
```

Logic programming in a general sense, giving procedural interpretations to logical formulas, aspires to an ideal of 'declarative' (or 'assertional') programming where the programmer merely specifies what is to be done, rather than how to do it. In practice, languages like Prolog impose particular search strategies that give quite different behaviour, or at least efficiency, on problem descriptions that are logically equivalent. For example, the following rules (Lloyd 1984) specify declaratively what it means for a list of 0-successor integers to be a sorted permutation of another:

```
let sortrules =
 ["sort(X,Y) :- perm(X,Y),sorted(Y)";
  "sorted(nil)";
  "sorted(X::nil)";
  "sorted(X::Y::Z) :- X <= Y, sorted(Y::Z)";
  "perm(nil,nil)";
  "perm(X::Y,U::V) :- delete(U,X::Y,Z), perm(Z,V)";
  "delete(X,X::Y,Y)";
  "delete(X,Y::Z,Y::W) :- delete(X,Z,W)";
  "0 <= X";
  "S(X) <= S(Y) :- X <= Y"];;
```

This is a good example of Prolog's power as a declarative programming language, since the standard strategy of unification and backtracking automatically turns this description into a sorting algorithm, albeit not a very efficient one.

```
# prolog sortrules
   "sort(S(S(S(S(0))))::S(0)::0::S(S(0))::S(0)::nil,X)";;
- : fol formula list =
[<<X = 0::S(0)::S(0)::S(S(0))::S(S(S(S(0))))::nil>>]
```

But note that the logically insignificant change of swapping the hypotheses in the first rule causes this example to loop indefinitely. In practice, Prolog programmers pay close attention to non-declarative aspects such as the ordering of rules, and sometimes use logically impure features such as 'cut' to control backtracking more explicitly. It's also notable that many Prolog implementations omit the *occurs check* for circular unification problems like $X = f(X)$, taking them further from the logical ideal.

SLD resolution

Prolog-style backchaining can be recast as a restricted form of resolution,[†] by identifying the current `goals` list $[p_1; \ldots; p_n]$, giving the 'fringe' of unsolved

---

[†] We can also consider the final Prolog-style proof tree as a bottom-up refutation of the initial clauses by positive hyperresolution. However, this turns upside down the way the proof is actually *found*.

goals, with the clause $-p_1 \lor \cdots \lor -p_n$. Now an extension step on the first subgoal with a rule $q_1 \land \cdots \land q_m \Rightarrow p'_1$, based on an MGU σ of p_1 and p'_1, can be considered simply as a resolution step with the clause $\neg q_1 \lor \cdots \lor -q_m \lor p'_1$ giving a new fringe of subgoals $\mathtt{subst}\ \sigma\ (-q_1 \lor \cdots \lor -q_m \lor -p_2 \lor \cdots \lor -p_n)$. Note that if we started with a clause $r_1 \land \cdots \land r_k \Rightarrow \bot$ the first nontrivial set of subgoals corresponds to the input clause $-r_1 \lor \cdots \lor -r_k$ from which the top rule was derived.

Thus, the entire Prolog backchaining proof can be considered as a refutation by linear resolution. But it places some additional restrictions on linear refutations, and hence shows that these preserve refutation completeness in the special case of Horn clauses: no ancestor resolution is performed, factoring is never implicitly applied, and we always resolve on the leftmost literal of the main branch at each stage. The corresponding restriction on linear resolution is often called SLD-resolution (linear resolution with selection function for definite clauses), or LUSH resolution (linear resolution with unrestricted selection for Horn clauses). It is very close to being a restriction of a more general procedure of SL-resolution developed by Kowalski and Kuehner (1971), which is itself a variant of the *model elimination* calculus that we consider next.

3.15 Model elimination

Can Prolog-style backward chaining be extended to cover non-Horn clauses? One trick that sometimes works is to transform a set of clauses into Horn form by appropriately 'renaming' predicate symbols. Consider for example the following unsatisfiable set of clauses:

$$\{P \lor Q,\ \neg P,\ \neg Q\}.$$

Although $P \lor Q$ is not Horn, one can introduce two new predicate symbols P' and Q' intended to denote the negations of P and Q. It is not too hard to see that the original clause set is equisatisfiable with:

$$\{\neg P' \lor \neg Q',\ P',\ Q'\}$$

which is Horn. However, this approach is quite limited in its scope (see Exercise 3.18). For example, the following set of clauses is also unsatisfiable:

$$\{P \lor Q,\ P \lor \neg Q,\ \neg P \lor Q,\ \neg P \lor \neg Q\},$$

yet, as one can see by symmetry, one of the clauses will remain non-Horn however the predicate symbols are renamed. A slight variant of this idea is to create Prolog-style rules by treating positive and negative literals symmetrically, and turning a clause with n literals into n different rules, picking each literal in turn to act as the head clause, regardless of which literals are positive and negative, e.g. converting

$$P \vee Q \vee \neg R$$

into the rules

$$\neg Q \wedge R \;\Rightarrow\; P,$$
$$\neg P \wedge R \;\Rightarrow\; Q,$$
$$\neg P \wedge \neg Q \;\Rightarrow\; \neg R,$$

together, perhaps, with the additional rule:

$$\neg P \wedge \neg Q \wedge R \Rightarrow \perp.$$

These rules are often said to be *contrapositives* of the original clause; note that they are all logically equivalent to the original clause and to each other. However, even treating all the contrapositives as Prolog-like rules, the set of clauses $\{P \vee Q, \quad P \vee \neg Q, \quad \neg P \vee Q, \quad \neg P \vee \neg Q\}$ will not be refuted, because there are no unit clauses to terminate branches of the proof tree. Thus, even a very liberalized notion of Prolog rule is insufficient as a proof procedure for non-Horn clauses. However, it turns out that just one small further extension is needed to give a complete proof procedure, and to understand what it might be we turn to the connection with tableaux.

Model elimination and connection tableaux

The model elimination method was invented by Loveland (1968), who later recast it (Loveland 1978) in a format similar to Prolog-like backchaining through subgoals. Loveland called the modified format MESON (model elimination, subgoal oriented), and it is mainly this that we'll be concerned with rather than model elimination in its original form. The Prolog connection was effectively exploited by Stickel (1988) in his influential 'Prolog technology theorem prover' (PTTP). Stickel not only presented MESON as a small perturbation of standard Prolog, but even compiled the input clauses to Prolog to take advantage of the advanced optimizations of existing Prolog compilers.

From a theoretical point of view, model elimination including MESON was originally analyzed via its relationship with linear resolution.[†] Since

---

[†] Donald Loveland has told the author that he developed model elimination before he had heard of resolution at all, and his later invention of linear resolution was in fact quite separate, even though in retrospect there are obvious parallels.

Prolog-style search corresponds to linear resolution without ancestor steps, it's natural to attempt to extend it to cover all of first-order logic by restoring a kind of ancestor resolution. This is just what MESON does, but it doesn't correspond exactly to any variant of resolution, since it is with individual literals on a branch of a Prolog-style search tree, rather than with clauses representing the whole fringe of the tree, that MESON allows ancestor unification. In fact full SL-resolution that we mentioned above was specifically designed as an adaptation of model elimination into a standard resolution format. However, it differs in non-trivial details, such as permitting factoring. Instead, it seems more natural to understand MESON as a refinement of tableaux, giving *connection tableaux* (Letz, Mayr and Goller 1994). This also emphasizes the fact that, unlike the usual refinements of resolution, MESON is a global method.

MESON works on formulas in clausal form, and we now consider the behaviour of the tableau prover from Section 3.10 on a conjunction of universally quantified clauses. It will simply proceed left-to-right across the conjunction, repeatedly instantiating each clause with fresh variables, then splitting the disjunctions to give multiple paths that will, subject to the variable limit, be expanded in a depth-first fashion. After a clause is used, it is put at the back of the list and will eventually be re-used unless a contradiction is reached on all paths. A major weakness of the tableau method is that clauses are split over in a round-robin fashion, expanding the number of paths, even if doing so makes no contribution. The following example, for instance:

```
# tab <<forall a. ~(P(a) /\ (forall y z. Q(y) \/ R(z)) /\ ~P(a))>>;;
...
- : int = 2
```

requires a variable limit of 2 and involves a pointless case-split over the instantiated second clause, even though if the order of the conjuncts is modified:

```
# tab <<forall a. ~(P(a) /\ ~P(a) /\ (forall y z. Q(y) \/ R(z)))>>;;
...
- : int = 0
```

no variable instantiation is needed, and the non-unit clause is never examined. This observation suggests that we might be able to make tableaux much more efficient if we could avoid using unnecessary clauses. Recognizing which clauses are unnecessary, however, requires some care if we want to retain completeness.

Let us first consider the refutation of a finite unsatisfiable set of purely propositional clauses. In the tableau prover from Section 3.10, at any point in the execution of some branch we have a list `lits` of literals and a list `fms` of other formulas, and the combined lists `lits` and `fms` are unsatisfiable. All the processing steps retain this invariant, implying that we must eventually terminate each branch by the time the list `fms` becomes empty. (In the full first-order case, things are more complicated, of course.) In *connection* tableaux we will retain a stronger invariant:

There exists a *minimal* unsatisfiable subset of the combined lists `lits` and `fms` that includes the most recently added literal in `lits` if any. (In the actual implementation, this literal is the head of `lits` if that list is nonempty.)

By a minimal unsatisfiable set of a set of formulas, we mean a subset that is unsatisfiable and such that each proper subset of it is satisfiable. Note that if a finite set S of formulas is unsatisfiable, then there must exist at least one minimal unsatisfiable subset $S_0 \subseteq S$. In the propositional case we could in principle find one by successively removing elements from S until the resulting set is satisfiable, then putting back the most recently removed element and trying to remove others until no further progress is possible.

At the beginning, `lits` is empty and the set `fms` is by hypothesis unsatisfiable, and so the combination of the lists is unsatisfiable and therefore contains a minimal unsatisfiable subset. The invariant thus holds initially. The steps of the connection tableau procedure are as follows.

(1) If `lits` is empty, pick an all-negative clause C from `fms`, say of the form $\neg P_1 \vee \cdots \vee \neg P_n$, and generate, for each $1 \leq i \leq n$, the new branches $\text{lits}' = \{\neg P_i\}$ and $\text{fms}' = \text{fms} - \{C\}$.

(2) Otherwise, if `lits` is nonempty with P the most recently added literal, try to find a complementary literal $-P$ in `lits` and terminate the branch if there is one.

(3) Otherwise, with `lits` nonempty and P the most recently added literal, pick a clause C from `fms` that includes a literal $-P$, say of the form $-P \vee P_1 \vee \cdots \vee P_n$, and generate, for each $1 \leq i \leq n$, the new branches $\text{lits}' = \{P_i\} \cup \text{lits}$ and $\text{fms}' = \text{fms} - \{C\}$.

Note that each step transforms a refutation problem into an equisatisfiable set of refutation problems, and either closes a branch or reduces the number of formulas in `fms`. Therefore, the propositional version of this procedure must terminate whatever choices are made at each stage, closing all branches if the original problem is unsatisfiable and otherwise running out of possible choices of clauses from `fms`, indicating satisfiability, just as for traditional tableaux.

Even at the propositional level, this involves some nondeterministic choices. We will prove that there is always *some* choice to be made that preserves the invariant, and in the actual implementation we will have to explore all the available possibilities in a backtracking search. Note that it is the fact that in (3) we require a 'connection' between the latest literal P and the chosen clause that explains the name 'connection tableaux'.

Trivially (2) preserves the invariant, since it terminates a branch. To prove that (3) preserves the invariant, we can assume not only that the invariant holds initially, but that `lits` alone is satisfiable, since (2) is always applied in preference to (3). We know by the invariant that the combined lists `lits` and `fms` have a minimal unsatisfiable subset S_0 that contains P. Since $S_0 - \{P\}$ is satisfiable, this set must contain a clause with the literal $-P$, otherwise modifying a satisfying assignment to map the literal P to 'true' would still satisfy $S_0 - \{P\}$, and therefore S_0 itself. This clause cannot be another unit clause in `lits` because that was assumed satisfiable. Thus $S_0 \cap$ `fms` contains a clause C of the form $-P \vee P_1 \vee \cdots \vee P_n$ for some $n \geq 0$. Now we claim that for any $1 \leq i \leq n$ the new values `lits'` $= \{P_i\} \cup$ `lits` and `fms'` $=$ `fms` $- \{C\}$ satisfy the invariant. The combination of `lits'` and `fms'` is a superset of $S_i = \{P_i\} \cup (S_0 - \{C\})$, so it suffices to show that there is a minimal unsatisfiable subset of this S_i containing P_i. Since P_i implies C, this set is certainly unsatisfiable, so there is a minimal unsatisfiable subset $T \subseteq \{P_i\} \cup (S_0 - \{C\})$. But we must have $P_i \in T$, otherwise $S_0 - \{C\}$ would be unsatisfiable, contradicting minimality.

The step (1) is a minor variation of (3), imagining P to be $\top$, and the previous argument is routinely adapted. The list `lits` is empty, and by the invariant `fms` has a minimal unsatisfiable subset S_0. This must contain an all-negative literal C, say $\neg P_1 \vee \cdots \vee \neg P_n$ for some $n \geq 1$, or the assignment to 'true' of all atoms would satisfy it. Now we show exactly as before that for any $1 \leq i \leq n$ the new values `lits'` $= \{P_i\}$ and `fms'` $=$ `fms` $- \{C\}$ satisfy the invariant.

At the first-order level, all we have to change, given a latest literal P, is to search not only for a clause exactly involving $-P$ but for one *unifiable* with $-P$. By Herbrand's theorem, if the set of clauses is unsatisfiable, so is a finite set of ground instances. These propositional clauses can be refuted by propositional connection tableaux, and unification will discover the necessary instances by a straightforward lifting argument.

Instead of actually implementing things in the tableaux setting, we will work in the context of Prolog-style backtracking search with an initial goal of $\bot$ and using contrapositives of the clauses as rules, giving exactly the PTTP-style presentation of MESON. In Prolog terms, we imagine reducing the initial goal $\perp$ to a collection of subgoals $G_1, \ldots, G_s$ on the fringe of the current tree, so that if we solve each goal we can conclude $\perp$. The connection tableau view is the contrapositive: we are performing nested case splits and concluding that at least *some* $-G_i$ holds, so if we can rule out all these possibilities, we will reach a contradiction. Not only that, but as well as each $-G_i$ we may assume the *negations of all ancestors* along the path leading from the root to $-G_i$, for in the tableau setting the current subgoal G_i is the negation of the most recent literal added to `lits` and the other literals on the path to G_i are the negations of the other literals in `lits`. Thus, the step (2) of connection tableaux, in our context, means to solve a goal G_i by finding a complementary literal $-G_i$ in its own ancestor list, which is the key addition compared with Prolog.

Let us also check that Prolog-style backchaining with contrapositives of rules corresponds to steps (1) and (3) of connection tableaux. We will only create contrapositives of the form $P_1 \wedge \cdots \wedge P_n \Rightarrow \perp$ for all-negative clauses $\neg P_1 \vee \neg \cdots \vee \neg P_n$. Thus, the starting step must be to reduce the initial goal $\perp$ to the set of subgoals $P_1, \ldots, P_n$ corresponding to some such clause, which in the tableau context means exactly to generate n paths each with a single literal $\neg P_i$ in the literals list. We create all contrapositives with literals as conclusions, so for each clause of the form $P \vee P_1 \ldots \vee P_n$ we obtain rules of the form $-P_1 \wedge \cdots \wedge -P_n \Rightarrow P$. Then the usual Prolog step, using this rule to reduce a goal P to subgoals $-P_1, \ldots, -P_n$, corresponds in the tableau setting to picking a clause $P \vee P_1 \ldots \vee P_n$ connected to the current literal $-P$ and generating the new paths with each P_i as the latest literal, i.e. step (3).

The restriction to such connection tableaux almost always leads to more efficient and directed proof search than with raw tableaux. However, in some cases, the initial transformation into CNF can complicate the formula sufficiently that it overwhelms this advantage. Actually, even if we start with a formula in CNF, there are rare cases where a connection tableau proof is longer than a naive one. For example, the following formula yields a very efficient tableau proof:

```
tab <<~p /\ (p \/ q) /\ (r \/ s) /\ (~q \/ t \/ u) /\
       (~r \/ ~t) /\ (~r \/ ~u) /\ (~q \/ v \/ w) /\
       (~s \/ ~v) /\ (~s \/ ~w) ==> false>>;;
```

However, in a MESON proof that starts by reducing the initial goal $\perp$ to p using the rule $p \Rightarrow \perp$, we need to solve each of the subgoals r and s more than once. This requires duplication of a non-trivial sub-proof, whereas had the unconnected clause $r \vee s$ been used earlier, one of these would exist as a complementary ancestor. Connection proofs not starting with p (even using clauses that are not all-negative) also turn out longer since they must duplicate the generation of a subgoal $\neg p$ from q.

Even when a MESON proof and a naive tableau counterpart have a similar size, their structures are often very different. This applies in particular to theorems naturally proved by case-splits, like $x \neq 0 \Rightarrow 0 < x^2$ by considering the cases $0 < x$ and $0 < -x$ separately. For example, if we have MESON-style chains of implications $P \Rightarrow \cdots \Rightarrow R$ and $Q \Rightarrow \cdots \Rightarrow R$, a refutation of R and $P \lor Q$ is typically the rather strange 'back-to-back' proof $\neg R \Rightarrow \cdots \Rightarrow \neg Q \Rightarrow P \Rightarrow \cdots \Rightarrow R$, with a final ancestor resolution solving $\neg R$ by unification with the complement of the starting goal.[†]

It is not just MESON that can be seen as a specialized variant of tableaux. Most top-down proof procedures can be understood starting with the naive `prawitz` procedure, as a way of arriving at a contradictory DNF but limiting the search space as much as possible by enforcing further requirements. One interesting top-down method that we do not discuss at length in this book was developed independently as the 'connection method' (Kowalski 1975; Bibel and Schreiber 1975; Bibel 1987) and the 'method of matings' (Andrews 1976; Andrews 1981). This is similar in principle to tableaux and model elimination, but avoids some of the inefficiency caused by the initial transformation into canonical forms.

Implementation

We start with a function to map a clause into all its contrapositives. In line with the discussion above, we only create an additional rule with $\bot$ as the conclusion if the original clause is all-negative:

```
let contrapositives cls =
  let base = map (fun c -> map negate (subtract cls [c]),c) cls in
  if forall negative cls then (map negate cls,False)::base else base;;
```

The main implementation is not far from Prolog, but to make later extensions easier we use the current goal `g` and a continuation function `cont` to solve remaining subgoals, rather than simply a list of subgoals. A triple consisting of the current instantiation `env`, the maximum number `n` of additional nodes in the proof tree permitted, and a counter `k` for variable renaming are passed through the chain of continuations. Each goal `g` also has associated with it the list of `ancestor` goals.

The actions required are simple. If the current size bound has been exceeded, we fail. Otherwise, we first try to unify the current goal with the

---

[†] This tendency towards long chains is a reason we prefer bounding proof size rather than depth below.

negation of one of its ancestors (not renaming variables of course since this is a global method) and call `cont` to solve the remaining goals under the new instantiation. If this fails, we try a normal Prolog-style extension with one of the rules, first unifying with a renamed rule and then iterating the same goal-solving operation over the list of subgoals, modifying the environment according to the results of unification, decreasing the permissible number of new nodes by the number of new subgoals created, and appropriately increasing the variable renaming counter.

```
let rec mexpand rules ancestors g cont (env,n,k) =
  if n < 0 then failwith "Too deep" else
  try tryfind (fun a -> cont (unify_literals env (g,negate a),n,k))
            ancestors
  with Failure _ -> tryfind
    (fun rule -> let (asm,c),k' = renamerule k rule in
               itlist (mexpand rules (g::ancestors)) asm cont
                    (unify_literals env (g,c),n-length asm,k'))
    rules;;
```

This can now be packaged up into the overall function with the usual iterative deepening. As with tableaux, we split the input problem into subproblems as much as possible. This is particularly worthwhile here when we reduce the problem to clausal form, since otherwise the translated form often becomes significantly more complicated.

```
let puremeson fm =
  let cls = simpcnf(specialize(pnf fm)) in
  let rules = itlist ((@) ** contrapositives) cls [] in
  deepen (fun n ->
     mexpand rules [] False (fun x -> x) (undefined,n,0); n) 0;;
```

The overall function starts with the usual generalization, negation and Skolemization, then attempts to refute the clauses using MESON:

```
let meson fm =
  let fm1 = askolemize(Not(generalize fm)) in
  map (puremeson ** list_conj) (simpdnf fm1);;
```

This simple procedure often compares quite favourably with tableaux. For example, the following is solved far faster than with tableaux:

```
# let davis_putnam_example = meson
    <<exists x. exists y. forall z.
        (F(x,y) ==> (F(y,z) /\ F(z,z))) /\
        ((F(x,y) /\ G(x,y)) ==> (G(x,z) /\ G(z,z)))>>;;
  ...
val davis_putnam_example : int list = [8]
```

Note also that for Horn clause problems, all atomic formulas considered will be positive, so MESON will never perform ancestor resolution and retains the attractive features of Prolog-style search. However, compared with general tableaux, MESON does have the handicap of requiring an initial transformation into clausal form, and on some formulas this can cause such an increase in complexity that MESON's superior goal-directedness cannot compensate. For example, Pelletier's (1986) problem **p38**, solved in a fraction of a second with tableaux above, takes longer with MESON.

Search optimization

Effective though it usually is, there are several ways in which the MESON implementation above can be improved. One simple observation is that we need never repeat a subgoal on a branch, so that if a current goal has an identical ancestor, we can always fail; any expansion done from the current goal could more efficiently be done starting from the identical ancestor. It is not difficult to test whether two literals are identical under an existing set of assignments. Rather than code it explicitly, we can simply call the unification function and see that no additional assignments are returned.[†]

```
let rec equal env fm1 fm2 =
  try unify_literals env (fm1,fm2) == env with Failure _ -> false;;
```

As well as incorporating this test, we can make some more substantial changes to the search strategy. One quite simple and effective alternative (Harrison 1996b) is to distribute the available size bound over subgoals more efficiently. Note that given a current size bound of n to solve two subgoals g_1 and g_2, one subgoal or the other must be solvable with size $\leq n/2$ (where division truncates downwards if n is odd). Thus, rather than immediately making the full bound of n available for g_1 then solving g_2 with what's left, we can try solving g_1 with size limit $n/2$ and then g_2 with what's left of the overall n, and if that fails (or the rest of the goals cannot be solved under any of the resulting instantiations), reverse the roles of g_1 and g_2 and try it that way round. This applies equally well if any number of subgoals are divided approximately equally into two lists of subgoals.

Since the search space typically grows exponentially, this optimization is likely to result in an overall saving even though solutions where both g_1 and g_2 are solvable with size $\leq n/2$ will be found twice. We just want to ensure that this duplication doesn't cause all the other goals to be attempted

---

[†] Recall that '==' is a pointer equality test; conventional equality could also be used, but we exploit our knowledge of the implementation of `unify`.

twice with the same instantiations, otherwise there could be an exponential explosion of duplicated work. Thus, the continuation must sometimes be ignored if a solution is found with too *few* steps. The following function is intended to take a basic expansion function `expfn` for lists of subgoals and apply it to `goals1` with size limit `n1`, then attempt `goals2` with whatever is left over from `goals1` plus an additional `n2`, yet force the continuation to fail unless the second takes more than `n3`.

```
let expand2 expfn goals1 n1 goals2 n2 n3 cont env k =
    expfn goals1 (fun (e1,r1,k1) ->
        expfn goals2 (fun (e2,r2,k2) ->
                        if n2 + r1 <= n3 + r2 then failwith "pair"
                        else cont(e2,r2,k2))
            (e1,n2+r1,k1))
        (env,n1,k);;
```

First, `goals1` is attempted with limit `n1` and the unused size `r1` is captured before proceeding to `goals2`. They are solved with limit `n2+r1`, leaving `r2` of this limit. Now, we want to ensure that more than `n3` steps *were* used for `goals2`, so we only call the continuation if $(n2 + r1) - r2 > n3$ and fail otherwise. The overall MESON expansion is now done via two mutually recursive procedures, `mexpand` dealing with a single subgoal and `mexpands` with a list of subgoals. The `mexpand` function starts as before with a check for exceeding the size bound and an attempt at ancestor unification, though it also makes a repetition check using `equal`. However, when expanding using a rule, control is then passed to `mexpands` to deal with the multiple subgoals.

```
let rec mexpand rules ancestors g cont (env,n,k) =
  if n < 0 then failwith "Too deep"
  else if exists (equal env g) ancestors then failwith "repetition" else
  try tryfind (fun a -> cont (unify_literals env (g,negate a),n,k))
              ancestors
  with Failure _ -> tryfind
    (fun r -> let (asm,c),k' = renamerule k r in
              mexpands rules (g::ancestors) asm cont
                    (unify_literals env (g,c),n-length asm,k'))
    rules
```

In `mexpands`, if there are too many new subgoals for the current size limit, we fail at once, and if there is at most one new subgoal, we deal with it in the same way as before. Only if there are at least two do we initiate the optimization. The total available limit `n` is split into two roughly equal parts `n1` and `n2`, and the list of subgoals is itself chopped in two, giving `goals1` and `goals2`. We try solving `goals1` first with size `n1` and then `goals2` with the remainder plus **n2**, with no lower limit (hence the **-1**), and if that fails, try it the other way round, this time imposing a lower limit **n1** to avoid running the continuation twice.

```
and mexpands rules ancestors gs cont (env,n,k) =
  if n < 0 then failwith "Too deep" else
  let m = length gs in
  if m <= 1 then itlist (mexpand rules ancestors) gs cont (env,n,k) else
  let n1 = n / 2 in
  let n2 = n - n1 in
  let goals1,goals2 = chop_list (m / 2) gs in
  let expfn = expand2 (mexpands rules ancestors) in
  try expfn goals1 n1 goals2 n2 (-1) cont env k
  with Failure _ -> expfn goals2 n1 goals1 n2 n1 cont env k;;
```

Generally, the improved version of MESON (redefining **puremeson** and **meson** to use the rewritten **mexpand**) performs much better. For example, we are finally able to solve the Schubert Steamroller (Stickel 1986) in a reasonable amount of time:

```
# let steamroller = meson
  <<((forall x. P1(x) ==> P0(x)) /\ (exists x. P1(x))) /\
    ((forall x. P2(x) ==> P0(x)) /\ (exists x. P2(x))) /\
    ((forall x. P3(x) ==> P0(x)) /\ (exists x. P3(x))) /\
    ((forall x. P4(x) ==> P0(x)) /\ (exists x. P4(x))) /\
    ((forall x. P5(x) ==> P0(x)) /\ (exists x. P5(x))) /\
    ((exists x. Q1(x)) /\ (forall x. Q1(x) ==> Q0(x))) /\
    (forall x. P0(x)
            ==> (forall y. Q0(y) ==> R(x,y)) \/
                ((forall y. P0(y) /\ S0(y,x) /\
                     (exists z. Q0(z) /\ R(y,z))
                     ==> R(x,y)))) /\
    (forall x y. P3(y) /\ (P5(x) \/ P4(x)) ==> S0(x,y)) /\
    (forall x y. P3(x) /\ P2(y) ==> S0(x,y)) /\
    (forall x y. P2(x) /\ P1(y) ==> S0(x,y)) /\
    (forall x y. P1(x) /\ (P2(y) \/ Q1(y)) ==> ~(R(x,y))) /\
    (forall x y. P3(x) /\ P4(y) ==> R(x,y)) /\
    (forall x y. P3(x) /\ P5(y) ==> ~(R(x,y))) /\
    (forall x. (P4(x) \/ P5(x)) ==> exists y. Q0(y) /\ R(x,y))
    ==> exists x y. P0(x) /\ P0(y) /\
                exists z. Q1(z) /\ R(y,z) /\ R(x,y)>>;;
...
steamroller : int list = [53]
```

There is still plenty of scope for further improvements, which can often cut runtimes dramatically. As Stickel (1988) emphasized, one can sometimes exploit the extensive body of experience with optimizing Prolog implementations. For example, it's often the case that various ways of solving some initial set of the subgoals give rise to the same instantiation. If the remaining goals have already failed once under this instantiation, there is no need to explore them again, unless a larger size bound is available. Inserting checks for this into the continuation functions is often very effective (Harrison 1996b). Other reasonable changes involve further restricting the proof procedure to cut down the search space (Plaisted 1990) or modifying it to avoid contrapositives (Baumgartner and Furbach 1993).

Retrospective: top-down vs. bottom-up

We have now developed two quite powerful first-order proof procedures that work on problems in clausal form, resolution and model elimination. At the level of the proofs that are eventually found, these are quite similar, and in fact MESON can almost be considered as a very restricted form of resolution. Nevertheless, the actual procedures are very different, with resolution being a local, bottom-up method and model elimination being a global top-down method. As hinted earlier, this affects the problems they can solve most effectively.

The fact that resolution accumulates a set (often very large) of derived clauses more or less forces one to use redundancy control and additional strategies to direct the proof in order to get satisfactory performance and avoid filling up memory. Note that even if virtually unlimited memory is available, the time taken to perform subsumption checking (even with less naive algorithms) can also grow with the number of derived clauses. By contrast, MESON works quite well without any special measures and uses minimal memory. The calculus also has a degree of goal-direction that contrasts with resolution, even if the latter is given a good set of support.

However, for tackling truly difficult problems, the very fact that redundancy control and strategy is *possible* is a strength of resolution-like systems. In MESON, it is difficult to take into account the large-scale structure of the proof, since the current goalstate only exists ephemerally. A particularly fundamental problem with all top-down procedures is that identical subgoals, or instances of a more general subgoal, are often solved more than once at different parts of the proof tree. Resolution, for example, dealt with the Łoś problem much more effectively, and this can be traced to the fact that MESON proves two almost identical subgoals that in resolution are just particular instances of a lemma.

At present, bottom-up provers seem to have been more effective at solving very hard problems. In particular, a research group at Argonne National Labs has enjoyed remarkable success in answering non-trivial open questions in various fields of mathematics or logic, using a line of highly engineered resolution-based theorem provers culminating in McCune's `Prover9`.[†] Of course, it is difficult to decide how much is owed to the talent and focus of the researchers, and how much to the bottom-up approach. However, it seems that the ability to direct the proof with individually tailored strategies depending on the problem domain is important to their success.

Despite the better record of bottom-up provers, research continues on retaining the strengths of top-down systems while ameliorating some of their weaknesses. One promising way to retain MESON's goal-directness while coming closer to resolution in the ability to re-use general results is to somehow remember lemmas encountered earlier in proof search (Astrachan and Stickel 1992; Letz, Mayr and Goller 1994). A particularly well-engineered system that incorporates techniques of this kind is SETHEO (Letz, Schumann, Bayerl and Bibel 1992). Some researchers have also examined judicious combinations of top-down and bottom-up theorem proving, with some success (Fuchs 1988; Schumann 1994).

3.16 More first-order metatheorems

We can extend Skolemization, at least as a theoretical device, to infinite sets of formulas. However, making sure that the Skolem functions for different formulas do not clash, either with each other or with existing function symbols, causes a few tiresome technical complications. We will assume that the function symbols are indexed by a string of characters, as in our OCaml implementation, but similar methods work for any infinite indexing set. The idea is to avoid clashes by first consistently renaming all the function symbols in the original set of formulas so that they start with 'old_', thus making symbols starting with 'f_' and 'c_' available for Skolem functions without fear of clashing with existing function symbols. (An infinite set of formulas might already use every possible name.) Here is an OCaml implementation:

```
let rec rename_term tm =
  match tm with
    Fn(f,args) -> Fn("old_"^f,map rename_term args)
  | _ -> tm;;

let rename_form fm =
  onatoms (fun (R(p,args)) -> Atom(R(p,map rename_term args))) fm;;
```

After that, we can enumerate the renamed formulas in some order, Skolemizing each in turn avoiding Skolem functions that have been previously used. We will show the coding for a finite list of formulas, but, from a theoretical

[†] `www.cs.unm.edu/~mccune/prover9/`

point of view, this can be iterated to map a countable set (enumerated in some order) to another countable set.

```
let rec skolems fms corr =
  match fms with
    [] -> [],corr
  | (p::ofms) ->
        let p',corr' = skolem (rename_form p) corr in
        let ps',corr'' = skolems ofms corr' in
        p'::ps',corr'';;

let skolemizes fms = fst(skolems fms []);;
```

For example:

```
# skolemizes [<<exists x y. x + y = 2>>;
              <<forall x. exists y. x + 1 = y>>];;
- : fol formula list =
[old_+(c_x,c_y) = old_2; forall x. old_+(x,old_1) = f_y(x)]
```

Theorem 3.46 *A countably infinite set Σ of formulas is satisfiable in domain D iff* skolemizes(Σ) *is also satisfiable in domain D.*

Proof One way is easy, since each model of skolemizes(Σ) gives rise to a model of Σ with the same domain. Conversely, suppose Σ is satisfiable. Then the set of formulas Σ' resulting from renaming the function symbols is also satisfiable in the same domain, for a model of Σ gives rise immediately to a corresponding model of Σ'. Call some such model M_0. Enumerate the formulas of Σ' in some order, as $p_1, p_2, p_3, \ldots$ Using Theorem 3.10, if we have a model M_n that satisfies skolemizes$\{p_1, \ldots, p_n\}$, we can derive a new model M_{n+1} of skolemizes$\{p_1, \ldots, p_n, p_{n+1}\}$ differing from M_n only in the interpretation of function symbols that do not occur in p_m for $m \leq n$. Thus we can form the interpretation M by taking the 'union' of all the M_n. This is a model of skolemizes(Σ). $\square$

Recall from the discussion after Theorem 3.24 that only in general for a quantifier-free formula is satisfiability equivalent to satisfiability in a Herbrand model. On the other hand, the consequent equivalence with satisfiability in a countable domain can be extended.

Theorem 3.47 *If every finite subset of a countable set Σ of formulas has a model, then Σ as a whole has a model whose domain is countable.*

Proof If every finite subset of Σ has a model, then so does every finite subset of skolemizes(Σ), because any such subset is contained in skolemizes(Δ)

for some finite $\Delta \subseteq \Sigma$. Consequently, any finite subset of the set of ground instances of formulas in `skolemizes`(Σ) is propositionally satisfiable. By propositional compactness, the set of all ground instances is propositionally satisfiable, so `skolemizes`(Σ) has a Herbrand model, just adapting the proof of Theorem 3.23 to an infinite set of formulas. The domain of the Herbrand model is countable, because a countable set of formulas can only use a countable language and hence has a countable Herbrand universe. But then by the previous theorem, Σ itself has a model with the same domain, which is therefore also countable. □

It's customary to split this up into two theorems, the compactness theorem for first-order logic:

Corollary 3.48 *If every finite subset of a countable set Σ of formulas has a model, then Σ as a whole has a model;*

and the downward Löwenheim–Skolem theorem:

Corollary 3.49 *If a countable set Σ of formulas has a model, it has a countable model.*

This latter result has some rather intriguing consequences. For example, one might try to write down a set of formulas characterizing the set of real numbers, e.g. various basic algebraic properties involving addition, multiplication and ordering, and perhaps some special functions like sin. Nevertheless, the downward Löwenheim–Skolem theorem assures us that if this holds in the usual system of real numbers (which is uncountable), it also holds in some countable model. Even more surprisingly, since the theorem still holds for an infinite set of formulas however it is defined, we can actually take the set of *all* formulas in our (countable) language that are true in the specific model $\mathbb{R}$ with the usual operations. Yet even that set has a countable model. This gives an indication that many characteristics of a model cannot be specified by first-order means, and we will consider this in more depth in Section 4.2.

Finally, it is worth pointing out explicitly that we also have an upward variant of the Löwenheim–Skolem theorem, but in the present context, without special treatment of the equality relation as in Chapter 4, it is rather trivial.

Theorem 3.50 *If a countable set Σ of formulas has a model, it has a model of arbitrarily larger cardinality.*

Proof Take any model M with domain D. Given any cardinal $\kappa \geq D$ we can find a set S such that $|S \cup D| = \kappa$. Extend the model from D to $S \cup D$ by picking an arbitrary element $a \in D$ and defining the interpretations of functions and predicates to treat every $b \in S - D$ the same as a. $\qquad\square$

Further reading

The basic theoretical results here can be found in most introductory logic texts, e.g. Enderton (1972), Mendelson (1987), Boolos and Jeffrey (1989), Goodstein (1971), Kreisel and Krivine (1971) and Andrews (1986), and are taken much further in advanced texts on model theory such as Bell and Slomson (1969), Chang and Keisler (1992), Hodges (1993b), Marcja and Toffalori (2003) and Poizat (2000). Davis, Sigal and Weyuker (1994) cover the material with more of a bias towards mechanization. Books giving more historical and philosophical background concerning the development of mathematical logic include Bocheński (1961), Dumitriu (1977) and Kneale and Kneale (1962), while Kneebone (1963) gives a blend of philosophy and technical results. Van Heijenoort (1967) is a selection of classic papers in the field including the seminal work of Löwenstein, Skolem, Gödel and Herbrand underlying most of the methods in this chapter. For a detailed study of Skolemization and reduction to clause normal form, with an emphasis on efficiency aspects that are relevant to automated proof, see Nonnengart and Weidenbach (2001).

First-order logic admits several generalizations, which we do not consider in any depth. The most radical is higher-order logic (HOL), where quantification over functions and predicates is permitted; of the above texts Andrews (1986) is the only one to cover higher-order logic extensively, but it is also mentioned in Boolos and Jeffrey (1989) and Enderton (1972). A more modest generalization allows branching scope of quantifiers; this can be seen as a more restricted form of higher-order logic. Hintikka (1996) argues that in some sense such an 'independence friendly' logic is more fundamental than normal first-order logic, but the validity problem for IF logic or HOL is no longer even semidecidable.[†]

[†] For HOL, this follows from the corresponding result for first-order arithmetic truth proved in Chapter 7, because the second-order Peano axioms PA (in sharp contrast to first-order approximations thereof) characterize $\mathbb{N}$ up to isomorphism and hence truth of p is equivalent to second-order validity of $PA \Rightarrow p$.

A less dramatic generalization is to *many-sorted* first-order logic, where terms are divided into distinct 'sorts'. This generalization is often natural, e.g. for formalizing geometry with separate classes of 'points' and 'lines'. We might state that any two distinct points determine a line as follows, where $x : T$ indicates 'a variable x of sort T':

$$\forall x : P,\ y : P.\ \neg(x = y) \Rightarrow \exists! l : L.\ \mathrm{On}(x, l) \wedge \mathrm{On}(y, l),$$

whereas in one-sorted logic we would need to add explicit predicates 'is a point' and 'is a line':

$$\forall x,\ y.\ P(x) \wedge P(y) \wedge \neg(x = y) \Rightarrow \exists! l.\ L(l) \wedge \mathrm{On}(x, l) \wedge \mathrm{On}(y, l).$$

All the main results of one-sorted logic extend to the many-sorted case, and indeed can often be stated in a sharper form (Feferman 1968; Feferman 1974; Kreisel and Krivine 1971). Moreover, sorts have significant benefits for automated theorem proving since the type discipline can avoid explicit inferences (Cohn 1985; Walther 1985) or cut the search space (Jereslow 1988) even from infinite to finite (Pnueli, Ruah and Zuck 2001; Fontaine 2004). However, we have avoided many-sortedness here because the machinery is more technical; interpretations need a separate domain D_σ for each sort σ, and functions and predicates acquire type annotations that restrict term formation. For more information see Manzano (1993) and also Kreisel and Krivine (1971).

The basic methods of automated theorem proving we have considered, namely tableaux, resolution and model elimination, are covered in various standard texts. Bundy (1983) is a basic survey of relevant material, while Robinson and Voronkov (2001) is a collection of more recent survey articles covering most of the main topics in this chapter in more depth. Siekmann and Wrightson (1983a) and Siekmann and Wrightson (1983b) are collections of some of the most significant papers in the field in the period 1957-1970. The classic text by Chang and Lee (1973) is still to be recommended as a general introduction to the field, focusing mainly on resolution but also mentioning some other approaches. Fitting (1990) is also a more modern text covering resolution and tableaux, and Bibel (1987) gives a distinctive treatment emphasizing the connection method. Newborn (2001) covers some automated theorem proving methods with more on implementation details. Duffy (1991) is a survey that, while it also gives few proofs, goes some way beyond our material in this chapter in the range of topics it considers. More technical books on resolution include Loveland (1978), which also covers model elimination in some depth, and Leitsch (1997), while Wos, Overbeek, Lusk and Boyle (1992) and several other books by the Argonne group are recommended for further guidance on actually solving non-trivial problems using (mainly resolution-based) automated reasoning. A thorough discussion of unification is given by Baader and Nipkow (1998), which is also the main text recommended in the next chapter.

Although unification-based methods similar to tableaux or resolution have generally supplanted naive Herbrand procedures, there are still some competitive 'instantiation-based' methods for first-order logic that work by generating ground instances, albeit in a more intelligent way, e.g. ordered semantic hyperlinking (Plaisted and Zhu 1997). Jacobs and Waldmann (2005) give a survey of several such techniques.

An introduction to tableaux and their historical development is given by Fitting (1999). Other papers in the same volume give extensive information about all aspects of the subject, from theoretical complexity results to implementation details. A presentation of model elimination in terms of connection tableaux, discussing many refinements and implementation details, is given by Letz and Stenz (2001).

Horn clauses were first isolated by McKinsey (1943), who noted several of their key properties; see Hodges (1993a) for a detailed study of their logical features. The use of theorem-provers for question-answering and problem-solving goes back to Green (1969). Languages like Absys (Elcock 1991) and the first version of Prolog (Colmerauer, Kanoi, Roussel and Pasero 1973), which we now think of as logic programming languages, were developed before the idea of logic programming in its general sense was thoroughly articulated, e.g. by Hayes (1973) and Kowalski (1974). There are numerous books on Prolog programming, e.g. Clocksin and Mellish (1987), while Lloyd (1984) discusses the theory behind Prolog. Two more recent and arguably purer logic programming languages in the Prolog tradition are Gödel (Hill and Lloyd 1994) and Mercury (Somogyi, Henderson and Conway 1994).

We have used a variety of examples in this chapter, including those from Pelletier (1986). A large and growing selection of problems, some very hard or even unsolved, can be found in the TPTP ('Thousands of Problems for Theorem Provers') problem library (Sutcliffe and Suttner 1998). This is the basis for the annual CASC competition between automated theorem provers, which in recent years has usually been dominated by the Vampire system.

Exercises

3.1   Show that the 'exists unique' quantifier $\exists!$ does not 'commute with' any other kind of quantifier, nor even with itself. For example, $\exists!x.\exists!y.P[x,y]$ is not in general logically equivalent to $\exists!y.\exists!x.P[x,y]$.

3.2   Modify the parser for first-order terms so that `-x^n` parses as `-(x^n)`.

3.3   Modify the basic syntax of first-order formulas to include a new quantifier 'existsunique' (traditional logic syntax $\exists!$ for 'there exists a unique...'). Modify the canonical form operations so that it is eliminated using an equivalent such as $(\exists!x.\,P[x]) = (\exists x.\,P[x] \wedge \forall y.\,P[y] \Rightarrow y = x)$.

3.4   Show how to construct, for every first-order formula p, another formula p^* in prenex normal form with all the universal formulas preceding the existential ones (i.e. of the form $\forall x_1, \ldots, x_n.\,\exists y_1, \ldots, y_m.\,q$ with q quantifier-free) such that p^* is satisfiable iff p is. You may find it helpful to consider introducing new predicate symbols to denote quantified subformulas by analogy with definitional CNF in propositional logic, e.g. $\forall x\ y.\,R(x, y) \Leftrightarrow \exists w.\,P[w, x, y]$ or $\forall x\ y\ z.\,R(x, y, z) \Leftrightarrow \forall w.\,P[w, x, y, z]$. Show also that one may make p^* free of function symbols by replacing each function with a new predicate symbol with an additional hypothesis $\forall x.\,\exists!y.\,R(x, y)$. This is often called *Skolem normal form* (Skolem 1920). Implement a function to perform the translation into Skolem NF, and test it on some examples.

3.5   We noted that the original Davis–Putnam procedure often examines many useless instances of the formula before arriving at a refutation, and that we could filter out many redundant ones using dp_refine. Is the result guaranteed to be minimal in the sense that no smaller number of ground instances gives a propositional contradiction? Are unification-based methods guaranteed to be minimal in this sense? Find a proof or counterexample.

3.6   Show that if two instantiations σ and τ each only affect finitely many variables, then $\sigma \leq \tau$ and $\tau \leq \sigma$ together imply that there is an instantiation δ with $\tau = \delta \circ \sigma$ that maps distinct variables to distinct variables. Deduce that most general unifiers are unique up to renaming. Show, however, that this fails if we allow instantiations to affect infinitely many variables.

3.7   Show that the '$\leq$' ordering on instantiations defines a lattice structure where unification can be used to find least upper bounds. Implement an algorithm for 'anti-unification', i.e. finding *greatest lower* bounds. What is the intuitive significance of these GLBs?

3.8   The tableau prover attempted to close each branch in various ways, effectively enumerating them by backtracking. An alternative to backtracking would be for each branch to return the set of all possible unifiers closing that branch, and at each branch-point, perform an appropriate 'intersection' operation on the sets of unifiers. Of course, it is still necessary to consider multiple instances of universal

formulas. Fill in the details of this idea and implement it; it may
help to consult Giese (2001). How does performance compare with
backtracking tableaux?

3.9   In the tableau prover, instead of Skolemizing at the start, we could
introduce a new tableau rule to deal with existential formulas by
transforming a formula $\exists x. P[x]$ on the current branch into $P[c]$,
where c is a new constant symbol. Work out such an approach that
maintains soundness and refutation completeness and implement it.
How does performance compare with the pre-Skolemizing version?
This exercise is non-trivial since one needs to keep track of variable
dependencies in a way that Skolemization does automatically; see
Section 6.8.

3.10   In the 'given clause algorithm' (the main loop of resolution), we
added the given clause `cls` to the `used` list before forming all resolvents of the `used` list with the given clause. This implies that each
given clause is resolved with itself. Can you prove whether this is
actually necessary? Does avoiding self-resolution significantly affect
efficiency on any interesting problems?

3.11   Implement (a) linear resolution and (b) hyperresolution, and test
them on some problems.

3.12   A unit clause P can be used to simplify any clause of the form
$\neg P' \vee Q$, with P' an instance of P, to Q (this can be seen as a
first-order generalization of the Davis–Putnam 1-literal rule). The
unit deletion feature of Otter can perform this kind of simplification.
Incorporate this into the main resolution loop and test its effectiveness on some problems. Can you guarantee that this feature will not
destroy refutation completeness?

3.13   Recall that a clause C *properly* subsumes a clause C' if $C \leq_{ss} C'$ and
$C' \not\leq_{ss} C$. Show that the 'properly subsumes' relation is wellfounded.

3.14   Horn clauses also have special features from the point of view of efficiency of deduction. Implement an algorithm to decide propositional
satisfiability of a set of Horn clauses in linear time in the size of the
input.

3.15   The 'Towers of Hanoi' puzzle (invented by Edouard Lucas in 1883
writing under the pen-name N. Lucas de Siam) consists of n discs
all of different sizes and three pegs. Initially all discs are on the
leftmost peg with the discs arranged in order of size, the largest at
the bottom and the smallest at the top. One is permitted at each
stage to move the topmost disc on any peg onto the top of another
peg, subject to the restriction that a disc may never be placed on top

of a smaller one. The objective is to finish a sequence of moves with all the n discs on the right-hand peg. Express these constraints as a set of Horn clauses and use Prolog to find a solution for particular n. You might like to start with $n = 3$. Arrange your Prolog program so that it finds the shortest solution. How does the number of moves necessary change with n? Could you predict this theoretically?

3.16 We argued in Section 3.13 that the set of all the all-negative clauses as the initial set of support retains refutation completeness. Is it true that at least one of the all-negative clauses must be a refutation-complete set of support in itself?

3.17 A clause is said to be provable by *input resolution* if it has a resolution proof in which at least one hypothesis in each resolution step is an input clause. (This is close to linear resolution but without ancestor steps.) A clause is said to be provable by *unit resolution* if it has a resolution proof in which at least one hypothesis in each resolution step is (possibly after factoring) a unit clause. Give counterexamples to show that neither input nor unit resolution is refutation complete. Prove in fact that the two are refutation equivalent, in the sense that there is an input refutation of a set of clauses S iff there is a unit refutation (Chang 1970). Is it true more generally that an arbitrary clause C is derivable by input resolution iff it is derivable by unit resolution?

3.18 Given the equivalent power of unit and input resolution (Exercise 3.17), show that both are refutation complete for Horn clauses. Show moreover that a partial converse holds: if a set of *ground* clauses has a unit or input refutation, then it has an unsatisfiable subset that can be made Horn by renaming as discussed at the start of Section 3.15, but this is not in general the case for non-ground clauses (Henschen and Wos 1974). For a more efficient algorithm for testing Horn renamability of clauses, see Lewis (1978).

3.19 In our resolution rule, with factoring included, possible factorings of both clauses were examined. Show, however, that it is only necessary to apply factoring to *one* of the input clauses to retain refutation completeness (Noll 1980). Does this affect efficiency on examples? Does it extend to all the refinements we have considered?

3.20 Modify `meson` so that it avoids repeated attempts to solve the same set of subgoals with the same set of instantiations that has already failed before, unless there is a larger size limit available. Show that this optimization greatly increases efficiency on many problems, in particular the Steamroller (Pelletier 1986 p47).

3.21   Modify `meson` so that it performs iterative deepening based on the maximum height of the proof tree. How does efficiency compare with the total size bound over a range of problems?

3.22   Prove that refutation completeness of `meson` is retained if only *positive* (or equally, only negative) ancestors are checked for unifiability with the complement of the current goal (Plaisted 1990). Implement this 'positive restriction' and compare its efficiency on some problems.

3.23   Our proof procedures usually start by first splitting up the input formula when it can be expressed as a disjunction of closed formulas. Show that, more generally, it is valid to refute a disjunction $p \vee q$ by separately refuting p and q provided p and q have no free variables in common. Implement this and see if there are interesting examples where it substantially improves performance. (This more powerful splitting rule is implemented in the Vampire theorem prover.)

3.24   The Davis–Putnam affirmative–negative rule can be extended to an analogous 'purity principle' for first-order logic. Show that if a set S of clauses contains a clause C that itself contains a literal P, then if there is no other literal N occurring in S that is unifiable with $-P$, the set S is satisfiable iff $S - \{C\}$ is. Does filtering out redundant clauses in this way have much practical impact on the difficulty of later proof using resolution or MESON? (This purity principle was already exploited in Robinson's original paper on resolution.)

3.25   Consider the '2-inverter' puzzle from the previous chapter (Exercise 2.9). Can you use one of our first-order provers to find the solution to the problem, rather than leaving the creativity to a human and merely confirming the correctness of the solution?

4

Equality

So far, equality has been treated as just another binary predicate that may be interpreted arbitrarily. However, the role of equality is so central that often we only want to consider interpretations where 'equality means equality'. The previous logical theory and programmed proof procedures are easily modified for the new circumstances, but there are also more efficient and specialized ways of handling equality.

4.1 Equality axioms

In many applications of logic, particularly to mathematical reasoning, equations play a central role. We've partly recognized this by supporting the usual infix notion '$s = t$' instead of '$= (s, t)$'. Moreover, we can define various handy syntax operations for testing if a formula is an equation and for creating and breaking apart equations, e.g.

```
let is_eq = function (Atom(R("=",_))) -> true | _ -> false;;

let mk_eq s t = Atom(R("=",[s;t]));;

let dest_eq fm =
  match fm with
    Atom(R("=",[s;t])) -> s,t
  | _ -> failwith "dest_eq: not an equation";;

let lhs eq = fst(dest_eq eq) and rhs eq = snd(dest_eq eq);;
```

But, logically speaking, equality has just been dealt with as an arbitrary binary predicate; the interpretations we consider when deciding questions of logical validity include those where '=' is interpreted quite differently from equality. In view of the claimed central role of equality, it's natural to investigate restricting the class of models to those where 'equality means equality', since it is those that we normally have in mind in, say, abstract algebra. We call an interpretation (or model of a particular set of sentences) *normal* if the equality predicate '=' is interpreted as equality on its domain.

Any normal interpretation must satisfy the formulas asserting that equality is an equivalence relation, i.e. is reflexive, symmetric and transitive:

$$\forall x.\, x = x,$$
$$\forall x\, y.\, x = y \Leftrightarrow y = x,$$
$$\forall x\, y\, z.\, x = y \wedge y = z \Rightarrow x = z,$$

as well as formulas asserting *congruence* for each n-ary function f in the language under consideration:

$$\forall x_1 \cdots x_n y_1 \cdots y_n.\, x_1 = y_1 \wedge \cdots \wedge x_n = y_n \Rightarrow f(x_1, \ldots, x_n) = f(y_1, \ldots, y_n),$$

and similarly for each n-ary predicate R:

$$\forall x_1 \cdots x_n y_1 \cdots y_n.\, x_1 = y_1 \wedge \cdots \wedge x_n = y_n \Rightarrow R(x_1, \ldots, x_n) \Rightarrow R(y_1, \ldots, y_n).$$

For a given set of first-order formulas Δ, we write $\mathtt{eqaxioms}(\Delta)$ ('the equality axioms for Δ') to mean the equivalence relation formulas together with the congruence formulas for all functions f and predicates R appearing in the formulas of Δ.

We have observed that any normal interpretation satisfies $\mathtt{eqaxioms}(\Delta)$, but it's not the case that any interpretation satisfying $\mathtt{eqaxioms}(\Delta)$ must be normal. Consider, for example, a language with just the two binary function symbols '+' and '·' and the constants 0 and 1. Interpreting all these in the usual way in $\mathbb{Z}$ but equality by the relation $x \equiv y \pmod{2}$, the equality axioms are still satisfied even though the interpretation is not normal. In fact, *no* set of formulas can constrain its models to be normal, because given any normal model, we can create a non-normal one by picking some a in the domain, adding arbitrarily many additional elements $b_i \in B$ and interpreting all the b_i in the same way as a. Despite this, we *do* have the following key result.

Theorem 4.1 *Any set Δ of first-order formulas has a normal model if and only if the set $\Delta \cup \mathtt{eqaxioms}(\Delta)$ has a model.*

Proof One direction is easy: if M is a normal interpretation, it is clear that $\mathtt{eqaxioms}(\Delta)$ holds in it; thus in any normal model of Δ, so does $\Delta \cup \mathtt{eqaxioms}(\Delta)$.

Conversely, suppose that $\Delta \cup \mathtt{eqaxioms}(\Delta)$ has a model M. Define a relation '$\sim$' on the domain D of M by setting $a \sim b$ precisely when $=_M (a,b)$, i.e. when a and b are 'equal' according to the interpretation $=_M$. Because the equivalence axioms hold in M, this is an equivalence relation, so we can partition D into equivalence classes where each $a \in D$ belongs to the equivalence class:

$$[a] = \{b \mid b \sim a\}$$

and $[a] = [b]$ iff $a \sim b$. We will use the set $D' = \{[a] \mid a \in D\}$ of equivalence classes as the domain of a new model M', and interpret each n-ary function symbol f as follows:

$$f_{M'}([a_1], \ldots, [a_n]) = [f_M(a_1, \ldots, a_n)].$$

Note that this is well-defined, i.e. independent of the particular representative of each equivalence class, because if $a_i' \sim a_i$ for $i = 1, \ldots, n$, we also have $f_M(a_1', \ldots, a_n') \sim f_M(a_1, \ldots, a_n)$ precisely because the functional congruence axiom holds in M. Similarly, we interpret each n-ary predicate symbol R by $R_{M'}([a_1], \ldots, [a_n]) = R_M(a_1, \ldots, a_n)$. Once again, this is independent of the particular choice of equivalence class representatives because the predicate congruence holds in M.

In particular we have $=_{M'} ([a], [b])$ precisely when $a \sim b$ and so when $[a] = [b]$. Thus M' is a normal interpretation. To see that it satisfies all the formulas in Δ, we essentially need to show that we can 'pull' the equivalence-class forming operation up the semantics of a formula. Note first that:

$$\mathtt{termval}\ M'\ \delta'\ t = [\mathtt{termval}\ M\ \delta\ t],$$

where $\delta'(x) = [\delta(x)]$ for all variables x. To prove this, simply proceed by structural induction on t. If t is the variable x then we have

$$\mathtt{termval}\ M'\ \delta'\ x$$
$$= \quad \delta'\ x$$
$$= \quad [\delta(x)]$$
$$= \quad [\mathtt{termval}\ M\ \delta\ x],$$

while if $t = f(s_1, \ldots, s_n)$, then using the inductive hypothesis and the definition of $f_{M'}$ we have:

$$\mathtt{termval}\ M'\ \delta'\ f(s_1, \ldots, s_n)$$
$$= \quad f_{M'}(\mathtt{termval}\ M'\ \delta'\ s_1, \ldots, \mathtt{termval}\ M'\ \delta'\ s_n)$$
$$= \quad f_{M'}([\mathtt{termval}\ M\ \delta\ s_1], \ldots, [\mathtt{termval}\ M\ \delta\ s_n])$$

$$= \quad [f_M(\texttt{termval } M \ \delta \ s_1, \dots, \texttt{termval } M \ \delta \ s_n)]$$
$$= \quad [\texttt{termval } M \ \delta \ f(s_1, \dots, s_n)].$$

Now we claim that for any formula p we have $\texttt{holds } M' \ \delta' \ p = \texttt{holds } M \ \delta$ p. Once again, the proof is by structural induction. This is trivial if p is $\bot$ or $\top$, while it holds by definition of $R_{M'}$ when p is an atomic formula. The propositional operations obviously preserve this property, which leaves the quantified formulas as the interesting case. Note that:

$$\texttt{holds } M' \ \delta' \ (\forall x. \, p)$$
$$= \quad \text{for all } A \in D', \texttt{holds } M' \ ((x \mapsto A)\delta') \ p$$
$$= \quad \text{for all } a \in D, \texttt{holds } M' \ ((x \mapsto [a])\delta') \ p$$
$$= \quad \text{for all } a \in D, \texttt{holds } M' \ ((x \mapsto a)\delta)' \ p$$
$$= \quad \text{for all } a \in D, \texttt{holds } M \ ((x \mapsto a)\delta) \ p$$
$$= \quad \texttt{holds } M \ \delta \ (\forall x. \, p),$$

and similarly for the existential quantifier. Thus, since each $p \in \Delta$ holds in M in all valuations δ, it also holds in M' for all valuations ϵ, since ϵ is necessarily of the form δ' for some valuation δ in M (just let $\delta(x)$ be any member of $\epsilon(x)$). □

In our practical applications, we will be concerned with a single formula. Define $\texttt{eqaxiom}(p)$ to be the conjunction of the (necessarily finitely many) equality axioms $\texttt{eqaxioms}(\{p\})$. Then:

Corollary 4.2 *Any formula p is satisfiable in a normal model iff $p \wedge$ $\texttt{eqaxiom}(p)$ is satisfiable.*

Proof By definition of the semantics of conjunction, an interpretation satisfies $p \wedge \texttt{eqaxiom}(p)$ iff it satisfies p and $\texttt{eqaxiom}(\{p\})$. □

We have the following dual result for validity.

Corollary 4.3 *A formula p holds in all normal models iff $\texttt{eqaxiom}(p) \Rightarrow p$ holds in all models.*

Proof Since p holds in a model iff its universal closure does, we can assume without loss of generality that p is closed. Thus it holds in all normal models iff $\neg p$ has no normal model, and so if $\neg p \wedge \texttt{eqaxiom}(\neg p)$ has no model. But $\texttt{eqaxiom}(\neg p) = \texttt{eqaxiom}(p)$ and so $\neg p \wedge \texttt{eqaxiom}(\neg p)$ is logically equivalent to $\neg(p \vee \neg(\texttt{eqaxiom}(p)))$ and so to $\neg(\texttt{eqaxiom}(p) \Rightarrow p)$. This is unsatisfiable iff $\texttt{eqaxiom}(p) \Rightarrow p$ is valid. □

In the abstract treatment above, the equality axioms included a predicate congruence property for equality itself:

$$\forall x_1 \; x_2 \; y_1 \; y_2. \; x_1 = y_1 \wedge x_2 = y_2 \Rightarrow x_1 = x_2 \Rightarrow y_1 = y_2.$$

But we can afford to omit it, because it's a logical consequence of the equivalence axioms. We can economize further by using only two equivalence axioms, reflexivity and a variant of transitivity $\forall x \; y \; z.x = y \wedge x = z \Rightarrow y = z$. (Symmetry follows by instantiating that axiom so that x and z are the same, then using reflexivity.)

OCaml implementation

In Skolemization we used **functions** to find all the functions in a term; similarly the following finds all predicates, again as name–arity pairs:

```
let rec predicates fm = atom_union (fun (R(p,a)) -> [p,length a]) fm;;
```

We can manufacture a congruence axiom for each function symbol by producing the appropriate number of arguments $x_1, \ldots, x_n$ and $y_1, \ldots, y_n$ and constructing the formula

$$\forall x_1 \ldots x_n \; y_1 \ldots y_n.x_1 = y_1 \wedge \cdots x_n = y_n \Rightarrow f(x_1, \ldots, x_n) = f(y_1, \ldots, y_n).$$

We return a list that normally has one member but is empty in the case of a nullary function (i.e. individual constant):

```
let function_congruence (f,n) =
  if n = 0 then [] else
  let argnames_x = map (fun n -> "x"^(string_of_int n)) (1 -- n)
  and argnames_y = map (fun n -> "y"^(string_of_int n)) (1 -- n) in
  let args_x = map (fun x -> Var x) argnames_x
  and args_y = map (fun x -> Var x) argnames_y in
  let ant = end_itlist mk_and (map2 mk_eq args_x args_y)
  and con = mk_eq (Fn(f,args_x)) (Fn(f,args_y)) in
  [itlist mk_forall (argnames_x @ argnames_y) (Imp(ant,con))];;
```

for example:

```
# function_congruence ("f",3);;
- : fol formula list =
[<<forall x1 x2 x3 y1 y2 y3.
    x1 = y1 /\ x2 = y2 /\ x3 = y3 ==> f(x1,x2,x3) = f(y1,y2,y3)>>]
# function_congruence ("+",2);;
- : fol formula list =
[<<forall x1 x2 y1 y2. x1 = y1 /\ x2 = y2 ==> x1 + x2 = y1 + y2>>]
```

An analogous function for predicates is almost the same, except that we use implication of formulas rather than equality of terms in the consequent:

```
let predicate_congruence (p,n) =
  if n = 0 then [] else
  let argnames_x = map (fun n -> "x"^(string_of_int n)) (1 -- n)
  and argnames_y = map (fun n -> "y"^(string_of_int n)) (1 -- n) in
  let args_x = map (fun x -> Var x) argnames_x
  and args_y = map (fun x -> Var x) argnames_y in
  let ant = end_itlist mk_and (map2 mk_eq args_x args_y)
  and con = Imp(Atom(R(p,args_x)),Atom(R(p,args_y))) in
  [itlist mk_forall (argnames_x @ argnames_y) (Imp(ant,con))];;
```

As planned, we use this variant of the equivalence properties:

```
let equivalence_axioms =
  [<<forall x. x = x>>; <<forall x y z. x = y /\ x = z ==> y = z>>];;
```

Now we define a function that returns $\text{eqaxiom}(p) \Rightarrow p$ for an input formula p. It leaves p alone if it doesn't involve equality at all, since there is then no distinction between its normal and non-normal models.

```
let equalitize fm =
  let allpreds = predicates fm in
  if not (mem ("=",2) allpreds) then fm else
  let preds = subtract allpreds ["=",2] and funcs = functions fm in
  let axioms = itlist (union ** function_congruence) funcs
                      (itlist (union ** predicate_congruence) preds
                              equivalence_axioms) in
  Imp(end_itlist mk_and axioms,fm);;
```

The upshot of Corollary 4.3 is that we can test the validity of p in first-order logic with equality by testing the validity of $\text{equalitize}(p)$ in ordinary first-order logic. Thus, we can just apply equalitize as a preprocessing step for any of our existing proof procedures. Note, by the way, that we will avoid creating congruence axioms for the Skolem functions, which only appear later in the underlying proof procedure. It's hard to predict whether it would be more efficient to add congruences for Skolem functions: it means more hypotheses, but perhaps allows shortcuts in proofs. Observe also that the equality axioms are Horn clauses (Section 3.14), so whenever Δ is a set of Horn clauses, so is $\Delta \cup \text{eqaxioms}(\Delta)$. Thus, we can also extend the Prolog-like proof procedure hornprove from Section 3.14 to a complete prover for Horn problems in logic with equality just by adding the equality axioms in a preprocessing step in the same way. And since meson reduces to Prolog-type search on Horn problems, it will continue to do so when combined with the preprocessing step.

For a first example, consider the following formula given by Dijkstra (1997), who shows how its validity underlies a proof of Morley's theorem in geometry.

```
# let ewd = equalitize
  <<(forall x. f(x) ==> g(x)) /\
    (exists x. f(x)) /\
    (forall x y. g(x) /\ g(y) ==> x = y)
    ==> forall y. g(y) ==> f(y)>>;;
...
```

We can prove it by any of the main methods developed earlier, including model elimination, resolution and even tableaux with splitting, e.g.

```
# meson ewd;;
...
- : int list = [6]
```

We thus conclude that the original formula is valid in first-order logic with equality, i.e. holds in all normal models. Another example, which the author learned from Wishnu Prasetya,[†] is that for any two functions $f : A \to B$ and $g : B \to A$ there is a unique x such that $x = f(g(x))$ iff there is a unique y such that $y = g(f(y))$.

```
let wishnu = equalitize
  <<(exists x. x = f(g(x)) /\ forall x'. x' = f(g(x')) ==> x = x') <=>
    (exists y. y = g(f(y)) /\ forall y'. y' = g(f(y')) ==> y = y')>>;;
```

The resulting formula is solvable by MESON, but already it takes a significant amount of time. So, although just adding equality axioms allows us to re-use existing procedures, one might wonder if there are more effective ways of dealing with equality. This is a matter to which we will return before too long.

4.2 Categoricity and elementary equivalence

Thanks to Theorem 4.1, the theoretical results in Chapter 3 can also be adapted quite easily to consider only normal models. Arguably, they are more interesting in this context, since it is usually normal models we have in mind when thinking about mathematical structures. In fact, many of the structures studied in abstract algebra are precisely the normal models of some first-order formula or set of first-order formulas. For example, a *group*

[†] See his message to the info-hol mailing list on 18 October 1993, available on the Web as ftp://ftp.cl.cam.ac.uk/.aftp/hvg/info-hol-archive/15xx/1574.

is essentially just a normal model of the following formula:

$$(\forall x\; y\; z.\; m(x, m(y, z)) = m(m(x, y), z)) \land$$
$$(\forall x.\; m(x, 1) = x \land m(1, x) = x) \land$$
$$(\forall x.\; m(x, i(x)) = 1 \land m(i(x), x) = 1).$$

It's not difficult to come up with similar axiomatizations for many other structures such as partial orders and rings. Thus, in the model theory of first-order logic, we have a suitable mathematical generalization taking in various specific mathematical structures. This enables us to define notions like 'substructure' and 'homomorphism', such that for example 'subgroup' and 'ring homomorphism' are special cases of the general concept. We give the general definition of 'isomorphism' shortly,[†] and starting in Section 5.6 we will take a closer look at various algebraic systems.

Metatheorems

First, we can easily adapt the compactness theorem to logic with equality.

Theorem 4.4 *If every finite subset Δ of a set Σ of formulas has a normal model, then Σ itself has a normal model.*

Proof If each finite $\Delta \subseteq \Sigma$ has a normal model, then each $\Delta \cup \mathtt{eqaxioms}(\Delta)$ for finite Δ has a model. However, every finite $\Delta' \subseteq \Sigma \cup \mathtt{eqaxioms}(\Sigma)$ is a subset of some such $\Delta \cup \mathtt{eqaxioms}(\Delta)$ for finite Δ, and consequently each finite $\Delta' \subseteq \Sigma \cup \mathtt{eqaxioms}(\Sigma)$ has a model. By the compactness theorem for arbitrary models, $\Sigma \cup \mathtt{eqaxioms}(\Sigma)$ has a model and therefore, by Theorem 4.1, Σ has a normal model. $\qquad\qquad\square$

The equalitarian version of the downward Löwenheim–Skolem theorem can be derived similarly.

Theorem 4.5 *If a countable set of formulas Σ has a normal model M, then it has a countable (either finite or countably infinite) normal model.*

Proof If Σ has a normal model, $\Sigma \cup \mathtt{eqaxioms}(\Sigma)$ has a model, and so by the original downward LS Theorem 3.49, it has a model with a countable domain D. The corresponding normal model of Σ that we constructed in the

---

[†] There is actually some divergence in general definitions of *homomorphism*, with two standard texts by Enderton (1972) and Mendelson (1987) differing over whether just implication or full equivalence is demanded between interpreted predicates. Also, note that in general these concepts can depend on whether the axioms contain operation symbols or just existence assertions (Hodges 1993b).

proof of Theorem 4.1 has as its domain equivalence classes of elements of D. The cardinality of this set of equivalence classes is at most the cardinality of D (since each equivalence class contains at least one element of D) and so is countable too. $\square$

Constructing *larger* models than a given model is no longer trivial, because we can't just add new domain elements and retain normality. However, by cleverly exploiting compactness, we can still find a way to grow models. For example:

Theorem 4.6 *If a set of sentences S has normal models of arbitrarily large finite cardinality, then it has an infinite normal model.*

Proof Consider the following sentences B_i, which intuitively mean 'there are at least i distinct elements'.

$$
\begin{aligned}
B_2 &= \exists x\, y.\, x \neq y, \\
B_3 &= \exists x\, y\, z.\, x \neq y \wedge x \neq z \wedge y \neq z, \\
B_4 &= \exists w\, x\, y\, z.\, w \neq x \wedge w \neq y \wedge w \neq z \wedge x \neq y \wedge x \neq z \wedge y \neq z, \\
B_5 &= \ldots
\end{aligned}
$$

Write $B = \bigcup_{i \in \mathbb{N}} B_i$. Since, by hypothesis, S has models of arbitrarily large finite cardinality, all finite subsets of $S \cup B$ are satisfiable. Therefore by compactness so is $S \cup B$, but clearly any model of these sentences must be infinite. $\square$

Using a closely related technique, one can prove the upward Löwenheim–Skolem theorem (actually due to Tarski), analogous to Theorem 3.50 but much more interesting: if a set of formulas Σ has a normal model with infinite domain D, then it has a model of any infinite cardinality $\geq |D|$. The proof is simply to add enough new constants c_i that do not already occur in Σ, and apply compactness to the set $\Sigma \cup \{c_i \neq c_j \mid i, j \in S,\ i \neq j\}$. However, we will not present this in detail since we have not proved compactness for uncountable languages. Indeed, the upward Löwenheim–Skolem theorem requires the machinery of the Axiom of Choice.[†]

We will, however, give an example of how to construct 'nonstandard' models using compactness. Consider some language for the real numbers, maybe including addition, multiplication, negation, inversion, the constants

[†] The formula $\forall x\, y\, x'\, y'.\, p(x, y) = p(x', y') \Rightarrow x = x' \wedge y = y'$ has a model with domain $\mathbb{N}$, e.g. interpreting p as the pairing function $\langle x, y \rangle$ in Section 7.2. The upward LS theorem then implies that this has models of arbitrary infinite cardinality, and hence that $\kappa^2 \leq \kappa$ for any infinite κ. This is known to be equivalent to AC (Jech 1973).

0 and 1, and special functions like sin. Let Σ be the set of all formulas in this language that are true in $\mathbb{R}$ with the intended interpretation, a.k.a. the 'standard model', Consider the set:

$$\Sigma' = \Sigma \cup \{1 < c, 1 + 1 < c, 1 + 1 + 1 < c, \ldots\},$$

where c is a constant symbol not appearing in Σ. Any finite set of these has a model, for the reals are a model of Σ and we can then interpret c by some suitably large number. Thus by compactness there is a 'nonstandard model' of Σ in which c behaves like an infinite number, with $n < c$ for each natural number n. Indeed, this gives rise to other larger infinite numbers like $c + c$ and infinitesimal numbers like $1/c$ (despite the fact that we can also, by the Downward Löwenheim–Skolem theorem, assume it to be countable). Yet this strange menagerie of numbers obeys all the first-order properties that the 'real reals' do. This observation is a possible starting point for non-standard analysis (A. Robinson 1966) which exploits nonstandard models to prove standard results using infinite and infinitesimal elements. For more on this, see Cutland (1988), Davis (1977) or Hurd and Loeb (1985).

Consequences

In the axiomatic approach to mathematics, one starts from a set of axioms and derives conclusions without making any additional assumptions. If we are concerned with properties expressible in first-order logic, we might formalize this idea by allowing from axioms Σ the deduction of any first-order consequence of the axioms Σ. We will sometimes abbreviate the set $\{p \mid \Sigma \models p\}$ of first-order consequences of a set of first-order 'axioms' Σ by $\mathrm{Cn}(\Sigma)$.

Part of the appeal of the axiomatic method is that it isolates the assumptions that are actually necessary, so that the full generality of the results is seen. For this to be significant, we actually want Σ to have several interesting models. For example, the group axioms are satisfied by addition of integers or reals, multiplication of nonzero reals, composition of permutations on a set and so on. Sometimes, however, we want to use a set of axioms almost as a *definition* of a particular structure, such that all structures obeying the axioms are essentially the same. In fact, this use of axioms predated the general idea of the axiomatic method. For example, it used to be believed that the traditional axioms for geometry (without the axioms of parallels) had this property, but it later turned out that there were unexpected non-Euclidean models.

Given two interpretations M and M' of a first-order language with respective domains D and D', we say that M and M' are *isomorphic* if there are mappings $i : D \to D'$ and $j : D' \to D$ such that for all $x \in D$, $j(i(x)) = x$, for all $x' \in D'$, $i(j(x')) = x'$, for each n-ary function symbol f in the language:

$$i(f_M(a_1, \ldots, a_n)) = f_{M'}(i(a_1), \ldots, i(a_n))$$

and for each n-ary predicate symbol

$$R_M(a_1, \ldots, a_n) = R_{M'}(i(a_1), \ldots, i(a_n))$$

for any $a_1, \ldots, a_n \in D$. The functions i and j are said to set up an *isomorphism*, or sometimes themselves to be *isomorphisms*. Intuitively, isomorphic interpretations are 'essentially the same' but for using a different underlying set, and indeed the word literally means something like 'equal shape'. A set of formulas (or 'axioms') Σ is said to be *categorical* if any two models are isomorphic. (One usually assumes also that it *has* at least one model.) The Löwenheim–Skolem theorems imply that if a set of first-order formulas has some infinite model, it has models of a different cardinality, which are therefore certainly not isomorphic (since an isomorphism is also a bijection). Thus, for first-order formulas, categoricity only arises for sets of formulas with just finite models, which are often the less interesting ones.

However there are at least two natural ways in which we can weaken the idea of categoricity. First, we might say that even though the cardinality of models of Σ may not be fixed, at least all models of some particular cardinality κ are determined up to isomorphism. In this case Σ is said to be κ-*categorical*. A number of interesting instances of this phenomenon are known, many predating the formal articulation of the concept using first-order logic. For example, Steinitz (1910) proved that any two algebraically closed fields of a given characteristic with the same uncountable cardinality are isomorphic. However, we will not dwell on the theory of κ-categoricity here.

Another idea is to say that since Σ consists only of first-order statements, it's unreasonable to expect to be able to prove that all its models are *isomorphic*. It's much more reasonable just to demand that all models satisfy the same first-order sentences, i.e. are all *elementarily equivalent*. (It's not too hard to show that isomorphic models are also elementarily equivalent, though the example of nonstandard models shows that the converse is false in general.) This is essentially the notion of *completeness of a theory*, which we study in detail in Section 5.6.

4.3 Equational logic and completeness theorems

Consider purely equational logic, where we start from a set Δ of (implicitly universally quantified) equations and ask whether another equation $s = t$ holds in all normal models of Δ, i.e. whether $\Delta \models s = t$ in first-order logic with equality. A famous theorem due to Birkhoff (1935) relates this to a set of *proof rules* or *inference rules* for generating equational conclusions. Given a set of equations Δ we define '$s = t$ is provable from Δ', written $\Delta \vdash s = t$, inductively (see Appendix 1) by the following rules:

$$\frac{(s = t) \in \Delta}{\Delta \vdash s = t}\text{AXIOM}$$

$$\frac{\Delta \vdash s = t}{\Delta \vdash \texttt{subst } i(s = t)}\text{INST}$$

$$\frac{}{\Delta \vdash t = t}\text{REFL}$$

$$\frac{\Delta \vdash s = t}{\Delta \vdash t = s}\text{SYM}$$

$$\frac{\Delta \vdash s = t \quad \Delta \vdash t = u}{\Delta \vdash s = u}\text{TRANS}$$

$$\frac{\Delta \vdash s_1 = t_1 \quad ... \quad \Delta \vdash s_n = t_n}{\Delta \vdash f(s_1, ..., s_n) = f(t_1, ..., t_n)}\text{CONG}$$

Theorem 4.7 $\Delta \models s = t$, *i.e. an equation $s = t$ holds in all normal models of a set Δ of equations, if and only if $\Delta \vdash s = t$, i.e. the equation $s = t$ is derivable from Δ by repeated use of Birkhoff's rules.*

Proof We first consider the right-to-left direction. Note that each proof rule applied to logically valid hypotheses gives logically valid conclusions; for example for transitivity we just need to observe that if $\Delta \models s = t$ and $\Delta \models t = u$ then also $\Delta \models s = u$. So by induction, whenever $\Delta \vdash s = t$ we also have $\Delta \models s = t$ in first-order logic with equality.

Conversely, if $\Delta \models s = t$, then $\Delta' = \Delta \cup \neg(s = t)$ has no normal model, and therefore $\Delta' \cup \texttt{eqaxioms}(\Delta')$ is unsatisfiable. As noted earlier, all these formulas are Horn clauses, so there is a Prolog-style proof of $\bot$ from them, as explained in Section 3.14. This must start with the formula $s = t \Rightarrow \bot$ to get the subgoal $s = t$, and thereafter divide into subgoals ending either in instances of reflexivity or (possibly instantiation of) formulas in Δ. The internal nodes simply apply transitivity, symmetry and congruence. They therefore correspond exactly to Birkhoff's rules; all we have done is consider instances of the equality axioms as inference rules in themselves. □

This vindicates a naive expectation that if one equational formula is a logical consequence of others, one can get it by rewriting forwards, backwards and at depth, the kind of manipulative techniques we learn at school. Birkhoff originally approached the problem more directly, and later Maltsev (1936) and others realized that many of the nice properties of equational logic discovered by Birkhoff still hold in the more general setting of Horn clauses.

Soundness and completeness

Birkhoff's theorem is an important case where a *semantic* notion $\Delta \models s = t$ is shown equivalent to a *syntactic* notion $\Delta \vdash s = t$ of 'provability'. In general, we say that such a provability relation '$\vdash$' is:

- *sound* if whenever $\Delta \vdash p$ we also have $\Delta \models p$;
- *complete* if whenever $\Delta \models p$ we also have $\Delta \vdash p$.

Birkhoff's theorem asserts that the rules above are both sound and complete provided we restrict ourselves just to equations. They are definitely incomplete if we consider first-order formulas in general, however, since they can only deduce equational conclusions. We can also consider the resolution rule from Section 3.11 as defining a proof system. However, the reader should register an important mathematical distinction and another, purely psychological, one.

Completeness and refutation completeness Birkhoff's theorem assures us that any equation that holds semantically can be derived syntactically. This is in contrast with, say, the resolution calculus, where we merely showed that if a set of clauses is unsatisfiable, we can derive the empty clause from it. This implies $\Delta \models p$ iff $\Delta \vdash p$ only for the special case $p = \bot$, a property we called *refutation* completeness. As noted in Section 3.11, the example of $P \models P \vee Q$ shows that resolution is not complete in the stronger sense.

Naturalness As mentioned earlier, Birkhoff's theorem confirms our natural intuition and the Birkhoff rules formalize steps that a human attempting to prove the same theorem might make. By contrast, the resolution calculus, which J. A. Robinson (1965b) explicitly categorized as a *machine-oriented* principle, is remote from the methods people typically use when proving theorems, with its Skolemizing steps and insistence on clausal form.[†]

We will describe a more human-oriented proof system that is complete for full first-order logic in Section 6.3.

The difficulty of equational proofs

Although in some respects equational logic has turned out to be 'tamer' than full first-order logic, there is a precise sense in which it is just as difficult, by virtue of an embedding of full first-order logic in equational logic due to McKenzie (1975).[‡] Indeed, the reader with any experience of finding equational proofs in relatively simple axiom systems will know that it can be astonishingly difficult (Kapur and Zhang 1991). For example, the following problem is often set as an exercise in courses on group theory. We are given '1-sided' versions of the identity and inverse axioms, and are required to deduce that left inverses are also right inverses. Our existing setup for equality handling can solve this problem, but it takes many hours; a more efficient approach is discussed in Section 4.8.

```
(meson ** equalitize)
<<(forall x y z. x * (y * z) = (x * y) * z) /\
  (forall x. 1 * x = x) /\
  (forall x. i(x) * x = 1)
  ==> forall x. x * i(x) = 1>>;;
```

The reader may like to try competing against the machine! Here is a reasonably human-oriented proof:

$$
\begin{aligned}
x \cdot i(x) &= 1 \cdot (x \cdot i(x)) \\
&= (i(i(x)) \cdot i(x)) \cdot (x \cdot i(x)) \\
&= i(i(x)) \cdot (i(x) \cdot (x \cdot i(x))) \\
&= i(i(x)) \cdot ((i(x) \cdot x) \cdot i(x)) \\
&= i(i(x)) \cdot (1 \cdot i(x)) \\
&= i(i(x)) \cdot i(x) \\
&= 1.
\end{aligned}
$$

We found this by tracing the proof MESON found, and rearranging the order of some of the Birkhoff rules to turn it into a simple transitivity chain for easier presentation in a linear format. In fact, Birkhoff proofs in some

[†] Note, however, the suggestion of A. Robinson (1957) that Skolem functions have their analogue in construction lines used in traditional geometrical proofs.

[‡] On the other hand, an embedding of first-order logic in the theory of Boolean rings was actually suggested by Hsiang (1985) as a workable approach to first-order proof.

stronger canonical form can be easier to find, just as, say, linear resolution can cut down the search space compared to unrestricted resolution (Section 3.13). And some of the results we present next can be proved using canonical transformations of Birkhoff proofs (Exercise 4.2).

4.4 Congruence closure

Consider equational logic in the special case of ground terms, i.e. deciding $E \models s = t$ where $s = t$ and all members of E are equations not containing variables. In the light of Birkhoff's Theorem 4.7, this is equivalent to $E \vdash s = t$. But since no variables are involved, the Birkhoff instantiation rule is clearly not necessary. The highlight of this section is the observation that we can further restrict the Birkhoff proofs to those where all terms appearing in intermediate equations are subterms of the terms in the original problem, which implies that the problem is decidable.

In what follows, we assume some set G of terms that is closed under subterms, i.e. if $t \in G$ and s is a subterm of t then $s \in G$. The following can serve as the implementation and the formal definition of the set of subterms of a term:

```
let rec subterms tm =
  match tm with
    Fn(f,args) -> itlist (union ** subterms) args [tm]
  | _ -> [tm];;
```

We say that a binary relation $\sim$ on G is a *congruence* if it is reflexive, symmetric and transitive (i.e. an equivalence relation) and satisfies the congruence property: for each n-ary function symbol f, if $s_1 \sim t_1, \ldots, s_n \sim t_n$ then also $f(s_1, \ldots, s_n) \sim f(t_1, \ldots, t_n)$, whenever all those terms are in G. Note that given any binary relation $R \subseteq G \times G$ there is a unique smallest congruence extending R, and this is known as the *congruence closure* of R. It can be defined inductively (see Appendix 1) by starting with R and adding rules for closure under the equivalence and congruence properties.

Theorem 4.8 *Suppose all s_i, t_i, s and t are ground terms, and G consists of those terms and all their subterms. Let '$\sim$' be the congruence closure on G of $\{(s_1, t_1), \ldots, (s_n, t_n)\}$. Then the following are equivalent:*

(i) $\{s_1 = t_1, \ldots, s_n = t_n\} \models s = t$;

(ii) $s \sim t$;

(iii) *there is a Birkhoff proof of $s = t$ from $s_1 = t_1, \ldots, s_n = t_n$ whose intermediate steps involve only terms in G;*

(iv) $\{s_1 = t_1, \ldots, s_n = t_n\} \vdash s = t$.

Proof By Birkhoff's Theorem 4.7, (i) and (iv) are equivalent. If (iii) then (iv), since it is just a more restricted case of the same thing. If (ii) then (iii), since the set of pairs (s, t) that have a restricted Birkhoff proof from $s_1 = t_1, \ldots, s_n = t_n$ contains $\{(s_1, t_1), \ldots, (s_n, t_n)\}$ and is closed under equivalence and congruence because of the Birkhoff rules, and therefore must include the smallest such relation '$\sim$'. To complete the circle of equivalents, we need to show that (ii) follows from (i).

In fact we show the contrapositive, assuming $s \not\sim t$ and exhibiting an interpretation M where each $s_i = t_i$ holds but $s = t$ does not. The domain of M is the set of equivalence classes of G under '$\sim$'. Each constant c is interpreted by itself. An n-ary function f for $n \geq 1$ is interpreted as $f_M(C_1, \ldots, C_n) = C$, where C is the equivalence class containing $f(u_1, \ldots, u_n)$ for some representatives $u_i \in C_i$ if such a class exists, and some fixed but arbitrary equivalence class otherwise. (There may indeed be no such C containing a suitable $f(u_1, \ldots, u_n)$, because we are restricted to terms in G, but if there is one, it is uniquely defined independent of the representatives u_i, precisely because $\sim$ is a congruence.) This is indeed a (normal) interpretation, and by induction on terms `termval` $M \sigma u \sim u$ for all $u \in G$. Therefore for all $u, v \in G$, `holds` $M \sigma (u = v)$ is equivalent to $u \sim v$. Consequently each $s_i = t_i$ holds in M but not $s = t$, so $\{s_1 = t_1, \ldots, s_n = t_n\} \not\models s = t$ as required. $\qquad\square$

Implementation of congruence closure

Our implementation of congruence closure will take an existing congruence relation and extend it to a new one including a given equivalence $s \sim t$. This can then be iterated starting with the empty congruence to find the congruence closure of $\{(s_1, t_1), \ldots, (s_n, t_n)\}$ as required. We will use a standard union-find data structure described in Appendix 2 to represent equivalences, so closure under the equivalence properties will be automatic and we'll just have to pay attention to closure under congruences. So suppose we have an existing congruence $\sim$ and we want to extend it to a new one $\sim'$ such that $s \sim' t$. We need to merge the corresponding equivalence classes $[s]$ and $[t]$, and may also need to merge others such as $[f(s, t, f(s, s))]$ and $[f(t, t, f(s, t))]$ to maintain the congruence property. We can test whether two terms 'should be' equated by a 1-step congruence by checking if all their immediate subterms are already equivalent:

```
let congruent eqv (s,t) =
  match (s,t) with
    Fn(f,a1),Fn(g,a2) -> f = g & forall2 (equivalent eqv) a1 a2
  | _ -> false;;
```

For the main algorithm, as well as the equivalence relation itself, `eqv`, we maintain a 'predecessor function' `pfn` mapping each canonical representative s of an equivalence class C to the set of terms of which some $s' \in C$ is an immediate subterm. We can then direct our attention at the appropriate terms each time equivalence classes are merged. It is this (`eqv`,`pfn`) pair that is updated by the following `emerge` operation for a new equivalence $s \sim t$.

First we normalize $s \to s'$ and $t \to t'$ based on the current equivalence relation, and if they are already equated, we need do no more. Otherwise we obtain the sets of predecessors, `sp` and `tp`, of the two terms. We update the equivalence relation to `eqv'` to take account of the new equation, and combine the predecessor sets to update the predecessor function to `pfn'` (mapped from the new canonical representative `st'` in the new equivalence relation). Then we run over all pairs from `sp` and `tp`, recursively performing an `emerge` operation on terms that should become equated as a result of a single congruence step.

```
let rec emerge (s,t) (eqv,pfn) =
  let s' = canonize eqv s and t' = canonize eqv t in
  if s' = t' then (eqv,pfn) else
  let sp = tryapplyl pfn s' and tp = tryapplyl pfn t' in
  let eqv' = equate (s,t) eqv in
  let st' = canonize eqv' s' in
  let pfn' = (st' |-> union sp tp) pfn in
  itlist (fun (u,v) (eqv,pfn) ->
              if congruent eqv (u,v) then emerge (u,v) (eqv,pfn)
              else eqv,pfn)
        (allpairs (fun u v -> (u,v)) sp tp) (eqv',pfn');;
```

At least this algorithm must terminate, because each time it gets past the initial $s' = t'$ test it reduces the total number of equivalence classes, of which there can only be a finite number. We need to show that if the initial `eqv` is a congruence and `pfn` maps canonical representatives to the predecessor sets, the resulting equivalence relation is the congruence closure of `eqv` and the new equivalence $s \sim t$, and `pfn` is correspondingly updated.

The last part is easy, since `pfn` is always modified in step with direct changes in the equivalence relation from `equate`. As for congruence closure, we can see that the new equivalence relation certainly includes the original `eqv`, since all we do is add to it, and it also contains (s, t) because unless these terms were already equated, the very first `equate` call equates them. Moreover, because of the representation of equivalence classes, it is automatically closed under equivalence properties. We only need to show that it is also closed under congruences. Supposing otherwise, there must be two terms of the form $f(s_1, \ldots, s_n)$ and $f(t_1, \ldots, t_n)$ that are not equivalent, yet each pair (s_i, t_i) for $1 \leq i \leq n$ is. Since, by hypothesis, the initial `eqv` was congruence closed, at least one of these equivalences $s_i = t_i$ must have resulted from a call to `equate` from within `emerge`, and there must have been some such `equate` call at which *all* the pairs (s_i, t_i) became equated for the first time. However, by construction, this would be followed by a congruence check that would equate $f(s_1, \ldots, s_n)$ and $f(t_1, \ldots, t_n)$, a contradiction.

Equality decision procedure

We can use congruence closure to give a complete decision procedure for validity of universal formulas $\forall x_1, \ldots, x_n. \, P[x_1, \ldots, x_n]$ where $P[x_1, \ldots, x_n]$ involves no predicates besides equality, but may involve arbitrary function symbols. Such a formula is valid iff its negation $\exists x_1, \ldots, x_n. \, \neg P[x_1, \ldots, x_n]$ is unsatisfiable, and so, by Skolemization as usual, if $\neg P[c_1, \ldots, c_n]$ is unsatisfiable for new constants $c_1, \ldots, c_n$. If we put $\neg P[c_1, \ldots, c_n]$ into DNF:

$$Q_1[c_1, \ldots, c_n] \vee \cdots \vee Q_k[c_1, \ldots, c_n],$$

then, since no variables are involved, the whole formula is satisfiable precisely if one of the $Q_i[c_1, \ldots, c_n]$ is. Each such formula is just a conjunction of equations and inequations:

$$s_1 = t_1 \wedge \cdots \wedge s_n = t_n \wedge u_1 \neq v_1 \wedge \cdots \wedge u_m \neq v_m.$$

Returning to validity by negation, we need to test validity of

$$s_1 = t_1 \wedge \cdots \wedge s_n = t_n \Rightarrow u_1 = v_1 \vee \cdots \vee u_m = v_m.$$

If $m = 1$, we know from Theorem 4.8 that this can be tested by forming the congruence closure of $\sim$ of $\{(s_1, t_1), \ldots, (s_n, t_n)\}$ and testing if $u_1 \sim v_1$. We now observe that for general m, the formula is valid precisely if for some $1 \leq i \leq m$ the formula $s_1 = t_1 \wedge \cdots \wedge s_n = t_n \Rightarrow u_i = v_i$ is valid, by the convexity property for Horn clauses (Theorem 3.43), since we can consider the problem as deduction in first-order logic without equality from the (Horn) equality axioms and the hypotheses $s_k = t_k$. Alternatively, the proof of Theorem 4.8 extends easily to cover this generalization.

To set up the initial 'predecessor' function we use the following, which updates an existing function `pfn` with a new mapping for each immediate subterm `s` of a term `t`:

```
let predecessors t pfn =
  match t with
    Fn(f,a) -> itlist (fun s f -> (s |-> insert t (tryapplyl f s)) f)
                      (setify a) pfn
  | _ -> pfn;;
```

Hence, the following tests if a list **fms** of ground equations and inequations is satisfiable. This list is partitioned into equations (**pos**) and inequations (**neg**), which are mapped into lists of pairs of terms **eqps** and **eqns** for easier manipulation. All the left-hand and right-hand sides are collected in **lrs**, and the predecessor function **pfn** is constructed to handle all their sub-terms. (Note that it is only **pfn** that determines the overall term set.) Then congruence closure is performed starting with the trivial equivalence relation **unequal**, and iteratively calling **emerge** over all the positive equations. Then it is tested whether all the lefts and rights of all the negated equations are inequivalent.

```
let ccsatisfiable fms =
  let pos,neg = partition positive fms in
  let eqps = map dest_eq pos and eqns = map (dest_eq ** negate) neg in
  let lrs = map fst eqps @ map snd eqps @ map fst eqns @ map snd eqns in
  let pfn = itlist predecessors (unions(map subterms lrs)) undefined in
  let eqv,_ = itlist emerge eqps (unequal,pfn) in
  forall (fun (l,r) -> not(equivalent eqv l r)) eqns;;
```

The overall decision procedure now becomes the following:

```
let ccvalid fm =
  let fms = simpdnf(askolemize(Not(generalize fm))) in
  not (exists ccsatisfiable fms);;
```

Let us try a few examples. In this one, the first disjunct always holds, but we include another disjunct to show that we can deal with arbitrary formulas.

```
# ccvalid <<f(f(f(f(f(f(c)))))) = c /\ f(f(f(c))) = c
          ==> f(c) = c \/ f(g(c)) = g(f(c))>>;;
- : bool = true
```

On the other hand, the following is not valid:

```
# ccvalid <<f(f(f(f(c)))) = c /\ f(f(c)) = c ==> f(c) = c>>;;
- : bool = false
```

The congruence closure algorithm and its proof that we have presented essentially follows Nelson and Oppen (1980). There are asymptotically faster algorithms for congruence closure (Downey, Sethi and Tarjan 1980), but the Nelson–Oppen algorithm seems adequate for most typical examples. One drawback is that we need to decide the term universe once and for all based on the hypotheses and the goal. For some applications, it's preferable to be able to maintain the equivalence relation incrementally so that the relation can be augmented with new equalities *and* the term universe expanded as new goals are encountered, in which case another algorithm due to Shostak (1978) may be preferable.

The earliest decision procedure for this problem was given by Ackermann (1954) using a slightly different technique. He observed that matters can be reduced to the theory of equality without functions by introducing new variables for all subterms and adding new constraints to reflect congruence properties. For example, given the problem $f(f(f(c))) = c \land f(f(c)) = c \Rightarrow f(c) = c$, we could introduce variables $x_k = f^k(c)$ for $0 \leq k \leq 3$ and consider the problem:

$$(x_0 = x_1 \Rightarrow x_1 = x_2) \land$$
$$(x_0 = x_2 \Rightarrow x_1 = x_3) \land$$
$$(x_1 = x_2 \Rightarrow x_2 = x_3) \land$$
$$\Rightarrow x_3 = x_0 \land x_2 = x_0 \Rightarrow x_1 = x_0.$$

This *Ackermann reduction* can be taken still further by replacing the equations $s = t$ between variables by propositional atoms $P_{s,t}$ and adding further constraints to reflect equivalence properties like $P_{s,t} \land P_{t,u} \Rightarrow P_{s,u}$, so reducing the problem simply to propositional tautology checking (Exercise 4.4).

4.5 Rewriting

In the more general case of nonground equations, matters are no longer so simple. In order to find a Birkhoff proof of $s = t$ from hypotheses E, we may have to use arbitrarily large and complex intermediate terms. However, a lot of everyday equational reasoning is very straightforward, mostly using equations in a predictable direction. For example, we would normally think of using the group axiom $i(x) \cdot x = 1$ left-to-right in order to make expressions 'simpler'. It's precisely when we have to use it backwards to make a larger intermediate term that proofs tend to become much harder. (See the group theory puzzle in Section 4.3 for an example.) Admittedly the definition of what is 'simpler' can be subtle. For instance, in algebra we often regard using distributive laws to transform:

$$(u + v)(x + y) \rightarrow \cdots \rightarrow ux + uy + vx + vy$$

as a simplification. This makes the term larger, but it does makes it easier to perform subsequent cancellation operations. Using equations in a directional fashion like this is called *rewriting*, because equations are used to 'rewrite' one term into another.[†] More precisely, if t is a term, and $l = r$ an equation, we say that t' results from rewriting t with $l = r$ if t' is t with a subterm that is an instance of l replaced by a corresponding instance of r. Note that a single rewriting step only transforms a *single* subterm. For instance, the equation $x + x = 2x$ can rewrite the term $(a + a) + (b + b)$ into either $2a + (b + b)$ or to $(a + a) + 2b$, but not (in a single step) to $2a + 2b$.

Given a set R of equations to be considered as left-to-right rewrite rules, we write $t \rightarrow_R t'$ iff there is some equation $(l = r) \in R$ which rewrites t to t'. When the set of rewrites R is clear from the context, we may just write $t \rightarrow t'$. Note that rewriting is logically sound, in the sense that $t = t'$ holds in any model of the equations R, and we could if we wish decompose each rewriting step into a series of Birkhoff rule applications.

If we're trying to prove that $E \Rightarrow s = t$ where E is closed (a conjunction of universally quantified equations in the present situation), then by Theorem 3.11 we're justified in replacing all free variables in s and t by new constants. So we can if we wish always assume that the terms we're rewriting are ground. In principle, rewrite rules might have variables on the RHS that do not occur in the LHS (e.g. $y \cdot 0 = 0 \cdot x$), and this could make intermediate terms non-ground. However, as the reader might expect, these tend to spoil the nice properties of rewriting, and we will never use rewriting with such terms. In fact, many authors define a *rewrite rule* to be an equation $l = r$ where $\mathrm{FV}(r) \subseteq \mathrm{FV}(l)$ and l is not a variable. (A term with a variable LHS could be applied to any term, and is hence not likely to be controllable.)

Nevertheless, it's quite convenient to be able to rewrite arbitrary terms, first so that we don't have to transform the initial problem, and also because we sometimes want to rewrite some of the rewrite rules themselves with others. On the other hand, even if it does involve variables, we *don't* want to permit instantiation of the term being rewritten, since that would spoil the idea that we are simplifying a fixed term. The extension of rewriting to allow instantiation of the term being rewritten is known as *narrowing* (Fay 1979; Hullot 1980); it is a special case of *paramodulation* which we consider later.

[†] The first explicit use of rewriting seems to have been described by Wos, Robinson, Carson and Shalla (1967), and the original term 'demodulation' from that paper is still used instead of 'rewriting' in some parts of the resolution theorem proving community; see Section 4.9.

Canonical rewrite systems

Sometimes, a simplification procedure has the property that all 'equivalent' expressions reduce to the *same* simplified form. In such cases we can decide whether s and t are equivalent by reducing both s and t to their simplified forms s' and t' and then comparing s' and t' syntactically (Evans 1951). In equational reasoning with hypotheses E, it is natural to call s and t equivalent iff $E \models s = t$. We call E a *canonical* or *convergent* rewrite system when it can be decided whether $E \models s = t$ by treating E as a set of rewrite rules, repeatedly rewriting s and t as much as possible to give s' and t' respectively, and comparing the results. That is, we can rewrite each term to a 'canonical' or 'normal' form, so that all terms s and s' with $E \models s = s'$ have the same normal form. For example, the following set of rewrite rules can be thought of as embodying evaluation rules for addition of numbers written in terms of 0 and a successor operation S, though they have other models:

$$\{m + 0 = m, 0 + n = n, m + S(n) = S(m + n), S(m) + n = S(m + n)\}.$$

No intelligence or creativity is required: even where there are several possible ways of reducing a term, we cannot make an irrevocable wrong decision that will lead us away from the canonical form, e.g. reducing $S(0) + S(S(0))$ in this way:

$$\begin{aligned} S(0) + S(S(0)) &\to S(0 + S(S(0))) \\ &\to S(S(S(0))), \end{aligned}$$

or another:

$$\begin{aligned} S(0) + S(S(0)) &\to S(S(0) + S(0)) \\ &\to S(S(S(0) + 0)) \\ &\to S(S(S(0 + 0))) \\ &\to S(S(S(0))). \end{aligned}$$

Of course, from the point of view of *efficiency*, it may matter which rewrite we choose (e.g. if we have a rule $0 \cdot x = 0$, it makes sense to apply it to a term $0 \cdot E$ without performing reductions on E). And there are surprisingly simple rewrite systems that, although terminating in principle, can lead to infeasibly lengthy reduction sequences, e.g. (Hofbauer and Lautemann 1989):

$$\begin{aligned} \{\ f(x) + (y + z) &= x + (f(f(y)) + z), \\ f(u) + (v + (w + x)) &= u + (w + (v + x))\}. \end{aligned}$$

Let us neglect efficiency for now, and ask how canonicality can fail completely. Using the singleton set $\{x + y = y + x\}$ any subterm $a + b$ can be rewritten indefinitely, and for this reason that set is not canonical:

$$a + b \rightarrow b + a \rightarrow a + b \rightarrow b + a \rightarrow a + b \rightarrow \cdots$$

Rewriting with the following rewrite set:

$$\{\ x \cdot (y + z) = x \cdot y + x \cdot z, (x + y) \cdot z = x \cdot z + y \cdot z\}$$

can never be continued indefinitely (we will prove this later), but we may not get a well-defined result in that even the same term can sometimes be rewritten to different irreducible forms, e.g.

$$
\begin{aligned}
(a + b) \cdot (c + d) \ &\rightarrow a \cdot (c + d) + b \cdot (c + d) \\
&\rightarrow (a \cdot c + a \cdot d) + b \cdot (c + d) \\
&\rightarrow (a \cdot c + a \cdot d) + (b \cdot c + b \cdot d)
\end{aligned}
$$

or

$$
\begin{aligned}
(a + b) \cdot (c + d) \ &\rightarrow (a + b) \cdot c + (a + b) \cdot d \\
&\rightarrow (a \cdot c + b \cdot d) + (a + b) \cdot d \\
&\rightarrow (a \cdot c + b \cdot d) + (a \cdot d + b \cdot d).
\end{aligned}
$$

Abstract reduction relations

The examples above hint at two critical properties we need, roughly speaking:

- termination – starting from any term, we must eventually reach a form that can no longer be further reduced;
- confluence – starting from any term, if we apply the simplification rules in different orders to get different intermediate results, we can subsequently 'rejoin' them by further reductions.

We will now define these more precisely and show that together they give us the results we need. However, it's convenient to work in the more general context of an arbitrary binary relation on a set, rather than merely rewrite relations over terms. This helps to clarify the essential theoretical features without introducing technical complications, and also allows us to re-use some of the key results in a different context later on.[†] Our view is fairly pragmatic and we only scratch the surface of the subject; for a more thorough treatment see, for example, Klop (1992).

[†] See Section 5.11 on Gröbner bases. Many of these concepts were first articulated in contexts other than rewriting, e.g. reductions in untyped lambda calculus (Barendregt 1984; Hindley and Seldin 1986).

An abstract reduction relation is simply a binary relation R on a set X, though we jog our intuition by writing $x \to y$ instead of $R(x, y)$, and the reader may like to keep in mind the special case of rewrite relations. In the following, we denote by $\to^+$ the transitive closure of $\to$ and by $\to^*$ its reflexive transitive closure (see Appendix 1). That is, $x \to^+ y$ if there is a possibly-empty sequence of elements $x_i \in X$ with $x \to x_1 \to \cdots \to x_n \to y$, and $x \to^* y$ if $x \to^+ y$ or $x = y$.

An $x \in X$ is said to be in *normal form* iff there is no $y \in X$ with $x \to y$. In the context of rewriting, a term is in normal form w.r.t. $\to_R$ precisely when no rewrites from R can be applied to it. A reduction relation is said to be *terminating, strongly normalizing* (SN) or *noetherian* iff there is no infinite reduction sequence $x_0 \to \cdots \to x_n \to \cdots$.[†]

Considering the reverse relation defined by $x < y =_{\text{def}} y \to x$, we see that x is in normal form iff it is minimal with respect to $<$, and $\to$ is terminating precisely if $<$ is wellfounded. Thus, the two concepts just defined are familiar in another guise, and we can take over corresponding theorems with trivial changes. For example, the transitive closure of a terminating relation is also terminating, and we can perform induction over a terminating relation: if $\to$ is terminating and we can establish that $P(x)$ holds whenever $P(y)$ holds for all y such that $x \to y$, then we may conclude $P(x)$ for all $x \in X$. We'll apply this principle shortly. (Note that this includes the degenerate case of establishing $P(x)$ for all x in normal form.)

An abstract reduction relation is said to have the *diamond property* iff whenever $x \to y$ and $x \to y'$, there is a z such that $y \to z$ and $y' \to z$. It is said to be *confluent* if $\to^*$ has the diamond property. It is said to be *weakly confluent* if whenever $x \to y$ and $x \to y'$, there is a z such that $y \to^* z$ and $y' \to^* z$. We say for short that x and y are *joinable*, and write $x \downarrow y$, to mean that there is a z with $x \to^* z$ and $y \to^* z$, so we can express confluence as 'if $x \to^* y_1$ and $x \to^* y_2$ then $y_1 \downarrow y_2$' and weak confluence as 'if $x \to y_1$ and $x \to y_2$ then $y_1 \downarrow y_2$'.

The name 'diamond property' comes from the convenient diagrammatic representation of reductions as descending diagonal lines moving from the first element to the second. Thus the forms of confluence all assert that given reductions from x to both y and y', there is a z with reductions from both y and y' to z; the forms only differ in whether we have $\to$ or $\to^*$ at the top or bottom.

[†] Weak normalization (WN) means that for each x there is a y in normal form such that $x \to^* y$. We won't use this concept but it seems worth noting the distinction in case the reader wants to delve deeper into such material.

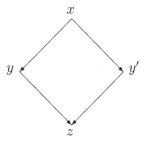

All the variations on a theme of confluence are closely interrelated. If
→ has the diamond property, it is weakly confluent, since $y \to z$ trivially
implies $y \to^* z$. For similar reasons, confluence implies weak confluence. It
is not much harder to see that the diamond property implies confluence, by
double induction on the lengths of the initial reduction sequences $x \to^* y$
and $x \to^* y'$. For example, if we have a 2-step reduction $x \to y_1 \to y_2$ and
a 3-step reduction $x \to y_3 \to y_4 \to y_5$ we can show that there is a z with
$y_2 \to^* z$ and $y_5 \to^* z$ by repeatedly using the diamond property to fill in
the internal lines in this diagram, starting at the top and ending with some
suitable z:

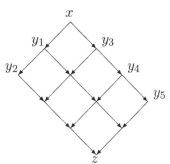

On the other hand, weak confluence does not in general imply confluence;
the following is a particularly simple counterexample due to Hindley. (One
can think of this as specifying a term rewriting system where a, b, c and
d are all constants, or simply as an exhaustive enumeration of an abstract
binary relation.)

$$b \;\to\; a$$
$$b \;\to\; c$$
$$c \;\to\; b$$
$$c \;\to\; d$$

Still, for a *terminating* reduction relation, weak confluence does imply confluence. This key result is known as *Newman's lemma*. The original proof (Newman 1942) was rather complicated, and it was only much later that Huet (1980) pointed out the following relatively straightforward proof, exploiting the fact that when $\rightarrow$ is terminating we can perform wellfounded induction.

Theorem 4.9 *If $\rightarrow$ is terminating and weakly confluent, then it is confluent.*

Proof Since $\rightarrow$ is terminating, all reduction sequences terminate, so we just need to prove that if $x \rightarrow^* y$ and $x \rightarrow^* y'$ with y and y' in normal form, then $y = y'$. We will prove this by wellfounded induction: suppose x is the minimal element such that for some y and y' this fails.

The assertion is vacuous if $x = y$ or $x = y'$, so we can assume the existence of w and w' such that $x \rightarrow w \rightarrow^* y$ and $x \rightarrow w' \rightarrow^* y'$. Weak confluence tells us that there's a z with $w \rightarrow^* z$ and $w' \rightarrow^* z$; by continuing the reduction as much as possible we can assume z to be in normal form. But by the fact that y and y' are successors of x and x was the minimal case where the key property fails, we have $y = z$ and $y' = z$, and so $y' = y$ as required. $\qquad\square$

Let us write $\leftrightarrow^*$ for the reflexive *symmetric* transitive closure of $\rightarrow$. We say that $\rightarrow$ is *Church–Rosser* if whenever $x \leftrightarrow^* y$ then $x \downarrow y$.[†] We will prove in fact that the Church–Rosser property is equivalent to confluence, so the two terms may be, and sometimes are, used synonymously. In one direction this is easy, since confluence is a special case of the Church–Rosser property: if $x \rightarrow^* y_1$ and $x \rightarrow^* y_2$ then $y_1 \leftrightarrow^* y_2$. In the other direction, if $x \leftrightarrow^* y$ then we can get from x to y by a series of steps that we can separate into alternating 'forward' and 'backward' segments,

$$x \cdots \rightarrow^* x_i \leftarrow^* x_{i+1} \rightarrow^* x_{i+2} \leftarrow^* \cdots y.$$

Because of confluence, we can at each stage find a suitable z_i such that $x_i \rightarrow^* z_i$ and $x_{i+2} \rightarrow^* z_i$ and hence successively reduce the number of segments, filling in the internal sides in the diagram until we eventually reach a final z with $x \rightarrow^* z$ and $y \rightarrow^* z$.

[†] The peculiar name 'Church–Rosser' arises from the fact that the first significant instance was proved for the case of β-reduction in lambda calculus by Church and Rosser (1936).

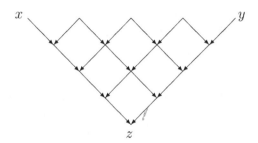

In what follows, we recast this argument as a formal induction. Note that we do *not* need to assume termination to show that interconvertible elements are joinable.

Theorem 4.10 *Confluence is equivalent to the Church–Rosser property, i.e. $\rightarrow$ is confluent if and only if for any x and y we have $x \leftrightarrow^* y$ iff $x \downarrow y$.*

Proof Since $x \downarrow y$ is a special case of $x \leftrightarrow^* y$, we just need to prove that confluence is equivalent to 'if $x \leftrightarrow^* y$ then $x \downarrow y$'. As noted above, the right-to-left direction is easy because confluence is a special case of the Church–Rosser property. For the other direction, we proceed by induction on the definition $x \leftrightarrow^* y$. If we actually have $x \rightarrow y$ then trivially $x \downarrow y$ because $x \rightarrow^* y$ and $y \rightarrow^* y$. Even more trivially, if x and y are identical, they are joinable. If $x \leftrightarrow^* y$ is obtained by symmetry from $y \leftrightarrow^* x$, then by the inductive hypothesis $y \downarrow x$, and since joinability is symmetric between x and y we have $x \downarrow y$. Finally, if $x \leftrightarrow^* y$ arises by transitivity from $x \leftrightarrow^* z$ and $z \leftrightarrow^* y$, we have by the inductive hypothesis some u and v with $x \rightarrow^* u$, $z \rightarrow^* u$ and $z \rightarrow^* v$, $y \rightarrow^* v$. Using confluence, there is a z such that $u \rightarrow^* z$ and $v \rightarrow^* z$. By transitivity of $\rightarrow^*$, we therefore have $x \rightarrow^* z$ and $y \rightarrow^* z$ as required.   □

Another useful lemma about joinability is the following.

Lemma 4.11 *A reduction relation $\rightarrow$ is confluent iff the corresponding joinability relation is transitive, i.e. for all x, y and z such that $x \downarrow y$ and $y \downarrow z$ we have $x \downarrow z$.*

Proof If $\rightarrow$ is confluent, the previous result shows that $x \downarrow y$ coincides with $x \leftrightarrow^* y$, and the latter is clearly transitive. (It's also easy to reason more directly.)

Conversely, suppose joinability is transitive. If $p \to^* q_1$ and $p \to^* q_2$ then $p \downarrow q_1$ and $p \downarrow q_2$. Using the obvious symmetry and assumed transitivity of $\downarrow$, we see that $q_1 \downarrow q_2$ so the relation is confluent.   □

We say that a reduction relation is *canonical* when it is both terminating and confluent. Note that if $\to$ is canonical, then whenever $x \to^* x'$ and $y \to^* y'$ with x' and y' in normal form, we have $x \leftrightarrow^* y$ iff $x' = y'$. In the special case of a rewrite relation, this justifies exactly the kind of process for testing $E \models s = t$ that we outlined at the start of this section, by virtue of the following theorem.

Theorem 4.12 *For a rewrite relation $\to_R$ generated by a set of rewrites R, for all terms s and t we have $s \leftrightarrow_R^* t$ iff $R \models s = t$.*

Proof One way is relatively easy: if $s \to_R t$ then $R \models s = t$ because t results from replacing s according to an equation in R. By induction, the same applies when $s \leftrightarrow_R^* t$.

Conversely, if $R \models s = t$ then by Theorem 4.7 we have $R \vdash s = t$. We will show by induction on the Birkhoff rules that if $R \vdash s = t$ then also $s \leftrightarrow_R^* t$. Closure of $\leftrightarrow_R^*$ under reflexivity, symmetry and transitivity is immediate, and if $(s = t) \in R$ then by a trivial rewrite step $s \leftrightarrow_R^* t$. We will be finished if we can establish that $\leftrightarrow_R^*$ is closed under congruence and instantiation. Both of these follow (formally, by another induction) by systematically applying the congruence or instantiation to all elements in the transitivity chain, since the core rewrite relation $\to_R$ is closed in this way.   □

Implementing rewriting

To rewrite a term t at the top level with an equation $l = r$ we just attempt to match l to t and apply the corresponding instantiation to r; the following does this with the first in a list of equations to succeed:

```
let rec rewrite1 eqs t =
  match eqs with
    Atom(R("=",[l;r]))::oeqs ->
      (try tsubst (term_match undefined [l,t]) r
      with Failure _ -> rewrite1 oeqs t)
  | _ -> failwith "rewrite1";;
```

Our interest is in rewriting at all subterms, and repeatedly, to normalize a term w.r.t. a set of equations. Although, for theoretical reasons, in particular for applying Newman's Lemma, it's important to single out the 'one-step' (though at depth) rewrite relation $\rightarrow_R$, from an implementation point of view we needn't bother isolating it. The following function simply applies rewrites at all possible subterms and repeatedly until no further rewrites are possible. The user is responsible for ensuring that the rewrites terminate, and if this is not the case this function may loop indefinitely. Where several rewrites could be applied, the leftmost outermost subterm in the term being rewritten is always preferred, and thereafter the first applicable equation in the list of rewrites. Alternative strategies such as choosing the innermost rewritable subterm would work equally well in our applications.

```
let rec rewrite eqs tm =
  try rewrite eqs (rewrite1 eqs tm) with Failure _ ->
  match tm with
    Var x -> tm
  | Fn(f,args) -> let tm' = Fn(f,map (rewrite eqs) args) in
                  if tm' = tm then tm else rewrite eqs tm';;
```

Here's a simple example, evaluating $3 * 2 + 4$ in the zero-successor representation of numerals:

```
rewrite [<<0 + x = x>>; <<S(x) + y = S(x + y)>>;
         <<0 * x = 0>>; <<S(x) * y = y + x * y>>]
        <<|S(S(S(0))) * S(S(0)) + S(S(S(S(0))))|>>;;
- : term = <<|S(S(S(S(S(S(S(S(S(S(0)))))))))|>>
```

It is in general undecidable whether a particular set of equations, used as a rewrite system, is terminating, either for some particular reduction strategy or for all strategies. Indeed, one can express arbitrary algorithms as rewrite systems in a manner not unlike the clausal pattern-matching that is typical in functional programming languages.[†] The analogy is not exact, since functional languages tend to have many additional constructs and a particular evaluation strategy. On the other hand, in one respect the standard clausal function definitions are simpler than general rewrite rules because they are *linear*, meaning that each variable occurs at most once on the left-hand side. (For example, OCaml will reject a function definition 'function (x,x) -> 0' because the variable x is bound twice in the pattern.) There is a substantial literature on the theory of linear rewrite rules; they turn out to be in certain respects 'better behaved' than general rewrite rules. In particular, it is more straightforward to analyze their

---

[†] To see that *any* algorithm can be suitably encoded, one can observe that SK combinator reduction is just a pair of rewrite rules, and it is known that SK combinators can encode all computable functions (Hindley and Seldin 1986). In practice one can often use more direct encodings (see Exercise 4.7).

confluence without assuming termination. The connection with functional programming is examined in detail by Huet and Lévy (1991).

4.6 Termination orderings

One way of showing that a reduction $\rightarrow$ is terminating is to show that it is included in another relation $>$ (i.e. whenever $s \rightarrow t$ we also have $s > t$) that is itself terminating. For a suitable $>$, this can be more tractable than a direct attack on $\rightarrow$. In particular, for a rewrite relation, things are much more straightforward when it suffices to consider $l > r$ for the equations $(l = r) \in R$ themselves, rather than the induced rewrite relationship, which may involve instantiations and substitution at an arbitrary (single) subterm. This motivates the following definition.

Definition 4.13 *A binary relation $>$ on terms is said to be a* rewrite order *if it is transitive and irreflexive and is closed under instantiation and simple congruences (within a fixed set of function symbols understood implicitly), i.e.*

- *it is never the case that $t > t$,*
- *if $s > t$ and $t > u$ then $s > u$,*
- *if $s > t$ then* tsubst $i\ s >$ tsubst $i\ t$,
- *if $s > t$ then*

$$f(u_1, \ldots, u_{i-1}, s, u_{i+1}, \ldots, u_n) > f(u_1, \ldots, u_{i-1}, t, u_{i+1}, \ldots, u_n).$$

A rewrite order that is terminating is said to be a *reduction order*. Note that in this case the irreflexivity clause is redundant since a wellfounded relation is automatically irreflexive (if $t > t$ then $t > t > t > \cdots$ would be an infinite descending chain).

Lemma 4.14 *If $>$ is a reduction order and $l > r$ for each equation $(l = r) \in R$, then the rewrite relation $\rightarrow_R$ is terminating.*

Proof By definition $s \rightarrow_R t$ if there is some instantiation $l' = r'$ of an equation $(l = r) \in R$ such that t results from s by replacing a single instance of l' with r'. By hypothesis, $l > r$, and since $>$ is closed under instantiation $l' > r'$. Repeatedly using the fact that $>$ is closed under simple congruences, we see that $s > t$. Therefore, the rewrite relation $\rightarrow_R$ is included in the relation $>$ and is consequently also terminating. $\qquad \square$

Measure-based orders

How do we find a suitable reduction order for a given rewrite set? One of the standard techniques for generating wellfounded relations is to use a measure function to map into a familiar wellfounded set such as $\mathbb{N}$, using the fact that if $<$ is wellfounded then so is the relation defined by $x \prec y =_{\text{def}} m(x) < m(y)$. In our context, a natural idea is to consider the 'size' of terms. Denote by $|t|$ the number of variables and function symbols in t, which we can compute like this:

```
let rec termsize tm =
  match tm with
    Var x -> 1
  | Fn(f,args) -> itlist (fun t n -> termsize t + n) args 1;;
```

We might hope to define a reduction order $s > t$ by $|s| > |t|$. Since the size is always a positive integer, this is wellfounded and is also transitive and obeys the congruence property. However, it fails the instantiation property; for example $f(x, x, x) > g(x, y)$ but if we instantiate y to $f(x, x, x)$ we have $f(x, x, x) \not> g(x, f(x, x, x))$. A little thought will convince the reader that it's the presence of variables that occur more often in the smaller term than the larger term that is the source of the problem. One can fix this by defining $s > t$ if both $|s| > |t|$ *and* $|s|_x \geq |t|_x$ for each $x \in \text{FVT}(t)$, where $|t|_x$ denotes the number of occurrences of x in t. However, although this does yield a reduction order (as the reader can confirm), it's poorly suited to the kinds of equations we often encounter in algebraic theories. Two typical examples are associative and distributive laws:

- $(x \cdot y) \cdot z = x \cdot (y \cdot z)$,
- $x \cdot (y + z) = x \cdot y + x \cdot z$.

Both sides of the associative law have equal measure, so we can't use the size-based ordering whichever way round it's written. And for the distributive law things are even worse: the right-hand side is larger than the left, despite the fact that we might want to consider expanding using it left-to-right.

Lexicographic path orders

These problems with simple measure-based orders suggest that to deal with typical algebraic examples, we need first to be able to:

- treat the arguments to functions asymmetrically, so that applying the associative law in one preferred direction is possible;

- treat the function symbols asymmetrically so that we can say, for example, that replacing the top-level function symbol f by g represents 'progress', even if the term grows in size.

It is possible to do both of these things with more elaborate measure-based orderings. However, the most direct method is simply to define an ordering on terms by recursion, explicitly designed to 'force' the required properties. To deal with the associative law, for example, we can say that:

- $f(s_1, \ldots, s_m) > f(t_1, \ldots, t_m)$ if the sequence $s_1, \ldots, s_m$ is lexicographically greater than $t_1, \ldots, t_m$, i.e. if $s_i = t_i$ for all $i < k \leq m$ and $s_k > t_k$ under the same ordering.

This ensures that $(x \cdot y) \cdot z > x \cdot (y \cdot z)$ provided $x \cdot y > x$. It's natural to also arrange more generally that $s > t$ whenever t is a proper subterm of s. It's more in keeping with the structurally recursive nature of the other clauses if we just specify it for immediate subterms; the general result then follows by induction. Note that this includes the special case that if t is a variable x we have $s > x$ whenever $x \in \mathrm{FVT}(s)$, excluding the reflexive case when $s = x$.

- $f(s_1, \ldots, s_n) > t$ whenever $s_i \geq t$.

Finally, in order to impose a precedence on function symbols, allowing us to deal with the distributive law by 'preferring' '$\cdot$' to '$+$' or vice versa, we can stipulate:

- $f(s_1, \cdots, s_m) > g(t_1, \ldots, t_n)$ if $f > g$ according to some specified precedence ordering of the function symbols, without further analysis of the s_i and t_i.

These desiderata are almost enough to allow us to define the ordering directly by recursion. However, as it stands the requirements are stated too bluntly and are not enough to ensure termination. For example, instead of the correct distributive law, consider $x \cdot (y + z) = x \cdot (z + y) + z$. The LHS is still greater than the RHS according to the ordering as specified so far, but it is nonterminating. We therefore refine things slightly to ensure that the proper subterms of the RHS must also be less than the starting term on the left, i.e. that $f(s_1, \ldots, s_m) > g(t_1, \ldots, t_n)$ (whether or not $f = g$) only if in addition $f(s_1, \ldots, s_m) > t_i$ for each $1 \leq i \leq n$. It isn't immediately obvious that this fix is enough to ensure termination, but we will prove it below. The resulting order is called the *lexicographic path order* (LPO). More properly, it specifies a whole class of LPOs parametrized by the particular 'weighting' of function symbols chosen. We can render the definition in OCaml quite directly. First we define the general lexicographic extension of an arbitrary relation ord. It always returns falsity when applied to lists of different lengths; this feature is exploited below.

```
let rec lexord ord l1 l2 =
  match (l1,l2) with
    (h1::t1,h2::t2) -> if ord h1 h2 then length t1 = length t2
                       else h1 = h2 & lexord ord t1 t2
  | _ -> false;;
```

Now we define the irreflexive and reflexive versions of the LPO, both of which are parametrized by a 'weighting' w on function symbols, where w (f, n) (g, m) decides whether the n-ary function f is 'bigger' than the m-ary function symbol g. We will sloppily write $f > g$ for this below, but note from a formal point of view that we treat as distinct function symbols with the same name but different arity.[†]

```
let rec lpo_gt w s t =
  match (s,t) with
    (_,Var x) ->
        not(s = t) & mem x (fvt s)
  | (Fn(f,fargs),Fn(g,gargs)) ->
        exists (fun si -> lpo_ge w si t) fargs or
        forall (lpo_gt w s) gargs &
        (f = g & lexord (lpo_gt w) fargs gargs or
         w (f,length fargs) (g,length gargs))
  | _ -> false

and lpo_ge w s t = (s = t) or lpo_gt w s t;;
```

Specifying the ordering on function symbols, arities and all, is quite a tedious business. We define the following function to generate a weight function from a more convenient starting point: a list of function symbols in increasing order of precedence. In the (unexpected) case when functions are identical but arities different, we disambiguate by treating functions with larger arity as 'greater':

```
let weight lis (f,n) (g,m) = if f = g then n > m else earlier lis g f;;
```

[†] This is just for theoretical reasons; we will never actually work with terms containing identically-named function symbols with different arities. In fact we could ignore arities for our present purposes. But for some applications, it is important that the LPO be total on ground terms, and $f(c, c)$ and $f(c)$ would be incomparable if we ignored arities. A common alternative is to use a more general notion of lexicographic extension.

Properties of the LPO

Although the LPO is a more or less natural embodiment of the desiderata we outlined, with fixes to counter the obvious failures of termination, it isn't at all obvious that the final result is terminating, or indeed satisfies other reduction order properties such as transitivity. In fact, if there are infinitely many function symbols with a nonterminating sequence of weights $w(f_1) > w(f_2) > \cdots$, then the LPO is not terminating, but we usually implicitly assume a finite set of function symbols, those that occur in the finitely many formulas we are dealing with. In this case, we will establish that the LPO is a reduction order. Most of the proofs that follow are by induction on the (total) sizes of the terms involved followed by an analysis of the cases in the LPO definition.

Lemma 4.15 *If $s > t$ then $FVT(t) \subseteq FVT(s)$.*

Proof By induction on $|s| + |t|$. If t is a variable x then $s > x$ means that $x \in FVT(s)$ and therefore $FVT(x) = \{x\} \subseteq FVT(s)$, so the result holds. If s is a variable then $s > t$ is false and the result holds trivially. Otherwise we can assume s is of the form $f(s_1, \ldots, s_n)$ and t of the form $g(t_1, \ldots, t_m)$. One way that $s > t$ can arise is if some $s_i \geq t$. But then $FVT(t) \subseteq FVT(s_i)$ by the inductive hypothesis and since $FVT(s_i) \subseteq FVT(s)$ we have $FVT(t) \subseteq FVT(s)$ as required. Otherwise, whatever the relation between f and g we always have $s > t_i$ for $1 \leq i \leq m$. Consequently, by the inductive hypothesis each $FVT(t_i) \subseteq FVT(s)$ and therefore $FVT(t) = \bigcup_{1 \leq i \leq n} FVT(t_i) \subseteq FVT(s)$ as required. $\square$

Theorem 4.16 *The LPO is transitive.*

Proof By induction on the total term size $|s| + |t| + |u|$, we show that if $s > t$ and $t > u$ then $s > u$. We sometime use variants of the inductive hypothesis such as the inference that if $s > t \geq u$ then $s > u$. This is an easy consequence since if $t \geq u$ either $t = u$ or $t > u$.

Suppose first that u is a variable x. In this case we have $x \in FVT(t)$ and $x \neq t$ by definition. But by Lemma 4.15 we also have $FVT(t) \subseteq FVT(s)$ and so $x \in FVT(s)$. We can also rule out $x = s$ because $x > t$ could not then hold. Consequently $s > u$ in this case.

Now assume u is of the form $h(u_1, \ldots, u_p)$. Since we never have $x > u$ it must be the case that t is also of the form $g(t_1, \ldots, t_n)$ and similarly s of the form $f(s_1, \ldots, s_m)$. We now consider the various ways in which $s > t$ and $t > u$ could arise.

First, suppose $f(s_1, \ldots, s_m) > g(t_1, \ldots, t_n)$ arises because for some $1 \le i \le m$ we have $s_i \ge g(t_1, \ldots, t_n) = t$. By the inductive hypothesis, $s_i \ge t > u$ implies $s_i > u$, so a fortiori $s_i \ge u$ and therefore also $s > u$ by the definition of the LPO. There now just remains the case where, whatever the relation between f and g, we have $s > t_i$ for each $1 \le i \le n$.

Now suppose $g(t_1, \ldots, t_n) > h(u_1, \ldots, u_p)$ arises because for some $1 \le i \le n$ we have $t_i \ge h(u_1, \ldots, u_p) = u$. Since $s > t_i$ the inductive hypothesis yields $s > u$ as required.

Otherwise, we may now assume $t > u_i$ for each $1 \le i \le p$, and also that $f \ge g \ge h$. By the inductive hypothesis we have $s > u_i$ for each $1 \le i \le p$, so the additional condition on $s > u$ is satisfied. If $f > h$, therefore, we have $s > u$ immediately. Otherwise we have $f = g = h$, $m = n = p$ and the lexicographic relations:

$$(s_1, \ldots, s_p) >_{\text{LEX}} (t_1, \ldots, t_p) >_{\text{LEX}} (u_1, \ldots, u_p).$$

By the inductive hypothesis, $s_i > t_j$ and $t_j > u_k$ implies $s_i > u_k$ for any such triple from these subterms. Therefore we also have transitivity of the lexicographic extension and $(s_1, \ldots, s_p) >_{\text{LEX}} (u_1, \ldots, u_p)$, yielding $s > u$ as required. $\qquad\square$

Theorem 4.17 *The LPO has the subterm property, i.e. if t is a proper subterm of s then $s > t$.*

Proof Now that we know $>$ is transitive, the result follows by induction on the size of s if we can prove the special case $f(s_1, \ldots, s_{i-1}, t, s_{i+1}, \ldots, s_n) > t$. If t is a variable this holds by definition. Otherwise it is also immediate from the definition since $t \ge t$. $\qquad\square$

Theorem 4.18 *The LPO is closed under substitutions, i.e. if $s > t$ then for any instantiation σ we have* tsubst σ s > tsubst σ t.

Proof Fix an instantiation σ; for any term u we will consistently abbreviate $u' = $ tsubst σ u. We proceed by induction on $|s| + |t|$. If t is a variable x we have $x \in \text{FVT}(s)$ so x' is a subterm of s'; since we also have $x \ne s$ it is a *proper* subterm and the result follows from the subterm property.

Otherwise, neither s nor t can be a variable, so we can suppose that s is of the form $f(s_1, \ldots, s_m)$ and t is also of the form $g(t_1, \ldots, t_n)$. Consider the ways in which $s > t$ can arise. If $s_i > t$ for $1 \le i \le m$ we have by the inductive hypothesis that $s_i' > t'$. Since s_i' is a proper subterm of s', it follows by transitivity that $s' > t'$. Otherwise the auxiliary condition $s > t_i$

for $1 \leq i \leq n$ implies by the inductive hypothesis that the corresponding condition $s' > t'_i$ holds. If $f > g$ then the required result is immediate. If $f = g$, $m = n$ then we have $(s_1, \ldots, s_m) >_{\text{LEX}} (t_1, \ldots, t_n)$. This means that there is some $1 \leq i \leq n$ such that $s_j = t_j$ for $j < i$ and $s_i > t_i$. Trivially, then $s'_j = t'_j$ for $j < i$ and by the inductive hypothesis $s'_i > t'_i$, thus showing $(s'_1, \ldots, s'_m) >_{\text{LEX}} (t'_1, \ldots, t'_n)$ and hence $s' > t'$ as required. $\qquad\square$

Theorem 4.19 *The LPO is a congruence w.r.t. the function symbols, i.e. if $t > u$ then* $f(s_1, \ldots, s_{i-1}, t, s_{i+1}, \ldots, s_n) > f(s_1, \ldots, s_{i-1}, u, s_{i+1}, \ldots, s_n)$

Proof $(s_1, \ldots, s_{i-1}, t, s_{i+1}, \ldots, s_n) >_{\text{LEX}} (s_1, \ldots, s_{i-1}, u, s_{i+1}, \ldots, s_n)$ since $t > u$ and all preceding terms are identical. Moreover, most of the auxiliary condition follows from the fact that $f(s_1, \ldots, s_{i-1}, t, s_{i+1}, \ldots, s_n) > s_j$ for $j \in \{1, \ldots, i-1, i+1, \ldots, n\}$, while $f(s_1, \ldots, s_{i-1}, t, s_{i+1}, \ldots, s_n) > u$ is immediate from transitivity given the hypothesis $t > u$ and the subterm property $f(s_1, \ldots, s_{i-1}, t, s_{i+1}, \ldots, s_n) > t$ proved previously. $\qquad\square$

Theorem 4.20 *The LPO is irreflexive, i.e. $t > t$ never holds.*

Proof By induction on the size of t. If t is a variable then $t > t$ is false by definition because of the $x \neq t$ clause in the definition. If on the other hand we have $t = f(t_1, \ldots, t_n)$, then $t > t$ can only arise because of lexicographic extension $(t_1, \ldots, t_n) >_{\text{LEX}} (t_1, \ldots, t_n)$. But by the inductive hypothesis we never have $t_i > t_i$ for $1 \leq i \leq n$ and there could be no 'first' i such that this holds. $\qquad\square$

Tedious as those proofs were, they were mostly a question of following one's nose. Termination, however, is a bit more subtle, though not much more difficult if approached in the right way, using a *minimality* trick. Our proof here is inspired by Ferreira and Zantema (1995); for another relatively short proof see Buchholz (1995).

Theorem 4.21 *The LPO, restricted to terms based on a finite set of function symbols, is terminating.*

Proof If there exists an infinite descending chain at all, there exists one $t_0 > t_1 > t_2 > \cdots$ that is *minimal* in the sense that each term has minimal size among those that could possibly appear at that point in an infinite descending chain. More precisely, let us say that a term t is *nonwellfounded* if there is an infinite descending chain starting with t. We will show that if there is a descending chain, then there is one $t_0 > t_1 > t_2 > \cdots$ with the following properties:

- $|t_0| \leq |s|$ for all nonwellfounded terms s,
- $|t_{i+1}| \leq |s|$ for all nonwellfounded terms s with $t_i > s$.

To show that such a chain exists, proceed by recursion on i. If there is an infinite descending chain, then there is some nonwellfounded element. Let t_0 be one of minimal size (this is not in general unique). Now, having defined a sequence $t_0 > t_1 > \cdots > t_i$ with t_i nonwellfounded, there must be some nonwellfounded s with $t_i > s$ (otherwise t_i would be wellfounded). Again, we can simply pick the minimal one as t_{i+1}.

Now, we never have $t > x$ for a variable x, and so no variable is nonwellfounded and so none of the t_i can be a variable. And since the number of function symbols is by hypothesis finite, there must be at least one function symbol (with particular arity n) that occurs infinitely often as the top-level function in the t_i. We can define a subsequence, i.e. an increasing function $k : \mathbb{N} \to \mathbb{N}$, such that each t_{k_i} is of the form $f(u_1^i, \ldots, u_n^i)$. Now, by the minimality hypothesis, none of the u_j^i can be nonwellfounded, and by transitivity we have $f(u_1^i, \ldots, u_n^i) > f(u_1^{i+1}, \ldots, u_n^{i+1})$ for each i.

Consider the ways in which this can happen according to the definition of the LPO. We cannot have any $u_j^i > f(u_1^{i+1}, \ldots, u_n^{i+1})$, for that would contradict minimality of t_{k_i}. Since the function symbols are the same, we must have $(u_1^i, \ldots, u_n^i) > (u_1^{i+1}, \ldots, u_n^{i+1})$ lexicographically for each i. However the LPO restricted to all the terms u_j^i is wellfounded, and therefore so is its lexicographic extension. We thus arrive at a contradiction. $\square$

A rewrite order with the subterm property ($s > t$ whenever t is a proper subterm of s) is said to be a *simplification order*. Surprisingly, a simplification order turns out to be automatically terminating and hence a reduction order (Dershowitz 1979); by appealing to this result, we could have avoided the direct proof that the LPO is terminating. Typically, one proves relations wellfounded by means of mappings into a wellfounded set like $\mathbb{N}$. But provided the properties of a simplification order hold, mappings into other sets like $\mathbb{R}$ can be useful.

4.7 Knuth–Bendix completion

Suppose we know, perhaps via a suitable ordering as in the previous section, that a rewrite system R is terminating. This is a great help in deciding confluence, because of Newman's lemma (Theorem 4.9): $\to_R$ is confluent, and hence canonical, iff it is locally confluent. Analyzing local confluence can be much more tractable than a direct attack on full confluence, because we only need to consider two individual rewrite steps $s \to_R t_1$ and $s \to_R t_2$ and decide whether $t_1 \downarrow_R t_2$. Consider, for example, the following axioms for groups, which can be seen to constitute a terminating rewrite set R using a suitable LPO:

$$(x \cdot y) \cdot z = x \cdot (y \cdot z),$$
$$1 \cdot x = x,$$
$$i(x) \cdot x = 1.$$

We can rewrite the term $(1 \cdot x) \cdot y$ in two different ways, either by the first equation to:

$$(1 \cdot x) \cdot y \to_R 1 \cdot (x \cdot y)$$

or by the second equation to:

$$(1 \cdot x) \cdot y \to_R x \cdot y.$$

However, these are joinable, because we can make an additional rewrite to the first result by the second equation and get $1 \cdot (x \cdot y) \to_R x \cdot y$. On the other hand, if we start from the term $(i(x) \cdot x) \cdot y$, we can rewrite with the first equation to get

$$(i(x) \cdot x) \cdot y \to_R i(x) \cdot (x \cdot y)$$

or by the third to get

$$(i(x) \cdot x) \cdot y \to_R 1 \cdot y.$$

The first term is already in R-normal form, and the only further reduct of the second term is $1 \cdot y \to y$, which is not the same. Consequently, the terms are not joinable so R is not (even locally) confluent.

This example suggests how, given any terminating rewrite set (with a finite number of equations) we can decide its local confluence. We need to discover whether any starting terms s give rise via $s \to_R t_1$ and $s \to_R t_2$ to non-joinable reducts t_1 and t_2. Because R is terminating, joinability of any given t_1 and t_2 can be shown to be decidable, since there are only finitely many possible terms to which each can be rewritten.[†] In fact, with confluence as the overall aim, the situation is even simpler: we need only reduce t_1 and t_2 in some arbitrary way to normal forms t_1' and t_2' and compare them. If they are the same, this particular pair of terms is

---

[†] This follows at once from König's lemma, which states that a finitely-branching tree without an infinite path has only finitely many nodes. This can be proved simply by wellfounded induction.

joinable, while if they are different we can conclude at once that the whole rewrite set is non-confluent (and hence not locally confluent either) without examining any other possibilities.

Critical pairs

At first sight, this still doesn't help much because we need to consider an arbitrary starting term s, of which there are infinitely many. However it turns out that we can decide local confluence by examining a finite number of critical situations where rewrites can interfere with each other and lead to the failure of local confluence. When $s \to_R t_1$ and $s \to_R t_2$ we can distinguish three possibilities.

- The two rewrites apply to disjoint subterms, for example $(1 \cdot x) \cdot (i(y) \cdot y)$ to $x \cdot (i(y) \cdot y)$ and to $(1 \cdot x) \cdot 1$,
- One rewrite applies to a term that is a (not necessarily proper) subterm of a term to which a variable is instantiated in the other rewrite. For example $((1 \cdot x) \cdot y) \cdot z$ can be rewritten either to $(1 \cdot x) \cdot (y \cdot z)$ or to $(x \cdot y) \cdot z$, but the subterm $1 \cdot x$ to which the second rewrite is applied is exactly the subterm to which x is instantiated in the first rewrite $(x \cdot y) \cdot z \to x \cdot (y \cdot z)$.
- One rewrite applies to a term that is inside the term to which the other rewrite applies, but is not at or below a variable position. Examples include the two rewrites to $(1 \cdot x) \cdot y$ given near the start of this section.

It is only the third situation, when the rewritten subterms are said to 'overlap',[†] that non-confluence can occur, because in the first two cases the subterm to which the other rewrite is applicable is not structurally changed by the chosen rewrite, though in the second case it may be removed or duplicated. Let us analyze this more precisely. Consider the application of two rewrite rules $l_1 = r_1$ and $l_2 = r_2$ to subterms l_1' and l_2' of a term s, replacing them with r_1' and r_2' respectively. Note that in general we need to consider the case where the two rewrites are identical or are applied to the same subterm. However, if the rewrites *and* the subterm are both identical, we evidently get the same results immediately so confluence is not an issue.

First, if the rewrites are applied to disjoint subterms of $s = s[l_1', \ldots, l_2']$ to give $t_1 = s[r_1', \ldots, l_2']$ and $t_2 = s[l_1', \ldots, r_2']$, we may rejoin t_1 and t_2 by applying the other rewrite to the undisturbed subterm. Thus, in the first case t_1 and t_2 are always joinable.

[†] The terminology is perhaps unfortunate. Despite the misleading impression the concrete syntax might give, two subterms are either disjoint or one is a subterm of the other.

Second, consider the case where one rewrite is applied below the variable position in another. Without loss of generality we will consider the case where $l_2 = r_2$ occurs inside $l_1 = r_1$, the other being symmetric. That is, there is some variable x occurring in $l_1[\ldots, x, \ldots, x, \ldots]$ that is instantiated in l_1' to some term $u[l_2']$:

$$l_1'[\ldots, u[l_2'], \ldots, u[l_2'], \ldots],$$

and the other rewrite is applied to one of the subterms (indeed, there may be several of them) $u[l_2']$. The result of applying $l_2 = r_2$ to one of these subterms, say the first, is:

$$l_1'[\ldots, u[r_2'], \ldots, u[l_2'], \ldots].$$

On the other hand, if we apply $l_1 = r_1$, at the top level we get the following term, where the number of instances of $u[l_2']$ depends on how many times x occurs in r_1; we choose three as a paradigmatic example:

$$r_1'[\ldots, u[l_2'], \ldots, u[l_2'], \ldots, u[l_2'], \ldots].$$

These two terms are always joinable. To the first we can apply $l_2 = r_2$ repeatedly until *all* the terms $u[l_2']$ substituted for x are modified to $u[r_2']$, then apply $l_1 = r_1$ to the whole term. To the second, we can apply $l_2 = r_2$ to all the subterms $u[l_2']$ and the end result is the same, namely:

$$r_1'[\ldots, u[r_2'], \ldots, u[r_2'], \ldots, u[r_2'], \ldots].$$

We see here the advantages of only needing to prove local confluence: we just make a single rewrite step from s to t_1 and t_2, but are allowed arbitrarily many subsequent steps to rejoin them.

Therefore, in order to decide confluence, we only need to consider non-variable 'critical overlaps', which as the initial examples showed may or may not turn out to be joinable. This is much more appealing, because there are only finitely many essentially different ways that one left-hand side can be overlapped with another: one LHS cannot go below the variable position of the other. The points of overlap may depend on the instantiation, but we can always find the most general instantiation that allows overlap at a given position, if any, via most general unifiers (MGUs), as we will now show.

Definition 4.22 *Suppose $l_1 = r_1$ and $l_2 = r_2$ are two rewrite rules (we assume the variables of the LHSs are disjoint, i.e. $FVT(l_1) \cap FVT(l_2) = \emptyset$). If l_2' occurs at least once as a non-variable subterm of $l_1 = l_1[l_2', \ldots, l_2', \ldots, l_2']$, and σ is a most general unifier of l_2 and l_2', then the pair of terms:*

$$(\mathtt{tsubst}\ \sigma\ r_1,\ \mathtt{tsubst}\ \sigma\ l_1[l_2', \ldots, r_2, \ldots, l_2'])$$

is said to be a critical pair *of* $l_1 = r_1$ *and* $l_2 = r_2$.

Critical pairs are intended to be 'most general' representatives of the ways in which two rewrites can overlap. Indeed, we have the following key properties.

Lemma 4.23 *Let* $l_1 = r_1$ *and* $l_2 = r_2$ *be two equations with no common variables. If* $s \to_{l_1=r_1} t_1$ *and* $s \to_{l_2=r_2} t_2$ *with* t_1 *and* t_2 *not joinable, then* t_1 *and* t_2 *differ only in two subterms* u_1 *and* u_2 *(i.e.* $t_1 = u[\ldots, u_1, \ldots]$ *and* $t_2 = u[\ldots, u_2, \ldots]$*) such that either* (u_1, u_2) *or* (u_2, u_1) *is an instance of a critical pair.*

Proof The above discussion makes clear that the two rewrites cannot be applied at disjoint positions, nor one at or below a variable subterm of another, for otherwise t_1 and t_2 would be joinable, contrary to hypothesis. Thus there is a nontrivial overlap in the rewrites; without loss of generality we will suppose that $l_2 = r_2$ rewrites inside l_1. Since the two equations have no variables in common, we can assume the same instantiation θ for both l_1 and l_2 in the rewrites. Thus, l_1 has a subterm l_2' that is unifiable with l_2, say $l_1 = l_1 = l_1[\ldots, l_2', \ldots]$, with $\texttt{tsubst } \theta\ l_2' = \texttt{tsubst } \theta\ l_2$. The two rewrites on the term $\texttt{tsubst } \theta\ l_1[\ldots, l_2', \ldots]$ result in $u_1 = \texttt{tsubst } \theta\ r_1$ and $u_2 = \texttt{tsubst } \theta\ l_1[\ldots, r_2, \ldots]$. Since l_2 and l_2' are unifiable, they have a most general unifier σ, and so $(\texttt{tsubst } \sigma\ r_1, \texttt{tsubst } \sigma\ l_1[\ldots, r_2, \ldots])$ is a critical pair. By the MGU property, (u_1, u_2) is an instance of this critical pair. □

Theorem 4.24 *A term rewriting system is locally confluent iff all its critical pairs are joinable.*

Proof If a system is locally confluent, then since critical pairs (t_1, t_2) all arise by applying two 1-step rewrites to some starting term s, i.e. $s \to t_1$ and $s \to t_2$, it follows at once that t_1 and t_2 are joinable.

Conversely, suppose all critical pairs are joinable. Now, given any term s, suppose $s \to u_1$ and $s \to u_2$; we will show that u_1 and u_2 are joinable. There are two equations (possibly the same) with $s \to_{l_1=r_1} u_1$ and $s \to_{l_2=r_2} u_2$. Now, by the previous lemma, either u_1 and u_2 are joinable, or u_1 and u_2 differ only in corresponding subterms v_1 and v_2 where (v_1, v_2) is an instance of a critical pair (t_1, t_2). By hypothesis t_1 and t_2 are joinable. Since reduction is closed under substitution (whenever $s \to t$ we also have $\texttt{tsubst } \theta\ s \to \texttt{tsubst } \theta\ t$), v_1 and v_2 are joinable. Since rewriting allows arbitrary subterms, so are u_1 and u_2. □

Corollary 4.25 *A terminating term rewriting system is confluent iff all its critical pairs are joinable.*

Proof Since the system is terminating, Newman's lemma shows that confluence and local confluence are equivalent, so the result is immediate from the previous theorem.   □

We now turn to implementation. As with resolution, we start with the tedious business of preparing for unification by renaming variables. For simplicity, we replace the variables in two given formulas by schematic variables of the form `x_n`:

```
let renamepair (fm1,fm2) =
  let fvs1 = fv fm1 and fvs2 = fv fm2 in
  let nms1,nms2 = chop_list(length fvs1)
                         (map (fun n -> Var("x"^string_of_int n))
                              (0--(length fvs1 + length fvs2 - 1))) in
  subst (fpf fvs1 nms1) fm1,subst (fpf fvs2 nms2) fm2;;
```

Now we come to finding all possible overlaps. This is a little bit trickier than it looks, because we want to ensure that the MGU discovered at depth eventually gets applied to the whole term. The following function defines all ways of overlapping an equation `l = r` with another term `tm`, where the additional argument `rfn` is used to create each overall critical pair from an instantiation `i`.

The function simply recursively traverses the term, trying to unify `l` with each non-variable subterm and applying `rfn` to any resulting instantiations to give the critical pair arising from that overlap. During recursive descent, the function `rfn` is itself modified correspondingly. For updating `rfn` across the list of arguments we define the auxiliary function `listcases`, which we will re-use later in a different situation:

```
let rec listcases fn rfn lis acc =
  match lis with
    [] -> acc
  | h::t -> fn h (fun i h' -> rfn i (h'::t)) @
            listcases fn (fun i t' -> rfn i (h::t')) t acc;;

let rec overlaps (l,r) tm rfn =
  match tm with
    Fn(f,args) ->
        listcases (overlaps (l,r)) (fun i a -> rfn i (Fn(f,a))) args
                (try [rfn (fullunify [l,tm]) r] with Failure _ -> [])
  | Var x -> [];;
```

In order to present a nicer interface, we accept equational formulas rather than pairs of terms, and return critical pairs in the same way, by appropriately setting up the initial `rfn`:

```
let crit1 (Atom(R("=",[l1;r1]))) (Atom(R("=",[l2;r2]))) =
  overlaps (l1,r1) l2 (fun i t -> subst i (mk_eq t r2));;
```

For the overall function, we need to rename the variables in the initial formula then find all overlaps of the first on the second and vice versa, unless the two input equations are identical, in which case only one needs to be done:

```
let critical_pairs fma fmb =
  let fm1,fm2 = renamepair (fma,fmb) in
  if fma = fmb then crit1 fm1 fm2
  else union (crit1 fm1 fm2) (crit1 fm2 fm1);;
```

As a simple example, which also illustrates how an equation can have non-trivial overlaps with itself, consider the following:

```
# let eq = <<f(f(x)) = g(x)>> in critical_pairs eq eq;;
- : fol formula list = [<<f(g(x0)) = g(f(x0))>>; <<g(x1) = g(x1)>>]
```

Because of the fairly naive implementation, which doesn't check the trivial case of overlapping identical equations on the same subterm, we get reflexive results. But the other critical pair $(f(g(x_0)), g(f(x_0)))$, arising from two rewrites to $f(f(f(x_0)))$, is non-trivial. Since both terms are in normal form, it shows that the initial 1-element rewrite set is not confluent.

Completion

We could now code up a function to decide if a terminating rewrite system is confluent by finding all the critical pairs $\{(s_i, t_i) \mid 1 \leq i \leq n\}$ between pairs of equations, and for each such (s_i, t_i) reducing the terms to some normal forms s_i' and t_i'. The resulting system is confluent iff all corresponding pairs of terms s_i' and t_i' are syntactically equal. However, rather than merely doing this, we can be more ambitious.

If (s_i', t_i') is a normalized critical pair, then it is a logical consequence of the initial equations, since it results from repeated rewriting with those equations of a common starting term. Thus, we could add $s_i' = t_i'$ or $t_i' = s_i'$ as a new equation, retaining logical equivalence with the old axiom set. It may turn out that with this addition, the set will become confluent. If not, we can repeat the process with remaining critical pairs and any arising from the new equation. This idea is known as *completion*, and was first systematically investigated by Knuth and Bendix (1970), who demonstrated that it can be a remarkably effective technique for arriving at a canonical rewrite set for many interesting algebraic theories such as groups. It should be noted, however, that success of the procedure is not guaranteed; two things can go wrong.

First, adding $s_i' = t_i'$ or $t_i' = s_i'$ may cause the resulting rewrite set to become nonterminating. To try and avoid this, we will keep a fixed term ordering in mind, and try to orient the equation so that it respects the ordering, but it may turn out that *neither* direction respects the ordering.

Second, although the new equation $s_i' = t_i'$ or $t_i' = s_i'$ trivially means that the originating critical pair (s_i, t_i) is now joinable in the new system, the new equation will in general create new critical pairs, with the existing equations and perhaps even with itself. It's entirely possible that the creation of new critical pairs will 'outrun' their processing into new rules, so that the overall process never terminates.

Despite these provisos, let us implement completion and see it in action. The central component is a procedure that takes an equation $s = t$, normalizes both s and t to give s' and t', and attempts to orient these terms into an equation respecting the given ordering ord, failing if this is impossible. We assume ord is the reflexive form of ordering, so failure will not occur in the case where s' and t' are identical.

```
let normalize_and_orient ord eqs (Atom(R("=",[s;t]))) =
  let s' = rewrite eqs s and t' = rewrite eqs t in
  if ord s' t' then (s',t') else if ord t' s' then (t',s')
  else failwith "Can't orient equation";;
```

The central completion procedure maintains a set of equations eqs and a set of pending critical pairs crits, and successively examines critical pairs, normalizing and orienting resulting equations and adding them to eqs. However, since the order in which we examine critical pairs is arbitrary, we try to avoid failing too hastily by storing equations that cannot as yet be oriented on a separate 'deferred' list def.

Only at the end, by which time these troublesome equations may normalize to the point of joinability, or at least orientability, do we reconsider them, putting the first orientable one back in the main list of critical pairs. The following auxiliary function is used to conditionally emit a report on current status, so that the user gets an idea what's going on.

```
let status(eqs,def,crs) eqs0 =
  if eqs = eqs0 & (length crs) mod 1000 <> 0 then () else
  (print_string(string_of_int(length eqs)^" equations and "^
                string_of_int(length crs)^" pending critical pairs + "^
                string_of_int(length def)^" deferred");
   print_newline());;
```

In the main completion loop, if there is a critical pair left to be examined, we attempt to normalize and orient it; if it is nontrivial (i.e. not of the form $t = t$) we add it to the equations, and augment the critical pairs (at the tail end) with new critical pairs from this new equation and itself plus those already present. If the orientation fails, then we just add the critical pair to the 'deferred' list. Finally, if there are no critical pairs left, we attempt to orient and deal with the deferred critical pairs, starting with any found to be orientable. If we are ultimately left with some that are non-orientable, we fail. Otherwise we terminate with success and return the new equations.

```
let rec complete ord (eqs,def,crits) =
  match crits with
    (eq::ocrits) ->
        let trip =
          try let (s',t') = normalize_and_orient ord eqs eq in
              if s' = t' then (eqs,def,ocrits) else
              let eq' = Atom(R("=",[s';t'])) in
              let eqs' = eq'::eqs in
              eqs',def,
              ocrits @ itlist ((@) ** critical_pairs eq') eqs' []
          with Failure _ -> (eqs,eq::def,ocrits) in
        status trip eqs; complete ord trip
  | _ -> if def = [] then eqs else
         let e = find (can (normalize_and_orient ord eqs)) def in
         complete ord (eqs,subtract def [e],[e]);;
```

The main loop maintains the invariant that all critical pairs from pairs of equations in `eqs` that are not joinable by `eqs` are contained in `crits` and `def` together, so when successful termination occurs, since `crits` and `def` are both empty, there are no non-joinable critical pairs, and so by Corollary 4.25 successful the system is confluent. Moreover, since the original equations are included in the final set and we have only added equational consequences of the original equations, they give a logically equivalent set. In order to get started, we just have to set `crits` to the critical pairs for the original equations and also `def = []`, so the invariant is true to start with.

Before considering refinements, let's try a simple example: the axioms for groups. For the ordering we choose the lexicographic path ordering, with 1 having smallest precedence and the inverse operation the largest. The intuitive reason for giving the inverse the highest precedence is that it will tend to cause the expansion $(x \cdot y)^{-1} = y^{-1} \cdot x^{-1}$ to be applied (when it is eventually derived), leading to more opportunities for cancellation of multiple inverse operations. Indeed, if we try this out:

```
# let eqs =
   [<<1 * x = x>>; <<i(x) * x = 1>>; <<(x * y) * z = x * y * z>>];;
...
# let ord = lpo_ge (weight ["1"; "*"; "i"]);;
...
# let eqs' = complete ord
   (eqs,[],unions(allpairs critical_pairs eqs eqs));;
```

the completion algorithm terminates successfully after a little computation, and the inverse property is one of the equations deduced as part of the final complete set (first in the list that follows):

```
val eqs' : fol formula list =
  [<<i(x4 * x5) = i(x5) * i(x4)>>; <<x1 * i(x5 * x1) = i(x5)>>;
   <<i(x4) * x1 * i(x3 * x1) = i(x4) * i(x3)>>;
   <<x1 * i(i(x4) * i(x3) * x1) = x3 * x4>>;
   <<i(x3 * x5) * x0 = i(x5) * i(x3) * x0>>;
   <<i(x4 * x5 * x6 * x3) * x0 = i(x3) * i(x4 * x5 * x6) * x0>>;
   <<i(x0 * i(x1)) = x1 * i(x0)>>; <<i(i(x2 * x1) * x2) = x1>>;
   <<i(i(x4) * x2) * x0 = i(x2) * x4 * x0>>;
   <<x1 * i(x2 * x1) * x2 = 1>>;
   <<x1 * i(i(x4 * x5) * x1) * x3 = x4 * x5 * x3>>;
   <<i(x3 * i(x1 * x2)) = x1 * x2 * i(x3)>>;
   <<i(i(x3 * i(x1 * x2)) * i(x5 * x6)) * x1 * x2 * x0 = x5 * x6 * x3 *
     x0>>;
   <<x1 * x2 * i(x1 * x2) = 1>>; <<x2 * x3 * i(x2 * x3) * x1 = x1>>;
   <<i(x3 * x4) * x3 * x1 = i(x4) * x1>>;
   <<i(x1 * x3 * x4) * x1 * x3 * x4 * x0 = x0>>;
   <<i(x1 * i(x3)) * x1 * x4 = x3 * x4>>;
   <<i(i(x5 * x2) * x5) * x0 = x2 * x0>>;
   <<i(x4 * i(x1 * x2)) * x4 * x0 = x1 * x2 * x0>>; <<i(i(x1)) = x1>>;
   <<i(1) = 1>>; <<x0 * i(x0) = 1>>; <<x0 * i(x0) * x3 = x3>>;
   <<i(x2 * x3) * x2 * x3 * x1 = x1>>; <<x1 * 1 = x1>>;
   <<i(1) * x1 = x1>>; <<i(i(x0)) * x1 = x0 * x1>>;
   <<i(x1) * x1 * x2 = x2>>; <<1 * x = x>>; <<i(x) * x = 1>>;
   <<(x * y) * z = x * y * z>>]
```

And, indeed, this complete set gives an effective canonical simplifier for groups based on rewriting, e.g.

```
# rewrite eqs' <<|i(x * i(x)) * (i(i((y * z) * u) * y) * i(u))|>>;;
- : term = <<|z|>>
```

Interreduction

Although eqs' does form a canonical rewrite set, it seems to be an unnecessarily large and redundant one. For example, the two sides of $i(x_3 \cdot x_5) \cdot x_0 = i(x_5) \cdot i(x_3) \cdot x_0$ are joinable from the simple inverse law noted above and the associative law. The fact that one equation is joinable by others may mean that the critical pair giving rise to it was processed before the equations that allow it to be joined were derived. Or, since we just blindly normalized them using an essentially arbitrary choice of rewrites at a time when the rewrite set was not confluent, we may just have been unlucky and taken the wrong path even when there was a way to join them.

Whatever their genesis, it's natural to filter out afterwards equations whose two sides are joinable by others. We might even go further by simplifying both sides of each equation using all the others. Plausible as this looks, we need first to satisfy ourselves that the result remains canonical. Indeed, reducing the LHS of an equation may cause it to become mis-oriented, or even non-orientable. Fortunately, however, it turns out that if the LHS of an equation in a canonical term rewriting system is reducible by the other equations, then both sides are automatically joinable by the other equations and it may be discarded. Thus (Métivier 1983) we can simply:

- discard any equation whose LHS is reducible by any of the others (excluding itself);
- reduce the RHS of any equation with all the equations (including itself).

Both these facts follow quite easily from the following general theorem about arbitrary reduction relations.

Theorem 4.26 *Let $\to_R$ be a canonical (terminating and confluent) reduction relation on a set X (this can be any relation, though the reader may care to think of it as a rewrite relation generated by R). Suppose another reduction relation $\to_S$ has the following two properties:*

- *for any $x, y \in X$, if $x \to_S y$ then $x \to_R^+ y$;*
- *for any $x, y \in X$, if $x \to_R y$ then there is a $y' \in X$ with $x \to_S y'$.*

Then $\to_S$ is also canonical and defines the same equivalence, i.e. two objects are joinable by $\to_R$ iff they are joinable by $\to_S$.

Proof First we will prove the lemma that if y is in normal form w.r.t. $\to_R$, then for any x with $x \to_R^* y$ we also have $x \to_S^* y$. Since $\to_R$ is terminating, we can prove this by wellfounded induction on x, keeping y fixed. Suppose $x \to_R^* y$. If $x = y$ the result follows at once; otherwise there is a $u \in X$

with $x \rightarrow_R u \rightarrow_R^* y$. Using the hypotheses relating $\rightarrow_R$ and $\rightarrow_S$, we deduce that there is some $v \in X$ with $x \rightarrow_S v$, and that $x \rightarrow_R^+ v$ and so a fortiori $x \rightarrow_R^* v$. Since $\rightarrow_R$ is confluent, there is therefore a $z \in X$ with $y \rightarrow_R^* z$ and $v \rightarrow_R^* z$. Since y is in normal form w.r.t. $\rightarrow_R$ we must in fact have $z = y$. Therefore we have $v \rightarrow_R^* y$. By the inductive hypothesis, $v \rightarrow_S^* y$ and by definition of reflexive transitive closure we have $x \rightarrow_S^* y$ as required.

Because $\rightarrow_S$ is a subrelation of the transitive closure $\rightarrow_R^+$, which is itself terminating because $\rightarrow_R$ is, $\rightarrow_S$ is terminating. To show that it is also confluent, then, we need only prove local confluence and appeal to Newman's lemma. So suppose $x \rightarrow_S y_1$ and $x \rightarrow_S y_2$. Then by hypothesis $x \rightarrow_R^+ y_1$ and $x \rightarrow_R^+ y_2$. Since $\rightarrow_R$ is confluent, we have some z, which we can by termination assume to be in normal form, such that $y_1 \rightarrow_R^* z$ and $y_2 \rightarrow_R^* z$. But by the lemma established at the beginning of this proof, $y_1 \rightarrow_S^* z$ and $y_2 \rightarrow_S^* z$, establishing local and hence full confluence of $\rightarrow_S$.

Finally, we need to show that for any $x, y \in X$, $x \downarrow_R y$ iff $x \downarrow_S y$. The right-to-left implication is almost immediate, because $\rightarrow_S$ is contained in $\rightarrow_R^+$ and therefore $\rightarrow_S^*$ is contained in $\rightarrow_R^*$. For the other direction, if $x \downarrow_R y$ we can assume by termination that there is a z in normal form w.r.t. $\rightarrow_R$ such that $x \rightarrow_R^* z$ and $y \rightarrow_R^* z$. But now by the lemma at the start of the proof, we also have $x \rightarrow_S^* z$ and $y \rightarrow_S^* z$. $\qquad\square$

Corollary 4.27 *If R is a canonical term rewriting system and $(l = r) \in R$, then if l is reducible by the other equations, the system $R - \{l = r\}$ is also canonical and is logically equivalent.*

Proof We simply need to check that the conditions of Theorem 4.26 are satisfied, with $\rightarrow_R$ generated by R and $\rightarrow_S$ by $S = R - \{l = r\}$. It is immediate that if $s \rightarrow_S t$ then $s \rightarrow_R t$, and hence $s \rightarrow_R^+ t$, since S is a subset of R. Moreover, if $s \rightarrow_R t$ then since l is reducible by $\rightarrow_S$, so is s. $\qquad\square$

Corollary 4.28 *If R is a canonical term rewriting system and $(l = r) \in R$, let S be the result of replacing the equation $l = r$ in R with $l = r'$ where r' is the R-normal form of r. Then S is also canonical and logically equivalent to R.*

Proof Again, we just need to check the conditions of Theorem 4.26. Suppose first that $s \rightarrow_S t$. If this reduction uses the new rule $l = r'$, then there is a transition $s \rightarrow_R u \rightarrow_R^* t$, where the first step corresponds to the original rewrite $l = r$ and the remaining steps to the normalization of r, with the appropriate subterm and instantiation. This exactly means that $s \rightarrow_R^+ t$. On the other hand, if the reduction does not use the new rule, then trivially $s \to_R t$ and so $s \to_R^+ t$. Now suppose $s \to_R t$. Either this reduction involves $l = r$, in which case it can also be reduced by $l = r'$ and hence by $\to_S$, or it does not, in which case $s \to_S t$ anyway. $\qquad \qquad \square$

To implement this, we just transfer equations from the input list `eqs` to the output list `dun` as needed, reversing at the end to maintain the order:

```
let rec interreduce dun eqs =
  match eqs with
    (Atom(R("=",[l;r]))):::oeqs ->
        let dun' = if rewrite (dun @ oeqs) l <> l then dun
                   else mk_eq l (rewrite (dun @ eqs) r)::dun in
        interreduce dun' oeqs
  | [] -> rev dun;;
```

Applying this to the complete set obtained above, we get a much more elegant and manageable result. In fact, it can be shown (Métivier 1983) that the interreduced set is essentially unique once the reduction ordering is fixed.

```
# interreduce [] eqs';;
- : fol formula list =
[<<i(x4 * x5) = i(x5) * i(x4)>>; <<i(i(x1)) = x1>>; <<i(1) = 1>>;
 <<x0 * i(x0) = 1>>; <<x0 * i(x0) * x3 = x3>>; <<x1 * 1 = x1>>;
 <<i(x1) * x1 * x2 = x2>>; <<1 * x = x>>; <<i(x) * x = 1>>;
 <<(x * y) * z = x * y * z>>]
```

Let us now set up a slightly more convenient interface to completion, so that input equations are oriented, the initial critical pairs are generated automatically, and interreduction is applied afterwards.

```
let complete_and_simplify wts eqs =
  let ord = lpo_ge (weight wts) in
  let eqs' = map (fun e -> let l,r = normalize_and_orient ord [] e in
                           mk_eq l r) eqs in
  (interreduce [] ** complete ord)
  (eqs',[],unions(allpairs critical_pairs eqs' eqs'));;
```

Instead of waiting till the end of the completion process to perform interreduction, it's usually significantly more efficient to simplify and perhaps delete or reorient equations *during* the completion process. Nevertheless, justifying such optimizations is significantly more complicated, particularly in connection with simplification of existing equations on the left (Huet 1981; Baader and Nipkow 1998). And our simple algorithm is already enough to handle most of the examples from the original paper by Knuth and Bendix (1970). One of the more surprising is the following single-axiom system. If one asserts $i(x) \cdot (x \cdot y) = y$, it also follows that $x \cdot (i(x) \cdot y) = y$, and vice versa, without any other assumptions such as associativity. Knuth and Bendix remark that 'this fact can be used to simplify several proofs which appear in the literature, for example in the algebraic structures associated with projective geometry'.

```
# complete_and_simplify ["1"; "*"; "i"]
  [<<i(a) * (a * b) = b>>];;
2 equations and 4 pending critical pairs + 0 deferred
3 equations and 9 pending critical pairs + 0 deferred
3 equations and 0 pending critical pairs + 0 deferred
- : fol formula list =
[<<x0 * i(x0) * x3 = x3>>; <<i(i(x0)) * x1 = x0 * x1>>;
<<i(a) * a * b = b>>]
```

Knuth and Bendix also demonstrate in their paper some techniques for extending the approach to non-equational axioms. Consider the quite typical 'cancellation' property $\forall x\ y\ z.\ x \cdot y = x \cdot z \Rightarrow y = z$. Although this isn't an equation, it is logically equivalent to $\forall x\ z.\ \exists w.\ \forall y.\ z = x \cdot y \Rightarrow w = y$, as we can confirm automatically:

```
# (meson ** equalitize)
   <<(forall x y z. x * y = x * z ==> y = z) <=>
     (forall x z. exists w. forall y. z = x * y ==> w = y)>>;;
...
- : int list = [5; 4]
```

If we Skolemize this equivalent form we get $\forall x\ y\ z.\ z = x \cdot y \Rightarrow f(x, z) = y$, which is logically equivalent to $\forall x\ y.\ f(x, x \cdot y) = y$, a purely equational property. Thus we can introduce a new operator f and an axiom $\forall x\ y.\ f(x, x \cdot y) = y$, and by the conservativity property of Skolemization (see Section 3.6) anything we can prove that does not involve f must still be true in the original system. Similarly, the language can sometimes be expanded to accommodate otherwise non-orientable rules. For example, if an equation $g(w, x, y) = g(w, x, z)$ is derived, this is an indication that the third argument is irrelevant and we can replace g with a binary function.

Dealing with commutativity

Despite tricks for extending the scope of completion, certain standard alge-braic axioms give rise to difficult problems. In particular the commutativity law $x \cdot y = y \cdot x$ cannot be oriented according to any rewrite order, since any such order has to be closed under the instantiation $x \mapsto y$, $y \mapsto x$. There are several approaches to dealing with commutativity, either on its own or in conjunction with other properties such as associativity.

The most sophisticated is to change the notions of matching and uni-fication to treat as equal all associative and commutative rearrangements of the same term. This process is usually called associative–commutative (AC) unification or matching. There are algorithms for these operations, but they are a bit more complicated than regular unification; indeed the first full AC-unification algorithm (Stickel 1981) was only proved to ter-minate some years after it was first introduced (Fages 1984). Moreover, in contrast to simple unification, single MGUs may not exist, though there are always finitely many; even in matching, for example, $1 \cdot (x \cdot y)$ can be matched to $(2 \cdot 1) \cdot 3$ either by $x \mapsto 2, y \mapsto 3$ or $x \mapsto 3, y \mapsto 2$, neither of which is an instance of the other. The idea of AC-unification can be generalized from unification modulo associative and commutative laws to unification modulo any set of equational axioms (regular unification being the special case of the empty set), and this was actually discussed by Plotkin (1972) some years before algorithms for specific cases like AC were developed. In the general case, however, unification may be undecidable and there may not even be an *infinite* set of most general unifiers (Fages and Huet 1986). Nevertheless, this is an important technique, playing a role in some of the most impressive achievements in automated equational reasoning such as the solution by McCune (1997) of the Robbins conjec-ture.

A simpler alternative is to re-examine a key idea motivating the definition of rewrite orderings, that we just need to orient an equation $l = r$ once and for all rather than separately considering each individual instance $l' = r'$. Appealing as this is, we can consider dropping it and constraining rewriting by an ordering on the *instances*. This idea seems to have first been used by Boyer and Moore (1977), who used a system like the following to implement associative–commutative normalization for an operator '+':

$$
\begin{aligned}
x + y &= y + x, \\
x + (y + z) &= y + (x + z), \\
(x + y) + z &= x + (y + z).
\end{aligned}
$$

Applying these rewrites subject to a suitable ordering constraint on the instances will normalize terms to be right-associated, and also ordered via a kind of 'bubblesort', e.g.

$$(1 + 4) + (3 + 2) \to 1 + (4 + (3 + 2)) \to 1 + (3 + (4 + 2))$$
$$\to 1 + (3 + (2 + 4)) \to 1 + (2 + (3 + 4)).$$

Assuming that the ordering we use is wellfounded, termination is assured, so to show confluence we just need to demonstrate local confluence. For many common orderings such as LPO, testing local confluence with ordering constraints on instances is decidable (Comon, Narendran, Nieuwenhuis and Rusinowitch 1998). In general it can still be difficult, though in typical cases a fairly straightforward approach based on analyzing all the possible orderings of the subterms in the instances works well; see Exercise 4.15 for the automation of such case analysis and checking. Martin and Nipkow (1990) demonstrate confluence of ordered rewrite systems for many important systems of algebraic axioms using such techniques.

Unfailing completion

Ordered rewriting can also be used to generalize completion to *unfailing completion* (Bachmair, Dershowitz and Plaisted 1989), which will never fail owing to non-orientable equations, but rather will use them with ordered rewriting based on some term ordering, typically an LPO.

Moreover, if implemented appropriately, one can show that even if it never finds a canonical rewrite system, it will eventually find a rewrite system capable of proving $s = t$ by rewriting whenever $s = t$ follows from the starting axioms. Thus, it can form a complete proof procedure for equational logic. This shift in emphasis from finding canonical systems to proving equations is quite natural. After all, if we try to complete the axioms for groups where $x^2 = 1$, then we do not meet with success:

```
complete_and_simplify ["1"; "*"; "i"]
 [<<(x * y) * z = x * (y * z)>>;
  <<1 * x = x>>; <<x * 1 = x>>; <<x * x = 1>>];;
```

If we trace through successive loops of the completion procedure (using `#trace complete;;` before execution), we find that the critical pair $x_2 \cdot x_0 = x_0 \cdot x_2$ is generated, and subsequently put in the deferred list since it is non-orientable. This immediately dooms the standard completion procedure to failure or nontermination, since this equation will never be oriented or rewritten away. Yet from the point of view of first-order theorem proving, we have rapidly drawn an interesting conclusion (such a group must be commutative) and so this should be considered a success rather than a failure.

4.8 Equality elimination

Many of the ideas from equational logic, such as orienting rewrites into a favoured direction and considering only proper overlaps, can be generalized to full first-order logic. However, the theoretical justification becomes significantly more difficult, and we will not dwell on it. However, we will consider a few approaches to equality handling other than just adding the equality axioms in a preprocessing step. In this section, we briefly consider avoiding equality altogether, then examine a more sophisticated way of preprocessing the input formulas to incorporate the necessary equality properties.

Predicate formulations

One technique that was popular for encoding group theory etc. in the early days of automated reasoning was to use, rather than a 2-argument function symbol, a 3-argument predicate symbol, the idea being that $P(x, y, z)$ stands for $x \cdot y = z$. Now we can render the axioms of identity and inverse as $\forall x.\ P(1, x, x)$ and $\forall x.\ P(i(x), x, 1)$. By introducing auxiliary variables for subexpressions, we can express the associative law, e.g. as

$$\forall u, v, w, x, y, z.\ P(x, y, u) \wedge P(y, z, w) \Rightarrow (P(x, w, v) \leftrightarrow P(u, z, v)).$$

Admittedly, there are several important properties of the group operation that aren't captured by the three axioms for P so far, e.g. $\forall x\ y.\exists! z.P(x, y, z)$. Nevertheless, it turns out that some properties of groups can still be derived just from these properties. The problem of proving that a group where $x^2 = 1$ is abelian ($x \cdot y = y \cdot x$) works particularly nicely, because we don't need to postulate an inverse operation, each element being its own inverse:

```
# meson
   <<(forall x. P(1,x,x)) /\
     (forall x. P(x,x,1)) /\
     (forall u v w x y z. P(x,y,u) /\ P(y,z,w)
                     ==> (P(x,w,v) <=> P(u,z,v)))
     ==> forall a b c. P(a,b,c) ==> P(b,a,c)>>;;
...
- : int list = [13]
```

Effective though this method can be, and interesting as it is to see how weaker axioms suffice for many purposes, it has a rather ad hoc flavour, and obliges us to code up the natural notions in a rather peculiar fashion. Indeed, it was mainly popular before more effective equality reasoning methods had been developed. Nevertheless, the idea of breaking down terms like $(x \cdot y) \cdot z$ by the introduction of auxiliary variables will reappear in a slightly different form below.

Equivalence elimination

Our main interest is in the equality relation, but we'll consider equality-like properties of an arbitrary binary relation R in what follows. Besides giving greater generality, it might actually be clearer since the notation won't tempt the reader to make special assumptions about equality. Note that in contrast to most of this chapter, we're concerned with arbitrary interpretations here, not necessarily normal ones.

Consider the axiom 'Equiv' asserting that a binary relation R is an equivalence relation, i.e. is reflexive, symmetric and transitive.

$$(\forall x.\ R(x, x)) \land$$
$$(\forall x\ y.\ R(x, y) \Rightarrow R(y, x)) \land$$
$$(\forall x\ y\ z.\ R(x, y) \land R(y, z) \Rightarrow R(x, z)).$$

This is equivalent to simply $\forall x\ y.\ R(x, y) \Leftrightarrow (\forall z.\ R(x, z) \Leftrightarrow R(y, z))$; the reader can verify this, or we can leave it to the machine:

```
# meson
   <<(forall x. R(x,x)) /\
     (forall x y. R(x,y) ==>  R(y,x)) /\
     (forall x y z. R(x,y) /\ R(y,z) ==> R(x,z))
     <=> (forall x y. R(x,y) <=> (forall z. R(x,z) <=> R(y,z)))>>;;
...
- : int list = [4; 3; 9; 3; 2; 7]
```

Similarly, an assertion of reflexivity and transitivity (without symmetry) is equivalent to $\forall x\ y.\ R(x, y) \Leftrightarrow (\forall z.\ R(y, z) \Rightarrow R(x, z))$, while symmetry of R alone is equivalent to $\forall x\ y.\ R(x, y) \Leftrightarrow R(x, y) \land R(y, x)$. These equivalences are all of the form

$$\forall x\ y.\ R(x, y) \Leftrightarrow R^*[x, y],$$

so we can think of them as rules for replacing each instance of $R(s, t)$ in a formula by $R^*[s, t]$. After making such replacements, we will prove shortly that the corresponding axioms about R are no longer needed. Consider the case of full equivalence; the reflexivity–transitivity and symmetry cases work similarly. Given an atomic formula $R(s,t)$, write $R^*[s,t]$ for $\forall w.\ R(s,w) \Leftrightarrow R(t,w)$ where $w \notin \text{FV}(s) \cup \text{FV}(t)$.

Theorem 4.29 $P \wedge Equiv$ *is satisfiable iff the formula P^* that results from replacing each subformula $R(s,t)$ in P with $R^*[s,t]$ is satisfiable.*

Proof We noted above that $Equiv \Leftrightarrow (\forall x\ y.\ R(x,y) \Leftrightarrow R^*[x,y])$ and so for any terms s and t we have $Equiv \Rightarrow (R(s,t) \Leftrightarrow R^*[s,t])$. Hence $Equiv \wedge P \Leftrightarrow Equiv \wedge P^*$. This means that if $Equiv \wedge P$ is satisfiable, so is $Equiv \wedge P^*$ and a fortiori P^*. Note that this works equally well if we choose only to replace *some* formulas $R(s,t)$ in P with $R^*[s,t]$, not necessarily all of them.

Now suppose that P^* is satisfiable, say in an interpretation M with domain D where R is interpreted by R_M. Define a new interpretation N that is the same except that $R_N(a,b)$ is defined to hold precisely when $R_M(a,c)$ and $R_M(b,c)$ are equivalent for all $c \in D$. By design, `holds` $N\ v\ (R(s,t)) =$ `holds` $M\ v\ (R^*[s,t])$, so since P^* holds in M, P holds in N. By construction R_N is an equivalence relation, so $Equiv$ also holds in N. □

This approach is generalized by Ohlbach, Gabbay and Plaisted (1994) to a large class of 'killer transformations', so called because they 'kill' certain axioms. The proofs here of the key equisatisfiability properties were suggested by Rob Arthan.

Brand's S- and T-modifications

An earlier equality elimination method (Brand 1975) similarly eliminates symmetry and transitivity, but keeps the reflexivity axiom $\forall x.\ R(x,x)$. The advantage of doing this is that one may then perform the expansive transformation only on *positive* occurrences of $R(s,t)$, while negative occurrences $\neg R(u,v)$ can be left alone. We can adapt the proof of Theorem 4.29 as follows. Assume the formula $P[\ldots, R(s,t), \ldots, \neg R(u,v), \ldots]$ whose satisfiability is at issue is in NNF, so we can distinguish positive and negative occurrences simply by whether they are directly covered by a negation operation. All are treated in the way indicated for the paradigmatic examples $R(s,t)$ and $\neg R(u,v)$. Write as before

$$P^* = P[\ldots, R^*[s,t], \ldots, \neg R^*[u,v], \ldots]$$

but also

$$P' = P[\ldots, R^*[s,t], \ldots, \neg R(u,v), \ldots].$$

The first part of the proof works equally well to show that if Equiv $\wedge\ P$ is satisfiable, so is Equiv $\wedge\ P'$ and therefore $(\forall x.\ R(x,x)) \wedge P'$. Conversely, $(\forall x.\ R(x,x)) \Rightarrow R^*[u,v] \Rightarrow R(u,v)$, so $(\forall x.\ R(x,x)) \Rightarrow \neg R(u,v) \Rightarrow \neg R^*[u,v]$ and therefore $(\forall x. R(x,x)) \wedge P' \Rightarrow (\forall x. R(x,x)) \wedge P^*$. Thus if $(\forall x. R(x,x)) \wedge P'$ is satisfiable, so is P^* and, by the same proof as before, so is P.

Restricted to the special case of a formula in clausal form with R being the equality relation, these ways of eliminating symmetry and transitivity give exactly Brand's S-modification and T-modification respectively. Doing these successively works out the same as doing equivalence-elimination once and for all, but we'll keep them separate both to emphasize the correspondence with Brand's work and to modularize the implementation. In the clausal context we can also recognize positivity or negativity trivially. If we keep the same predicate symbol, namely $=$, then we can just leave negative literals untouched in each case, and only modify positive equations. The S-transformation on a clause with n positive equations (written at the beginning for simplicity):

$$s_1 = t_1 \vee \cdots \vee s_n = t_n \vee C$$

leads to

$$(s_1 = t_1 \wedge t_1 = s_1) \vee \cdots \vee (s_n = t_n \wedge t_n = s_n) \vee C.$$

This is no longer in clausal form, but we can redistribute and arrive at 2^n resulting clauses:

$$s_1 = t_1 \vee \cdots \vee s_{n-1} = t_{n-1} \vee s_n = t_n \vee C,$$
$$s_1 = t_1 \vee \cdots \vee s_{n-1} = t_{n-1} \vee t_n = s_n \vee C,$$
$$s_1 = t_1 \vee \cdots \vee t_{n-1} = s_{n-1} \vee s_n = t_n \vee C,$$
$$s_1 = t_1 \vee \cdots \vee t_{n-1} = s_{n-1} \vee t_n = s_n \vee C,$$
$$\cdots$$
$$t_1 = s_1 \vee \cdots \vee t_{n-1} = s_{n-1} \vee t_n = s_n \vee C,$$

which essentially cover all possible combinations of forward and backward equations in the original clause. Admittedly, if n is large, this exponential blowup in the number of clauses is not very appealing, but it can be made manageable using a few extra tricks (see Exercise 4.4). Here is the implementation on a clause represented as a list of literals:

```
let rec modify_S cl =
  try let (s,t) = tryfind dest_eq cl in
      let eq1 = mk_eq s t and eq2 = mk_eq t s in
      let sub = modify_S (subtract cl [eq1]) in
      map (insert eq1) sub @ map (insert eq2) sub
  with Failure _ -> [cl];;
```

For the T-modification, we need to replace each equation $s_i = t_i$ in a clause:

$$s_1 = t_1 \lor \cdots \lor s_n = t_n \lor C$$

as follows:

$$(\forall w.\, t_1 = w \Rightarrow s_1 = w) \lor \cdots \lor (\forall w.\, t_n = w \Rightarrow s_n = w) \lor C.$$

We can pull out the universal quantifiers to retain clausal form, but we then need to use distinct variable names w_i instead of a single w in each equation. We also transform $t_1 = w \Rightarrow s_1 = w$ into $\neg(t_1 = w) \lor s_i = w$ to return to clausal form, resulting in:

$$\neg(t_1 = w_1) \lor s_1 = w_1 \lor \cdots \lor \neg(t_n = w_n) \lor s_n = w_n \lor C.$$

We can implement this directly, just running through the literals successively, recursively transforming the tail and picking a new variable w that is neither in the transformed tail nor the unmodified literal being considered:

```
let rec modify_T cl =
  match cl with
    (Atom(R("=",[s;t]))) as eq)::ps ->
        let ps' = modify_T ps in
        let w = Var(variant "w" (itlist (union ** fv) ps' (fv eq))) in
        Not(mk_eq t w)::(mk_eq s w)::ps'
  | p::ps -> p::(modify_T ps)
  | [] -> [];;
```

Brand's E-modification

We have shown how the equivalence axioms can be eliminated by incorporating new structure into the other formulas. We now proceed to do the same with the congruence axioms

$$\forall x_1 \cdots x_n y_1 \cdots y_n.\, x_1 = y_1 \land \cdots \land x_n = y_n \Rightarrow f(x_1, \ldots, x_n) = f(y_1, \ldots, y_n)$$

and

$$\forall x_1 \cdots x_n y_1 \cdots y_n.\, x_1 = y_1 \land \cdots \land x_n = y_n \Rightarrow P(x_1, \ldots, x_n) \Rightarrow P(y_1, \ldots, y_n)$$

for the function symbols f and predicates P appearing in the initial formulas. We will actually perform this transformation first, and so we can assume the equivalence axioms. The basic idea is to repeatedly pull out non-variable immediate subterms t of function and predicate symbols (other than equality) using the following, which are clearly equivalences in the presence of the congruence and reflexivity axioms:

$$f(\ldots, t, \ldots) = s \quad \Leftrightarrow \quad \forall w.\, t = w \Rightarrow f(\ldots, w, \ldots) = s,$$
$$s = f(\ldots, t, \ldots) \quad \Leftrightarrow \quad \forall w.\, t = w \Rightarrow s = f(\ldots, w, \ldots),$$
$$P(\ldots, t, \ldots) \quad \Leftrightarrow \quad \forall w.\, t = w \Rightarrow P(\ldots, w, \ldots).$$

We can repeat this transformation until function symbols (including constants) only appear as arguments to the equality predicate, not other predicates nor other functions. A formula with this property is said to be *flat* and we will describe the transformation as *flattening*. For example, we might transform the associative law as follows, assuming all free variables to be implicitly universally quantified:

$$(x \cdot y) \cdot z = x \cdot (y \cdot z),$$
$$x \cdot y = w_1 \Rightarrow w_1 \cdot z = x \cdot (y \cdot z),$$
$$x \cdot y = w_1 \wedge y \cdot z = w_2 \Rightarrow w_1 \cdot z = x \cdot w_2.$$

It turns out that for flat quantifier-free formulas, the congruence axioms are not necessary, in the following precise sense.

Theorem 4.30 *Suppose a quantifier-free formula P is flat, E asserts the equivalence properties of equality and C is the collection of congruences for the functions and predicates appearing in P. Then $P \wedge E \wedge C$ is satisfiable iff $P \wedge E$ is.*

Proof One way is immediate. So suppose $P \wedge E$ is satisfiable; we will show that $P \wedge E \wedge C$ is too. If M is a model of $P \wedge E$ with domain D, then since it is a fortiori a model of E, the interpretation $=_M$ of equality is an equivalence relation. For any $a \in D$, let $\bar{a}$ be some fixed canonical representative of the equivalence class $[a]_{=_M}$. Thus, for any $a, b \in D$ we have $=_M (a, b)$ iff $\bar{a} = \bar{b}$. We now define a new model M' with the same domain D interpreting the function symbols as follows:

$$f_{M'}(a_1, \ldots, a_n) = f_M(\overline{a_1}, \ldots, \overline{a_n}),$$

equality in the same way, $=_M$, and the other predicate symbols like this:

$$P_{M'}(a_1, \ldots, a_n) = P_M(\overline{a_1}, \ldots, \overline{a_n}).$$

We claim that M' is a model of $P \wedge E \wedge C$. It is a model of E since we have not changed the interpretation of the equality symbol nor the domain, and no function symbols or other predicates appear in E. To see that it is also a model of C, note that the function congruence axiom

$$x_1 = y_1 \wedge \cdots \wedge x_n = y_n \Rightarrow f(x_1, \ldots, x_n) = f(y_1, \ldots, y_n)$$

holds in M' under a valuation mapping each $x_i \mapsto a_i$ and $y_i \mapsto b_i$ precisely if whenever $a_i =_M b_i$ for $1 \leq i \leq n$, then $f_{M'}(a_1, \ldots, a_n) = f_{M'}(b_1, \ldots, b_n)$. But $a_i = b_i$ implies, as noted above, that $\overline{a_i} = \overline{b_i}$, and since by definition $f_{M'}(a_1, \ldots, a_n) = f_M(\overline{a_1}, \ldots, \overline{a_n})$ and similarly for b_i, the result follows. The predicate congruences hold for similar reasons.

All that remains is to show that M' is a model of P as well, and this is where the flatness of P is critical. Let v be any valuation, and define $\overline{v}(x) = \overline{v(x)}$. We claim that for any flat atomic formula p we have $\mathtt{holds}\ M'\ v\ p = \mathtt{holds}\ M\ \overline{v}\ p$. Note first that for each term consisting of a function applied to (not necessarily distinct) variables we have

$$
\begin{aligned}
&\mathtt{termval}\ M'\ v\ (f(x_1, \ldots, x_n)) \\
=\ &f_{M'}(\mathtt{termval}\ M'\ v\ x_1, \ldots, \mathtt{termval}\ M'\ v\ x_n) \\
=\ &f_{M'}(v(x_1), \ldots, v(x_n)) \\
=\ &f_M(\overline{v(x_1)}, \ldots, \overline{v(x_n)}) \\
=\ &f_M(\overline{v}(x_1), \ldots, \overline{v}(x_n)) \\
=\ &f_M(\mathtt{termval}\ M\ \overline{v}\ x_1, \ldots, \mathtt{termval}\ M\ \overline{v}\ x_n) \\
=\ &\mathtt{termval}\ M\ \overline{v}\ (f(x_1, \ldots, x_n)).
\end{aligned}
$$

The same result does not hold for variables alone, but at least the two values $\mathtt{termval}\ M'\ v\ x = v(x)$ and $\mathtt{termval}\ M\ \overline{v}\ x = \overline{v}(x) = \overline{v(x)}$ are equivalent under $=_M$ by definition. Thus if t is a 'flat term', either a variable or function applied to variables, we have

$$=_M\ (\mathtt{termval}\ M'\ v\ t, \mathtt{termval}\ M\ \overline{v}\ t).$$

Consequently, since $=_M$ is an equivalence relation we can see that for an equation between two such terms:

$$
\begin{aligned}
& \texttt{holds } M' \ v \ (s = t) \\
=\ & =_M (\texttt{termval } M' \ v \ s, \texttt{termval } M' \ v \ t) \\
=\ & =_M (\texttt{termval } M \ \overline{v} \ s, \texttt{termval } M \ \overline{v} \ t) \\
=\ & \texttt{holds } M \ \overline{v} \ (s = t).
\end{aligned}
$$

For other predicate symbols applied to variables, we similarly have:

$$
\begin{aligned}
& \texttt{holds } M' \ v \ (P(x_1, \ldots, x_n)) \\
=\ & P'_M(\texttt{termval } M' \ v \ x_1, \ldots, \texttt{termval } M' \ v \ x_n)) \\
=\ & P'_M(v(x_1), \ldots, v(x_n)) \\
=\ & P_M(\overline{v(x_1)}, \ldots, \overline{v}(x_n)) \\
=\ & P_M(\overline{v}(x_1), \ldots, \overline{v}(x_n)) \\
=\ & P_M(\texttt{termval } M \ \overline{v} \ x_1, \ldots, \texttt{termval } M \ \overline{v} \ x_n) \\
=\ & \texttt{holds } M \ \overline{v} \ (P(x_1, \ldots, x_n)).
\end{aligned}
$$

It now follows by induction on the structure of P that we can extend the basic result to the whole formula (which is quantifier-free by hypothesis):

$$
\texttt{holds } M' \ v \ P = \texttt{holds } M \ \overline{v} \ P
$$

However, since M is a model of P, the RHS is simply 'true', and therefore so is the left. But v was arbitrary, and therefore the theorem is proved. $\qquad\square$

Brand's 'E-modification' applies the flattening transformation to clauses, adding new negative literals $\neg(t = w_i)$ for the extra variable definitions included. It follows that if we perform E-modification and then S- and T-modifications, the resulting set of clauses plus the reflexive law $x = x$ has a model iff the original formula has a normal model. We have thus succeeded in transforming the input clauses to eliminate the need for any equality axioms besides reflexivity.

Implementation

First we define functions to identify non-variables:

```
let is_nonvar = function (Var x) -> false | _ -> true;;
```

and hence find a nested non-variable subterm where possible:

```
let find_nestnonvar tm =
  match tm with
    Var x -> failwith "findnvsubt"
  | Fn(f,args) -> find is_nonvar args;;
```

Now we can identify a non-variable subterm that we want to pull out in flattening; in the case of equality this is a *nested* non-variable subterm, while for the other predicate symbols it is any non-variable subterm:

```
let rec find_nvsubterm fm =
  match fm with
    Atom(R("=",[s;t])) -> tryfind find_nestnonvar [s;t]
  | Atom(R(p,args)) -> find is_nonvar args
  | Not p -> find_nvsubterm p;;
```

Having found such a non-variable subterm, we want to replace it with a new variable. We don't have a general function to replace subterms (tsubst and subst only replace *variables*), so we define one, first for terms:

```
let rec replacet rfn tm =
  try apply rfn tm with Failure _ ->
  match tm with
    Fn(f,args) -> Fn(f,map (replacet rfn) args)
  | _ -> tm;;
```

and then for other formulas (here we only care about literals, and can treat quantified formulas without regard to variable capture):

```
let replace rfn = onformula (replacet rfn);;
```

To *E*-modify a clause, we try to find a nested non-variable subterm; if we fail we are already done, and otherwise we replace that term with a fresh variable w, add the new disjunct $\neg(t = w)$ and call recursively:

```
let rec emodify fvs cls =
  try let t = tryfind find_nvsubterm cls in
      let w = variant "w" fvs in
      let cls' = map (replace (t |=> Var w)) cls in
      emodify (w::fvs) (Not(mk_eq t (Var w))::cls')
  with Failure _ -> cls;;
```

The fvs parameter tracks the free variables in the clause so far, so we just need to set its initial value:

```
let modify_E cls = emodify (itlist (union ** fv) cls []) cls;;
```

The overall Brand transformation now applies E-modification, then S-modification and T-modification, then finally includes the reflexive clause $x = x$:

```
let brand cls =
  let cls1 = map modify_E cls in
  let cls2 = itlist (union ** modify_S) cls1 [] in
  [mk_eq (Var "x") (Var "x")]::(map modify_T cls2);;
```

We insert Brand's transformation into MESON's clausal framework to give `bmeson`:

```
let bpuremeson fm =
  let cls = brand(simpcnf(specialize(pnf fm))) in
  let rules = itlist ((@) ** contrapositives) cls [] in
  deepen (fun n ->
    mexpand rules [] False (fun x -> x) (undefined,n,0); n) 0;;

let bmeson fm =
  let fm1 = askolemize(Not(generalize fm)) in
  map (bpuremeson ** list_conj) (simpdnf fm1);;
```

For easy comparison, we'll define a similar version of MESON that just uses the equality axioms.

```
let emeson fm = meson (equalitize fm);;
```

The relative performance of these two methods depends on the application. For example, on the `wishnu` problem from the end of Section 4.1, Brand's transformation is substantially slower than just adding the equality axioms. But on our group theory examples, Brand's transformation is much better, e.g. only a few minutes here while `emeson` takes far longer:

```
# bmeson
   <<(forall x y z. x * (y * z) = (x * y) * z) /\
     (forall x. e * x = x) /\
     (forall x. i(x) * x = e)
     ==> forall x. x * i(x) = e>>;;
- : int list = [19]
```

Since Brand's original work, several variant methods have been proposed that are often more efficient. Moser and Steinbach (1997) suggest a version that avoids equations with variables on their left-hand sides, which tends to reduce the number of possible unifications. However, this comes at the cost of needing to split negative equations as well as positive ones in the analogue of the T-modification. A further refinement based on imposing term ordering constraints was proved complete by Bachmair, Ganzinger and

Voronkov (1997) and shown to be substantially more efficient on a number of examples.

4.9 Paramodulation

So far we have handled equality by using standard first-order proof methods on modified formulas, resulting either from adding equality axioms or using the more sophisticated modification methods in the previous section. Pre-processing has several advantages: we can re-use proof procedures intended for pure first-order logic without internal modification, and can also transfer results like compactness to the equality case without new theoretical difficulties. However, it is also possible to augment one of the standard first-order theorem proving techniques with additional rules for equality, rather than modifying the input formulas themselves. It seems more straightforward to add new inference rules in the context of bottom-up procedures like resolution, though some authors have also introduced special equality-handling methods for top-down methods such as tableaux (Fitting 1990), model elimination (Moser, Lynch and Steinbach 1995), model evolution (Baumgartner and Tinelli 2005) and others.

The first equality-based inference rule to be introduced was *demodulation* (Wos, Robinson, Carson and Shalla 1967), which uses unit equality clauses like $x + 0 = x$ as rewrite rules to simplify other clauses. The name arises because it is typically used to remove 'modulations' of essentially the same fact, e.g. $P(x)$, $P(0 + x)$, $P(x - 0)$ etc. Although useful in practice, it is not complete. However, the more general rule of *paramodulation* introduced a little later (G. Robinson and Wos 1969) gives, when used together with the standard resolution rule, a theoretically complete method of handling equality. Even in its unrestricted initial form it was often found to be far more effective than adding equality axioms, and it has subsequently been extensively refined, in particular by introducing ordering notions from term rewriting. Paramodulation is the following inference rule, where $s \doteq t$ may be either $s = t$ or $t = s$:

$$\frac{C \lor s \doteq t \quad D \lor P[s']}{\textsf{subst } \sigma \ (C \lor D \lor P[t])} \text{ Paramodulation,}$$

where σ is a MGU of s and the indicated term instance s'. Paramodulation generalizes rewriting in several respects that make it look more like the resolution rule itself: we can use equations that occur disjoined with additional literals C to rewrite with, the rewrite may be applied in either direction, and the identification of the terms s and s' is done by full unification, not just matching. It's relatively easy to see that the rule is sound, i.e that the conclusion holds in any normal model in which the hypotheses do. The issue of its refutation completeness as a method of equality handling is subtler.

Refutation completeness of paramodulation

It is *not* the case that if a set of clauses has no normal model then it can be refuted by resolution plus paramodulation, as the example of $\{\neg(x = x)\}$ shows. This suggests that, as with Brand's method, we may not need all the equality axioms but we *do* at least need to add reflexivity to the input clauses. In fact, we will demonstrate refutation completeness on the stronger assumption that we also add all the *functional reflexive axioms* of the form:

$$f(x_1, \ldots, x_n) = f(x_1, \ldots, x_n),$$

one for each function symbol f appearing in the input clauses. (This looks strange, but the reason will become clearer below.) Our proof of refutation completeness rests on the fact that a hyperresolution proof assuming equality axioms can be simulated by resolution and paramodulation with the functional reflexive axioms. In order to simplify the proof, we will adopt instead of the usual congruence rules the 1-instance variants:

$$\neg(x = x') \lor f(x_1, \ldots, x_{i-1}, x, x_{i+1}, \ldots, x_n) = f(x_1, \ldots, x_{i-1}, x', x_{i+1}, \ldots, x_n)$$

for each n-ary function f in the clauses S and for each $1 \le i \le n$, and similarly:

$$\neg(x = x') \lor \neg P(x_1, \ldots, x_{i-1}, x, x_{i+1}, \ldots, x_n) \lor P(x_1, \ldots, x_{i-1}, x', x_{i+1}, \ldots, x_n)$$

for each n-ary predicate P in the clauses S and for each $1 \le i \le n$, together with the usual combined symmetry–transitivity rule:

$$\neg(x = y) \lor \neg(x = z) \lor (y = z)$$

and simple reflexivity

$$x = x.$$

We refer to these collectively as $\mathtt{eqaxioms'}(S)$. They are logically equivalent to $\mathtt{eqaxioms}(S)$, since we can derive the multiple-instance congruence rules by repeated use of the one-instance rule put together by transitivity, while the converse follows by reflexivity. We let R be simple reflexivity together with the functional reflexive axioms, one for each function symbol in S:

$$f(x_1, \ldots, x_n) = f(x_1, \ldots, x_n).$$

Theorem 4.31 *If S has no normal model, then $S \cup R$ has a refutation by resolution and paramodulation.*

Proof Since S has no normal model, $S \cup$ eqaxioms$'(S)$ is unsatisfiable (by the above remarks and Theorem 4.1). It therefore has a refutation by positive hyperresolution (see Section 3.13). We will show that all conclusions obtainable by positive hyperresolution from $S \cup$ eqaxioms$'(S)$ can also be obtained by resolution and paramodulation from $S \cup R$.

We will establish this by induction on the steps of a hyperresolution proof. We need only consider hyperresolution steps where at least one input clause is taken from the set $R' =$ eqaxioms$'(S) - R$, since otherwise the conclusion holds at once. And since there are no all-positive clauses in R', we must by the definition of positive hyperresolution have *exactly* one input clause from R'. If this input clause is a function-congruence axiom, then the resolution must be of the following form. (In such cases, we can assume that only the left-hand hypothesis is instantiated, in this case with a unifier $x \mapsto s$ and $x' \mapsto t$, because x and x' are just variables.)

$$\frac{\neg(x = x') \vee f(\ldots, x, \ldots) = f(\ldots, x', \ldots) \quad C \vee s = t}{C \vee f(\ldots, s, \ldots) = f(\ldots, t, \ldots)}$$

This can be simulated by a paramodulation inference using the functional reflexive axiom:

$$\frac{f(\ldots, x, \ldots) = f(\ldots, x, \ldots) C \vee s = t}{C \vee f(\ldots, s, \ldots) = f(\ldots, t, \ldots)}.$$

Now, if the input is a predicate-congruence axiom, then any hyperresolution consisting of two successive positive resolution steps (in the order shown here or vice versa):

$$\frac{\dfrac{\neg(x = x') \vee \neg P(\ldots, x, \ldots) \vee P(\ldots, x', \ldots) \quad C \vee s = t}{C \vee \neg P(\ldots, s, \ldots) \vee P(\ldots, t, \ldots)} \quad D \vee P(\ldots, s', \ldots)}{\mathbf{subst}\ \sigma\ (C \vee D \vee P(\ldots, t, \ldots))},$$

where σ is an MGU of s and s', can be simulated directly by a single paramodulation:

$$\frac{C \vee s = t \quad D \vee P(\ldots, s', \ldots))}{\mathbf{subst}\ \sigma(C \vee D \vee P(\ldots, t, \ldots))},$$

Finally, a hyperresolution with the symmetry–transitivity axiom, again either in the order shown here or vice versa:

$$\frac{\neg(x = y) \vee \neg(x = z) \vee (y = z) \quad C \vee s = t}{\dfrac{C \vee \neg(s = z) \vee (t = z) \qquad\qquad D \vee s' = t'}{\texttt{subst}\ \sigma\ (C \vee D \vee t = t')}},$$

with σ a MGU of s and s', can be simulated by a single paramodulation as follows:

$$\frac{C \vee s = t \quad D \vee s' = t'}{\texttt{subst}\ \sigma\ (C \vee D \vee t = t')}.$$

□

This proof exploits the fact that many conclusions can be derived by paramodulation with the functional reflexive axioms. But for exactly the same reason, it's not clear that this combination in practice is actually any better controlled than direct hyperresolution with the equality axioms (Kowalski 1970a). Moreover, the apparent need for the functional reflexive axioms, all of which are just instances of $x = x$, shows that the kind of 'lifting' arguments underlying resolution do not generalize, and suggests that subsumption for paramodulation may be subtle.

For a long time it was an open question whether simple reflexivity $x = x$ is enough to ensure refutation completeness of resolution with paramodulation.[†] Eventually Brand (1975) presented an analogous simulation argument based on his equality transformation (Section 4.8), showing not only that simple reflexivity suffices but also that paramodulation can be restricted in other ways without losing refutation completeness. In particular, there is almost no need to paramodulate into variables, i.e. unify the left of the paramodulating equation with a variable subterm of the literal being paramodulated. However, when using many of the most effective refinements of resolution like set-of-support, the functional reflexive axioms are necessary once again for refutation completeness. Consider, for example, the following set of clauses, including simple reflexivity:

$$\{\neg(x < x), f(a) < f(b), a = b, x = x\}.$$

The entire set is unsatisfiable, but the set with $\neg(x < x)$ removed is satisfiable. However, if we attempt to find a proof by resolution and paramodulation with set of support $\neg(x < x)$, no proof can be found. On the other hand,

---

[†] A footnote in G.G. Robinson and Wos (1969) remarks: 'In the two years that paramodulation has been under study, no counterexample has been found to the *R*-refutation completeness of paramodulation and resolution for simply-reflexive systems'.

if we add the functional reflexive axiom $f(x) = f(x)$, we can paramodulate with $\neg(x < x)$ to yield $\neg(f(x) < f(x))$ and quickly arrive at a refutation. Despite such examples, it is common to leave the functional reflexive axioms out when attempting theorem proving in the hope that their theoretical necessity will not arise in the particular case under consideration. In our implementation, we will just use simple reflexivity and also disallow paramodulation into variables, in line with Brand's result.

Implementation

The key operation in paramodulation is not unlike that of finding a critical pair in Knuth–Bendix completion (Section 4.7), except that we need to consider overlaps inside an arbitrary literal, not just another term. It's similar enough that we can re-use some of the code such as the `overlaps` function. (To allow paramodulation into variables the last line 'Var x -> []' could be replaced by 'Var x -> [rfn (fullunify [l,tm]) r]'.) We then define an analogous function to find overlaps within literals. The code is very similar, the main change being that we don't attempt overlaps at the top level (which is a formula, not a term) and include a separate clause for negations.

```
let rec overlapl (l,r) fm rfn =
  match fm with
    Atom(R(f,args)) -> listcases (overlaps (l,r))
                             (fun i a -> rfn i (Atom(R(f,a)))) args []
  | Not(p) -> overlapl (l,r) p (fun i p -> rfn i (Not(p)))
  | _ -> failwith "overlapl: not a literal";;
```

We lift this to an operation on a whole clause, i.e. a list of literals:

```
let overlapc (l,r) cl rfn acc = listcases (overlapl (l,r)) rfn cl acc;;
```

Now to apply paramodulation to a clause `ocl` using all the positive equations in a paramodulating clause `pcl`, we treat each positive equation `eq` in turn, considering it as both $l = r$ and $r = l$. In each case we apply `overlapc`, with the reconstruction function set up to disjoin the other clauses and apply the final instantiation to each.

```
let paramodulate pcl ocl =
  itlist (fun eq -> let pcl' = subtract pcl [eq] in
                    let (l,r) = dest_eq eq
                    and rfn i ocl' = image (subst i) (pcl' @ ocl') in
                    overlapc (l,r) ocl rfn ** overlapc (r,l) ocl rfn)
         (filter is_eq pcl) [];;
```

Now to generate all paramodulants between clauses, we just rename the clauses to avoid variable clashes in unification, as usual, and then perform paramodulation of each clause within the other.

```
let para_clauses cls1 cls2 =
  let cls1' = rename "x" cls1 and cls2' = rename "y" cls2 in
  paramodulate cls1' cls2' @ paramodulate cls2' cls1';;
```

Now we modify the main resolution loop from Section 3.11 to incorporate both resolution and paramodulation:

```
let rec paraloop (used,unused) =
  match unused with
    [] -> failwith "No proof found"
  | cls::ros ->
        print_string(string_of_int(length used) ^ " used; "^
                     string_of_int(length unused) ^ " unused.");
        print_newline();
        let used' = insert cls used in
        let news =
           itlist (@) (mapfilter (resolve_clauses cls) used')
             (itlist (@) (mapfilter (para_clauses cls) used') []) in
        if mem [] news then true else
        paraloop(used',itlist (incorporate cls) news ros);;
```

and then set up the top-level function as before, remembering to add simple reflexivity to the clause set:

```
let pure_paramodulation fm =
  paraloop([],[mk_eq (Var "x") (Var "x")]::
              simpcnf(specialize(pnf fm)));;

let paramodulation fm =
  let fm1 = askolemize(Not(generalize fm)) in
  map (pure_paramodulation ** list_conj) (simpdnf fm1);;
```

This implementation is at least enough to deal with some simple equality problems we've already encountered, as well as some others like the following (Dijkstra 1996):

```
# paramodulation
   <<(forall x. f(f(x)) = f(x)) /\ (forall x. exists y. f(y) = x)
   ==> forall x. f(x) = x>>;;
...
- : bool list = [true]
```

However, our rather simple-minded implementation cannot really demonstrate the full power of paramodulation. It works best in conjunction with strong restrictions on applicability, e.g. applying equations in a preferred direction based on orderings in the style of term rewriting. Moreover, resolution itself, and paramodulation even more so, work best with more intelligent strategies for choosing the next application rather than the naive round-robin approach that we have implemented. In fact, by encoding atomic formulas $P(t_1, \ldots, t_n)$ as equations $f_P(t_1, \ldots, t_n) = \mathrm{T}$ (where 'T' is thought of as 'true'; see Exercise 4.3), one can essentially perform all logical inference via equational techniques like paramodulation, obviating the need for resolution or similar principles. This idea underlies the *superposition* method (Bachmair and Ganzinger 1994), implemented efficiently in the E theorem prover (Schulz 1999).

Further reading

The branch of model theory focusing on equational logic is also known as *universal algebra*, and there are several texts on the subject such as Cohn (1965) and Burris and Sankappanavar (1981). Almost all books on model theory cited in the last chapter also contain something about the theoretical material described here. More information, historical and otherwise, on the concept of categoricity is given by Corcoran (1980). Two more difficult theorems about κ-categoricity are Morley's theorem, which asserts that a theory categorical in one uncountable cardinal is categorical in them all, and the Ryll–Nardzewski theorem, which gives an attractive algebraic characterization of $\aleph_0$-categorical theories. Both these theorems can be found in Hodges (1993b).

For pure equational reasoning based on rewriting techniques, see the book by Baader and Nipkow (1998) and the survey articles by Huet and Oppen (1980), Klop (1992) and Plaisted (1993). Dershowitz's result that a simplification order is terminating is usually deduced from (a simple case of) *Kruskal's theorem* (Kruskal 1960; Nash-Williams 1963); an accessible account can be found in Baader and Nipkow (1998). In implementing the LPO we paid no attention to efficiency, but this question is carefully analyzed by Löchner (2006).

Methods for deciding validity of universal formulas in logic with equality have significant applications in verification (Burch and Dill 1994). This has led to the exploration of various alternative algorithms to congruence closure. For further refinements of the approach based on Ackermann reduction, see Goel, Sajid, Zhou, Aziz and Singhal (1998), Velev and Bryant (1999) and Lahiri, Bryant, Goel and Talupur (2004).

Paramodulation is discussed in some of the automated theorem proving texts already mentioned, including Chang and Lee (1973) and Loveland

(1978). Again, books such as Wos, Overbeek, Lusk and Boyle (1992) by the Argonne group cover the use of paramodulation to solve non-trivial problems. Bachmair and Ganzinger (1994) is a survey of paramodulation and related ideas, and Degtyarev and Voronkov (2001) of equality reasoning in top-down free-variable calculi like tableaux.

The TPTP problem library (Sutcliffe and Suttner 1998) includes many equational problems, and provides tools to add equality axioms for provers that do not handle equality directly. Some of the most impressive applications of automated reasoning to hard problems are in the general area of equational logic. The most famous example is the Robbins conjecture, which resisted proof attempts by many notable mathematicians including Tarski, yet was solved automatically by McCune (1997) using the EQP prover. This is just one particularly well-known case where automated reasoning programs have answered open questions. Some more can be found in the monographs by McCune and Padmanabhan (1996) and Wos and Pieper (2003), and on the Web.[†]

Exercises

4.1   Recall that a set of formulas is said to be κ-categorical if (it has a model and) all its models of cardinality κ are isomorphic. Prove a version of the *Loś–Vaught test*: if a countable set of formulas is κ-categorical for some infinite κ then all models are elementarily equivalent. (You may find it useful to use the upward Löwenheim-Skolem theorem.)

4.2   Show that a Birkhoff proof can be rearranged so that all instantiation and symmetry is applied immediately above the leaves, then congruence rules where necessary and at the top level a right-associated transitivity chain such that no two adjacent equations in a transitivity chain are derived by a congruence. Hence deduce in another way that congruence closure of the subterms in the input problem is a complete approach to the equational theory of a set of ground equations.

4.3   We can reduce validity of arbitrary formulas in first-order logic with equality to a language with equality as the only predicate by the device of turning each $P(t_1, \ldots, t_n)$ to a term $f_P(t_1, \ldots, t_n) = \mathrm{T}$ for some new n-ary function symbol f_P and a new constant T for 'true'. For example, this allows us to decide the full universal theory of first-order logic with equality using standard congruence closure. Under

---

[†] See `http://www-unix.mcs.anl.gov/AR/new_results/`

what circumstances does this transformation preserve validity? (Take care over 1-element interpretations!)

4.4 Rigorously justify the Ackermann reduction from universal formulas in logic with equality to the corresponding problem without functions, and so all the way to propositional logic. Implement this idea, using some method such as DPLL to solve the resulting formulas, and test it against congruence closure on examples.

4.5 We say that two abstract reduction relations $\rightarrow_\alpha$ and $\rightarrow_\beta$ on a set X *commute* if whenever $a \rightarrow_\alpha^* b$ and $a \rightarrow_\beta^* b'$ there is a c with $b \rightarrow_\beta^* c$ and $b' \rightarrow_\alpha^* c$. Thus, in particular, a reduction relation is confluent iff it commutes with itself. Prove that if a set of reduction relations $\{\rightarrow_\alpha | \alpha \in A\}$ on a set X has the property that any two (not necessarily distinct) $\rightarrow_\alpha$ and $\rightarrow_\beta$ commute, then the union relation $\rightarrow$, defined by $a \rightarrow b$ iff there is an $\alpha \in A$ with $a \rightarrow_\alpha b$, is confluent (Hindley 1964).

4.6 Prove that if two abstract reduction relations $\rightarrow_\alpha$ and $\rightarrow_\beta$ on a set X are such that the union relation $\rightarrow$, i.e. $a \rightarrow b$ iff either $a \rightarrow_\alpha b$ or $a \rightarrow_\beta b$, is transitive, then $\rightarrow$ is terminating iff both $\rightarrow_\alpha$ and $\rightarrow_\beta$ are (Geser 1990). You may find Ramsey's theorem useful. Extend this to the case of n different component relations. For an application to termination analysis of programs see Cook, Podelski and Rybalchenko (2006).

4.7 The Collatz conjecture (Lagarias 1985) is that the following recursive function (assuming unlimited range for the integer n) always terminates. Encode this definition as a rewrite system:

```
let rec collatz n =
  if n <= 1 then n
  else if n mod 2 = 0 then collatz (n / 2) else collatz(3 * n + 1);;
```

4.8 Show that the singleton set of rewrite rules $\{f(f(x)) = f(g(f(x)))\}$ is terminating, but this cannot be shown via any simplification order.

4.9 Complete the following rewrite sets taken from Baader and Nipkow (1998): (a) $\{f(g(f(x))) = g(x)\}$ and (b) $\{f(f(x)) = f(x), g(g(x)) = f(x), f(g(x)) = g(x), g(f(x)) = f(x)\}$. Can you characterize the normal forms? You may like to analyze the examples by hand before running completion.

4.10 Suppose E_1 and E_2 are two separate sets of equations, considered as rewrite rules, that have disjoint signatures, i.e. such that the function (including constant) symbols in E_1 do not occur in E_2 and vice versa. Show that if E_1 and E_2 both have the weak normalization property (every term has a normal form), then so does the combined set $E_1 \cup E_2$. However, give a counterexample to show that even if E_1 and E_2 are terminating (*strongly* normalizing) $E_1 \cup E_2$ may fail to be (Toyama 1987a). Also prove (more difficult) that if E_1 and E_2 are confluent, so is $E_1 \cup E_2$ (Toyama 1987b).

4.11   You will probably find that our present implementation cannot complete the following axioms for 'near rings' in a reasonable time:

$$
\begin{aligned}
0 + x &= x, \\
-x + x &= 0, \\
(x + y) + z &= x + (y + z), \\
(x \cdot y) \cdot z &= x \cdot (y \cdot z), \\
(x + y) \cdot z &= x \cdot z + y \cdot z.
\end{aligned}
$$

Nevertheless, finding a completion is quite feasible (Aichinger 1994). Try optimizing our completion algorithm so that left-reducible rules are put back into the critical pair list, and see if you can then solve it. Can you justify the completeness of this refinement?

4.12   Instead of running completion with a simple queue of critical pairs, an alternative (Lescanne 1984) would be to run the procedure for a while, select the most 'interesting' equations derived – perhaps those with the simplest structure, e.g. $i(i(x)) = x$ above $i(i(x \cdot i(y))) = i(y \cdot i(x))$ – and restart the procedure with the original equations and the interesting ones selected. Implement this idea and see how it works on typical examples. This idea is not restricted to equational reasoning, but could be used for any bottom-up procedure. Try implementing a similar approach to resolution theorem proving and test its effectiveness.

4.13   Although we've exclusively used versions of the LPO as the ordering in rewriting and completion, Knuth and Bendix (1970) originally used somewhat different orderings, now known as Knuth–Bendix orderings. Try these out following Knuth and Bendix's original paper, and try to convince yourselves theoretically that they have the required properties for a simplification order. Take care over the restrictions on the 'weights'.

4.14   Prove that the LPO is total on ground terms (or terms where weights are assigned to the variables as if they were constants).

4.15   Implement basic automated confluence analysis for ordered rewrite systems as follows. Generate all the possible orderings for the (terms substituted for) the variables on the left of a rewrite rule, e.g. for

$(x + y) + z = x + (y + z)$ the orders include $x = y = z$, $x = y < z$, $y < x = z$ and $y < z < z$. Implement a variant of `lpo_gt` that uses these orderings as hypotheses and deduces the ordering of terms built up from them. For each case, analyze critical pairs, exclude those that are ruled out by orderings and try to verify that the feasible critical pairs are joinable subject to the same constraints. Try your code out on the examples from Martin and Nipkow (1990).

4.16   Paramodulation was based on the idea of a special rule for equality, rather than modification of the input formula. We might also consider modifying top-down methods such as tableaux with special equality-handling methods. Study the methods presented by Fitting (1990) and implement and test them on some equality problems. Can you use similar techniques with model elimination?

5

Decidable problems

We've considered various algorithms (tableaux, resolution, etc.) for verifying that a first-order formula is logically valid, if indeed it is. But these will not in general tell us when a formula is not valid. We'll see in Chapter 7 that there is no systematic procedure for doing so. However, there are procedures that work for certain special classes of formulas, or for validity in certain special (classes of) models, and we discuss some of the more important ones in this chapter. Often these naturally generalize common decision problems in mathematics and universal algebra such as equation-solving or the 'word problem'.

5.1 The decision problem

There are three natural and closely connected problems for first-order logic for which we might want an algorithmic solution. By negating the formula, we can according to taste present them in terms of validity or unsatisfiability.

(1) Confirm that a logically valid (or unsatisfiable) formula is indeed valid (resp. unsatisfiable), and never confirm an invalid (satisfiable) one.

(2) Confirm that a logically invalid (or satisfiable) formula is indeed invalid (resp. satisfiable), and never confirm a valid (unsatisfiable) one.

(3) Test whether a formula is valid or invalid (or whether it is satisfiable or unsatisfiable).

Evidently (3) encompasses both (1) and (2). Conversely, solutions to both (1) and (2) could be used together to solve (3): just run the verification procedures for validity and invalidity (or satisfiability and unsatisfiability) in parallel. Now, we have presented explicit solutions to (1), such as tableaux or resolution. But these do *not* solve (3). Given a satisfiable formula, these algorithms, while at least not incorrectly claiming they are unsatisfiable, will not always terminate. For example, these attempts to prove an invalid formula just keep fruitlessly searching:

```
# tab <<forall x. p(x)>>;;
# meson <<forall x. p(x)>>;;
```

Trying `resolution` instead we *do* get a termination with failure. But one can concoct slightly more complicated examples where that too will loop indefinitely. In fact, a key limitative result due to Church (1936) and Turing (1936), which we will prove in Chapter 7, shows that *no general solution to (2) or (3) is possible.*

However, we can frequently find a full decision procedure for limited or modified forms of the same problem. First, we can restrict in some way the nature of the formula considered, e.g. the arrangement of nested quantifiers when it is placed in prenex normal form. Secondly, we can consider, instead of validity in *all* interpretations, validity in a more limited class of interpretations. Often this means all models of some standard set of axioms Δ, so instead of a decision procedure for $\models p$ we seek one for $\Delta \models p$.

5.2 The AE fragment

All the proof procedures for first-order logic that we've mechanized are ultimately justified by Herbrand's theorem: the Skolemized, quantifier-free form of a formula is unsatisfiable iff some finite conjunction of ground instances is propositionally unsatisfiable. In general, the set of possible ground instances is infinite, and the use of unification to guide our search through it does not alter that fundamental fact. However, in the special case when the Skolemized form contains no functions except nullary ones (i.e. constants), the number of ground instances is bounded. For example, recall the Łoś formula:

```
let los =
 <<(forall x y z. P(x,y) /\ P(y,z) ==> P(x,z)) /\
   (forall x y z. Q(x,y) /\ Q(y,z) ==> Q(x,z)) /\
   (forall x y. P(x,y) ==> P(y,x)) /\
   (forall x y. P(x,y) \/ Q(x,y))
   ==> (forall x y. P(x,y)) \/ (forall x y. Q(x,y))>>;;
```

If we Skolemize its negation as a prelude to refutation, the result contains four constant symbols and three variables, but no non-nullary functions:

```
# skolemize(Not los);;
- : fol formula =
<<(((~P(x,y) \/ ~P(y,z)) \/ P(x,z)) /\
   ((~Q(x,y) \/ ~Q(y,z)) \/ Q(x,z)) /\
   (~P(x,y) \/ P(y,x)) /\ (P(x,y) \/ Q(x,y))) /\
  ~P(c_x,c_y) /\ ~Q(c_x',c_y')>>
```

Each of the three variables can be replaced only by one of the four constants, so there are just $4^3 = 64$ ground instances. Thus the unsatisfiability of the Skolemized form is equivalent to propositional unsatisfiability of the conjunction of these 64 ground instances. Our earlier procedure `davisputnam` proves it reasonably quickly by trying only 45 of these possibilities:

```
# davisputnam los;;
0 ground instances tried; 0 items in list
...
44 ground instances tried; 109 items in list
- : int = 45
```

However, we now know that we could have just conjoined all ground instances and tested for propositional satisfiability once and for all. This general approach can be implemented as follows:

```
let aedecide fm =
  let sfm = skolemize(Not fm) in
  let fvs = fv sfm
  and cnsts,funcs = partition (fun (_,ar) -> ar = 0) (functions sfm) in
  if funcs <> [] then failwith "Not decidable" else
  let consts = if cnsts = [] then ["c",0] else cnsts in
  let cntms = map (fun (c,_) -> Fn(c,[])) consts in
  let alltuples = groundtuples cntms [] 0 (length fvs) in
  let cjs = simpcnf sfm in
  let grounds = map
   (fun tup -> image (image (subst (fpf fvs tup))) cjs) alltuples in
  not(dpll(unions grounds));;
```

For our implementations, tested on the Loś formula, `aedecide` happens to be significantly faster than `davisputnam`. But we're not really interested in this, or indeed the relative performance of intermediate possibilities like testing on every tenth ground instance (considered in Davis and Putnam's original paper). Rather, the crucial point is that by placing a bound on the number of ground instances, `aedecide` always gives a yes/no answer; if the original formula is *not* valid, it tells us, rather than simply carrying on forever.

We could quite easily ensure termination in such cases for many general theorem–proving procedures too. For instance, we could modify the inner loop of our Davis-Putnam procedure so that it returns 'true' if the formula is valid (instead of the number of ground instances) and 'false' if the set of ground instances is exhausted. Even some unification-based procedures are guaranteed to terminate for problems with no function symbols in the Skolemized negated input formula. The same can be true, by accident or design, for formulas in other significant subsets (Fermueller, Leitsch, Tammet and Zamov 1993; de Nivelle 1995).

How can we anticipate, based on the original problem, that the Skolemized form will have only nullary function symbols? For simplicity, suppose that the formula, to be tested for satisfiability, is in NNF. First of all, the initial formula must have no non-nullary functions, since Skolemization isn't going to *remove* any. Secondly, we must have no subformulas of the form $\exists y. P[x, y]$ with another free or universally quantified variable x in its scope, since this will result in a Skolem function with (at least) x as an argument. For a sentence, a simple sufficient condition for this not to happen is that all the existential quantifiers occur before the universal quantifiers in any path to a subformula:

$$\exists x_1. \cdots \exists x_n. \cdots \forall y_1. \cdots \forall y_m.$$

It's rather hard to state this precisely because of the complicated ways quantifiers and propositional connectives can be nested inside each other. It becomes easier to describe if we put the formula into prenex normal form first, since then we can say that a formula is in the required subset iff it has the form:

$$\exists x_1, \ldots, x_n. \forall y_1, \ldots, y_m. P[x_1, \ldots, x_n, y_1, \ldots, y_m]$$

(where n or m may be zero). Since all the '$\exists$'s come before the '$\forall$'s, such a formula is said to be in the 'EA subset'. However, we are speaking here of the satisfiability problem, which is applied to the negation of the formula we want to prove. We need the *original* formula that we are testing for validity to be of the form:

$$\forall x_1, \ldots, x_n. \exists y_1, \ldots, y_m. P[x_1, \ldots, x_n, y_1, \ldots, y_m],$$

that is, in the 'AE subset' or just 'AE'. The remarks above indicate that validity for AE formulas is decidable, or equivalently, that satisfiability for EA formulas is decidable.

While the systematic use of prenex normal form simplifies categorization of formulas, it's preferable in the actual implementation to Skolemize directly. If one does make a PNF transformation first, some finesse can be needed in the order of transformations. For example, if the original formula when put in NNF is of the form:

$$(\forall x.\, P(x)) \vee (\exists y.\, Q(y))$$

we must first pull out the universal quantifier, then the existential:

$$(\forall x.\, P(x)) \vee (\exists y.\, Q(y)) \longrightarrow \forall x.\, P(x) \vee \exists y.\, Q(y) \longrightarrow \forall x.\, \exists y.\, P(x) \vee Q(y)$$

rather than vice versa:

$$(\forall x.\, P(x)) \vee (\exists y.\, Q(y)) \longrightarrow \exists y.\, (\forall x.\, P(x)) \vee Q(y) \longrightarrow \exists y.\, \forall x.\, P(x) \vee Q(y)$$

even though both are logically valid transitions on the way to PNF. Luckily, we ordered the subcases of `pullquants` with the universal quantifier matches first, so we'll get the desired effect. But this must be applied to the formula *before it is negated for refutation*, or the opposite will happen.

```
# let fm = <<(forall x. p(x)) \/ (exists y. p(y))>>;;
val fm : fol formula = <<(forall x. p(x)) \/ (exists y. p(y))>>
# pnf fm;;
- : fol formula = <<forall x. exists y. p(x) \/ p(y)>>
```

The earlier group theory problem (a group where $x^2 = 1$ is abelian), in its predicate formulation, also lies in the AE subset, because we didn't use the inverse axiom:

```
# aedecide
  <<(forall x. P(1,x,x)) /\ (forall x. P(x,x,1)) /\
    (forall u v w x y z.
        P(x,y,u) /\ P(y,z,w) ==> (P(x,w,v) <=> P(u,z,v)))
    ==> forall a b c. P(a,b,c) ==> P(b,a,c)>>;;
- : bool = true
```

Admittedly, MESON solves it more rapidly, because the large number of variables in the associativity axiom gives rise to many ground instances ($4^6 = 4096$). But a decision procedure allows us, at least in principle, to confirm that certain similar assertions are *not* valid. For example, in case we were in doubt we can confirm that the identity axiom is necessary:

```
# aedecide
  <<(forall x. P(x,x,1)) /\
    (forall u v w x y z.
        P(x,y,u) /\ P(y,z,w) ==> (P(x,w,v) <=> P(u,z,v)))
    ==> forall a b c. P(a,b,c) ==> P(b,a,c)>>;;
- : bool = false
```

5.3 Miniscoping and the monadic fragment

We have noted that Skolemizing first usually avoids the problem of introducing quantifier nesting of an undesirable kind. For example, `aedecide` can easily settle the validity of the following, Pelletier problem 29:

```
# aedecide
   <<(exists x. P(x)) /\ (exists x. G(x))
     ==> ((forall x. P(x) ==> H(x)) /\ (forall x. G(x) ==> J(x)) <=>
         (forall x y. P(x) /\ G(y) ==> H(x) /\ J(y)))>>;;
- : bool = true
```

However, the wrong kind of quantifier nesting present from the start precludes the use of `aedecide`, even on examples that `davisputnam` can prove very easily, like Pelletier problem 18:

```
# aedecide <<exists y. forall x. P(y) ==> P(x)>>;;
Exception: Failure "Not decidable".
```

Nevertheless, we can massage the formula into AE form by applying some of the PNF transformations in reverse order, to push quantifiers in rather than pulling them out.

$$\exists y.\, \forall x.\, P(y) \Rightarrow P(x)$$
$$\longrightarrow\quad \exists y.\, \forall x.\, \neg P(y) \vee P(x)$$
$$\longrightarrow\quad \exists y.\, \neg P(y) \vee (\forall x.\, P(x))$$
$$\longrightarrow\quad (\exists y.\, \neg P(y)) \vee (\forall x.\, P(x))$$
$$\longrightarrow\quad \neg(\forall y.\, P(y)) \vee (\forall x.\, P(x))$$

The modified formula is AE, and if it is now prenexed the order of the quantifiers will have been reversed. In fact, the formula as it stands is, if we ignore bound variable names, a propositional tautology.

Thus, by performing some initial transformations, we can decide a broader class of formulas than those ostensibly in AE. It's hard to give any definite limit to the class of formulas that *can* be reduced to AE form, since after all any valid formula has an AE equivalent ('⊤'), as does every unsatisfiable one ('⊥'). We will present an algorithm that follows the pattern of the above example by trying, fairly straightforwardly, to push quantifiers as far inwards as possible. This converse to the PNF procedure is usually known as *miniscoping* because it minimizes the scope of the quantifier. First we define a function `separate` intended to transform a formula $\exists x.\, p_1 \wedge \cdots \wedge p_n$ into $(\exists x.\, p_i \wedge \cdots p_j) \wedge (p_k \wedge \cdots \wedge p_l)$ where the $p_i, \ldots, p_j$ are the formulas with x free and the $p_k, \ldots, p_l$ are the others. The conjuncts in the input formula are presented as a set `cjs`.

```
let separate x cjs =
  let yes,no = partition (mem x ** fv) cjs in
  if yes = [] then list_conj no
  else if no = [] then Exists(x,list_conj yes)
  else And(Exists(x,list_conj yes),list_conj no);;
```

Now we define a function **pushquant**, which given a variable x and formula p transforms the formula $\exists x.\, p$ into an equivalent with the scope of the quantifier reduced. First of all, if x is not free in p, the answer is just p. Otherwise the formula p is put into disjunctive normal form so the formula is:

$$\exists x.\, C_1 \vee \cdots \vee C_n,$$

where each C_i is a conjunction of literals. We then transform this to:

$$(\exists x.\, C_1) \vee \cdots \vee (\exists x.\, C_n)$$

and then each disjunct is dealt with by **separate** and the results disjoined:

```
let rec pushquant x p =
  if not (mem x (fv p)) then p else
  let djs = purednf(nnf p) in
  list_disj (map (separate x) djs);;
```

Now the overall function is a straightforward recursion. To avoid coding an essentially dual function for the universal quantifier, we transform $\forall x.\, p$ into $\neg(\exists x.\, \neg p)$. Note that we assume the initial formula is in NNF and hence avoid dealing with some cases:

```
let rec miniscope fm =
  match fm with
    Not p -> Not(miniscope p)
  | And(p,q) -> And(miniscope p,miniscope q)
  | Or(p,q) -> Or(miniscope p,miniscope q)
  | Forall(x,p) -> Not(pushquant x (Not(miniscope p)))
  | Exists(x,p) -> pushquant x (miniscope p)
  | _ -> fm;;
```

This handles the simple example we used above:

```
# miniscope(nnf <<exists y. forall x. P(y) ==> P(x)>>);;
- : fol formula = <<(exists y. ~P(y)) \/ (forall x. P(x))>>
```

as well as various more complicated examples such as Pelletier problem 20. Here the miniscoping restricts the scope of the quantifiers very successfully, right down to the level of the literals:

```
# let fm = miniscope(nnf
    <<(forall x y. exists z. forall w. P(x) /\ Q(y) ==> R(z) /\ U(w))
      ==> (exists x y. P(x) /\ Q(y)) ==> (exists z. R(z))>>);;
val fm : fol formula =
  <<((exists x. P(x)) /\
     (forall z. ~R(z)) /\ (exists w. ~U(w)) /\ (exists y. Q(y)) \/
     (exists x. P(x)) /\ (forall z. ~R(z)) /\ (exists y. Q(y)) \/
     (exists x. P(x)) /\ (exists w. ~U(w)) /\ (exists y. Q(y))) \/
    ~((exists x. P(x)) /\ (exists y. Q(y))) \/ (exists z. R(z))>>
```

and then the original prenexing procedure will give an AE result:

```
# pnf(nnf fm);;
#  pnf(nnf fm);;
- : fol formula =
<<forall z z' x y.
    exists x' w y'.
      (P(x') /\ ~R(z) /\ ~U(w) /\ Q(y') \/
       P(x') /\ ~R(z') /\ Q(w) \/ P(x') /\ ~U(w) /\ Q(y')) \/
      (~P(x) \/ ~Q(y)) \/ R(x')>>
```

It's hard to give an immediately graspable description of the class of problems where this miniscoping procedure, followed by prenexing, will give an AE formula. However, it does include a class of formulas that is very easy to describe, namely the *monadic* formulas. These are formulas (like the above example) that may have arbitrary quantifier nesting but involve no function symbols and just monadic (unary) predicate symbols, that is, those with only one argument. (The Łoś formula is not in this class because the predicate R it involves takes two arguments.) Even for a monadic formula, the miniscoping procedure may not always push quantifiers down to the level of literals; consider as a counterexample $\exists x.\ P(x) \wedge Q(x)$. Nevertheless, we claim that `miniscope` applied to a monadic formula yields a result that has the following property:

The body of each quantifier '$\forall x.\ \cdots$' or '$\exists x.\ \cdots$' has (i) no other quantifiers, and (ii) no free variables other than x.

We can prove this by induction on the size of the input formula, considering the cases in the definition of `miniscope`. The property above is preserved by propositional combinations, and the universal quantifier is transformed away. So the interesting case is the existential quantifier, and by the inductive hypothesis, it suffices to prove the following lemma: if p has this property so does `pushquant` $x\ p$. (In this application p is the result from the nested call to `miniscope`.) If we hit the trivial case where x is not free in p and the returned formula is p, the result is immediate. Otherwise, the DNF transformation of p yields a formula $C_1 \vee \cdots \vee C_n$ (maybe just one disjunct) over which we distribute the existential quantifier. Every C_i is a conjunction of terms:

$$p_1 \wedge \cdots \wedge p_n$$

and the formulas p_i are separated into two groups, those with x free and those not. Only the former group are in the scope of the final quantifier, and so the other formulas retain the assumed property. But those with x free must be literals, not quantified formulas, since by the inductive hypothesis quantified subformulas have no free variables (this is not changed by the propositional operations used in generating the DNF). And since all predicates are monadic, they can have no variable *other* than x free, and so the final quantified formula will have no free variables and no quantifier nesting.

Hence, by incorporating miniscoping we extend the scope of the `aedecide` function to a broader class of problems that includes at least all monadic formulas. We call the procedure `wang`, in honour of Hao Wang, who first implemented a theorem prover for this subset (Wang 1960).[†]

```
let wang fm = aedecide(miniscope(nnf(simplify fm)));;
```

This will, in principle, solve all monadic formulas, such as the following, Pelletier problem 20:

```
# wang
  <<(forall x y. exists z. forall w. P(x) /\ Q(y) ==> R(z) /\ U(w))
  ==> (exists x y. P(x) /\ Q(y)) ==> (exists z. R(z))>>;;
- : bool = true
```

In practice, however, our simple miniscoping transformations can cause an explosion in the size of the formula, because in the case of alternating quantifiers, the body is alternately transformed into DNF and CNF. Thus there is no guarantee that the method is acceptably efficient in practice. A particularly bad example is 'Andrews's challenge', which already blows up quite a lot just when transformed to NNF, even though the nesting of quantifiers is modest.

```
# pnf(nnf(miniscope(nnf
  <<((exists x. forall y. P(x) <=> P(y)) <=>
    ((exists x. Q(x)) <=> (forall y. Q(y)))) <=>
    ((exists x. forall y. Q(x) <=> Q(y)) <=>
    ((exists x. P(x)) <=> (forall y. P(y))))>>)));;
```

[†] Wang also discussed a general first-order proof procedure based on sequent calculus at much the same time as the other pioneers such as Gilmore and Prawitz. However, he did not actually implement this fuller procedure.

The resulting formula is AE, but it has 19 universal quantifiers followed by 10 existentials. There are thus no fewer than 10^{19} ground instances, of quite a large body. It is simply not feasible to test them all.

5.4 Syllogisms

One of the earliest and most influential works of logic was the analysis of *syllogisms* introduced by Aristotle in his *Prior Analytics*. Aristotelian syllogisms are constructed from three 'premises', each of one of the following forms (the letters A, E, I and O are now standard but were not introduced by Aristotle):

- A – all S are P (universal affirmative),
- E – no S are P (universal negative),
- I – some S are P (particular affirmative),
- O – some S are not P (particular negative).

Examples of premises include 'all men are mortal' (A) and 'some philosophers are not Greek' (O). The constructs S and P inside premises are traditionally called *terms*, but they are nothing like terms in first-order logic, and in fact we will shortly formalize them using first-order predicates. Aristotelian syllogisms are certain logical implications of the form 'if A and B then C' where A, B and C are premises. They are restricted to involve just three terms, the *subject S* and *predicate P*, which occur in that order in the consequent, and a *middle term M* which occurs in both antecedents together with either S or P. A concrete example given by Aristotle in the *Posterior Analytics* is:[†]

If all broad-leafed plants are deciduous, and all vines are broad-leafed plants, then all vines are deciduous.

There are four different 'figures' of the syllogism, depending on how the two antecedents are arranged. Actually, Aristotle only laid out the first three figures, but he gave several examples belonging to the fourth figure and it was therefore natural to add it later – for more information about the development of Aristotelian syllogisms, see Łukasiewicz (1951).

[†] Aristotle only used variables to denote terms used as general predicates, not to identify specific individuals, so the popular example 'Socrates is mortal' is not a premiss, strictly speaking, though one may interpret 'Socrates' as a predicate applying to those individuals identical with Socrates. Note also that syllogisms are implications with hypothetical antecedents, not deductions from premises assumed to be true, so should not be read 'A and B, therefore C'. Thus, the example right at the beginning of section 1.1 was not properly speaking a syllogism.

	I	II	III	IV
if	MP	PM	MP	PM
and	SM	SM	MS	MS
then	SP	SP	SP	SP

Now, we have four different figures, and each of the three premisses can be of one of the forms A, E, I and O; thus we can form $4 \times 4^3 = 256$ different assertions of the syllogistic form. However, only some of these are valid, and we will use our theorem proving apparatus to decide which. First we express the basic premisses in first-order logic, with first-order predicates for the terms and quantified sentences that appear to capture the intended meaning of the premisses:

- A (all S are P): $\forall x.\, S(x) \Rightarrow P(x)$,
- E (no S are P): $\forall x.\, S(x) \Rightarrow \neg P(x)$,
- I (some S are P): $\exists x.\, S(x) \wedge P(x)$,
- O (some S are not P): $\exists x.\, S(x) \wedge \neg P(x)$.

The following syntax functions construct these formulas for given terms p and q:

```
let atom p x = Atom(R(p,[Var x]));;

let premiss_A (p,q) = Forall("x",Imp(atom p "x",atom q "x"))
and premiss_E (p,q) = Forall("x",Imp(atom p "x",Not(atom q "x")))
and premiss_I (p,q) = Exists("x",And(atom p "x",atom q "x"))
and premiss_O (p,q) = Exists("x",And(atom p "x",Not(atom q "x")));;
```

while the following decomposes such a premiss and produces the corresponding English reading:

```
let anglicize_premiss fm =
  match fm with
    Forall(_,Imp(Atom(R(p,_)),Atom(R(q,_)))) ->   "all "^p^" are "^q
  | Forall(_,Imp(Atom(R(p,_)),Not(Atom(R(q,_))))) ->   "no "^p^" are "^q
  | Exists(_,And(Atom(R(p,_)),Atom(R(q,_)))) ->   "some "^p^" are "^q
  | Exists(_,And(Atom(R(p,_)),Not(Atom(R(q,_))))) ->
        "some "^p^" are not "^q;;
```

Regarding a syllogism itself as simply a formula $P_1 \wedge P_2 \Rightarrow P_3$ where the P_i are premisses, we can describe them in English using the following:

```
let anglicize_syllogism (Imp(And(t1,t2),t3)) =
  "If " ^ anglicize_premiss t1 ^ " and " ^ anglicize_premiss t2 ^
  ", then " ^ anglicize_premiss t3;;
```

Now let us generate all 256 possible syllogisms:

```
let all_possible_syllogisms =
  let sylltypes = [premiss_A; premiss_E; premiss_I; premiss_O] in
  let prems1 = allpairs (fun x -> x) sylltypes ["M","P"; "P","M"]
  and prems2 = allpairs (fun x -> x) sylltypes ["S","M"; "M","S"]
  and prems3 = allpairs (fun x -> x) sylltypes ["S","P"] in
  allpairs mk_imp (allpairs mk_and prems1 prems2) prems3;;
```

Note that these are all in the monadic fragment, hence decidable. In fact the quantifiers already have the minimum possible scope, so the formulas can be tested for validity with `aedecide`. Let us filter out all the logically valid syllogisms:

```
# let all_valid_syllogisms = filter aedecide all_possible_syllogisms;;
...
# length all_valid_syllogisms;;
- : int = 15
```

We get 15, which is perhaps a little surprising given that in the traditional Aristotelian syllogistic, 24 have been regarded as valid. (Sometimes only 19 are listed, but others are regarded as implicitly following by 'subalternation'.)

```
# map anglicize_syllogism all_valid_syllogisms;;
- : string list =
["If all M are P and all S are M, then all S are P";
 "If all M are P and some S are M, then some S are P";
 "If all M are P and some M are S, then some S are P";
 "If all P are M and no S are M, then no S are P";
 "If all P are M and no M are S, then no S are P";
 "If all P are M and some S are not M, then some S are not P";
 "If no M are P and all S are M, then no S are P";
 "If no M are P and some S are M, then some S are not P";
 "If no M are P and some M are S, then some S are not P";
 "If no P are M and all S are M, then no S are P";
 "If no P are M and some S are M, then some S are not P";
 "If no P are M and some M are S, then some S are not P";
 "If some M are P and all M are S, then some S are P";
 "If some P are M and all M are S, then some S are P";
 "If some M are not P and all M are S, then some S are not P"]
```

Comparison of this list with the traditional ones shows that we have recognized a proper subset of the traditional syllogisms, excluding several such as Darapti:[†] 'if all M are P and all M are S, then some S are P'. In our formulation this is clearly invalid: we can easily derive bogus instances such

---

[†] Syllogisms are traditionally allocated mnemonic names, with vowels that indicate the kinds of the three premises (A, E, I or O), and consonants that show in a rather complicated way how to convert the syllogism to those of the first figure.

as 'if all immortals will live forever and all immortals are people then some people will live forever'.

So the correspondence between Aristotle's logic and the first-order readings is not quite as straightforward as it first appeared. The problems seem to arise in cases where one or more of the predicates involved is identically false – i.e. there is nothing that satisfies it. One interpretation of the traditional list is that all terms are implicitly supposed to be applicable to something. If we add this hypothesis, then we *do* recover the classic list:

```
# let all_possible_syllogisms' =
    let p =
      <<(exists x. P(x)) /\ (exists x. M(x)) /\ (exists x. S(x))>> in
    map (fun t -> Imp(p,t)) all_possible_syllogisms;;
...
# let all_valid_syllogisms' = filter aedecide all_possible_syllogisms';;
...
# length all_valid_syllogisms';;
- : int = 24
# map (anglicize_syllogism ** consequent) all_valid_syllogisms';;
...
```

Still, it's not clear that this is really a faithful exegesis of how Aristotle and/or the medieval logicians really thought about syllogistic reasoning. To be at all confident about that, we need to consider not only the validity of the syllogisms themselves, but also of the various conversion rules that were used to manipulate them. For a more detailed examination of the relationship between Aristotle's logic and various first-order readings, see Strawson (1952).

In any case, since there are only finitely many possible syllogisms, Aristotle's logic is decidable, if only by fiat. And the other major logical system handed down from the Ancient Greeks, the Megarian–Stoic logic, can be regarded as a subset of propositional logic and so is also decidable. Perhaps this fact was unduly influential in forming Leibniz's expectations that a general *calculus ratiocinator* could be found.

5.5 The finite model property

For another perspective on first-order decidability, it's fruitful to consider the possible sizes of (the domains of) models of a formula. This can naturally explain the decidability of various fragments of first-order logic, and give rise to alternative decision procedures.

Note first that whether a formula p has a model M with domain D can depend only on the *size* (cardinality) of D. For given a model M with domain

D, and another set D' with the same cardinality, we know there are mutually inverse bijections $i : D \to D'$ and $j : D' \to D$ (see Appendix 1). We can then construct a model M' of p with domain D' by interpreting functions and predicates so that i and j determine an isomorphism (see Section 4.2) by construction: $f_{M'}(y_1, y_2) = i(f_M(j(y_1), j(y_2)))$, $P_{M'}(y) = P_M(j(y))$ etc.

Now the Löwenheim–Skolem theorems tell us that if a first-order formula has a model of any cardinality (any infinite cardinality, for logic with equality), it has a model of any other infinite cardinality. But formulas can place strong constraints on the sizes of *finite* models, even if we consider logic without equality. For example, $\exists x\, y.\, P(x) \wedge \neg P(y)$ is satisfiable, but any model must have size ≥ 2. If we consider logic with equality, i.e. restrict ourselves to normal models, we can get specific size constraints; for example $\exists x\, y.\, \neg(x = y) \wedge \forall z.\, z = x \vee z = y$ is only satisfiable in models of size *exactly* 2.

More generally, for syntactically restricted classes of formulas, it often turns out that satisfiability, i.e. having a model at all, is equivalent to having a finite model. (Or dually, validity is equivalent to holding in all finite models.)

Definition 5.1 *A formula is said to have the* finite model property *for validity precisely when it is valid in all models iff it is valid in all finite models. Similarly, it is said to have the finite model property for satisfiability precisely when it is satisfiable iff it is satisfiable in a finite model.*

As well as coining the phrase 'finite model property', Harrop (1958) made the following observation, in a somewhat more general context.

Theorem 5.2 *There is a systematic procedure for deciding the validity (satisfiability) of all formulas with the finite model property for validity (resp. satisfiability)*

Proof We will prove the 'validity' version, the 'satisfiability' one being essentially the same. We already have procedures that will verify the validity of a formula if it is indeed valid – any of the major methods like resolution will do. Moreover, because of the finite model property, we have a systematic procedure for verifying if it is *not* valid: just enumerate larger and larger finite interpretations till we find one in which it doesn't hold. To get a decision procedure we simply need to interleave these procedures, and one or the other will terminate successfully and make the decision. □

The proof can be considered just a special case of a general result in computability theory (see Theorem 7.13 later on). But to make the reasoning quite concrete and explicit we will really implement the interleaving posited in the previous proof. First, we implement functions to create the set of all interpretations with a domain $\{1, \ldots, n\}$, in a series of steps. The following constructs all tuples of size n with members chosen from the list l:

```
let rec alltuples n l =
  if n = 0 then [[]] else
  let tups = alltuples (n - 1) l in
  allpairs (fun h t -> h::t) l tups;;
```

The following produces all possible functions out of a finite domain dom and into a finite range ran, making it undefined outside dom:

```
let allmappings dom ran =
  itlist (fun p -> allpairs (valmod p) ran) dom [undef];;
```

To construct all interpretations, we need to enumerate all ways of interpreting function symbols. The intended domain depends on the arity of the function symbol, so we define a 'dependent domain' variant of the above:

```
let alldepmappings dom ran =
  itlist (fun (p,n) -> allpairs (valmod p) (ran n)) dom [undef];;
```

We can create all possible interpretations of n-ary functions and predicates over a domain dom:

```
let allfunctions dom n = allmappings (alltuples n dom) dom;;

let allpredicates dom n = allmappings (alltuples n dom) [false;true];;
```

Finally, we can now decide whether a formula holds in all interpretations of size n. First, we set the domain to be the set $\{1, \ldots, n\}$ and construct all possible interpretations of the functions and predicate symbols involved in the formula. Then we generalize the formula over all free variables (simpler than constructing all possible valuations of them) and test whether the generalized formula holds in all the interpretations constructed (the valuation is irrelevant for a closed formula so we make it undefined).

```
let decide_finite n fm =
  let funcs = functions fm and preds = predicates fm and dom = 1--n in
  let fints = alldepmappings funcs (allfunctions dom)
  and pints = alldepmappings preds (allpredicates dom) in
  let interps = allpairs (fun f p -> dom,f,p) fints pints in
  let fm' = generalize fm in
  forall (fun md -> holds md undefined fm') interps;;
```

Now, for a decision procedure we can interleave calls to this function for larger and larger **n** with the search process in some validity-proving procedure for the formula. This is quite straightforward using methods like `tab` and MESON where we already use iterative deepening to separate search into stages, each of which is itself certain to terminate. We just adapt MESON slightly to place a fixed proof size bound **n** on the search, essentially just removing the use of `deepen`:

```
let limmeson n fm =
  let cls = simpcnf(specialize(pnf fm)) in
  let rules = itlist ((@) ** contrapositives) cls [] in
  mexpand rules [] False (fun x -> x) (undefined,n,0);;
```

and construct a theorem-proving function from it as before:

```
let limited_meson n fm =
  let fm1 = askolemize(Not(generalize fm)) in
  map (limmeson n ** list_conj) (simpdnf fm1);;
```

The decision procedure works as follows. Try to prove the formula using MESON with a size limit n. If that succeeds, it is valid so we return 'true'. If not, we test whether the formula holds in all interpretations of size n. If it does not, it's not valid so we return 'false'. Otherwise we increase n by 1 and repeat:

```
let decide_fmp fm =
  let rec test n =
    try limited_meson n fm; true with Failure _ ->
    if decide_finite n fm then test (n + 1) else false in
  test 1;;
```

This can indeed be used to prove formulas either valid or invalid, and its results are always correct when it terminates.

```
# decide_fmp
    <<(forall x y. R(x,y) \/ R(y,x)) ==> forall x. R(x,x)>>;;
- : bool = true
# decide_fmp
    <<(forall x y z. R(x,y) /\ R(y,z) ==> R(x,z)) ==> forall x. R(x,x)>>;;
- : bool = false
```

Termination is guaranteed for formulas with the finite model property, but not if the formula has a countermodel (i.e. an interpretation that does not satisfy it) but no finite countermodel, as here (this example is discussed in more detail below):

```
decide_fmp
 <<~((forall x. ~R(x,x)) /\
     (forall x. exists z. R(x,z)) /\
     (forall x y z. R(x,y) /\ R(y,z) ==> R(x,z)))>>;;
```

Moreover, even when termination is guaranteed in principle, in practice the number of possible interpretations explodes dramatically as n increases, so this is hardly a feasible approach. Still, some such procedure is not a bad thing to try when faced with a reasonably simple formula whose validity is open. A generally more efficient alternative algorithm that avoids explicit enumeration of all interpretations by using propositional validity checking as a subroutine is suggested in Exercise 5.1 below. There are a number of more heavyweight tools that are designed to find (counter)models for first-order formulas, e.g. Mace4 and Paradox.[†]

Instances of the finite model property

For certain classes of formulas, one can not only demonstrate the finite model property abstractly, but exhibit some definite finite size that is all we need to check. In this case we say that the class of formulas has the *small model property*. Monadic formulas are a relatively easy example.

Theorem 5.3 *If a formula p involves k distinct monadic predicates (predicates of arity 1) and none of higher arity (in particular, not equality) and also involves no function symbols, then p has a model iff it has a model of size 2^k.*

Proof (sketch) The basic idea is that in any interpretation, the k predicates can distinguish at most 2^k distinct subsets, so all the information in such a model can be conveyed by a model of at most size 2^k, collapsing each such subset to a single element. The formal details are left to the reader.   □

The small model property yields a decision algorithm with a definite bound on its runtime, albeit sometimes not a very practical one, rather than merely an abstract assurance that it will eventually terminate. For example, to decide a monadic formula, we just need to test it in all interpretations of size 2^k, where k is the number of monadic predicate symbols involved.

```
let decide_monadic fm =
  let funcs = functions fm and preds = predicates fm in
  let monadic,other = partition (fun (_,ar) -> ar = 1) preds in
  if funcs <> [] or exists (fun (_,ar) -> ar > 1) other
  then failwith "Not in the monadic subset" else
  let n = funpow (length monadic) (( * ) 2) 1 in
  decide_finite n fm;;
```

This disposes of the Andrews Challenge very quickly:

```
# decide_monadic
    <<((exists x. forall y. P(x) <=> P(y)) <=>
      ((exists x. Q(x)) <=> (forall y. Q(y)))) <=>
      ((exists x. forall y. Q(x) <=> Q(y)) <=>
      ((exists x. P(x)) <=> (forall y. P(y))))>>;;
- : bool = true
```

On the other hand, the new procedure is inefficient when there are many predicates, so different methods are often preferable in other situations. For example, Pelletier problem 20, which is trivial for the **wang** procedure, is not feasible, since it involves constructing all 2^{64} possible interpretations of four predicates with a domain of size 16:

```
decide_monadic
  <<(forall x y. exists z. forall w. P(x) /\ Q(y) ==> R(z) /\ U(w))
    ==> (exists x y. P(x) /\ Q(y)) ==> (exists z. R(z))>>;;
```

Decidable and undecidable prefix classes

There are also straightforward small model bounds for the AE fragment that we have already considered, as first shown by Bernays and Schönfinkel (1928); see Exercise 5.4. Besides being independently interesting and proving decidability, such a theorem can be used to show definitively that certain formulas have no AE equivalent, by showing that they do not have the corresponding instances of the finite model property. Ackermann (1928) also showed that formulas of the form:

$$\forall x_1, \ldots, x_n. \exists y. \forall z_1, \ldots, z_m. P[x_1, \ldots, x_n, y, z_1, \ldots, z_m]$$

have the finite model property for validity. A still further generalization to formulas of the form:

$$\forall x_1, \ldots, x_n. \exists y_1, y_2. \forall z_1, \ldots, z_m. P[x_1, \ldots, x_n, y_1, y_2, z_1, \ldots, z_m]$$

was proved by Gödel (1932). This set of prefixes exhausts the cases where the decision problem can be solved by use of the finite model property. For consider these two formulas, having the simplest quantifier prefixes that fail to fit in the subsets with the finite model property discussed so far:

- $\exists x\, y\, z.\, \forall u.\, R(x,x) \vee \neg R(x,u) \vee (R(x,y) \wedge R(y,z) \wedge \neg R(x,z))$,
- $\exists x.\, \forall y.\, \exists z.\, R(x,x) \vee \neg R(x,y) \vee (R(y,z) \wedge \neg R(x,z))$.

We put them in prenex form to display the quantifier prefix, but they are perhaps more perspicuous in the following logically equivalent forms, which the reader may verify using, say, meson:

- $\neg((\forall x.\, \neg R(x,x)) \wedge (\forall x.\, \exists z.\, R(x,z)) \wedge (\forall x\, y\, z.\, R(x,y) \wedge R(y,z) \Rightarrow R(x,z)))$,
- $\neg((\forall x.\, \neg R(x,x)) \wedge (\forall x.\, \exists y.\, R(x,y) \wedge \forall z.\, R(y,z) \Rightarrow R(x,z)))$.

Interpreting $R(x,y)$ as the strict inequality relation $x < y$ over the real numbers makes both formulas false. (This is not hard to see, and in the next section we will develop tools that can verify it automatically.) Thus neither is logically valid. On the other hand, we will show that they *do* both hold in all finite interpretations, and hence the finite model property fails. It suffices to establish this for the second formula because that implies the first:

```
meson
  <<~((forall x. ~R(x,x)) /\
      (forall x. exists y. R(x,y) /\ forall z. R(y,z) ==> R(x,z)))
    ==> ~((forall x. ~R(x,x)) /\
          (forall x. exists z. R(x,z)) /\
          (forall x y z. R(x,y) /\ R(y,z) ==> R(x,z)))>>;;
...
- : int list = [1; 5]
```

Suppose the second formula is false in some finite interpretation M; being closed this means that its negation holds in M:

$$(\forall x.\, \neg R(x,x)) \wedge (\forall x.\, \exists y.\, R(x,y) \wedge \forall z.\, R(y,z) \Rightarrow R(x,z)).$$

Pick an arbitrary $a_0 \in M$. The second conjunct shows that there is an $a_1 \in M$ with $R_M(a_0, a_1)$ and also $R_M(a_0, z)$ for any other z with $R_M(a_1, z)$. Using the second conjunct again, we deduce that there is some a_2 with $R(a_1, a_2)$, and by the auxiliary property we also have $R(a_0, a_2)$. Continuing in this way we can generate a sequence of elements (a_i) with $R_M(a_i, a_j)$ for all $i < j$. Since the model is finite, we must eventually get a repetition, say $a_k = a_l$ for some $k < l$. But then $R_M(a_k, a_l)$ means $R_M(a_k, a_k)$, violating the first, irreflexivity, conjunct.

The failure of the finite model property for these prefix classes doesn't a priori rule out some other kind of solution to the decision problem, but in fact it was shown by, respectively, Surányi (1950) and Kahr, Moore and Wang (1962) that the decision problems for these prefixes are not solvable.

Hence, the quantifier prefix $\forall^n \exists \exists \forall^m$ represents the most complex class that is decidable in general. We will discuss the undecidability results in a little more detail in Chapter 7.

Adding equality

We have assumed above that we are dealing with first-order logic without equality, i.e. allowing non-normal interpretations. If we pass to first-order logic with equality, the boundary between the decidable and undecidable prefix classes is slightly different. We can deduce that the AE subset is still decidable even with equality, simply because if a formula p is AE, i.e. of the form:

$$\forall x_1 \ldots x_n. \, \exists y_1 \ldots y_m. \, q$$

with q quantifier-free, we have $\models p$ in first-order logic with equality iff $\models$ eqaxiom$(p) \Rightarrow p$ in pure first-order logic. But eqaxiom(p) is always, after prenexing in any reasonable way, purely universal, say $\forall z_1, \ldots, z_p. \, e$, and consequently: $\models$ eqaxiom$(p) \Rightarrow p$ is equivalent to

$$\forall x_1 \ldots x_n. \, \exists y_1 \ldots y_m \, z_1 \ldots z_p. \, e \Rightarrow q$$

and this is still AE, hence decidable. It's worth noting that the solvability of this class with equality was the main result of the paper in which Ramsey (1930) introduced his famous combinatorial theorem.[†]

Gödel (1932) asserted that his class $\forall^n \exists \exists \forall^m$ with equality could be decided using the same method he introduced for the non-equality case. However it seems that this was one of Gödel's rare mistakes, for the claim was never subsequently backed up and eventually Goldfarb (1984) proved that the class is in fact undecidable. However, it was proved by Ackermann (1954) that the class with prefix $\forall^n \exists \forall^m$ with equality is decidable. The class with prefix $\exists \forall \exists$ is undecidable even without equality, so a fortiori, with equality. Once again this gives a complete classification of decidability according to quantifier prefix.

Formulas involving only two variables (and no functions) also have the finite model property. We do not insist on prenex form here, so the two variables can be 're-used' quite extensively and the fragment is surprisingly expressive. Decidability was first demonstrated by Scott (1962), who reduced the problem to the Gödel prefix class $\forall^n \exists \exists \forall^m$. This reduction doesn't help

---

[†] Ramsey's proof of the decidability result appears laborious compared with the simple one we have given, but he proves a stronger result that the *spectrum* (set of possible cardinalities of models) is either finite or cofinite.

for the class with equality, but Mortimer (1975) showed that it also has the finite model property, and a much sharper bound was proved by Grädel, Kolaitis and Vardi (1997).

5.6 Quantifier elimination

In search of further interesting cases where a decision method is possible, we turn our attention away from pure logical validity in all interpretations and towards a couple of related questions (still for logic with equality):

- validity in a particular class of interpretations, i.e. whether $\models_M p$ for all interpretations M in a class K;
- logical consequence from a set of axioms Σ, i.e. whether $\Sigma \models p$.

For the examples we treat below (but not in general – see Exercises 5.5 and 5.6) which of these formulation is preferred is inconsequential because the class K is anyway defined to be exactly the collection of models of a set of axioms Σ:

$$\mathrm{Mod}(\Sigma) = \{M \mid \text{for all } \psi \in \Sigma, \ \models_M \psi\}.$$

For example, K might be the class of all groups, which is exactly[†] the class of models of:

$$(\forall x\, y\, z.\, x \cdot (y \cdot z) = (x \cdot y) \cdot z) \wedge (\forall x.\, 1 \cdot x = x) \wedge (\forall x.\, i(x) \cdot x = 1).$$

We can define a kind of converse to Mod, by defining the *theory* of a class of interpretations K to be the set of all sentences holding in all interpretations in the class K:

$$\mathrm{Th}(K) = \{\psi \mid \text{for all } I \in K, \ \models_I \psi\}.$$

When we want to talk about the theory of a specific structure (i.e. a 1-element class of interpretations), we will use the same terminology. For example the 'theory of real numbers', which with a slight abuse of notation we may write $\mathrm{Th}(\mathbb{R})$, is defined to be exactly the set of first-order sentences that hold in the specific structure $\mathbb{R}$. When we want to be precise about the language, as we often do, it's common to further abuse notation by bundling the list of functions and predicates in to boot, e.g. $\mathrm{Th}(\mathbb{R}, 0, 1, -, +, <)$ for a purely additive theory of reals with '$<$' as the only predicate besides equality. Moreover, we sometimes emphasize that we are using first-order

---

[†] We neglect subtleties over the choice of language, e.g. whether we actually have constants like 1 or just existential axioms. Although this doesn't matter much in the case of groups, where identities and inverses are unique, the choice of language can in general significantly affect whether algebraic notions are instantiations of their model-theoretic generalizations (Hodges 1993b).

logic instead of some richer language by stressing 'the *first-order* theory of ...' or 'the *elementary* theory of ...'.

We have $\Sigma \subseteq \mathrm{Th}(\mathrm{Mod}(\Sigma))$, with equality holding precisely when Σ is closed under logical consequence. A set of formulas with this property has a special name, one we use so routinely below that the reader may forget that it has a precise technical meaning:

Definition 5.4 *A theory is a set of formulas T closed under logical consequence, i.e. such that for any formula p we have $T \models p$ iff $p \in T$.*

As we might expect, $\mathrm{Th}(K)$ is always a theory. So also is the set of logical consequences $\mathrm{Cn}(\Sigma) = \{p \mid \Sigma \models p\}$ of any set of formulas Σ. In the latter case we say that the theory T is *axiomatized* by Σ and say that the theory is *axiomatizable*.[†] If there is a finite set of axioms, we say that the theory is *finitely axiomatizable*. Some other important characteristics a theory may have are listed below. (We phrase them in terms of $T \models p$ rather than the equivalent $p \in T$ so that we can forgive loosely applying them to a set of axioms for a theory rather than the theory itself.)

- Consistent – we never have both $T \models p$ and $T \models \neg p$. (Equivalently, we do not have $T \models \bot$, or *some* formula is not a logical consequence of T.)
- Complete – for any sentence p, either $T \models p$ or $T \models \neg p$. (Note that p is a *sentence*: with free variables this property could hardly be expected.)
- Decidable – there is an algorithm that takes as input a formula p and decides whether $T \models p$.

Note that 'consistent' is synonymous with 'satisfiable' when applied to a theory, but it's more common to use the former in this case.[‡] The reader should also take particular care over the use of the word 'complete' as applied to a *theory*, since it is used with a significantly different meaning when applied to a *proof system* as in Section 4.3 and Chapter 6; see also Section 7.3. Another characterization of completeness is that the first-order consequences are completely determined.

Theorem 5.5 *A theory is complete iff all its models are elementarily equivalent.*

[†] Take care: some authors require the set of axioms to be recursively enumerable.
[‡] Some authors use *satisfiable* for the semantic notion $T \not\models \bot$ and *consistent* for a corresponding syntactic notion $T \not\vdash \bot$ for a suitable proof system. But still, for first-order logic and a complete proof system of the kind we consider in chapter 6 they coincide anyway.

Proof Both properties hold trivially if the theory is unsatisfiable, since then there are no models and the theory contains ⊥ and all other formulas. So we can restrict ourselves to theories T with at least one model, say M.

If theory T is complete, take any formula p that holds in M and consider its universal closure $p^* = \texttt{generalize}(p)$. Since T is complete, we either have $p^* \in T$ or $\neg p^* \in T$. The latter is impossible because M is a model of T in which $\neg p^*$ does not hold, so $p^* \in T$ and hence $T \models p$, so p holds in *all* models.

Suppose now that all models of T are elementarily equivalent, and let p be any sentence. Either p or $\neg p$ holds in M (in all valuations, since p is a sentence) and so by elementary equivalence in all models, i.e. either $T \models p$ or $T \models \neg p$. □

It's useful to remember that a complete theory with a finite set of axioms, which we can collect by conjunction into a single axiom A, is automatically decidable. This is simply because for any sentence p we can search in parallel for verifications of $A \Rightarrow p$ and $A \Rightarrow \neg p$, knowing by completeness that one or the other will terminate (perhaps both if the theory is inconsistent). With a little more care, this argument generalizes, using the compactness theorem, to cases where the axiom set is recursively enumerable. On the other hand, this is usually not a very practical approach, so we will focus on more direct methods of proving decidability.

Quantifier elimination

A theory T in a first-order language L admits *quantifier elimination* if for each formula p of L, there is a quantifier-free formula q with $\mathrm{FV}(q) \subseteq \mathrm{FV}(p)$ such that $T \models p \Leftrightarrow q$ (or as we sometimes say, p and q are T-equivalent).[†] As usual, we are interested in constructing quantifier-free equivalents by an algorithmic process, rather than merely showing that they exist in principle.

Quantifier elimination in the case of arithmetical theories is a natural and far-reaching generalization of testing the solvability of equations, which is quantifier elimination for formulas of the particular form $\exists x.\ E[x] = 0$. If a theory admits quantifier elimination, we can reduce many logical questions that seem difficult to the special case of quantifier-free formulas, where they can be much easier. We are particularly interested in (completeness and) decidability. If we start with a sentence, its quantifier-free T-equivalent must be ground, i.e. contain no variables at all. For many, though not all, theories

---

† When the language contains at least one constant, the condition on free variables is no real additional restriction since we could always instantiate any new variables while retaining the validity of $T \models p \Leftrightarrow q$.

of practical interest, the ground formulas have the same truth-values in all models and can be evaluated to 'true' or 'false' algorithmically; for example, in arithmetic theories they are just concrete arithmetic assertions like $2+2 = 5 \Rightarrow 7 < 3$. Any such theory that admits a quantifier elimination algorithm is therefore complete and decidable, and an effective decision procedure is to reduce a formula to a quantifier-free equivalent and evaluate the latter.

Quite generally, to establish quantifier elimination for arbitrary first-order formulas, it suffices to demonstrate it for formulas with the following rather special form:

$$\exists x.\, \alpha_1 \wedge \cdots \wedge \alpha_n$$

with each α_i a literal (either an atomic formula or the negation of an atomic formula) containing x. The basic idea is that we can apply this elimination successively from the innermost quantifier to the outermost, transforming $\forall x. P[x]$ into $\neg(\exists x. \neg P[x])$ and always putting the body in disjunctive normal form and distributing the existential quantifier over it.

We will now expand this terse explanation into an OCaml function taking a quantifier elimination procedure for formulas of this special form and returning a general quantifier elimination procedure.

The first function accepts the core quantifier elimination procedure `bfn` and generalizes it slightly to work for $\exists x.\, p$ where p is any conjunction of literals, some perhaps not involving x. The method is simply to partition the literals into those containing x (`ycjs`) and those not (`ncjs`) and separate off the latter before calling `bfn` on the rest, implicitly using the equivalence $(\exists x.\, p \wedge q[x]) \Leftrightarrow p \wedge \exists x.\, q[x]$:

```
let qelim bfn x p =
  let cjs = conjuncts p in
  let ycjs,ncjs = partition (mem x ** fv) cjs in
  if ycjs = [] then p else
  let q = bfn (Exists(x,list_conj ycjs)) in
  itlist mk_and ncjs q;;
```

Now we define the main function, with a somewhat intricate parametrization. For the moment, assume `afn vars fm` simply returns its second argument `fm` unchanged, while `nfn` performs a transformation into disjunctive normal form. The core quantifier elimination is `qfn`, which takes as an additional parameter the list of quantifiers passed through so far; this information is sometimes useful. Before anything else we miniscope the formula, to make the core quantifier elimination apply to as small a formula as possible.

```
let lift_qelim afn nfn qfn =
  let rec qelift vars fm =
    match fm with
    | Atom(R(_,_)) -> afn vars fm
    | Not(p) -> Not(qelift vars p)
    | And(p,q) -> And(qelift vars p,qelift vars q)
    | Or(p,q) -> Or(qelift vars p,qelift vars q)
    | Imp(p,q) -> Imp(qelift vars p,qelift vars q)
    | Iff(p,q) -> Iff(qelift vars p,qelift vars q)
    | Forall(x,p) -> Not(qelift vars (Exists(x,Not p)))
    | Exists(x,p) ->
          let djs = disjuncts(nfn(qelift (x::vars) p)) in
          list_disj(map (qelim (qfn vars) x) djs)
    | _ -> fm in
  fun fm -> simplify(qelift (fv fm) (miniscope fm));;
```

For the propositional connectives, the same procedure is recursively applied at depth. A universally quantified formula is mapped into an existential one using the infinite De Morgan law. Thus, the interesting case is when the formula is existentially quantified. In this case, we recursively apply the overall quantifier elimination procedure to the body, with an augmented list of variables, which should result in a quantifier-free equivalent for the body. We transform this into DNF by a call to `nfn`, then split the result into its disjuncts and deal with each of them by `qelim`, implicitly using the equivalence:

$$(\exists x.\ D_1[x] \lor \cdots \lor D_n[x]) \Leftrightarrow (\exists x.\ D_1[x]) \lor \cdots \lor (\exists x.\ D_n[x]).$$

It is sometimes convenient to pass as `nfn` an enhanced version of the usual DNF conversion, performing the initial NNF transformation with a couple of tweaks.

First, we may wish to apply a function to modify literals, for example to transform negated inequalities into other forms, say $\neg(s < t)$ to $t \leq s$.

Second, our quantifier elimination functions will often perform case-splits according to some property p of the other variables, yielding a formula of the form $p \land q_0 \lor \neg p \land q_1$. If we subsequently negate this and perform DNF transformation, we tend to get an explosion in size. However, we can exploit the fact that $\neg(p \land q_0 \lor \neg p \land q_1) \Leftrightarrow p \land \neg q_0 \lor \neg p \land \neg q_1$. This wrinkle, together with an extra parameter for a 'literal modification' function `lfn`, is incorporated into a 'clever NNF' function `cnnf`. We incorporate simplification at the beginning, and at the end too in case the literal modification function `lfn` creates additional opportunities.

```
let cnnf lfn =
  let rec cnnf fm =
    match fm with
      And(p,q) -> And(cnnf p,cnnf q)
    | Or(p,q) -> Or(cnnf p,cnnf q)
    | Imp(p,q) -> Or(cnnf(Not p),cnnf q)
    | Iff(p,q) -> Or(And(cnnf p,cnnf q),And(cnnf(Not p),cnnf(Not q)))
    | Not(Not p) -> cnnf p
    | Not(And(p,q)) -> Or(cnnf(Not p),cnnf(Not q))
    | Not(Or(And(p,q),And(p',r))) when p' = negate p ->
          Or(cnnf (And(p,Not q)),cnnf (And(p',Not r)))
    | Not(Or(p,q)) -> And(cnnf(Not p),cnnf(Not q))
    | Not(Imp(p,q)) -> And(cnnf p,cnnf(Not q))
    | Not(Iff(p,q)) -> Or(And(cnnf p,cnnf(Not q)),
                          And(cnnf(Not p),cnnf q))
    | _ -> lfn fm in
  simplify ** cnnf ** simplify;;
```

Example: dense linear orders

The theory of 'dense linear orders without end points' (DLOs) is based on a language containing the binary predicate '<' as well as equality, but no function symbols. It can be axiomatized by the following finite set of sentences:

$$\forall x\, y.\, x = y \vee x < y \vee y < x,$$
$$\forall x\, y\, z.\, x < y \wedge y < z \Rightarrow x < z,$$
$$\forall x.\, \neg(x < x),$$
$$\forall x\, y.\, x < y \Rightarrow \exists z.\, x < z \wedge z < y,$$
$$\forall x.\, \exists y.\, x < y,$$
$$\forall x.\, \exists y.\, y < x.$$

The first three are fairly usual axioms for an irreflexive total (linear) order. The next one asserts 'denseness', i.e. that between each pair of elements there is another, while the last two assert that there is no greatest or least element. Two natural and significantly different models of these axioms are $\mathbb{R}$ and $\mathbb{Q}$ with the predicate '<' interpreted in the usual way. ($\mathbb{Z}$, by contrast, does not satisfy the denseness axiom and so is not a model of the DLO axioms.)

As shown by Langford (1927), this theory admits quantifier elimination, and we will demonstrate an explicit algorithm for it. By the above reduction result, it suffices to consider a formula $\exists x.\, l_1[x] \wedge \cdots \wedge l_n[x]$ where each $l_i[x]$ is a literal containing x. In fact, by giving the following negated literal modifier to the cnnf function, we can eliminate negated literals based on the equivalences $\neg(s < t) \Leftrightarrow s = t \vee t < s$ and $\neg(s = t) \Leftrightarrow s < t \vee t < s$:

```
let lfn_dlo fm =
  match fm with
    Not(Atom(R("<",[s;t]))) -> Or(Atom(R("=",[s;t])),Atom(R("<",[t;s])))
  | Not(Atom(R("=",[s;t]))) -> Or(Atom(R("<",[s;t])),Atom(R("<",[t;s])))
  | _ -> fm;;
```

Thus the core function may assume that all the literals are atoms, which since there are no function symbols must simply be of the form $x < y$ or $x = y$ for variables x and y. Any atom of the form $x = x$ is trivially true and can be ignored; other atoms are collected into a list `cjs`. If any of these is an equation, then it must (because all literals contain the quantified variable) be of the form $x = y$ or $y = x$ where x is the existentially quantified variable to be eliminated and y is another variable. In this case we can get a logically equivalent formula by removing the quantifier and substituting y for x throughout the other conjuncts – this just reflects logical equivalences such as $(\exists x.\, x = y \wedge P[x, y]) \Leftrightarrow P[y, y]$.

If this step is not applicable, then all atoms must be inequalities. If one is of the form $x < x$, it and hence the whole formula is trivially false. Otherwise we collect together as `ls` the set of terms s_i appearing in inequalities $s_i < x$ and as `rs` those t_j appearing in inequalities $x < t_j$. Now, note that in the theory the existential formula

$$\exists x.\, \left(\bigwedge_i s_i < x\right) \wedge \left(\bigwedge_j x < t_j\right)$$

has the quantifier-free equivalent

$$\bigwedge_{i,j} s_i < t_j$$

and so the algorithm forms this conjunction. For the justification of this step, note that $s_i < x \wedge x < t_j$ implies that $s_i < t_j$, while, conversely, if $\bigwedge_{i,j} s_i < t_j$, then in the model the largest s_i and the smallest t_j – and since the ordering is total there must be such – are in the relation $s_i < t_j$ and so by denseness there is an x between them and hence by transitivity between all other pairs. In cases where there are no inequalities of one kind or another (`ls` or `rs` is empty), the formula is equivalent to 'true' since the DLO axioms assert that there are no endpoints. Note that `list_conj` returns '⊤' for the empty list, so these degenerate cases work without special-case logic:

```
let dlobasic fm =
  match fm with
    Exists(x,p) ->
      let cjs = subtract (conjuncts p) [Atom(R("=",[Var x;Var x]))] in
      try let eqn = find is_eq cjs in
          let s,t = dest_eq eqn in
          let y = if s = Var x then t else s in
          list_conj(map (subst (x |=> y)) (subtract cjs [eqn]))
      with Failure _ ->
          if mem (Atom(R("<",[Var x;Var x]))) cjs then False else
          let lefts,rights =
            partition (fun (Atom(R("<",[s;t]))) -> t = Var x) cjs in
          let ls = map (fun (Atom(R("<",[l;_]))) -> l) lefts
          and rs = map (fun (Atom(R("<",[_;r]))) -> r) rights in
          list_conj(allpairs (fun l r -> Atom(R("<",[l;r]))) ls rs)
  | _ -> failwith "dlobasic";;
```

Now the overall quantifier elimination procedure is simple. We add an initial conversion to allow us to use other inequality relations and translate them into the core language ($s \leq t \Leftrightarrow \neg(t < s)$ etc.):

```
let afn_dlo vars fm =
  match fm with
    Atom(R("<=",[s;t])) -> Not(Atom(R("<",[t;s])))
  | Atom(R(">=",[s;t])) -> Not(Atom(R("<",[s;t])))
  | Atom(R(">",[s;t])) -> Atom(R("<",[t;s]))
  | _ -> fm;;
```

and then exploit the usual lifting function:

```
let quelim_dlo =
  lift_qelim afn_dlo (dnf ** cnnf lfn_dlo) (fun v -> dlobasic);;
```

For example:

```
# quelim_dlo <<forall x y. exists z. z < x /\ z < y>>;;
- : fol formula = <<true>>
```

We can also apply quantifier elimination to formulas with free variables. Sometimes these still simplify to a Boolean constant:

```
# quelim_dlo <<exists z. z < x /\ z < y>>;;
- : fol formula = <<true>>
```

while others give non-trivial formulas, sometimes in their simplest form, sometimes not:

```
# quelim_dlo <<exists z. x < z /\ z < y>>;;
- : fol formula = <<x < y>>
# quelim_dlo <<(forall x. x < a ==> x < b)>>;;
- : fol formula = <<~(b < a \/ b < a)>>
```

We can always prove equivalence to a simpler form we have thought up for ourselves by eliminating all quantifiers from the claimed equivalence:

```
# quelim_dlo <<forall a b. (forall x. x < a ==> x < b) <=> a <= b>>;;
- : fol formula = <<true>>
# quelim_dlo <<forall a b. (forall x. x < a <=> x < b) <=> a = b>>;;
- : fol formula = <<true>>
```

The following less obvious example confirms that the two formulas we gave in connection with the finite model property (Section 5.5) do indeed fail over a dense linear order. (We only check one because the other one implies it, but both work equally well.)

```
# quelim_dlo <<exists x y z. forall u.
               x < x \/ ~x < u \/ (x < y /\ y < z /\ ~x < z)>>;;
- : fol formula = <<false>>
```

Since the only ground formulas in the language are $\top$ and $\bot$ (there being no constants), this implies that the theory of DLOs is complete and decidable. By Theorem 5.5 we also see that all models of the DLO axioms are elementarily equivalent, and so no sentence in the first-order language considered here can distinguish two models of the theory, such as $\mathbb{R}$ and $\mathbb{Q}$. Of course, by using a language with a multiplication operator we can make such distinctions, e.g. via the formula $\exists x. \, x \cdot x = 2$.

5.7 Presburger arithmetic

We now consider the theory of linear integer arithmetic, which is roughly the set of formulas true in $\mathbb{Z}$ that are expressible *without* using multiplication. (In this context *linear* signifies the lack of multiplication, not the presence of a total/linear order.) For example, $\forall x. \, \exists q \, r. \, x = q + q + r \wedge 0 \le r \wedge r < 2$ is in this theory; it asserts that every integer x has a quotient and nonnegative remainder when divided by 2. But $\forall x. \, x \le x \cdot x$ is not included because it involves multiplication, even though it does hold in $\mathbb{Z}$.

In the most obvious formulation, with the language including just numeric constants, addition and subtraction functions and inequality predicates, the theory does *not* admit quantifier elimination; for example $\exists x. \, x + x = y$ has no quantifier-free equivalent. However, if we include in the language divisibility predicates D_k for all integers $k \geq 2$, we will see that quantifier elimination does hold, even if the original formula itself involves these divisibility predicates. Note that ground instances of divisibility predicates are always decidable – for example $D_5(7)$ is false and $D_5(15)$ is true – so a quantifier elimination algorithm will still give us a decision procedure for sentences. In principle, then, we are fixing the following first-order language, which has infinitely many predicate symbols:

- constants 0 and 1;
- functions of unary negation ('−'), addition ('+') and subtraction ('−');
- equality ('=') and all the usual inequality predicates ($\leq$, $<$, $\geq$ and $>$) as well as unary predicates D_k ('is divisible by k') for all integers $k \geq 2$.

We will not bother to spell out an explicit set of axioms for the theory, but will work directly with properties that clearly hold true in the usual model $\mathbb{Z}$. This theory is usually called 'Presburger arithmetic', in honour of Presburger (1930), who first demonstrated quantifier elimination and decidability for it. In the actual implementation, we are a bit more liberal with the language; our procedure will simply fail if this liberality is exploited to express things that could not be expressed in the 'pure' language like $x \cdot x$.

- We allow arbitrary positive and negative integer constants. This makes no difference in principle because we could always write -3 as $-(1 + 1 + 1)$, etc.
- We allow the multiplication function provided that it is only used to express multiplication by constants. Again, this is a convenience and we could avoid $4 \cdot x$ by writing $x + x + x + x$, etc.
- We use a single binary divisibility predicate `divides`, but we only allow the left-hand argument to be a (positive) integer constant. In discussions we sometimes use the conventional notation $d|x$ for 'd divides x'.

We have a special abbreviation `zero` for the integer constant term 0, since we use it quite often.

```
let zero = Fn("0",[]);;
```

The following functions convert between terms that are integer constants and OCaml unlimited-precision numbers, and test whether a term is indeed an integer constant.

```
let mk_numeral n = Fn(string_of_num n,[]);;

let dest_numeral t =
  match t with
    Fn(ns,[]) -> num_of_string ns
  | _ -> failwith "dest_numeral";;

let is_numeral = can dest_numeral;;
```

Using these functions we can take an arbitrary unary or binary operation on OCaml numbers, such as negation or addition, and lift it to an operation on numeral constants:

```
let numeral1 fn n = mk_numeral(fn(dest_numeral n));;

let numeral2 fn m n = mk_numeral(fn (dest_numeral m) (dest_numeral n));;
```

Canonical forms

As noted, we allow multiplication by numeral constants. Indeed, it makes the transformations involved in quantifier elimination easier to implement if we always keep terms in a canonical form:

$$c_1 \cdot x_1 + \cdots + c_n \cdot x_n + k,$$

where $n \geq 0$, c_i and k are integer constants, and the x_i are distinct variables, with a fixed order. We insist that c_i are present even if they are 1, but that they are never 0, and that k is present even if it is 0. Thus, a canonical term is a constant precisely if the top-level operator is not addition.

We need two main operations on terms in canonical form: multiplication by an integer constant, and addition. The former just amounts to multiplying up all the coefficients:

$$n \cdot (c_1 \cdot x_1 + \cdots + c_n \cdot x_n + k) = (n \cdot c_1) \cdot x_1 + \cdots + (n \cdot c_n) \cdot x_n + (n \cdot k)$$

unless $n = 0$, in which case we should just return 0. This can be implemented as a simple recursion:

```
let rec linear_cmul n tm =
  if n =/ Int 0 then zero else
  match tm with
    Fn("+",[Fn("*",[c; x]); r]) ->
        Fn("+",[Fn("*",[numeral1(( */ ) n) c; x]); linear_cmul n r])
  | k -> numeral1(( */ ) n) k;;
```

For addition, we need to merge together the sequences of variables, maintaining the fixed order. We assume that this order is defined by a list of variable names, and use `earlier` to tell us whether element x comes earlier than element y in such a list. The first clause corresponds to a term addition $(c_1 \cdot x_1 + r_1) + (c_2 \cdot x_2 + r_2)$ and the action taken depends on the relationship of the variables x_1 and x_2. If they are equal, then the coefficients are added and the remainders dealt with recursively. (Note that if the coefficients cancel, we do not include that term in the result, since we wanted all the c_i to be nonzero.) Otherwise, whichever variable takes precedence is put at the head of the output term and recursion proceeds; this is also the action on the other clauses where one term or the other is a constant term. Finally, if both terms are constants they are just added as numerals.

```
let rec linear_add vars tm1 tm2 =
  match (tm1,tm2) with
   (Fn("+",[Fn("*",[c1; Var x1]); r1]),
    Fn("+",[Fn("*",[c2; Var x2]); r2])) ->
        if x1 = x2 then
          let c = numeral2 (+/) c1 c2 in
          if c = zero then linear_add vars r1 r2
          else Fn("+",[Fn("*",[c; Var x1]); linear_add vars r1 r2])
        else if earlier vars x1 x2 then
          Fn("+",[Fn("*",[c1; Var x1]); linear_add vars r1 tm2])
        else
          Fn("+",[Fn("*",[c2; Var x2]); linear_add vars tm1 r2])
  | (Fn("+",[Fn("*",[c1; Var x1]); r1]),k2) ->
        Fn("+",[Fn("*",[c1; Var x1]); linear_add vars r1 k2])
  | (k1,Fn("+",[Fn("*",[c2; Var x2]); r2])) ->
        Fn("+",[Fn("*",[c2; Var x2]); linear_add vars k1 r2])
  | _ -> numeral2(+/) tm1 tm2;;
```

Using these basic functions, it's easy to define negation and subtraction on canonical forms:

```
let linear_neg tm = linear_cmul (Int(-1)) tm;;

let linear_sub vars tm1 tm2 = linear_add vars tm1 (linear_neg tm2);;
```

and we can even define multiplication of any two canonical terms, though it will fail unless at least one is just a constant:

```
let linear_mul tm1 tm2 =
  if is_numeral tm1 then linear_cmul (dest_numeral tm1) tm2
  else if is_numeral tm2 then linear_cmul (dest_numeral tm2) tm1
  else failwith "linear_mul: nonlinearity";;
```

In order to convert any permissible term into canonical form, we proceed by recursion, applying one of the arithmetic operations just defined to the translated subexpressions (allowing multiplication only if one side is simply a numeral), leaving numeral constants unchanged and converting variables from x into their canonical form $1 \cdot x + 0$:

```
let rec lint vars tm =
  match tm with
    Var(_) -> Fn("+",[Fn("*",[Fn("1",[]); tm]); zero])
  | Fn("-",[t]) -> linear_neg (lint vars t)
  | Fn("+",[s;t]) -> linear_add vars (lint vars s) (lint vars t)
  | Fn("-",[s;t]) -> linear_sub vars (lint vars s) (lint vars t)
  | Fn("*",[s;t]) -> linear_mul (lint vars s) (lint vars t)
  | _ -> if is_numeral tm then tm else failwith "lint: unknown term";;
```

We next extend this linearization to atomic formulas; this will eventually be plugged into lift_qelim as the parameter afn. We force both equations and inequalities to have zero on the LHS, e.g. transforming $s = t$ to $0 = s - t$ and $s < t$ to $0 < t - s$; this makes some later code more regular since in the case of $d \mid t$ the 'interesting' term is also the right-hand argument. Because the integers are a discrete structure, we take the chance to rewrite all the atomic inequality formulas in terms of $<$, e.g. $s \leq t$ as $0 < (t+1) - s$. And finally, we also force the left-hand constants in divisibility assertions to be positive. We start with a simple helper function mkatom to linearize a term and create an atom with that as the left-hand argument and zero as the other:

```
let mkatom vars p t = Atom(R(p,[zero; lint vars t]));;
```

Now the main function is straightforward case-by-case modification of the input formula.

```
let linform vars fm =
  match fm with
    Atom(R("divides",[c;t])) ->
      Atom(R("divides",[numeral1 abs_num c; lint vars t]))
  | Atom(R("=",[s;t])) -> mkatom vars "=" (Fn("-",[t;s]))
  | Atom(R("<",[s;t])) -> mkatom vars "<" (Fn("-",[t;s]))
  | Atom(R(">",[s;t])) -> mkatom vars "<" (Fn("-",[s;t]))
  | Atom(R("<=",[s;t])) ->
      mkatom vars "<" (Fn("-",[Fn("+",[t;Fn("1",[])]);s]))
  | Atom(R(">=",[s;t])) ->
      mkatom vars "<" (Fn("-",[Fn("+",[s;Fn("1",[])]);t]))
  | _ -> fm;;
```

In the main body of the procedure, we'll now be able to assume that the only inequality predicate is '$<$'. It may still occur negated, but if so we transform it into an unnegated equivalent using the code below. In the DLO procedure the analogous transformation involves a case-split such as

$\neg(s < t) \Leftrightarrow s = t \lor t < s$, but, because of the discreteness of the integers, we can just use $\neg(0 < t) \Leftrightarrow 0 < 1 - t$:

```
let rec posineq fm =
  match fm with
  | Not(Atom(R("<",[Fn("0",[]); t]))) ->
      Atom(R("<",[Fn("0",[]); linear_sub [] (Fn("1",[])) t]))
  | _ -> fm;;
```

Cooper's algorithm

Presburger's original algorithm is fairly straightforward, and follows the classic quantifier elimination pattern of dealing with the special case of an existentially quantified conjunction of literals. However, we will present a clever optimized version due to Cooper (1972), which is hardly more complicated and allows us to eliminate an existential quantifier whose body is an arbitrary quantifier-free NNF formula. This can be much more efficient since it avoids the blowup often caused by the transformation to DNF, especially in the presence of many quantifier alternations. For an in-depth discussion of Presburger's original procedure, the reader can consult Enderton (1972) and Smoryński (1980), or indeed the original article, which is quite readable – Stansifer (1984) gives an annotated English translation. Presburger's algorithm has additional historical significance for us, since the implementation by Davis (1957) was arguably the first logical decision procedure actually to be implemented on a computer.

Consider the task of eliminating the existential quantifier from $\exists x.p$ where p is quantifier-free. We will assume that all the atoms have been maintained in the standard form with 0 on the left and a linearized term on the right, and only strict inequalities using '<' present. Using `cnnf` with the parameter `posineq` to eliminate negated inequalities, we may assume in the core procedure that p is in NNF, i.e. built up from conjunction and disjunction from literals of the forms $0 = t$, $\neg(0 = t)$, $0 < t$, $d \mid t$ or $\neg(d \mid t)$, with each term t normalized so that if x occurs in it, it is of the form $c \cdot x + s$. (Note that `lift_qelim` produces the `vars` parameter in such a way that the innermost quantified variable, the one we want to eliminate first, is at the head of the list, and hence will appear first in the canonical form of any term involving it.) In order to correlate the various instances of x multiplied by different coefficients, we find the (positive) least common multiple of all the coefficients of x, returning 1 if there are no instances of x:

```
let rec formlcm x fm =
  match fm with
    Atom(R(p,[_;Fn("+",[Fn("*",[c;y]);z])]))) when y = x ->
        abs_num(dest_numeral c)
  | Not(p) -> formlcm x p
  | And(p,q) | Or(p,q) -> lcm_num (formlcm x p) (formlcm x q)
  | _ -> Int 1;;
```

(Note that the atom clause works uniformly for divisibility and other predicates, because the 'interesting' term is always the right-hand argument.) Now, having computed the LCM, say l, by this method, we can make the coefficient of x equal to $\pm l$ everywhere by taking each atomic formula whose right-hand argument is of the form $c \cdot x + z$, and consistently multiplying it through by an appropriate m. For all but inequalities this is $m = l/c$ and so the resulting coefficient of x will be l; for inequalities we use $m = |l/c|$, since we cannot multiply by negative numbers without changing their sense. Actually, as part of this transformation we force the coefficients of x from $\pm l \cdot x$ to $\pm 1 \cdot x$, in anticipation of the next stage:

```
let rec adjustcoeff x l fm =
  match fm with
    Atom(R(p,[d; Fn("+",[Fn("*",[c;y]);z])]))) when y = x ->
        let m = l // dest_numeral c in
        let n = if p = "<" then abs_num(m) else m in
        let xtm = Fn("*",[mk_numeral(m // n); x]) in
        Atom(R(p,[linear_cmul (abs_num m) d;
                    Fn("+",[xtm; linear_cmul n z])]))
  | Not(p) -> Not(adjustcoeff x l p)
  | And(p,q) -> And(adjustcoeff x l p,adjustcoeff x l q)
  | Or(p,q) -> Or(adjustcoeff x l p,adjustcoeff x l q)
  | _ -> fm;;
```

The next stage, which we have partly folded in above, is to replace $l \cdot x$ with just x and add a new divisibility clause, justified by the following equivalence:

$$(\exists x.\ P[l \cdot x]) \Leftrightarrow (\exists x.\ l \mid x \wedge P[x]).$$

The following code implements the entire transformation, reducing the coefficient of x to be ± 1 using the above functions, then adding the additional conjunct $l \mid x$, or actually, to retain canonicality, $l \mid 1 \cdot x + 0$. We make the slight optimization of not including the trivially true divisibility formula if $l = 1$, but we still call `adjustcoeff` since it might be needed to transform, say, $0 = -1 \cdot x + 3$ into $0 = 1 \cdot x + -3$ which is the form we expect later on.

```
let unitycoeff x fm =
  let l = formlcm x fm in
  let fm' = adjustcoeff x l fm in
  if l =/ Int 1 then fm' else
  let xp = Fn("+",[Fn("*",[Fn("1",[]);x]); zero]) in
  And(Atom(R("divides",[mk_numeral l; xp])),adjustcoeff x l fm);;
```

Now we come to the main quantifier elimination step for the transformed formula $\exists x.\, P[x]$. Note that since the integers are discrete and any set of integers bounded below has a minimal element, $\exists x.\, P[x]$ holds iff either (i) there are arbitrarily large and negative x such that $P[x]$, or (ii) there is a minimal x such that $P[x]$. So we'll separately consider how to find quantifier-free equivalents for the two cases on the right of this equivalence:

$$(\exists x.\, P[x]) \Leftrightarrow (\forall y.\, \exists x.\, x < y \wedge P[x]) \vee (\exists x.\, P[x] \wedge \forall y.\, y < x \Rightarrow \neg P[y]).$$

Arbitrarily large and negative x

Consider first the case where there are arbitrarily large and negative x such that $P[x]$. For sufficiently large and negative x, we claim that $P[x]$ must be equivalent to $P_{-\infty}[x]$, the formula that results from replacing the atoms in $P[x]$ as follows:

In $P[x]$	In $P_{-\infty}[x]$
$0 = x + a$	$\perp$
$0 < x + a$	$\perp$
$0 < -x + a$	$\top$

and leaving other atoms, i.e. divisibility assertions and those not involving x, unchanged.

Lemma 5.6 *For sufficiently large and negative x, $P[x]$ and $P_{-\infty}[x]$ are equivalent, i.e. $\exists y.\, \forall x.\, x < y \Rightarrow (P[x] \Leftrightarrow P_{-\infty}[x])$ holds.*

Proof Consider the possible atomic formulas first, starting with $P[x]$ of the form $0 = x + a$ or $0 < x + a$. In these cases $P_{-\infty}[x]$ is $\perp$ and we have $\forall x.\, x < -a \Rightarrow (P[x] \Leftrightarrow \perp)$. The required result follows, with $-a$ the witness for the existentially quantified variable y. The $0 < -x + a$ case is similar: $P_{-\infty}[x]$ is $\top$ and indeed $\forall x.x < a \Rightarrow (P[x] \Leftrightarrow \top)$. For other atomic formulas, $P_{-\infty}[x]$ is the same as $P[x]$ and so the result holds trivially.

Intuitively, we can now take the minimum of all the y values for the atoms contained in the formula. More formally, we can proceed by induction on its structure. If $P[x]$ is of the form $\neg Q[x]$, then by the inductive hypothesis $\exists y.\forall x.x < y \Rightarrow (Q[x] \Leftrightarrow Q_{-\infty}[x])$, so $\exists y.\forall x.x < y \Rightarrow (\neg Q[x] \Leftrightarrow \neg Q_{-\infty}[x])$ as required. If $P[x]$ is of the form $Q[x] \wedge R[x]$, then by the inductive hypothesis $\exists y.\forall x.\, x < y \Rightarrow (Q[x] \Leftrightarrow Q_{-\infty}[x])$ and $\exists z.\forall x.\, x < z \Rightarrow (R[x] \Leftrightarrow R_{-\infty}[x])$ hold, so $\exists w.\forall x.\, x < w \Rightarrow (P[x] \Leftrightarrow P_{-\infty}[x])$ (given y and z we can choose w to be their minimum). The case where $P[x]$ is of the form $Q[x] \vee R[x]$ is very similar. $\qquad\square$

Here is the 'minus infinity' transformation coded in OCaml, assuming that we have already used the canonical form conversions:

```
let rec minusinf x fm =
  match fm with
    Atom(R("=",[Fn("0",[]); Fn("+",[Fn("*",[Fn("1",[]);y]);a])]))
        when y = x -> False
  | Atom(R("<",[Fn("0",[]); Fn("+",[Fn("*",[pm1;y]);a])])) when y = x ->
        if pm1 = Fn("1",[]) then False else True
  | Not(p) -> Not(minusinf x p)
  | And(p,q) -> And(minusinf x p,minusinf x q)
  | Or(p,q) -> Or(minusinf x p,minusinf x q)
  | _ -> fm;;
```

The next key point is that all divisibility terms $d \mid \pm x + a$ are unchanged if x is altered by an integer multiple of d. Let us find the (positive) least common multiple D of *all* ds occurring in formulas of the form $d \mid c \cdot x + a$ (we know in fact that $c = \pm 1$ at this stage) using the following code:

```
let rec divlcm x fm =
  match fm with
    Atom(R("divides",[d;Fn("+",[Fn("*",[c;y]);a])])) when y = x ->
        dest_numeral d
  | Not(p) -> divlcm x p
  | And(p,q) | Or(p,q) -> lcm_num (divlcm x p) (divlcm x q)
  | _ -> Int 1;;
```

Then all divisibility atoms in the formula are invariant if x is changed to $x \pm kD$. Indeed, in the case of $P_{-\infty}[x]$, divisibility atoms and other atoms not involving x are all that's left, so $P_{-\infty}[x \pm kD] \Leftrightarrow P_{-\infty}[x]$ always holds. Thus we can find a simpler equivalent for our current target formula $\forall y.\, \exists x.\, x < y \wedge P[x]$.

Theorem 5.7 *For any $P[x]$ quantifier-free and in NNF we have*

$$(\forall y.\, \exists x.\, x < y \wedge P[x]) \Leftrightarrow \bigvee_{i=1}^{D} P_{-\infty}[i].$$

Proof By Lemma 5.6, $P[x]$ and $P_{-\infty}[x]$ are equivalent for sufficiently negative x, so the left-hand side of this formula is equivalent to $\forall y. \exists x. x < y \wedge P_{-\infty}[x]$. Since, by the above remarks, $P_{-\infty}[x]$ is invariant when x changes by any multiple of D, this is equivalent simply to $\exists x. P_{-\infty}[x]$, for given any x with $P_{-\infty}[x]$ we can find an arbitrarily large and negative one by subtracting a multiple of D. Finally, again by the invariance of $P_{-\infty}[x]$ under multiples of D, this is equivalent to $\bigvee_{i=1}^{D} P_{-\infty}[i]$, since any x is congruent to one of those values modulo D. (The use of $1, \ldots, D$ is inessential; we could have used $0, \ldots, D-1$ or any other D numbers that are pairwise incongruent modulo D.) □

A minimal x

We now turn to the other possibility, of a minimal x satisfying $P[x]$. In this case $P[x]$ holds but $P[x - D]$ does not. Since divisibility formulas do not change under translation by D, this implies that the change from true to false must have arisen from one of the other literals changing from true to false in the step from x to a smaller value. For such a literal, we can always identify a 'boundary point' b such that the literal is false for $x = b$ but true for $x = b + 1$. For example, for $0 < x + a$, the boundary point is $b = -a$ since $0 < x + a$ is false for $x = -a$ but true for $x = 1 - a$. Here are all the boundary points for literals that can change from true to false as x decreases by D, where applicable.

Literal	Boundary point
$0 = x + a$	$-(a + 1)$
$\neg(0 = x + a)$	$-a$
$0 < x + a$	$-a$
$0 < -x + a$	none
$d \mid x + a$	none
$\neg(d \mid x + a)$	none
literals without x	none

The collection of such boundary points for the relevant literals is called the B-set for the formula in question.[†] In OCaml:

[†] There is no reason to suppose that Cooper meant the 'B' to stand for boundary, since he used 'A' for the dual notion. But it is perhaps a good way of thinking of it.

```
let rec bset x fm =
  match fm with
    Not(Atom(R("=",[Fn("0",[]); Fn("+",[Fn("*",[Fn("1",[]);y]);a])])))
    when y = x -> [linear_neg a]
  | Atom(R("=",[Fn("0",[]); Fn("+",[Fn("*",[Fn("1",[]);y]);a])]))
    when y = x -> [linear_neg(linear_add [] a (Fn("1",[])))]
  | Atom(R("<",[Fn("0",[]); Fn("+",[Fn("*",[Fn("1",[]);y]);a])]))
    when y = x -> [linear_neg a]
  | Not(p) -> bset x p
  | And(p,q) -> union (bset x p) (bset x q)
  | Or(p,q) -> union (bset x p) (bset x q)
  | _ -> [];;
```

This is the crucial property of the B-set.

Theorem 5.8 *If D is the LCM of all relevant divisors in a quantifier-free NNF formula $P[x]$ with no logically negated inequality literals and a B-set B, and $P[x]$ holds while $P[x - D]$ does not, then $x = b + j$ for some $b \in B$ and $1 \leq j \leq D$.*

Proof First consider the literals for which the B-set is nonempty. If $P[x]$ is a literal $0 = x + a$, then $P[x]$ holding means $x = -a$. Since the B-set is $\{-(a + 1)\}$ and $x = -a = -(a + 1) + j$ for $j = 1$, the result follows. If $P[x]$ is $\neg(0 = x + a)$ then $\neg P[x - D]$ means $x = -a + D$. Since the B-set is $\{-a\}$ and $-a + D = -a + j$ for $j = D$, the result follows. Finally, if $P[x]$ is a literal $0 < x + a$ then since $P[x]$ holds but not $P[x - D]$, we must have $(x - D) + a \leq 0 < x + a$, or in other words $-a + 1 \leq x \leq -a + D$. Since the B-set is $\{-a\}$ this implies $x = -a + j$ for some $1 \leq j \leq D$ as required.

No other literals can satisfy the precondition of the theorem, that $P[x]$ holds but $P[x - D]$ does not. Divisibility relations are invariant modulo D, literals $0 < -x + a$ cannot possibly satisfy the assumed property since $0 < -x + a \Rightarrow 0 < -(x - D) + a$, and by hypothesis we have no logically negated inequality literals.

Having established the result for literals, we can proceed by induction on the structure of the NNF formula. Suppose $P[x]$ is of the form $Q[x] \wedge R[x]$ or $Q[x] \vee R[x]$, and that $P[x]$ holds while $P[x - D]$ does not. Whichever form $P[x]$ has, this means either that $Q[x]$ holds and $Q[x - D]$ does not, or that $R[x]$ holds and $R[x - D]$ does not. Then the inductive hypothesis, together with the fact that the B-set of $P[x]$ contains those of both $Q[x]$ and $R[x]$, implies that the result holds. $\qquad\square$

At last we arrive at the main theorem justifying quantifier elimination.

Corollary 5.9 *If $P[x]$ is a formula in the subset being discussed with B-set B, and D is the positive lowest common multiple of all the relevant divisors, then the following equivalence holds:*

$$(\exists x.\, P[x]) \Leftrightarrow \bigvee_{j=1}^{D} (P_{-\infty}[j] \vee \bigvee_{b \in B} P[b+j]).$$

Proof Redistributing the disjunction on the right a bit, we need to show that:

$$(\exists x.\, P[x]) \Leftrightarrow (\bigvee_{j=1}^{D} P_{-\infty}[j]) \vee (\bigvee_{j=1}^{D} \bigvee_{b \in B} P[b+j]).$$

Suppose first that $\exists x.\, P[x]$ holds. Then, as noted above, we either have $\forall y.\, \exists x.\, x < y \wedge P[x]$ (there are arbitrarily large and negative x with $P[x]$) or $\exists x.\, P[x] \wedge \forall y.\, y < x \Rightarrow \neg P[y]$ (there is a minimal x with $P[x]$). In the former case, we immediately have $\bigvee_{j=1}^{D} P_{-\infty}[j]$ by Theorem 5.7, while in the latter case there is an x with $P[x]$ but $\neg P[x-D]$, and therefore by Theorem 5.8 we have $x = b+j$ for some $b \in B$ and $1 \leq j \leq D$, from which $\bigvee_{j=1}^{D} \bigvee_{b \in B} P[b+j]$ follows immediately.

Conversely, suppose that the disjunction on the right holds. If $\bigvee_{j=1}^{D} P_{-\infty}[j]$, then by Theorem 5.7 we have arbitrarily large and negative x with $P[x]$ and so a fortiori $\exists x.\, P[x]$ holds. And trivially if $\bigvee_{j=1}^{D} \bigvee_{b \in B} P[b+j]$ holds then so does $\exists x.\, P[x]$. $\qquad\square$

In order to apply the main theorem, we need to be able to form the substitution instances like $P[b+j]$ while retaining canonical form. Thus we implement a function that replaces the top variable x in atoms by another term t (assumed not to involve x), restoring canonicality:

```
let rec linrep vars x t fm =
  match fm with
    Atom(R(p,[d; Fn("+",[Fn("*",[c;y]);a])])) when y = x ->
        let ct = linear_cmul (dest_numeral c) t in
        Atom(R(p,[d; linear_add vars ct a]))
  | Not(p) -> Not(linrep vars x t p)
  | And(p,q) -> And(linrep vars x t p,linrep vars x t q)
  | Or(p,q) -> Or(linrep vars x t p,linrep vars x t q)
  | _ -> fm;;
```

Now for the overall inner quantifier elimination step, we just perform the transformation corresponding to the equivalence in Corollary 5.9:

```
let cooper vars fm =
  match fm with
   Exists(x0,p0) ->
        let x = Var x0 in
        let p = unitycoeff x p0 in
        let p_inf = simplify(minusinf x p) and bs = bset x p
        and js = Int 1 --- divlcm x p in
        let p_element j b =
          linrep vars x (linear_add vars b (mk_numeral j)) p in
        let stage j = list_disj
          (linrep vars x (mk_numeral j) p_inf ::
           map (p_element j) bs) in
        list_disj (map stage js)
  | _ -> failwith "cooper: not an existential formula";;
```

If we eventually eliminate all quantifiers from an initially closed formula, the result will contain no variables at all and each atom can be evaluated to true (e.g. $0 < 5$, $2|4$) or false (e.g. $0 = 7$). It's convenient to define the function to perform such evaluation now, since we can also apply it at intermediate stages as a useful simplification; for example, if we have a subformula of the form $0 < -4 \wedge P$, we can simplify it to $\perp$ and never need to worry about P. The following auxiliary function just associates atoms with corresponding operations on rational numbers (we will use this later in other contexts, hence the incorporation of other inequalities):

```
let operations =
  ["=",(=/); "<",(</); ">",(>/); "<=",(<=/); ">=",(>=/);
   "divides",(fun x y -> mod_num y x =/ Int 0)];;
```

Now the main evaluation function is straightforward. Note that unless an atom has numerals as both of its two arguments, the inner **dest_numeral** calls will fail and the atom will be returned unchanged by the error trap.

```
let evalc = onatoms
  (fun (R(p,[s;t]) as at) ->
        (try if assoc p operations (dest_numeral s) (dest_numeral t)
            then True else False
          with Failure _ -> Atom at));;
```

The overall quantifier elimination procedure is built in the usual way, inserting **evalc** into the intermediate normalization steps and at the end. We use an NNF rather than DNF transformation, since Cooper's algorithm can cope with any NNF formula.

```
let integer_qelim =
  simplify ** evalc **
  lift_qelim linform (cnnf posineq ** evalc) cooper;;
```

For example, we can confirm or refute closed formulas:

```
# integer_qelim <<forall x y. ~(2 * x + 1 = 2 * y)>>;;
- : fol formula = <<true>>
# integer_qelim <<forall x. exists y. 2 * y <= x /\ x < 2 * (y + 1)>>;;
- : fol formula = <<true>>
# integer_qelim <<exists x y. 4 * x - 6 * y = 1>>;;
- : fol formula = <<false>>
# integer_qelim <<forall x. ~divides(2,x) /\ divides(3,x-1) <=>
                           divides(12,x-1) \/ divides(12,x-7)>>;;
- : fol formula = <<true>>
```

and eliminate quantifiers from formulas with free variables:

```
# integer_qelim <<forall x. b < x ==> a <= x>>;;
- : fol formula = <<~0 < 1 * a + -1 * b + -1>>
```

Optimizations

There are many ways in which the efficiency of Cooper's algorithm can be improved. One already considered in Cooper's original paper is to sometimes use a dual expansion based on a 'plus infinity' variant of the formula and corresponding 'A-sets' instead of B-sets (Exercise 5.13). A subtly improved treatment of the coefficient homogenization part of Cooper's algorithm due to Reddy and Loveland (1978) is also worth considering.

It has long been known that the arithmetical problems arising in program verification applications mostly fall within a small fragment of Presburger arithmetic. Typically, they are entirely universally quantified and do not depend on subtle divisibility properties. Indeed, Pratt (1977) observed that most involve just inequalities of the form $x \le y + c$. For this fragment, often called *difference logic* or *separation logic*,[†] a very efficient decision method is possible using the Bellman–Ford graph algorithm. Efficient algorithms for the slightly more general 'unit two variable per inequality' (UTVPI) case allowing $ax \le by + c$ for $a, b \in \{-1, 0, 1\}$ are given by Jaffar, Maher, Stuckey and Yap (1994), Harvey and Stuckey (1997) and Lahiri and Musuvathi (2005), while Ball, Cook, Lahriri and Rajamani (2004) give some statistics on how well it handles the demands of applications.

[†] The phrase 'separation logic' is now also used for something completely different (Reynolds 2002), so 'difference logic' is probably less ambiguous.

Natural numbers

This quantifier elimination procedure for the integers can easily be used to yield one for the natural numbers too. We can make the identification $\mathbb{N} = \{x \in \mathbb{Z} \mid 0 \leq x\}$, or if we prefer to leave out zero, $\mathbb{N} = \{x \in \mathbb{Z} \mid 0 < x\}$. Therefore, given a formula to be interpreted in $\mathbb{N}$, we can obtain a corresponding one whose meaning in $\mathbb{Z}$ is the same by systematically *relativizing* all the quantifiers:

$$\forall x. \, P[x] \quad \longrightarrow \quad \forall x. \, 0 \leq x \Rightarrow P[x],$$
$$\exists x. \, P[x] \quad \longrightarrow \quad \exists x. \, 0 \leq x \wedge P[x].$$

This relativization, for an arbitrary constraint formula, can be implemented as:

```
let rec relativize r fm =
  match fm with
    Not(p) -> Not(relativize r p)
  | And(p,q) -> And(relativize r p,relativize r q)
  | Or(p,q) -> Or(relativize r p,relativize r q)
  | Imp(p,q) -> Imp(relativize r p,relativize r q)
  | Iff(p,q) -> Iff(relativize r p,relativize r q)
  | Forall(x,p) -> Forall(x,Imp(r x,relativize r p))
  | Exists(x,p) -> Exists(x,And(r x,relativize r p))
  | _ -> fm;;
```

and we can apply it to the special case $0 \leq x$ as an initial step before integer quantifier elimination to yield a natural number version:

```
let natural_qelim =
  integer_qelim ** relativize(fun x -> Atom(R("<=",[zero; Var x])));;
```

The difference is exemplified by an instance of Bezout's theorem; we can think of the natural number version as claiming that we can make any value from 3-cent and 5-cent stamps. This is false:

```
# natural_qelim <<forall d. exists x y. 3 * x + 5 * y = d>>;;
- : fol formula = <<false>>
# integer_qelim <<forall d. exists x y. 3 * x + 5 * y = d>>;;
- : fol formula = <<true>>
```

but we do have:

```
# natural_qelim <<forall d. d >= 8 ==> exists x y. 3 * x + 5 * y = d>>;;
- : fol formula = <<true>>
# natural_qelim <<forall d. exists x y. 3 * x - 5 * y = d>>;;
- : fol formula = <<true>>
```

Skolem arithmetic and other variants

Quantifier elimination for essentially the same integer theory was arrived at independently by Skolem (1931), who also sketched a proof of decidability (not full quantifier elimination) for an analogous theory of nonzero natural numbers with multiplication (and no addition), often called 'Skolem arithmetic'. There's a natural correspondence between models of Skolem arithmetic and certain 'weak direct products' of models of Presburger arithmetic via the prime factorization $n \mapsto 2^{n_1} 3^{n_2} 5^{n_3} \cdots$, multiplication corresponding to pointwise addition and divisibility to pointwise ordering. Using general theorems about decidability of such products, Mostowski (1952) gave a clear proof of decidability for Skolem arithmetic. A generalization of Mostowski's result due to Feferman and Vaught (1959) was later applied by Cegielski (1981) to give full quantifier elimination for Skolem arithmetic.

As we shall see in Section 7.2, things change dramatically when one has both addition *and* multiplication together: the theory does not admit quantifier elimination, is not complete and, in a precise sense, is far from being decidable. And the extension of Presburger arithmetic to allow a general divisibility relation, not just divisibility by constants, is equally difficult because one can define (see Section 7.2) multiplication in terms of divisibility as follows (Tarski, Mostowski and Robinson 1953):

- define the relation 'l is a least common multiple of m and n' by $m|l \wedge n|l \wedge (\forall l'. \, m|l' \wedge n|l' \Rightarrow l|l')$
- define the relation $m = n^2$ by '$m + n$ is a least common multiple of n and $n + 1$ and $m - n$ is a least common multiple of n and $n - 1$'; (This is for $\mathbb{Z}$; over $\mathbb{N}$ just the fact that $m + n$ is a least common multiple of n and $n + 1$ suffices.)
- define the relation $m = n \cdot p$ by $(n + p)^2 = n^2 + p^2 + 2m$.

Indeed, with a little more ingenuity multiplication can be defined in terms of divisibility, successor and 1 only (J. Robinson 1949), so even that theory is undecidable. On the other hand, the validity of purely *universal* formulas *is* decidable for Presburger arithmetic with divisibility (Beltyokov 1974; Lipshitz 1978). A surprising positive result in another direction is that adding exponentiation, i.e. a function $E(x) = 2^x$, to Presburger arithmetic gives a decidable theory: Semënov (1984) proves this based on a variant of quantifier elimination. By contrast, a general binary exponentiation function immediately leads to undecidability since we can define the multiplication relation $mn = p$ by $(x^m)^n = x^p$ and then addition $m + n = p$ by $x^m x^n = x^p$, for any $x > 1$.

Even though basic Presburger arithmetic is decidable, the worst-case complexity of any algorithm is known to be at least doubly exponential in the size of the formula (Fischer and Rabin 1974). However, the more restricted case of deciding formulas without quantifier alternations is 'only' NP-complete (Papadimitriou 1981), and the still more special case of satisfiability of conjunctions of linear equations over the integers can be solved in polynomial time, e.g. via Hermite normal form (Nemhauser and Wolsey 1999).

5.8 The complex numbers

The complex numbers $\mathbb{C}$ include the imaginary unit i with $i^2 = -1$, a solution of the polynomial equation $x^2 + 1 = 0$. Indeed, the Fundamental Theorem of Algebra tells us that $\mathbb{C}$ is 'algebraically closed', meaning that *any* polynomial equation $a_n x^n + \cdots + a_1 x + a_0 = 0$ has a solution over $\mathbb{C}$, except for the degenerate case of a nonzero constant ($n = 0$ and $a_0 \neq 0$).[†] Using this property, we will demonstrate full quantifier elimination for $\mathbb{C}$ with both addition and multiplication.

Polynomial manipulation

Just as with Cooper's algorithm, it's convenient to maintain terms in a canonical form. All terms built up using constants, negation, subtraction and multiplication can be considered as multivariate polynomials, and we will choose a particular canonical form for them.[‡] We consider a multivariate polynomial as a polynomial in one variable whose coefficients are themselves polynomials in the other variables. Our canonical form will be equivalent to $a_n x^n + \cdots + a_0$, but expressed slightly differently in what is known as *Horner* form:

$$a_0 + x \cdot (a_1 + x \cdot (a_2 + x \cdots \cdot (a_{n-1} + x \cdot a_n))$$

with each coefficient a_i a canonical polynomial in the remaining variables. We will maintain a list with the innermost variable at the head, and this will determine the arrangement of variables in the canonical form. For example, if the variables from the inside out are x, y and z, we consider the polynomial

---

[†] For a clear proof of the Fundamental Theorem of Algebra see Ebbinghaus et al. (1990); this is an inductive refinement (Littlewood 1941; Estermann 1956) of Argand's classic 'minimum modulus' proof.

[‡] Formally, polynomials can be defined as terms in this normal form, though we will later adopt a different definition closer to the usual one in algebra. For the present, readers may if they wish think of polynomials as functions; since we will be concerned only with infinite base rings, two polynomials have the same canonical form iff they determine the same function.

$3xy^2 + 2x^2yz + zx + 3yz$ as:

$$[0 + y \cdot (0 + z \cdot 3)] + x \cdot ([(0 + z \cdot 1) + y \cdot (0 + y \cdot 3)] + x \cdot [0 + y \cdot (0 + z \cdot 2)]),$$

where the items in square brackets are considered as coefficients when eliminating x. Although not very nice for human reading, this representation suits the organization of the algorithm with variables eliminated from the inside out.

First we define arithmetic operations on canonical polynomials, subject to a list `vars` defining the variable ordering. For addition, the main case is adding $c + x \cdot p$ and $d + y \cdot q$. If x and y are different, one or other is added to the constant coefficient of the other, via the mutually recursive function `poly_ladd`. Otherwise we just compute $(c+x\cdot p)+(d+x\cdot q) = (c+d)+x\cdot(p+q)$, taking care to handle the case $p + q = 0$ by just returning $c + d$.

```
let rec poly_add vars pol1 pol2 =
  match (pol1,pol2) with
    (Fn("+",[c; Fn("*",[Var x; p])]),Fn("+",[d; Fn("*",[Var y; q])])) ->
        if earlier vars x y then poly_ladd vars pol2 pol1
        else if earlier vars y x then poly_ladd vars pol1 pol2 else
        let e = poly_add vars c d and r = poly_add vars p q in
        if r = zero then e else Fn("+",[e; Fn("*",[Var x; r])])
  | (_,Fn("+",_)) -> poly_ladd vars pol1 pol2
  | (Fn("+",_),pol2) -> poly_ladd vars pol2 pol1
  | _ -> numeral2 (+/) pol1 pol2
and poly_ladd vars =
  fun pol1 (Fn("+",[d; Fn("*",[Var y; q])])) ->
        Fn("+",[poly_add vars pol1 d; Fn("*",[Var y; q])]);;
```

For negation, we don't need the variable order, but can just recursively negate the coefficients

```
let rec poly_neg =
  function (Fn("+",[c; Fn("*",[Var x; p])])) ->
              Fn("+",[poly_neg c; Fn("*",[Var x; poly_neg p])])
         | n -> numeral1 minus_num n;;
```

and subtraction is an easy combination of addition and negation:

```
let poly_sub vars p q = poly_add vars p (poly_neg q);;
```

We can base a recursive definition of polynomial multiplication on the following equation, solving the simpler sub-problems $p \cdot d$ and $p \cdot q$ in the same way:

$$p \cdot (d + y \cdot q) = (p \cdot d) + (0 + y \cdot (p \cdot q)).$$

However, for $0+y\cdot(p\cdot q)$ to be in canonical form we need y to be the topmost variable overall, with p including no variables strictly earlier in the list. Hence we check which polynomial has the earlier topmost variable, and call the mutually recursive function `poly_lmul` to apply the main transformation with the arguments switched as necessary:

```
let rec poly_mul vars pol1 pol2 =
  match (pol1,pol2) with
    (Fn("+",[c; Fn("*",[Var x; p])]),Fn("+",[d; Fn("*",[Var y; q])])) ->
        if earlier vars x y then poly_lmul vars pol2 pol1
        else poly_lmul vars pol1 pol2
  | (Fn("0",[]),_) | (_,Fn("0",[])) -> zero
  | (_,Fn("+",_)) -> poly_lmul vars pol1 pol2
  | (Fn("+",_),_) -> poly_lmul vars pol2 pol1
  | _ -> numeral2 ( */ ) pol1 pol2
and poly_lmul vars =
  fun pol1 (Fn("+",[d; Fn("*",[Var y; q])])) ->
      poly_add vars (poly_mul vars pol1 d)
                    (Fn("+",[zero;
                            Fn("*",[Var y; poly_mul vars pol1 q])])));;
```

Powers p^n (for fixed n) are just repeated multiplication:

```
let poly_pow vars p n = funpow n (poly_mul vars p) (Fn("1",[]));;
```

We can even do division when the quotient polynomial is just a constant:

```
let poly_div vars p q = poly_mul vars p (numeral1((//) (Int 1)) q);;
```

and it is also handy to have a base case to put a variable x into canonical form $0 + 1 \cdot x$:

```
let poly_var x = Fn("+",[zero; Fn("*",[Var x; Fn("1",[])])]);;
```

Any term can now be translated into canonical form by transforming constants and variables then recursively applying the appropriate canonical form operations:

```
let rec polynate vars tm =
  match tm with
    Var x -> poly_var x
  | Fn("-",[t]) -> poly_neg (polynate vars t)
  | Fn("+",[s;t]) -> poly_add vars (polynate vars s) (polynate vars t)
  | Fn("-",[s;t]) -> poly_sub vars (polynate vars s) (polynate vars t)
  | Fn("*",[s;t]) -> poly_mul vars (polynate vars s) (polynate vars t)
  | Fn("/",[s;t]) -> poly_div vars (polynate vars s) (polynate vars t)
  | Fn("^",[p;Fn(n,[])]) ->
                  poly_pow vars (polynate vars p) (int_of_string n)
  | _ -> if is_numeral tm then tm else failwith "lint: unknown term";;
```

and we can apply this to put each equation into an equivalent form $t = 0$

with t a canonical polynomial. We ignore the predicate, which will always be equality, so this function can be re-used for inequalities in other contexts.

```
let polyatom vars fm =
  match fm with
    Atom(R(a,[s;t])) -> Atom(R(a,[polynate vars (Fn("-",[s;t]));zero]))
  | _ -> failwith "polyatom: not an atom";;
```

We are already in a position to check simple polynomial identities:[†]

```
# polyatom ["w"; "x"; "y"; "z"]
    <<((w + x)^4 + (w + y)^4 + (w + z)^4 +
       (x + y)^4 + (x + z)^4 + (y + z)^4 +
       (w - x)^4 + (w - y)^4 + (w - z)^4 +
       (x - y)^4 + (x - z)^4 + (y - z)^4) / 6 =
      (w^2 + x^2 + y^2 + z^2)^2>>;;
- : fol formula = <<0 = 0>>
```

Properties of univariate polynomials

When we assert some arithmetical or relational property of polynomials, we mean it in terms of the operations defined above. For example, to say that a polynomial s is divisible by another polynomial t means that there is a third polynomial q so that $qt = s$. By that equation, we mean that applying poly_mul to q and t will give s, or equivalently that both sides of the equation have the same canonical form under polynate. Occasionally, however, multivariate polynomials will be thought of as univariate polynomials with parameters. For example, it is not the case that $x^2 y - zx$ is divisible by $x - 1$ as a multivariate polynomial, but considered as a univariate polynomial in x, it is divisible for some values of the other parameters (e.g. when $y = z$) and not for others.

For a univariate polynomial p, the largest n for which the polynomial involves a term ax^n with $a \neq 0$ is called its *degree*, sometimes written $\partial(p)$. With slight abuse of notation, we write $p(a)$ for the result of 'evaluating' the polynomial $p(x)$ by plugging a in place of its variable; for example if $p(x) = x^2 - 2x + 1$ we have $p(2) = 1$. We also identify values with constant polynomials like $p(x) = 2$. An elementary fact that will be central in what follows is the following, which applies to polynomials over various number systems, not just $\mathbb{C}$.

[†] This identity is connected with Waring's problem in number theory (Nathanson 1996).

Theorem 5.10 *For any polynomial $p(x)$ and value a, the polynomial $p(x) - p(a)$ is divisible by $x - a$, and the quotient polynomial has a degree one less than the degree of $p(x)$.*

Proof Just observe that $x^0 - a^0 = 1 - 1 = (x - a) \cdot 0$ while for any $k \geq 1$ we have $x^k - a^k = (x - a) \cdot (x^{k-1} + ax^{k-2} + \cdots + a^{k-2}x + a^{k-1})$. Since we can write any polynomial as $p(x) = a_n x^n + \cdots + a_0$ the result follows. $\square$

A *root* or *zero* of a univariate polynomial $p(x)$ is a value a such that $p(a) = 0$. We deduce from the above theorem that:

Corollary 5.11 *If $p(a) = 0$ then $p(x)$ is divisible by $x - a$.*

An immediate corollary is:

Corollary 5.12 *A univariate polynomial $p(x)$ of degree n can have at most n roots.*

Proof By induction over the degree. If $p(x)$ has no roots, the result is trivially true. Otherwise, taking any root a we know $p(x) = (x - a)q(x)$ for some quotient polynomial $q(x)$ of degree $n - 1$. The roots of $p(x)$ are therefore those of $q(x)$ plus $x = a$ if it is not already a root of $q(x)$. Since by the inductive hypothesis $q(x)$ has at most $n - 1$ roots, the result follows. $\square$

In the special case of the complex numbers, algebraic closure gives us something more.

Corollary 5.13 *A univariate polynomial $p(x)$ of degree n over $\mathbb{C}$ has a decomposition into linear factors: for some $a_1, \ldots, a_n$, not necessarily distinct, $p(x) = k \cdot (x - a_1) \cdots (x - a_n)$. In other words, a polynomial over $\mathbb{C}$ splits.*

Proof By induction on the degree of $p(x)$. If $p(x)$ is a constant, the result holds trivially. Otherwise, algebraic closure tells us that there is a root a, and we then know there is a $q(x)$ of lower degree with $p(x) = (x - a) \cdot q(x)$. By the inductive hypothesis, $q(x)$ splits into linear factors. $\square$

Quantifier elimination method

We'll now describe a fairly simple quantifier elimination algorithm for the complex numbers, originally due to Tarski and apparently first mentioned in print by Seidenberg (1954). Imagine for the moment that all polynomials are univariate. By applying the polynomial normalization conversions, we may assume that all atomic formulas are of the form $p(x) = 0$, and as usual (see Section 5.6), it suffices to be able to eliminate a single existential quantifier from a conjunction of literals:

$$\exists x.\, p_1(x) = 0 \wedge \cdots \wedge p_n(x) = 0 \wedge q_1(x) \neq 0 \wedge \cdots q_m(x) \neq 0.$$

The first step is to reduce this to a similar case where $m \leq 1$ and $n \leq 1$. We may assume that none of the $p_i(x)$ or $q_j(x)$ is the zero polynomial, since in the former case we can just delete the equation $p_i(x) = 0$, and in the latter case the entire formula reduces to $\bot$ and we are finished. Now, to reduce n we can use one equation of minimal degree to substitute for higher powers appearing in the others, iterating the process until at most one equation is left, e.g.

$$
\begin{aligned}
2x^2 + 5x + 3 = 0 \wedge x^2 - 1 = 0 \quad &\Leftrightarrow \quad 5x + 5 = 0 \wedge x^2 - 1 = 0 \\
&\Leftrightarrow \quad 5x + 5 = 0 \wedge 0 = 0 \\
&\Leftrightarrow \quad 5x + 5 = 0.
\end{aligned}
$$

To reduce m, we may simply multiply all the $q_i(x)$ together since $q_i(x) \neq 0 \wedge q_{i+1}(x) \neq 0 \Leftrightarrow q_i(x) \cdot q_{i+1}(x) \neq 0$. Now, if we just have a single equation left, $\exists x.\, p(x) = 0$, there is by the Fundamental Theorem of Algebra a quantifier-free equivalent, namely $\bot$ or $\top$, depending on whether $p(x)$ is a nonzero constant polynomial. If we have just one inequation, $\exists x.\, q(x) \neq 0$, this is definitely equivalent to $\top$ since there are infinitely many complex numbers and a polynomial can only have finitely many roots. The more interesting case is where we have both equations and inequations for some non-trivial $p(x)$ and $q(x)$:

$$\exists x.\, p(x) = 0 \wedge q(x) \neq 0,$$

or equivalently $\neg(\forall x.\, p(x) = 0 \Rightarrow q(x) = 0)$. Consider the core formula:

$$\forall x.\, p(x) = 0 \Rightarrow q(x) = 0.$$

Since $\mathbb{C}$ is algebraically closed, we know that the polynomials $p(x)$ and $q(x)$ split into linear factors, whatever they may be (we can assume $k \neq 0$ and $l \neq 0$ because both polynomials were supposed not to be identically zero):

$$
\begin{aligned}
p(x) &= k \cdot (x - a_1) \cdot (x - a_2) \cdots (x - a_n), \\
q(x) &= l \cdot (x - b_1) \cdot (x - b_2) \cdots (x - b_m).
\end{aligned}
$$

Now $p(x) = 0$ is equivalent to $\bigvee_{1 \leq i \leq n} x = a_i$ and $q(x) = 0$ is equivalent to $\bigvee_{1 \leq j \leq m} x = b_j$. Thus, the formula $\forall x. \, p(x) = 0 \Rightarrow q(x) = 0$ says precisely that

$$\forall x. \bigvee_{1 \leq i \leq n} x = a_i \Rightarrow \bigvee_{1 \leq j \leq m} x = b_j,$$

or in other words, all the a_i appear among the b_j. However, since there are just n linear factors in the antecedent, a given factor $(x - a_i)$ cannot occur more than n times and thus the polynomial divisibility relation $p(x)|q(x)^n$ holds. Conversely, if this divisibility relation holds for $n > 0$, then clearly $\forall x. \, p(x) = 0 \Rightarrow q(x) = 0$ holds. Thus, the key quantified formula can be reduced to a polynomial divisibility relation, and as we will soon see in more detail, it's not difficult to express this as a quantifier-free formula in the coefficients, thus eliminating the quantification over x. In what follows, we present this sketch-proof in more detail and implement it.

Polynomial utilities

Before proceeding further, it's useful to have some additional utility functions on canonical polynomials. The `coefficients` function converts a polynomial $c_0 + c_1 x + c_2 x^2 + \cdots + c_n x^n$ into a list of coefficients $[c_0; c_1; c_2; \ldots; c_n]$. Note that we need to be explicit about the variable x, otherwise we couldn't tell whether, say, $1 + 2 \cdot y$ is a degree 1 polynomial in y or a degree 0 (constant) polynomial in x.

```
let rec coefficients vars =
  function Fn("+",[c; Fn("*",[Var x; q])]) when x = hd vars ->
              c::(coefficients vars q)
        | p -> [p];;
```

We define several other functions in terms of `coefficients`, though a direct implementation would be slightly more efficient. The `degree` function tells us the degree $\deg(p)$ of a polynomial p:

```
let degree vars p = length(coefficients vars p) - 1;;
```

`is_constant` tells us if the polynomial is constant in the top variable:

```
let is_constant vars p = degree vars p = 0;;
```

and `head` returns the head coefficient, i.e. the coefficient of the highest power of the top variable:

```
let head vars p = last(coefficients vars p);;
```

We might have used the terminology *formal* degree, to emphasize that the head coefficient could still be zero for certain values of the other variables. In situations where it is known to be zero, we often want to just remove that term, and this is done by the **behead** function. We must take care to maintain the canonical form, not, say, transforming $1 + x \cdot a$ into $1 + x \cdot 0$:

```
let rec behead vars =
  function Fn("+",[c; Fn("*",[Var x; p])]) when x = hd vars ->
        let p' = behead vars p in
        if p' = zero then c else Fn("+",[c; Fn("*",[Var x; p'])])
  | _ -> zero;;
```

To avoid redundant calculations later, we'd like to eliminate constant multiples of the same polynomial, e.g. $2x^2 - 4y$ and $6y - 3x^2$. To multiply a polynomial through by a (nonzero) constant k we use a special function:

```
let rec poly_cmul k p =
  match p with
    Fn("+",[c; Fn("*",[Var x; q])]) ->
        Fn("+",[poly_cmul k c; Fn("*",[Var x; poly_cmul k q])])
  | _ -> numeral1 (fun m -> k */ m) p;;
```

For definiteness, we pick the coefficient of the 'maximal' term:

```
let rec headconst p =
  match p with
    Fn("+",[c; Fn("*",[Var x; q])]) -> headconst q
  | Fn(n,[]) -> dest_numeral p;;
```

and multiply through by its inverse to put the polynomial in what we might call 'monic' form, with head coefficient 1. This **monic** function also returns a Boolean value indicating whether the multiplying constant was negative, and hence whether the normalization process has made a sign change:

```
let monic p =
  let h = headconst p in
  if h =/ Int 0 then p,false else poly_cmul (Int 1 // h) p,h </ Int 0;;
```

Pseudo-division

In the earlier sketch, we used one polynomial equation $p(x) = 0$ with degree n to substitute in other polynomials $s(x)$ of degree $\geq n$. By doing so repeatedly as necessary we are able to reduce $s(x)$ to an equivalent $r(x)$ with

$\deg(r) < \deg(p)$. The general process underlying this operation is *pseudo-division* of a polynomial $s(x)$ by a polynomial $p(x)$, resulting in quotient and remainder polynomials $q(x)$ and $r(x)$ and a 'constant' c (i.e. polynomial not involving x) such that:

$$cs(x) = p(x)q(x) + r(x)$$

and $\deg(r) < \deg(p)$. If we are considering univariate polynomials with rational coefficients, we may ensure $c = 1$, giving true division. Our 'coefficients' will in general be polynomials in other variables, so we can't do that. However, as will become clear from the algorithm that follows, we may always assume that c is a power of the leading coefficient of $p(x)$.

Suppose we isolate the leading terms of the polynomials to give $p(x) = ax^n + p_0(x)$ and $s(x) = bx^m + s_0(x)$. If $m < n$ already, then we can just set $c = 1$, $q(x) = 0$ and $r(s) = s(x)$ and the conditions for pseudo-division are trivially satisfied. Otherwise, if $n \le m$ we have:

$$as(x) = bx^{m-n}p(x) + (as_0(x) - bx^{m-n}p_0(x)).$$

Note that $s'(x) = as_0(x) - bx^{m-n}p_0(x)$ has lower degree than $s(x)$ because the leading terms cancel. We can proceed recursively to pseudo-divide it by p, giving, say:

$$a^k s'(x) = q'(x)p(x) + r'(x)$$

and then we have a quotient and remainder as required:

$$
\begin{aligned}
a^{k+1}s(x) &= a^k(bx^{m-n}p(x) + s'(x)) \\
&= a^k bx^{m-n}p(x) + a^k s'(x) \\
&= a^k bx^{m-n}p(x) + q'(x)p(x) + r'(x) \\
&= (a^k bx^{m-n} + q'(x))p(x) + r'(x).
\end{aligned}
$$

Thus we have a recursive pseudo-division algorithm, where the multiplying constant that results is always a power of a, the leading coefficient of $p(x)$. Actually, if it happens that the two leading coefficients a and b of the polynomials are the same, we can make their leading terms match without the multiplications by a and b, which seems a worthwhile optimization. (For more sophisticated enhancements, see Exercise 5.17 below.)

```
let pdivide =
  let shift1 x p = Fn("+",[zero; Fn("*",[Var x; p])]) in
  let rec pdivide_aux vars a n p k s =
    if s = zero then (k,s) else
    let b = head vars s and m = degree vars s in
    if m < n then (k,s) else
    let p' = funpow (m - n) (shift1 (hd vars)) p in
    if a = b then pdivide_aux vars a n p k (poly_sub vars s p')
    else pdivide_aux vars a n p (k+1)
             (poly_sub vars (poly_mul vars a s) (poly_mul vars b p')) in
  fun vars s p -> pdivide_aux vars (head vars p) (degree vars p) p 0 s;;
```

The auxiliary function `shift1` is used to multiply a polynomial by x, and `pdivide_aux` implements the main recursion sketched above, with `a` and `n` the head coefficient and degree of `p`, respectively. We return a pair giving the power of the leading coefficient used and the remainder. We don't even bother to compute the quotient explicitly, because we don't need it for our applications. For example, to use this function to simplify $p(x) = 0 \wedge s(x) = 0$ where $\deg(p) \leq \deg(s)$, we will pseudo-divide $s(x)$ by $p(x)$ to get:

$$a^k s(x) = q(x)p(x) + s'(x),$$

where a is the leading coefficient of $p(x)$. From this we have $a^k s(x) = s'(x)$ whenever $p(x) = 0$ and so, provided $a \neq 0$, we have

$$p(x) = 0 \wedge s(x) = 0 \Leftrightarrow p(x) = 0 \wedge s'(x) = 0.$$

The same approach works when we have many other polynomials:

$$p(x) = 0 \wedge \bigwedge_i s_i(x) = 0 \Leftrightarrow p(x) = 0 \wedge \bigwedge_i s_i'(x) = 0.$$

Now we can repeat the process, pseudo-dividing by whichever polynomial in the new conjunction has the lowest degree, and so on, until at most one polynomial is non-constant (with respect to x).

Sign determination

However, as we noted, we can only perform this sort of cancellation if the leading coefficient of the cancelling polynomial is nonzero; note that without $a \neq 0$ the main equivalence above breaks down. In general, whether a coefficient is nonzero depends on values of the other variables, so we often have to perform a case-split, considering the $a = 0$ and $a \neq 0$ cases separately. In the $a = 0$ case, we can at least delete the leading term and so we've made the degree of one of the polynomials smaller, while in the $a \neq 0$ case we can use it for cancellation to reduce the degree of others. Starting with a formula P, if under the assumption $a = 0$ we can reduce it to P_0, i.e.

$$a = 0 \Rightarrow (P \Leftrightarrow P_0),$$

while in the case $a \neq 0$ we can reduce it to P_1:

$$a \neq 0 \Rightarrow (P \Leftrightarrow P_1),$$

then we have overall:

$$P \Leftrightarrow a = 0 \wedge P_0 \vee a \neq 0 \wedge P_1.$$

To make explicit such 'local assumptions', we use a data structure associating coefficients with signs, represented via the following datatype.

```
type sign = Zero | Nonzero | Positive | Negative;;
```

At present we will only use `Zero` and `Nonzero`, but `Positive` and `Negative` will be useful for the reals later. For the same reason, we define a function to optionally swap a sign. Given a sign for a, it returns one for $-a$ if `swf` is true and otherwise returns the original sign unchanged.

```
let swap swf s =
  if not swf then s else
  match s with
    Positive -> Negative
  | Negative -> Positive
  | _ -> s;;
```

We store the assumptions about signs for *monic* polynomials, so that we don't, for example, have separate entries for a and $3a$. Thus the context is implemented as an association list of monic polynomials with their signs, and signs are tested by converting to monic form, with a sign flip afterwards if necessary:

```
let findsign sgns p =
  try let p',swf = monic p in swap swf (assoc p' sgns)
  with Failure _ -> failwith "findsign";;
```

Adding a new sign assumption to an existing context works similarly, but is a little more involved because it is permissible to refine an existing assumption of `Nonzero` to one of `Positive` or `Negative` (again, this will be useful for the reals):

```
let assertsign sgns (p,s) =
  if p = zero then if s = Zero then sgns else failwith "assertsign" else
  let p',swf = monic p in
  let s' = swap swf s in
  let s0 = try assoc p' sgns with Failure _ -> s' in
  if s' = s0 or s0 = Nonzero & (s' = Positive or s' = Negative)
  then (p',s')::(subtract sgns [p',s0]) else failwith "assertsign";;
```

Case-splits are organized by a higher-order function `split_zero` taking a sign context `sgns`, a polynomial `pol`, and two functions returning formulas, `cont_z` for the zero case and `cont_n` for the nonzero case. If the zero or nonzero status of `pol` can be determined immediately from the context, then the appropriate continuation is just called directly. Otherwise, the two continuations are both called on appropriately expanded sign contexts. The call of `cont_z` with the extra assumption that `pol` is zero returns some formula P_0, and similarly `cont_n` with the extra assumption that it's nonzero returns P_1. The splitting function then returns the final formula which will be $pol = 0 \wedge P_0 \vee pol \neq 0 \wedge P_1$.

```
let split_zero sgns pol cont_z cont_n =
  try let z = findsign sgns pol in
      (if z = Zero then cont_z else cont_n) sgns
  with Failure "findsign" ->
      let eq = Atom(R("=",[pol; zero])) in
      Or(And(eq,cont_z (assertsign sgns (pol,Zero))),
          And(Not eq,cont_n (assertsign sgns (pol,Nonzero))));;
```

Main algorithm

We start with a few supporting functions, the first of which produces a formula asserting that a polynomial is not the zero polynomial with respect to the current top variable, i.e. that at least one coefficient is nonzero. We could just create a disjunction $\neg(c_1 = 0) \vee \cdots \vee \neg(c_l = 0)$ for all the coefficients c_i, but we optimize things a bit by exploiting the sign context. First, we partition the coefficients `cs` into those that are immediately decidable (`dcs`) and undecidable (`ucs`) from the context. If any decidable coefficient is nonzero, we can just return the formula $\top$, while otherwise if there are no undecidable ones they must all be zero and so we can return $\bot$. Otherwise we take the undecidable coefficients $c_1, \ldots, c_k$ and create the formula $\neg(c_1 = 0) \vee \cdots \vee \neg(c_k = 0)$ asserting that one of them is nonzero.

```
let poly_nonzero vars sgns pol =
  let cs = coefficients vars pol in
  let dcs,ucs = partition (can (findsign sgns)) cs in
  if exists (fun p -> findsign sgns p <> Zero) dcs then True
  else if ucs = [] then False
  else end_itlist mk_or (map (fun p -> Not(mk_eq p zero)) ucs);;
```

The next function tests if one polynomial $s(x)$ is non-divisible by another one $p(x)$, treating both as univariate with the coefficients parametrized by other variables. We will assume that the leading coefficient a of $p(x)$ is nonzero when this function is used. We simply pseudo-divide to obtain a remainder r such that $a^k s(x) = p(x)q(x) + r(x)$ and $\partial(r) < \partial(p)$. Since a is a nonzero constant, $p(x)|s(x)$ is equivalent to $p(x)|r(x)$, and the latter, since $r(x)$ has lower degree than $p(x)$, holds precisely if $r(x)$ is the zero polynomial.

```
let rec poly_nondiv vars sgns p s =
  let _,r = pdivide vars s p in poly_nonzero vars sgns r;;
```

Now we are ready for the main quantifier elimination from

$$\exists x.\, p_1(x) = 0 \wedge \cdots \wedge p_k(x) = 0 \wedge q_1(x) \neq 0 \wedge \cdots \wedge q_l(x) \neq 0,$$

assuming some initial processing so that eqs holds the list $[p_1; \ldots; p_k]$ and neqs the list $[q_1; \ldots; q_l]$, while sgns is the sign context. The first step is to check if there are any constant polynomials (with respect to the top variable) in the list eqs. If so, we can pull them outside, since $\exists x.\, c = 0 \wedge p[x]$ is equivalent to $c = 0 \wedge (\exists x.\, P[x])$. We're free to add $c = 0$ to the context for the sub-problem $\exists x.\, P[x]$, but when doing so we check for failure, meaning that $c \neq 0$ already follows from the context. In this case we can just return $\bot$ for the entire problem.

Otherwise, if there are no equations the problem is just $\exists x.\, q_1(x) \neq 0 \wedge \cdots \wedge q_l(x) \neq 0$. Since any univariate polynomial has only finitely many roots, this will be true precisely if none of the q_i is the zero polynomial, so we generate the appropriate formula by applying poly_nonzero to each and conjoining the results. Otherwise, we have at least one equation, and we pick one $p(x) = 0$ where $p(x)$ has minimal degree n. We want to use this equation for elimination, but first we need to ensure that its head coefficient a is nonzero. Hence we case-split, and in the case where $a = 0$ just proceed recursively with that coefficient removed.

Once we know $a \neq 0$ together with $p(x) = 0$, it is legitimate to pseudo-divide any polynomial by $p(x)$ without changing its zero/nonzero status, because then if $a^k s(x) = p(x)q(x) + r(x)$ we have $s(x) = 0 \Leftrightarrow r(x) = 0$; this pseudo-division is implemented by **cfn**. If there are equations besides $p(x) = 0$, we just pseudo-divide all of them by $p(x)$ and recurse: now some other equation will have smaller degree. Otherwise, if there are no inequations, the problem is simply $\exists x.\, p(x) = 0$. Since we know $p(x)$ is nonconstant (that was checked first), this is trivially true by the Fundamental Theorem of Algebra. Otherwise we multiply all the inequations together to get $q(x) = q_1(x) \ldots q_l(x)$, and we need to solve the problem $\exists x.\, p(x) = 0 \wedge q(x) \neq 0$. As noted in the initial sketch, this is equivalent to $\neg(\forall x.\, p(x) = 0 \Rightarrow q(x) = 0)$ and so to the non-divisibility of $q(x)^{\partial(p)}$ by $p(x)$, so we create that formula:

```
let rec cqelim vars (eqs,neqs) sgns =
  try let c = find (is_constant vars) eqs in
    (try let sgns' = assertsign sgns (c,Zero)
         and eqs' = subtract eqs [c] in
         And(mk_eq c zero,cqelim vars (eqs',neqs) sgns')
     with Failure "assertsign" -> False)
  with Failure _ ->
      if eqs = [] then list_conj(map (poly_nonzero vars sgns) neqs) else
      let n = end_itlist min (map (degree vars) eqs) in
      let p = find (fun p -> degree vars p = n) eqs in
      let oeqs = subtract eqs [p] in
      split_zero sgns (head vars p)
        (cqelim vars (behead vars p::oeqs,neqs))
        (fun sgns' ->
           let cfn s = snd(pdivide vars s p) in
           if oeqs <> [] then cqelim vars (p::(map cfn oeqs),neqs) sgns'
           else if neqs = [] then True else
           let q = end_itlist (poly_mul vars) neqs in
           poly_nondiv vars sgns' p (poly_pow vars q (degree vars p)));;
```

Our initial sign hypothesis will assert that 1 is positive and 0 is zero; by handling the constants like this we avoid a separate path in **findsign**.

```
let init_sgns = [Fn("1",[]),Positive; Fn("0",[]),Zero];;
```

The core quantifier elimination function now breaks up the existential formula into the appropriate list of zero and nonzero assertions, and calls **cqelim** appropriately:

```
let basic_complex_qelim vars (Exists(x,p)) =
  let eqs,neqs = partition (non negative) (conjuncts p) in
  cqelim (x::vars) (map lhs eqs,map (lhs ** negate) neqs) init_sgns;;
```

We package this core algorithm using a full DNF transformation:

```
let complex_qelim =
  simplify ** evalc **
  lift_qelim polyatom (dnf ** cnnf (fun x -> x) ** evalc)
          basic_complex_qelim;;
```

Examples

Here is a simple example of quantifier elimination in action; one can understand why this formula holds by observing that $x^4 + 1 = (x^2 + \sqrt{2}x + 1)(x^2 - \sqrt{2}x + 1)$:

```
# complex_qelim
    <<forall a x. a^2 = 2 /\ x^2 + a * x + 1 = 0 ==> x^4 + 1 = 0>>;;
- : fol formula = <<true>>
```

The procedure works equally well in the context of parameters:

```
# complex_qelim
    <<forall a x. a^2 = 2 /\ x^2 + a * x + 1 = 0 ==> x^4 + c = 0>>;;
- : fol formula = <<~(~1 + c * (-4 + c * (6 + c * (-4 + c * 1)))) = 0)>>
```

and we can check any simplified form of the equivalence by more quantifier elimination:

```
complex_qelim
 <<forall c.
     (forall a x. a^2 = 2 /\ x^2 + a * x + 1 = 0 ==> x^4 + c = 0)
     <=> c = 1>>;;
```

The following proves the formulas for the sum and product of distinct roots of a quadratic equation:

```
# complex_qelim
    <<forall a b c x y.
        a * x^2 + b * x + c = 0 /\ a * y^2 + b * y + c = 0 /\ ~(x = y)
        ==> a * x * y = c /\ a * (x + y) + b = 0>>;;
- : fol formula = <<true>>
```

5.9 The real numbers

We now consider a similar theory of *real* arithmetic with addition and multiplication. A decision procedure for this theory, based on quantifier elimination, was first demonstrated by Tarski (1951).[†] However, Tarski's procedure, a generalization of the classical technique due to Sturm (1835) for finding the number of real roots of a univariate polynomial, was both difficult to understand and highly inefficient in practice. Seidenberg (1954) gave a simpler algorithm; indeed the possibility of quantifier elimination for this theory is often dually attributed as 'Tarski–Seidenberg'. Other relatively simple algorithms were given by Cohen (1969) and by Kreisel and Krivine (1971). Perhaps the most efficient general algorithm currently known, and the first actually to be implemented on a computer, is the Cylindrical Algebraic Decomposition (CAD) method. This was introduced by Collins (1976) and has subsequently been refined and improved, e.g. by the introduction of *partial* CAD (Hong 1990).[‡] The rather simple algorithm we describe here is from Hörmander (1983) based on an unpublished manuscript by Paul Cohen.

In our language we will allow both equations $s = t$ and inequalities $s < t$, $s \leq t$, $s > t$ and $s \geq t$. Our algorithm necessarily has a somewhat different flavour from the complex number procedure, not just because of the presence of inequalities, but because the reals are not algebraically closed. For example, since the quadratic equation $x^2 + 1 = 0$ has no solution over $\mathbb{R}$, the following are both valid, yet there is no simple divisibility relation between powers of the antecedent and consequent polynomials:

$$\forall x.\ x^2 + 1 = 0 \Rightarrow x + 2 = 0,$$
$$\forall x.\ x^3 + 2x^2 + x + 2 = 0 \Rightarrow x^2 + 4x + 4 = 0.$$

The algorithm will essentially use ordering properties, and we will freely exploit basic facts about polynomials over the reals.[§] Some of our reasoning will involve derivatives, so we start with a function to differentiate a polynomial with respect to the top variable. The derivative of $p(x) = c_0 + c_1 x + c_2 x^2 + \cdots + c_n x^n$ is just $p'(x) = c_1 + 2c_2 + \cdots + nc_n x^{n-1}$, but we need to operate on the canonical form. This auxiliary function takes as

---

[†] Tarski actually discovered the procedure in 1930, but it remained unpublished for many years afterwards. Tarski's procedure, and the one we will describe, work not only for the reals but for any 'real closed field'.

[‡] A technique related to CAD was earlier proposed by Łojasiewicz (1964). Another relatively efficient method was developed at much the same time as CAD by Monk (1975), working with Solovay; for a brief description see Rabin (1991).

[§] Most of these are familiar from elementary calculus. With more work, the properties we need can be deduced just from the real-closed field axioms, proving that they are complete for formulas in this language.

additional parameters the top variable x (as a term) and the implicit power of x by which the polynomial is multiplied; this determines the multiplier for the first coefficient:

```
let rec poly_diffn x n p =
  match p with
    Fn("+",[c; Fn("*",[y; q])]) when y = x ->
        Fn("+",[poly_cmul(Int n) c; Fn("*",[x; poly_diffn x (n+1) q])])
  | _ -> poly_cmul(Int n) p;;
```

Now to differentiate a polynomial $p(x) = c + x \cdot q(x)$, we just apply the auxiliary function to $q(x)$ with $n = 1$; if $p(x)$ is constant we just return zero.

```
let poly_diff vars p =
  match p with
    Fn("+",[c; Fn("*",[Var x; q])]) when x = hd vars ->
        poly_diffn (Var x) 1 q
  | _ -> zero;;
```

The key component of the quantifier elimination algorithm is a procedure to obtain a 'sign matrix' for a set of univariate polynomials $p_1(x), \ldots, p_n(x)$. Such a matrix is based on a division of the real line into a (possibly empty) ordered sequence of m points $x_1 < x_2 < \cdots < x_m$ representing precisely the roots of the polynomials, with the rows of the matrix representing, in alternating fashion, the points themselves and the intervals between adjacent pairs and the two intervals at the ends:

$$(-\infty, x_1), x_1, (x_1, x_2), x_2, \ldots, x_{m-1}, (x_{m-1}, x_m), x_m, (x_m, +\infty)$$

using the common shorthand for intervals $(a, b) = \{x \mid a < x \land x < b\}$, and columns representing the polynomials $p_1(x), \ldots, p_n(x)$, with the matrix entries giving the signs, either positive $(+)$, negative $(-)$ or zero (0), of each polynomial p_i at the points and on the intervals. For example, for the collection of polynomials:

$$
\begin{aligned}
p_1(x) &= x^2 - 3x + 2, \\
p_2(x) &= 2x - 3,
\end{aligned}
$$

the sign matrix looks like this:

Point/interval	p_1	p_2
$(-\infty, x_1)$	$+$	$-$
x_1	0	$-$
(x_1, x_2)	$-$	$-$
x_2	$-$	0
(x_2, x_3)	$-$	$+$
x_3	0	$+$
$(x_3, +\infty)$	$+$	$+$

Here x_1 and x_3 represent the roots 1 and 2 of $p_1(x)$ while x_2 represents $3/2$, the root of $p_2(x)$. However, the sign matrix contains no numerical information about the location of the points x_i, merely specifying their order and what signs the various polynomials take on each point and each intermediate interval. Crucially, the sign matrix for a set of univariate polynomials $p_1(x), \ldots, p_n(x)$ is sufficient to answer any question of the form $\exists x. \, P[x]$ where the body $P[x]$ is quantifier-free and all atoms are of the form $p_i(x) \bowtie_i 0$ for any of the relations $=, <, >, \leq, \geq$. Each relation $\bowtie$ is associated with a set of signs for p for which $p \bowtie 0$ holds:

```
let rel_signs =
  ["=",[Zero]; "<=",[Zero;Negative]; ">=",[Zero;Positive];
   "<",[Negative]; ">",[Positive]];;
```

Now, given an association list `pmat` of polynomials with their signs, we can evaluate a formula by just:

```
let testform pmat fm =
  eval fm (fun (R(a,[p;z])) -> mem (assoc p pmat) (assoc a rel_signs));;
```

As we will see, the generalization to multivariate polynomials is straightforward, so being able to find the sign matrix is the core of our enterprise. And a fairly simple recursive algorithm to find sign matrices can be based on the following observation. We can construct the sign matrix for the polynomials:

$$p, p_1, \ldots, p_n$$

given a sign matrix for the following polynomials, where p' is the derivative of p, and each q_i is the remainder on dividing p by p_i (with p_0 meaning p'):

$$p', p_1, \ldots, p_n, q_0, q_1, \ldots, q_n.$$

The procedure for deriving the sign matrix for the first set, given one for the second, is as follows. First, we split the sign matrix into two equally-sized parts, one for the $p', p_1, \ldots, p_n$ and one for the $q_0, q_1, \ldots, q_n$, but for the moment keeping all the points, even if no polynomial in one set has a root at some of them. We can now infer the sign of $p(x_i)$ for each point x_i that is a root of one of the polynomials p_k, as follows. Since q_k is the remainder on dividing p by p_k, we have $p(x) = s_k(x)p_k(x) + q_k(x)$ for some $s_k(x)$. Therefore, if $p_k(x_i) = 0$ we have $p(x_i) = q_k(x_i)$ and so we can derive the sign of p at x_i from that of the corresponding q_k. If the point x_i is not a root of one of the $p', p_1, \ldots, p_n$, or we are dealing with an interval, we just assign Nonzero; these will be eliminated in the next step. The following code implements this process for two corresponding rows pd and qd of the sign matrices for $p', p_1, \ldots, p_n$ and $q_0, \ldots, q_n$ respectively.

```
let inferpsign (pd,qd) =
  try let i = index Zero pd in el i qd :: pd
  with Failure _ -> Nonzero :: pd;;
```

Having applied this to all rows, we throw away the second sign matrix, giving signs for the $q_0, \ldots, q_n$, and retain the (partial) matrix for $p, p', p_1, \ldots, p_n$, which we 'condense' to remove points that are not roots of one of the $p', p_1, \ldots, p_n$. The signs of the $p', p_1, \ldots, p_n$ in an interval from which some other points have been removed can be read off from any of the subintervals in the original subdivision – they cannot change because there are no roots for the relevant polynomials there.

```
let rec condense ps =
  match ps with
    int::pt::other -> let rest = condense other in
                      if mem Zero pt then int::pt::rest else rest
  | _ -> ps;;
```

Now we have a sign matrix for $p, p', p_1, \ldots, p_n$ with correct signs at all the points, but undetermined signs for p on the intervals, and the possibility that there may be additional roots of p inside these intervals. However, note that there can be *at most one* root of p in each interval, even including its endpoint(s). For if there were two roots, then p would reach a maximum or minimum somewhere in between them, contradicting the fact that p' is nonzero on the interior of the interval.

Consider first an internal interval (x_i, x_{i+1}). By the observation above, if $p(x_i) = 0$ or $p(x_{i+1}) = 0$ we know that there can be no other root in the interval. If both $p(x_i)$ and $p(x_{i+1})$ are nonzero and their signs are different then there *is* a root of p in the interval, by the intermediate value property. Finally, if the signs are both nonzero but are the same, there is no root in the interval, because in that case p would reach a maximum or minimum there (whether it crosses or just touches the x-axis), and this is impossible since $p' \neq 0$. To summarize, there is one root of p inside the interval if the signs of $p(x_i)$ and $p(x_{i+1})$ are both nonzero and different, and there is no root otherwise.

What about the two semi-infinite intervals? For sufficiently large $|x|$, a polynomial is dominated by the term of highest degree, and if $p(x) \sim a_n x^n$ we have $p'(x) \sim na_n x^{n-1}$, so the ratio between the two eventually has positive sign as $x \to +\infty$ and negative sign as $x \to -\infty$. Let us temporarily introduce pseudo-endpoints $-\infty$ and $+\infty$ to denote 'points at infinity'. Based on the above observation, we define the sign of $p(-\infty)$ by flipping the sign of p' on the lowest interval $(-\infty, x_1)$ and the sign of $p(+\infty)$ by copying the sign of p' on the highest interval $(x_n, +\infty)$. Now exactly the same decision method works for this case too, which makes the implementation more regular.

The following function implements these observations to complete the sign matrix, assuming that the 'points at infinity' have been added first. When this is called, the first three elements of ps are the lists of polynomial signs for respectively the leftmost point, the interval following it, and the next point to its right. We pick out the signs of p (the head of each list) at the left (l) and right (r) endpoints of the interval. It should actually be impossible for both signs to be zero, since that would imply a point of zero derivative between. And we hope never to encounter just Nonzero; by design we will always have a more precise sign whenever inferisign function is used. Otherwise, if just one sign is zero, we infer the sign on the interval from the sign at the nonzero end. If both are negative or both positive, we infer the sign from l (we could equally well use r). The more complex case is where l and r are opposites, and we insert a new point and its surrounding intervals. The signs of p on the new subintervals are taken from the corresponding endpoints, and it is zero at the new point. Nothing changes for the other polynomials throughout the original interval, so we just duplicate ints for them. In each case we recursively call inferisign to deal with the remaining points and intervals. And finally, when there are fewer than three elements, we assume we have reached the rightmost endpoint, so there are no intervals to infer the sign of p on, and we return the original sign matrix unchanged.

```
let rec inferisign ps =
  match ps with
    ((l::ls) as x)::(_::ints)::((r::rs)::xs as pts) ->
        (match (l,r) with
            (Zero,Zero) -> failwith "inferisign: inconsistent"
          | (Nonzero,_)
          | (_,Nonzero) -> failwith "inferisign: indeterminate"
          | (Zero,_) -> x::(r::ints)::inferisign pts
          | (_,Zero) -> x::(l::ints)::inferisign pts
          | (Negative,Negative)
          | (Positive,Positive) -> x::(l::ints)::inferisign pts
          | _ -> x::(l::ints)::(Zero::ints)::(r::ints)::inferisign pts)
  | _ -> ps;;
```

Now we're ready for the overall function to convert a sign matrix `mat` for $p', p_1, \ldots, p_n, q_0, q_1, \ldots, q_n$ into one for $p, p_1, \ldots, p_n$. Rather than returning the result, it applies the given continuation function `cont` to it, since this fits in with the later code structure. Otherwise it's just a question of putting together the earlier pieces. We set $l = n + 1$, and apply `inferpsign` to all rows of the matrix, first splitting them into the pieces for $p', p_1, \ldots, p_n$ and for $q_0, q_1, \ldots, q_n$. After condensation to remove extraneous points, we get a partial sign matrix `mat1` for $p, p', p_1, \ldots, p_n$. The points at infinity are added, just for p since nothing else will be looked at, to give `mat2`. We then infer the signs on the intervals and remove the points at infinity again to give `mat3`. Finally, we remove p' from this matrix, condense again to remove points that were just roots of p', and apply the continuation to the result.

```
let dedmatrix cont mat =
  let l = length (hd mat) / 2 in
  let mat1 = condense(map (inferpsign ** chop_list l) mat) in
  let mat2 = [swap true (el 1 (hd mat1))]::mat1@[[el 1 (last mat1)]] in
  let mat3 = butlast(tl(inferisign mat2)) in
  cont(condense(map (fun l -> hd l :: tl(tl l)) mat3));;
```

The reasoning underlying `dedmatrix` is based on fairly straightforward observations of real analysis. Essentially the same procedure can be used even for multivariate polynomials, treating other variables as parameters while eliminating one variable. The only complication is that instead of literally dividing one polynomial s by another one p:

$$s(x) = p(x)q(x) + r(x)$$

we may instead have only a pseudo-division

$$a^k s(x) = p(x)q(x) + r(x),$$

where a is the leading coefficient of p, in general a polynomial in the other variables. As with the complex numbers, we will need to perform case-splits over polynomials in other variables to make sure $a \neq 0$. Even then, to infer the sign of r from that of s, we need to know the sign of a^k. Our solution is an enhanced pseudo-division function ensuring that r has the same sign as s. We obtain the head coefficient a of $p(x)$ and perform pseudo-division as usual, say $a^k s(x) = p(x)q(x) + r(x)$. We then examine what we know from the context about the sign of a. If it is zero, we fail, and if the context does not determine it, `findsign` will fail. Otherwise if we know either that $a > 0$ or that k is even, we have $a^k > 0$ and can safely return $r(x)$. Otherwise, k must be odd. If we know $a < 0$, then also $a^k < 0$ so we need to return $-r(x)$. Otherwise, all we know is $a \neq 0$, so we implicitly multiply through again by a and return $ar(x)$; note that $a^{k+1} s(x) = ap(x)q(x) + ar(x)$, and since k is odd, $k + 1$ is even.

```
let pdivide_pos vars sgns s p =
  let a = head vars p and (k,r) = pdivide vars s p in
  let sgn = findsign sgns a in
  if sgn = Zero then failwith "pdivide_pos: zero head coefficient"
  else if sgn = Positive or k mod 2 = 0 then r
  else if sgn = Negative then poly_neg r else poly_mul vars a r;;
```

We will also need to case-split over positive/negative status of coefficients, and the following function is analogous to the function `split_zero` that we wrote for the complex numbers and will shortly use again. It is assumed that by the time we use this function, we already know from the context at least that the polynomial concerned is nonzero.

```
let split_sign sgns pol cont =
  match findsign sgns pol with
    Nonzero -> let fm = Atom(R(">",[pol; zero])) in
               Or(And(fm,cont(assertsign sgns (pol,Positive))),
                  And(Not fm,cont(assertsign sgns (pol,Negative))))
  | _ -> cont sgns;;
```

In the later algorithm, the most convenient thing is to perform a three-way case-split over the zero, positive or negative cases, but call the same continuation on the positive and negative cases:

```
let split_trichotomy sgns pol cont_z cont_pn =
  split_zero sgns pol cont_z (fun s' -> split_sign s' pol cont_pn);;
```

Sign matrix determination is now implemented by a set of three mutually recursive functions. The first function `casesplit` takes two lists of polynomials: `dun` (so named because 'done' is a reserved word in OCaml) is the list whose head coefficients have known sign, and `pols` is the list to be checked. As soon as we have determined all the head coefficient signs, we call `matrix`. For each polynomial `p` in the list `pols` we perform appropriate case-splits. In the zero case we chop off its head coefficient and recurse, and in the other cases we just add it to the 'done' list. But if any of the polynomials is a constant with respect to the top variable, we recurse to a `delconst` function to remove it.

```
let rec casesplit vars dun pols cont sgns =
  match pols with
    [] -> matrix vars dun cont sgns
  | p::ops -> split_trichotomy sgns (head vars p)
                    (if is_constant vars p then delconst vars dun p ops cont
                     else casesplit vars dun (behead vars p :: ops) cont)
                    (if is_constant vars p then delconst vars dun p ops cont
                     else casesplit vars (dun@[p]) ops cont)
```

The `delconst` function just removes the polynomial from the list and returns to case-splitting, except that it also modifies the continuation appropriately to put the sign back in the matrix before calling the original continuation:

```
and delconst vars dun p ops cont sgns =
  let cont' m = cont(map (insertat (length dun) (findsign sgns p)) m) in
  casesplit vars dun ops cont' sgns
```

Finally, we come to the main function `matrix`, where we assume that all the polynomials in the list `pols` are non-constant and have a head coefficient of known nonzero sign. If the list of polynomials is empty, then trivially the empty sign matrix is the right answer, so we call the continuation on that. Note the exception trap, though! Because of our rather naive case-splitting, we may reach situations where an inconsistent set of sign assumptions is made – for example $a < 0$ and $a^3 > 0$ or just $a^2 < 0$. This can in fact lead to the 'impossible' situation that the sign matrix has two roots of some $p(x)$ with no root of $p'(x)$ in between them – in which case `inferisign` will generate an exception. We don't actually want to fail here, but we're at liberty to return whatever formula we like, such as $\bot$.

Otherwise, we pick a polynomial `p` of maximal degree, so that we make definite progress in the recursive step: we remove at least one polynomial of maximal degree and replace it only with polynomials of lower degree. One can show that the recursion is therefore terminating, via the wellfoundedness of the multiset order (Appendix 1) or using a more direct argument. We reshuffle the polynomials slightly to move `p` from position `i` to the head of the list, and add its derivative in front of that, giving `qs`. Then we form all the remainders `gs` from pseudo-division of `p` by each member of the `qs`, and recurse again on the new list of polynomials, starting with the case-splits. The continuation is modified to apply `dedmatrix` and also to compensate for the shuffling of `p` to the head of the list:

```
and matrix vars pols cont sgns =
  if pols = [] then try cont [[]] with Failure _ -> False else
  let p = hd(sort(decreasing (degree vars)) pols) in
  let p' = poly_diff vars p and i = index p pols in
  let qs = let p1,p2 = chop_list i pols in p'::p1 @ tl p2 in
  let gs = map (pdivide_pos vars sgns p) qs in
  let cont' m = cont(map (fun l -> insertat i (hd l) (tl l)) m) in
  casesplit vars [] (qs@gs) (dedmatrix cont') sgns;;
```

To perform quantifier elimination from an existential formula, we first pick out all the polynomials (we assume atoms have already been normalized), set up the continuation to test the body on the resulting sign matrix, and call `casesplit` with the initial sign context.

```
let basic_real_qelim vars (Exists(x,p)) =
  let pols = atom_union
    (function (R(a,[t;Fn("0",[])])) -> [t] | _ -> []) p in
  let cont mat = if exists (fun m -> testform (zip pols m) p) mat
                 then True else False in
  casesplit (x::vars) [] pols cont init_sgns;;
```

Note that we can test *any* quantifier-free formula using the matrix, not just a conjunction of literals. So we may elect to do no logical normalization of the formula at all, certainly not a full DNF transformation. We will however evaluate and simplify all the time:

```
let real_qelim =
  simplify ** evalc **
  lift_qelim polyatom (simplify ** evalc) basic_real_qelim;;
```

Examples

We can try out the algorithm by testing if univariate polynomials have solutions:

```
# real_qelim <<exists x. x^4 + x^2 + 1 = 0>>;;
- : fol formula = <<false>>
# real_qelim <<exists x. x^3 - x^2 + x - 1 = 0>>;;
- : fol formula = <<true>>
```

and even, though not very efficiently, count them:

```
# real_qelim <<exists x y. x^3 - x^2 + x - 1 = 0 /\
                          y^3 - y^2 + y - 1 = 0 /\ ~(x = y)>>;;
- : fol formula = <<false>>
```

If the reader is still a bit puzzled by all the continuation-based code, it might be instructive to *see* the sign matrix that gets passed to `testform`. One way is to switch on tracing; e.g. compare the output here with the example of a sign matrix we gave at the beginning:

```
# #trace testform;;
# real_qelim <<exists x. x^2 - 3 * x + 2 = 0 /\ 2 * x - 3 = 0>>;;
# #untrace testform;;
```

We can eliminate quantifiers however they are nested, e.g.

```
# real_qelim
    <<forall a f k. (forall e. k < e ==> f < a * e) ==> f <= a * k>>;;
- : fol formula = <<true>>
```

and we can obtain parametrized solutions to root existence questions, albeit not very compact ones:

```
# real_qelim <<exists x. a * x^2 + b * x + c = 0>>;;
- : fol formula =
<<0 + a * 1 = 0 /\
  (0 + b * 1 = 0 /\ 0 + c * 1 = 0 \/
   ~0 + b * 1 = 0 /\ (0 + b * 1 > 0 \/ ~0 + b * 1 > 0)) \/
  ~0 + a * 1 = 0 /\
  (0 + a * 1 > 0 /\
   (0 + a * ((0 + b * (0 + b * -1)) + a * (0 + c * 4)) = 0 \/
    ~0 + a * ((0 + b * (0 + b * -1)) + a * (0 + c * 4)) = 0 /\
    ~0 + a * ((0 + b * (0 + b * -1)) + a * (0 + c * 4)) > 0) \/
   ~0 + a * 1 > 0 /\
   (0 + a * ((0 + b * (0 + b * -1)) + a * (0 + c * 4)) = 0 \/
    ~0 + a * ((0 + b * (0 + b * -1)) + a * (0 + c * 4)) = 0 /\ 0 + a *
    ((0 + b * (0 + b * -1)) + a * (0 + c * 4)) > 0))>>
```

Moreover, we can check our own simplified condition by eliminating all quantifiers from a claimed equivalence, perhaps first guessing:

```
# real_qelim <<forall a b c. (exists x. a * x^2 + b * x + c = 0) <=>
                             b^2 >= 4 * a * c>>;;
- : fol formula = <<false>>
```

and then realizing we need to consider the degenerate case $a = 0$:

```
# real_qelim <<forall a b c. (exists x. a * x^2 + b * x + c = 0) <=>
                     a = 0 /\ (b = 0 ==> c = 0) \/
                     ~(a = 0) /\ b^2 >= 4 * a * c>>;;
- : fol formula = <<true>>
```

In Section 4.7 we derived a canonical term rewriting system for groups, and we can prove that it is terminating using the following polynomial interpretation (Huet and Oppen 1980). With each term t in the language of groups we associate an integer value $v(t) > 1$, by assigning some arbitrary integer > 1 to each variable and then calculating the value of a composite term according to the following rules:

$$
\begin{aligned}
v(s \cdot t) &= v(s)(1 + 2v(t)), \\
v(i(t)) &= v(t)^2, \\
v(1) &= 2.
\end{aligned}
$$

We should first verify that this is indeed 'closed', i.e. that if $v(s)$ and $v(t)$ are both > 1, so are $v(s \cdot t)$, $v(i(t))$ and $v(1)$. (The other required property, being an integer, is preserved by addition and multiplication.) We can do this pretty quickly:

```
# real_qelim <<1 < 2 /\ (forall x. 1 < x ==> 1 < x^2) /\
               (forall x y. 1 < x /\ 1 < y ==> 1 < x * (1 + 2 * y))>>;;
- : fol formula = <<true>>
```

To avoid tedious manual transcription, we automatically translate terms to their corresponding 'valuations', where the variables in a term are simply mapped to similarly-named variables in the value polynomial.

```
let rec grpterm tm =
  match tm with
    Fn("*",[s;t]) -> let t2 = Fn("*",[Fn("2",[]); grpterm t]) in
                     Fn("*",[grpterm s; Fn("+",[Fn("1",[]); t2])])
  | Fn("i",[t]) -> Fn("^",[grpterm t; Fn("2",[])])
  | Fn("1",[]) -> Fn("2",[])
  | Var x -> tm;;
```

Now to show that a set of equations $\{s_i = t_i \mid 1 \le i \le n\}$ terminates, it suffices to show that $v(s_i) > v(t_i)$ for each one. So let us map an equation

$s = t$ to a new formula $v(s) > v(t)$, then generalize over all variables, relativized to reflect the assumption that they are all > 1:

```
let grpform (Atom(R("=",[s;t])))) =
  let fm = generalize(Atom(R(">",[grpterm s; grpterm t]))) in
  relativize(fun x -> Atom(R(">",[Var x;Fn("1",[])]))) fm;;
```

After running completion to regenerate the set of equations:

```
let eqs = complete_and_simplify ["1"; "*"; "i"]
  [<<1 * x = x>>; <<i(x) * x = 1>>; <<(x * y) * z = x * y * z>>];;
```

we can create the critical formula and test it:

```
# let fm = list_conj (map grpform eqs);;
val fm : fol formula =
  <<(forall x4.
        x4 > 1 ==>
        (forall x5.
           x5 > 1 ==> (x4 * (1 + 2 * x5))^2 > x5^2 * (1 + 2 * x4^2))) /\
    (forall x1. x1 > 1 ==> x1^2^2 > x1) /\
    ...
  >>;;
# real_qelim fm;;
- : fol formula = true
```

Improvements

The decidability of the theory of reals is a remarkable and theoretically useful result. In principle, we could use `real_qelim` to settle unsolved problems such as finding kissing numbers for spheres in various dimensions (Conway and Sloane 1993). In practice, such a course is completely hopeless. The natural algorithms based on CAD are doubly exponential in the size of the formula, and Davenport and Heintz (1988) have shown that this is a lower bound in general, though an algorithm due to Grigor'ev (1988) that is 'only' doubly exponential in the number of *alternations* of quantifiers may be advantageous for formulas with a limited quantifier structure. These bad theoretical complexity bounds are matched by real practical difficulties, even on such simple-looking examples as $\forall x.\, x^4 + px^2 + qx + r \geq 0$ (Lazard 1988). Motivated by the 'feeling that a single algorithm for the full elementary theory of **R** can hardly be practical' (van den Dries 1988), many authors have investigated special heuristic mixtures of algorithms for restricted subcases.

One particularly notable failing of our algorithm is that it does not exploit equations in the initial problem to perform cancellation by pseudo-division, yet in many cases this would be a dramatic improvement – see Exercise 5.20

below. Indeed, even Collins's original CAD algorithm, according to Loos and Weispfenning (1993), performed badly on the following:

$$\exists c. \forall b. \forall a. (a = d \wedge b = c) \vee (a = c \wedge b = 1) \Rightarrow a^2 = b.$$

We do poorly here too, but if we first split the formula up into DNF:

```
let real_qelim' =
  simplify ** evalc **
  lift_qelim polyatom (dnf ** cnnf (fun x -> x) ** evalc)
                 basic_real_qelim;;
```

the situation is much better:

```
# real_qelim'
  <<forall d.
      (exists c. forall a b. (a = d /\ b = c) \/ (a = c /\ b = 1)
                  ==> a^2 = b)
      <=> d^4 = 1>>;;
 - : fol formula = <<true>>
```

A refinement of this idea of elimination using equations, developed and successfully applied by Weispfenning (1997), is to perform 'virtual term substitution' to replace other instances of x constrained by a polynomial $p(x) = 0$ by expressions for the roots of that polynomial. In the purely linear case, where the language does not include multiplication except by constants, things are better still: we can slightly elaborate the DLO procedure from Section 5.6 to rearrange equations or inequalities using arithmetic normalization. We just put the variable to be eliminated alone on one side of each equation or inequality (e.g. transforming $0 < 3x + 2y - 6z$ into $-2/3y + 2z < x$ when eliminating x) then proceed with the same elimination step:

$$\left(\exists x. \left(\bigwedge_i s_i < x\right) \wedge \left(\bigwedge_j x < t_j\right)\right) \Leftrightarrow \bigwedge_{i,j} s_i < t_j.$$

This gives essentially the classic 'Fourier–Motzkin' elimination method, first described by Fourier (1826) but then largely forgotten until being rediscovered much later by Dines (1919) and Motzkin (1936); Ferrante and Rackoff (1975) give a refinement inspired by Cooper's algorithm avoiding the need for DNF conversion. Note that each such variable elimination can roughly square the number of inequalities, leading to exponential complexity even for a prenex existential formula with a conjunctive body, and this cost is known to be unavoidable in general for full quantifier elimination (Fischer and Rabin 1974). But the special case of deciding a closed existentially quantified conjunction of linear constraints is essentially linear programming. For this, the classic simplex method (Dantzig 1963) often works well in practice, and more recent interior-point algorithms following Karmarkar (1984) even have provable polynomial-time bounds.[†]

5.10 Rings, ideals and word problems

The algorithm for complex quantifier elimination in Section 5.8 is often inefficient because eliminating one quantifier tends to make the formula substantially larger and blow up the degrees of the other variables. If we restrict ourselves to a more limited goal of testing validity over $\mathbb{C}$ of *purely universal* formulas:

$$\forall x_1 \ldots x_n. \, P[x_1, \ldots, x_n]$$

we can use a quite different approach that deals with all the variables at once. We first generalize such problems from $\mathbb{C}$ to broader classes of interpretations.

Word problems

Suppose K is a class of algebraic structures, e.g. all groups. The *word problem* for K asks whether a set E of ground equations in some agreed language implies another such equation $s = t$ in all structures of class K. More precisely, we may wish to distinguish:

- the uniform word problem for K: deciding given any E and $s = t$ whether $E \models_M s = t$ for all models M in K;
- the word problem for K, E: with E fixed, deciding given any $s = t$ whether $E \models_M s = t$ for all models M in K;
- the free word problem for K: deciding given any $s = t$ whether $\models_M s = t$ for all models M in K.

We've already developed an algorithm to solve the *free* word problem for groups: rewrite both sides of the equation $s = t$ with the canonical term rewriting system for groups produced by Knuth–Bendix completion (Section 4.7) and see if the results are the same. Yet it turns out that there are finite E such that the word problem for groups and E is undecidable (Novikov 1955; Boone 1959). Somewhat more obscurely, there are classes K for which

---

[†] The linear programming problem was famously proved to be solvable in polynomial time by Khachian (1979), using a reduction to approximate convex optimization, solvable in polynomial time using the ellipsoid algorithm. However, the implicit algorithm was seldom competitive with simplex in practice. See Grotschel, Lovsz and Schrijver (1993) for a detailed discussion of the ellipsoid algorithm and its remarkable generality.

there is no uniform decision algorithm with E and $s = t$ as inputs, even though for any specific finite E there is a decision algorithm taking $s = t$ as input (Mekler, Nelson and Shelah 1993).

Assuming that the class K can be axiomatized by Σ, the word problem asks whether $\Sigma \cup E \models s = t$. If we further assume that E is finite, and replace constants not appearing in the axioms by variables, we can express the word problem as deciding whether the following holds, where all terms involve only constants and function symbols that occur in the axioms Σ:

$$\Sigma \models \forall x_1 \ldots x_n. \bigwedge_i s_i = t_i \Rightarrow s = t.$$

Rings

Rings are algebraic structures that have both an addition and a multiplication operation, with respective identities 0 and 1, satisfying the following axioms:

$$
\begin{aligned}
x + y &= y + x, \\
x + (y + z) &= (x + y) + z, \\
x + 0 &= x, \\
x + (-x) &= 0, \\
x \cdot y &= y \cdot x, \\
x \cdot (y \cdot z) &= (x \cdot y) \cdot z, \\
x \cdot 1 &= x, \\
x \cdot (y + z) &= x \cdot y + x \cdot z.
\end{aligned}
$$

We will consider deductions in first-order logic without equality. For this reason, we denote by Ring the above axioms together with the following equivalence and congruence properties:

$$
\begin{aligned}
&x = x, \\
&x = y \Rightarrow y = x, \\
&x = y \wedge y = z \Rightarrow x = z, \\
&x = x' \Rightarrow -x = -x', \\
&x = x' \wedge y = y' \Rightarrow x + y = x' + y', \\
&x = x' \wedge y = y' \Rightarrow x \cdot y = x' \cdot y'.
\end{aligned}
$$

so that p holds in all rings exactly if Ring $\models p$. Many familiar structures are rings, e.g. the integers, rationals, real numbers and complex numbers with the symbols interpreted in the obvious way. Also, for any $n > 0$ we can define a finite ring $\mathbb{Z}/n\mathbb{Z}$ with domain $\{0, \ldots, n-1\}$ interpreting the operations modulo n, e.g. $-5 = 1$, $3 + 5 = 2$ and $3 \cdot 5 = 3$ in $\mathbb{Z}/6\mathbb{Z}$. Another interesting example can be defined on $\wp(A)$, the set of all subsets of an arbitrary set A, with $0 = \emptyset$, $1 = A$, $-S = A - S$, $S + T = (S - T) \cup (T - S)$ ('symmetric difference') and $S \cdot T = S \cap T$.

Various other equations follow just from the ring axioms, notably $0 \cdot x = x \cdot 0 = 0$:

$$0 \cdot x = x \cdot 0 = x \cdot 0 + 0 = x \cdot 0 + (x \cdot 0 + -(x \cdot 0)) =$$
$$(x \cdot 0 + x \cdot 0) + -(x \cdot 0) = x \cdot (0 + 0) + -(x \cdot 0) = x \cdot 0 + -(x \cdot 0) = 0.$$

Similarly, one can show that $(-1) \cdot x = -x$. We use the binary subtraction notation $s - t$ to abbreviate $s + -t$. Note that the ring axioms imply $s = t \Leftrightarrow s - t = 0$. (If $s = t$ then $s - t = s + -t = t + -t = 0$, while if $s - t = 0$ then $s = s + 0 = s + (t + -t) = s + (-t + t) = (s + -t) + t = (s - t) + t = 0 + t = t$.) This allows us to state many results just for equations of the form $t = 0$ without real loss of generality. Just as we use the conventional symbols 1 and 0 for arbitrary rings, we abuse notation a little and write n to mean the ring element:

$$\overbrace{1 + \cdots + 1}^{n \text{ times}}.$$

However, it is important to realize that these values may not all be distinct. The smallest positive n such that $n = 0$ is called the *character-istic* of the ring, while if there is is no such n we say that the ring has characteristic zero. For example $\mathbb{Z}/6\mathbb{Z}$ has characteristic 6, $\wp(A)$ has characteristic 2 (even if A and hence $\wp(A)$ is infinite) and $\mathbb{R}$ has characteristic 0. Note that $k = 0$ in a ring R exactly if k is divisible by the ring's characteristic $\text{char}(R)$. If $\text{char}(R) = 0$ this is immediate since only 0 is divisible by 0, while for positive characteristic we can write $k = q \cdot \text{char}(R) + r$ where $0 \leq r < \text{char}(R)$, and $q \cdot \text{char}(R) = q \cdot 0 = 0$ so $k = 0$ iff $r = 0$. When we wish to restrict ourselves to rings of some specific characteristic n for $n > 0$ we can add a suitable set of axioms C_n:

$$\neg(1 = 0),$$
$$\neg(2 = 0),$$
$$\ldots$$
$$\neg(n - 1 = 0),$$
$$n = 0.$$

or specify that it has characteristic 0 by the infinite set of axioms $C_0 = \{\neg(n = 0) \mid n \in \mathbb{N} \wedge n \geq 1\}$. At the very least we may freely choose to add the axiom $C_1 = \{\neg(1 = 0)\}$ to indicate that the ring is non-trivial, since it makes little difference to the decision problem.

Theorem 5.14 *Ring* $\cup \Gamma \models \forall x_1, \ldots, x_n.\, \bigwedge_i s_i = t_i \Rightarrow s = t$ *iff Ring* $\cup \Gamma \cup C_1 \models \forall x_1, \ldots, x_n.\, \bigwedge_i s_i = t_i \Rightarrow s = t$.

Proof The left-to-right direction is immediate. In the other direction, note that any equation $s = t$ follows from the ring axioms and $1 = 0$. $\qquad\square$

The ring of polynomials

Given a ring R, we want to define a set $R[x_1, \ldots, x_n]$ of polynomials in n variables with coefficients in R. The appropriate definition in abstract algebra is neither of the following.

- The set of expressions generating the polynomials. This fails to identify expressions like $x + 1$ and $1 + x$ that we want to think of as the same. (One can, however, define the polynomials as an appropriate quotient structure on the set of expressions, as Theorem 5.16 below indicates.)
- The functions resulting from evaluating a polynomial. This may identify too *many* polynomials, such as $x^2 + x$ and 0 over a 2-element base ring.

Rather, we will define a polynomial formally as a mapping $p : \mathbb{N}^n \to R$ such that $\{i \in \mathbb{N}^n \mid p(i) \neq 0\}$ is finite. Intuitively we think of $(i_1, \ldots, i_n) \in \mathbb{N}^n$ as representing a monomial $x_1^{i_1} \cdots \cdot x_n^{i_n}$ and the function p as giving the coefficient of that monomial. For example, the polynomial normally written $x_1^2 x_2 + 3 x_1 x_2$ is the function that maps $(2, 1) \mapsto 1$, $(1, 1) \mapsto 3$ and all other pairs $(i, j) \mapsto 0$.

We define operations on $R[x_1, \ldots, x_n]$ in terms of those in the base ring R. Intuitively, the arithmetic operations correspond to expanding out and collecting like terms, e.g. $(x + 1) \cdot (x - 1) = x^2 - 1$. It is a little tedious but not fundamentally difficult to verify that these operations make the polynomials themselves into a ring; for a more detailed discussion of all this construction and other aspects of ring theory that we treat somewhat cursorily below, see Weispfenning and Becker (1993).

- 0 is the constant function with value 0;
- 1 is the function mapping $(0, \ldots, 0) \mapsto 1$ and all other tuples to 0;
- $-p$ is defined by $(-p)(m) = -p(m)$;

- $p + q$ is defined by $(p+q)(m) = p(m) + q(m)$;
- $(p \cdot q)$ is defined by $(p \cdot q)(m) = \sum_{\{(m_1,m_2)|m_1 \cdot m_2 = m\}} p(m_1) \cdot q(m_2)$, where monomial multiplication is defined by $(i_1, \ldots, i_n) \cdot (j_1, \ldots, j_n) = (i_1 + j_1, \ldots, i_n + j_n)$.

We will implement the ring $\mathbb{Q}[x_1, \ldots, x_n]$ of polynomials with rational coefficients in OCaml, where for convenience we adopt a list-based representation of the graph of the function p, containing exactly the pairs $(c, [i_1; \ldots; i_n])$ such that $p(i_1, \ldots, i_n) = c$ with $c \neq 0$. (The zero polynomial is represented by the empty list.) From now on we will sometimes use the word 'monomial' in a more general sense for a pair (c, m) including a constant multiplier.[†] We can multiply monomials in accordance with the definition as follows:

```
let mmul (c1,m1) (c2,m2) = (c1*/c2,map2 (+) m1 m2);;
```

Indeed, we can divide one monomial by another in some circumstances:

```
let mdiv =
  let index_sub n1 n2 = if n1 < n2 then failwith "mdiv" else n1-n2 in
  fun (c1,m1) (c2,m2) -> (c1//c2,map2 index_sub m1 m2);;
```

and even find a 'least common multiple' of two monomials:

```
let mlcm (c1,m1) (c2,m2) = (Int 1,map2 max m1 m2);;
```

To avoid multiple list representations of the same function $p : \mathbb{N}^n \to \mathbb{Q}$, we ensure that the monomials are sorted according to a fixed total order $\ll$, with the largest elements under this ordering appearing first in the list. We adopt the following order, which compares monomials first according to their *multidegree* (the sum of the degrees of all the variables), breaking ties by ordering them reverse lexicographically.

```
let morder_lt m1 m2 =
  let n1 = itlist (+) m1 0 and n2 = itlist (+) m2 0 in
  n1 < n2 or n1 = n2 & lexord(>) m1 m2;;
```

For example, $x_2^2 \ll x_1^2 x_2$ because the multidegrees are 2 and 3, while $x_1^2 x_2 \ll x_2^3$ because powers of x_1 are considered first in the lexicographic ordering. The attractions of this ordering are considered below; here we just note that it is *compatible* with monomial multiplication: if $m_1 \ll m_2$ then also $m \cdot m_1 \ll m \cdot m_2$. This means that we can multiply a polynomial by

---

[†] Sometimes 'term' is used, but in our context that might be more confusing.

a monomial without reordering the list, which is both simpler and more efficient:

```
let mpoly_mmul cm pol = map (mmul cm) pol;;
```

Similarly, a polynomial can be negated by a mapping operation:

```
let mpoly_neg = map (fun (c,m) -> (minus_num c,m));;
```

Note that the formal definition of the ring of polynomials renders 'variables' anonymous, but if we have some particular list of variables $x_1, \ldots, x_n$ in mind, we can regard x_i as a shorthand for $(0, \ldots, 0, 1, 0, \ldots, 0)$ where only the ith entry is nonzero:

```
let mpoly_var vars x =
  [Int 1,map (fun y -> if y = x then 1 else 0) vars];;
```

To create a constant polynomial, we use **vars** too, but only to determine how many variables we're dealing with. If the constant is zero, we give the empty list, otherwise a list mapping the constant monomial to an appropriate value:

```
let mpoly_const vars c =
  if c =/ Int 0 then [] else [c,map (fun k -> 0) vars];;
```

To add two polynomials, we can run along them recursively, putting the 'larger' of the two head monomials first in the output list, or when two head monomials have the same degree, merging them by adding coefficients and if the resulting coefficient is zero, removing it.

```
let rec mpoly_add l1 l2 =
  match (l1,l2) with
    ([],l2) -> l2
  | (l1,[]) -> l1
  | ((c1,m1)::o1,(c2,m2)::o2) ->
        if m1 = m2 then
           let c = c1+/c2 and rest = mpoly_add o1 o2 in
           if c =/ Int 0 then rest else (c,m1)::rest
        else if morder_lt m2 m1 then (c1,m1)::(mpoly_add o1 l2)
        else (c2,m2)::(mpoly_add l1 o2);;
```

Addition and negation together give subtraction:

```
let mpoly_sub l1 l2 = mpoly_add l1 (mpoly_neg l2);;
```

For multiplication, we just multiply the second polynomial by the various monomials in the first one, adding the results together:

```
let rec mpoly_mul l1 l2 =
  match l1 with
    [] -> []
  | (h1::t1) -> mpoly_add (mpoly_mmul h1 l2) (mpoly_mul t1 l2);;
```

and we can get powers by iterated multiplication:

```
let mpoly_pow vars l n =
  funpow n (mpoly_mul l) (mpoly_const vars (Int 1));;
```

We can also permit inversion of constant polynomials:

```
let mpoly_inv p =
  match p with
    [(c,m)] when forall (fun i -> i = 0) m -> [(Int 1 // c),m]
  | _ -> failwith "mpoly_inv: non-constant polynomial";;
```

and hence also perform division subject to the same constraint:

```
let mpoly_div p q = mpoly_mul p (mpoly_inv q);;
```

We can convert any suitable term in the language of rings into a polynomial by the usual process of recursion:

```
let rec mpolynate vars tm =
  match tm with
    Var x -> mpoly_var vars x
  | Fn("-",[t]) -> mpoly_neg (mpolynate vars t)
  | Fn("+",[s;t]) -> mpoly_add (mpolynate vars s) (mpolynate vars t)
  | Fn("-",[s;t]) -> mpoly_sub (mpolynate vars s) (mpolynate vars t)
  | Fn("*",[s;t]) -> mpoly_mul (mpolynate vars s) (mpolynate vars t)
  | Fn("/",[s;t]) -> mpoly_div (mpolynate vars s) (mpolynate vars t)
  | Fn("^",[t;Fn(n,[])]) ->
            mpoly_pow vars (mpolynate vars t) (int_of_string n)
  | _ -> mpoly_const vars (dest_numeral tm);;
```

Then we can convert any suitable equational formula $s = t$, which we think of as $s - t = 0$, into a corresponding polynomial:

```
let mpolyatom vars fm =
  match fm with
    Atom(R("=",[s;t])) -> mpolynate vars (Fn("-",[s;t]))
  | _ -> failwith "mpolyatom: not an equation";;
```

In later discussions, we will write 'norm' to abbreviate `mpolynate vars` where `vars` contains all the variables in any of the polynomials under consideration. We also write $s \approx t$ to mean $\mathrm{norm}(s) = \mathrm{norm}(t)$, i.e. that the terms s and t in the language of rings define the same polynomial.

The word problem for rings

To state the next result, it's helpful to introduce the concept of an *ideal* in a polynomial ring.[†] If $p_1, \ldots, p_n$ are polynomials in $R[x_1, \ldots, x_k]$ (we often abbreviate such a finite sequence of variables x_i as $\overline{x}$) we write $\mathrm{Id}_R \langle p_1, \ldots, p_n \rangle$ (read 'the ideal generated by $p_1, \ldots, p_n$') for the set of polynomials that can be expressed as follows:

$$p_1 \cdot q_1 + \cdots + p_n \cdot q_n,$$

where q_i (sometimes referred to as *cofactors*) are arbitrary polynomials with coefficients in R, allowing the empty sum 0. With slight abuse of language, we will also use the ideal expression $p \in \mathrm{Id}_R \langle p_1, \ldots, p_n \rangle$ for terms in the language of rings, when we should more properly write $\mathrm{norm}(p) \in \mathrm{Id}_R \langle \mathrm{norm}(p_1), \ldots, \mathrm{norm}(p_n) \rangle$. Let us note the following closure properties.

(i) $0 \in \mathrm{Id}_R \langle p_1, \ldots, p_n \rangle$, because we can take each $q_i = 0$.

(ii) Each $p_i \in \mathrm{Id}_R \langle p_1, \ldots, p_n \rangle$, because we can take $q_i = 1$ and all other $q_j = 0$.

(iii) If $p \in \mathrm{Id}_R \langle p_1, \ldots, p_n \rangle$ and $q \in \mathrm{Id}_R \langle p_1, \ldots, p_n \rangle$ then also $(p + q) \in \mathrm{Id}_R \langle p_1, \ldots, p_n \rangle$, because if $\sum_i p_i \cdot q_i = p$ and $\sum_i p_i \cdot q_i' = q$ we have $\sum_i p_i \cdot (q_i + q_i') = p + q$.

(iv) If $p \in \mathrm{Id}_R \langle p_1, \ldots, p_n \rangle$ and q is any other polynomial with coefficients in R, then $(pq) \in \mathrm{Id}_R \langle p_1, \ldots, p_n \rangle$, because if $\sum_i p_i \cdot q_i = p$ then $\sum_i p_i \cdot (q \cdot q_i) = p \cdot q$.

(v) If $p \in \mathrm{Id}_R \langle p_1, \ldots, p_n \rangle$ then $(-p) \in \mathrm{Id}_R \langle p_1, \ldots, p_n \rangle$. This follows from (iv) since $-p = p \cdot (-1)$.

(vi) If $p \in \mathrm{Id}_R \langle p_1, \ldots, p_n \rangle$ and $q \in \mathrm{Id}_R \langle p_1, \ldots, p_n \rangle$ then also $(p - q) \in \mathrm{Id}_R \langle p_1, \ldots, p_n \rangle$. This follows from (iii) and (v) since since $p - q = p + (-q)$.

Using the Horn nature of the ring axioms, we can find a reduction to ideal membership of the uniform word problem for rings (Scarpellini 1969; Simmons 1970).[‡]

[†] Ideals were originally introduced by Kummer as a way of restoring unique factorization in algebraic number fields. Note that for a principal ideal, i.e. one generated by a single element, we have $x \in \mathrm{Id} \langle y \rangle$ precisely if x is divisible by y. Ideals can be considered as a way of augmenting the 'real' divisors with additional 'ideal' ones, hence the name.

[‡] The proof works slightly more directly using the Birkhoff rules from Section 4.3, in which case we don't need to consider the equality axioms as separate hypotheses. However, we emphasize a

Theorem 5.15 *Ring* $\models \forall \overline{x}. \, p_1(\overline{x}) = 0 \wedge \cdots \wedge p_n(\overline{x}) = 0 \Rightarrow q(\overline{x}) = 0$ *iff* $q \in \mathrm{Id}_{\mathbb{Z}} \langle p_1, \ldots, p_n \rangle$, *i.e. there exist terms* $q_1, \ldots, q_n$ *in the language of rings with* $p_1 \cdot q_1 + \cdots + p_n \cdot q_n \approx q$.

Proof We will replace Ring $\models \forall \overline{x}. \, p_1(\overline{x}) = 0 \wedge \cdots \wedge p_n(\overline{x}) = 0 \Rightarrow q(\overline{x}) = 0$ by the logically equivalent Ring $\cup \{p_1 = 0, \ldots, p_n = 0\} \models q = 0$, considering the $\overline{x}$ as Skolem constants.

The right-to-left direction is the easier one: if there are q_i with Ring $\models p_1 \cdot q_1 + \cdots + p_n \cdot q_n = q$, then using hypotheses $p_i = 0$ and ring properties $0 \cdot q_i$ and $0 + 0 = 0$ repeatedly, we can derive $q = 0$.

For the other direction, note that all the formulas Ring and $p_i = 0$ are Horn clauses. By the results of Section 3.14, this means that if Ring $\cup \{p_1 = 0, \ldots, p_n = 0\} \models q = 0$ there is a Prolog-style deduction of $q = 0$ from the hypotheses Ring $\cup \{p_1 = 0, \ldots, p_n = 0\}$. We will show by induction on this proof that for each equation $s = t$ in the proof tree, we have $(s - t) \in \mathrm{Id}_{\mathbb{Z}} \langle p_1, \ldots, p_n \rangle$.

Each leaf $s = t$ is either a ring axiom or reflexivity of equality, in which case $s - t \approx 0 \in \mathrm{Id}_{\mathbb{Z}} \langle p_1, \ldots, p_n \rangle$, or one of the p_i, and we know $p_i \in \mathrm{Id}_{\mathbb{Z}} \langle p_1, \ldots, p_n \rangle$. For the inner nodes, we need to verify that the property is preserved when using equality and congruence rules, and all those follow immediately from the closure properties of ideals noted above. For example, if an internal node $s = u$ uses transitivity of equality from subnodes $s = t$ and $t = u$, we know by the inductive hypothesis that $(s-t) \in \mathrm{Id}_{\mathbb{Z}} \langle p_1, \ldots, p_n \rangle$ and $(t - u) \in \mathrm{Id}_{\mathbb{Z}} \langle p_1, \ldots, p_n \rangle$. By closure of ideals under addition we have $(s - u) = ((s - t) + (t - u)) \in \mathrm{Id}_{\mathbb{Z}} \langle p_1, \ldots, p_n \rangle$. $\square$

In the special case of the free word problem we have:

Theorem 5.16 *Ring* $\models s = t$ *iff* $s \approx t$, *i.e.* s *and* t *define the same polynomial.*

Proof Apply the previous theorem in the degenerate case $n = 0$ to $p = s - t$. $\square$

In a more general direction, the Horn nature of the ring axioms allows us to relate the validity of an arbitrary universal formula in the language of rings to the special case of the word problem. We can put the body of the formula into CNF, distributing the universal quantifiers over the

general first-order deduction and the Horn nature of the ring axioms here to clarify the contrast with the word problem for integral domains considered below.

conjuncts and splitting the problem up, then write each resulting clause
in the form

$$\forall x_1, \ldots, x_n. \bigwedge_i p_i(\overline{x}) = 0 \Rightarrow \bigvee_j q_j(\overline{x}) = 0.$$

If there are no $q_j(\overline{x})$ then the formula is equivalent to $\bot$, since all the
ring axioms and $p_i(\overline{x}) = 0$ are definite clauses and therefore cannot be
unsatisfiable. If there is exactly one $q_j(\overline{x})$ then we have the word problem.
If there are several $q_j(\overline{x})$, we can use the fact that theories defined by Horn
clauses are convex (Theorem 3.39) and therefore the above is equivalent to
the disjunction of word problems

$$\bigvee_j (\forall x_1, \ldots, x_n. \bigwedge_i p_i(\overline{x}) = 0 \Rightarrow q_j(\overline{x}) = 0).$$

Thus, we can solve the entire universal theory of rings if we can solve the
word problem, and we can solve that if we can solve ideal membership.

The word problem for torsion-free rings

We say that a ring is *torsion-free* if it satisfies the infinite set of axioms:

$$T = \{\forall x. \, nx = 0 \Rightarrow x = 0 \mid n \geq 1\}.$$

We can arrive at a satisfying ideal membership equivalence for the word
problem in torsion-free rings (Simmons 1970).

Theorem 5.17 $Ring \cup T \models \forall \overline{x}. \, p_1(\overline{x}) = 0 \wedge \cdots \wedge p_n(\overline{x}) = 0 \Rightarrow q(\overline{x}) = 0$ *iff*
$q \in \mathrm{Id}_{\mathbb{Q}} \langle p_1, \ldots, p_n \rangle$.

Proof A minor adaptation of the proof of Theorem 5.15. Note that $q \in$
$\mathrm{Id}_{\mathbb{Q}} \langle p_1, \ldots, p_n \rangle$ iff there is a nonzero integer c such that $cq \in \mathrm{Id}_{\mathbb{Z}} \langle p_1, \ldots, p_n \rangle$.
Now, the right-to-left direction follows as before, also using the non-torsion
axiom $cq = 0 \Rightarrow q = 0$. In the other direction, note that the axioms T are
still Horn, and in the same way we can prove the result by induction on a
Prolog-style proof. $\qquad\square$

Note that a non-trivial torsion-free ring must have characteristic zero
because $n = 0$ for $n \geq 2$ implies $n \cdot 1 = 0$ and so $1 = 0$. The converse
is not true in general, though it is true in integral domains, considered next.

The word problem for integral domains

A ring is called an *integral domain* if it is non-trivial $(1 \neq 0)$ and satisfies the following axiom I:

$$x \cdot y = 0 \Rightarrow x = 0 \vee y = 0.$$

If R is an integral domain, then either $\text{char}(R) = 0$ or $\text{char}(R) = p$ for some prime number p, because if $p = m \cdot n = 0$ the axiom I implies that either $m = 0$ or $n = 0$.

We will show that $\text{Ring} \cup \{I\} \models \forall \overline{x}.\, p_1(\overline{x}) = 0 \wedge \cdots \wedge p_n(\overline{x}) = 0 \Rightarrow q(\overline{x}) = 0$ iff there is some nonnegative integer k such that $q^k \in \text{Id}_{\mathbb{Z}} \langle p_1, \ldots, p_n \rangle$; it is only in the power k that the result differs from the one for general rings. In fact we consider the more general assertion, where we keep variables $\overline{x}$ for familiarity but assume they are really Skolem constants:

$$\text{Ring} \cup \{I\} \cup \{p_1(\overline{x}) = 0, \ldots, p_n(\overline{x}) = 0\} \cup \{q_1(\overline{x}) \neq 0, \ldots, q_m(\overline{x}) \neq 0\} \models \bot.$$

As with rings, we will consider a proof of such a statement, and show by recursion on proofs that it implies a corresponding ideal membership property. But this time we have a non-Horn axiom I, so we need a more general proof format than Prolog-style trees; roughly following Lifschitz (1980), we use binary resolution. This is refutation complete, so if the assertion above holds there is a proof of it by resolution. We may assume that all hypotheses are instantiated and consider a refutation of the instantiations by propositional resolution. Each clause in the refutation is a set of negated and unnegated literals that is implicitly a disjunction of the form:

$$\bigvee_{i=1}^{r} (e_i \neq e_i') \vee \bigvee_{j=1}^{s} f_j = f_j'.$$

For simplicity, we implicitly regard an equation $s = t$ as $s - t = 0$ when we consider ideal membership assertions, so we often just consider the special case

$$\bigvee_{i=1}^{r} (e_i \neq 0) \vee \bigvee_{j=1}^{s} f_j = 0.$$

We will show by induction on the proof that for all such clauses in such a refutation, there is a nonnegative integer k such that

$$\left(\left(\prod_{i=1}^{m} q_i \right) \left(\prod_{j=1}^{s} f_j \right) \right)^k \in \text{Id}_{\mathbb{Z}} \langle e_1, \ldots, e_r, p_1, \ldots, p_n \rangle.$$

For the purely equational ring axioms $l = r$, including reflexivity of equality, we always have $l - r \approx 0$ so trivially $(l - r) \in \mathrm{Id}_{\mathbb{Z}} \langle p_1, \ldots, p_n \rangle$. Equally trivially, for each unit clause $p_i = 0$ we have $p_i \in \mathrm{Id}_{\mathbb{Z}} \langle p_1, \ldots, p_n \rangle$. In both cases it was sufficient to take $k = 1$. The same is true of the equivalence and congruence properties of equality, as we can check systematically.

- For $x = y \Rightarrow y = x$ we need to show $(y - x) \in \mathrm{Id}_{\mathbb{Z}} \langle x - y, p_1, \ldots, p_n \rangle$, which is true since $(y - x) \approx -1 \cdot (x - y)$.
- For $x = y \wedge y = z \Rightarrow x = z$ we need $(x - z) \in \mathrm{Id}_{\mathbb{Z}} \langle x - y, y - z, p_1, \ldots, p_n \rangle$, which is true since $(x - z) \approx 1 \cdot (x - y) + 1 \cdot (y - z)$.
- For $x = x' \Rightarrow -x = -x'$ we need $(-x - -x') \in \mathrm{Id}_{\mathbb{Z}} \langle x - x', p_1, \ldots, p_n \rangle$, which is true since $(-x - -x') \approx -1 \cdot (x - x')$.
- For $x = x' \wedge y = y' \Rightarrow x + y = x' + y'$ we need to show $((x + y) - (x' + y')) \in \mathrm{Id}_{\mathbb{Z}} \langle x - x', y - y', p_1, \ldots, p_n \rangle$, which is true since $((x + y) - (x' + y')) \approx 1 \cdot (x - x') + 1 \cdot (y - y')$.
- For $x = x' \wedge y = y' \Rightarrow x \cdot y = x' \cdot y'$ we need to show $(x \cdot y - x' \cdot y') \in \mathrm{Id}_{\mathbb{Z}} \langle x - x', y - y', p_1, \ldots, p_n \rangle$, which is true since $x \cdot y - x' \cdot y' \approx y \cdot (x - x') + x' \cdot (y - y')$.

For a unit clause $q_i \neq 0$, we have trivially $q_i \in \mathrm{Id}_{\mathbb{Z}} \langle q_i, p_1, \ldots, p_n \rangle$, so by closure of ideals under multiplication we have $\prod_{i=1}^{m} q_i \in \mathrm{Id}_{\mathbb{Z}} \langle q_i, p_1, \ldots, p_n \rangle$, where again we can take $k = 1$. The axiom I, which when put in clause form is $xy \neq 0 \vee x = 0 \vee y = 0$ is slightly subtler. In the simple case we have $xy \in \mathrm{Id}_{\mathbb{Z}} \langle xy, p_1, \ldots, p_n \rangle$ and therefore we can take $k = 1$:

$$\left(\prod_{i=1}^{m} q_i \right) xy \in \mathrm{Id}_{\mathbb{Z}} \langle xy, p_1, \ldots, p_n \rangle,$$

but we need to distinguish the special case where x and y receive the same instantiation: since we think of clauses as sets, this is technically a 2-element clause $x^2 \neq 0 \vee x = 0$ and we need $k = 2$:

$$\left(\left(\prod_{i=1}^{m} q_i \right) x \right)^2 \in \mathrm{Id}_{\mathbb{Z}} \langle x^2, p_1, \ldots, p_n \rangle.$$

Now we just need to show that the claimed property is preserved by resolution steps. We decompose each resolution step into a pseudo-resolution step, producing a 'clause' with possible duplicates, followed by a series of factoring steps. Let's look at the factoring steps first. If we factor two instances of a negated equation

$$\frac{e \neq 0 \vee e \neq 0 \vee \Gamma}{e \neq 0 \vee \Gamma},$$

the result follows because $\mathrm{Id}_{\mathbb{Z}}\langle e, e, \ldots \rangle$ is the same as $\mathrm{Id}_{\mathbb{Z}}\langle e, \ldots \rangle$. If we factor two instances of a positive equation

$$\frac{f = 0 \vee f = 0 \vee \Gamma}{f = 0 \vee \Gamma},$$

then we have by hypothesis an ideal membership of the form:

$$(p \cdot f \cdot f)^k \in I$$

which implies (because ideals are closed under multiplication by other terms):

$$(p \cdot f)^{2k} \in I$$

as required. The most complicated case is a pseudo-resolution step on $e = 0$:

$$\frac{e \neq 0 \vee \bigvee_{i=1}^{r} e_i \neq 0 \vee \bigvee_{j=1}^{s} f_j = 0 \quad e = 0 \vee \bigvee_{i=1}^{t} g_i \neq 0 \vee \bigvee_{j=1}^{u} h_j = 0}{\bigvee_{i=1}^{r} e_i \neq 0 \vee \bigvee_{i=1}^{t} g_i \neq 0 \vee \bigvee_{j=1}^{s} f_j = 0 \vee \bigvee_{j=1}^{u} h_j = 0}.$$

By the inductive hypothesis applied to the two input clauses we have ideal memberships

$$
\begin{aligned}
(QF)^k &\in \mathrm{Id}_{\mathbb{Z}}\langle e, e_1, \ldots, e_r, p_1, \ldots, p_n \rangle, \\
(QeH)^l &\in \mathrm{Id}_{\mathbb{Z}}\langle g_1, \ldots, g_t, p_1, \ldots, p_n \rangle,
\end{aligned}
$$

where we write $Q = \prod_{i=1}^{m} q_i$, $F = \prod_{j=1}^{s} f_j$ and $H = \prod_{j=1}^{u} h_j$. We can separate the cofactor r of e in the first ideal membership:

$$(QF)^k - re \in \mathrm{Id}_{\mathbb{Z}}\langle e_1, \ldots, e_r; p_1, \ldots, p_n \rangle$$

and therefore (since $x^l - y^l$ is always divisible by $x - y$):

$$(QF)^{kl} - r^l e^l \in \mathrm{Id}_{\mathbb{Z}}\langle e_1, \ldots, e_r, p_1, \ldots, p_n \rangle.$$

Using closure under multiplication again, we have

$$(QF)^{kl}(QH)^l - r^l(QeH)^l \in \mathrm{Id}_{\mathbb{Z}}\langle e_1, \ldots, e_r, p_1, \ldots, p_n \rangle$$

and therefore using the second ideal membership assertion

$$(QF)^{kl}(QH)^l \in \mathrm{Id}_{\mathbb{Z}}\langle e_1, \ldots, e_r, g_1, \ldots, g_t, p_1, \ldots, p_n \rangle$$

and using closure under multiplication we can reach a common exponent as required:

$$(QFH)^{kl+l} \in \mathrm{Id}_{\mathbb{Z}}\langle e_1, \ldots, e_r, g_1, \ldots, g_t, p_1, \ldots, p_n \rangle.$$

We are finally ready to conclude:

Theorem 5.18

$$Ring \cup \{I\} \models \forall \overline{x}.\, p_1(\overline{x}) = 0 \wedge \cdots \wedge p_n(\overline{x}) = 0 \Rightarrow q_1(\overline{x}) = 0 \vee \cdots \vee q_m(\overline{x}) = 0$$

if and only if there is a nonnegative integer k *such that*

$$\left(\prod_{i=1}^{m} q_i \right)^k \in \mathrm{Id}_{\mathbb{Z}} \langle p_1, \ldots, p_n \rangle \, .$$

Proof If the logical assertion holds, then since resolution is refutation complete, there is a derivation of $\bot$ from the axioms

$$Ring \cup \{I\} \cup \{p_1(\overline{x}) = 0, \ldots, p_n(\overline{x}) = 0\} \cup \{q_1(\overline{x}) \neq 0, \ldots, q_m(\overline{x}) \neq 0\}.$$

Applying the property deduced above to the empty clause yields the result. Conversely, if the ideal membership holds, then whenever all the $p_i(\overline{x}) = 0$ we have $\left(\prod_{i=1}^m q_i \right)^k = 0$. If k is nonzero, it follows from axiom I that $\prod_{i=1}^m q_i = 0$ and then that some $q_i(\overline{x}) = 0$, contradicting one of the hypotheses. If all k_i are zero we have deduced $1 = 0$ and therefore any $q_i(\overline{x}) = 0$ at once. □

Several results on word problems are corollaries, most straightforwardly:

Theorem 5.19 $\forall \overline{x}.\, p_1(\overline{x}) = 0 \wedge \cdots \wedge p_n(\overline{x}) = 0 \Rightarrow q(\overline{x}) = 0$ *holds in all integral domains, i.e.* $Ring \cup \{I\} \cup C_1 \models \forall \overline{x}.\, p_1(\overline{x}) = 0 \wedge \cdots \wedge p_n(\overline{x}) = 0 \Rightarrow q(\overline{x}) = 0$, *iff there is a nonnegative integer* k *such that* $q^k \in \mathrm{Id}_{\mathbb{Z}} \langle p_1, \ldots, p_n \rangle$.

Proof Combine Theorem 5.14 and the $m = 1$ case of the previous theorem. □

More specifically, we might ask about the word problem for integral domains of a particular characteristic p.

Theorem 5.20 $\forall \overline{x}.\, p_1(\overline{x}) = 0 \wedge \cdots \wedge p_n(\overline{x}) = 0 \Rightarrow q(\overline{x}) = 0$ *holds in all integral domains of characteristic* p, *i.e.* $Ring \cup \{I\} \cup C_p \models \forall \overline{x}.\, p_1(\overline{x}) = 0 \wedge \cdots \wedge p_n(\overline{x}) = 0 \Rightarrow q(\overline{x}) = 0$, *iff there is a nonnegative integer* k *and an integer* c *not divisible by* p *such that such that* $cq^k \in \mathrm{Id}_{\mathbb{Z}} \langle p, p_1, \ldots, p_n \rangle$, *where* p *is the constant polynomial corresponding to the integer* p.

Proof As usual, the right-to-left direction is straightforward. Conversely, if the logical assertion holds then we have

$$Ring \cup \{I\} \cup C_1 \cup \{c_1 \neq 0, \ldots, c_m \neq 0, p = 0\}$$
$$\models \forall \overline{x}.\, p_1(\overline{x}) = 0 \wedge \cdots \wedge p_n(\overline{x}) = 0 \Rightarrow q(\overline{x}) = 0$$

for a finite set of integers $c_1, \ldots, c_m$, none divisible by p. (In the case of nonzero characteristic, $p = 0$ and the various $c_i \neq 0$ make up exactly the axiom C_p. In the case of zero characteristic, $p = 0$ is trivially derivable anyway, and by compactness only finitely many instances of $c \neq 0$ are used.) This is equivalent to:

$$\text{Ring} \cup \{I\} \cup C_1 \models p_1(\overline{x}) = 0 \wedge \cdots \wedge p_n(\overline{x}) = 0 \wedge p = 0 \Rightarrow c_1 \cdots c_m q(\overline{x}) = 0$$

By the main theorem we have $(c_1 \cdots c_m \cdot q)^k \in \text{Id}_{\mathbb{Z}} \langle p, p_1, \ldots, p_n \rangle$, and the result follows by writing $c = (c_1 \cdots c_m)^k$. The characteristic p is zero or a prime, so if it doesn't divide any c_i, and thus neither does it divide this c. $\qquad \blacksquare$

As we will see later, this is equivalent to a famous theorem in algebraic geometry, the (strong) Hilbert Nullstellensatz. We will use the term 'Nullstellensatz' to refer to all the variants above, for integral domains in general or those of specified characteristic. In the special case of characteristic zero:

Theorem 5.21 $\forall \overline{x}. \; p_1(\overline{x}) = 0 \wedge \cdots \wedge p_n(\overline{x}) = 0 \Rightarrow q(\overline{x}) = 0$ *holds in all integral domains of characteristic 0 iff there is a nonnegative integer k such that such that $q^k \in \text{Id}_{\mathbb{Q}} \langle p_1, \ldots, p_n \rangle$.*

Proof As with torsion-free rings, note that $q^k \in \text{Id}_{\mathbb{Q}} \langle p_1, \ldots, p_n \rangle$ iff there is a nonzero integer c such that $cq^k \in \text{Id}_{\mathbb{Z}} \langle p_1, \ldots, p_n \rangle$. As usual, the right-to-left direction is straightforward: if all the $p_i = 0$ are zero, so is $cq^k = 0$ and hence $q = 0$, trivially if $k = 0$ so we get an immediate contradiction. Conversely, apply the previous theorem in the case $p = 0$; we don't need to include p in the ideal since 0 is already a member of every ideal. $\qquad \blacksquare$

Fields

A *field* is a non-trivial ring where each nonzero element x has a multiplicative inverse x^{-1} such that $x^{-1} \cdot x = 1$. Logically, the axioms for fields are just those for non-trivial rings together with

$$\neg(x = 0) \Rightarrow x^{-1} x = 1,$$

where x^{-1} is syntactic sugar for the application of a new unary function symbol. Note that a field is automatically an integral domain, because if $x \cdot y = 0$ yet $x \neq 0$ then

$$y = 1 \cdot y = (x^{-1} \cdot x) \cdot y = x^{-1} \cdot (x \cdot y) = x^{-1} \cdot 0 = 0.$$

The converse is not true; $\mathbb{Q}$, $\mathbb{R}$ and $\mathbb{C}$ are fields but $\mathbb{Z}$ is not (there is no element such that $2 \cdot x = 1$). The ring $\mathbb{Z}/n\mathbb{Z}$ is a field iff it is an integral domain iff n is a prime number (Section 3.3). However, every integral domain R can be extended to a field (R's 'field of fractions'), whose elements are equivalence classes of pairs (p, q) of elements of R such that $q \neq 0$, under the equivalence relation $(p_1, q_1) \sim (p_2, q_2) \Leftrightarrow p_1 q_2 = q_1 p_2$. Intuitively, we think of a pair (p, q) as representing the 'fraction' p/q, and the equivalence classes as taking into account the multiple pairs corresponding to the same fraction (e.g. $1/2 = 2/4 = 3/6$). The operations are defined in accordance with that intuition:

$$
\begin{aligned}
0 &= (0, 1), \\
1 &= (1, 1), \\
-(p, q) &= (-p, q), \\
(p, q)^{-1} &= (q, p), \\
(p_1, q_1) + (p_2, q_2) &= (p_1 \cdot q_2 + p_2 \cdot q_1, q_1 \cdot q_2), \\
(p_1, q_1) \cdot (p_2, q_2) &= (p_1 \cdot p_2, q_1 \cdot q_2);
\end{aligned}
$$

but, independent of any intuition, one can show directly that these operations are well-defined with respect to the equivalence relation and satisfy the field axioms; this is worked out in detail in many textbooks on abstract algebra (Cohn 1974; Jacobson 1989; Lang 1994). From the embeddability of integral domains in fields, we can conclude that integral domains and fields are equivalent w.r.t. universal formulas.

Theorem 5.22 *A universal formula in the language of rings holds in all fields [of characteristic p] iff it holds in all integral domains [of characteristic p].*

Proof If a formula holds in all integral domains, then it also holds in all fields, because a field is a kind of integral domain. Conversely, if a property holds in all fields, then given an integral domain R, it holds in the field of fractions of R and hence, since it is a universal formula, in the subset corresponding to R. □

The Rabinowitsch trick

If we can solve the word problem for fields or integral domains, we can solve the whole universal theory. To decide:

$$\forall \overline{x}.\, p_1(\overline{x}) = 0 \wedge \cdots \wedge p_n(\overline{x}) = 0 \Rightarrow q_1(\overline{x}) = 0 \vee \cdots q_m(\overline{x}) = 0$$

we can't rely on convexity as we did for rings (the axiom I is non-Horn). But the integral domain axiom justifies our condensing the disjunction of equations into one:

$$\forall \overline{x}.\, p_1(\overline{x}) = 0 \wedge \cdots \wedge p_n(\overline{x}) = 0 \Rightarrow q_1(\overline{x}) \cdots\cdots q_m(\overline{x}) = 0.$$

In fact, in a field we can reduce matters to a degenerate case of the word problem. Because all nonzero field elements have multiplicative inverses, and $0 \cdot y = 0$ in any ring, we have:

$$\neg(x = 0) \Leftrightarrow \exists y.\, xy = 1.$$

This means that we can replace negated equations by unnegated ones, at the cost of adding new variables. For example, we can rewrite the standard word problem

$$\forall \overline{x}.\, p_1(\overline{x}) = 0 \wedge \cdots \wedge p_n(\overline{x}) = 0 \Rightarrow q(\overline{x}) = 0$$

as

$$\forall \overline{x}\, z.\, p_1(\overline{x}) = 0 \wedge \cdots \wedge p_n(\overline{x}) = 0 \wedge 1 - q(\overline{x})z = 0 \Rightarrow \bot.$$

For the general universal case, we can condense the conclusion to one equation as noted above, or if we prefer introduce separate variables for every negated equation:

$$\forall \overline{x}\, z_1 \ldots z_m.\ p_1(\overline{x}) = 0 \wedge \cdots \wedge p_n(\overline{x}) = 0 \wedge$$
$$1 - q_1(\overline{x})z_1 = 0 \wedge \cdots \wedge 1 - q_m(\overline{x})z_m = 0$$
$$\Rightarrow \bot.$$

This method of replacing negated equations by unnegated ones is known as the *Rabinowitsch trick*. Since $\bot$ is equivalent to $1 = 0$ in any field, we can reduce such an assertion to membership of 1 in an ideal. (Note that if an ideal contains 1 then it is in fact a 'trivial' ideal consisting of the entire ring of polynomials, since ideals are closed under multiplication.) A Nullstellensatz in this special case of triviality is referred to as a *weak* Nullstellensatz. For example:

Theorem 5.23 $\forall \overline{x}.\, p_1(\overline{x}) = 0 \wedge \cdots \wedge p_n(\overline{x}) = 0 \Rightarrow \bot$ *holds in all integral domains / fields, i.e.* $\mathrm{Ring} \cup \{I\} \cup C_1 \models \forall \overline{x}.\, p_1(\overline{x}) = 0 \wedge \cdots \wedge p_n(\overline{x}) = 0 \Rightarrow \bot$, *iff* $1 \in \mathrm{Id}_{\mathbb{Z}} \langle p_1, \ldots, p_n \rangle$.

Proof Apply the strong Nullstellensatz with $q(\overline{x}) = 1$, noting that $q^k = 1$.
□

Similarly:

Theorem 5.24 $\forall \overline{x}.\, p_1(\overline{x}) = 0 \wedge \cdots \wedge p_n(\overline{x}) = 0 \Rightarrow \bot$ *holds in all integral domains / fields of characteristic* 0 *iff* $1 \in \mathrm{Id}_{\mathbb{Q}} \langle p_1, \ldots, p_n \rangle$.

Proof Apply the strong Nullstellensatz with $q(\overline{x}) = 1$, noting that $q^k = 1$.
□

Using the Rabinowitsch trick plus a weak Nullstellensatz (Kapur 1988) is more attractive for automated theorem proving than a strong Nullstellensatz because we don't have to search through all possible powers of the conclusion polynomial. However, the trick was first used as a theoretical device to show that one can deduce a strong Nullstellensatz from the corresponding weak one. Indeed, given explicit cofactors for an ideal membership $1 \in \mathrm{Id}_{\mathbb{Z}} \langle p_1, \ldots, p_n, 1 - qz \rangle$ one can explicitly construct an l such that $q^l \in \mathrm{Id}_{\mathbb{Z}} \langle p_1, \ldots, p_n \rangle$ (see Exercise 5.23). This also shows that one can treat the Rabinowitsch trick as a purely formal transformation without reference to inverses. (Since we have noted that fields and integral domains are equivalent w.r.t. universal formulas in the language of rings, this observation is perhaps supererogatory.)

Algebraically closed fields

The existence of multiplicative inverses in fields implies that a linear equation $a \cdot x + b = 0$ in a field has a solution unless $a = 0$ and $b \neq 0$; if $a \neq 0$ the solution is simply $x = -b \cdot a^{-1}$. However, polynomial equations of higher degree such as quadratics may not have a solution; for instance $x^2 + 1 = 0$ has no solution in the field of real numbers. Recall that a field is said to be *algebraically closed* when every polynomial other than a nonzero constant has a root.

A fundamental result in algebra states that any field can be extended to an algebraically closed field. (As it is an extension, it necessarily has the same characteristic.) The proof is not too hard but uses a certain amount of algebraic machinery (Lang 1994); for a sketch of an alternative proof using results of logic see Exercise 5.25. So just as we related universal formulas for integral domains and fields, we can conclude:

a universal formula in the language of rings holds in all algebraically closed fields [of characteristic p] iff it holds in all fields [of characteristic p].

The Fundamental Theorem of Algebra, which we exploited to justify quantifier elimination in Section 5.8, states exactly that the field of complex numbers is algebraically closed. In fact, re-examining how the quantifier elimination procedure was justified, the reader can observe that we use no properties beyond the fact that $\mathbb{C}$ is an algebraically closed field of characteristic zero (see Exercise 5.18). Thus we conclude that any sentence has the same truth-value in all algebraically closed fields of characteristic zero. This means that the theory of algebraically closed fields of characteristic zero is complete, and in particular that:

a closed formula holds in $\mathbb{C}$ iff it holds in all algebraically closed fields of characteristic zero.

Combining all our results we see that all the following are equivalent for a *universal* formula in the language of rings.

- it holds in all integral domains of characteristic 0,
- it holds in all fields of characteristic 0,
- it holds in all algebraically closed fields of characteristic 0,
- it holds in any given algebraically closed field of characteristic 0,
- it holds in $\mathbb{C}$.

(The Nullstellensatz, for example, is most commonly stated for a fixed but arbitrary algebraically closed field.) Thus, despite the lengthy detour into general algebraic structures, we have arrived back at the complex numbers. Modifying the quantifier elimination procedure from Section 5.8 to take into account the characteristic (see Exercise 5.18), we can likewise see that it works identically for *any* algebraically closed field of characteristic p. Thus, the theory of algebraically closed fields of a particular characteristic p is also complete.

Abelian monoids and groups

We started with the word problem for general rings, then considered rings with additional axioms and/or operations (integral domains, fields, algebraically closed fields). We can proceed towards structures with fewer axioms as well. A *monoid* is an algebraic structure with a distinguished element 1 and a binary operator · satisfying the axioms of associativity and identity (so a group is a monoid with an inverse operation). An *abelian* monoid also satisfies commutativity of the operation, i.e:

$$x \cdot (y \cdot z) = (x \cdot y) \cdot z,$$
$$x \cdot y = y \cdot x,$$
$$1 \cdot x = x.$$

Recall that universal formulas hold in all integral domains iff they hold in all fields, because every field is an integral domain, while every integral domain can be extended to a field. Similarly we have:

Theorem 5.25 *A universal formula in the multiplicative language of monoids holds in all abelian monoids iff it holds in all rings.*

Proof Every ring is in particular an abelian monoid with respect to its multiplication operation, since the ring axioms include the abelian monoid axioms. So if any formula holds in all abelian monoids it holds in all rings. Conversely, every abelian monoid M can be extended, given any starting ring R such as $\mathbb{Z}$, to a ring $R(M)$ called the *monoid ring*. This is based on the set of functions $f : M \to R$ such that $\{x|f(x) \neq 0\}$ is finite. The operators are defined just as for the polynomial ring $R[\overline{X}]$, using elements of the monoid rather than monomials, and monoid operations in place of monomial operations. We leave it to the reader to check that all details of the construction generalize straightforwardly. (Indeed, we could have regarded the polynomial ring as a special case of a monoid ring, based on the monoid of monomials.) Thus if a universal formula holds in all rings, it holds in all monoid rings and hence in the substructure of monoid elements ('polynomials with at most one monomial'). ☐

Corollary 5.26 $\forall \overline{x}. \, s_1 = t_1 \wedge \cdots \wedge s_n = t_n \Rightarrow s = t$ *holds in all monoids iff* $s - t \in \mathrm{Id}_{\mathbb{Z}} \langle s_1 - t_1, \ldots, s_n - t_n \rangle$.

Proof Combine the previous theorem and Theorem 5.15. ☐

We can do something similar for abelian groups, but this time piggybacking off the additive structure of the ring. (The 'abelian' is crucial: as we have already remarked the word problem for groups in general is undecidable.) We'll therefore consider abelian groups additively, with the axioms:

$$x + (y + z) = (x + y) + z,$$
$$x + y = y + x,$$

$$0 + x = x,$$
$$-x + x = 0.$$

We will once again argue that the word problems for abelian groups and rings (in the common additive language) are equivalent. One can prove this similarly based on the fact that every abelian group can be embedded in the additive structure of a ring (Exercise 5.26), but the following proof is perhaps more illuminating.

Theorem 5.27 *The following are equivalent for a word problem in the additive language of abelian groups:*

(i) $\forall \overline{x}.\, s_1 = t_1 \wedge \cdots \wedge s_n = t_n \Rightarrow s = t$ *holds in all abelian groups;*

(ii) $\forall \overline{x}.\, s_1 = t_1 \wedge \cdots \wedge s_n = t_n \Rightarrow s = t$ *holds in all rings;*

(iii) $s - t \in \mathrm{Id}_{\mathbb{Z}} \langle s_1 - t_1, \ldots, s_n - t_n \rangle$;

(iv) *there are integers $c_1, \ldots, c_n$ such that $s - t = c_1 \cdot (s_1 - t_1) + \cdots + c_n \cdot (s_n - t_n)$.*

Proof (i) $\Rightarrow$ (ii) because every ring is an additive abelian group. (ii) $\Rightarrow$ (iii) is Theorem 5.15. It is easy to see that (iv) $\Rightarrow$ (i) because the linear combination of terms gives rise to a proof in group theory just as it does (with more general cofactors) in ring theory. It just remains to prove (iii) $\Rightarrow$ (iv). If the ideal membership holds, separate the cofactors into constant terms c_i and those of higher degree q_i:

$$s - t = (c_1 + q_1) \cdot (s_1 - t_1) + \cdots + (c_n + q_n) \cdot (s_n - t_n).$$

Since all monomials in the polynomials $s - t$ and all $s_i - t_i$ have multidegree 1, comparing coefficients of the terms of multidegree 1 shows that $s - t = c_1 \cdot (s_1 - t_1) + \cdots + c_1 \cdot (s_n - t_n)$ as required. $\square$

5.11 Gröbner bases

The previous section showed that we can reduce several logical decision problems to questions of ideal membership, even the triviality of ideals, over polynomial rings. To recap, a formula $\forall \overline{x}.\, p_1(\overline{x}) = 0 \wedge \cdots \wedge p_n(\overline{x}) \Rightarrow q(\overline{x}) = 0$ in the language of rings:

- holds in all rings (or in all non-trivial rings) iff $q \in \mathrm{Id}_{\mathbb{Z}} \langle p_1, \ldots, p_n \rangle$;
- holds in all torsion-free rings (or in all non-trivial torsion-free rings) iff $q \in \mathrm{Id}_{\mathbb{Q}} \langle p_1, \ldots, p_n \rangle$;

- holds in all integral domains (or in all fields, or in all algebraically closed fields) iff $q^k \in \mathrm{Id}_{\mathbb{Z}} \langle p_1, \ldots, p_n \rangle$ for some $k \geq 0$, or iff for some variable z not among the $\overline{x}$ we have $1 \in \mathrm{Id}_{\mathbb{Z}} \langle p_1, \ldots, p_n, 1 - qz \rangle$;
- holds in all integral domains of characteristic 0 (or in all fields of characteristic 0, or in all algebraically closed fields of characteristic 0, or in $\mathbb{C}$) iff $q^k \in \mathrm{Id}_{\mathbb{Q}} \langle p_1, \ldots, p_n \rangle$ for some $k \geq 0$, or iff for some variable z not among the $\overline{x}$ we have $1 \in \mathrm{Id}_{\mathbb{Q}} \langle p_1, \ldots, p_n, 1 - qz \rangle$.

But how do we solve such ideal membership questions? To be explicit, given multivariate polynomials $q(\overline{x}), p_1(\overline{x}), \ldots p_n(\overline{x})$ we want to test whether there exist 'cofactor' polynomials $q_1(\overline{x}), \ldots q_n(\overline{x})$ such that:

$$p_1(\overline{x}) q_1(\overline{x}) + \cdots + p_n(\overline{x}) q_n(\overline{x}) = q(\overline{x}).$$

If we know that we only need to consider a limited class of monomials in the cofactors, a workable approach is to parametrize general polynomials of that form and test solvability of the linear constraints that arise from comparing coefficients. For example, to show that $x^4 + 1$ is in the ideal generated by $x^2 + xy + 1$ and $y^2 - 2$ we might postulate that we only need terms of multidegree ≤ 2 in the cofactors:

$$
\begin{aligned}
&(x^2 + xy + 1) \cdot (a_1 x^2 + a_2 y^2 + a_3 xy + a_4 x + a_5 y + a_6) \\
&+ (y^2 - 2) \cdot (b_1 x^2 + b_2 y^2 + b_3 xy + b_4 x + b_5 y + b_6) \\
&= x^4 + 1.
\end{aligned}
$$

If we expand out and compare coefficients w.r.t. the original variables, we get the following linear constraints (for example, $b_6 - 2b_2 + a_2$ by considering the coefficient of y^2):

$a_1 - 1 = 0$	$b_2 = 0$	$b_3 + a_2 = 0$
$b_1 + a_2 + a_3 = 0$	$a_3 + a_1 = 0$	$a_4 = 0$
$b_5 = 0$	$b_4 + a_5 = 0$	$a_5 + a_4 = 0$
$-2b_1 + a_6 + a_1 = 0$	$b_6 - 2b_2 + a_2 = 0$	$-2b_3 + a_6 + a_3 = 0$
$-2b_4 + a_4 = 0$	$-2b_5 + a_5 = 0$	$-2b_6 + a_6 - 1 = 0$

These equations are solvable, so the polynomial is indeed in the ideal. Moreover, from the solutions to the equations, which can be expressed in terms of a parameter t:

$$
\begin{aligned}
&a_1 = 1, a_2 = t, a_3 = -1, a_4 = 0, a_5 = 0, a_6 = 1 - 2t, \\
&b_1 = 1 - t, b_2 = 0, b_3 = -t, b_4 = 0, b_5 = 0, b_6 = -t
\end{aligned}
$$

we can explicitly obtain suitable cofactors:

$$(x^2 + xy + 1) \cdot (x^2 + ty^2 - xy + (1 - 2t)) + (y^2 - 2) \cdot ((1 - t)x^2 - txy - t) = x^4 + 1,$$

such as the instance with $t = 0$:

$$(x^2 + xy + 1) \cdot (x^2 - xy + 1) + (y^2 - 2) \cdot (x^2) = x^4 + 1.$$

Despite a certain crudity, this approach can work well, since solving systems of linear equations is a well-studied topic for which polynomial-time and practically efficient algorithms exist, not only over $\mathbb{Q}$ but also over $\mathbb{Z}$ (Nemhauser and Wolsey 1999). But a serious defect is the need to place a bound on the monomials considered in the cofactors. (One special case where this is unproblematical is solving the word problem for abelian groups: as noted we only need to consider constant cofactors.) We can perform iterative deepening, searching for increasingly 'complicated' cofactors. But this is only a semi-decision procedure like first-order proof search: if the polynomial *is* in the ideal we will prove it, but if not we may search forever. In fact there are theoretical bounds on the multidegrees we need to consider, and this formed the basis of early decision procedures for the problem (Hermann 1926). However, this approach is rather pessimistic since even over $\mathbb{Q}$ the bounds are doubly exponential ('only' singly exponential for triviality of an ideal) and over $\mathbb{Z}$ the situation is worse; see Aschenbrenner (2004) for a detailed discussion.

We will present instead a completely different method of *Gröbner bases*, giving algorithmic solutions not only for ideal membership but for several related problems. This approach was originally developed by Buchberger (1965) in his PhD thesis – see also Buchberger (1970) – and in retrospect it has much in common with Knuth–Bendix completion, which it predated by some years. We will present it emphasizing this connection and re-using some of the general theoretical results about abstract reduction relations from Section 4.5. Our focus will be on ideal membership in $\mathbb{Q}[\overline{x}]$, which by the previous section allows us to decide universal formulas over $\mathbb{C}$, or over all fields of characteristic 0. With a little care, Gröbner bases can be generalized to $\mathbb{Z}[\overline{x}]$ and other polynomial rings (Kandri-Rody and Kapur 1984).

Polynomial reduction

A polynomial equation $m_1 + m_2 + \cdots + m_p = 0$, where m_1 is the *head* monomial (the maximal one according to the ordering `morder_lt` from Section 5.10) can be rewritten as

$$m_1 = -m_2 + \cdots + -m_p.$$

The idea in what follows is to use this as a 'rewrite rule' to simplify other polynomials: any polynomial multiple $p = qm_1$ of m_1 can be replaced by

$-qm_2 + \cdots + -qm_p$. For technical simplicity, we define one-step reduction as applying this replacement to a single monomial in the target polynomial. Explicitly, we write $p \rightarrow_S p'$ if p contains a monomial m such that for some polynomial $h+q$ in S with head monomial h we have $p' = p - m'(h+q) = (p - m) - m'q$, where $m = h \cdot m'$. For example, if $S = \{x^2 - xy + y\}$ and our variable order makes x^2 the head monomial, we can repeatedly apply $x^2 = xy - y$ to reduce $x^4 + 1$ as follows. (We show the actual reductions followed by a restoration of the canonical polynomial representation with like monomials collected together, to make it easier to grasp what is happening. Abstractly, though, we consider these folded together in the reduction relation.)

$$
\begin{aligned}
x^4 + 1 \quad &\rightarrow \quad x^2(xy - y) + 1 \\
&= \quad x^3y - x^2y + 1 \\
&\rightarrow \quad xy(xy - y) - x^2y + 1 \\
&= \quad x^2y^2 - x^2y - xy^2 + 1 \\
&\rightarrow \quad y^2(xy - y) - x^2y - xy^2 + 1 \\
&= \quad -x^2y + xy^3 - xy^2 - y^3 + 1 \\
&\rightarrow \quad -y(xy - y) + xy^3 - xy^2 - y^3 + 1 \\
&= \quad xy^3 - 2xy^2 - y^3 + y^2 + 1.
\end{aligned}
$$

We have thus shown $x^4 + 1 \rightarrow^* xy^3 - 2xy^2 - y^3 + y^2 + 1$. Moreover, x appears only linearly in the result, so no further reductions are possible. Indeed, we will show that polynomial reduction is *always* terminating, whatever the set S and the initial polynomial. A reduction step with $h + q$ removes a monomial $m'h$, replacing it by the various monomials $m'(-q)$. Since h is the head monomial, all monomials in q are below h in the ordering, so by compatibility of the ordering with multiplication, all monomials in $m'q$ are below $m'h = m$. We have thus replaced one monomial by a finite number of monomials that are smaller according to $\ll$. Moreover, the monomial order is wellfounded; indeed, given a monomial m there are only finitely many m' with $m' \ll m$, since we only need to consider those with at most the same multidegree. It follows at once from the wellfoundedness of the multiset ordering (see Appendix 1) that the reduction process is terminating.

There may in general be several different p' such that $p \rightarrow_S p'$, either because more than one polynomial in S is applicable, or because several monomials in p could be reduced. This means that confluence is a non-trivial question, and we will return to it before long. But first we will implement polynomial reduction as a function, making natural but arbitrary choices where nondeterminism arises. The following code attempts to apply `pol` as a reduction rule to a monomial `cm`:

```
let reduce1 cm pol =
  match pol with
    [] -> failwith "reduce1"
  | hm::cms -> let c,m = mdiv cm hm in mpoly_mmul (minus_num c,m) cms;;
```

and the following generalizes this to an entire set `pols`:

```
let reduceb cm pols = tryfind (reduce1 cm) pols;;
```

We use this to reduce a target polynomial repeatedly until no further reductions are possible; by the above remark, we know that this will always terminate.

```
let rec reduce pols pol =
  match pol with
    [] -> []
  | cm::ptl -> try reduce pols (mpoly_add (reduceb cm pols) ptl)
               with Failure _ -> cm::(reduce pols ptl);;
```

Confluence

Since polynomial reduction is terminating, confluence is equivalent, by Newman's lemma (Theorem 4.9), to just local confluence. As with rewriting, we can reduce local confluence to the consideration of a finite number of critical situations. Suppose that a polynomial p can be reduced in one step either to q_1 or to q_2. Rather as with rewriting, we can distinguish two distinct possibilities.

- The reductions result from rewriting different monomials, i.e. $p = m_1 + m_2 + p_0$ such that one rewrite maps $m_1 \to r_1$ and the other maps $m_2 \to r_2$. Thus, $q_1 = r_1 + m_2 + p_0$ and $q_2 = m_1 + r_2 + p_0$.
- The reductions result from rewriting the same monomial, i.e. $p = m + p_0$ and one reduction rewrites $m \to r_1$ and the other maps $m \to r_2$.

In the first case, it looks clear that we can join q_1 and q_2 just by applying $m_2 \to r_1$ to q_1 and $m_1 \to r_2$ to q_2, giving a common result $r_1 + r_2 + p_0$. It's not *quite* that simple, because one of the reducts r_i may contain a rational multiple of the other monomial m_j, changing the coefficient of m_j in p_i. However, since the monomial order is wellfounded, we cannot have both $m_1 \gg m_2$ and $m_2 \gg m_1$, so either r_2 does not involve m_1 or r_1 does not involve m_2. By symmetry, it suffices to consider one of these possibilities. So suppose that r_2 does not involve m_1, while $r_1 = am_2 + s_2$ for some constant

a (possibly 0) and another polynomial s_2 not involving the monomial m_2. We have:

$$
\begin{aligned}
q_1 &= r_1 + m_2 + p_0 \\
&= (am_2 + s_2) + m_2 + p_0 \\
&= (a+1)m_2 + s_2 + p_0 \\
&\to^* (a+1)r_2 + s_2 + p_0,
\end{aligned}
$$

while

$$
\begin{aligned}
q_2 &= m_1 + r_2 + p_0 \\
&\to r_1 + r_2 + p_0 \\
&= (am_2 + s_2) + r_2 + p_0 \\
&= am_2 + s_2 + r_2 + p_0 \\
&\to^* ar_2 + s_2 + r_2 + p_0 \\
&= (a+1)r_2 + s_2 + p_0.
\end{aligned}
$$

Thus q_1 and q_2 are joinable. (We use $\to^*$ rather than $\to$ in some steps to take in the possibility that $a = 0$ or $a + 1 = 0$.)

This shows that non-confluence can only occur in the second situation, with rewrites to the same monomial m. Just as with Knuth–Bendix completion, where we were able to cover all such situations with a finite number of critical pairs based on most general unifiers, for Gröbner bases we can cover all situations by considering a 'most general' monomial to which both rewrites are applicable, namely the lowest common multiple (LCM) of m_1 and m_2. This is indeed 'most general' because reduction is closed under monomial multiplication:

Lemma 5.28 *If $p \to q$ and m is a nonzero monomial, then also $mp \to mq$.*

Proof By definition, if $p \to q$, the reduction arises from some equation $m' = r$ such that $p = m'm'' + p'$ and $q = rm'' + p'$. But then $mp = m(m'm'' + p') = m'(mm'') + mp'$ and so a reduction to $r(mm'') + mp'$ is possible; this however is exactly $m(rm'' + p') = mq$. $\square$

Corollary 5.29 *If $p \to^* q$ and m is a monomial or zero, then also $mp \to^* mq$.*

Proof By rule induction on the reduction sequence $p \to^* q$, applying the lemma repeatedly. The case $m = 0$ is trivial since we are permitted an empty reduction sequence in $mp \to^* mq$. $\square$

We might be tempted to conclude that it suffices to analyze confluence of the two rewrites to a single monomial $\text{LCM}(m_1, m_2)$. Such a conclusion would be too hasty, however, because although the previous corollary shows that '$\rightarrow^*$', and hence joinability, is closed under monomial multiplication, the same is not true of addition. For example, consider the rewrite rules:

$$F = \{w = x + y, w = x + z, x = z, x = y\}.$$

We have $x + y \downarrow_F x + z$, since both terms are immediately reducible to $y + z$, yet we do *not* have $y \downarrow_F z$. So although the two possible rewrites to the monomial w give joinable results, they lead to non-confluence when applied to w within a polynomial $w - x$.

So instead of focusing on $p \downarrow q$ (Exercise 5.29 pursues this idea) it is simpler to consider the relation $p - q \rightarrow^* 0$. This is also closed under monomial multiplication since if $p - q \rightarrow^* 0$ we have by Corollary 5.29 that $m(p - q) \rightarrow^* 0$ and hence $mp - mq \rightarrow^* 0$. Moreover, its closure under addition of another polynomial is a triviality, since $(p + r) - (q + r)$ and $p - q$ are the very same polynomial. Although this new relation does not coincide with joinability, it does imply it.

Theorem 5.30 *If $p - q \rightarrow^* 0$ then also $p \downarrow q$.*

Proof By induction on the length of the reduction sequence in $p - q \rightarrow^* 0$. If $p - q = 0$ then $p = q$ and the result is trivial. Otherwise, suppose $p - q \rightarrow r \rightarrow^* 0$. The rewrite $p - q \rightarrow r$ must arise from some multiple of a monomial m in the polynomial $p - q$, say to s. Let a and b be the coefficients of this monomial in p and q respectively. Thus we have:

$$
\begin{aligned}
p &= am + p_1, \\
q &= bm + q_1, \\
p - q &= (a - b)m + (p_1 - q_1), \\
r &= (a - b)s + (p_1 - q_1).
\end{aligned}
$$

Note that $a - b \neq 0$ because we assumed m actually occurs in $p - q$. Now we have $p \rightarrow^* p' = as + p_1$ and $q \rightarrow^* q' = bs + p_1$, using either zero or one instances of the same rewrite, depending on whether $a = 0$ and $b = 0$ respectively. But now $p' - q' = (a - b)s + (p_1 - p_2) = r \rightarrow^* 0$. By the inductive hypothesis, therefore, $p' \downarrow q'$ and this shows that $p \downarrow q$.   □

The converse is not true in general, as the example F above shows. There we have $x + y \downarrow_F x + z$ yet $(x + y) - (x + z) = y - z$ is irreducible and nonzero. However, *if* the rewrites F define a confluent relation, many more nice properties hold, including this converse. We lead up to this via a few lemmas.

Lemma 5.31 *If $p \to q$ then $p + r \downarrow q + r$.*

Proof Suppose the reduction $p \to q$ arises from reducing a monomial m in $p = m + p'$ to s, so $q = s + p'$. Note that the monomial m does not occur in p' by construction and does not occur in s because of the ordering restriction in polynomial rewrites. Let a be the coefficient of the monomial m in r, i.e. $r = am + r'$ (this a may be zero). We have:

$$
\begin{aligned}
p + r &= (a + 1)m + p' + r', \\
q + r &= am + s + p' + r'.
\end{aligned}
$$

Thus we have the following rewrites, possibly zero-step if $a = 0$ or $a + 1 = 0$: first $p + r \to^* (a + 1)s + p' + r'$ and also $q + r \to as + s + p' + r'$. But these results are equal, so $p + r \downarrow q + r$ as required. □

Lemma 5.32 *If $\to$ is confluent and $p \to^* q$ then $p + r \downarrow q + r$.*

Proof By induction on the reduction sequence $p \to^* q$. If $p = q$ then $p + r$ and $q + r$ are the same polynomial, so trivially $p + r \downarrow q + r$. Otherwise we have $p \to p' \to^* q$ for some p'. By Lemma 5.31 we have $p + r \downarrow p' + r$, while the inductive hypothesis tells us that $p' + r \downarrow q + r$. But by Lemma 4.11, the confluence of $\to$ implies the transitivity of $\downarrow$, and thus $p + r \downarrow q + r$ as required. □

Theorem 5.33 *If $\to$ is confluent and $p \downarrow q$ then also $p + r \downarrow q + r$ for any other polynomial r.*

Proof We will prove by induction on a reduction sequence $p \to^* s$ that for any $q \to^* s$ we have $p + r \downarrow q + r$. If the reduction sequence $p \to^* s$ is empty, we have $q \to^* p$ and the result is immediate by the previous lemma. Otherwise we have $p \to p' \to^* s$. By Lemma 5.31, $p + r \downarrow p' + r$, while the inductive hypothesis yields $p' + r \downarrow q + r$. Again appealing to Lemma 4.11 for the transitivity of joinability, we have $p + r \downarrow q + r$. □

Corollary 5.34 *If $\to$ is a confluent polynomial reduction and $p \downarrow q$ then also $p - q \to^* 0$.*

Proof Since $p \downarrow q$ the previous theorem yields $p - q \downarrow q - q$, i.e. $p - q \downarrow 0$. Since 0 is in normal form w.r.t. $\rightarrow$, this shows that $p - q \rightarrow^* 0$. □

Now we can arrive at an analogous theorem to Theorem 4.24 for rewriting. Given two polynomials p and q, defining reduction rules $m_1 = p_1$ and $m_2 = p_2$ according to the chosen ordering, define their *S-polynomial*[†] as follows:

$$S(p, q) = p_1 m_1' - p_2 m_2',$$

where $\mathrm{LCM}(m_1, m_2) = m_1 m_1' = m_2 m_2'$. In OCaml this becomes:

```
let spoly pol1 pol2 =
  match (pol1,pol2) with
    ([],p) -> []
  | (p,[]) -> []
  | (m1::ptl1,m2::ptl2) ->
      let m = mlcm m1 m2 in
      mpoly_sub (mpoly_mmul (mdiv m m1) ptl1)
                (mpoly_mmul (mdiv m m2) ptl2);;
```

We have:

Theorem 5.35 *A set of polynomial reductions F defines a confluent reduction relation $\rightarrow_F$ iff for any two polynomials $p, q \in F$ we have $S(p, q) \rightarrow_F^* 0$.*

Proof If $\rightarrow_F$ is confluent, then since both $\mathrm{LCM}(m_1, m_2) \rightarrow p_1 m_1'$ and $\mathrm{LCM}(m_1, m_2) \rightarrow p_2 m_2'$ are permissible reductions, we have $p_1 m_1' \downarrow p_2 m_2'$. But this and confluence again, by Corollary 5.34, yields $S(p, q) = p_1 m_1' - p_2 m_2' \rightarrow^* 0$.

Conversely, suppose all S-polynomials reduce to zero; we will show that the reduction relation is confluent. We have shown that the only possibility for non-confluence is when two rewrites apply to the same monomial m in a polynomial $p = m + p'$. Since this monomial m is a multiple both of m_1 and m_2, it must be a multiple of $\mathrm{LCM}(m_1, m_2)$. So we can write $p = m'\mathrm{LCM}(m_1, m_2) + p'$ and see that the two reductions give $m'p_1 m_1' + p'$ and $m'p_2 m_2' + p'$. But since by hypothesis $p_1 m_1' - p_2 m_2' \rightarrow^* 0$, we have $m'p_1 m_1' - m'p_2 m_2' \rightarrow^* 0$ and so $(m'p_1 m_1' + p') - (m'p_2 m_2' + p') \rightarrow^* 0$. However, by Theorem 5.30, this implies that $m'p_1 m_1' + p' \downarrow m'p_2 m_2' + p'$ as required. □

[†] The S stands for syzygy, a concept that is explained in many books on commutative algebra and algebraic geometry such as Weispfenning and Becker (1993).

Gröbner bases

We've produced a decidable criterion for confluence of a set of polynomial rewrites, but haven't yet explained the relevance to the ideal membership problem. We say that a set of polynomials F is a *Gröbner basis* for an ideal J if $J = \mathrm{Id}_\mathbb{Q}\langle F\rangle$ (i.e. J is the ideal generated by F) and F defines a confluent reduction system. (The basic theory of Gröbner bases was developed by Buchberger, who was at the time a Ph.D. student supervised by Gröbner.) To see the significance of the concept, we first note a few more simple lemmas.

Lemma 5.36 *If $\to$ is a confluent polynomial rewrite system, then if $p \downarrow q$ and $r \downarrow s$, we also have $p + r \downarrow q + s$.*

Proof Using Theorem 5.33 twice we see that $p + r \downarrow q + r$ and $q + r \downarrow q + s$. Using transitivity of '$\downarrow$' (Lemma 4.11) we have $p + r \downarrow q + s$ as required. ☐

Lemma 5.37 *If $\to$ is a confluent polynomial rewrite system, then if $p \downarrow q$ then also $rp \downarrow rq$ for any polynomial r.*

Proof We can write r as a sum of monomials $m_1 + \cdots + m_k$. By Lemma 5.29 we have $m_i p \downarrow m_i q$ for $1 \le i \le k$ and so by using the previous result repeatedly $m_1 p + \cdots + m_k p \downarrow m_1 q + \cdots + m_k q$, i.e. $rp \downarrow rq$ as required. ☐

Now we are ready to see how Gröbner bases allow us to decide ideal membership.

Theorem 5.38 *The following are equivalent:*

(i) *F is a Gröbner basis for $\mathrm{Id}_\mathbb{Q}\langle F\rangle$, i.e. $\to_F$ is confluent;*
(ii) *for any polynomial p, we have $p \to_F^* 0$ iff $p \in \mathrm{Id}_\mathbb{Q}\langle F\rangle$;*
(iii) *for any polynomials p and q, we have $p \downarrow_F q$ iff $p - q \in \mathrm{Id}_\mathbb{Q}\langle F\rangle$.*

Proof First note the triviality that if $p \to_F^* q$ then $p - q \in \mathrm{Id}_\mathbb{Q}\langle F\rangle$. Since ideals contain zero and are closed under addition, it suffices to prove that if $p \to_F q$ then $p - q \in \mathrm{Id}_\mathbb{Q}\langle F\rangle$. But this is clear since if if $p \to_F q$ then by definition, q arises from subtracting a multiple of a polynomial in q. Similarly, if $p \downarrow_F q$ then there is an r with $p \to_F^* r$ and $q \to_F^* r$. By the remarks at the beginning, $p - r \in \mathrm{Id}_\mathbb{Q}\langle F\rangle$ and $q - r \in \mathrm{Id}_\mathbb{Q}\langle F\rangle$, but then by the closure properties of ideals, $p - q = (p - r) - (q - r) \in \mathrm{Id}_\mathbb{Q}\langle F\rangle$. This shows that the 'only if' parts of (ii) and (iii) are immediate regardless of whether

F is a Gröbner basis. And since $p - q \rightarrow^* 0$ implies $p \downarrow q$ by Theorem 5.30, we have $(ii) \Rightarrow (iii)$ at once. Now we will prove the other implications.

$(i) \Rightarrow (ii)$. Suppose that F is a Gröbner basis. As noted above, if $p \rightarrow^*_F 0$ then $p = p - 0 \in \mathrm{Id}_{\mathbb{Q}} \langle F \rangle$. Conversely, if $p \in \mathrm{Id}_{\mathbb{Q}} \langle F \rangle$ then we can write $p = \sum_{i=1}^{k} q_i p_i$ where each $p_i \in F$. Since trivially each $p_i \rightarrow_F 0$ (rewrite its head monomial), we see by the lemmas above that $p \rightarrow^*_F 0$. (Note that $p \rightarrow^* 0$ and $p \downarrow 0$ are always equivalent since 0 is irreducible.)

$(iii) \Rightarrow (i)$. Now suppose $p \downarrow_F q$ iff $p - q \in \mathrm{Id}_{\mathbb{Q}} \langle F \rangle$. Note that the relation on the right is trivially transitive, by the closure of ideals under addition. Consequently, the joinability relation $\downarrow_F$ is also transitive, but by Lemma 4.11 this is equivalent to confluence. $\qquad\square$

This result shows that a Gröbner basis allows us to decide the ideal membership problem just by rewriting a given polynomial p to a normal form and comparing the normal form with zero. In particular, we can test if 1 is in the ideal by checking if $1 \rightarrow^*_F 0$. Evidently this can only happen if there is a constant polynomial in the Gröbner basis.

Buchberger's algorithm

The above result shows the value of Gröbner bases in solving (among others) our original problem, membership of 1 in a polynomial ideal. Moreover, Theorem 5.35 allows us to implement a decidable test whether a given set of polynomials constitutes a Gröbner basis. As we shall see, Buchberger's algorithm allows us to go further and create a Gröbner basis for (the ideal generated by) any finite set of polynomials.

Suppose that given a set F of polynomials, some $f, g \in F$ are such that $S(f, g) \rightarrow^*_F h$ where h is in normal form but nonzero. Just as with Knuth–Bendix completion, we can add the new polynomial h to the set to obtain $F' = F \cup \{h\}$. Trivially, we have $h \rightarrow_{F'} 0$, but to test F' for confluence we need also to consider the new S-polynomials of the form $\{S(h, k) \mid k \in F\}$. (Note that we only need to consider one of $S(h, k)$ and $S(k, h)$ since one reduces to zero iff the other does.) Thus, the following algorithm maintains the invariant that all S-polynomials of pairs of polynomials from **basis** are joinable by the reduction relation induced by **basis** except possibly those in **pairs**. Moreover, since each $S(f, g)$ is of the form $hf + kg$, the set **basis** always defines exactly the same ideal as the original set of polynomials:

```
let rec grobner basis pairs =
  print_string(string_of_int(length basis)^" basis elements and "^
               string_of_int(length pairs)^" pairs");
  print_newline();
  match pairs with
    [] -> basis
  | (p1,p2)::opairs ->
        let sp = reduce basis (spoly p1 p2) in
        if sp = [] then grobner basis opairs
        else if forall (forall ((=) 0) ** snd) sp then [sp] else
        let newcps = map (fun p -> p,sp) basis in
        grobner (sp::basis) (opairs @ newcps);;
```

So, if this process eventually terminates with no unjoinable S-polynomials, we know that the resulting set is confluent and defines the same ideal, i.e. is a Gröbner basis for the ideal defined by the initial polynomials. And in fact, we are in the happy situation, in contrast to completion, that termination is guaranteed. Note that each S-polynomial is reduced with the existing **basis** before it is added to that basis. Consequently, each polynomial added to **basis** has no monomial divisible by the head monomial of any existing polynomial in **basis**. So nontermination of the algorithm would imply the existence of an infinite sequence of monomials (m_i) such that m_j is never divisible by m_i for $i < j$. However, we will show that such an infinite sequence is impossible.[†] Since the divisibility of $dx_1^{n_1} \cdots x_k^{n_k}$ by $cx_1^{m_1} \cdots x_k^{m_k}$ is equivalent to $m_i \le n_i$ for all $1 \le i \le k$, this is an immediate consequence of the following result known as *Dickson's lemma* (Dickson 1913).

Lemma 5.39 *Define the ordering $\le_n$ on $\mathbb{N}^n$ by $(x_1, \ldots, x_n) \le_n (y_1, \ldots, y_n)$ iff $x_i \le y_i$ for all $1 \le i \le n$. Then there is no infinite sequence (t_i) of elements of $\mathbb{N}^n$ such that $t_i \not\le_n t_j$ for all $i < j$.*

Proof By induction on n. The result is trivial for $n = 0$, or an immediate consequence of wellfoundedness of $\mathbb{N}$ for $n = 1$. So it suffices to assume the result established for n, and prove it for $n + 1$. We use the same kind of 'minimal bad sequence' argument used in the proof that the lexicographic path order is terminating (Theorem 4.21).

Suppose we have a sequence (t_i) of elements of $\mathbb{N}^{n+1}$ that is 'bad', i.e. such that $t_i \not\le_{n+1} t_j$ for any $i < j$. We will show that there is also a mini-

---

[†] The reader who knows some commutative algebra can prove this more directly by observing that the sequence of ideals $I_k = \text{Id} \langle m_1, \ldots, m_k \rangle$ would form a strictly increasing chain, contradicting Hilbert's Basis Theorem in the form of the ascending chain condition. A fairly simple proof of the Hilbert Basis Theorem due to Sarges (1976) can be found in Weispfenning and Becker (1993).

mal bad sequence. Since $\mathbb{N}$ is wellfounded, there must be a minimal $a \in \mathbb{N}$ that can occur as the left component of the start (a, s) of a bad sequence (where $s \in \mathbb{N}^n$). Let a_0 be such a number. Similarly, for later elements, let a_{k+1} be the smallest number $a \in \mathbb{N}$ such that there is a bad sequence beginning $(a_0, s_0), \ldots, (a_{k+1}, s_{k+1})$ for some $s_0, \ldots, s_{k+1}$. This is the minimal bad sequence.

However, the existence of a minimal bad sequence $((a_i, s_i))$ is contradictory. By the inductive hypothesis, there are no bad sequences in $\leq_n$, so we must have some $i < j$ such that $s_i \leq_n s_j$. Since $((a_i, s_i))$ is assumed bad, we cannot have $(a_i, s_i) \leq_{n+1} (a_j, s_j)$, and therefore we cannot have $a_i \leq a_j$. But then $a_j < a_i$, and so there is a bad sequence $(a_0, s_0), \ldots, (a_{i-1}, s_{i-1})$, $(a_j, s_j), \ldots$, but this contradicts the minimality of a_i. $\square$

In order to start Buchberger's algorithm off, we just collect the initial set of S-polynomials, exploiting symmetry to avoid considering both $S(f, g)$ *and* $S(g, f)$ for each pair f and g:

```
let groebner basis = grobner basis (distinctpairs basis);;
```

Universal decision procedure

Although we could create some polynomials at once and start experimenting, it's better to fulfil our original purpose of producing a decision procedure for universal formulas over the complex numbers (or over all fields of characteristic 0) based on Gröbner bases, since that provides a more flexible input format. In the core quantifier elimination step, we need to eliminate some block of existential quantifiers from a conjunction of literals. For the negative equations, we will use the Rabinowitsch trick. The following maps a variable v and a polynomial p to $1 - vp$ as required:

```
let rabinowitsch vars v p =
   mpoly_sub (mpoly_const vars (Int 1))
            (mpoly_mul (mpoly_var vars v) p);;
```

The following takes a set of formulas (equations or inequations) and returns **true** if they have no common solution. We first separate the input formulas into positive and negative equations. New variables **rvs** are created for the Rabinowitsch transformation of the negated equations, and the negated polynomials are appropriately transformed. We then find a Gröbner basis for the resulting set of polynomials and test whether 1 is in the ideal (i.e. reduces to 0).

```
let grobner_trivial fms =
  let vars0 = itlist (union ** fv) fms [] 
  and eqs,neqs = partition positive fms in
  let rvs = map (fun n -> variant ("_"^string_of_int n) vars0)
                (1--length neqs) in
  let vars = vars0 @ rvs in
  let poleqs = map (mpolyatom vars) eqs
  and polneqs = map (mpolyatom vars ** negate) neqs in
  let pols = poleqs @ map2 (rabinowitsch vars) rvs polneqs in
  reduce (groebner pols) (mpoly_const vars (Int 1)) = [];;
```

For an overall decision procedure for universal formulas, we first perform some simplification and prenexing, in case some effectively universal quantifiers are internal. Then we negate, break the formula into DNF and apply `grobner_trivial` to each disjunct:

```
let grobner_decide fm =
  let fm1 = specialize(prenex(nnf(simplify fm))) in
  forall grobner_trivial (simpdnf(nnf(Not fm1)));;
```

We can try one of our earlier examples:

```
# grobner_decide
    <<a^2 = 2 /\ x^2 + a*x + 1 = 0 ==> x^4 + 1 = 0>>;;
3 basis elements and 3 pairs
3 basis elements and 2 pairs
- : bool = true
```

On the other hand, if we change $x^4 + 1$ to $x^4 + 2$ we get **false**, as expected. Moreover, on universal formulas, the Gröbner basis algorithm is generally significantly faster than the earlier quantifier elimination procedure, especially when many variables are involved. Even the following simple example is solved in a fraction of the time taken by the earlier procedure:

```
# grobner_decide
    <<(a * x^2 + b * x + c = 0) /\
      (a * y^2 + b * y + c = 0) /\
      ~(x = y)
      ==> (a * x * y = c) /\ (a * (x + y) + b = 0)>>;;
...
21 basis elements and 190 pairs
- : bool = true
```

There are numerous refinements to the basic Gröbner basis algorithm, which can be found in the standard texts listed near the end of this chapter. For example, the guaranteed termination of Buchberger's algorithm means we don't need to have the same kind of worries about fairness that beset us when we considered completion. Thus, one can employ heuristics for which S-polynomial to consider next, rather than just processing them in round-robin fashion, without affecting incompleteness. There are also various criteria that justify ignoring many S-polynomials, e.g. Buchberger's first and second criteria (see Exercise 5.30 for the former) and methods of Faugère (2002).

5.12 Geometric theorem proving

A seminal event in the development of modern mathematics was the introduction of coordinates into geometry, mainly by Fermat and Descartes (hence *Cartesian* coordinates). For each point p in the original assertion we consider its coordinates, two real numbers p_x and p_y (for two-dimensional geometry). Geometrical assertions about the points can then be translated into equations in the coordinates. For example, three points a, b and c are collinear (on some common line) iff:

$$(a_x - b_x)(b_y - c_y) = (a_y - b_y)(b_x - c_x),$$

while a is the midpoint of the line joining b and c iff:

$$2a_x = b_x + c_x \land 2a_y = b_y + c_y.$$

Here's a list of correspondences between assertions about points (numbered 1, 2, ...) and the corresponding equations, which we will use to automate such translation. Note that we don't define 'length' or 'angle', since the translations would involve square roots and arctangents. However, we do define *equality* of lengths as equality of their squares, and we could likewise express most relationships among angles algebraically via the addition formula for tangents (see Exercise 5.37). It has even been suggested (Wildberger 2005) that geometry should be phrased in terms of *quadrance* and *spread* instead of length and angle, precisely to stick with algebraic functions of the coordinates.[†]

[†] In terms of the more familiar concepts, quadrance is the square of distance and spread is the square of the sine of an angle.

```
let coordinations =
  ["collinear", (** Points 1, 2 and 3 lie on a common line **)
    <<(1_x - 2_x) * (2_y - 3_y) = (1_y - 2_y) * (2_x - 3_x)>>;
   "parallel", (** Lines (1,2) and (3,4) are parallel **)
    <<(1_x - 2_x) * (3_y - 4_y) = (1_y - 2_y) * (3_x - 4_x)>>;
   "perpendicular", (** Lines (1,2) and (3,4) are perpendicular **)
    <<(1_x - 2_x) * (3_x - 4_x) + (1_y - 2_y) * (3_y - 4_y) = 0>>;
   "lengths_eq", (** Lines (1,2) and (3,4) have the same length **)
    <<(1_x - 2_x)^2 + (1_y - 2_y)^2 = (3_x - 4_x)^2 + (3_y - 4_y)^2>>;
   "is_midpoint", (** Point 1 is the midpoint of line (2,3) **)
    <<2 * 1_x = 2_x + 3_x /\ 2 * 1_y = 2_y + 3_y>>;
   "is_intersection", (** Lines (2,3) and (4,5) meet at point 1 **)
    <<(1_x - 2_x) * (2_y - 3_y) = (1_y - 2_y) * (2_x - 3_x) /\
      (1_x - 4_x) * (4_y - 5_y) = (1_y - 4_y) * (4_x - 5_x)>>;
   "=", (** Points 1 and 2 are the same **)
    <<(1_x = 2_x) /\ (1_y = 2_y)>>];;
```

To translate a quantifier-free formula we just use these templates as a
pattern to modify atomic formulas. (To be applicable to general first-order
formulas, we should also expand each quantifier over points into two quantifiers over coordinates.)

```
let coordinate fm = onatoms
  (fun (R(a,args)) ->
    let xtms,ytms = unzip
      (map (fun (Var v) -> Var(v^"_x"),Var(v^"_y")) args) in
    let xs = map (fun n -> string_of_int n^"_x") (1--length args)
    and ys = map (fun n -> string_of_int n^"_y") (1--length args) in
    subst (fpf (xs @ ys) (xtms @ ytms)) (assoc a coordinations));;
```

For example:

```
# coordinate <<collinear(a,b,c) ==> collinear(b,a,c)>>;;
- : fol formula =
<<(a_x - b_x) * (b_y - c_y) = (a_y - b_y) * (b_x - c_x) ==>
  (b_x - a_x) * (a_y - c_y) = (b_y - a_y) * (a_x - c_x)>>
```

We can optimize the translation process somewhat by exploiting the invariance of geometric properties under certain kinds of spatial transformation.
The following generates an assertion that one of our geometric properties is
unchanged if we systematically map each $x \mapsto x'$ and $y \mapsto y'$:

```
let invariant (x',y') ((s:string),z) =
  let m n f =
    let x = string_of_int n^"_x" and y = string_of_int n^"_y" in
    let i = fpf ["x";"y"] [Var x;Var y] in
    (x |-> tsubst i x') ((y |-> tsubst i y') f) in
  Iff(z,subst(itlist m (1--5) undefined) z);;
```

We will check the invariance of our properties under various transformations of this sort. (We check them over the complex numbers for efficiency; if a universal formula holds over $\mathbb{C}$ it also holds over $\mathbb{R}$.) Under a spatial translation $x \mapsto x + X$, $y \mapsto y + Y$:

```
let invariant_under_translation = invariant (<<|x + X|>>,<<|y + Y|>>);;
```

all geometric properties above are invariant, as one would expect from the intended geometric meaning:

```
# forall (grobner_decide ** invariant_under_translation) coordinations;;
...
- : bool = true
```

Thus we may without loss of generality assume that one of the points, say the first in the free variable list of the initial formula, is $(0, 0)$. Moreover, the geometric properties are also unchanged under rotation about the origin. We can describe this algebraically by a transformation $x \mapsto cx - sy$, $y \mapsto sx + cy$ with $s^2 + c^2 = 1$. (Intuitively we think of s and c as the sine and cosine of the angle of rotation, but we treat it purely algebraically.)

```
let invariant_under_rotation fm =
  Imp(<<s^2 + c^2 = 1>>,
      invariant (<<|c * x - s * y|>>,<<|s * x + c * y|>>) fm);;
```

and confirm:

```
# forall (grobner_decide ** invariant_under_rotation) coordinations;;
...
- : bool = true
```

Given any point (x, y), we can choose s and c subject to $s^2 + c^2 = 1$ to make $sx + cy = 0$. (The application of our real quantifier elimination algorithm shown here works, but takes a little time.)

```
# real_qelim
   <<forall x y. exists s c. s^2 + c^2 = 1 /\ s * x + c * y = 0>>;;
- : fol formula = true
```

Thus, given two points A and B in the original problem, we may take them to be $(0, 0)$ and $(x, 0)$ respectively:

```
let originate fm =
  let a::b::ovs = fv fm in
    subst (fpf [a^"_x"; a^"_y"; b^"_y"] [zero; zero; zero])
          (coordinate fm);;
```

Two other important transformations are *scaling* and *shearing*. Any combination of translation, rotation, scaling and shearing is called an *affine transformation*.

```
let invariant_under_scaling fm =
  Imp(<<~(A = 0)>>,invariant(<<|A * x|>>,<<|A * y|>>) fm);;

let invariant_under_shearing = invariant(<<|x + B * y|>>,<<|y|>>);;
```

Because all our geometric properties are invariant under scaling:

```
# forall (grobner_decide ** invariant_under_scaling) coordinations;;
- : bool = true
```

we might be tempted to go further and use $(1,0)$ for the point B, but we can only do this if we are happy to rule out the possibility that $A = B$. Similarly, we might want to use shearing invariance to justify taking three of the points as $(0,0)$, $(x,0)$ and $(0,y)$, but this is problematic if the three points may be collinear. In any case, while some properties are invariant under shearing, perpendicularity and equality of lengths are not, as the reader can confirm thus:

```
# partition (grobner_decide ** invariant_under_shearing) coordinations;;
```

Thus, the special choice of coordinates based on invariance under scaling and shearing seems best left to the user setting up the problem.

Complex coordinates

Once we've translated the assertion into its algebraic form, we just need to decide whether that statement is true for all real numbers. In principle, as Tarski (1951) already noted, we could use a quantifier elimination procedure for the reals. In practice it's hard to prove nontrivial geometric properties in this fashion, because even sophisticated algorithms for real quantifier elimination, let alone the simple one from Section 5.9, are relatively inefficient. Indeed, the best-known early work on automated theorem proving in geometry (Gelerntner 1959) wasn't based on algebraic reduction, but attempted to mimic traditional Euclidean proofs. For some time after this, the subject of automated geometry theorem proving received little attention. Then Wu Wen-tsün (1978) demonstrated an algebraic method capable of proving automatically a wide class of geometrical theorems, as its implementation by Chou (1988) convincingly demonstrated. Wu's first basic insight was simply this.

Remarkably many geometrical theorems, when formulated as universal algebraic statements in terms of coordinates, are also true for all *complex* values of the 'coordinates'.

This means that instead of using the highly inefficient methods for deciding real algebra, we can try the much more practical methods for the complex numbers. Provided the statement is universal, we can use Gröbner bases, knowing that validity over $\mathbb{C}$ implies validity over $\mathbb{R}$. The converse is false (consider $\forall x.\ x^2 + 1 \neq 0$), so even if a statement is false in $\mathbb{C}$ it might still be true in the intended domain. Nevertheless, it turns out in practice that most geometrical statements remain valid in the extended interpretation; see Exercise 5.38 for some rare exceptions. Another drawback is that we cannot express ordering of points using the complex numbers, which places some restrictions on the geometric problems we can formulate. Even so, with a few tricks in formulation, the approach using complex numbers is remarkably flexible.

Degenerate cases

We can successfully prove a few simple geometry theorems based on this idea. For example, if the line joining the midpoint of a side of a triangle to the opposite vertex is actually perpendicular to the line, the triangle must be isosceles:

```
# (grobner_decide ** originate)
    <<is_midpoint(m,a,c) /\ perpendicular(a,c,m,b)
      ==> lengths_eq(a,b,b,c)>>;;
...
- : bool = true
```

However, we can immediately see some difficulties with this approach if we try to prove the parallelogram theorem, which asserts that the diagonals of an arbitrary parallelogram intersect at their midpoints:

```
# (grobner_decide ** originate)
    <<parallel(a,b,d,c) /\ parallel(a,d,b,c) /\
      is_intersection(e,a,c,b,d)
      ==> lengths_eq(a,e,e,c)>>;;
...
- : bool = false
```

One might guess that this failure results from the use of complex coordinates. However, this is not the case; rather the failure results from neglecting the possibility that what we have called a 'parallelogram' might be trivial, for example all the points a, b, c and d being collinear:

```
# (grobner_decide ** originate)
    <<parallel(a,b,d,c) /\ parallel(a,d,b,c) /\
      is_intersection(e,a,c,b,d) /\ ~collinear(a,b,c)
      ==> lengths_eq(a,e,e,c)>>;;
...
- : bool = true
```

This hints at a general problem: the formulation of geometric theorems is usually based on some unstated assumptions about non-degeneracy that may be vital to their truth. Sometimes this doesn't matter – the isosceles triangle theorem above remains true if the 'triangle' is is flat or even a single point. However, in general some non-degeneracy conditions are necessary, and they may be difficult to anticipate when looking at the 'naive' form of a complicated theorem. Wu's second major achievement was to realize that these non-degenerate conditions are usually necessary, and to develop a way of producing them automatically as part of the proof of a theorem.

Wu's method

Many geometry theorems are of the 'constructive type': one starts with an initial set of arbitrary points $P_1, \ldots, P_k$ and successively 'constructs' new points $P_{k+1}, \ldots, P_n$ based on geometric constraints involving *previously defined points* (including initial points). The conclusion of the theorem is then some assertion about this configuration of points. The crucial point is the presence of a particular order of construction, with each point P_i satisfying constraints involving only the set of points $\{P_j \mid j < i\}$. Exploiting this 'natural' ordering of points appropriately – for example when choosing the variable ordering for Gröbner bases – can make the theorem-proving process much more efficient.

Instead of pursing this, we will explain a somewhat different approach developed by Wu, which exploits the initial constructive order and sharpens it to put the set of equations in *triangular* form, i.e.

$$p_m(x_1, \ldots, x_k, x_{k+1}, x_{k+2}, \ldots, x_{k+m}) = 0,$$
$$\ldots$$
$$p_2(x_1, \ldots, x_k, x_{k+1}, x_{k+2}) = 0,$$
$$p_1(x_1, \ldots, x_k, x_{k+1}) = 0,$$
$$p_0(x_1, \ldots, x_k) = 0.$$

where the polynomial p_m involves a variable x_{k+m} that does not appear in any of the successive polynomials, and then if we exclude that one, the next polynomial in sequence contains a variable that does not appear in the rest, and so on. The appeal of a triangular set is that it can be used to successively 'eliminate' variables in another polynomial, though not in such a simple way as with simultaneous linear equations.

Suppose we assume the equations in such a triangular set as hypotheses. Given another polynomial $p(x_1, \ldots, x_{k+m})$, we will use the triangular set to obtain a conjunction of conditions that are a sufficient (though not in general necessary) condition for $p(x_1, \ldots, x_{k+m}) = 0$ to follow from the equations in the triangular set. First we pseudo-divide $p(x_1, \ldots, x_{k+m})$ by $p_m(x_1, \ldots, x_{k+m})$, considering both as polynomials in x_{k+m} with the other variables as parameters:

$$a_m(x_1, \ldots, x_{k+m-1})^k p(x_1, \ldots, x_{k+m})$$
$$= p_m(x_1, \ldots, x_{k+m}) s_m(x_1, \ldots, x_{k+m}) + p'(x_1, \ldots, x_{k+m}).$$

Given $p_m(x_1, \ldots, x_{k+m}) = 0$, a sufficient condition for $p(x_1, \ldots, x_{k+m}) = 0$ is $a_m(x_1, \ldots, x_{k+m-1}) \neq 0 \land p'(x_1, \ldots, x_{k+m}) = 0$. (If $k = 0$ we can omit the first conjunct.) Writing $p'(x_1, \ldots, x_{k+m})$ in terms of powers of x_{k+m} with 'coefficients' in other variables:

$$c_0(x_1, \ldots, x_{k+m-1}) + c_1(x_1, \ldots, x_{k+m-1}) x_{k+m} + \cdots + c_r(x_1, \ldots, x_{k+m-1}) x_{k+m}^r$$

we get a further sufficient condition that does not involve x_{k+m}:

$$a_m(x_1, \ldots, x_{k+m-1}) \neq 0 \land$$
$$c_0(x_1, \ldots, x_{k+m-1}) = 0 \land \cdots \land c_r(x_1, \ldots, x_{k+m-1}) = 0.$$

We can then proceed to replace each $c_i(x_1, \ldots, x_{k+m-1}) = 0$ in turn by its sufficient conditions using $p_{m-1}(x_1, \ldots, x_{k+m-1}) = 0$, and so on. The following function implements this idea: it takes a triangular set `triang` and a starting polynomial `p`, augmenting an initial set of conditions `degens` with a new set that together are sufficient for `p` to be zero whenever all the `triang` are. We assume that the list of variables `vars` defines the order of elimination, and the polynomials in `triang` are arranged in the appropriate order.

```
let rec pprove vars triang p degens =
  if p = zero then degens else
  match triang with
    [] -> (mk_eq p zero)::degens
  | (Fn("+",[c;Fn("*",[Var x;_])]) as q)::qs ->
        if x <> hd vars then
          if mem (hd vars) (fvt p)
          then itlist (pprove vars triang) (coefficients vars p) degens
          else pprove (tl vars) triang p degens
        else
          let k,p' = pdivide vars p q in
          if k = 0 then pprove vars qs p' degens else
          let degens' = Not(mk_eq (head vars q) zero)::degens in
          itlist (pprove vars qs) (coefficients vars p') degens';;
```

Any set of polynomials can be transformed into a triangular set of polynomials that are all zero whenever all the initial polynomials are. If the desired 'top' variable x_{k+m} occurs in at most one polynomial, we set that one aside and triangulate the rest with respect to the remaining variables. Otherwise, we can pick the polynomial p with the lowest degree in x_{k+m} and pseudo-divide all the other polynomials by p, then repeat. We must reach a stage where x_{k+m} is confined to one polynomial, since each time we run pseudo-division we reduce the aggregate degree of x_{k+m}. This is implemented in the following function, where we assume that polynomials in the list **consts** do not involve the head variable in **vars**, but those in **pols** may do:

```
let rec triangulate vars consts pols =
  if vars = [] then pols else
  let cns,tpols = partition (is_constant vars) pols in
  if cns <> [] then triangulate vars (cns @ consts) tpols else
  if length pols <= 1 then pols @ triangulate (tl vars) [] consts else
  let n = end_itlist min (map (degree vars) pols) in
  let p = find (fun p -> degree vars p = n) pols in
  let ps = subtract pols [p] in
  triangulate vars consts (p::map (fun q -> snd(pdivide vars q p)) ps);;
```

Because geometry statements tend to be of the constructive type, they are already in 'almost triangular' form and the triangulation tends to be quick and efficient. Constructions like 'M is the midpoint of the line AB' or 'P is the intersection of lines AB and CD' define points by one or two constraints on their coordinates. Assuming all coordinates introduced later have been triangulated, we now only need to triangulate the two equations defining these constraints by pseudo-division within this pair, and need not modify other equations. Thus, forming a triangular set tends to be much more efficient than forming a Gröbner basis. However, when it comes to actually reducing with the set, a Gröbner basis is often much more efficient.

Now we will implement the overall procedure that returns a set of sufficient conditions for one conjunction of polynomial equations to imply another. The user is expected to list the variables in elimination order in `vars`, and specify which coordinates are to be set to zero in `zeros`. We could attempt to infer an order automatically, and rely on `originate` for the choice of zeros, but since both these parameters can affect efficiency dramatically, a finer degree of control is useful.

```
let wu fm vars zeros =
  let gfm0 = coordinate fm in
  let gfm = subst(itlist (fun v -> v |-> zero) zeros undefined) gfm0 in
  if not (set_eq vars (fv gfm)) then failwith "wu: bad parameters" else
  let ant,con = dest_imp gfm in
  let pols = map (lhs ** polyatom vars) (conjuncts ant)
  and ps = map (lhs ** polyatom vars) (conjuncts con) in
  let tri = triangulate vars [] pols in
  itlist (fun p -> union(pprove vars tri p [])) ps [];;
```

Examples

Let us try the procedure out on Simson's theorem, which asserts that given four points A, B, C and D on a circle with centre O, the points where the perpendiculars from D meet the (possibly produced) sides of the triangle ABC are all collinear.

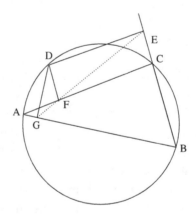

We can express this as follows:

```
let simson =
 <<lengths_eq(o,a,o,b) /\ lengths_eq(o,a,o,c) /\ lengths_eq(o,a,o,d) /\
   collinear(e,b,c) /\ collinear(f,a,c) /\ collinear(g,a,b) /\
   perpendicular(b,c,d,e) /\ perpendicular(a,c,d,f) /\
   perpendicular(a,b,d,g)
   ==> collinear(e,f,g)>>;;
```

We choose a coordinate system with A as the origin and O on the x-axis, ordering the remaining variables according to one possible construction sequence:

```
let vars =
  ["g_y"; "g_x"; "f_y"; "f_x"; "e_y"; "e_x"; "d_y"; "d_x"; "c_y"; "c_x";
   "b_y"; "b_x"; "o_x"]
and zeros = ["a_x"; "a_y"; "o_y"];;
```

Wu's algorithm produces a result quite rapidly:

```
#   wu simson vars zeros;;
- : fol formula list =
[<<~(((0 + b_x * (0 + b_x * 1)) + b_y * (0 + b_y * 1)) + c_x *
     ((0 + b_x * -2) + c_x * 1)) +
   c_y * ((0 + b_y * -2) + c_y * 1) = 0>>;
 <<~(0 + b_x * (0 + b_x * 1)) + b_y * (0 + b_y * 1) = 0>>;
 <<~(0 + b_x * -1) + c_x * 1 = 0>>;
 <<~(0 + c_x * (0 + c_x * 1)) + c_y * (0 + c_y * 1) = 0>>;
 <<~0 + b_x * 1 = 0>>; <<~0 + c_x * 1 = 0>>; <<~-1 = 0>>]
```

Our expectation is that these correspond to non-degeneracy conditions. We can rewrite them more tidily as:

$$(b_x - c_x)^2 + (b_y - c_y)^2 \; \neq \; 0,$$
$$b_x^2 + c_x^2 \; \neq \; 0,$$
$$b_x - c_x \; \neq \; 0,$$
$$c_x^2 + c_y^2 \; \neq \; 0,$$
$$b_x \; \neq \; 0,$$
$$c_x \; \neq \; 0,$$
$$-1 \; \neq \; 0.$$

The last is trivially true. The others do indeed express various non-degeneracy conditions: the points B and C are distinct, the points B and A are distinct, and the points C and A are distinct. (Remember that A is the origin in this coordinate system.) In the intended interpretation as real numbers, there is some redundancy, since $b_x - c_x \neq 0$ implies $(b_x - c_x)^2 + (b_y - c_y)^2 \neq 0$. However, this is not in general the case over the complex numbers, and indeed there are non-Euclidean geometries (e.g. Minkowski geometry) in which non-trivial isotropic lines (lines perpendicular to themselves) may exist.

To see how significant the choice of coordinates can be for the efficiency of the method, it's worth trying the same example without the special choice

of coordinates. It takes much longer, though the output is the same, after
allowing for the different coordinate systems:

```
# wu simson (vars @ zeros) [];;
```

An even trickier choice of coordinate system can be used for Pappus's
theorem, which asserts that given three collinear points A_1, A_2 and A_3 and
three other collinear points B_1, B_2 and B_3, the points of intersection of the
pairs of lines joining the A_i and B_j are collinear. Exploiting the invariance of
incidence properties under arbitrary affine transformations, we can choose
the two lines to be the axes, and hence set the x-coordinates of all the B_i
and the y-coordinates of all the A_i to zero:

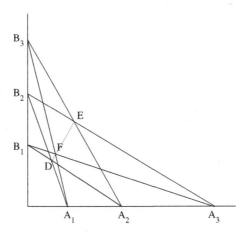

```
let pappus =
 <<collinear(a1,b2,d) /\ collinear(a2,b1,d) /\ collinear(a2,b3,e) /\
   collinear(a3,b2,e) /\ collinear(a1,b3,f) /\ collinear(a3,b1,f)
   ==> collinear(d,e,f)>>;;

let vars = ["f_y"; "f_x"; "e_y"; "e_x"; "d_y"; "d_x";
            "b3_y"; "b2_y"; "b1_y"; "a3_x"; "a2_x"; "a1_x"]
and zeros = ["a1_y"; "a2_y"; "a3_y"; "b1_x"; "b2_x"; "b3_x"];;
```

We get a quick solution:

```
# wu pappus vars zeros;;
- : fol formula list =
[<<~(0 + b1_y * (0 + a1_x * 1)) + b2_y * (0 + a2_x * -1) = 0>>;
 <<~(0 + b1_y * (0 + a1_x * 1)) + b3_y * (0 + a3_x * -1) = 0>>;
 <<~(0 + b2_y * (0 + a2_x * 1)) + b3_y * (0 + a3_x * -1) = 0>>;
 <<~0 + a1_x * -1 = 0>>; <<~0 + a2_x * -1 = 0>>]
```

The first three degenerate conditions express precisely the conditions that the pairs of lines whose intersections we are considering are not in fact parallel. The others assert that the points A_1 and A_2 are not in fact the origin of the clever coordinate system we chose, i.e. the intersection of the two lines considered.

Our examples above closely follow Chou (1984), and numerous other examples can be found in Chou (1988). Theoretically, Wu's method is related to the characteristic set method (Ritt 1938) in the field of *differential algebra* (Ritt 1950). For comparative surveys of various approaches to geometric theorem proving, including Wu's method, Gröbner bases and Dixon resultants, see Kapur (1998) and Robu (2002).

5.13 Combining decision procedures

In many applications, such as program verification, we want decision procedures that work even in the presence of 'alien' terms. For example, instead of proving over $\mathbb{N}$ that $n < 1 \Rightarrow n = 0$, one might want to prove $el(a, i) < 1 \Rightarrow el(a, i) = 0$, where $el(a, i)$ denotes `a[i]`, the ith element of some array a. This problem involves a function symbol el that is not part of the language of Presburger arithmetic. In this case, the solution is straightforward. Since $\forall n \in \mathbb{N}.\, n < 1 \Rightarrow n = 0$ holds, we can specialize n to any term whatsoever, including $el(a, i)$, and so derive the desired theorem. Thus, when faced with a problem involving functions or predicates not considered by a given decision procedure, we can simply try to generalize the problem by replacing them with fresh variables, solve the generalized problem and specialize it again to obtain the desired result. However, sometimes this process of generalization leads from a valid initial claim to a false generalization, even if the additional symbols are completely uninterpreted (i.e. if we assume no axioms for them). For example, the validity of the following (interpreting the arithmetic symbols in the usual way)

$$m \leq n \wedge n \leq m \Rightarrow f(m - n) = f(0)$$

only depends on basic substitutivity properties of f that will be valid for any normal interpretation of f. Yet the naive generalization replacing instances of $f(\cdots)$ by new variables,

$$m \leq n \wedge n \leq m \Rightarrow x = y,$$

is clearly not valid. Thus, there arises the problem of finding an efficient complete generalization of decision procedures for such situations.

Limitations

Unfortunately, the freedom to generalize existing decision procedures by introducing new symbols is quite limited. For example, consider the theory of reals with addition and multiplication, which we know is decidable (Section 5.9). If we add just one new monadic predicate symbol P, we can consider the following hypothesis H:

$$(\forall n.\ P(n+1) \Leftrightarrow P(n)) \wedge (\forall n.\ 0 \leq n \wedge n < 1 \Rightarrow (P(n) \Leftrightarrow n = 0)).$$

Over $\mathbb{R}$, this constrains P to define exactly the class of integers. Thus given any problem over the integers involving addition and multiplication, we can reduce it to an equivalent statement over $\mathbb{R}$ by adding the hypothesis H and systematically relativizing all quantifiers using P. As we will see in Section 7.2, the theory of integers with addition and multiplication is highly undecidable, and hence so is the theory of $\mathbb{R}$ with one additional monadic predicate symbol. In fact, the theory is even more spectacularly undecidable than this reasoning implies (see Exercise 5.40).

Presburger (linear integer) arithmetic with one new monadic predicate symbol is also undecidable (Downey 1972), and so is Presburger arithmetic with one new unary function symbol f. For the latter, consider a hypothesis:

$$(\forall n.\ f(-n) = f(n)) \wedge (f(0) = 0) \wedge (\forall n.\ 0 \leq n \Rightarrow f(n+1) = f(n)+n+n+1).$$

This constrains f to be the squaring function, so we can define multiplication as noted in Section 5.7:

$$m = n \cdot p \Leftrightarrow (n+p)^2 = n^2 + p^2 + 2m$$

and again get into the realm of the undecidable theory of integer addition and multiplication. Halpern (1991) gives a detailed analysis of just how extremely undecidable the various extensions of Presburger arithmetic with new symbols are.

All this might suggest that the idea of extending decision procedures to accommodate new symbols is a hopeless cause. However, provided we stick to validity of *quantifier-free* or explicitly *universally quantified* statements, several standard decision procedures can be extended to allow uninterpreted function and predicate symbols of arbitrary arities, and we can even combine multiple decision procedures for various sets of symbols. The limitation to universal formulas may seem a severe restriction, but it still covers a large proportion of the problems that arise in many applications.

We will present a general method for combining decision procedures due to Nelson and Oppen (1979). It is applicable in most situations when we have separate decision procedures for (universal formulas in) several theories

$T_1, \ldots, T_n$ whose axioms involve disjoint languages, i.e. such that no two distinct T_i and T_j have axioms involving the same function or predicate symbol, except for equality.

Craig's interpolation theorem

Underlying the completeness of the Nelson–Oppen combination method is a classic result in pure logic due to Craig (1957), known as *Craig's interpolation theorem*. This holds for logic with equality and logic without equality, and we will prove both forms below. The traditional formulation is:

If $\models \phi_1 \Rightarrow \phi_2$ then there is an 'interpolant' ψ, whose free variables and function and predicate symbols occur in *both* ϕ_1 and ϕ_2, such that $\models \phi_1 \Rightarrow \psi$ and $\models \psi \Rightarrow \phi_2$.

We will find it more convenient to prove the following equivalent, which treats the two starting formulas symmetrically and fits more smoothly into our refutational approach.[†]

If $\models \phi_1 \wedge \phi_2 \Rightarrow \perp$ then there is an 'interpolant' ψ whose only variables and function and predicate symbols occur in *both* ϕ_1 and ϕ_2, such that $\models \phi_1 \Rightarrow \psi$ and $\models \phi_2 \Rightarrow \neg\psi$.

The starting-point is the analogous result for propositional formulas, which is relatively easy to prove.

Theorem 5.40 *If* $\models A \wedge B \Rightarrow \perp$, *where A and B are propositional formulas, then there is an interpolant C with* $\mathtt{atoms}(C) \subseteq \mathtt{atoms}(A) \cap \mathtt{atoms}(B)$, *such that* $\models A \Rightarrow C$ *and* $\models B \Rightarrow \neg C$.

Proof By induction on the number of elements in $\mathtt{atoms}(A) - \mathtt{atoms}(B)$. If this set is empty, we can just take the interpolant to be A; this satisfies the atom set requirement since $\models A \Rightarrow A$ holds trivially, and since $\models A \wedge B \Rightarrow \perp$ we have $\models B \Rightarrow \neg A$. Otherwise, consider any atom p in A but not B and let $A' = \mathtt{psubst}\ (p \mapsto \perp)\ A \vee \mathtt{psubst}\ (p \mapsto \top)\ A$. Since A' has fewer atoms not in B than A does, the inductive hypothesis means that there is an interpolant C such that $\models A' \Rightarrow C$ and $\models B \Rightarrow \neg C$. But note that $\models A \Rightarrow A'$ and so $\models A \Rightarrow C$ too. Moreover, since $\mathtt{atoms}(C) \subseteq \mathtt{atoms}(A') \cap \mathtt{atoms}(B)$ and $\mathtt{atoms}(A') = \mathtt{atoms}(A) - \{p\} \subseteq \mathtt{atoms}(A)$, this has the atom inclusion property as required. $\qquad\square$

[†] This is often referred to as the Craig–Robinson theorem, since as well as Craig's theorem it is equivalent to a result in pure logic known as *Robinson's consistency theorem* (A. Robinson 1956).

This proof can easily be converted into an algorithm; we add simplification at the end, to get rid of the new 'true' and 'false' atoms:

```
let pinterpolate p q =
  let orify a r = Or(psubst(a|=>False) r,psubst(a|=>True) r) in
  psimplify(itlist orify (subtract (atoms p) (atoms q)) p);;
```

We will proceed to full first-order logic with equality in a number of steps of increasing generality. First:

Lemma 5.41 *Let* $\forall x_1 \ldots x_n.\, P[x_1, \ldots, x_n]$ *and* $\forall y_1 \ldots y_m.\, Q[y_1, \ldots, y_m]$ *be two closed universal formulas such that:*

$$\models (\forall x_1 \cdots x_n.\, P[x_1, \ldots, x_n]) \wedge (\forall y_1 \cdots y_m.\, Q[y_1, \ldots, y_m]) \Rightarrow \bot.$$

Then there is a quantifier-free ground formula C *such that:*

$$\models (\forall x_1 \cdots x_n.\, P[x_1, \ldots, x_n]) \Rightarrow C$$

and

$$\models (\forall y_1 \cdots y_m.\, Q[x_1, \ldots, x_n]) \Rightarrow \neg C$$

such that the only predicate symbols appearing in C *are those that appear in both the starting formulas.*

Proof By Herbrand's theorem, there are sets of ground terms (possibly after adding a new nullary constant to the language if there are none already) such that:

$$\models (P[t_1^1, \ldots, t_n^1] \wedge \cdots \wedge P[t_1^k, \ldots, t_n^k]) \wedge (Q[s_1^1, \ldots, s_m^1] \wedge \cdots \wedge Q[s_1^k, \ldots, s_m^k]) \Rightarrow \bot.$$

Consider now the propositional interpolant C, containing only atomic formulas that occur in both the original propositional expansions, and such that:

$$\models P[t_1^1, \ldots, t_n^1] \wedge \cdots \wedge P[t_1^k, \ldots, t_n^k] \Rightarrow C$$

and

$$\models Q[s_1^1, \ldots, s_m^1] \wedge \cdots \wedge Q[s_1^k, \ldots, s_m^k] \Rightarrow \neg C$$

By straightforward first-order logic, we therefore have:

$$\models (\forall x_1 \ldots x_n.\, P[x_1, \ldots, x_n]) \Rightarrow C$$

and

$$\models (\forall y_1 \ldots y_m.\, Q[y_1, \ldots, y_m]) \Rightarrow \neg C.$$

Moreover, if $R(t_1, \ldots, t_l)$ appears in C, this atom must appear in the propositional expansions of both starting formulas, and therefore R must appear in both starting formulas. □

Again we can express the proof as an algorithm, for simplicity using the Davis–Putnam procedure from Section 3.8 to find the set of ground instances. (This will usually loop indefinitely unless the user does indeed supply formulas p and q such that $\models p \wedge q \Rightarrow \bot$.)

```
let urinterpolate p q =
  let fm = specialize(prenex(And(p,q))) in
  let fvs = fv fm and consts,funcs = herbfuns fm in
  let cntms = map (fun (c,_) -> Fn(c,[])) consts in
  let tups0 = dp_loop (simpcnf fm) cntms funcs fvs 0 [] [] [] in
  let tups = dp_refine_loop (simpcnf fm) cntms funcs fvs 0 [] [] [] in
  let fmis = map (fun tup -> subst (fpf fvs tup) fm) tups in
  let ps,qs = unzip (map (fun (And(p,q)) -> p,q) fmis) in
  pinterpolate (list_conj(setify ps)) (list_conj(setify qs));;
```

For example:

```
# let p = prenex
    <<(forall x. R(x,f(x))) /\ (forall x y. S(x,y) <=> R(x,y) \/ R(y,x))>>
  and q = prenex
    <<(forall x y z. S(x,y) /\ S(y,z) ==> T(x,z)) /\ ~T(0,0)>>;;
...
# let c = urinterpolate p q;;
...
val c : fol formula =
  <<S(0,f(0)) /\ S(f(0),0) \/ S(0,f(0)) /\ S(f(0),0)>>
```

Note that, as expected, c involves only the common predicate symbol S, not the unshared ones R and T, and we can confirm by running, say, meson that $\models p \Rightarrow c$ and $\models q \Rightarrow \neg c$. However, c contains the unshared function symbols 0 and f, and indeed combinations of the two, so is not yet a full interpolant. (We could also simplify it to just $S(0, f(0)) \wedge S(f(0), 0)$, but we won't worry about that.) To show how we can always eliminate unshared function symbols from our partial interpolants, we note a few lemmas.

Lemma 5.42 *Consider the formula* $\forall x_1 \cdots x_n . C[x_1, \ldots, x_n, z]$ *with free variable* z. *Suppose that* $t = h(t_1, \ldots, t_m)$ *is a ground term such that for all terms* $h(u_1, \ldots, u_m)$ *in* $C[x_1, \ldots, x_n, z]$, *the* u_i *are ground (in other words, there are no terms built by* h *from formulas involving variables). Then if:*

$$\models (\forall x_1 \cdots x_n. \, C[x_1, \ldots, x_n, t]) \Rightarrow \bot$$

we also have:

$$\models (\exists z.\, \forall x_1 \cdots x_n.\, C[x_1, \ldots, x_n, z]) \Rightarrow \bot.$$

Proof From the main hypothesis, Herbrand's theorem asserts that there are substitution instances s_i^j such that the following is a propositional tautology:

$$\models C[s_1^1, \ldots, s_n^1, t] \wedge \cdots \wedge C[s_1^k, \ldots, s_n^k, t] \Rightarrow \bot.$$

Since this is a propositional tautology, it remains so if we consistently replace t by a new variable z, a mapping of terms and formulas we schematically denote by $s \mapsto s'$, to obtain:

$$\models C[s_1^1, \ldots, s_n^1, t]' \wedge \cdots \wedge C[s_1^k, \ldots, s_n^k, t]' \Rightarrow \bot$$

for appropriately replaced instances. But note that since there are no terms in $C[x_1, \ldots, x_n, z]$ with topmost function symbol h involving variables, replacement within the formula is equivalent to replacement of each substituting term, where of course $t' = z$:

$$\models C[s_1^{1'}, \ldots, s_n^{1'}, z] \wedge \cdots \wedge C[s_1^{k'}, \ldots, s_n^{k'}, z] \Rightarrow \bot.$$

By simple first-order logic, therefore:

$$\models (\forall x_1 \cdots x_n.\, C[x_1, \ldots, x_n, z]) \Rightarrow \bot$$

and so:

$$\models (\exists z.\, \forall x_1 \cdots x_n.\, C[x_1, \ldots, x_n, z]) \Rightarrow \bot$$

as required.   □

We lift this to general formulas using Skolemization.

Lemma 5.43 *Consider any formula $P[z]$ with free variable z only. Suppose $t = h(t_1, \ldots, t_m)$ is a ground term such that for all terms $h(u_1, \ldots, u_m)$ in $P[z]$, the u_i are ground. Then if $\models P[t] \Rightarrow \bot$ we also have $\models (\exists z.\, P[z]) \Rightarrow \bot$.*

Proof We may suppose that $P[z]$ is in prenex normal form, since the transformation to PNF does not affect the function symbols or free variables. We will now prove the result by induction on the number of existential quantifiers in this formula. If there are none, then the result follows from the previous lemma. Otherwise, we can write:

$$P[z] =_{\text{def}} \forall x_1 \cdots x_m.\, \exists y.\, Q[x_1, \ldots, x_m, y, z].$$

Let us Skolemize this using a function symbol f that does not occur in $P[z]$:

$$P^*[z] =_{\text{def}} \forall x_1 \cdots x_m.\, Q[x_1, \ldots, x_m, f(x_1, \ldots, x_m), z].$$

Since by hypothesis $\models P[t] \Rightarrow \bot$ we also have $\models P^*[t] \Rightarrow \bot$. The inductive hypothesis now tells us that $\models (\exists z.\, P^*[z]) \Rightarrow \bot$, and so $\models P^*[c] \Rightarrow \bot$, where c is a constant symbol not appearing in $P^*[z]$. But by the basic equisatisfiability property of Skolemization, this means $\models P[c] \Rightarrow \bot$, and so $\models (\exists z.\, P[z]) \Rightarrow \bot$. $\qquad\square$

We can use this repeatedly to refine a partial interpolant so that it contains only shared function symbols. Consider a partial interpolant C with:

$$\models (\forall x_1 \ldots x_n.\, P[x_1, \ldots, x_n]) \Rightarrow C$$

and

$$\models (\forall y_1 \ldots y_m.\, Q[y_1, \ldots, y_m]) \Rightarrow \neg C.$$

Suppose it is not yet an interpolant, i.e. it contains at least one term built from a function symbol h that occurs in only one of the starting formulas. In order to apply replacement repeatedly, we need to be careful over the order in which we eliminate terms. Let $t = h(t_1, \ldots, t_m)$ be a *maximal* term in C starting with an unshared function symbol h, i.e. one that does not appear as a proper subterm of any other such term in C. Let $D[z]$ result from C by replacing all instances of t with some variable z not occurring in C, so $C = D[t]$. Now, since h is non-shared, there are two cases. If h occurs in $P[x_1, \ldots, x_n]$ but not $Q[y_1, \ldots, y_m]$, then since

$$\models (\forall y_1 \ldots y_m.\, Q[y_1, \ldots, y_m]) \Rightarrow \neg C$$

we also have

$$\models (\forall y_1 \ldots y_m.\, Q[y_1, \ldots, y_m]) \wedge D[t] \Rightarrow \bot,$$

and so by the previous lemma

$$\models (\exists z.\, (\forall y_1 \ldots y_m.\, Q[y_1, \ldots, y_m]) \wedge D[z]) \Rightarrow \bot,$$

i.e.

$$\models (\forall y_1 \ldots y_m.\, Q[y_1, \ldots, y_m]) \Rightarrow \neg \exists z.\, D[z].$$

On the other hand, since

$$\models (\forall x_1 \ldots x_n.\, P[x_1, \ldots, x_n]) \Rightarrow D[t]$$

we trivially have

$$\models (\forall x_1 \ \ldots \ x_n. \ P[x_1, \ldots, x_n]) \Rightarrow \exists z. \ D[z].$$

Thus, we have succeeded in eliminating one term involving an unshared function symbol by replacing it with an existentially quantified variable. Dually, if h occurs in $Q[y_1, \ldots, y_m]$ but not $P[x_1, \ldots, x_n]$, then we have

$$\models (\forall x_1 \ \ldots \ x_n. \ P[x_1, \ldots, x_n]) \wedge \neg D[t] \Rightarrow \bot,$$

and so by the lemma

$$\models (\exists z. \ (\forall x_1 \ \ldots \ x_n. \ P[x_1, \ldots, x_n]) \wedge \neg D[z]) \Rightarrow \bot,$$

i.e.

$$\models (\forall x_1 \ \ldots \ x_n. \ P[x_1, \ldots, x_n]) \Rightarrow \forall z. \ D[z],$$

while again the counterpart is straightforward:

$$\models (\forall y_1 \ \ldots \ y_m. \ Q[y_1, \ldots, y_m]) \Rightarrow \neg(\forall z. \ D[z]).$$

This time, we have eliminated one term involving an unshared function symbol by replacing it with a universally quantified variable. We can now iterate this step over all terms involving unshared function symbols, existentially or universally quantifying over the new variable depending on which of the starting terms the top function appears in. Eventually we will eliminate all such terms and arrive at an interpolant. To turn this into an algorithm we first define a function to obtain all the topmost terms whose head function is in the list **fns**, first for terms:

```
let rec toptermt fns tm =
  match tm with
    Var x -> []
  | Fn(f,args) -> if mem (f,length args) fns then [tm]
                  else itlist (union ** toptermt fns) args [];;
```

and then for formulas:

```
let topterms fns = atom_union
  (fun (R(p,args)) -> itlist (union ** toptermt fns) args []);;
```

For the main algorithm, we find the pre-interpolant using **urinterpolate**, find the top terms in it starting with non-shared function symbols, sort them in decreasing order of size (so no earlier one is a subterm of a later one), then iteratively replace them by quantified variables.

```
let uinterpolate p q =
  let fp = functions p and fq = functions q in
  let rec simpinter tms n c =
    match tms with
      [] -> c
    | (Fn(f,args) as tm)::otms ->
        let v = "v_"^(string_of_int n) in
        let c' = replace (tm |=> Var v) c in
        let c'' = if mem (f,length args) fp
                  then Exists(v,c') else Forall(v,c') in
        simpinter otms (n+1) c'' in
  let c = urinterpolate p q in
  let tts = topterms (union (subtract fp fq) (subtract fq fp)) c in
  let tms = sort (decreasing termsize) tts in
  simpinter tms 1 c;;
```

Note that while an individual step of the generalization procedure is valid regardless of whether we choose a maximal subterm, we do need to observe the ordering restriction to allow repeated application, otherwise we might end up with a term involving an unshared function h where one of the subterms is non-ground, when the lemma is not applicable. If we try this on our current example, we now get a true interpolant as expected. It uses only the common language of p and q:

```
# let c = uinterpolate p q;;
...
val c : fol formula =
  <<forall v_2.
      exists v_1. S(v_2,v_1) /\ S(v_1,v_2) \/ S(v_2,v_1) /\ S(v_1,v_2)>>
```

and has the logical properties:

```
meson(Imp(p,c));;
meson(Imp(q,Not c));;
```

Now we need to lift interpolation to arbitrary formulas. Once again we use Skolemization. Let us suppose first that the two formulas p and q have no common free variables. Since $\models p \wedge q \Rightarrow \bot$ we also have $\models (\exists u_1 \cdots u_n . p \wedge q) \Rightarrow \bot$ where the u_i are the free variables. If we Skolemize $\exists u_1 \cdots u_n . p \wedge q$ we get a closed universal formula of the form $p^* \wedge q^*$, with $\models p^* \wedge q^* \Rightarrow \bot$. Thus we can apply `uinterpolate` to obtain an interpolant. Recall that different Skolem functions are used for the different existential quantifiers in p and q,[†] while there are no common free variables that would make any of the Skolem constants for the u_i common. Thus, none of the newly introduced Skolem

---

[†] This is an instance where the logically sound optimization of using the same Skolem function for the same formula would spoil the implementation.

functions are common to p^* and q^* and will not appear in the interpolant c. And since $\models p^* \Rightarrow c$ and $\models q^* \Rightarrow \neg c$ with c containing none of the Skolem functions, the basic conservativity result (Section 3.6) assures us that $\models p \Rightarrow c$ and $\models q \Rightarrow \neg c$, and it is also an interpolant for the original formulas. This is realized in the following algorithm:

```
let cinterpolate p q =
  let fm = nnf(And(p,q)) in
  let efm = itlist mk_exists (fv fm) fm
  and fns = map fst (functions fm) in
  let And(p',q'),_ = skolem efm fns in
  uinterpolate p' q';;
```

To deal with shared variables we could introduce Skolem constants by existential quantification before the core operation. The only difference is that we need to replace them by variables again in the final result to respect the conditions for an interpolant. We elect to 'manually' replace the common variables by new constants c_i and then restore them afterwards.

```
let interpolate p q =
  let vs = map (fun v -> Var v) (intersect (fv p) (fv q))
  and fns = functions (And(p,q)) in
  let n = itlist (max_varindex "c_" ** fst) fns (Int 0) +/ Int 1 in
  let cs = map (fun i -> Fn("c_"^(string_of_num i),[]))
               (n---(n+/Int(length vs-1))) in
  let fn_vc = fpf vs cs and fn_cv = fpf cs vs in
  let p' = replace fn_vc p and q' = replace fn_vc q in
  replace fn_cv (cinterpolate p' q');;
```

We can test this on a somewhat elaborated version of the same example using a common free variable and existential quantifiers.

```
# let p =
  <<(forall x. exists y. R(x,y)) /\
    (forall x y. S(v,x,y) <=> R(x,y) \/ R(y,x))>>
  and q =
  <<(forall x y z. S(v,x,y) /\ S(v,y,z) ==> T(x,z)) /\
    (exists u. ~T(u,u))>>;;
```

Indeed, the procedure works, and we leave it to the reader to confirm that the result is indeed an interpolant:

```
# let c = interpolate p q;;
...
val c : fol formula =
  <<forall v_2.
      exists v_1.
        S(v,v_2,v_1) /\ S(v,v_1,v_2) \/ S(v,v_2,v_1) /\ S(v,v_1,v_2)>>
```

There are yet two further generalizations to be made. First, note that interpolation applies equally to logic with equality, where now the interpolant may contain the equality symbol (even if only one of the formulas p and q does). We simply note that $\models p \wedge q \Rightarrow \bot$ in logic with equality iff $\models (p \wedge \mathtt{eqaxiom}(p)) \wedge (q \wedge \mathtt{eqaxiom}(q)) \Rightarrow \bot$ in standard first-order logic. Since the augmentations $a \wedge \mathtt{eqaxiom}(a)$ have the same language as a plus equality, the interpolant will involve only shared symbols in the original formulas and possibly the equality sign. To implement this, we can extract the equality axioms from `equalitize` (which is designed for validity-proving and hence adjoins them as hypotheses):

```
let einterpolate p q =
  let p' = equalitize p and q' = equalitize q in
  let p'' = if p' = p then p else And(fst(dest_imp p'),p)
  and q'' = if q' = q then q else And(fst(dest_imp q'),q) in
  interpolate p'' q'';;
```

By using compactness, we reach the most general form of the Craig–Robinson theorem for logic with equality, where it is generalized to infinite sets of sentences.

Theorem 5.44 *If $T_1 \cup T_2 \models \bot$ for two sets of formulas T_1 and T_2, there is a formula C in the common language plus the equality symbol, and with only free variables appearing in $T_1 \cap T_2$, such that $T_1 \models C$ and $T_2 \models \neg C$.*

Proof If $T_1 \cup T_2 \models \bot$, then, by compactness, there are finite subsets $T_1' \subseteq T_1$ and $T_2' \subseteq T_2$ such that $T_1' \cup T_2' \models \bot$. Form the conjunctions of their universal closures p and q and apply the basic result for logic with equality. $\qquad\Box$

The Nelson–Oppen method

To combine decision procedures for theories $T_1, \ldots, T_n$ (with axiomatizations using pairwise disjoint sets of function and predicate symbols), the Nelson–Oppen method doesn't need any special knowledge about the implementation of those procedures, but just the procedures themselves and some characterization of their languages. In order to permit languages with an infinite signature (e.g. all numerals n), we will characterize the language by discriminator functions on functions and predicates, rather than lists of them. All the information is packaged up into a triple. For example, the following is the information needed by the Nelson–Oppen for the theory of reals with multiplication:

```
let real_lang =
  let fn = ["-",1; "+",2; "-",2; "*",2; "^",2]
  and pr = ["<=",2; "<",2; ">=",2; ">",2] in
  (fun (s,n) -> n = 0 & is_numeral(Fn(s,[])) or mem (s,n) fn),
  (fun sn -> mem sn pr),
  (fun fm -> real_qelim(generalize fm) = True);;
```

Almost identical is the corresponding information for the linear theory of integers, decided by Cooper's method. Note that we still include multiplication (though not exponentiation) in the language though its application is strictly limited; this can be considered just the acceptance of syntactic sugar rather than an expansion of the language.

```
let int_lang =
  let fn = ["-",1; "+",2; "-",2; "*",2]
  and pr = ["<=",2; "<",2; ">=",2; ">",2] in
  (fun (s,n) -> n = 0 & is_numeral(Fn(s,[])) or mem (s,n) fn),
  (fun sn -> mem sn pr),
  (fun fm -> integer_qelim(generalize fm) = True);;
```

We might also want to use congruence closure or some other decision procedure for functions and predicates that are not interpreted by any of the specified theories. The following takes an explicit list of languages `langs` and adds on another one that treats all other functions as uninterpreted and handles equality as the only predicate using congruence closure. This could be extended to treat other predicates as uninterpreted, either by direct extension of congruence closure to the level of formulas or by using Exercise 4.3.

```
let add_default langs =
  langs @ [(fun sn -> not (exists (fun (f,p,d) -> f sn) langs)),
           (fun sn -> sn = ("=",2)),ccvalid];;
```

A special procedure for universal Presburger arithmetic plus uninterpreted functions and predicates was once given by Shostak (1979), before his own work on general combination methods to be discussed later. We will use as a running example the following formula valid in this combined theory:

$$u + 1 = v \land f(u) + 1 = u - 1 \land f(v - 1) - 1 = v + 1 \Rightarrow \bot.$$

Homogenization

The Nelson–Oppen method starts by assuming the negation of the formula to be proved, reducing it to DNF, and attempting to refute each disjunct.

We will simply retain the original free variables in the formula in the negated form, for convenience of implementation, but note that logically all the 'variables' below should be considered as Skolem constants. In the running example, we have just one disjunct that we need to refute:

$$u + 1 = v \wedge f(u) + 1 = u - 1 \wedge f(v - 1) - 1 = v + 1.$$

The next step is to introduce new variables for subformulas in such a way that we arrive at an equisatisfiable conjunction of literals, each of which except for equality uses symbols from only a single theory, a procedure known as *homogenization* or *purification*. For our example we might get:

$$u + 1 = v \wedge v_1 + 1 = u - 1 \wedge v_2 - 1 = v + 1 \wedge v_2 = f(v_3) \wedge v_1 = f(u) \wedge v_3 = v - 1.$$

This introduction of fresh 'variables' is satisfiability-preserving, since they are really constants. To implement the transformation, we wish to choose given each atom a language for it based on a 'topmost' predicate or function symbol. Note that in the case of an equation there may be a choice of which topmost function symbol to choose, e.g. for $f(x) = y + 1$. Note also that in the case of an equation between variables we need a language including the equality symbol in our list (e.g. the one incorporated by **add_default**).

```
let chooselang langs fm =
  match fm with
    Atom(R("=",[Fn(f,args);_])) | Atom(R("=",[_;Fn(f,args)])) ->
        find (fun (fn,pr,dp) -> fn(f,length args)) langs
  | Atom(R(p,args)) ->
        find (fun (fn,pr,dp) -> pr(p,length args)) langs;;
```

Once we have fixed on a language for a literal, the topmost subterms not in that language are replaced by new variables, with their 'definitions' adjoined as new equations, which may themselves be homogenized later. To handle the recursion replacing non-homogeneous subterms, we use a continuation-passing style where the continuation handles the replacement within the current context and accumulates the new definitions. The following general function maps a continuation-based operator over a list, modifying the list elements successively:

```
let rec listify f l cont =
  match l with
    [] -> cont []
  | h::t -> f h (fun h' -> listify f t (fun t' -> cont(h'::t')));;
```

The continuations take as arguments the new term, the current variable index and the list of new definitions. The following homogenizes a term, given a language with its function and predicate discriminators `fn` and `pr`. In the case of a variable, we apply the continuation to the current state. In the case of a function in the language, we keep it but recursively modify the arguments, while for a function not in the language, we replace it with a new variable v_n, with n picked at the outset to avoid existing variables:

```
let rec homot (fn,pr,dp) tm cont n defs =
  match tm with
    Var x -> cont tm n defs
  | Fn(f,args) ->
        if fn(f,length args) then
          listify (homot (fn,pr,dp)) args (fun a -> cont (Fn(f,a))) n defs
        else cont (Var("v_"^(string_of_num n))) (n +/ Int 1)
              (mk_eq (Var("v_"^(string_of_num n))) tm :: defs);;
```

Homogenizing a literal is similar, using `homot` to deal with the arguments of predicates.

```
let rec homol langs fm cont n defs =
  match fm with
    Not(f) -> homol langs f (fun p -> cont(Not(p))) n defs
  | Atom(R(p,args)) ->
        let lang = chooselang langs fm in
        listify (homot lang) args (fun a -> cont (Atom(R(p,a)))) n defs
  | _ -> failwith "homol: not a literal";;
```

This only covers a single pass of homogenization, and the new definitional equations may also have non-homogeneous subterms on their right-hand sides, so we need to pass those along for another iteration as long as there are any pending definitions:

```
let rec homo langs fms cont =
  listify (homol langs) fms
          (fun dun n defs ->
              if defs = [] then cont dun n defs
              else homo langs defs (fun res -> cont (dun@res)) n []);;
```

The overall procedure just picks the appropriate variable index to start with:

```
let homogenize langs fms =
  let fvs = unions(map fv fms) in
  let n = Int 1 +/ itlist (max_varindex "v_") fvs (Int 0) in
  homo langs fms (fun res n defs -> res) n [];;
```

Partitioning

The next step is to partition the homogenized literals into those in the various languages. The following tells us whether a formula belongs to a given language, allowing equality in all languages:

```
let belongs (fn,pr,dp) fm =
  forall fn (functions fm) &
  forall pr (subtract (predicates fm) ["=",2]);;
```

and using that, the following partitions up literals according to a list of languages:

```
let rec langpartition langs fms =
  match langs with
    [] -> if fms = [] then [] else failwith "langpartition"
  | l::ls -> let fms1,fms2 = partition (belongs l) fms in
             fms1::langpartition ls fms2;;
```

In our example, we will separate the literals into two groups, which we can consider as a conjunction:

$$(u + 1 = v \wedge v_1 + 1 = u - 1 \wedge v_2 - 1 = v + 1 \wedge v_3 = v - 1) \wedge$$
$$(v_2 = f(v_3) \wedge v_1 = f(u))$$

Interpolants and stable infiniteness

Once those preliminary steps are done with, we enter the interesting phase of the algorithm. In general, the problem is to decide whether a conjunction of literals, partitioned into groups ϕ_k of homogeneous literals in the language of T_k, is unsatisfiable:

$$T_1, \ldots, T_n \models \phi_1 \wedge \cdots \wedge \phi_n \Rightarrow \bot.$$

It will in general not be the case that any individual $T_i \models \phi_i \Rightarrow \bot$, just as in the example at the beginning of this section where naive generalization failed. The key idea underlying the Nelson–Oppen method is to use the kinds of interpolants guaranteed by Craig's theorem as the only means of communication between the various decision procedures. In our example, where we have two theories (Presburger arithmetic and uninterpreted functions), a suitable interpolant is $u = v_3 \wedge \neg(v_1 = v_2)$. Once we know that, we can just use the constituent decision procedures in their respective domains:

```
# (integer_qelim ** generalize)
    <<(u + 1 = v /\ v_1 + 1 = u - 1 /\ v_2 - 1 = v + 1 /\ v_3 = v - 1)
       ==> u = v_3 /\ ~(v_1 = v_2)>>;;
- : fol formula = <<true>>
# ccvalid
    <<(v_2 = f(v_3) /\ v_1 = f(u)) ==> ~(u = v_3 /\ ~(v_1 = v_2))>>;;
- : bool = true
```

and conclude that the original conjunction is unsatisfiable. (If we have more
than two theories, we need an iterated version of the same procedure.) However, there remains the problem of *finding* an interpolant. The interpolation
theorem assures us that an interpolant exists, and that it is built from variables using the equality relation. However, it may in general contain quantifiers, and this presents two problems: there are infinitely many logically
inequivalent possibilities, and we may not even be able to test prospective
interpolants for suitability. (We would prefer to assume only component
decision procedures for universal formulas, and indeed this is all we have for
the theory of uninterpreted functions and equality.)

Things would be much better if we could guarantee the existence of
quantifier-free interpolants involving just variables and equality. And indeed
we *almost* have quantifier elimination for the theory of equality, using a variant of the DLO decision procedure of Section 5.6. As usual we only need to
eliminate one existential quantifier from a conjunction of literals involving
it. If there is any positive equation then we have $(\exists x.\, x = y \land P[x]) \Leftrightarrow P[y]$,
so the only difficulty is a formula of the form

$$\exists x.\, x \neq y_1 \land \cdots \land x \neq y_k.$$

In an interpretation with an infinite domain (or one with more than k
elements), this is trivially equivalent to $\top$, but unfortunately it has no
quantifier-free equivalent in general. If we assume that all models of the
component theories are infinite, we will have no problems. But while this is
certainly valid for arithmetic theories, it isn't for some others, such as the
theory of uninterpreted functions. Instead, a weaker condition suffices.[†]

Definition 5.45 *A theory T is said to be* stably infinite *iff any quantifier-
free formula holds in all models of T iff it holds in all infinite models of
T.*

[†] Stable infiniteness is often defined in the dual satisfiability form. However, one needs to interpret
satisfiability with an implicit existential quantification over valuations, the opposite of the
convention we have chosen.

Let us write $\Gamma \models_\infty \phi$ to mean that ϕ holds in all models of Γ with an infinite domain. Stable-infiniteness of a theory T is therefore assertion that $T \models_\infty \phi$ iff $T \models \phi$ whenever ϕ is quantifier-free.

Let C be any equality formula and C' be the quantifier-free form resulting from applying the quantifier elimination procedure sketched above. This is equivalent in all infinite models, i.e. $\models_\infty C \Leftrightarrow C'$. Therefore, if we can deduce

$$T \models \phi[C_1, \ldots, C_n],$$

where ϕ is quantifier-free except for the equality formulas $C_1, \ldots, C_n$, then a fortiori

$$T \models_\infty \phi[C_1, \ldots, C_n],$$

and so

$$T \models_\infty \phi[C'_1, \ldots, C'_n],$$

Therefore, by stable infiniteness of T,

$$T \models \phi[C'_1, \ldots, C'_n].$$

Consequently, when dealing with validity in a stably infinite theory, we can replace equality formulas in an otherwise propositional formula with quantifier-free forms. We will use this below. Our arithmetic theories, for example, are trivially stably infinite, since they have *only* infinite models. The theory of uninterpreted functions is also stably infinite. For if a formula p fails to hold in some finite model, there is a finite model of its Skolemized negation. Since this is a ground formula, we can extend the domain of the model arbitrarily without affecting its validity, since it is ground and therefore that validity does not involve any quantification over the domain.

Naive combination algorithm

We'll follow Oppen (1980a) in first considering a naive way in which we could decide combinations of stably infinite theories, and only then consider more efficient implementations along the lines originally suggested by Nelson and Oppen. Recall that our general problem is to decide whether

$$T_1, \ldots, T_n \models \phi_1 \wedge \cdots \wedge \phi_n \Rightarrow \bot.$$

Suppose that the formulas $\phi_1, \ldots, \phi_n$ involve k variables (properly Skolem constants) $x_1, \ldots, x_k$. Let us consider all possible ways in which an interpretation can set them equal or unequal to each other, i.e. can partition the interpretations into equivalence classes. For each partitioning P of the $x_1, \ldots, x_k$, we define the *arrangement* $ar(P)$ to be the conjunction of (i) all equations $x_i = x_j$ such that x_i and x_j are in the same class, and (ii) all negated equations $\neg(x_i = x_j)$ such that x_i and x_j are not in the same class. For example, if the partition P identifies x_1, x_2 and x_3 but x_4 is different:

$$\begin{aligned} \text{ar}(P) = \quad & x_1 = x_2 \wedge x_2 = x_1 \wedge x_1 = x_3 \wedge x_3 = x_1 \wedge x_2 = x_3 \wedge x_3 = x_2 \wedge \\ & \neg(x_1 = x_4) \wedge \neg(x_4 = x_1) \wedge \neg(x_2 = x_4) \wedge \\ & \neg(x_4 = x_2) \wedge \neg(x_3 = x_4) \wedge \neg(x_4 = x_3). \end{aligned}$$

Although this is our abstract characterization of $\text{ar}(P)$, for the actual implementation we can be a bit more economical, provided the formula we produce is equivalent in first-order logic with equality. For every equivalence class $\{x_1, \ldots, x_k\}$ within a partition we include

$$x_1 = x_2 \wedge x_2 = x_3 \wedge \cdots \wedge x_{k-1} = x_k,$$

which is done by the following code:

```
let rec arreq l =
  match l with
    v1::v2::rest -> mk_eq (Var v1) (Var v2) :: (arreq (v2::rest))
  | _ -> [];;
```

and then for each pair of equivalence class representatives (chosen as the head of the list) x_i and x_j, we include $\neg(x_i = x_j)$ in one direction:

```
let arrangement part =
  itlist (union ** arreq) part
         (map (fun (v,w) -> Not(mk_eq (Var v) (Var w)))
              (distinctpairs (map hd part)));;
```

Note that any $\text{ar}(P)$ implies either the truth or falsity of any equation between the k variables. And since the disjunction of all the possible arrangements is valid in first-order logic with equality, the original assertion is equivalent to the validity, for all the possible partitions P, of

$$T_1, \ldots, T_n \models \phi_1 \wedge \cdots \wedge \phi_n \wedge \text{ar}(P) \Rightarrow \bot.$$

Now, we claim that if the above holds, then subject to stable infiniteness, we actually have

$$T_i \models \phi_i \wedge \text{ar}(P) \Rightarrow \bot$$

for some $1 \leq i \leq n$. This gives us, in principle, a decision method. Set up all the possible $\text{ar}(P)$ and for each one try to find an i so $T_i \models \phi_i \wedge \text{ar}(P) \Rightarrow \bot$, using the various component decision procedures. Now let us justify the claim.

Since T_1 and $T_2 \cup \cdots \cup T_n$ have no symbols in common, the Craig Interpolation Theorem 5.44 implies the existence of an interpolant C, which we can assume thanks to stable infiniteness to be a quantifier-free Boolean combination of equations, such that

$$T_1 \models \phi_1 \wedge \operatorname{ar}(P) \Rightarrow C,$$
$$T_2, \ldots, T_n \models \phi_2 \wedge \cdots \wedge \phi_n \wedge \operatorname{ar}(P) \Rightarrow \neg C.$$

Since $\operatorname{ar}(P)$ includes all equations either positively or negatively, either $\models \operatorname{ar}(P) \Rightarrow \neg C$ or $\models \operatorname{ar}(P) \Rightarrow C$. In the former case, we actually have $T_1 \models \phi_1 \wedge \operatorname{ar}(P) \Rightarrow \bot$ as required. Otherwise we have

$$T_2, \ldots, T_n \models \phi_2 \wedge \cdots \wedge \phi_n \wedge \operatorname{ar}(P) \Rightarrow \bot$$

and by using the same argument repeatedly, we see that eventually we do indeed reach a stage where some $T_i \models \phi_i \wedge \operatorname{ar}(P) \Rightarrow \bot$, so validity can be decided by one of the component decision procedures.

It's not hard to implement this, but one initial optimization seems worthwhile. Most of our component decision procedures are notably poor at dealing with equations $x = t$, but the Nelson–Oppen procedure naturally generates many such equations, both by the initial homogenization process and the positive equations generated by the arrangements. It's useful to provide a wrapper that repeatedly uses such equations (with $x \notin \operatorname{FVT}(t)$ of course) to eliminate the variable by substituting it into the other equations.[†]

```
let dest_def fm =
  match fm with
    Atom(R("=",[Var x;t])) when not(mem x (fvt t)) -> x,t
  | Atom(R("=",[t; Var x])) when not(mem x (fvt t)) -> x,t
  | _ -> failwith "dest_def";;

let rec redeqs eqs =
  try let eq = find (can dest_def) eqs in
      let x,t = dest_def eq in
        redeqs (map (subst (x |=> t)) (subtract eqs [eq]))
  with Failure _ -> eqs;;
```

Now, we start with a procedure that, given a set of theory triples and list of assumptions `fms0`, checks if they are consistent with a new set of assumptions `fms`:

```
let trydps ldseps fms =
  exists (fun ((_,_,dp),fms0) -> dp(Not(list_conj(redeqs(fms0 @ fms)))))
         ldseps;;
```

[†] Another way of avoiding the set of equations arising from homogenization is not to *actually* perform homogenization, but regard alien subterms as variables only implicitly (Barrett 2002).

The following auxiliary function generates all partitions of a set of objects:

```
let allpartitions =
  let allinsertions x l acc =
    itlist (fun p acc -> ((x::p)::(subtract l [p])) :: acc) l
           (([x]::l)::acc) in
  fun l -> itlist (fun h y -> itlist (allinsertions h) y []) l [[]];;
```

Now we can decide whether every arrangement leads to inconsistency within at least one component theory:

```
let nelop_refute vars ldseps =
  forall (trydps ldseps ** arrangement) (allpartitions vars);;
```

The overall procedure for one branch of the DNF merely involves homogenization followed by separation and this process of refutation. Note that since the arrangements only need to be able to decide the nominal interpolants considered above, we may restrict ourselves to considering variables that appear in at least two of the homogenized conjuncts (Tinelli and Harandi 1996).

```
let nelop1 langs fms0 =
  let fms = homogenize langs fms0 in
  let seps = langpartition langs fms in
  let fvlist = map (unions ** map fv) seps in
  let vars = filter (fun x -> length (filter (mem x) fvlist) >= 2)
                    (unions fvlist) in
  nelop_refute vars (zip langs seps);;
```

The obvious refutation wrapper turns it into a general validity procedure:

```
let nelop langs fm = forall (nelop1 langs) (simpdnf(simplify(Not fm)));;
```

Indeed, our running example works:

```
# nelop (add_default [int_lang])
    <<f(v - 1) - 1 = v + 1 /\ f(u) + 1 = u - 1 /\ u + 1 = v ==> false>>;;
- : bool = true
```

However, for larger examples, enumerating all arrangements can be slow. The number of ways $B(k)$ of partitioning k objects into equivalence classes is known as the *Bell number* (Bell 1934), and it grows exponentially with k:

```
# let bell n = length(allpartitions (1--n)) in map bell (1--10);;
- : int list = [1; 2; 5; 15; 52; 203; 877; 4140; 21147; 115975]
```

The Nelson–Oppen procedure

The original Nelson–Oppen method is a reformulation of the above procedure that can be much more efficient. After homogenization, we repeatedly try the following.

- Try to deduce $T_i \models \phi_i \Rightarrow \bot$ in one of the component theories. If this succeeds, the formula is unsatisfiable.
- Otherwise, try to deduce a new disjunction of equations between variables in one of the component theories, i.e. $T_i \models \phi_i \Rightarrow x_1 = y_1 \vee \cdots \vee x_n = y_n$ where none of the equations $x_j = y_j$ already occurs in ϕ_i.
- If no such disjunction is deducible, conclude that the original formula is satisfiable. Otherwise, for each $1 \leq j \leq n$, case-split over the disjuncts, adding $x_j = y_j$ to every ϕ_i and repeating.

Since there are only finitely many disjunctions of equations, this process must eventually terminate, since we cannot perform the final case-split and augmentation indefinitely. We can justify concluding satisfiability in much the same way as before. If we reach a stage where no further disjunctions of equations are deducible, then we must retain consistency by adding $x_j \neq y_j$ for every pair of variables not already assumed equal in the ϕ_i. But now, as with the arrangements in the previous algorithm, we have assumptions that decide all quantifier-free equality formulas, so by the same argument, the original formula must be satisfiable.

To generate the disjunctions, we could simply enumerate all subsets of the set of equations. But in case this set is infeasibly large, we use a more refined approach. We start with a function to consider subsets of `l` of size `m` and return the result of applying `p` to the first one possible:

```
let rec findasubset p m l =
  if m = 0 then p [] else
  match l with
    [] -> failwith "findasubset"
  | h::t -> try findasubset (fun s -> p(h::s)) (m - 1) t
            with Failure _ -> findasubset p m t;;
```

We can then use this to return the first subset, enumerated in order of size, on which a predicate `p` holds:

```
let findsubset p l =
  tryfind (fun n ->
    findasubset (fun x -> if p x then x else failwith "") n l)
      (0--length l);;
```

Now the overall Nelson–Oppen refutation procedure uses the method of deduction and case-splits spelled out above. Because subsets are enumerated in order of size, and include the empty subset, we check satisfiability within each existing theory first without any separate code.

```
let rec nelop_refute eqs ldseps =
  try let dj = findsubset (trydps ldseps ** map negate) eqs in
      forall (fun eq ->
        nelop_refute (subtract eqs [eq])
                     (map (fun (dps,es) -> (dps,eq::es)) ldseps)) dj
  with Failure _ -> false;;
```

Now `nelop1` is very similar to the version before, except that it first constructs the set of equations to pass to `nelop_refute`:

```
let nelop1 langs fms0 =
  let fms = homogenize langs fms0 in
  let seps = langpartition langs fms in
  let fvlist = map (unions ** map fv) seps in
  let vars = filter (fun x -> length (filter (mem x) fvlist) >= 2)
                    (unions fvlist) in
  let eqs = map (fun (a,b) -> mk_eq (Var a) (Var b))
                (distinctpairs vars) in
  nelop_refute eqs (zip langs seps);;
```

and `nelop` is defined in exactly the same way. We find this is much faster on many examples than the naive procedure, e.g.

```
# nelop (add_default [int_lang])
    <<y <= x /\ y >= x + z /\ z >= 0 ==> f(f(x) - f(y)) = f(z)>>;;
- : bool = true
# nelop (add_default [int_lang])
    <<x = y /\ y >= z /\ z >= x ==> f(z) = f(x)>>;;
- : bool = true
# nelop (add_default [int_lang])
    <<a <= b /\ b <= f(a) /\ f(a) <= 1
      ==> a + b <= 1 \/ b + f(b) <= 1 \/ f(f(b)) <= f(a)>>;;
- : bool = true
```

Convexity

It's not immediately clear that the Nelson–Oppen method is faster in general than the straightforward case split over all variable arrangements. However, if we trace through the previous examples, we find that in fact we never performed a non-trivial case-split, but actually deduced an equation (a disjunction of size 1) at each stage. Thus, it's not so surprising that the procedure worked relatively quickly. This wasn't just a lucky fluke. One can prove that in certain situations no case-splits are ever needed.

A theory T is said to be *convex* if whenever $T \models L_1 \wedge \cdots \wedge L_n \Rightarrow A_1 \vee \cdots \vee A_m$ for literals L_i and atomic formulas A_i, then there is a particular k with $1 \leq k \leq m$ such that $T \models L_1 \wedge \cdots \wedge L_n \Rightarrow A_k$. We will consider here just the special case where all the A_i are equations between variables. Even then, none of the arithmetic theories we have considered so far is convex. The theory of reals with multiplication is not:

```
# map (real_qelim ** generalize)
   [<<x * y = 0 /\ z = 0 ==> x = z \/ y = z>>;
    <<x * y = 0 /\ z = 0 ==> x = z>>;
    <<x * y = 0 /\ z = 0 ==> y = z>>];;
- : fol formula list = [<<true>>; <<false>>; <<false>>]
```

and neither is the linear theory of integers:

```
# map (integer_qelim ** generalize)
   [<<0 <= x /\ x < 2 /\ y = 0 /\ z = 1 ==> x = y \/ x = z>>;
    <<0 <= x /\ x < 2 /\ y = 0 /\ z = 1 ==> x = y>>;
    <<0 <= x /\ x < 2 /\ y = 0 /\ z = 1 ==> x = z>>];;
- : fol formula list = [<<true>>; <<false>>; <<false>>]
```

This might seem a bit discouraging. However the *linear* theory of reals is convex for equations between variables (see Exercise 5.42), so it's only in the cases where discreteness is used essentially that non-convexity arises for the linear theory of integers. And the theory of uninterpreted functions is also convex, as more generally is any theory axiomatizable by Horn clauses (Theorem 3.39). Of course, since we enumerated disjunctions of equations in order of size anyway, there's not much advantage in restricting ourselves to only single equations when proving unsatisfiability. However, if we know all our theories are convex, we can conclude *satisfiability* (and hence invalidity of the universally quantified starting formula before negation) without running through the potentially huge numbers of disjunctions of equations, which can be a dramatic improvement.

Shostak's method

The Nelson–Oppen approach is quite general, and has an appealing modularity, in that we can combine component decision procedures without any knowledge of their internal working. On the other hand, using decision procedures speculatively on all the possible equations or disjunctions of equations between variables is crude. It would be beneficial to tweak individual decision procedures where possible so that they can produce the implied equations by a more intelligent approach than trial-and-error. Another popular way

of combining decision procedures is derived from a method developed by
Shostak (1984b). Shostak's method is less generally applicable, in that it
requires each component theory to have a *canonizer* and a *solver*. Roughly
speaking:

- A *canonizer* 'can' for a theory T maps each term t to a T-equivalent
  canonical (normal) form. This canonizer must satisfy some fairly natural
  technical restrictions, in particular the fact that if $can(t) = f(s_1, \ldots, s_n)$
  then the s_i are themselves canonical, i.e. $can(s_i) = s_i$ for $1 \leq i \leq n$.
- A *solver* σ for a theory T maps equations $s = t$ to a set S of equations of
  the form $x_i = t_i$ whose conjunction is T-equivalent to the original, again
  with some technical restrictions like non-circularity ($x_i \notin \text{FVT}(t_j)$ for
  any of the i and j). A simple example is linear arithmetic over $\mathbb{R}$ where
  an equation like $x + 3y + z = 2x$ can be reduced to $\{x = 3y + z\}$, or
  $\{y = \frac{1}{3}x + \frac{-1}{3}z\}$.

Shostak's procedure then uses the canonizers and solvers for the component theories and ties them into a central algorithm that is a generalization of
congruence closure using the component solvers and canonizers. Experience
indicates that this tighter integration can result in significantly improved
efficiency on many examples, as one might expect. On the other hand, it
has a narrower range of applicability. The Nelson–Oppen method can apply
to any decidable theories, and even in its simple form (only communicat-
ing equations not disjunctions of equations) applies to any convex theory.
Shostak's method, on the other hand, is complete iff the theory is both convex *and* solvable; the presence of a canonizer is not actually theoretically
necessary (Ganzinger 2002).

Despite its practical popularity over the years since Shostak's original
publication, the algorithm has until recently steadfastly resisted a clearly
correct proof of completeness, despite numerous attempts to explicate the
theory. Shostak's original paper has a number of significant errors. For example, it was first noticed by Levitt (1999) that in general, multiple solvers for
the constituent theories cannot be combined as Shostak claimed. Reuß and
Shankar (2001) subsequently showed that Shostak's original algorithm and
all the known later refinements were in fact incomplete and potentially nonterminating. Concretely, they fail to prove our first running example:

```
# nelop (add_default [int_lang])
    <<f(v - 1) - 1 = v + 1 /\ f(u) + 1 = u - 1 /\ u + 1 = v ==> false>>;;
- : bool = true
```

and go into an infinite loop on:

```
# nelop (add_default [int_lang])
   <<f(v) = v /\ f(u) = u - 1 /\ u = v ==> false>>;;
- : bool = true
```

The authors go on to present what is claimed to be a fully corrected version of Shostak's method, a version of which has even been subjected to machine checking (Ford and Shankar 2002). The corrected method has been used as the basis for a real implementation of the combined procedure called `Yices`.[†] Note that there is an important difference between (i) combining *one* Shostak theory with non-trivial axioms and the theory of uninterpreted functions and (ii) combining multiple Shostak theories with non-trivial axioms. In the latter case, it is essentially *never* the case that solvers can be combined (Krstić and Conchon 2003), and the recent complete methods in Shostak style can be considered merely as optimizations of a Nelson–Oppen combination using canonizers.

Modern SMT systems

At the time of writing, there is intense interest in decision procedures for combinations of (mainly, but not entirely quantifier-free) theories. The topic has become widely known as *satisfiability modulo theories* (SMT), emphasizing the perspective that it is a generalization of the standard propositional SAT problem. Indeed, most of the latest SMT systems use methods strongly influenced by the leading SAT solvers, and are usually organized around a SAT-solving core.

The idea of basing other decision procedures around SAT appeared in several places and in several slightly different contexts, going back at least to Armando, Castellini and Giunchiglia (1999). The simplest approach is to use the SAT checker as a 'black box' subcomponent. Given a formula to be tested for satisfiability, just treat each atomic formula as a propositional atom and feed the formula to the SAT checker. If the formula is propositionally unsatisfiable, then it is trivially unsatisfiable as a first-order formula and we are finished. If on the other hand the SAT solver returns a satisfying assignment for the propositional formula, test whether the implicit conjunction of literals is also satisfiable within our theory or theories. If it is satisfiable, then we can conclude that so is the whole formula and terminate. However, if the putative satisfying valuation is *not* satisfiable in our theories, we conjoin its negation with the input formula, just like a conflict clause in

† yices.csl.sri.com.

a modern SAT solver (see Section 2.9) and repeat the procedure. Since all propositional assignments only involve atoms in the original formula, and in each iteration we eliminate at least one satisfying assignment, this process must terminate.

In this framework, we still need to test satisfiability within our theory of various conjunctions of literals. In some sense, all this approach does is replace the immediate explosion of cases caused by an expansion into DNF with the possibly more efficient and intelligent enumeration of satisfying assignments given by the SAT solver. Flanagan, Joshi, Ou and Saxe (2003) contrast this *offline* approach with the *online* alternative where the theory solvers are integrated with the SAT solver in a more sophisticated way, so that the SAT solver can retain most of its context (e.g. conflict clauses or other useful state information) instead of starting afresh each time.

Most modern SMT systems use a form of this online approach, with numerous additional refinements. For example, it is probably worthwhile to standardize atomic formulas as much as possible w.r.t. the theories, e.g. putting terms in normal form, to give more information to the SAT solver. And although we have presented the theory solver as a separate entity that may itself use a Nelson–Oppen combinations scheme, it may be preferable to reimplement the theory combination scheme itself in the same SAT-based framework, e.g. via *delayed theory combination* (Bozzano, Bruttomesso, Cimatti, Junttila, Ranise, van Rossum and Sebastiani 2005).

These general approaches to SMT are often called *lazy*, because the underlying theory decision procedures are only called upon when matters cannot be resolved by propositional reasoning. A contrasting *eager* approach is to reduce the various theories directly to propositional logic in a preprocessing step and then call the SAT checker just once (Bryant, Lahiri and Seshia 2002). It is also possible to combine lazy and eager techniques, e.g. by eliminating the need for congruence closure using the Ackermann reduction (Section 4.4) at the outset, but otherwise proceeding lazily.

Further reading

Many logic texts discuss the decision problem. For solvable and unsolvable cases of the decision problem for logical validity, see Börger, Grädel and Gurevich (2001), Ackermann (1954) and Dreben and Goldfarb (1979), plus the brief treatment is given by Hilbert and Ackermann (1950). Note that the decision problem is often treated from the dual point of view of satisfiability rather than validity, so one needs to swap the role of $\forall$ and $\exists$ in the quantifier prefixes to correlate such writings with our discussion. A survey of decidable theories is given by Rabin (1991), some of which we have considered in this chapter.

Syllogisms are discussed extensively in texts on the history of logic such as Bocheński (1961), Dumitriu (1977), Kneale and Kneale (1962) and Kneebone (1963).

There are a number of other quantifier elimination results for mathematical theories known from the literature. Two fairly difficult examples are the theories of abelian groups (Szmielew 1955) and Boolean algebras (Tarski 1949). A chapter of Kreisel and Krivine (1971) is devoted to quantifier elimination, and includes the theory of separable Boolean algebras (and so atomic Boolean algebras as a special case). Other standard textbooks on model theory such as Chang and Keisler (1992), Hodges (1993b) and Marcja and Toffalori (2003) also discuss quantifier elimination as well as related ideas like model completeness and *o-minimality*; one formulation of model completeness (A. Robinson 1963; MacIntyre 1991) for a theory T is that every formula is T-equivalent to a purely universal (or equivalently, purely existential) one. A survey of theories to which quantifier elimination has been successfully applied is towards the end of Ershov, Lavrov, Taimanov and Taitslin (1965). Soloray (private communication) has also described to the present author a quantifier elimination procedure for various kinds of real and complex vector space.

A treatment of Presburger arithmetic and some other related theories is given by Enderton (1972), and a detailed treatment of the different quantifier elimination procedures of Presburger and Skolem by Smoryński (1980). This book contains a lot of information about related topics, including a discussion of the corresponding theory of multiplication. A nice application of quantifier elimination for Presburger arithmetic is given by Smoryński (1981). Yap (2000) goes further into related decidability questions and has much other relevant material. Other approaches to Presburger arithmetic include the *Omega test* (Pugh 1992) and the method of Williams (1976). A quantifier elimination procedure for linear arithmetic with a *mixture* of reals and integers is given by Weispfenning (1999).

Basu, Pollack and Roy (2006) is a standard reference for quantifier elimination and related questions for the reals, including CAD. Caviness and Johnson (1998) is a collection of important papers in the area including Tarski's original article (which is otherwise quite hard to find). The classical Sturm theory is treated in numerous practically-oriented books on algorithmic algebra such as Mignotte (1991) and Mishra (1993) as well as books specializing in real algebraic geometry such as Benedetti and Risler (1990) and Bochnak, Coste and Roy (1998). The Artin–Schreier theory of

real closed fields is also discussed in many classic algebra texts like van der
Waerden (1991) and Jacobson (1989). Discussion of the full quantifier elimination results (or their equivalent in other formulations) can also be found
in many of these texts, and as already noted our decision procedure follows
Hörmander (1983) based on an unpublished manuscript by Paul Cohen.[†]
Bochnak, Coste and Roy (1998) and Gårding (1997) give other presentations, while Schoutens (2001) and Michaux and Ozturk (2002) describe a
very similar algorithm due to Muchnik. For more leisurely presentations
of the Seidenberg and Kreisel–Krivine algorithms, see Jacobson (1989) and
Engeler (1993) respectively. Two of the most powerful implementations of
real quantifier elimination available are QEPCAD[‡] and REDLOG[§]; the latter needs the REDUCE computer algebra system.

In his original article, Tarski raised the question of whether the theory
of reals remains complete and decidable when one adds to the language the
exponential function $x \mapsto e^x$. This is still unknown, and analysis of related
questions is still a hot research topic at the time of writing. One certainly
needs to further expand the signature (rather as divisibility was needed to
give quantifier elimination for Presburger arithmetic) since the unexpanded
language does *not* admit quantifier elimination: in fact the following formula
(Osgood 1916) has no quantifier-free equivalent even in a language expanded
with arbitrarily many total analytic functions:

$$y > 0 \wedge \exists w. \, x = yw \wedge z = ye^w.$$

What is known (Wilkie 1996) is that this theory and various similar ones
are all *model complete* (see above). Moreover, Macintyre and Wilkie (1996)
have shown decidability of the real exponential field *assuming* the truth of
Schanuel's conjecture, a generalization of the Lindemann–Weierstrass theorem in transcendental number theory. In addition there are extensions of
the *linear* theory of reals with transcendental functions that are known to
be decidable (Weispfenning 2000).

Another extension of the reals that *is* known to be decidable is with a
unary predicate for the algebraic numbers (A. Robinson 1959). But adding
periodic functions such as sin to the reals immediately leads to undecidability, because one can constrain variables to be integers, e.g. by $\sin(n \cdot p) = 0 \wedge$
$\sin(p) = 0 \wedge 3 < p \wedge p < 4$. It follows easily from the undecidability of Hilbert's
tenth problem (Matiyasevich 1970), which we shall see in Chapter 7, that

---

[†] 'A simple proof of Tarski's theorem on elementary algebra', mimeographed manuscript, Stanford University 1967.

[‡] See www.cs.usna.edu/~qepcad/B/QEPCAD.html.

[§] See www.fmi.uni-passau.de/~redlog/.

even the universal fragment of this theory is undecidable, though this was actually proved earlier using a more direct argument (Richardson 1968). Since $\sin(z) = (e^{iz} - e^{-iz})/2$, adding an exponential function to the *complex* numbers leads at once to undecidability.

Considering geometrically the subsets of $\mathbb{R}^n$ or $\mathbb{C}^n$ defined by formulas (see Section 7.2 for a precise definition of definability by a formula) yields some connections with algebraic geometry. Note that existential quantification over x corresponds to projection onto a hyperplane $x = $ constant, and so, for example, (van den Dries 1988) Chevalley's constructibility theorem 'the projection of a constructible set is constructible', is essentially just quantifier elimination in another guise; this even applies to the generalization by Grothendieck (1964). And 'Lefschetz's principle' in algebraic geometry, pithily but imprecisely stated by Weil (1946) as 'There is but one algebraic geometry of characteristic p' has a formal counterpart in the fact that the first-order theory of algebraically closed fields of given characteristic is complete, and this formal version can be further generalized (Eklof 1973). These and other examples of applications of mathematical logic to pure mathematics are surveyed by Kreisel (1956), A. Robinson (1963), Kreisel and Krivine (1971) and Cherlin (1976).

The phrase 'word problem' arises because terms in algebra are sometimes called 'words'; it is quite unrelated to its use in elementary algebra for a problem formulated in everyday language where part of the challenge is to translate it into mathematical terms; see Watterson (1988), p.116. For more relationships between word problems and ideal membership, see Kandri-Rody, Kapur and Narendran (1985). There are several books on Gröbner bases including Adams and Loustaunau (1994) and Weispfenning and Becker (1993), as well as other treatments of algebraic geometry that cover the topic extensively, e.g. Cox, Little and O'Shea (1992), while a short treatment of the basic theory and its applications is given by Buchberger (1998). The text on rewriting methods by Baader and Nipkow (1998) also has a brief treatment of the subject, which like ours re-uses some of the results developed for rewriting.

There is an approach to the universal theory of $\mathbb{R}$ analogous to the use of Gröbner bases for $\mathbb{C}$. The starting-point is an analogue of the Nullstellensatz for the reals, which likewise can be considered as a result about properties true in all ordered fields or in the particular structure $\mathbb{R}$. (The Artin–Schreier theorem asserts that all ordered fields have a real closure, and one can show that all real-closed fields are elementarily equivalent.) Sums of squares of polynomials feature heavily in the various versions of the real Nullstellensatz; for example, the simplest version says that a conjunction $p_1(\overline{x}) = 0 \wedge \cdots \wedge$

$p_n(\overline{x}) = 0$ has no solution over $\mathbb{R}$ iff there are polynomials such that $s_1(\overline{x})^2 + \cdots + s_m(\overline{x})^2 + 1 \in \text{Id} \langle p_1, \ldots, p_n \rangle$. In order to find the appropriate polynomials in practice, the most effective approach seems to be based on *semidefinite programming* (Parrilo 2003). For interesting related material about sums of squares and Hilbert's 17th problem see Reznick (2000) and Roy (2000).

For logical or 'metamathematical' approaches to geometry in general, see Tarski (1959) and Schwabhäuser, Szmielev and Tarski (1983). Important aspects of Wu's method are anticipated in a more limited mechanization theorem given by Hilbert (1899), while extensive practical applications of Wu's method are reported by Chou (1988). A modern survey of Wu's method and many other approaches to geometry theorem proving is given by Chou and Gao (2001). For a general perspective on the theory behind triangular sets see Hubert (2001). Narboux (2007) describes a graphical system that among other things can be used as an interface to the the code in this book.

The proof of Craig's theorem here is taken from Kreisel and Krivine (1971). Extending combination methods to theories that are not stably infinite is problematical (Tinelli and Zarba 2005). In practice, most theories of interest that are not stably infinite have natural domains with a specific finite size (e.g. machine words, with 2^{32} elements). It's arguably better to formulate theory combination in many-sorted logic, where we can still assume quantifier elimination for equality formulas owing to the fixed size for each domain (Ranise, Ringeissen and Zarba 2005). Even better, perhaps, is a parametric sort system (Krstic, Goel, Grundy and Tinelli 2007). Moreover, sort distinctions can even justify some extensions with richer quantifier structure (Fontaine 2004). On the other hand, there are situations where a 1-sorted approach is needed, e.g. the ingenious combination of additive and multiplicative theories of arithmetic suggested by Avigad and Friedman (2006). There are some known cases of decidable combined theories that do not fit into the Nelson–Oppen framework. A notable example is 'BAPA', the combination of the Boolean algebra of sets of uninterpreted elements with Presburger arithmetic, allowing any quantifier structure and including a cardinality operator from sets to numbers. The decidability of this theory is arguably a direct consequence of results of Feferman and Vaught (1959), but was made explicit by Revesz (2004) and, in a more general form, Kuncak, Nguyen and Rinard (2005).

For more on modern SMT systems see the survey by Barrett, Sebastiani, Seshia and Tinelli (2008), and rule-based presentations by Nieuwenhuis, Oliveras and Tinelli (2006) and Krstić and Goel (2007). The practical applications in the computer industry that have driven the current interest in SMT have also suggested other 'computer-oriented' theories whose decidability is of interest. For example, to verify hardware or low-level programs using machine integers, one may want to reason about operations on fixed-size groups of bits such as bytes and words. One approach is via 'bit-blasting', using a propositional variable for each bit and encoding arithmetic operations bitwise. Primitive as this seems, it is very flexible and, thanks to the power of modern SAT solvers, often effective.[†] Other approaches, e.g. the Shostak-like approach of Cyrluk, Möller and Reuß (1997) or the use of modular arithmetic by Babić and Musuvathi (2005) are more elegant and can be more efficient for large word sizes, but are also less general. Other interesting theories for programming include arrays (Stump, Dill, Barrett and Levitt 2001; Bradley, Manna and Sipma 2006) and recursive data types (Barrett, Shikanian and Tinelli 2007). Kroening and Strichman (2008) give a systematic overview of many of these topics, their integration into modern SMT systems and some of their practical applications. Bradley and Manna (2007) describe the key ideas of program verification and how decision procedures can be applied to it, and they also provide a discussion of some important decision procedures and other logical material.

Although it lies somewhat outside the topics we have considered, there are several quite effective algorithms for automated summation of hypergeometric functions, which can automatically prove impressive-looking identities such as $\sum_{k=0}^{n} \binom{n}{k}^2 = \binom{2n}{n}$. Indeed, computer implementations of these algorithms are usually much more effective than people. See Petkovšek, Wilf and Zeilberger (1996) for an introduction. Another slightly peripheral but interesting topic is deciding whether an equation in a language with addition, multiplication and exponentiation holds for the natural numbers (i.e. the free word problem for the structure $\mathbb{N}$). This is known to be decidable (Macintyre 1981; Gurevič 1985), but contrary to a well-known conjecture (Doner and Tarski 1969) it does not coincide with the equational theory of a basic set of 'high school algebra' identities (Wilkie 2000) and in fact the equational theory is not finitely axiomatizable (Gurevič 1990; Di Cosmo and Dufour 2004).

Exercises

5.1   Roughly speaking, in a model of size k, we can think of $\forall x. P[x]$ as equivalent to $P[a_1] \wedge \cdots \wedge P[a_k]$ for some constants a_i interpreted by elements of the model. Likewise we can think of existential quantifiers

---

[†] For example, most of the collection of bit-level hacker tricks à la Warren (2002) listed in the page graphics.stanford.edu/~seander/bithacks.html have been verified for 32-bit words using this technique.

as disjunctions. Make precise the observation that we can implement first-order validity in finite models by expanding quantifiers in this way and using propositional logic – effectively, we bypass part of the enumeration of possible models by relying on non-enumerative methods available for propositional logic. Implement it and compare its performance with the earlier function `decide_finite`. Now experiment with reducing the nesting of quantifiers, and hence the possible blowup, by first transforming into Skolem normal form (see Exercise 3.4) using definitions for subformulas. Does this improve performance? Prove that this is a sound approach.

5.2   As we noted, some standard methods for first-order proof turn out to be decision procedures for restricted subsets. Prove in particular that hyperresolution is complete for the AE fragment (Leitsch 1997).

5.3   Show how to deduce the decidability of the prefix class $\forall^n \exists \exists \forall^m$ from that for $\exists \exists \forall^m$.

5.4   Consider a formula that is in the EA subset we defined, i.e. is of the form $\exists x_1, \ldots, x_n. \forall y_1, \ldots, y_m. P[x_1, \ldots, x_n, y_1, \ldots, y_m]$ with P quantifier-free and without function symbols. (We even exclude constants, though we can just reconsider them as additional variables x_i). Show that it has a model iff it has a model of size n (or 1 in the case $n = 0$), for logic without equality. What about logic with equality?

5.5   The *Friendship theorem* asserts that in a set of people in which any two distinct people have exactly one common friend, there is one person who is everybody else's friend. For a proof that it holds for any *finite* set of friends, see Aigner and Ziegler (2001). Show that the finiteness is essential, and hence that the following formula does not have the finite model property:

```
<<(forall x. ~friend(x,x)) /\
  (forall x y. friend(x,y) ==> friend(y,x)) /\
  (forall x y. ~(x = y)
             ==> exists z. friend(x,z) /\ friend(y,z) /\
                           forall w. friend(x,w) /\ friend(y,w)
                           ==> w = z)
  ==> exists u. forall v. ~(v = u) ==> friend(u,v)>>;;
```

5.6   A class of models that can be expressed as $\mathrm{Mod}(\Sigma)$ (the set of all models of Σ) for some set of first-order axioms Σ is said to be 'Δ-elementary', and if there is some such *finite* set Σ, simply 'elementary'. Show that a class K is elementary precisely if both K and its complement $\overline{K}$ are Δ-elementary. Show that the class of models with infinite domain is elementary, but the class of models with a finite domain is not.

5.7 Use the definitions of 'Δ-elementary' and 'elementary' from the previous exercise. Show that the class of fields of characteristic zero is Δ-elementary but not elementary, while the class of Archimedean fields is not even Δ-elementary.

5.8 Show that if a theory is finitely axiomatizable, any axiomatization of it has a finite subset that axiomatizes the same theory. That is, if $\mathrm{Cn}(\Gamma) = \mathrm{Cn}(\Delta)$ with Δ finite, then there's a finite $\Gamma' \subseteq \Gamma$ with $\mathrm{Cn}(\Gamma') = \mathrm{Cn}(\Gamma)$.

5.9 Show that if a theory is κ-categorical and finitely axiomatizable, then it is decidable. Hint: suppose the conjunction of the axioms is A. Add axioms B_i asserting that there are at least i distinct objects. Now apply the Łoś–Vaught test (Exercise 4.1) to $A \cup \{B_i\}$.

5.10 The theories of dense linear order *with* endpoints also admits quantifier elimination. Implement such a quantifier elimination procedure.

5.11 Show that the theory of dense linear orders without endpoints is $\aleph_0$-categorical. (If you get stuck, look for the classic 'back and forth' proof of this due to Cantor.) Hence show by the Łoś–Vaught test (Exercise 4.1) that the theory is complete, without any use of a concrete quantifier elimination procedure.

5.12 Give a quantifier elimination procedure for the theory of arithmetic truths in a language including the successor function S and the ordering predicate $<$ but not addition. Show that, by contrast to the version without $<$, this theory is finitely axiomatizable, and not κ-categorical for any infinite κ. Show that while the same subsets of $\mathbb{N}$ are definable as without $<$, there are more subsets of $\mathbb{N} \times \mathbb{N}$, including $\{(m, n) \mid m < n\}$. Show that $\{(m, n, p) \mid m + n = p\}$ is still not definable.

5.13 Instead of basing Cooper's algorithm on the existence of minimal or arbitrarily negative solutions, we could have based it on maximal or arbitrarily large and positive ones. Define a notion of 'A-set' dual to the 'B-set' in our presentation and implement Cooper's algorithm based on that. Now implement an 'adaptive' version that uses either the A-set or the B-set depending on which one yields a simpler result.

5.14 Implement an optimization suggested by Cooper: instead of actually expanding out the formulas of the form $\bigvee_{j=1}^{d} \cdots$, introduce j as a new parameter while dealing with the remaining quantifiers. You will then need to deal with them at the end, but this is relatively straightforward. See whether this dramatically improves performance on problems, especially those with many quantifiers of the same kind.

5.15   A set $D \subseteq \mathbb{Z}$ is said to be 'eventually periodic' iff there are positive numbers n and p such that for all $x \geq n$, we have $x + p \in D \Leftrightarrow x \in D$. Show that all sets of integers definable in the language of Presburger arithmetic are eventually periodic. Use this result to show that the set of squares $\{x^2 \mid x \in \mathbb{Z}\}$ is not definable, and hence neither is the graph of the multiplication relation $\{(m, n, p) \mid mn = p\}$.

5.16   Implement one of the algorithms from Harvey and Stuckey (1997) or Lahiri and Musuvathi (2005) for the UTVPI subset of Presburger arithmetic.

5.17   A central component of the complex and real decision procedures was pseudo-division by repeated cancellation of polynomials, i.e. given $p(x) = ax^n + p_1(x)$ and $q(x) = bx^m + q_1(x)$, forming $bx^{m-n}p(x) - aq(x)$ in order to cancel the leading terms. However, it would be more economical to avoid multiplying by common factors of a and b. For example, in the common operation of cancelling $p(x) = ax^n + \cdots$ and $p'(x) = nax^{n-1} + \cdots$ it's clearly unnecessary to multiply both $p(x)$ and $p'(x)$ by a in order to cancel them. Modify the complex and real decision procedures so that they use $a' = a/\gcd(a, b)$ and $b' = b/\gcd(a, b)$ instead. Algorithms for multivariate GCDs based on repeated pseudo-division would give a nice simple implementation based on interlocking recursion – see, for example, Section 4.6.1 of Knuth (1969). Test the improvement on some examples. Take care that you do not violate sign constraints in the case of the reals – if $a = bc$ then $a \neq 0$ implies $b \neq 0$ and $c \neq 0$, but $a > 0$ does not imply either $b > 0$ or $c > 0$. Can you similarly improve sign determination so it takes into account sign information for factors or multiples of the requested polynomial?

5.18   Modify the complex quantifier elimination procedure to work over algebraically closed fields of arbitrary characteristic p. The main place where we implicitly relied on characteristic zero is that we start with the hypothesis that 1 is nonzero (actually positive), and deduce that any multiple of a nonzero number is nonzero. In a field of characteristic p, we need to check divisibility by p. Generalize it to work in unspecified characteristic, case-splitting over $c = 0$ even for constants as need be. How does efficiency change?

5.19   Show that if for arbitrarily large p, a given set of sentences holds in some algebraically closed field of characteristic p, then it holds in some algebraically closed field of characteristic 0. Hence show that every injective polynomial map $f : \mathbb{C}^n \to \mathbb{C}^n$ is also surjective. This requires quite a bit of algebra; for a proof see Weiss and D'Mello (1997), p23.

5.20 The algorithm we presented for reals does not exploit the possibility of using an equation as part of a conjunction to simplify other conjuncts. Implement this feature and test the resulting algorithm on some otherwise difficult examples.

5.21 Augment the DLO procedure from Section 5.6 so that it performs Fourier–Motzkin elimination for the linear theory of reals, as sketched near the end of Section 5.9. Optimize it so that both strict ($<$) and non-strict ($\leq$) inequalities are handled directly instead of transforming $s \leq t \Leftrightarrow s < t \vee s = t$ as we did with the DLO procedure. Implement the further non-DNF optimization from Ferrante and Rackoff (1975) and compare the two procedures on some examples.

5.22 Enhance the Hörmander implementation so that it attempts to find simple factorizations when constructing the sign matrix, e.g. inferring the sign of $x^5 y^4$ from the sign of x and y. Try the result out on examples. Also consider reducing the number of polynomials considered in the complex and real quantifier elimination by maintaining them in monic form to avoid rational multiples.

5.23 Show how to take explicit cofactors for an ideal membership of the form $1 \in \mathrm{Id} \langle p_1, \ldots, p_n, 1 - qz \rangle$ and explicitly find an l and cofactor expansion showing $q^l \in \mathrm{Id} \langle p_1, \ldots, p_n \rangle$. Hint: intuitively we have $z = 1/q$, so consider multiplying the first equation by q^l where l is the largest power of z in the cofactors.

5.24 A ring is said to be *reduced* when it has no nilpotent elements, i.e. satisfies the axioms $\forall x. x^n = 0 \Rightarrow x = 0$ for all $n \geq 1$. A ring is called a *Boolean ring* when it satisfies the axiom $\forall x. x^2 = x$. (Note that a Boolean ring is automatically reduced, even though it may have zero-divisors.) Show how to reduce the word problems for reduced rings, non-trivial reduced rings (also satisfying $1 \neq 0$), and Boolean rings to equivalent ideal membership assertions.

5.25 This exercise is intended for readers who know a bit of algebra; it shows that the usual 'Zornication' in the proof that every field has an algebraic closure can be replaced by the compactness theorem (Kreisel and Krivine 1971). Note that given any field F and polynomial p with coefficients in F, one can construct a field extension F' of F such that p has a root in F', by forming the quotient of $F[x]$ by a maximal ideal containing p. Thus, we can form an extension where any finite set of polynomials all have a root, and hence by compactness where all polynomials in F have a root. We can then take a minimal subfield of elements algebraic over F and this is an algebraically closed extension of F.

5.26 Show that if G is any abelian group, then it can be embedded in the ring on $\mathbb{Z} \times G$ with the operations defined as $(m, a) + (n, b) = (m+n, a+b)$ and $(m, a) \cdot (n, b) = (m \cdot n, m \cdot b + n \cdot a)$, where $m \cdot x$ is just $x + \cdots + x$ repeated m times (Cohn 1974). In fact, many additive abelian groups can be given a ring structure without increasing the domain. Show however that the additive group of rational numbers p/q where q is squarefree (not divisible by n^2 for $n > 1$) cannot be turned into a ring based on the existing domain.

5.27 Show that the word problem for abelian groups can be reduced to that for abelian monoids by pushing down inversion to the variables using $(xy)^{-1} = x^{-1}y^{-1}$, introducing a new variable z_i for each term y_i^{-1} and testing the monoid word problem with the additional equations $z_i y_i = 1$.

5.28 Implement code to solve ideal membership goals using the approach set out at the beginning of Section 5.11, parametrizing general cofactors polynomials and comparing coefficients. How does performance compare with our Gröbner basis approach?

5.29 By considering the rewrite set $F = \{w = x + y, w = x + z, x = z, x = y\}$ we pointed out that joinability of the 'critical pair' $(x + y, x + z)$ arising from w was not in itself enough to imply confluence of rewrites to w in the polynomial $w - x$. However, there is another unjoinable critical pair in this rewrite set, namely (y, z), so this does not provide a counterexample to the global assertion 'joinability of all critical pairs under $\rightarrow_F$ is a necessary and sufficient condition for F to be a Gröbner basis'. Can you find such a counterexample, or else prove that the assertion is in fact true?

5.30 Show that if $p = \sum_{i=1}^{k} p_i$ and $q = \sum_{j=1}^{l} q_i$ are two polynomials, with the monomials p_i arranged in decreasing order ($p_i \gg p_{i+1}$) in the monomial ordering, and likewise for the q_j, then if $\mathrm{LCM}(p_1 q_1) = p_1 q_1$ up to a constant multiple, $S(f, g) \rightarrow_{\{p,q\}} 0$. This observation, known as Buchberger's first criterion, justifies a change to `spoly` so that if two rewrites to a monomial are 'orthogonal' (`snd(m) = snd(mmul m1 m2)`) it just returns the zero polynomial `[]`. How does that optimization improve performance?

5.31 Show that a polynomial $P[\sin(\theta), \cos(\theta)]$ is identically zero iff $x^2 + y^2 = 1 \Rightarrow P[x, y] = 0$ is valid over the complex numbers.

5.32   Enhance the Cooper and Hörmander algorithms in a uniform way so that they handle a unary absolute value function $\mathrm{abs}(x) = |x|$ by performing suitable case-splits, e.g. expanding $\mathrm{abs}(x + y) \leq a$ to $x + y \leq a \wedge -(x + y) \leq a$. Test this function on simple properties of absolute values, e.g. $||x| - |y|| \leq |x - y|$, then see whether you can handle the following. Consider a sequence of integers (or indeed reals) with the property that $x_i + x_{i+2} = |x_{i+1}|$ for all $i \geq 0$ (the values of x_0 and x_1 can be chosen arbitrarily). Such a sequence has the at first sight surprising property that it is periodic with period 9.[†] Can you find an attractive argument to show this? Are any of our algorithms capable of verifying it by brute force, showing $\bigwedge_{i=0}^{8} x_i + x_{i+2} = |x_{i+1}| \Rightarrow x_0 = x_9 \wedge x_1 = x_{10}$? Do any of the optimizations considered in other exercises help?

5.33   Complex quantifier elimination for universal formulas (e.g. Gröbner bases) can be used to solve combinatorial problems, as the following graph-colouring example due to Bayer (1982) indicates. Let z be a primitive cube root of unity, i.e. $z^3 = 1$ but $z^k \neq 1$ for $0 < k < 3$. Represent colours by 1, z and z^2. Each vertex, represented by variables x_i, has one of these colours, so we assert $x_i^3 - 1 = 0$. Now if two vertices represented by x_i, x_j have an edge between them, we want to constrain them to have different colours. We can do this by forcing one of the other roots, i.e. asserting $x_i^2 + x_i x_j + x_j^2 = 0$. Show that a graph is 3-colourable iff these equations are all satisfiable; try some concrete examples. Can you extend this to 4-colourability?

5.34   Show that the subsets of $\mathbb{C}$ definable using addition, multiplication and equations, with arbitrary propositional and quantifier structure, are either finite or cofinite, and hence that the set of reals is not definable.

5.35   We mentioned the two possibilities of introducing a separate Rabinowitsch variable for each negated equation, or combining them all into one negated equation by multiplication then using a single Rabinowitsch variable. We adopted the former; try the latter and see how performance compares on examples.

5.36   Implement a combination of `complex_qelim` and the generally faster method for universal formulas using Gröbner bases, so that outer universal quantifiers are handled by the latter but general quantifier

---

[†] See M. Brown in 'Problems and solutions', *American Mathematical Monthly* **90**, p.569, 1983. Colmerauer (1990) gives a solution using Prolog III.

elimination is used internally as necessary. A typical example you might want to try is the following:

```
<<forall a b c x y.
    ~(a = 0) /\
    (forall z. a * z^2 + b * z + c = 0 <=> z = x \/ z = y)
    ==> a * x * y = c /\ a * (x + y) + b = 0>>;;
```

5.37   Show how to encode equality of angles in algebraic terms using the coordinates. Implement an OCaml function that generates an assertion, using algebraic functions of the coordinates only, that one angle is the sum of two others, and that one angle is n times another one, for an arbitrary positive integer n.

5.38   If three distinct points in the plane all lie on a circle with centre O, and also all lie on a circle with centre O', then $O = O'$. Show by an explicit counterexample that when formulated in terms of coordinates, this fails when the coordinates are allowed to be complex. Look up the '8_3 theorem' of Mac Lane (1936) and show that it also fails for complex 'coordinates'. Show also that the Steiner–Lehmus theorem fails over the complex numbers.[†]

5.39   One can imagine a more ambitious project of not merely verifying geometric theorems, but discovering new ones, perhaps by guessing and testing via some specific numerical instances, then attempting to prove the ones that pass the first test (Davis and Cerutti 1976). Implement a program to do this.

5.40   The system of second-order arithmetic extends the usual first-order arithmetic of natural numbers by having a separate class of unary predicate (or set) variables over which quantification is permitted. For example, one can state the principle of mathematical induction by $\forall P.P(0) \wedge (\forall n.P(n) \Rightarrow P(n+1)) \Rightarrow \forall n.P(n)$, whereas in first-order arithmetic the quantification over P is not possible. Show that in the first-order theory of reals with a predicate for the integers, one can interpret second-order arithmetic. That is, there is an (injective) function $\mathcal{I}$ from formulas in the language of second-order arithmetic to those in the language of the first-order theory of reals with an integer predicate, such that each ϕ is true in arithmetic iff the corresponding $\mathcal{I}(\phi)$ is true over the reals. The author does not know a precise reference for this 'folklore' result, which he learned from Robert Solovay, though see Exercises 8B.2 and 8B.3 of Moschovakis (1980) for a related result. Hint: you might map the predicate (set)

[†] See `groups.google.com/group/geometry.college/msg/323a597e9348ba50` for a note on this by Conway.

P to the digits in a real number's positional expansion, e.g. the set $\{1, 3, 5, \ldots\}$ of odd numbers to the real number $0.1010101 \ldots$.

5.41 Prove a refinement of Craig's interpolation theorem due to Lyndon (1959), which asserts that if $\models A \Rightarrow B$ we can choose the interpolant C such that $\models A \Rightarrow C$ and $\models C \Rightarrow B$ with all the usual conditions *and* the fact that predicate symbols appear only with a particular sign if they appear with that sign in both A and B.

5.42 Prove that the linear theory of reals is convex for equations between variables.

5.43 Prove that for theories with no 1-element models, convexity implies stable infiniteness (Barrett, Dill and Levitt 1996).

5.44 Show that the SAT problem can be reduced with only linear blowup to deciding satisfiability of a conjunction of literals in the combination of (i) the UTVPI fragment of linear integer arithmetic and (ii) uninterpreted function symbols. (Hint: consider transforming a clause $p \vee \neg q \vee r$ into a literal $f(p, q, r) \neq f(0, 1, 0)$.) This shows that even if two theories have an efficient decision procedure, their combination may not (unless the theories are convex).

6

Interactive theorem proving

Our efforts so far have been aimed at making the computer prove theorems completely automatically. But the scope of fully automatic methods, subject to any remotely realistic limitations on computing power, covers only a very small part of present-day mathematics. Here we develop an alternative: an interactive proof assistant that can help to precisely state and formalize a proof, while still dealing with some boring details automatically. Moreover, to ensure its reliability, we design the proof assistant based on a very simple logical kernel.

6.1 Human-oriented methods

We've devoted quite a lot of energy to making computers prove statements completely automatically. The methods we've implemented are fairly powerful and can do some kinds of proofs better than (most) people. Still, the enormously complicated chains of logical reasoning in many fields of mathematics are seldom likely to be discovered in a reasonable amount of time by systematic algorithms like those we've presented. In practice, human mathematicians find these chains of reasoning using a mixture of intuition, experimentation with specific instances, analogy with or extrapolation from related results, dramatic generalization of the context (e.g. the use of complex-analytic methods in number theory) and of course pure luck – see Lakatos (1976), Polya (1954) and Schoenfeld (1985) for varied attempts to subject the process of mathematical discovery to methodological analysis. It's probably true to say that very few human mathematicians approach the task of proving theorems with methods like those we have developed.

One natural reaction to the limitations of systematic algorithmic methods is to try to design computer programs that reason in a more human-like style. Even before the methods we've discussed so far were properly developed, some researchers instinctively felt that systematic methods would be of little practical use and embarked on more human-oriented approaches. For example, Newell and Simon (1956) designed a program that could prove many of the simple logic theorems in *Principia Mathematica* (see Section 6.4). At about the same time Gelerntner (1959) designed a prover that could prove facts in Euclidean geometry using human-style diagrams to direct or restrict the proofs. However, it turned out that their rationale, in particular their pessimism about systematic methods, was not entirely vindicated. For example, the systematic approaches to geometry theorem proving starting with Wu (see Section 5.12) have been remarkably effective and certainly go beyond anything achieved by Gelerntner or others using human-oriented approaches. As Wang (1960) remarked when presenting his simple systematic program for the AE fragment of first-order logic (Section 5.2) that was dramatically more effective than Newell and Simon's:

The writer [...] cannot help feeling, all the same, that the comparison reveals a fundamental inadequacy in their approach. There is no need to kill a chicken with a butcher's knife. Yet the net impression is that Newell–Shore–Simon failed even to kill the chicken with their butcher's knife.

In fairness to those pursuing the human-oriented approach, however, their primary objective was often not to make an effective theorem prover, incidentally appealing though that might be. Rather it was to understand, by formally reconstructing it, the human thought process. Mediocrity may indicate success rather than failure in pursuit of that goal, since people are generally not very good at solving logic puzzles!

After these initial explorations in the 1950s with both 'systematic' and 'human-oriented' approaches to theorem proving, the former won out almost completely. Only a few researchers pursued human-oriented approaches, notably Bledsoe, who, for example, attempted to formalize methods often used by humans for proving theorems about limits in analysis (Bledsoe 1984). Bledsoe's student Boyer together with Moore developed the remarkable NQTHM prover (Boyer and Moore 1979) which can often perform automatic generalization of suggested theorems and prove the generalizations by induction. The success of NQTHM, and the contrasting difficulty of fitting its methods into a simple conceptual framework, has led Bundy (1991) to reconstruct its methods in a general science of reasoning based on *proof planning*.

A more hawkish reaction to the limited success of human-oriented methods when computerized is to observe that in some situations, systematic methods are better *even for people*. For instance, Knuth and Bendix (1970) suggest that completion (Section 4.7) is a useful systematization of the ways mathematicians experiment with equational axioms. Dislike of anthropomorphism in computing generally (Dijkstra 1982b) has perhaps spurred a drive in some quarters towards making human proof more systematically organized and syntax-driven – in short more machine-like (Dijkstra and Scholten 1990). And Wos attributes his considerable success in applying automated reasoning to the fact that he plays to a computer's strengths instead of attempting to make it emulate human thought:

Simply put, differences abound between the way a person reasons and the way a program of the type featured here reasons. Those differences may in part explain why OTTER has succeeded in answering questions that were unanswered for decades, and also explain why its use has produced proofs far more elegant than those previously known. (Even if I knew what was needed, I would not redesign OTTER to function as a mathematician, logician, or any other person does, and not because of a lack of respect for people's reasoning.) (Wos and Pieper 1999)

6.2 Interactive provers and proof checkers

Experience suggests that neither approach, systematically algorithmic or heuristic and human-oriented, is capable of proving a wide range of difficult mathematical theorems automatically. Moreover, there is no indication that incremental improvements in such methods together with advances in technology will change this fact. Some might even argue that it is hardly *desirable* to automate proofs that humans are incapable of developing themselves.

[...] I consider mathematical proofs as a reflection of my understanding and 'understanding' is something we cannot delegate, either to another person or to a machine. (Dijkstra 1976b)

A more modest goal is to create a system that can verify a proof found by a human, or assist in a limited capacity under human guidance. At the very least the computer should act as a humble clerical assistant checking the correctness of the proof, guarding against typical human errors such as implicit assumptions and forgotten special cases. At best the computer might help the process substantially by automating certain parts of the proof; after all, proofs often contain parts that are just routine verifications or are amenable to automation, such as algebraic identities. This idea of a machine and human working together to prove theorems from sketches was already envisaged by Wang (1960), whose work on automated theorem proving was merely intended to lay the groundwork for such a system:

The original aim of the writer was to take mathematical textbooks such as Landau on the number system, Hardy–Wright on number theory, Hardy on the calculus,

Veblen–Young on projective geometry, the volumes by Bourbaki, as outlines and make the machine formalize all the proofs (fill in the gaps).

Early proof assistants

Early computers only supported batch working with a long turnaround time. But by the 1960s, a more interactive style was becoming widespread. Thanks to this, and perhaps motivated by a feeling that the abilities of fully automated systems were starting to plateau, there was increasing interest in the idea of a proof assistant. The first effective realization was the SAM (semi-automated mathematics) family of provers:

Semi-automated mathematics is an approach to theorem-proving which seeks to combine automatic logic routines with ordinary proof procedures in such a manner that the resulting procedure is both efficient and subject to human intervention in the form of control and guidance. Because it makes the mathematician an essential factor in the quest to establish theorems, this approach is a departure from the usual theorem-proving attempts in which the computer *unaided* seeks to establish proofs. (Guard, Oglesby, Bennett and Settle 1969)

In 1966, the fifth in the series of systems, SAM V, was used to construct a proof of a hitherto unproven conjecture in lattice theory (Bumcrot 1965). This was indubitably a success for the semi-automated approach because the computer automatically proved a result now called 'SAM's lemma' and the mathematician recognized that it easily yielded a proof of Bumcrot's conjecture.

Not long after the SAM project, two other important proof-checking systems appeared: AUTOMATH (de Bruijn 1970; de Bruijn 1980; Nederpelt, Geuvers and Vrijer 1994) and Mizar (Trybulec 1978; Trybulec and Blair 1985). Both of these have been highly influential in different ways, and both have been used to check non-trivial pieces of mathematics. Although we will refer to these systems too as 'interactive', we use this term loosely as an antonym of 'automatic'. Both AUTOMATH and Mizar were oriented around batch usage. However, the files that they process consist of a *proof*, or a proof sketch, which they *check* the correctness of, rather than a statement that they attempt to prove automatically.

LCF

Many successful proof checkers, including Mizar, have relatively weak automation, and oblige the user to describe the proof in a rather detailed manner with only small gaps for the machine to fill in. For example, Mizar's automated abilities are quite restricted, to steps that are 'obvious' in a precise logical sense (Davis 1981; Rudnicki 1987). To some extent this weakness is a conscious design choice. If the gaps in a proof sketch are too large, that sketch is difficult to understand for a human reader working without machine assistance – and now that the emphasis is on helping a human mathematician rather than automated *tours de force*, that seems an undesirable feature. This restriction also sharply circumscribes the search needed to fill a gap in the proof or decide that the inference implicit in that gap is non-obvious, so the proof-checking process can be made quite efficient. Since Mizar is designed for batch usage, where a potentially large proof text is checked in a single interaction, this is especially important.

However, the Mizar definition of an obvious inference often fails to coincide with the human definition of what is obvious, and some such dissonance seems inevitable. A particular difficulty is that what a person considers obvious may include domain-specific knowledge about the branch of mathematics being formalized. For example, algebraic identities are often obvious or routine, yet decomposing them to steps that Mizar will accept as obvious can be tedious. Moreover, there seems no end in sight to the new facts that may come to be considered obvious once a certain result has been formalized (Zammit 1999b). For example, one might establish that a certain binary operator '$\otimes$' arising in an abstract branch of mathematics is associative and commutative. From that point on it might be considered obvious that, say, $w \otimes (x \otimes (y \otimes z)) = (x \otimes z) \otimes (w \otimes y)$, and one wouldn't interrupt the flow of a more interesting proof to belabour this point. However, a purely logical deduction of this from the associative and commutative law requires several instances of these laws, and so it turns out not to be obvious in the Mizar sense.

The initial designer(s) of a proof checker can hardly be expected to anticipate all its future applications and the new facts that may come to be regarded as 'obvious' in consequence. This suggests that the ideal proof checker should be *programmable*, i.e. that ordinary users should be able to extend the built-in automation as much as desired. Provided the basic mechanisms of the theorem prover are straightforward and well-documented and the source code is made available, there's no reason why a user shouldn't extend or modify it – we hope that many readers will do something similar with the code discussed in this book. However, difficulties arise if we want to restrict the user to extensions that are logically sound, since unsoundness renders questionable the whole idea of machine-checking supposedly more fallible human proofs. Even the isolated automated theorem proving programs we've implemented in this book are often subtler than they appear, and we wouldn't be surprised to find that they contain occasional bugs rendering them incorrect. The difficulty of integrating a large body of special proof methods into a powerful interactive system without compromising soundness is considerably greater.

One influential solution to this difficulty was introduced in the Edinburgh LCF project led by Robin Milner (Gordon, Milner and Wadsworth 1979). The original Edinburgh LCF system was designed to support proofs in a logic $PP\lambda$ based on the 'Logic of Computable Functions' (Scott 1993) – hence the name LCF. But the key idea, as Gordon (1982) emphasizes, is equally applicable to more orthodox logics supporting conventional mathematics, and subsequently many 'LCF-style' proof checkers were designed using the same principles (Gordon 2000). Two key ideas underlie the LCF approach, one of which permits flexible programmability and one of which enforces logical soundness.

- The system is implemented within an interactive programming language, and the user interacts via the top-level loop of that programming language. Consequently, the user has the full power of a general-purpose programming language available to implement new proof procedures.
- A special type (say thm) of proven theorems is distinguished, such that anything of type thm must by construction have been *proved* rather than merely asserted. This is enforced by making thm an *abstract type* whose only constructors correspond to approved methods of inference.

The original LCF project introduced a completely new programming language called ML (meta language) specifically designed for implementing LCF-style provers – our own implementation language, Objective CAML, is a direct descendant of it. We will implement in OCaml a prover for first-order logic using the LCF approach, but first we need to fix a suitable set of approved inference rules.

6.3 Proof systems for first-order logic

A formal language like first-order logic is intended to be a precise version of informal mathematical notation. Given such a language, a formal proof system should formalize and systematize the permissible steps in a mathematical proof. (These are exactly the *characteristica* and *calculus* that Leibniz dreamed of.) Abstractly, we can consider a proof system as simply a relation of 'provability', defined inductively via a set of rules that we think of as permissible proof steps. We will always write $\Gamma \vdash p$ to mean 'p is provable from assumptions Γ', occasionally attaching a subscript to the 'turnstile' symbol ⊢ when we want to make the particular proof system explicit.

For purely equational reasoning, a natural proof system is the one defined by Birkhoff's rules (see Section 4.3). These nicely formalize the way one typically reasons with equations, and even though using them to prove theorems may require great subtlety, the individual rules themselves are all fairly simple. In addition, the rules are complete: $\Delta \vdash s = t$ ('$s = t$ is provable from Δ') if and only if $\Delta \models s = t$ ('$s = t$ is a logical consequence of Δ'). We would naturally wish for all these properties in a proof system for first-order logic in general.

The first proof system adequate for first-order logic was developed by Frege (1879). While this work is now regarded as crucial in the modern evolution of logic, it was little appreciated in Frege's lifetime, and similar ideas were developed partly independently by others such as Peano, Peirce and Russell. Frege's proof system actually went far beyond first-order logic, and was used to support his 'logicist' thesis that all mathematics is reducible to logic. On studying Frege's work, it became apparent to Russell how much of his philosophical analysis had already been anticipated, often in more refined form, by Frege's own formal development of arithmetic (Frege 1893). But Russell noticed that Frege's work had a serious flaw: the logical system was inconsistent, and could actually be used to prove any fact, true or false, by exploiting a logical antinomy now commonly known as *Russell's paradox* (see Section 7.1). Despite Peano's limited articulation of a formal system, Zermelo (1908), who independently discovered Russell's paradox, claimed that Peano's approach was also subject to it.

It was really Hilbert and Ackermann (1950) in the original 1928 edition of their short textbook who isolated first-order logic, presented a precise system of formal rules for it and raised the question of the completeness of those rules. Arguably, completeness was implicit in an earlier paper by Skolem (1922), but it was first proved explicitly by Gödel (1930). Subsequently, many different kinds of formal proof system for first-order logic were introduced and proved complete. We can roughly distinguish three kinds:

- Hilbert or Frege systems (Frege 1879; Hilbert and Ackermann 1950),
- natural deduction (Gentzen 1935; Prawitz 1965),
- sequent calculus (Gentzen 1935).

We will see in more detail later how Hilbert systems work, since we are going to make one the foundation of our LCF implementation. But let us now devote a few words to the other two approaches, presenting both of them in terms of *sequents*. A sequent $\Gamma \to p$, where p is a formula and Γ a set of formulas, is thought of intuitively as meaning 'if all the Γ hold then p holds', synonymous in the finite case $\Gamma = \{p_1, \ldots, p_n\}$ with $p_1 \wedge \cdots \wedge p_n \Rightarrow p$.[†]

In the modern literature, one usually sees $\Gamma \vdash p$ rather than Gentzen's original notation $\Gamma \to p$. However, we will avoid that, since we want to emphasize the equivalence between the notion of provability $\vdash$ defined below and semantic entailment $\models$. The latter has the feature that quantification over valuations is done per formula, not once over the whole assertion. For example, just as it's not the case that $P(x) \Rightarrow P(y)$ is valid, the sequent $P(x) \to P(y)$ will not be derivable, yet $P(x) \models P(y)$; see the discussion in Section 3.3. In fact, we will for simplicity focus on deducibility without hypotheses $\vdash p$, but since in Section 6.8 we consider the general case, it seems better to avoid any risk of confusion.

As the word 'natural' suggests, natural deduction systems are supposed to be closer than Hilbert systems to intuitive reasoning, in particular when reasoning from assumptions. They are based on a set of 'introduction' and 'elimination' rules for each logical connective, which introduce or eliminate the top-level connective in the conclusion. For example, the implication-introduction rule is

$$\frac{\Gamma \cup \{p\} \to q}{\Gamma \to p \Rightarrow q},$$

while the implication-elimination rule is:[‡]

$$\frac{\Gamma \to p \Rightarrow q \quad \Gamma \to p}{\Gamma \to q}.$$

The or-introduction rule has both a left and a right variant:

$$\frac{\Gamma \to p}{\Gamma \to p \vee q} \quad \frac{\Gamma \to q}{\Gamma \to p \vee q}.$$

The or-elimination rule is a little more complicated:

$$\frac{\Gamma \to p \vee q \quad \Gamma \cup \{p\} \to r \quad \Gamma \cup \{q\} \to r}{\Gamma \to r}.$$

[†] In (classical) sequent calculus, sequents are further generalized so that the right-hand side may be a set of formulas, and $\Gamma \to \Delta$ means 'if all the Γ hold then at least one of the Δ holds'. However, using single-conclusion sequents is enough to show the essential flavour of natural deduction and sequent calculus. Natural deduction systems are often presented with the hypotheses Γ implicit, but the 'trivial reformulation' (Prawitz 1971) in terms of sequents makes it easier to give a precise statement of the rules and stresses the similarities and differences with sequent calculus.

[‡] For simplicity we always assume that there is a fixed set of assumptions. In many formulations, the two theorems above the line may have different sets of assumptions Γ and Δ and the final theorem inherits $\Gamma \cup \Delta$.

Natural deduction systems are indeed relatively good for formalizing typical human proofs. However, the formulation of some rules such as or-elimination is rather messy. Instead of both introduction and elimination rules for the conclusion, Gentzen's sequent calculus systems have only introduction rules, but both left (assumption) and right (conclusion) versions. For example, the right or-introduction rules are as in natural deduction, but there is a left-introduction rule:

$$\frac{\Gamma \cup \{p\} \to r \quad \Gamma \cup \{q\} \to r}{\Gamma \cup \{p \vee q\} \to r}.$$

Similarly, the implication-introduction rule is as in natural deduction,[†] but instead of a right-elimination rule we have a left-introduction rule

$$\frac{\Gamma \to p \quad \Gamma \cup \{q\} \to r}{\Gamma \cup \{p \Rightarrow q\} \to r}.$$

In order to perform proofs in practice, it's convenient to use the *cut* rule:

$$\frac{\Gamma \cup \{p\} \to q \quad \Gamma \cup \{q\} \to r}{\Gamma \cup \{p\} \to r}.$$

However, the *Hauptsatz* (major theorem) in Gentzen (1935) shows that the cut rule is inessential: any proof involving cut can be transformed into a *cut-free* one, albeit possibly at the cost of unfeasibly large blowup.

The particular appeal of cut-free sequent calculus proofs is that all the other rules build up the formula without introducing any logical connectives not involved in the result. This allows proofs to be found in a syntax-directed way, just as with semantic tableaux. In fact, although the original motivations of Beth and Hintikka were semantic, tableaux can be considered a reformulation of sequent calculus. The approaches of several pioneers of automated theorem proving like Prawitz, Prawitz and Voghera (1960) and Wang (1960) were founded on Gentzen's proof methods, rather than semantic considerations. And the *inverse method*, developed by Maslov (1964), while closely related to resolution, was motivated by searching for proofs in sequent calculus using not the obvious top-down syntax-directed approach, but working from the bottom upwards – hence the name.[‡]

Pioneers like Frege, Peano and Russell clearly *used* their formal proof systems. But while proof in natural deduction systems does tend to be more

---

[†] For simplicity, we are ignoring here the possibility of multiple formulas on the right of the sequent.

[‡] Note that variables in the inverse method are essentially metavariables, so it is not restricted to finding cut-free proofs. Therefore, the inverse method is quite dissimilar to tableaux despite their common roots in sequent calculus.

natural than in Hilbert systems, proof theorists like Gentzen were more intent on bringing out structure and symmetry in logic than with developing practical tools. Indeed, most mathematicians do not even formalize statements in logic, let alone prove them using formal rules because it is 'too complicated in practice' (Rasiowa and Sikorski 1970). Dijkstra (1985) has remarked that 'as far as the mathematical community is concerned George Boole has lived in vain'.

6.4 LCF implementation of first-order logic

Like Frege, Russell was interested in establishing a 'logicist' thesis that all mathematics could in principle be reduced to pure logic. To this end, he derived in *Principia Mathematica* (Whitehead and Russell 1910) a body of elementary mathematical theorems by explicit formal proofs. This was an extraordinarily painstaking task, and Russell (1968) remarks that his intellect 'never quite recovered from the strain'. However, with computer assistance, the length and tedium of formal proofs need no longer be such a serious obstacle.[†] Our first priority is that the basic inference rules should be simple, so we can really feel confident in our logical foundations and their computer implementation. If this comes at the cost of lengthier formal proofs, we are undismayed, since most of the low-level proof generation will be hidden by additional layers of programming.

Usually, first-order proof systems have at least one rule or axiom scheme involving substitution, e.g. a rule allowing us to pass from a universal theorem $\vdash \forall x. P[x]$ to any substitution instance $\vdash P[t]$. But, as we saw in Section 3.4, a correct implementation of substitution is not entirely trivial. We will avoid building any such intricate code into our logical core by setting up simpler rules from which substitution is derivable (Tarski 1965; Monk 1976).[‡] We have two 'proper' rules that take theorems and produce new theorems. One is modus ponens :

$$\frac{\vdash p \Rightarrow q \quad \vdash p}{\vdash q}$$

[†] Russell reacted enthusiastically to some early experiments in automated theorem proving, remarking 'I am delighted to know that *Principia Mathematica* can now be done by machinery' (O'Leary 1991).

[‡] In other respects our setup is not unlike the system P_1 given by Church (1956), but with elimination axioms for connectives that Church uses as metalogical abbreviations.

and the other is generalization, allowing us to universally quantify a theorem over any variable:

$$\frac{\vdash p}{\vdash \forall x.\, p}\,.$$

Each 'axiom' is really a *schema* of axioms, stated for arbitrary formulas p, q and r, terms s, s_i, t, t_i and variable x. For each one, there are infinitely many specific instances:

$$\vdash \; p \Rightarrow (q \Rightarrow p),$$
$$\vdash \; (p \Rightarrow q \Rightarrow r) \Rightarrow (p \Rightarrow q) \Rightarrow (p \Rightarrow r),$$
$$\vdash \; ((p \Rightarrow \bot) \Rightarrow \bot) \Rightarrow p,$$
$$\vdash \; (\forall x.\, p \Rightarrow q) \Rightarrow (\forall x.\, p) \Rightarrow (\forall x.\, q),$$
$$\vdash \; p \Rightarrow \forall x.\, p \quad [\textbf{provided } x \notin \mathrm{FV}(p)],$$
$$\vdash \; (\exists x.\, x = t) \quad [\textbf{provided } x \notin \mathrm{FVT}(t)],$$
$$\vdash \; t = t,$$
$$\vdash \; s_1 = t_1 \Rightarrow \cdots \Rightarrow s_n = t_n \Rightarrow f(s_1, ..., s_n) = f(t_1, ..., t_n),$$
$$\vdash \; s_1 = t_1 \Rightarrow \cdots \Rightarrow s_n = t_n \Rightarrow P(s_1, ..., s_n) \Rightarrow P(t_1, ..., t_n).$$

Those would in fact suffice if we were content to express all theorems just using '$\bot$', '$\Rightarrow$' and '$\forall$'. However, this is rather unnatural, so we add additional axiom schemas that amount to 'definitions' of the other connectives. Since these are stated as equivalences, we also need to add some properties of equivalence in order to make use of those definitions:

$$\vdash \; (p \Leftrightarrow q) \Rightarrow p \Rightarrow q,$$
$$\vdash \; (p \Leftrightarrow q) \Rightarrow q \Rightarrow p,$$
$$\vdash \; (p \Rightarrow q) \Rightarrow (q \Rightarrow p) \Rightarrow (p \Leftrightarrow q),$$
$$\vdash \; \top \Leftrightarrow (\bot \Rightarrow \bot),$$
$$\vdash \; \neg p \Leftrightarrow (p \Rightarrow \bot),$$
$$\vdash \; p \wedge q \Leftrightarrow (p \Rightarrow q \Rightarrow \bot) \Rightarrow \bot,$$
$$\vdash \; p \vee q \Leftrightarrow \neg(\neg p \wedge \neg q),$$
$$\vdash \; (\exists x.\, p) \Leftrightarrow \neg(\forall x.\, \neg p).$$

At least one property of this proof system is relatively easy to check.

Theorem 6.1 *If ⊢ p then ⊨ p, i.e. anything provable using these rules is logically valid in first-order logic with equality. In other words, the inference rules are* sound.

Proof One simply needs to check that each instance of the axiom schemas is logically valid, and that the two proper inference rules when applied to logically valid formulas also produce logically valid formulas. The overall result follows by rule induction. □

In the LCF approach, abstract logical inference rules are implemented as ML functions manipulating objects of the special type `thm`. We declare a suitable OCaml *signature* to enforce the type discipline, giving names to the *primitive rules* and fixing them as the only basic operations on type `thm`:

```
module type Proofsystem =
  sig type thm
      val modusponens : thm -> thm -> thm
      val gen : string -> thm -> thm
      val axiom_addimp : fol formula -> fol formula -> thm
      val axiom_distribimp :
          fol formula -> fol formula -> fol formula -> thm
      val axiom_doubleneg : fol formula -> thm
      val axiom_allimp : string -> fol formula -> fol formula -> thm
      val axiom_impall : string -> fol formula -> thm
      val axiom_existseq : string -> term -> thm
      val axiom_eqrefl : term -> thm
      val axiom_funcong : string -> term list -> term list -> thm
      val axiom_predcong : string -> term list -> term list -> thm
      val axiom_iffimp1 : fol formula -> fol formula -> thm
      val axiom_iffimp2 : fol formula -> fol formula -> thm
      val axiom_impiff : fol formula -> fol formula -> thm
      val axiom_true : thm
      val axiom_not : fol formula -> thm
      val axiom_and : fol formula -> fol formula -> thm
      val axiom_or : fol formula -> fol formula -> thm
      val axiom_exists : string -> fol formula -> thm
      val concl : thm -> fol formula
  end;;
```

The functions `modusponens` and `gen` implement proper inference rules, so they take theorems as arguments and produce new theorems. The functions implementing axiom schemas also mostly take arguments, but only to indicate the desired instance of the schema. Finally, the `concl` ('conclusion') function maps a theorem back to the formula it proves. This has no logical role, but we often want to 'look inside' a theorem, for example to decide on what kind of inference rules to apply to it. Of course, we *don't* allow the reverse operation mapping any formula to a corresponding theorem, since that would defeat the whole purpose of using a limited set of rules.

A guiding principle in the choice of primitive rules is that they should admit a simple and transparent implementation. The only non-trivial part involves checking the side-conditions $x \notin \mathrm{FV}(p)$ and $x \notin \mathrm{FVT}(t)$. Although these are hardly difficult, the most straightforward implementations presuppose some set operations, which we choose to sidestep by coding the tests directly. The following function decides whether a term s occurs as a subterm of another term t; we allow any term s, not just a variable, though this generality is not exploited:

```
let rec occurs_in s t =
  s = t or
  match t with
    Var y -> false
  | Fn(f,args) -> exists (occurs_in s) args;;
```

Now we define a similar function for deciding whether a term t occurs *free* in a formula fm. When t is a variable Var x, this means the same as $x \in \mathrm{FV}(\mathrm{fm})$, but it is expressed more directly. The free_in function actually allows an arbitrary term t, not just a variable, extending the concept in a natural way to say that there is a subterm t of fm *none* of whose variables are in the scope of a quantifier. As it happens, we will only use this when t is a variable, but the extra generality does not make the code any longer.

```
let rec free_in t fm =
  match fm with
    False| True -> false
  | Atom(R(p,args)) -> exists (occurs_in t) args
  | Not(p) -> free_in t p
  | And(p,q)|Or(p,q)|Imp(p,q)|Iff(p,q) -> free_in t p or free_in t q
  | Forall(y,p)|Exists(y,p) -> not(occurs_in (Var y) t) & free_in t p;;
```

Besides being more direct and more general, this function can be significantly more efficient in some cases than first computing the free-variable set then testing membership. For example, if we ask whether x is free in $P(x) \wedge Q$ or in $\forall x. Q$, we never need to examine Q but can return 'true' and 'false' respectively by looking at the other part of the formula.

Using these ingredients, we can now implement the proof system itself. While this chunk of code might not look particularly beautiful, a side-by-side examination shows that it is a direct transliteration of the logical rules. These few dozen lines, together with occurs_in and free_in and a few auxiliary functions like exists and itlist2, constitute the *entire* logical core of our theorem prover. Provided we got this right, we can be confident that anything of type **thm** we derive later really has been proved.[†]

```
module Proven : Proofsystem =
  struct
    type thm = fol formula
    let modusponens pq p =
      match pq with
        Imp(p',q) when p = p' -> q
      | _ -> failwith "modusponens"
    let gen x p = Forall(x,p)
    let axiom_addimp p q = Imp(p,Imp(q,p))
    let axiom_distribimp p q r =
      Imp(Imp(p,Imp(q,r)),Imp(Imp(p,q),Imp(p,r)))
    let axiom_doubleneg p = Imp(Imp(Imp(p,False),False),p)
    let axiom_allimp x p q =
      Imp(Forall(x,Imp(p,q)),Imp(Forall(x,p),Forall(x,q)))
    let axiom_impall x p =
      if not (free_in (Var x) p) then Imp(p,Forall(x,p))
      else failwith "axiom_impall: variable free in formula"
    let axiom_existseq x t =
      if not (occurs_in (Var x) t) then Exists(x,mk_eq (Var x) t)
      else failwith "axiom_existseq: variable free in term"
    let axiom_eqrefl t = mk_eq t t
    let axiom_funcong f lefts rights =
        itlist2 (fun s t p -> Imp(mk_eq s t,p)) lefts rights
                (mk_eq (Fn(f,lefts)) (Fn(f,rights)))
    let axiom_predcong p lefts rights =
        itlist2 (fun s t p -> Imp(mk_eq s t,p)) lefts rights
                (Imp(Atom(R(p,lefts)),Atom(R(p,rights))))
    let axiom_iffimp1 p q = Imp(Iff(p,q),Imp(p,q))
    let axiom_iffimp2 p q = Imp(Iff(p,q),Imp(q,p))
    let axiom_impiff p q = Imp(Imp(p,q),Imp(Imp(q,p),Iff(p,q)))
    let axiom_true = Iff(True,Imp(False,False))
    let axiom_not p = Iff(Not p,Imp(p,False))
    let axiom_and p q = Iff(And(p,q),Imp(Imp(p,Imp(q,False)),False))
    let axiom_or p q = Iff(Or(p,q),Not(And(Not(p),Not(q))))
    let axiom_exists x p = Iff(Exists(x,p),Not(Forall(x,Not p)))
    let concl c = c
  end;;
```

To proceed further, we'll open the module and set up a printer as usual:

[†] Bugs in derived rules may indeed lead to the deduction of the *wrong* theorem, i.e. not the one that was intended. But they cannot lead to an *invalid* one. And, needless to say, we are tacitly assuming the correctness of the OCaml type system, OCaml implementation, operating system, and underlying hardware! In fact, by subverting the OCaml type system or using mutability of strings, it is possible to derive false results even in our LCF prover, but we restrict ourselves to 'normal' functional programming.

```
include Proven;;

let print_thm th =
  open_box 0;
  print_string "|-"; print_space();
  open_box 0; print_formula print_atom 0 (concl th); close_box();
  close_box();;

#install_printer print_thm;;
```

6.5 Propositional derived rules

Our proof system with its strange-looking menagerie of axioms will turn out to be complete for first-order logic, while being technically simple (the code implementing it is short). But, in stark contrast to natural deduction, explicit proofs in the system tend to be very *un*-natural. For example, consider proving the apparent triviality $\vdash p \Rightarrow p$ for some arbitrary p. Readers who haven't seen something similar before will probably find it a bit of a puzzle. Either by a flash of inspiration or with computer assistance (see Exercise 6.5) one can arrive at the following:

$1 \vdash (p \Rightarrow (p \Rightarrow p) \Rightarrow p) \Rightarrow (p \Rightarrow (p \Rightarrow p)) \Rightarrow (p \Rightarrow p)$ [second axiom],
$2 \vdash p \Rightarrow (p \Rightarrow p) \Rightarrow p$ [first axiom],
$3 \vdash (p \Rightarrow (p \Rightarrow p)) \Rightarrow (p \Rightarrow p)$ [modus ponens, 1 and 2],
$4 \vdash p \Rightarrow (p \Rightarrow p)$ [first axiom],
$5 \vdash p \Rightarrow p$ [modus ponens, 3 and 4].

The above sequence of steps can be considered a proof of the following metatheorem *about* our deductive system: for any formula p we have $\vdash p \Rightarrow p$, each instance of which for a particular p is a formal theorem *in* the system. We give the proof a computational twist in our LCF implementation, by implementing an OCaml function taking a formula p as its argument and proving the corresponding $\vdash p \Rightarrow p$:

```
let imp_refl p =
  modusponens (modusponens (axiom_distribimp p (Imp(p,p)) p)
                           (axiom_addimp p (Imp(p,p))))
              (axiom_addimp p p);;
```

We can thereafter use `imp_refl` as another inference rule. It is a *derived* one, not a primitive one like `modusponens`, but works equally well:

```
# imp_refl <<r>>;;
- : thm = |- r ==> r
# imp_refl <<exists x y. ~(x = y)>>;;
- : thm = |- (exists x y. ~x = y) ==> (exists x y. ~x = y)
```

As in standard logic texts – Mendelson (1987) and Andrews (1986) are typical – we will build up a sequence of more interesting metatheorems, using earlier metatheorems as lemmas. But we'll always have an explicitly computational implementation of the metatheorems, using earlier ones as subcomponents. For example, consider the metatheorem that if $p \Rightarrow p \Rightarrow q$ is provable then so is $p \Rightarrow q$. We can represent this as an inference rule:

$$\frac{\vdash p \Rightarrow p \Rightarrow q}{\vdash p \Rightarrow q}$$

and prove it appealing to $\vdash p \Rightarrow p$ as a lemma:

$1 \vdash (p \Rightarrow p \Rightarrow q) \Rightarrow (p \Rightarrow p) \Rightarrow (p \Rightarrow q)$ [second axiom],
$2 \vdash p \Rightarrow p \Rightarrow q$ [assumed],
$3 \vdash (p \Rightarrow p) \Rightarrow (p \Rightarrow q)$ [modus ponens, 1 and 2],
$4 \vdash p \Rightarrow p$ [from the lemma],
$5 \vdash p \Rightarrow q$ [modus ponens, 3 and 4].

This proof can be expressed as a derived inference rule in OCaml, using `imp_refl` as a subcomponent:

```
let imp_unduplicate th =
  let p,pq = dest_imp(concl th) in
  let q = consequent pq in
  modusponens (modusponens (axiom_distribimp p p q) th) (imp_refl p);;
```

Elementary derived rules

The first three axioms and the modus ponens inference rule suffice for all propositional reasoning, provided one is prepared to express all formulas in terms of $\{\Rightarrow, \bot\}$. We will often prove formulas by mapping them into this subset and dealing with them there. So instead of negation $\neg p$ we will often use the logically equivalent $p \Rightarrow \bot$, and the following variants of the usual syntax functions handle this form:

```
let negatef fm =
  match fm with
    Imp(p,False) -> p
  | p -> Imp(p,False);;

let negativef fm = match fm with Imp(p,False) -> true | _ -> false;;
```

Our next derived rule is a rather simple one: given a theorem $\vdash q$ and a formula p, it produces the theorem $\vdash p \Rightarrow q$, i.e. adds an additional antecedent to something already proved. This might not appear enormously useful, but it comes in handy later on. The rule works by forming the axiom instance $\vdash q \Rightarrow p \Rightarrow q$ and then performing modus ponens with that and the input theorem $\vdash q$ to obtain $\vdash p \Rightarrow q$.

```
let add_assum p th = modusponens (axiom_addimp (concl th) p) th;;
```

This is used as a component in a slightly more interesting rule which, given a theorem $\vdash q \Rightarrow r$ and a formula p returns the theorem $\vdash (p \Rightarrow q) \Rightarrow (p \Rightarrow r)$. It does it by using **add_assum** to add a new hypothesis p to the input theorem to give $\vdash p \Rightarrow q \Rightarrow r$. Modus ponens is then performed with this and the axiom instance $\vdash (p \Rightarrow q \Rightarrow r) \Rightarrow (p \Rightarrow q) \Rightarrow (p \Rightarrow r)$ to obtain the desired theorem.

```
let imp_add_assum p th =
  let (q,r) = dest_imp(concl th) in
  modusponens (axiom_distribimp p q r) (add_assum p th);;
```

We will leave the reader to understand the proofs underlying many of the rules that follow, letting the code speak for itself.[†] One way is to run through the code line-by-line in an OCaml session picking some arbitrary formulas as inputs.[‡] Alternatively, one can simply sketch out the steps on paper. The next rule, much used in what follows, is for transitivity of implication: from $\vdash p \Rightarrow q$ and $\vdash q \Rightarrow r$ obtain $\vdash p \Rightarrow r$.

```
let imp_trans th1 th2 =
  let p = antecedent(concl th1) in
  modusponens (imp_add_assum p th2) th1;;
```

We can use this to define other simple rules for implication, such as passing from $\vdash p \Rightarrow r$ to $\vdash p \Rightarrow q \Rightarrow r$:

[†] Not much will be lost by ignoring the details; the proofs are mainly technical puzzles without any deeper significance.

[‡] This is trickier for rules that take theorems as inputs, since we can't create any desired theorem, by design. One could temporarily add an **axiom** function to the primitive basis to create arbitrary theorems.

```
let imp_insert q th =
  let (p,r) = dest_imp(concl th) in
  imp_trans th (axiom_addimp r q);;
```

and from $\vdash p \Rightarrow q \Rightarrow r$ to $\vdash q \Rightarrow p \Rightarrow r$:

```
let imp_swap th =
  let p,qr = dest_imp(concl th) in
  let q,r = dest_imp qr in
  imp_trans (axiom_addimp q p)
            (modusponens (axiom_distribimp p q r) th);;
```

The following is a derived axiom schema (derived rule with no theorem arguments) producing $\vdash (q \Rightarrow r) \Rightarrow (p \Rightarrow q) \Rightarrow (p \Rightarrow r)$:

```
let imp_trans_th p q r =
   imp_trans (axiom_addimp (Imp(q,r)) p)
            (axiom_distribimp p q r);;
```

If $\vdash p \Rightarrow q$ then $\vdash (q \Rightarrow r) \Rightarrow (p \Rightarrow r)$:

```
let imp_add_concl r th =
  let (p,q) = dest_imp(concl th) in
  modusponens (imp_swap(imp_trans_th p q r)) th;;
```

$\vdash (p \Rightarrow q \Rightarrow r) \Rightarrow (q \Rightarrow p \Rightarrow r)$:

```
let imp_swap_th p q r =
  imp_trans (axiom_distribimp p q r)
            (imp_add_concl (Imp(p,r)) (axiom_addimp q p));;
```

and if $\vdash (p \Rightarrow q \Rightarrow r) \Rightarrow (s \Rightarrow t \Rightarrow u)$ then $\vdash (q \Rightarrow p \Rightarrow r) \Rightarrow (t \Rightarrow s \Rightarrow u)$:

```
let imp_swap2 th =
  match concl th with
    Imp(Imp(p,Imp(q,r)),Imp(s,Imp(t,u))) ->
        imp_trans (imp_swap_th q p r) (imp_trans th (imp_swap_th s t u))
  | _ -> failwith "imp_swap2";;
```

We can also easily derive a 'right' version of modus ponens, passing from $\vdash p \Rightarrow q \Rightarrow r$ and $\vdash p \Rightarrow q$ to $\vdash p \Rightarrow r$. (This could be obtained more efficiently using `axiom_distribimp`, but the code is slightly longer.)

```
let right_mp ith th =
  imp_unduplicate(imp_trans th (imp_swap ith));;
```

That gives us enough basic properties of implication to make further progress. However, since we need to use the axioms of the form $p \otimes q \Leftrightarrow \cdots$

for expressing propositional connectives $\otimes$ in terms of others, it's convenient to define operations that map $\vdash p \Leftrightarrow q$ to $\vdash p \Rightarrow q$ and to $\vdash q \Rightarrow p$:

```
let iff_imp1 th =
  let (p,q) = dest_iff(concl th) in
  modusponens (axiom_iffimp1 p q) th;;

let iff_imp2 th =
  let (p,q) = dest_iff(concl th) in
  modusponens (axiom_iffimp2 p q) th;;
```

and conversely to map $\vdash p \Rightarrow q$ and $\vdash q \Rightarrow p$ together to $\vdash p \Leftrightarrow q$:

```
let imp_antisym th1 th2 =
  let (p,q) = dest_imp(concl th1) in
  modusponens (modusponens (axiom_impiff p q) th1) th2;;
```

Now we consider some rules for dealing with falsity and 'negation' (in the sense of $p \Rightarrow \bot$). We often want to eliminate double 'negation' from the consequent of an implication, passing from $\vdash p \Rightarrow (q \Rightarrow \bot) \Rightarrow \bot$ to $\vdash p \Rightarrow q$:

```
let right_doubleneg th =
  match concl th with
    Imp(_,Imp(Imp(p,False),False)) -> imp_trans th (axiom_doubleneg p)
  | _ -> failwith "right_doubleneg";;
```

An immediate application is the classic rule $\vdash \bot \Rightarrow p$, traditionally called *ex falso quodlibet* ('from falsity, anything goes'):

```
let ex_falso p = right_doubleneg(axiom_addimp False (Imp(p,False)));;
```

Also useful is a variant of `imp_trans` that copes with an extra level of implication in the first theorem, from $\vdash p \Rightarrow q \Rightarrow r$ and $\vdash r \Rightarrow s$ to $\vdash p \Rightarrow q \Rightarrow s$:

```
let imp_trans2 th1 th2 =
  let Imp(p,Imp(q,r)) = concl th1 and Imp(r',s) = concl th2 in
  let th = imp_add_assum p (modusponens (imp_trans_th q r s) th2) in
  modusponens th th1;;
```

A generalization in a different direction allows us to map a list of theorems $\vdash p \Rightarrow q_i$ for $1 \leq i \leq n$ and another theorem $\vdash q_1 \Rightarrow \cdots \Rightarrow q_n \Rightarrow r$ to a result $\vdash p \Rightarrow r$:

```
let imp_trans_chain ths th =
  itlist (fun a b -> imp_unduplicate (imp_trans a (imp_swap b)))
         (rev(tl ths)) (imp_trans (hd ths) th);;
```

Finally, a couple more rules for implication will be useful later for technical reasons, one for deriving $\vdash (q \Rightarrow \bot) \Rightarrow p \Rightarrow (p \Rightarrow q) \Rightarrow \bot$:

```
let imp_truefalse p q =
  imp_trans (imp_trans_th p q False) (imp_swap_th (Imp(p,q)) p False);;
```

and the other producing a kind of monotonicity theorem for implication of the form $\vdash (p' \Rightarrow p) \Rightarrow (q \Rightarrow q') \Rightarrow (p \Rightarrow q) \Rightarrow p' \Rightarrow q'$:

```
let imp_mono_th p p' q q' =
  let th1 = imp_trans_th (Imp(p,q)) (Imp(p',q)) (Imp(p',q'))
  and th2 = imp_trans_th p' q q'
  and th3 = imp_swap(imp_trans_th p' p q) in
  imp_trans th3 (imp_swap(imp_trans th2 th1));;
```

Derived connectives

Most derived inference rules so far have involved the 'primitive' logical constants implication and falsity. But we can equally well define derived rules to encapsulate properties of other connectives. The simplest example is the theorem $\vdash \top$:

```
let truth = modusponens (iff_imp2 axiom_true) (imp_refl False);;
```

For negation, contraposition passes from $\vdash p \Rightarrow q$ to $\vdash \neg q \Rightarrow \neg p$:

```
let contrapos th =
  let p,q = dest_imp(concl th) in
  imp_trans (imp_trans (iff_imp1(axiom_not q)) (imp_add_concl False th))
            (iff_imp2(axiom_not p));;
```

Some rules for conjunction will also be useful later. There are several important features of this connective, for instance that $\vdash p \wedge q \Rightarrow p$:

```
let and_left p q =
  let th1 = imp_add_assum p (axiom_addimp False q) in
  let th2 = right_doubleneg(imp_add_concl False th1) in
  imp_trans (iff_imp1(axiom_and p q)) th2;;
```

and that symmetrically $\vdash p \wedge q \Rightarrow q$:

```
let and_right p q =
  let th1 = axiom_addimp (Imp(q,False)) p in
  let th2 = right_doubleneg(imp_add_concl False th1) in
  imp_trans (iff_imp1(axiom_and p q)) th2;;
```

More generally, we can get the list of theorems $p_1 \wedge \cdots \wedge p_n \Rightarrow p_i$ for $1 \le i \le n$:

```
let rec conjths fm =
  try let p,q = dest_and fm in
      (and_left p q)::map (imp_trans (and_right p q)) (conjths q)
  with Failure _ -> [imp_refl fm];;
```

Conversely, p and q together imply $p \wedge q$, i.e. $\vdash p \Rightarrow q \Rightarrow p \wedge q$:

```
let and_pair p q =
  let th1 = iff_imp2(axiom_and p q)
  and th2 = imp_swap_th (Imp(p,Imp(q,False))) q False in
  let th3 = imp_add_assum p (imp_trans2 th2 th1) in
  modusponens th3 (imp_swap (imp_refl (Imp(p,Imp(q,False)))));;
```

Also useful are two rules to 'shunt' between conjunctive antecedents and iterated implication, passing from $\vdash p \wedge q \Rightarrow r$ to $\vdash p \Rightarrow q \Rightarrow r$:

```
let shunt th =
  let p,q = dest_and(antecedent(concl th)) in
  modusponens (itlist imp_add_assum [p;q] th) (and_pair p q);;
```

and from $\vdash p \Rightarrow q \Rightarrow r$ to $\vdash p \wedge q \Rightarrow r$:

```
let unshunt th =
  let p,qr = dest_imp(concl th) in
  let q,r = dest_imp qr in
  imp_trans_chain [and_left p q; and_right p q] th;;
```

6.6 Proving tautologies by inference

The derived rules defined so far can make certain propositional steps easier to perform by inference. Now we will define a more ambitious rule that can automatically prove any propositional tautology. Unlike the previous derived rules, this will require non-trivial control flow. Our plan is to implement a version of the tableau procedure considered in Section 3.10, systematically modified to use inference instead of ad hoc formula manipulation. That is, rather than simply *asserting* that lists of formulas $p_1, \ldots, p_n$ and literals $l_1, \ldots, l_m$ lead to a contradiction, the main function will actually *prove* the following theorem:

$$\vdash p_1 \Rightarrow \cdots \Rightarrow p_n \Rightarrow l_1 \Rightarrow \cdots \Rightarrow l_m \Rightarrow \perp.$$

The pattern of recursion, breaking apart the first formula p_1 and making recursive calls for the new problem(s), is very close to the implementation of `tableau`, and it is instructive to look at their code side-by-side.

The principal difference is that we need to justify all steps in terms of inference rules. Other notable differences are:

- the core inference steps are presented in terms of implication and falsity, with other propositional connectives immediately eliminated;
- we do not handle quantifiers and unification, only propositional structure.

Eliminating defined connectives

Our first order of business is the elimination of connectives other than falsity and implication. Most of the other connectives are defined by axioms of the form $\vdash p \otimes q \Leftrightarrow \cdots$. The exception is '$\Leftrightarrow$' itself, so for uniformity we implement a derived rule for $\vdash (p \Leftrightarrow q) \Leftrightarrow (p \Rightarrow q) \wedge (q \Rightarrow p)$:

```
let iff_def p q =
  let th = and_pair (Imp(p,q)) (Imp(q,p))
  and th1 = [axiom_iffimp1 p q; axiom_iffimp2 p q] in
  imp_antisym (imp_trans_chain th1 th) (unshunt (axiom_impiff p q));;
```

Now we can produce an equivalent for any formula built with a 'defined' connective at the top level:

```
let expand_connective fm =
  match fm with
    True -> axiom_true
  | Not p -> axiom_not p
  | And(p,q) -> axiom_and p q
  | Or(p,q) -> axiom_or p q
  | Iff(p,q) -> iff_def p q
  | Exists(x,p) -> axiom_exists x p
  | _ -> failwith "expand_connective";;
```

The formula we are considering will always be a hypothesis in a refutation, so we want to prove that it implies its expanded form. On the other hand, the formula may be positive, in which case we want to produce $\vdash p \otimes q \Rightarrow \cdots$, or negative, in which case we want $\vdash (p \otimes q \Rightarrow \bot) \Rightarrow (\cdots) \Rightarrow \bot$:

```
let eliminate_connective fm =
  if not(negativef fm) then iff_imp1(expand_connective fm)
  else imp_add_concl False (iff_imp2(expand_connective(negatef fm)));;
```

Simulating tableau steps

So now we just need to implement the key steps underlying tableaux as inference rules. The first one corresponds to conjunctive splitting: we can obtain a contradiction from $p \wedge q$, or in our context $(p \Rightarrow -q) \Rightarrow \bot$, by obtaining one from p and q separately. The following inference rule gives a list containing the two theorems $\vdash ((p \Rightarrow q) \Rightarrow \bot) \Rightarrow p$ and $\vdash ((p \Rightarrow q) \Rightarrow \bot) \Rightarrow (q \Rightarrow \bot)$:

```
let imp_false_conseqs p q =
  [right_doubleneg(imp_add_concl False (imp_add_assum p (ex_falso q)));
   imp_add_concl False (imp_insert p (imp_refl q))];;
```

which we can use to pass from $\vdash p \Rightarrow (q \Rightarrow \bot) \Rightarrow r$ to $\vdash ((p \Rightarrow q) \Rightarrow \bot) \Rightarrow r$:

```
let imp_false_rule th =
  let p,r = dest_imp (concl th) in
  imp_trans_chain (imp_false_conseqs p (funpow 2 antecedent r)) th;;
```

The dual step is disjunctive splitting: if we can obtain a contradiction from p separately and also from q separately, then we can obtain one from $p \lor q$, in our context $-p \Rightarrow q$. So we need to pass from $\vdash (p \Rightarrow \bot) \Rightarrow r$ and $\vdash q \Rightarrow r$ to $\vdash (p \Rightarrow q) \Rightarrow r$:

```
let imp_true_rule th1 th2 =
  let p = funpow 2 antecedent (concl th1) and q = antecedent(concl th2)
  and th3 = right_doubleneg(imp_add_concl False th1)
  and th4 = imp_add_concl False th2 in
  let th5 = imp_swap(imp_truefalse p q) in
  let th6 = imp_add_concl False (imp_trans_chain [th3; th4] th5)
  and th7 = imp_swap(imp_refl(Imp(Imp(p,q),False))) in
  right_doubleneg(imp_trans th7 th6);;
```

Ultimately, we will need to obtain a contradiction from two complementary literals; in fact the following will allow us to deduce $\vdash p \Rightarrow -p \Rightarrow q$ for any q:

```
let imp_contr p q =
  if negativef p then imp_add_assum (negatef p) (ex_falso q)
  else imp_swap (imp_add_assum p (ex_falso q));;
```

In the original tableau procedure, we add a literal to the `lits` list when there is currently no complementary literal. To maintain the correspondence between those lists and the iterated implications in the present version, we need to be able to justify the same step by inference: if we can derive a contradiction from a 'shuffled' implication, we can also derive one from the unshuffled version. To get a smoother recursion, we first implement a rule producing the implicational theorem $\vdash (p_0 \Rightarrow p_1 \Rightarrow \cdots \Rightarrow p_{n-1} \Rightarrow p_n \Rightarrow q) \Rightarrow (p_n \Rightarrow p_0 \Rightarrow p_1 \Rightarrow \cdots \Rightarrow p_{n-1} \Rightarrow q)$, where q may itself be an iterated implication:

```
let rec imp_front_th n fm =
  if n = 0 then imp_refl fm else
  let p,qr = dest_imp fm in
  let th1 = imp_add_assum p (imp_front_th (n - 1) qr) in
  let q',r' = dest_imp(funpow 2 consequent(concl th1)) in
  imp_trans th1 (imp_swap_th p q' r');;
```

Now to pull the nth component of an iterated implication to the front:

```
let imp_front n th = modusponens (imp_front_th n (concl th)) th;;
```

Tableaux by inference

All the pieces are now in place for an inferential version of tableaux. The basic pattern of recursion is the same as in the plain version, with lists of formulas (`fms`) and literals (`lits`), but the function returns the canonical theorem rather than just quietly succeeding. So we usually need to perform inference rules to get us back to a solution of the initial problem from the solutions to modified problem(s) resulting from recursive calls. We will go through the cases in the following code one at a time.

```
let rec lcfptab fms lits =
  match fms with
    False::fl ->
        ex_falso (itlist mk_imp (fl @ lits) False)
  | (Imp(p,q) as fm)::fl when p = q ->
        add_assum fm (lcfptab fl lits)
  | Imp(Imp(p,q),False)::fl ->
        imp_false_rule(lcfptab (p::Imp(q,False)::fl) lits)
  | Imp(p,q)::fl when q <> False ->
        imp_true_rule (lcfptab (Imp(p,False)::fl) lits)
                      (lcfptab (q::fl) lits)
  | (Atom(_)|Forall(_,_)|Imp((Atom(_)|Forall(_,_)),False) as p)::fl ->
        if mem (negatef p) lits then
            let l1,l2 = chop_list (index (negatef p) lits) lits in
            let th = imp_contr p (itlist mk_imp (tl l2) False) in
            itlist imp_insert (fl @ l1) th
        else imp_front (length fl) (lcfptab fl (p::lits))
  | fm::fl ->
        let th = eliminate_connective fm in
        imp_trans th (lcfptab (consequent(concl th)::fl) lits)
  | _ -> failwith "lcfptab: no contradiction";;
```

The first two cases are needed because using the minimalist set of connectives $\{\bot, \Rightarrow\}$ we can end up with either $\bot$ or $\bot \Rightarrow \bot$ as an assumption.

In the former case, we can obtain a contradiction directly, but we must remember to add all the assumptions to maintain the pattern. The latter assumption is thrown away in the recursive call and put back into the final theorem afterwards. Actually we ignore *all* implications $p \Rightarrow p$ since no such implication can contribute to finding a contradiction.

The next couple of cases implement conjunctive and disjunctive splitting. Thanks to the work we did above embodying these steps in special inference procedures, the implementation is straightforward. We just need a guard to make sure that disjunctive splitting of $p \Rightarrow q$ doesn't break up implications $p \Rightarrow \perp$ into subgoals $p \Rightarrow \perp$ and $\perp$, since then we'd get into an infinite loop; these are always dealt with by other cases.

The fifth case applies to literals, and first attempts to find a complementary literal in the list. If it succeeds, it uses `imp_contr` to construct an implication, remembering to add all the additional assumptions to maintain the pattern using `imp_insert` etc. Otherwise the literal is shuffled back in the list and a recursive call made; afterwards `imp_front` is used to bring it back to the front if the whole function terminates successfully.

The sixth case deals with non-primitive logical connectives, and makes a recursive call after expanding them, and the last case applies when nothing else works and therefore no refutation will be achieved.

Proving tautologies

Now to prove that p is a tautology, we apply the above procedure to $p \Rightarrow \perp$ to obtain a theorem $\vdash (p \Rightarrow \perp) \Rightarrow \perp$ and then apply double-negation elimination to get $\vdash p$:

```
let lcftaut p =
  modusponens (axiom_doubleneg p) (lcfptab [negatef p] []);;
```

for example:

```
# lcftaut <<(p ==> q) \/ (q ==> p)>>;;
- : thm = |- (p ==> q) \/ (q ==> p)
# lcftaut <<p /\ q <=> ((p <=> q) <=> p \/ q)>>;;
- : thm = |- p /\ q <=> (p <=> q) <=> p \/ q
# lcftaut <<((p <=> q) <=> r) <=> (p <=> (q <=> r))>>;;
- : thm = |- ((p <=> q) <=> r) <=> p <=> q <=> r
```

Performing inference certainly makes things complicated and markedly slower – the last example above takes an appreciable fraction of a second. However, it is reassuring to reflect that we can be more confident in any results we get from this procedure.

6.7 First-order derived rules

One of the most fundamentally useful inference steps in first-order logic is 'specialization', passing from $\vdash \forall x.\, P[x]$ to $\vdash P[t]$. In most presentations of first-order logic, it's taken as a primitive inference rule; we must derive it. The key idea (due to Tarski) underlying our axiomatization is that we can deduce $\vdash x = t \Rightarrow P[x] \Rightarrow P[t]$ using congruence rules, and so proceed in a few more basic steps to

$$\vdash (\forall x.\, P[x]) \Rightarrow (\forall x.\, x = t \Rightarrow P[t])$$

and hence to

$$\vdash (\forall x.\, P[x]) \Rightarrow (\exists x.\, x = t) \Rightarrow P[t].$$

Now using the basic axiom $\vdash \exists x.\, x = t$ we get the required result:

$$\vdash (\forall x.\, P[x]) \Rightarrow P[t].$$

We will see shortly that this is something of an oversimplification, but it shows the basic idea. It also makes clear that the rules for manipulating equality are very important, and we now turn to these.

Basic equality properties

We already have an axiom `axiom_eqrefl` for reflexivity of equality. In combination with that, others properties of equality follow from `axiom_predcong`, which is applicable to equality as well as other predicates. Symmetry is implemented as a rule `eq_sym` that, given terms s and t, yields a theorem $\vdash s = t \Rightarrow t = s$:

```
let eq_sym s t =
  let rth = axiom_eqrefl s in
  funpow 2 (fun th -> modusponens (imp_swap th) rth)
           (axiom_predcong "=" [s; s] [t; s]);;
```

and the following implements transitivity, returning $\vdash s = t \Rightarrow t = u \Rightarrow s = u$ given terms s, t and u:

```
let eq_trans s t u =
  let th1 = axiom_predcong "=" [t; u] [s; u] in
  let th2 = modusponens (imp_swap th1) (axiom_eqrefl u) in
  imp_trans (eq_sym s t) th2;;
```

We also want to be able to derive theorems of the form $\vdash s = t \Rightarrow u[s] = u[t]$. Such theorems can be built up recursively by composing the basic congruence rules. The following function takes the terms `s` and `t` as well as the two terms `stm` and `ttm` to be proven equal by replacing `s` by `t` inside `stm` as necessary.

```
let rec icongruence s t stm ttm =
  if stm = ttm then add_assum (mk_eq s t) (axiom_eqrefl stm)
  else if stm = s & ttm = t then imp_refl (mk_eq s t) else
  match (stm,ttm) with
    (Fn(fs,sa),Fn(ft,ta)) when fs = ft & length sa = length ta ->
        let ths = map2 (icongruence s t) sa ta in
        let ts = map (consequent ** concl) ths in
        imp_trans_chain ths (axiom_funcong fs (map lhs ts) (map rhs ts))
  | _ -> failwith "icongruence: not congruent";;
```

Our formulation allows replacement to be applied only to *some* of the possible instances of `s`, for example:

```
# icongruence <<|s|>> <<|t|>> <<|f(s,g(s,t,s),u,h(h(s)))|>>
                                  <<|f(s,g(t,t,s),u,h(h(t)))|>>;;
- : thm =
|- s = t ==> f(s,g(s,t,s),u,h(h(s))) = f(s,g(t,t,s),u,h(h(t)))
```

More quantifier rules

In order to realize the implementation of specialization sketched above, we need some more rules for the quantifiers. The following is a variant of `axiom_allimp` for the case when x does not appear free in the antecedent p, giving $\vdash (\forall x.\, p \Rightarrow Q[x]) \Rightarrow p \Rightarrow (\forall x.\, Q[x])$:

```
let gen_right_th x p q =
  imp_swap(imp_trans (axiom_impall x p) (imp_swap(axiom_allimp x p q)));;
```

Now `axiom_allimp` is used to map $\vdash P[x] \Rightarrow Q[x]$ to $\vdash (\forall x.\, P[x]) \Rightarrow (\forall x.\, Q[x])$:

```
let genimp x th =
  let p,q = dest_imp(concl th) in
  modusponens (axiom_allimp x p q) (gen x th);;
```

and similarly using the variant `gen_right_th` we obtain a version applicable only when x is not free in p, mapping $\vdash p \Rightarrow Q[x]$ to $\vdash p \Rightarrow (\forall x.\, Q[x])$:

```
let gen_right x th =
  let p,q = dest_imp(concl th) in
  modusponens (gen_right_th x p q) (gen x th);;
```

The following derivation of $\vdash (\forall x.\, P[x] \Rightarrow q) \Rightarrow (\exists x.\, P[x]) \Rightarrow q$ is a bit more complicated, but is obtained from `gen_right_th` by systematic contraposition and expansion of the definition of the existential quantifier:

```
let exists_left_th x p q =
  let p' = Imp(p,False) and q' = Imp(q,False) in
  let th1 = genimp x (imp_swap(imp_trans_th p q False)) in
  let th2 = imp_trans th1 (gen_right_th x q' p') in
  let th3 = imp_swap(imp_trans_th q' (Forall(x,p'))) False) in
  let th4 = imp_trans2 (imp_trans th2 th3) (axiom_doubleneg q) in
  let th5 = imp_add_concl False (genimp x (iff_imp2 (axiom_not p))) in
  let th6 = imp_trans (iff_imp1 (axiom_not (Forall(x,Not p)))) th5 in
  let th7 = imp_trans (iff_imp1(axiom_exists x p)) th6 in
  imp_swap(imp_trans th7 (imp_swap th4));;
```

and the 'rule' form maps $\vdash P[x] \Rightarrow q$ where $x \notin \mathrm{FV}(q)$ to $\vdash (\exists x.\, P[x]) \Rightarrow q$

```
let exists_left x th =
  let p,q = dest_imp(concl th) in
  modusponens (exists_left_th x p q) (gen x th);;
```

Congruence rules for formulas

We can now realize our plan for specialization: given a theorem $\vdash x = t \Rightarrow P[x] \Rightarrow P[t]$ with $x \notin \mathrm{FVT}(t)$ we can derive $\vdash (\forall x.\, P[x]) \Rightarrow P[t]$. In fact, the following inference rule is slightly more general, taking $\vdash x = t \Rightarrow P[x] \Rightarrow q$ for $x \notin \mathrm{FVT}(t)$ and $x \notin \mathrm{FV}(q)$ and yielding $\vdash (\forall x.\, P[x]) \Rightarrow q$:

```
let subspec th =
  match concl th with
    Imp(Atom(R("=",[Var x;t])) as e,Imp(p,q)) ->
        let th1 = imp_trans (genimp x (imp_swap th))
                            (exists_left_th x e q) in
        modusponens (imp_swap th1) (axiom_existseq x t)
  | _ -> failwith "subspec: wrong sort of theorem";;
```

However, we still need to obtain that theorem $\vdash x = t \Rightarrow P[x] \Rightarrow P[t]$ in the first place, by extending the substitution rule from *terms* (**icongruence**) to *formulas*. This is a bit trickier than it seems, because to substitute in a formula containing quantifiers, we may need to alpha-convert (change the names of bound variables), e.g. to obtain:

$$\vdash x = y \Rightarrow (\forall y.\, P[y] \Rightarrow y = x) \Rightarrow (\forall y'.\, P[y'] \Rightarrow y' = y).$$

The key to alpha-conversion is passing from $\vdash x = x' \Rightarrow P[x] \Rightarrow P[x']$ to $\vdash (\forall x.\, P[x]) \Rightarrow (\forall x'.\, P[x'])$. This just needs a slight elaboration of **subspec**, following it up with **gen_right**. Once again, the scope of the inference rule is somewhat wider, passing from $\vdash x = y \Rightarrow P[x] \Rightarrow Q[y]$ to $\vdash (\forall x.\, P[x]) \Rightarrow$

$(\forall y. Q[y])$ whenever $x \notin \mathrm{FV}(Q[y])$ and $y \notin \mathrm{FV}(P[x])$. Moreover, we also deal with the special case where x and y are the same variable:

```
let subalpha th =
  match concl th with
    Imp(Atom(R("=",[Var x;Var y])),Imp(p,q)) ->
        if x = y then genimp x (modusponens th (axiom_eqrefl(Var x)))
        else gen_right y (subspec th)
  | _ -> failwith "subalpha: wrong sort of theorem";;
```

Since we still need a congruence theorem as a starting-point, this may look circular, but the congruence instance we need is for a simpler formula than the one we are trying to construct, with a quantifier removed. We can therefore implement a recursive procedure to produce $\vdash s = t \Rightarrow P[s] \Rightarrow P[t]$ as follows.

```
let rec isubst s t sfm tfm =
  if sfm = tfm then add_assum (mk_eq s t) (imp_refl tfm) else
  match (sfm,tfm) with
    Atom(R(p,sa)),Atom(R(p',ta)) when p = p' & length sa = length ta ->
        let ths = map2 (icongruence s t) sa ta in
        let ls,rs = unzip (map (dest_eq ** consequent ** concl) ths) in
        imp_trans_chain ths (axiom_predcong p ls rs)
  | Imp(sp,sq),Imp(tp,tq) ->
        let th1 = imp_trans (eq_sym s t) (isubst t s tp sp)
        and th2 = isubst s t sq tq in
        imp_trans_chain [th1; th2] (imp_mono_th sp tp sq tq)
  | Forall(x,p),Forall(y,q) ->
        if x = y then
            imp_trans (gen_right x (isubst s t p q)) (axiom_allimp x p q)
        else
            let z = Var(variant x (unions [fv p; fv q; fvt s; fvt t])) in
            let th1 = isubst (Var x) z p (subst (x |=> z) p)
            and th2 = isubst z (Var y) (subst (y |=> z) q) q in
            let th3 = subalpha th1 and th4 = subalpha th2 in
            let th5 = isubst s t (consequent(concl th3))
                                 (antecedent(concl th4)) in
            imp_swap (imp_trans2 (imp_trans th3 (imp_swap th5)) th4)
  | _ ->
            let sth = iff_imp1(expand_connective sfm)
            and tth = iff_imp2(expand_connective tfm) in
            let th1 = isubst s t (consequent(concl sth))
                                 (antecedent(concl tth)) in
      imp_swap(imp_trans sth (imp_swap(imp_trans2 th1 tth)));;
```

Most of the cases are straightforward. If the two formulas are the same, we simply use `imp_refl`, but add the antecedent $s = t$ to maintain the pattern. For atomic formulas, we string together congruence theorems obtained by `icongruence` much as in that function's own recursive call. For implications, we use the fact that implication is respectively antimonotonic and monotonic in its arguments, i.e. $\vdash (p' \Rightarrow p) \Rightarrow (q \Rightarrow q') \Rightarrow ((p \Rightarrow q) \Rightarrow (p' \Rightarrow q'))$, and hence construct the result from appropriately oriented subcalls on the antecedent and consequent. We deal with all 'defined' connectives as usual, by writing them away in terms of their definitions and making a recursive call on the translated call.

The complicated case is the universal quantifier, where we want to deduce $\vdash s = t \Rightarrow (\forall x.\ P[x, s]) \Rightarrow (\forall y.\ P[y, t])$. In the case where x and y are the same, it's quite easy: a recursive call yields $\vdash s = t \Rightarrow P[x, s] \Rightarrow P[x, t]$ and we then universally quantify antecedent and consequent. When the bound variables are different, we pick yet a third variable z chosen not to cause any clashes, and using recursive calls and `subalpha` produce

$$\texttt{th3} \quad = \quad \vdash (\forall x.\ P[x, s]) \Rightarrow (\forall z.\ P[z, s]),$$
$$\texttt{th4} \quad = \quad \vdash (\forall z.\ P[z, t]) \Rightarrow (\forall y.\ P[y, t]),$$
$$\texttt{th5} \quad = \quad \vdash s = t \Rightarrow (\forall z.\ P[z, s]) \Rightarrow (\forall z.\ P[z, t]).$$

Although `th5` requires a recursive call on a formula with the same size, we know that this time it will be dealt with in the 'easy' path where both variables are the same; hence the overall recursion is terminating. To get the final result, we just need to string together these theorems by transitivity of implication.

The hard work is done. We can set up a standalone alpha-conversion routine that given a term $\forall x.\ P[x]$ and a desired new variable name $z \notin \mathrm{FV}(P[x])$ will produce $\vdash (\forall x.\ P[x]) \Rightarrow (\forall z.\ P[z])$, simply by appropriate instances of earlier functions:

```
let alpha z fm =
  match fm with
    Forall(x,p) -> let p' = subst (x |=> Var z) p in
                   subalpha(isubst (Var x) (Var z) p p')
  | _ -> failwith "alpha: not a universal formula";;
```

Now we can finally achieve our original goal of a specification rule, which given a term $\forall x.\ P[x]$ and a term t produces $\vdash (\forall x.\ P[x]) \Rightarrow P[t]$. Once again it's mostly a matter of instantiating earlier functions correctly. But note that our entire infrastructure for specialization developed so far required $x \notin \mathrm{FVT}(t)$. We certainly don't want to restrict the specialization rule in this way, so if $x \in \mathrm{FVT}(t)$ we use a two-step process, first alpha-converting to get $\forall z.\ P[z]$ for some suitable z and then using specialization.[†]

[†] Note that we use `var` rather than `fvt` to ensure that z does not even clash with *bound* variables. Although logically inessential, this makes sure that the alpha-conversion does not cause any 'knock-on' renaming deeper in the term, for example when specializing $\forall x\ x'.\ x + x' = x' + x$ with $2 \cdot x$.

```
let rec ispec t fm =
  match fm with
    Forall(x,p) ->
      if mem x (fvt t) then
        let th = alpha (variant x (union (fvt t) (var p))) fm in
        imp_trans th (ispec t (consequent(concl th)))
      else subspec(isubst (Var x) t p (subst (x |=> t) p))
    | _ -> failwith "ispec: non-universal formula";;
```

Here is this rather involved derived rule in action. Note how it correctly renames bound variables as necessary. Since this is implemented as a derived rule, we aren't likely to be perturbed by doubts that this is done in a sound way.

```
# ispec <<|y|>> <<forall x y z. x + y + z = z + y + x>>;;
- : thm =
|-
(forall x y z. x + y + z = z + y + x) ==>
(forall y' z. y + y' + z = z + y' + y)
```

As usual, we also set up a 'rule' version that from a theorem $\vdash \forall x.\ P[x]$ yields $P[t]$:

```
let spec t th = modusponens (ispec t (concl th)) th;;
```

6.8 First-order proof by inference

We've now produced a reasonable stock of derived rules, which among other things can prove all propositional tautologies. But we haven't established that our rules are complete for all of first-order logic with equality, i.e. that if p is logically valid then we can derive it in our system. We know that we can derive all the equational axioms (by **eq_trans**, **icongruence**, etc.), so it would suffice to show that we can simulate by inference any method that is complete for first-order logic. We plan to recast the full first-order tableaux in Section 3.10 using the methodology of proof generation from Section 6.6. As there, we will reduce other propositional connectives to implication and falsity, so complementary literals are now those of the form p and $p \Rightarrow \bot$ (rather than p and $\neg p$). We tweak the core literal unification function correspondingly:

```
let unify_complementsf env =
  function (Atom(R(p1,a1)),Imp(Atom(R(p2,a2)),False))
         | (Imp(Atom(R(p1,a1)),False),Atom(R(p2,a2)))
             -> unify env [Fn(p1,a1),Fn(p2,a2)]
         | _ -> failwith "unify_complementsf";;
```

Main tableau code

We will now encounter universally quantified formulas, replace them with fresh variables, and later try to find instantiations of those variables to reach a contradiction. So we use the same backtracking method as in Section 3.10, passing an environment of instantiations to a continuation function. But the end result passed to the top-level continuation in the event of overall success should somehow yield a *theorem* as in Section 6.6, showing that the collection of formulas $p_1, \ldots, p_n$ and literals $l_1, \ldots, l_m$ lead to a contradiction:

$$\vdash p_1 \Rightarrow \cdots \Rightarrow p_n \Rightarrow l_1 \Rightarrow \cdots \Rightarrow l_m \Rightarrow \bot.$$

The most straightforward approach would be to produce that theorem and pass it to the continuation function. However, this creates some difficulties. Suppose we are faced with a universally quantified formula at the head of the list, so we want to prove:

$$\vdash (\forall x.\ P[x]) \Rightarrow p_2 \Rightarrow \cdots \Rightarrow p_n \Rightarrow l_1 \Rightarrow \cdots \Rightarrow l_m \Rightarrow \bot.$$

The inference-free code in Section 3.10 first replaces x by a fresh variable y, and at some later time discovers an instantiation t to reach a contradiction. If we successfully produce the corresponding theorem:

$$\vdash P[t] \Rightarrow p_2 \Rightarrow \cdots \Rightarrow p_n \Rightarrow l_1 \Rightarrow \cdots \Rightarrow l_m \Rightarrow \bot,$$

then using `ispec` we can get the theorem we originally wanted. The difficulty is that we don't in general know what t is at the time we break down the quantified formula. In an inference context, we can't just replace it with a fresh variable, since the following doesn't hold in general:

$$\vdash P[y] \Rightarrow p_2 \Rightarrow \cdots \Rightarrow p_n \Rightarrow l_1 \Rightarrow \cdots \Rightarrow l_m \Rightarrow \bot.$$

So rather than having our main function pass a *theorem* to the continuation function, we make it pass an OCaml *function* that *returns* a theorem; the arguments to this function include a representation of the final instantiation. An advantage of this approach is that we do essentially no inference until right at the end when success is achieved and we get the final instantiation, so we don't waste time simulating fruitless search paths by inference.

We also need to consider existentially quantified formulas, which in our reduced set of connectives will be those of the form $(\forall y.\ P[y]) \Rightarrow \bot$. In the original tableau procedure, these were removed by an initial Skolemization step. Our plan is to do essentially the same Skolemization dynamically, replacing $(\forall y.\ P[x_1, \ldots, x_n, y]) \Rightarrow \bot$ by $P[x_1, \ldots, x_n, f(x_1, \ldots, x_n)] \Rightarrow \bot$, for the appropriately determined Skolem function f, whenever we deal with the formula in proof search. But whether Skolemization is done statically or dynamically, it presents serious problems for proof reconstruction. Even given

$$\vdash (P[x_1, \ldots, x_n, f(x_1, \ldots, x_n)] \Rightarrow \bot)$$
$$\Rightarrow p_2 \Rightarrow \cdots \Rightarrow p_n \Rightarrow l_1 \Rightarrow \cdots \Rightarrow l_m \Rightarrow \bot$$

there's no straightforward way of applying inference rules to get the 'un-Skolemized' counterpart to that theorem, which is what we eventually want:

$$\vdash ((\forall y.\, P[x_1, \ldots, x_n, y]) \Rightarrow \bot)$$
$$\Rightarrow p_2 \Rightarrow \cdots \Rightarrow p_n \Rightarrow l_1 \Rightarrow \cdots \Rightarrow l_m \Rightarrow \bot.$$

The problem is that while the Skolemized and un-Skolemized formulas are equisatisfiable (one is satisfiable iff the other one is), there is only a logical *implication* between them in one direction, and not the direction we really want:

$$\nvdash P[x_1, \ldots, x_n, f(x_1, \ldots, x_n)] \Rightarrow (\forall y.\, P[x_1, \ldots, x_n, y]).$$

We will evade this difficulty in a way that may seem reckless, but will turn out to be adequate: we just add to the final theorem the hypotheses that all those implications *do* hold. More precisely, the final theorem will not be

$$\vdash p_1 \Rightarrow \cdots \Rightarrow p_n \Rightarrow l_1 \Rightarrow \cdots \Rightarrow l_m \Rightarrow \bot$$

but rather

$$\vdash p_1 \Rightarrow \cdots \Rightarrow p_n \Rightarrow l_1 \Rightarrow \cdots \Rightarrow l_m \Rightarrow s,$$

where s is of the form $s_1 \Rightarrow \cdots \Rightarrow s_k \Rightarrow \bot$, each s_k being a (ground-instantiated, as usual) implication between Skolemized and un-Skolemized formulas we encountered during proof search:

$$P[t_1, \ldots, t_n, f(t_1, \ldots, t_n)] \Rightarrow (\forall y.\, P[t_1, \ldots, t_n, y]).$$

The proof reconstruction needs to be able to 'use' an implication that occurs later in the chain like this. The following inference rule passes from $\vdash (q \Rightarrow f) \Rightarrow \cdots \Rightarrow (q \Rightarrow p) \Rightarrow r$ to $\vdash (p \Rightarrow f) \Rightarrow \cdots \Rightarrow (q \Rightarrow p) \Rightarrow r$, where the first argument i identifies the later implication $q \Rightarrow p$ in the chain to use, since there might be more than one with antecedent q. (In our application, we will always have $f = \bot$, but the rule works whatever it may be.)

```
let rec use_laterimp i fm =
  match fm with
    Imp(Imp(q',s),Imp(Imp(q,p) as i',r)) when i' = i ->
        let th1 = axiom_distribimp i (Imp(Imp(q,s),r)) (Imp(Imp(p,s),r))
        and th2 = imp_swap(imp_trans_th q p s)
        and th3 = imp_swap(imp_trans_th (Imp(p,s)) (Imp(q,s)) r) in
        imp_swap2(modusponens th1 (imp_trans th2 th3))
  | Imp(qs,Imp(a,b)) ->
        imp_swap2(imp_add_assum a (use_laterimp i (Imp(qs,b))));;
```

Since the final Skolemization formula s will also not be known until the proof is completed, we make that an argument to the theorem-producing functions, as well as the instantiation. More precisely, each of our theorem-producing functions has the OCaml type (term -> term) * term -> thm, where the first component represents the instantiation[†] and the second is the Skolemization formula s.

The fact that we're always manipulating functions that return theorems, rather than simply theorems, makes things more involved and confusing, of course. It helps a bit if we define 'lifted' variants of the relevant inference rules. Some of these just feed their arguments through to the input theorem-producers, then apply the usual inference rule to the result, for inference rules with one theorem argument:

```
let imp_false_rule' th es = imp_false_rule(th es);;
```

or two theorem arguments:

```
let imp_true_rule' th1 th2 es = imp_true_rule (th1 es) (th2 es);;
```

or one non-theorem and one theorem argument:

```
let imp_front' n thp es = imp_front n (thp es);;
```

In other cases we actually need to apply the instantiation to the terms used in inference rules. For example, when adding a new assumption to a theorem, we need to instantiate, using **onformula** to convert it from a mapping on terms to a mapping on formulas:

```
let add_assum' fm thp (e,s as es) =
  add_assum (onformula e fm) (thp es);;
```

[†] We make it a general term mapping rather than just a mapping on variables since replacement of non-variable subterms will later be necessary to get rid of the Skolemization assumptions.

We make some of our lifted inference rules richer than the primitives on which they are based, to reflect the use they will be put to in the tableau procedure. For example, we fold into `eliminate_connective'` the transitivity step in proof reconstruction:

```
let eliminate_connective' fm thp (e,s as es) =
  imp_trans (eliminate_connective (onformula e fm)) (thp es);;
```

and make `spec'` handle the way a universally quantified formula is copied to the back of the list as well as instantiated at the front, so it passes from $\vdash P[t] \Rightarrow p_2 \Rightarrow \cdots \Rightarrow p_n \Rightarrow (\forall x.\ P[x]) \Rightarrow r$ to $\vdash (\forall x.\ P[x]) \Rightarrow p_2 \Rightarrow \cdots \Rightarrow p_n \Rightarrow r$:

```
let spec' y fm n thp (e,s) =
  let th = imp_swap(imp_front n (thp(e,s))) in
  imp_unduplicate(imp_trans (ispec (e y) (onformula e fm)) th);;
```

The two terminal steps that produce a theorem rather than modifying another one need to create a theorem with all the appropriate instantiated assumptions in the chain of implications, and with s as the conclusion. For immediate contradiction where we have a head formula $\bot$ we just do the following; we assume that the instantiation e has already been applied to s and we don't do it again:

```
let ex_falso' fms (e,s) =
  ex_falso (itlist (mk_imp ** onformula e) fms s);;
```

For complementary literals, we need the full lists of formulas and literals, plus the index i in the literals list for the complement p' of the head formula p:

```
let complits' (p::fl,lits) i (e,s) =
  let l1,p'::l2 = chop_list i lits in
  itlist (imp_insert ** onformula e) (fl @ l1)
         (imp_contr (onformula e p)
                    (itlist (mk_imp ** onformula e) l2 s));;
```

Finally, handling Skolemization is simple because all we do is use the later hypothesis to eliminate it:

```
let deskol' (skh:fol formula) thp (e,s) =
  let th = thp (e,s) in
  modusponens (use_laterimp (onformula e skh) (concl th)) th;;
```

We are now ready for the main refutation recursion `lcftab`. The first argument `skofun` determines what Skolem term $f(x_1, \ldots, x_n)$ to use on a given formula $(\forall y.\ P[x_1, \ldots, x_n, y]) \Rightarrow \bot$. The formulas (`fms`), literals (lits) and depth limit (n) come next, just as in Section 3.10. Then we have the continuation (cont) and finally the current instantiation environment (env), list of Skolem hypotheses needed so far (sks) and the counter for fresh variable naming (k). As before, the last triple of arguments is the one that is passed 'horizontally' across the sequence of continuations. With reference to Sections 3.10 and 6.6 the structure of the code should now be understandable.

```
let rec lcftab skofun (fms,lits,n) cont (env,sks,k as esk) =
  if n < 0 then failwith "lcftab: no proof" else
  match fms with
    False::fl -> cont (ex_falso' (fl @ lits)) esk
  | (Imp(p,q) as fm)::fl when p = q ->
      lcftab skofun (fl,lits,n) (cont ** add_assum' fm) esk
  | Imp(Imp(p,q),False)::fl ->
      lcftab skofun (p::Imp(q,False)::fl,lits,n)
                    (cont ** imp_false_rule') esk
  | Imp(p,q)::fl when q <> False ->
      lcftab skofun (Imp(p,False)::fl,lits,n)
        (fun th -> lcftab skofun (q::fl,lits,n)
                          (cont ** imp_true_rule' th)) esk
  | ((Atom(_)|Imp(Atom(_),False)) as p)::fl ->
      (try tryfind (fun p' ->
          let env' = unify_complementsf env (p,p') in
          cont(complits' (fms,lits) (index p' lits)) (env',sks,k)) lits
        with Failure _ ->
          lcftab skofun (fl,p::lits,n)
                        (cont ** imp_front' (length fl)) esk)
  | (Forall(x,p) as fm)::fl ->
      let y = Var("X_"^string_of_int k) in
      lcftab skofun ((subst (x |=> y) p)::fl@[fm],lits,n-1)
                    (cont ** spec' y fm (length fms)) (env,sks,k+1)
  | (Imp(Forall(y,p) as yp),False))::fl ->
      let fx = skofun yp in
      let p' = subst(y |=> fx) p in
      let skh = Imp(p',Forall(y,p)) in
      let sks' = (Forall(y,p),fx)::sks in
      lcftab skofun (Imp(p',False)::fl,lits,n)
                    (cont ** deskol' skh) (env,sks',k)
  | fm::fl ->
      let fm' = consequent(concl(eliminate_connective fm)) in
      lcftab skofun (fm'::fl,lits,n)
                    (cont ** eliminate_connective' fm) esk
  | [] -> failwith "lcftab: No contradiction";;
```

Assigning Skolem functions

The previous function relied on the argument **skofun** to determine the Skolem term to use for a given subformula. (We are implicitly using the same Skolem function for any instances of the same formula, which we noted is permissible in Section 3.6.) We need to set up some such function based on the initial formula. The following function returns the set of appropriately quantified subformulas of a formula `fm`, existentially quantified if `e` is true and universally quantified if `e` is false. This determination respects the implicit parity of the subformula, had we done an initial NNF conversion; for example when looking for existentially quantified subformulas of $p \Rightarrow q$ we search for existentially quantified subformulas of q and *universally* quantified subformulas of p.

```
let rec quantforms e fm =
  match fm with
    Not(p) -> quantforms (not e) p
  | And(p,q) | Or(p,q) -> union (quantforms e p) (quantforms e q)
  | Imp(p,q) -> quantforms e (Or(Not p,q))
  | Iff(p,q) -> quantforms e (Or(And(p,q),And(Not p,Not q)))
  | Exists(x,p) -> if e then fm::(quantforms e p) else quantforms e p
  | Forall(x,p) -> if e then quantforms e p else fm::(quantforms e p)
  | _ -> [];;
```

Hence we can identify all the 'existential' subformulas of `fm` of the form $(\forall y.\ P[x_1, \ldots, x_n, y]) \Rightarrow \bot$ that we may encounter during proof search and need to 'Skolemize'. We create a Skolem function for each one, and return an association list with pairs consisting of the formula $\forall y.\ P[x_1, \ldots, x_n, y]$ and the corresponding term $f(x_1, \ldots, x_n)$:

```
let skolemfuns fm =
  let fns = map fst (functions fm)
  and skts = map (function Exists(x,p) -> Forall(x,Not p) | p -> p)
                 (quantforms true fm) in
  let skofun i (Forall(y,p) as ap) =
    let vars = map (fun v -> Var v) (fv ap) in
    ap,Fn(variant("f"^"_"^string_of_int i) fns,vars) in
  map2 skofun (1--length skts) skts;;
```

However, during proof search, we will not normally encounter these subformulas themselves, but rather instantiations of them (quite possibly several different ones) with fresh variables. To deduce these instantiations we use an extension of `term_match` from terms to formulas; note that we require corresponding bound variables to be the same in both terms:

```
let rec form_match (f1,f2 as fp) env =
  match fp with
    False,False | True,True -> env
  | Atom(R(p,pa)),Atom(R(q,qa)) -> term_match env [Fn(p,pa),Fn(q,qa)]
  | Not(p1),Not(p2) -> form_match (p1,p2) env
  | And(p1,q1),And(p2,q2)| Or(p1,q1),Or(p2,q2) | Imp(p1,q1),Imp(p2,q2)
  | Iff(p1,q1),Iff(p2,q2) -> form_match (p1,p2) (form_match (q1,q2) env)
  | (Forall(x1,p1),Forall(x2,p2) |
     Exists(x1,p1),Exists(x2,p2)) when x1 = x2 ->
        let z = variant x1 (union (fv p1) (fv p2)) in
        let inst_fn = subst (x1 |=> Var z) in
        undefine z (form_match (inst_fn p1,inst_fn p2) env)
  | _ -> failwith "form_match";;
```

We can now incorporate this Skolem-finder into `lcftab` and further specialize it: `lcfrefute` will attempt to refute a formula `fm` using a variable limit of `n`, and pass the overall theorem-producing function, as well as the final triple `(env,sks,k)` containing the instantiation, list of Skolem hypotheses and number of variables used, to the continuation `cont`:

```
let lcfrefute fm n cont =
  let sl = skolemfuns fm in
  let find_skolem fm =
    tryfind(fun (f,t) -> tsubst(form_match (f,fm) undefined) t) sl in
  lcftab find_skolem ([fm],[],n) cont (undefined,[],0);;
```

All we need to make the prover work is a continuation that derives the appropriate replacement function and Skolem term from the second argument and passes them to the theorem-producer. To construct each Skolem hypothesis $P[t] \Rightarrow \forall y.\, P[y]$ from the corresponding pair of $(\forall y.\, P[y])$ and t and add it as an antecedent to another formula q we use:

```
let mk_skol (Forall(y,p),fx) q =
  Imp(Imp(subst (y |=> fx) p,Forall(y,p)),q);;
```

and then our continuation is:

```
let simpcont thp (env,sks,k) =
  let ifn = tsubst(solve env) in
  thp(ifn,onformula ifn (itlist mk_skol sks False));;
```

Let's test it on a couple of very simple first-order refutation problems:

```
# lcfrefute <<p(1) /\ ~q(1) /\ (forall x. p(x) ==> q(x))>> 1 simpcont;;
- : thm = |- p(1) /\ ~q(1) /\ (forall x. p(x) ==> q(x)) ==> false
# lcfrefute <<(exists x. ~p(x)) /\ (forall x. p(x))>> 1 simpcont;;
- : thm =
|-
(exists x. ~p(x)) /\ (forall x. p(x)) ==>
(~(~p(f_1)) ==> (forall x. ~(~p(x)))) ==> false
```

In each case it works fine. But since the second problem required Skolemization, we don't get the direct refutation, but rather a refutation *assuming* the given property of Skolem functions.

Eliminating Skolem functions

To finish the job, we need to get rid of those Skolem hypotheses. At first sight, it's not at all clear how to do that post hoc, because none of them are logically valid! However, note that they are all the final ground instances, and inside proof generation they are used 'as is' without any breakdown or instantiation. So the entire proof would work equally well if we systematically replaced all the Skolem terms $f(t_1, \ldots, t_n)$ with variables. Since the theorem-producing function takes any term mapping as an argument, we can easily modify the continuation to make it perform such a replacement. How does this help? Suppose that without replacement we would end up with a Skolem assumption $P[f(t_1, \ldots, t_n)] \Rightarrow \forall y.\, P[y]$ in the final theorem:

$$\vdash \phi \Rightarrow (P[f(t_1, \ldots, t_n)] \Rightarrow \forall y.\, P[y]) \Rightarrow \cdots \Rightarrow \bot.$$

If we replace the Skolem term with a variable v then we get:

$$\vdash \phi \Rightarrow (P[v] \Rightarrow \forall y.\, P[y]) \Rightarrow \cdots \Rightarrow \bot$$

and so one application of `imp_swap` gives:

$$\vdash (P[v] \Rightarrow \forall y.\, P[y]) \Rightarrow \phi \Rightarrow \cdots \Rightarrow \bot.$$

Provided v does not occur free in any other part of the theorem (ϕ or any of the other terms in the chain of implications), we can eliminate this assumption using the 'drinker's principle' (Section 3.3): there is always a v such that if $P[v]$ holds then $\forall y.\, P[y]$ holds. The derivation is fairly straightforward; note that we infer v from the formula but take care to pick a default in the case where the formula $P[v]$ does not actually have v free:

```
let elim_skolemvar th =
  match concl th with
    Imp(Imp(pv,(Forall(x,px) as apx)),q) ->
        let [th1;th2] = map (imp_trans(imp_add_concl False th))
                            (imp_false_conseqs pv apx) in
        let v = hd(subtract (fv pv) (fv apx) @ [x]) in
        let th3 = gen_right v th1 in
        let th4 = imp_trans th3 (alpha x (consequent(concl th3))) in
        modusponens (axiom_doubleneg q) (right_mp th2 th4)
  | _ -> failwith "elim_skolemvar";;
```

By using this repeatedly, we can eliminate all the variable-replaced Skolem hypotheses. We need a bit of care, because when eliminating v from $\vdash (P[v] \Rightarrow \forall y. \, P[y]) \Rightarrow q$ using `elim_skolemvar`, we need $v \notin \mathrm{FV}(q)$. We can easily ensure that v doesn't occur in the initial formula by starting off with its universal closure. And although it's perfectly possible for a Skolem variable to appear in Skolem hypotheses other than its own 'defining' one, we can find an order to list the Skolem hypotheses so that no Skolem variable occurs in a hypothesis later than its own defining one, which is enough for the iterated elimination to work. We simply need to sort according to the sizes of the Skolem terms that we're replacing by variables. For each Skolem hypothesis for a Skolem term $f(t_1, \ldots, t_n)$

$$P[t_1, \ldots, t_n, f(t_1, \ldots, t_n)] \Rightarrow \forall y. \, P[t_1, \ldots, t_n, y]$$

arises from instantiating (by matching) a formula that characterizes the Skolem function f and involves no others:

$$P[x_1, \ldots, x_n, f(x_1, \ldots, x_n)] \Rightarrow \forall y. \, P[x_1, \ldots, x_n, y].$$

Therefore, if the Skolem hypothesis above involves any other Skolem term $g(s_1, \ldots, s_m)$, that term must occur in one of the terms to which some x_i is instantiated, and hence must also occur inside $f(t_1, \ldots, t_n)$ as a (proper) subterm and so be smaller in size.

The plan for a de-Skolemizing continuation is now clear. We start as before by creating an instantiation function `ifn` for the basic variable instantiation. We then apply this to all the data for the Skolem hypotheses and sort them in decreasing order (after eliminating any duplicates) to give `ssk`. We then construct a further instantiation `vfn` to replace all the Skolem terms with variables, apply the theorem-creator to the composed replacement and the appropriate Skolem term, then finally remove all the Skolem hypotheses from the resulting theorem:

```
let deskolcont thp (env,sks,k) =
  let ifn = tsubst(solve env) in
  let isk = setify(map (fun (p,t) -> onformula ifn p,ifn t) sks) in
  let ssk = sort (decreasing (termsize ** snd)) isk in
  let vs = map (fun i -> Var("Y_"^string_of_int i)) (1--length ssk) in
  let vfn =
    replacet(itlist2 (fun (p,t) v -> t |-> v) ssk vs undefined) in
  let th = thp(vfn ** ifn,onformula vfn (itlist mk_skol ssk False)) in
  repeat (elim_skolemvar ** imp_swap) th;;
```

Now for a first-order prover with similar power to `tab`, we just need to wrap this up appropriately on the negated universal closure of the starting formula:

```
let lcffol fm =
  let fvs = fv fm in
  let fm' = Imp(itlist mk_forall fvs fm,False) in
  let th1 = deepen (fun n -> lcfrefute fm' n deskolcont) 0 in
  let th2 = modusponens (axiom_doubleneg (negatef fm')) th1 in
  itlist (fun v -> spec(Var v)) (rev fvs) th2;;
```

For example, here is a first-order problem with a fairly rich quantifier structure:

```
# let p58 = lcffol
    <<forall x. exists v. exists w. forall y. forall z.
      ((P(x) /\ Q(y)) ==> ((P(v) \/ R(w))  /\ (R(z) ==> Q(v))))>>;;
Searching with depth limit 0
Searching with depth limit 1
Searching with depth limit 2
Searching with depth limit 3
Searching with depth limit 4
val p58 : thm =
  |-
  forall x.
    exists v w.
      forall y z. P(x) /\ Q(y) ==> (P(v) \/ R(w)) /\ (R(z) ==> Q(v))
```

and here is another old favourite:

```
# let ewd1062_1 = lcffol
    <<(forall x. x <= x) /\
      (forall x y z. x <= y /\ y <= z ==> x <= z) /\
      (forall x y. f(x) <= y <=> x <= g(y))
      ==> (forall x y. x <= y ==> f(x) <= f(y))>>;;
...
val ewd1062_1 : thm =
  |-
  (forall x. x <= x) /\
  (forall x y z. x <= y /\ y <= z ==> x <= z) /\
  (forall x y. f(x) <= y <=> x <= g(y)) ==>
  (forall x y. x <= y ==> f(x) <= f(y))
```

Completeness of first-order logic

The automated prover using the primitive logical steps is a useful tool. Moreover, the supporting arguments we have given yield a crucial *completeness theorem* for our first-order deductive system, complementing the *soundness* Theorem 6.1.

Theorem 6.2 *If p is valid in first-order logic (without equality), then it is provable using the primitive rules set out in Section 6.4 and can be (in* *principle without time or space limitations) proved automatically by the prover* lcffol.

Proof Note first that although our derived rules use equality internally, none of the actual proof search treats the equality relation specially, so we can assume without loss of generality that p does not involve the equality relation.

If p is logically valid, the discussion in Section 3.10 shows that negation, Skolemization and tableaux will prove it. The arguments set out in this section imply that this process will be accurately simulated by lcffol using only the primitive rules. ◻

Sometimes, it is useful to generalize the idea of provability to cover reasoning from a (possibly infinite) set of assumptions Γ. We simply define $\Gamma \vdash p$ by the same set of inference rules plus:

$$\frac{p \in \Gamma}{\Gamma \vdash p},$$

It is straightforward to prove by rule induction that if $\Gamma \vdash p$ and $\Gamma \subseteq \Delta$ then also $\Delta \vdash p$. We can extend soundness and completeness to the new notion.

Theorem 6.3
$\Gamma \vdash p$ *iff* $\Gamma \models p$.

Proof As before, the left-to-right direction is straightforward. Each $p \in \Gamma$ satisfies $\Gamma \models p$ by definition, all the logical axioms also hold in all interpretations, in particular models of Γ, while the two proper inference rules preserve validity. The result follows by rule induction.

Conversely, suppose $\Gamma \models p$. By the compactness theorem, there is a finite subset $\{p_1, \ldots, p_n\} \subseteq \Gamma$ with $\{p_1, \ldots, p_n\} \models p$. By definition, this is equivalent to $\{\forall(p_1), \ldots, \forall(p_n)\} \models p$ where $\forall(p_i)$ is the generalization of p_i over its free variables. This in turn is equivalent to $\models \forall(p_1) \Rightarrow \cdots \Rightarrow \forall(p_n) \Rightarrow p$. By completeness, we have $\vdash \forall(p_1) \Rightarrow \cdots \Rightarrow \forall(p_n) \Rightarrow p$. Clearly this also implies $\Gamma \vdash \forall(p_1) \Rightarrow \cdots \Rightarrow \forall(p_n) \Rightarrow p$, since all the old inference rules are still present. But since $\Gamma \vdash \forall(p_i)$ for $1 \leq i \leq n$, we obtain after n more instances of modus ponens the theorem $\Gamma \vdash p$. ◻

As a corollary we obtain the *deduction theorem*:

Corollary 6.4
$\Gamma \vdash \forall(p) \Rightarrow q$ *if and only if* $\Gamma \cup \{p\} \vdash q$.

Proof The same property holds by definition for '$\models$', and by completeness this coincides with '$\vdash$'. (For a more algorithmic way of establishing this result, see Exercise 6.6 below.)   □

Sometimes we only want to consider provability of formulas in a particular language L. In this case it's important to note that we may similarly restrict the function and predicate symbols that appear in all the axioms, including logical axioms like $p \Rightarrow (q \Rightarrow p)$, while retaining completeness. This isn't immediately obvious just looking at the inference rules, since in modus ponens we could imagine that it might be necessary to use some p not in the language in order to conclude $\vdash q$ for q in the language from $\vdash p$ and $\vdash p \Rightarrow q$. To see that such excursions, while quite possible, are not necessary, simply observe that all instantiations of axioms and inference rules in `lcffol` involve terms in the original language. Although the Skolem functions were used as an auxiliary device, they played no role in any inference steps.

6.9 Interactive proof styles

We seem to have the key components needed to realize the dream of interactive theorem proving set out at the beginning of this chapter. We can compose and modify theorems interactively using the inference rules, and can fill in simple steps automatically using something like `lcffol`. However, this is still a bit painful because Hilbert-style proof systems aren't very convenient for reasoning with assumptions. A natural deduction system is much better, since we can locally use p as an assumption to help us to derive q, then apply the rule of implication-introduction (see Section 6.3) to deduce $p \Rightarrow q$.[†] Moreover, it's sometimes more convenient to work *backwards* (top-down), breaking down the goal into simpler subgoals, rather than starting with the assumptions and working forwards.

Tactics

Both the use of a different deductive system and the mixing of forward and backward proof can be supported very elegantly in LCF-style theorem provers using the idea of a *tactic*, due to Milner (Gordon, Milner and Wadsworth 1979). Although different implementations of the idea are possible, we will present something close to the original LCF approach. We first define a notion of *goal*, which is a desired 'conclusion' formula q together with a set of hypotheses $p_1, \ldots, p_n$, each of which may be assigned a name for ease of reference.

[†] Also interesting is structured calculational proof (Back, Grundy and Wright 1996), which has even more refined notions of local scope.

Intuitively, a goal corresponds to a theorem $p_1 \wedge \cdots \wedge p_n \Rightarrow q$, or if $n = 0$ just $\top \Rightarrow q$, logically equivalent to q. In fact, to *solve* such a goal is precisely to produce a theorem $\vdash p_1 \wedge \cdots \wedge p_n \Rightarrow q$. We now define a type `goals` to be a set (actually list) of such goals together with a *justification function*, which, given theorems solving each subgoal, produces the theorem solving the original starting goal.

```
type goals =
   Goals of ((string * fol formula) list * fol formula)list *
            (thm list -> thm);;
```

Most of the time, we will operate on the first goal in the list, and we set up the printer so that it only prints this goal:

```
let print_goal =
  let print_hyp (l,fm) =
    open_hbox(); print_string(l^":"); print_space();
    print_formula print_atom fm; print_newline(); close_box() in
  fun (Goals(gls,jfn)) ->
    match gls with
      (asl,w)::ogls ->
        print_newline();
        (if ogls = [] then print_string "1 subgoal:" else
         (print_int (length gls);
          print_string " subgoals starting with"));
        print_newline();
        do_list print_hyp (rev asl);
        print_string "---> ";
        open_hvbox 0; print_formula print_atom w; close_box();
        print_newline()
    | [] -> print_string "No subgoals";;

#install_printer print_goal;;
```

Now, a *tactic* is simply a function of type `:goals->goals`.[†] It modifies the list of goals in some way, (e.g. replacing a single goal whose conclusion is $a \wedge b$ by two goals with conclusions a and b) and appropriately modifies the justification function to work from the modified goals. The idea is that one sets up an initial goal, refines it using tactics until the list of subgoals is empty, and then applies the final justification function to the empty list of theorems in order to obtain the final theorem.

To start the process with an initial formula p to be proved, we set up a singleton list of goals with just p as conclusion and no antecedent. By

---

[†] This differs slightly from the original LCF notion where a tactic maps a single goal to a list of goals and corresponding justification function. However, the present notion is slightly more regular to describe.

the organizational plan set out above, the justification function is expected to return a theorem $\top \Rightarrow p$, and so at the end we just want to perform modus ponens with $\vdash \top$ to get the final theorem. However, since there is no guarantee that the justification function did its job properly,[†] we confirm that the conclusion is as expected.

```
let set_goal p =
  let chk th = if concl th = p then th else failwith "wrong theorem" in
  Goals([[],p],fun [th] -> chk(modusponens th truth));;
```

At the other end, once we have the empty list of subgoals, we can terminate the proof and (we hope) get the intended theorem by:

```
let extract_thm gls =
  match gls with
    Goals([],jfn) -> jfn []
  | _ -> failwith "extract_thm: unsolved goals";;
```

We can solve goals **g** by applying tactics in the list **prf** in sequence:

```
let tac_proof g prf = extract_thm(itlist (fun f -> f) (rev prf) g);;
```

and in particular prove **p** using a sequence of tactics:

```
let prove p prf = tac_proof (set_goal p) prf;;
```

So much for the overall setup: what of the actual tactics? We can view a goal as a 'desired sequent', and design our tactics to apply natural deduction rules 'in reverse'. For example, the natural deduction rule of conjunction introduction can be written:

$$\frac{\Gamma \rightarrow p \quad \Gamma \rightarrow q}{\Gamma \rightarrow p \wedge q} .$$

We can turn it into a tactic that breaks down a goal with conclusion $p \wedge q$ into two subgoals with conclusions p and q. We need to modify the justification function correspondingly; the original justification function expects a list of theorems starting with $\vdash a \Rightarrow p \wedge q$, whereas we need one where the list starts with two theorems $\vdash a \Rightarrow p$ and $\vdash a \Rightarrow q$:

```
let conj_intro_tac (Goals((asl,And(p,q))::gls,jfn)) =
  let jfn' (thp::thq::ths) =
    jfn(imp_trans_chain [thp; thq] (and_pair p q)::ths) in
  Goals((asl,p)::(asl,q)::gls,jfn'));;
```

[†] In customary LCF jargon, a tactic may be 'invalid'.

Many tactics just take the first of the goals and modify it, without changing the total number. In this case the following idiom often occurs when constructing the modified justification function:

```
let jmodify jfn tfn (th::oths) = jfn(tfn th :: oths);;
```

A tactic corresponding to the natural deduction rule of '$\forall$-introduction' is similar to the generalization rule in our axiomatization:

$$\frac{\Gamma \to P[x]}{\Gamma \to \forall x.\, P[x]} \;.$$

In fact, with our encoding of a sequent $a_1, \ldots, a_n \to P[x]$ as $\vdash a_1 \land \cdots \land a_n \Rightarrow P[x]$, it is exactly the `gen_right` rule. The rule is only sound when x does not occur free in any of the a_i, which matches the circumstances under which `gen_right` works. We can consider a slight generalization to include an implicit bound variable change:

$$\frac{\Gamma \to P[y]}{\Gamma \to \forall x.\, P[x]} \;,$$

where again we assume that y does not occur in any of the assumptions Γ, nor indeed in $\forall x.\, P[x]$. This can be implemented as:

```
let gen_right_alpha y x th =
  let th1 = gen_right y th in
  imp_trans th1 (alpha x (consequent(concl th1)));;
```

Now we can implement a corresponding tactic that reverses this process: given a first goal with conclusion $\forall x.\, P[x]$, we replace it by a similar subgoal with conclusion $P[y]$.

```
let forall_intro_tac y (Goals((asl,(Forall(x,p) as fm))::gls,jfn)) =
  if mem y (fv fm) or exists (mem y ** fv ** snd) asl
  then failwith "fix: variable already free in goal" else
  Goals((asl,subst(x |=> Var y) p)::gls,
        jmodify jfn (gen_right_alpha y x));;
```

Similarly there is a natural deduction rule of '$\exists$-introduction':

$$\frac{\Gamma \to P[t]}{\Gamma \to \exists x.\, P[x]} \;.$$

The core of such an inference rule, taking a variable x, a term t and a formula $P[x]$ and yielding a theorem $\vdash P[t] \Rightarrow \exists x.\, P[x]$, can be derived by contraposing the result from `ispec`:

```
let right_exists x t p =
  let th = contrapos(ispec t (Forall(x,Not p))) in
  let Not(Not p') = antecedent(concl th) in
  end_itlist imp_trans
    [imp_contr p' False; imp_add_concl False (iff_imp1 (axiom_not p'));
     iff_imp2(axiom_not (Not p')); th; iff_imp2(axiom_exists x p)];;
```

and then we can implement the corresponding tactic that reduces a goal with conclusion $\exists x.\, P[x]$ to a new goal $P[t]$ with user-specified t:

```
let exists_intro_tac t (Goals((asl,Exists(x,p))::gls,jfn)) =
  Goals((asl,subst(x |=> t) p)::gls,
        jmodify jfn (fun th -> imp_trans th (right_exists x t p)));;
```

Another characteristic natural deduction rule is '$\Rightarrow$-introduction'. Indeed, the ability to use an assumption p to help establish q and then use this rule to obtain $p \Rightarrow q$ is one of the strengths of natural deduction compared with Hilbert-style systems:

$$\frac{\Gamma \to q}{\Gamma - \{p\} \to p \Rightarrow q}.$$

Assuming we have p as the head of the list of assumptions Γ, this just amounts to passing from $\vdash p \wedge a \Rightarrow q$ to $\vdash a \Rightarrow p \Rightarrow q$, or just from $\vdash p \Rightarrow q$ to $\vdash \top \Rightarrow p \Rightarrow q$ in the degenerate case of no other assumptions. So a corresponding tactic to break a goal with conclusion $p \Rightarrow q$ down to a similar goal with q as the conclusion and p added as a new assumption (with a chosen label) is:

```
let imp_intro_tac s (Goals((asl,Imp(p,q))::gls,jfn)) =
  let jmod = if asl = [] then add_assum True else imp_swap ** shunt in
  Goals(((s,p)::asl,q)::gls,jmodify jfn jmod);;
```

Justifications

In some cases, facts are justified by a previously proved theorem that does not depend on the current context of assumptions. It's often convenient to turn such a theorem $\vdash p$ into $\vdash a_1 \wedge \cdots \wedge a_n \Rightarrow p$, where the a_i are the current assumptions; even though this weakens the theorem it makes it fit better into a framework where most theorems have that hypothesis.

```
let assumptate (Goals((asl,w)::gls,jfn)) th =
  add_assum (list_conj (map snd asl)) th;;
```

Hence we can 'import' (the universal closures of) a list of theorems, giving them the right assumptions for the current goal. (The reason for the redundant argument p will become clear later.)

```
let using ths p g =
  let ths' = map (fun th -> itlist gen (fv(concl th)) th) ths in
  map (assumptate g) ths';;
```

Similarly, we often want to turn the assumptions into theorems of that form, i.e. produce $\vdash a_1 \wedge \cdots \wedge a_n \Rightarrow a_i$ for all $1 \leq i \leq n$. Note that we can't just create a big conjunction and call `conjths` because some of the a_i may themselves be conjunctions, so we need something more elaborate.

```
let rec assumps asl =
  match asl with
    [] -> []
  | [l,p] -> [l,imp_refl p]
  | (l,p)::lps ->
        let ths = assumps lps in
        let q = antecedent(concl(snd(hd ths))) in
        let rth = and_right p q in
        (l,and_left p q)::map (fun (l,th) -> l,imp_trans rth th) ths;;
```

Sometimes we only need the first assumption, in which case the following is much more efficient than using `assumps` then taking the head:

```
let firstassum asl =
  let p = snd(hd asl) and q = list_conj(map snd (tl asl)) in
  if tl asl = [] then imp_refl p else and_left p q;;
```

To get the standardized theorems corresponding to a list of assumption labels we use the following:

```
let by hyps p (Goals((asl,w)::gls,jfn)) =
  let ths = assumps asl in map (fun s -> assoc s ths) hyps;;
```

It's also convenient to be able to produce, in the same standardized form, more or less trivial consequences of some other theorems. In this `justify` function it is assumed that `byfn` applied to the arguments `hyps`, p and g, returns a list of canonical theorems. Then p is deduced from those theorems using first-order automation (with special treatment of the case where the only theorem matches the desired conclusion), and the final result put in standard form too:

```
let justify byfn hyps p g·=
  match byfn hyps p g with
    [th] when consequent(concl th) = p -> th
  | ths ->
       let th = lcffol(itlist (mk_imp ** consequent ** concl) ths p) in
       if ths = [] then assumptate g th else imp_trans_chain ths th;;
```

We can define other ways of justifying a result that fit into the same framework. For example we can prove it by a nested subproof (this is why we carried through the argument p):

```
let proof tacs p (Goals((asl,w)::gls,jfn)) =
 [tac_proof (Goals([asl,p],fun [th] -> th)) tacs];;
```

The degenerate case is justifying the empty list of theorems, using a little hack so we can write 'at once':

```
let at once p gl = [] and once = [];;
```

Thus we are able to write any of the following in justification of a claim:

- 'justify by ["lab1"; ...; "labn"]' (deduce from assumptions);
- 'justify using [th1; ...; thm]' (deduce from external theorems);
- 'justify proof [tac1; ...; tacp]' (deduce by applying sequence of tactics using current assumptions);
- 'justify at once' (deduce by pure first-order reasoning).

The most basic use of this automated justification is to solve the entire first goal:

```
let auto_tac byfn hyps (Goals((asl,w)::gls,jfn) as g) =
  let th = justify byfn hyps w g in
  Goals(gls,fun ths -> jfn(th::ths));;
```

We can also use it to justify adding a new, appropriately labelled, assumption that we can regard as a lemma on the way to the main result:

```
let lemma_tac s p byfn hyps (Goals((asl,w)::gls,jfn) as g) =
  let tr = imp_trans(justify byfn hyps p g) in
  let mfn = if asl = [] then tr else imp_unduplicate ** tr ** shunt in
  Goals(((s,p)::asl,w)::gls,jmodify jfn mfn);;
```

We can also naturally implement some of the elimination rules of natural deduction. We have already implemented a rule for existential introduction

(`exists_intro_tac`); one simple formulation of the existential elimination
rule is:

$$\frac{\Gamma \vdash \exists x.\, P[x] \quad \Gamma \cup \{P[x]\} \to Q}{\Gamma \to Q},$$

where we assume that x does not appear free in Q nor in any formula in Γ.
A corresponding tactic to reduce $\Gamma \to Q$ to $\Gamma \cup \{P[x]\} \to Q$, with the proof
of $\Gamma \vdash \exists x.\, P[x]$ being performed by the given justification function, is:

```
let exists_elim_tac l fm byfn hyps (Goals((asl,w)::gls,jfn) as g) =
  let Exists(x,p) = fm in
  if exists (mem x ** fv) (w::map snd asl)
  then failwith "exists_elim_tac: variable free in assumptions" else
  let th = justify byfn hyps (Exists(x,p)) g in
  let jfn' pth =
    imp_unduplicate(imp_trans th (exists_left x (shunt pth))) in
  Goals(((l,p)::asl,w)::gls,jmodify jfn jfn');;
```

Similarly, for the natural deduction disjunction elimination rule:

$$\frac{\Gamma \to p \vee q \quad \Gamma \cup \{p\} \to r \quad \Gamma \cup \{q\} \to r}{\Gamma \to r}$$

we first implement the basic inference rule getting us from $\vdash p \Rightarrow r$ and
$\vdash q \Rightarrow r$ to $\vdash p \vee q \Rightarrow r$:

```
let ante_disj th1 th2 =
  let p,r = dest_imp(concl th1) and q,s = dest_imp(concl th2) in
  let ths = map contrapos [th1; th2] in
  let th3 = imp_trans_chain ths (and_pair (Not p) (Not q)) in
  let th4 = contrapos(imp_trans (iff_imp2(axiom_not r)) th3) in
  let th5 = imp_trans (iff_imp1(axiom_or p q)) th4 in
  right_doubleneg(imp_trans th5 (iff_imp1(axiom_not(Imp(r,False)))));;
```

and hence derive a tactic that, given a formula `fm` of the form $p \vee q$, proves it
using the justification provided and then requires us to prove two subgoals
resulting from adding p and q respectively as new assumptions:

```
let disj_elim_tac l fm byfn hyps (Goals((asl,w)::gls,jfn) as g) =
  let th = justify byfn hyps fm g and Or(p,q) = fm in
  let jfn' (pth::qth::ths) =
    let th1 = imp_trans th (ante_disj (shunt pth) (shunt qth)) in
    jfn(imp_unduplicate th1::ths) in
  Goals(((l,p)::asl,w)::((l,q)::asl,w)::gls,jfn');;
```

We can illustrate the framework we have set up with a simple example.
Let us set up a goal:

```
let g0 = set_goal
<<(forall x. x <= x) /\
  (forall x y z. x <= y /\ y <= z ==> x <= z) /\
  (forall x y. f(x) <= y <=> x <= g(y))
  ==> (forall x y. x <= y ==> f(x) <= f(y)) /\
      (forall x y. x <= y ==> g(x) <= g(y))>>;;
```

We might start the proof by making the antecedent a new hypothesis:

```
# let g1 = imp_intro_tac "ant" g0;;
val g1 : goals =
1 subgoal:
ant: (forall x. x <= x) /\
     (forall x y z. x <= y /\ y <= z ==> x <= z) /\
     (forall x y. f(x) <= y <=> x <= g(y))
---> (forall x y. x <= y ==> f(x) <= f(y)) /\
     (forall x y. x <= y ==> g(x) <= g(y))
```

Now, we could in principle just solve the goal by pure first-order automation, i.e. `auto_tac by ["ant"] g1`. In practice, our rather limited first-order prover takes too much time. But we can break the goal down into two subgoals:

```
# let g2 = conj_intro_tac g1;;
val g2 : goals =
2 subgoals starting with
ant: (forall x. x <= x) /\
     (forall x y z. x <= y /\ y <= z ==> x <= z) /\
     (forall x y. f(x) <= y <=> x <= g(y))
---> forall x y. x <= y ==> f(x) <= f(y)
```

and now we can solve the two subgoals separately using automation:

```
# let g3 = funpow 2 (auto_tac by ["ant"]) g2;;
...
val g3 : goals = No subgoals
```

and then we can recover the theorem with `extract_thm g3`. We can also put together the whole proof:

```
prove <<(forall x. x <= x) /\
        (forall x y z. x <= y /\ y <= z ==> x <= z) /\
        (forall x y. f(x) <= y <=> x <= g(y))
        ==> (forall x y. x <= y ==> f(x) <= f(y)) /\
            (forall x y. x <= y ==> g(x) <= g(y))>>
    [imp_intro_tac "ant";
     conj_intro_tac;
     auto_tac by ["ant"];
     auto_tac by ["ant"]];;
```

Admittedly this was a somewhat trivial proof, but it illustrates the philosophy of the tactic setup: we can systematically break down the goals until they become accessible to efficient automation.

Declarative proof

A tactic proof like the one above is reminiscent of an imperative program: it is a sequence of instructions (tactics) specifying how to change the state (goals). Indeed, many LCF systems provide operations on tactics, often called tacticals, analogous to typical imperative programming constructs, such as 'repeat a tactic until it is no longer applicable'. We will therefore call such proofs *procedural*: they emphasize *how* to perform proof steps. Although this approach to proof can be quite efficient, it has some drawbacks, most notably inscrutability. Without replaying the steps interactively at the computer, it's hard to visualize the intermediate goalstates, just as it's hard when given the moves of a chess game to visualize the position on the board at various points.

We could try to make tactic proofs more readable by annotating them with comments showing the intermediate goalstates at various critical junctures, just as a sequence of chess moves is often supplemented with diagrams. Helpful as this can be, there's a danger that the comments and the proof may fail to correspond, as they sometimes do for programs in general. But we can do better by making the additional annotation an integral part of the proof, checked for correctness when the proof is run.

First we'll enhance `imp_intro_tac` so that the user needs to state the facts being added to the assumption list. When run, the tactic will check that these do indeed correspond to the antecedent p of the conclusion $p \Rightarrow q$ of the goal. While we're about it, we'll allow the enhanced tactic, given a goal $p_1 \wedge \cdots \wedge p_k \Rightarrow q$, to split the conjunctive antecedent into separately labelled assumptions $p_1, \ldots, p_k$. The following inference rule is necessary to support this: it maps $\vdash p_1 \wedge \cdots \wedge p_n \Rightarrow q$ to $\vdash p_{i+1} \wedge \cdots \wedge p_n \Rightarrow p_1 \wedge \cdots \wedge p_i \Rightarrow q$, hence allowing us to modify the justification function to compensate for multiple new assumptions:

```
let multishunt i th =
  let th1 = imp_swap(funpow i (imp_swap ** shunt) th) in
  imp_swap(funpow (i-1) (unshunt ** imp_front 2) th1);;
```

Now our tactic, which we give the friendlier name `assume`, just takes a list of label–term pairs for the conjuncts of the assumption:

```
let assume lps (Goals((asl,Imp(p,q))::gls,jfn)) =
  if end_itlist mk_and (map snd lps) <> p then failwith "assume" else
  let jfn' th = if asl = [] then add_assum True th
              else multishunt (length lps) th in
  Goals((lps@asl,q)::gls,jmodify jfn jfn'));;
```

This is our first step in pursuit of a more *declarative*[†] approach to proof, where the emphasis is on stating at each stage *what* is being proved rather than *how*. In its simplest form, a declarative proof might simply be a sequence of intermediate assertions, acting as stepping-stones between the assumptions and conclusion. This is the approach taken by the NQTHM prover (Boyer and Moore 1979), which attempts to bridge the gaps between steps using powerful automation. Our notion of declarative proof, inspired by Mizar (Trybulec 1978; Trybulec and Blair 1985; Rudnicki 1992),[‡] is a little different in two respects:

- the step-bridging automation is guided/constrained by an indication of which assumptions to use;
- proofs can be structured using local introduction of variables and assumptions.

We will, moreover, implement these declarative proof constructs within our existing tactic framework. To prove an intermediate assertion p and add it to the assumptions with label `lab`, we use `note("lab",p) byfn hyps`, with a justification function `byfn` and arguments `hyps` as used in several tactics above.

```
let note (l,p) = lemma_tac l p;;
```

When the trivial label suffices, we use **have p** as an abbreviation:

```
let have p = note("",p);;
```

Very often we will want to automatically include the previously deduced assumption, labelled or not, in the list of theorems produced by a justification. The **so** function modifies a tactic to add the head of the list of assumptions to the theorems produced by its justification:

```
let so tac arg byfn =
  tac arg (fun hyps p (Goals((asl,w)::_,_) as gl) ->
                  firstassum asl :: byfn hyps p gl);;
```

Although the core of a declarative proof will be a series of such intermediate assertions, we will also impose some block structure so that variables and assumptions can be introduced and a series of steps can take place locally

---

[†] This terminology (Harrison 1996c) was suggested by Mike Gordon based on the analogy with programming languages.

[‡] Mizar in turn was inspired by natural deduction in the particular style of Jaskowski (1934) and Fitch (1952), as well as the block structure in the Pascal programming language (Jensen and Wirth 1974).

in that context. For introducing assumptions we use **assume**, defined above. For introducing new variables, we use either:

- **fix "v"** to reduce a goal $\forall x.\,P[x]$ to $P[v]$, introducing the variable v, or
- **consider("v",<<P[v]>>)** ('consider a v such that $P[v]$') to introduce a new variable v and an assumption $P[v]$, given some justification for $\exists x.\, P[x]$.

The implementations are little more than friendlier names for existing tactics:

```
let fix = forall_intro_tac;;

let consider (x,p) = exists_elim_tac "" (Exists(x,p));;
```

A couple of other handy constructs respectively provide a witness for an existential quantifier and perform a case-split over a disjunctive theorem:

```
let take = exists_intro_tac;;

let cases = disj_elim_tac "";;
```

We also need some way of indicating that we're finished: **conclude p**, with appropriate justification, will try to deduce **p**, and if that matches the conclusion of the goal will reduce it to the trivial $\top$. More generally (following Mizar), if the goal has conclusion $p \wedge q$ then it is reduced to q, allowing us to nibble away at a conjunctive goal one conjunct at a time:

```
let conclude p byfn hyps (Goals((asl,w)::gls,jfn) as gl) =
   let th = justify byfn hyps p gl in
   if p = w then Goals((asl,True)::gls,jmodify jfn (fun _ -> th)) else
   let p',q = dest_and w in
 / if p' <> p then failwith "conclude: bad conclusion" else
   let mfn th' = imp_trans_chain [th; th'] (and_pair p q) in
   Goals((asl,q)::gls,jmodify jfn mfn);;
```

Although it arguably compromises our ideal of forcing explicit quotation of all facts, it's convenient to be able to conclude the entire goal by writing **our thesis**:

```
let our thesis byfn hyps (Goals((asl,w)::gls,jfn) as gl) =
   conclude w byfn hyps gl
and thesis = "";;
```

We choose to have **conclude** leave a trivial goal $\top$ rather than just solving it so that we need an explicit end-marker **qed**:

```
let qed (Goals((asl,w)::gls,jfn) as gl) =
  if w = True then Goals(gls,fun ths -> jfn(assumptate gl truth :: ths))
  else failwith "qed: non-trivial goal";;
```

Here is a simple example taken from Dijkstra's EWD954,[†] where we define
a 'less than or equal' operation in terms of 'multiplication' (as is done in
Boolean rings) and prove that a function f that has a homomorphism property for multiplication is therefore monotonic with respect to the ordering.

```
let ewd954 = prove
<<(forall x y. x <= y <=> x * y = x) /\
  (forall x y. f(x * y) = f(x) * f(y))
  ==> forall x y. x <= y ==> f(x) <= f(y)>>
[note("eq_sym",<<forall x y. x = y ==> y = x>>)
   using [eq_sym <<|x|>> <<|y|>>];
 note("eq_trans",<<forall x y z. x = y /\ y = z ==> x = z>>)
   using [eq_trans <<|x|>> <<|y|>> <<|z|>>];
 note("eq_cong",<<forall x y. x = y ==> f(x) = f(y)>>)
   using [axiom_funcong "f" [<<|x|>>] [<<|y|>>]];
 assume ["le",<<forall x y. x <= y <=> x * y = x>>;
         "hom",<<forall x y. f(x * y) = f(x) * f(y)>>];
 fix "x"; fix "y";
 assume ["xy",<<x <= y>>];
 so have <<x * y = x>> by ["le"];
 so have <<f(x * y) = f(x)>> by ["eq_cong"];
 so have <<f(x) = f(x * y)>> by ["eq_sym"];
 so have <<f(x) = f(x) * f(y)>> by ["eq_trans"; "hom"];
 so have <<f(x) * f(y) = f(x)>> by ["eq_sym"];
 so conclude <<f(x) <= f(y)>> by ["le"];
 qed];;
```

The proof is not very deep, but it requires the deployment of some equality properties and is not feasible with our tableau procedure directly. The
proof starts by assembling the general properties of equality we need, then
makes the appropriate assumptions and systematically proceeds through a
sequence of lemmas until the goal is reached. We will see a more extended
application of declarative proofs in the next chapter. The reader may like
to step through these proofs one or two tactics at a time as we did with our
first example ('let g2 = conj_intro_tac g1;;' etc.)

LCF and efficiency

Proving theorems in the LCF style can be quite slow, even on a fast modern
computer, because everything has to proceed under the surface using the
very simple primitive rules. This can be much less efficient than a direct

---

[†] http://www.cs.utexas.edu/users/EWD/ewd09xx/EWD954.PDF

implementation by term manipulations. Even if the performance only differs by a constant factor, a constant factor of 500 (see Exercise 6.12) may be important for large problems. In general, is it possible to implement a wide variety of traditional theorem proving algorithms so that they produce theorems by inference in a traditional logical system, with acceptable efficiency? There are essentially two approaches one can consider:

- directly rephrasing the existing algorithms to work by inference and produce theorems at each stage;
- modifying the existing algorithms so that they produce some kind of trace of their activity from which a proof using inference rules can be created.

Our propositional prover `lcfptab` uses the first approach: the steps of a conventional tableau prover are directly mimicked by inference steps. The first-order extension `lcftab` looks similar but is arguably closer to the second approach: almost all inference is delayed until a successful path to a refutation is found, avoiding inference steps for the blind alleys in proof search. We could make the separation more obvious by producing a real 'proof' or *certificate* data structure from the search phase, and processing it separately. If this certificate is substantially more efficient just to verify than to find in the first place, the additional overhead of performing inference in the verification phase may not change things much overall. For example, in first-order proof search, the search space is often very large but the eventual proof found is usually relatively short and simple. The same can apply to a number of other algorithms such as Knuth–Bendix completion (Section 4.7) and refutation of systems of real or complex equations and inequalities using the real or complex Nullstellensatz (Section 5.11).

Where there is no easily exploited finding–checking separation, one must seek other optimizations. Sometimes the central transformations of proof procedures can be expressed as very general theorems that can later be instantiated quickly to the case in hand. Our inference system hardly lends itself to this kind of approach – for example we cannot 'instantiate' atomic subformulas as an atomic operation, going say from $P \Rightarrow P$ to $Q[x] \Rightarrow Q[x]$, but rather must 'replay' a modified version of the original proof. However, in suitable logical systems this method is very effective and has been used extensively in practice – see Melham (1989) for an early example.

If one finds that certain inference rules cannot feasibly be implemented in the LCF style, but one is still wary of trusting complex code, what can be done? One popular idea (Davis and Schwartz 1979; Weyhrauch 1980) is to use metatheoretic extensibility or 'reflection principles', starting with a trusted core system and only extending it with new code when (some formal version of) that code has been proven correct using the existing system. Although this is an enticing idea, it requires rigorous correctness proofs, which are often significantly harder than a direct LCF-style implementation.

Further reading

Interactive theorem proving, and human-oriented proving too for that matter, are hardly covered at all in textbooks. Doubtless the main reason is that they do not so easily lend themselves to discussion in terms of some standard collection of theorems and methods; perhaps to some extent they are considered less intellectually exciting. However, there is a discussion of interactive theorem proving in the 'logic for computer science' text by Reeves and Clarke (1990), and an extended example in the book on SML programming by Paulson (1991). MacKenzie (2001) gives an account of the history of interactive theorem proving and its applications, while Wiedijk (2006) is a survey of some of the main interactive theorem provers showing proofs of the irrationality of $\sqrt{2}$ in each.

There are, however, numerous books about *particular* interactive systems, many in the LCF family. The first book on Edinburgh LCF (Gordon, Milner and Wadsworth 1979) describes the original innovative ideas, and Paulson (1987) describes Cambridge LCF, a version with greatly rationalized organization. Constable (1986), Gordon and Melham (1993) and Paulson (1994) describe the LCF-descended provers Nuprl, HOL and Isabelle respectively. Boyer and Moore (1979) discuss NQTHM, the Boyer–Moore prover, which can, despite its powerful automation, be considered as an interactive system in the way it's normally used. ACL2 is a more modern system based on similar principles (Kaufmann, Manolios and Moore 2000).

The study of formal calculi for deduction is a large part of contemporary logic. Many logic texts (Enderton 1972; Mendelson 1987) present and prove completeness for Hilbert systems, whereas others such as van Dalen (1994) use natural deduction. *Proof theory* is the study of proof systems in themselves; Troelstra and Schwichtenberg (1996), Prawitz (1965) and Girard, Lafont and Taylor (1989) are introductions to the field in somewhat different styles. Girard (1987) is an introduction to more advanced topics, while Goubault-Larrecq and Mackie (1997) discuss automated theorem proving in more proof-theoretic style.

The original LCF publication (Gordon, Milner and Wadsworth 1979) is still worth reading for more information on tactics. Others have generalized tactics in various directions; for example Sokołowski (1983) enhanced tactics to maintain a list of instantiable 'metavariables' that can be instantiated gradually. This allows the instantiation of existential terms to be done more freely at various points in the proof. A similar mechanism is supported, via a more direct implementation in terms of theorems, by Isabelle (Paulson 1994), which also supports nondeterministic tactics with an unlimited number of possible successor goalstates. Boulton (1992) extends the idea of delaying inference to the whole of an LCF-style prover. Mizar-style declarative proofs within LCF-style systems are described by Harrison (1996a), Syme (1997), Wenzel (1999), Zammit (1999a), Wiedijk (2001) and Corbineau (2008), while Harrison (1996c) is a more detailed comparison of declarative and procedural proving.

For a more detailed analysis of efficiency in LCF-style provers, see Boulton (1993) and Harrison (1995). The latter also contains a more detailed explanation of reflection in theorem proving and related fields of logic and computer science, though its survey of work in the field is now out of date. Many useful high-level derived rules have been written in the LCF style. For example, LCF implementation of arithmetical decision procedures goes back at least to Boulton (1993), and recent LCF-style implementations of Hörmander's algorithm for the reals are described by Mahboubi and Pottier (2002) and McLaughlin and Harrison (2005). Complex LCF-style derived rules for making inductive or recursive definitions are described by Melham (1991) and Slind (1996). Chaieb (2008) describes the implementation of several decision procedures, both in the LCF style and using reflection.

The alternatives of verifying code once and for all and checking correctness of particular results (step-by-step as the program runs or from a log or a more compact certificate that it creates) can be generalized beyond theorem proving. Blum (1993) suggests that, in many situations, checking results may be more practical and effective than verifying code – Mehlhorn *et al.* (1996) is a concrete example of incorporating result checking into a library for computational geometry. Harrison and Théry (1998) describe checking 'answers' from a computer algebra system, and Hurd (1999) describes checking 'proofs' from first-order provers by LCF inference.

There are at present two main application areas for interactive theorem proving: (i) formalizing pure mathematics, and (ii) verifying the correctness of computer programs, hardware, protocols, etc. Formalization of mathematics may be undertaken purely for its intellectual interest (Shankar 1994; Fleuriot 2001), or to support applications in verification (Harrison 1998; Hurd 2001), or because there is genuine doubt or scepticism about an informal proof (Gonthier 2005). The largest single corpus of formalized mathematics at present is the Mizar Mathematical Library,[†] and Wiedijk (2006)

[†] mizar.org/library/

gives a good short survey of other recent activity in the area. The Fly-speck project (Hales 2006), which aims for a complete formal proof of the Kepler sphere-packing conjecture, is perhaps the most ambitious formalization project to date, and is making good progress at the time of writing. As for verification, it is impossible in a reasonable space to summarize the many impressive applications of interactive theorem proving. To give a rough sample, a non-exhaustive list of verifications of real industrial hardware, software or microcode *just* in the particular domain of floating-point arithmetic would include Moore, Lynch and Kaufmann (1998), Russinoff (1998), O'Leary, Zhao, Gerth and Seger (1999), Harrison (2000), Kaivola and Aagaard (2000), Kaivola and Kohatsu (2001) and Slobodová (2007).

Exercises

6.1   Try out our earlier methods on the logical problems considered by Newell and Simon (1956). Are they all easy for our methods? How about the geometry theorems given by Gelerntner (1959)? Can we solve them easily via Gröbner bases or Wu's method?

6.2   Implement a version of tableaux with a Mizar-style restriction to obvious inferences, with at most one instantiation of each universal variable. How many of our usual stock of test problems, e.g. the Pelletier problems, turn out to be obvious in this sense? How does this match your intuitive feelings about what is obvious?

6.3   Implement a simple LCF-style prover with the Birkhoff rules for equational reasoning (see Section 4.3) as the primitive inferences. Re-implement Knuth–Bendix completion so that all theorems are derived using this system. For a similar project, see Slind (1991).

6.4   Enderton (1972) presents a somewhat different proof system for first-order logic. The inference rule **gen** that allows us to pass from $\vdash p$ to $\vdash \forall x.\, p$ is absent, and only modus ponens gives new theorems for old. But any of the axioms may be generalized over an arbitrary (possibly empty) subset of its free variables. Formulate a proof system close to ours with this restriction, and build up an LCF-style system from this foundation. Prove that p is deducible or first-order valid iff $\Gamma \models p$ in the sense of propositional logic, where Γ is the set of all (perhaps partially generalized) axioms.

6.5   Finding proofs of even fairly trivial facts in our Hilbert-style proof system, without the kinds of systematic principles embodied in **taut**, is often challenging. However, it is possible to use automated theorem provers on the 'meta' level to search for ways of proving them. For example here's a proof that $\vdash p \Rightarrow p$ is derivable:

```
meson <<(forall p q. Pr(Imp(p,q)) /\ Pr(p) ==> Pr(q)) /\
        (forall p q. Pr(Imp(p,Imp(q,p)))) /\
        (forall p q r. Pr(Imp(Imp(p,Imp(q,r)),
                             Imp(Imp(p,q),Imp(p,r)))))
        ==> forall p. Pr(Imp(p,p))>>;;
```

Set up some appropriate proof-tracing for some procedure such as `meson` so you can figure out the proof it found. See if you can thus find nicer proofs than ours of some of the simpler logical results. To avoid difficulties over free variable side-conditions, you may prefer to restrict yourself to propositional logic. Note that Otter has been applied to this sort of problem with great success, often finding proofs substantially shorter and more elegant than those in standard textbooks; see Wos (1994) for a detailed case study using powerful strategies. Try experimenting with other axiomatizations, using the machine to help you decide whether certain arrangements are complete.

6.6 Prove by induction on the inference steps in the proof that if $\Gamma \vdash q$ then also $\Gamma - \{p\} \vdash \forall(p) \Rightarrow q$ where $\forall(p)$ is the universal closure of p. This gives a more 'algorithmic' way of converting a proof of $\Gamma \vdash q$ into one of $\Gamma - \{p\} \vdash \forall(p) \Rightarrow q$. However, it still does not give any nice algorithmic way of implementing it as a derived inference rule since as input we need the *proof* of $\Gamma \vdash q$.

6.7 Another popular proof of the completeness of a proof system for propositional logic, due to Kalmár (1935) and presented by Mendelson (1987), is an adaptation of the usual truth-table method. Instead of considering a valuation as a model-theoretic concept, we encode the same information in a formula $l_1 \wedge \cdots \wedge l_n$, where each l_i is either p_i or $p_i \Rightarrow \perp$ (i.e. $\neg p_i$) for each propositional variable p_i in the formula. For example, if the propositional letters are p, q and r we represent the valuation v with $v(p) = \text{true}$, $v(q) = \text{false}$, $v(r) = \text{true}$ as $p \wedge (q \Rightarrow \perp) \wedge r$. We can prove a formula valid by showing that it holds for all valuations in this sense. Implement this and compare performance with `lcftaut`.

6.8 Implement an LCF core for a formulation of natural deduction, taking the rules from some standard text such as van Dalen (1994) or Troelstra and Schwichtenberg (1996). Write derived rules corresponding to the primitive rules of our Hilbert system, hence showing completeness.

6.9 Modify `lcffol` to perform initial splitting of the formula as done by `splittab`. Make sure that it also introduces Skolem constants (though not non-nullary Skolem functions). How much of the code can be re-used unchanged or easily adapted?

6.10 Although `lcftab` mostly avoids inference until a path to a refutation is found, the expansion of derived connectives still uses inference rules. Change the code so that this is no longer the case. Would you expect the efficiency to improve significantly, and does it seem to?

6.11 The case-splitting process in Mizar itself is somewhat different from ours. The user initiates a case-split by **per cases** *justification* and then begins various blocks with **suppose** p_i. Only when the case block is terminated is the proof of $p_1 \vee \cdots \vee p_n$ attempted using *justification*. Can you support this kind of case-splitting within our tactic framework?

6.12 Extend the LCF prover to add a primitive rule equivalent to **spec** that operates by directly using **subst** on the conclusion of the theorem. Compare its performance against the existing derived rule on increasingly large examples, and see how they compare. One might expect, at least in cases where complex renaming is not needed, that the runtime of either implementation would grow linearly with the size of the input theorem, but that one would be much faster than the other. Do your experiments bear this out?

6.13 Extend the LCF primitive inference system so that each inference rule maintains a 'counter' incremented on each call. Use this to see how many inference rules get used in some interesting proofs.

6.14 Extend the type of theorems to keep a tree structure recording the proof. Note that because of the LCF encapsulation, only the primitive inferences should need changing (Wong 1993). This opens up the possibility of taking proofs in an LCF system and feeding them to an independent proof-checker (Gordon, Hale, Herbert, Wright and Wong 1994) or using them in another prover (Obua and Skalberg 2006; McLaughlin 2006). You might even try translating the proofs and feeding them to an LCF prover using a different deductive system, of the kind suggested in Exercise 6.8.

6.15 For usefulness of `lcfptab` in higher-level derived rules, it would be desirable if we could constrain inference by a 'pattern'. For example, we would want $\vdash p \Rightarrow p$ to be provable in essentially the same way whatever the formula p might be, yet as things stand, a large formula p with a complex logical structure will generate a much larger proof. Generalize `lcfptab` so that it takes two arguments, the first a pattern

term, and the second an instance of that term, and uses the pattern
to constrain inferences. One way of doing this might be inspired by
the way `lcftaut` takes a mapping to modify terms; you could do
likewise for formulas.

6.16   Set up a more convenient interactive environment for developing
tactic proofs (declarative or otherwise) step-by-step. For example,
you might maintain a reference variable with the current goalstate
and set up commands to apply a tactic to it. Even better, you might
make a script to process a proof in the batch style of Mizar: take a
proof script in a file, and either run it or report any errors.

6.17   Create some 'tacticals' to operate on tactics corresponding to typical programming constructs such as 'then' (perform one tactic then
another), 'orelse' (try one tactic, and if it failed use another) and
'repeat' (apply a tactic repeatedly till it fails).

7

Limitations

Most of this book is about positive results: certain logical problems can in principle be automated. Here we consider the limits of automation, showing that algorithms in the usual sense cannot exist for certain logical problems. In particular we show that pure first-order logic is not decidable, and that the theory of natural numbers with addition and multiplication is, in a precise sense, nowhere near decidable. In making our way to these results, we prove Gödel's famous first incompleteness theorem.

7.1 Hilbert's programme

The idea of mechanizing reasoning fascinated people long before computers. Specific questions about the scope and limits of mechanization were investigated systematically in the early part of the twentieth century, largely due to the influence of *Hilbert's programme* to place mathematics on firm foundations. To appreciate the full cultural significance of the results that follow, it's worth examining the intellectual ferment over the foundations of mathematics that made these questions so significant at the time.

At various points in history, mathematicians have become concerned over apparent problems in the accepted foundations of their subject. For example, the Pythagoreans tried to base mathematics just on the rational numbers, and so were disturbed by the discovery that $\sqrt{2}$ must be irrational. Subsequently, the apparently self-contradictory treatment of infinitesimals in Newton and Leibniz's calculus disturbed many (Berkeley 1734), as later did the use of complex numbers and the discovery of non-Euclidean geometries. Later still, when the theory of infinite sets began to be pursued for its own sake and generalized, mainly by Cantor, renewed foundational worries appeared.

Many mathematicians, while accepting the idea of a 'potential infinity' (for example that every natural number has a successor), felt that mathematics must nevertheless remain rooted in concrete calculation. For example, Kronecker was happy to work with *algebraic* numbers, i.e. those like $\sqrt{2}+\sqrt{3}$ that are roots of polynomial equations with integer coefficients ($x^4 - 10x^2 + 1$ in this case), but he rejected *transcendental* (non-algebraic) numbers because they did not seem amenable to explicit computation with finite representations. Reputedly, he said that the proof by Lindemann (1882) that π is transcendental was 'interesting, except that π does not exist'.[†] Mathematicians with this point of view tended to reject most of the Cantorian apparatus, as well as nonconstructive existence proofs: Gordan greeted Hilbert's solution of a key problem in invariant theory via what is now called the Hilbert basis theorem with the remark 'That is not mathematics, it is theology!'.[‡] To understand what is meant by 'constructive' and 'nonconstructive' in this context, consider the following.

Theorem 7.1 *There are algebraic irrational numbers x and y such that x^y is rational.*

Proof If $\sqrt{2}^{\sqrt{2}}$ is rational, then $x = \sqrt{2}$ and $y = \sqrt{2}$ works. If it's irrational then $x = \sqrt{2}^{\sqrt{2}}$ and $y = \sqrt{2}$ works. $\qquad\square$

This proof is said to be nonconstructive because although it justifies the claim by apparently unimpeachable (and indeed rather slick) logical reasoning, it doesn't allow us to exhibit specific x and y. A similar remark applies to the following proof.

Theorem 7.2 *Either* $e + \pi$ *or* $e - \pi$ *is irrational, where* $e = 2.71828\dots$ *is the base of natural logarithms.*

Proof If $e + \pi$ and $e - \pi$ are both rational, then so is their sum $2e$. But this is a contradiction since e is known to be irrational. $\qquad\square$

Careful analysis of such proofs shows that constructivity tends to be lost because of a few specific principles of reasoning. In the proof of Theorem 7.1 it is the 'law of the excluded middle' $p \vee \neg p$, while for Theorem 7.2 it is the 'principle of contradiction' $(\neg p \Rightarrow \bot) \Rightarrow p$ or 'double negation elimination'

[†] Kronecker might have been satisfied with a representation of computable reals by approximating programs, though equality even of primitive recursive reals is undecidable.

[‡] This theorem was shown by Simpson (1988a) to be equivalent, in a precise sense, to the assumption that $\mathbb{N}^{\mathbb{N}}$ can be wellordered, and hence to be highly nonconstructive.

$\neg\neg p \Rightarrow p$. A constructivist would counsel against the careless use of such principles, making sure that they do not affect the constructivity of the overall result.

Brouwer, known as one of the founders of modern topology, went much further, starting a radical constructivist movement known as *intuitionism*. He claimed that nonconstructive proofs are not just in bad taste but are not even valid proofs at all. In particular, he asserted that both the law of the excluded middle and the principle of contradiction, in their full generality, are *invalid*. His student Heyting developed an intuitionistic logic to formalize intuitionistically acceptable reasoning, and traditional logic is now known as 'classical logic' in contradistinction.

At first sight it looks astonishing to question such elementary principles of reasoning. But Brouwer argued that the everyday laws of logic are unjustified extrapolations from simple reasoning about finite objects. For example, intuitionism accepts $p \vee \neg p$ in cases where the truth or falsity of p could, at least in principle, be determined – for example, whether a particular number is prime. But to claim $p \vee \neg p$ for *every* mathematical proposition p, even one that is currently unsolved and perhaps never will be solved, assumes a particular view of mathematical truth that Brouwer found objectionable: 'arithmetic as the natural history (mineralogy) of numbers' in the words of Wittgenstein (1956). It's clear that Hilbert (1922) accepted a considerable part of this critique, but he found Brouwer's mutilation of traditional mathematics unacceptable and suggested that it might be justified based on careful analysis of proofs:

But if we thoughtlessly apply to infinite totalities a procedure which is permissible in the finite case, then we open gate and door to errors. It is the same source of error that we see in analysis; in the latter field the carrying over, to infinite sums and products, of theorems which are valid for the corresponding finite sums and products is permissible only if special convergence conditions, etc., are satisfied. Similarly we cannot treat the infinite logical sums and products [existentially and universally quantified assertions, in our terminology] in the same manner as the finite, unless our proof theory reveals such treatment to be justified.

The similarities and contrasts with earlier foundational controversies is instructive, for example over the complex numbers, which were used in formulas for solving cubic and quartic equations as early as the sixteenth century. For many years afterwards the 'imaginary unit' i was frequently used in algebraic calculations, following the usual rules for real numbers together with $i^2 = -1$. Such uses of i often considerably streamlined calculations, but there was no convincing justification for it. Nevertheless, when a conclusion not involving complex numbers was reached, it did always seem to be correct, and after a while mathematicians began to take it for granted. In the same way, Hilbert wanted to regard infinite sets and the other non-constructive paraphernalia as 'ideal' elements, and prove that any concrete results (say, elementary facts of number theory) reached with the help of infinite sets were still valid.

In the case of complex numbers, by Hilbert's time their validity had already been established by creating a *model* of the complex numbers using pairs of real numbers. Similarly, one can create a model for Euclidean, and non-Euclidean, geometries using real numbers as coordinates. There are slightly more complicated schemes due to Klein and Cayley for giving a model of non-Euclidean geometries in terms of Euclidean, interpreting the plane as the interior of a circle and lines as chords. This technique of using models to prove one theory sound using another accepted theory was well-known. However, it seems impossible to justify Cantorian set theory in the same way – how can we create a model for infinite sets out of finite sets or natural numbers?

Hilbert's ingenious idea was to base the justification not on *models* but on *proofs*. Thanks to the work of Whitehead and Russell (1910) and others, it was possible to express axioms and deductions completely formally. These deductions could be identified with concrete objects like sequences of characters, or even (large) numbers. They could themselves become the object of mathematical study (often called *metamathematics*),[†] and this study could aim at proving properties of deductions in such systems – for example, that concrete results proved using infinite sets were nevertheless true, or even that they could also be proved without using infinite sets. Since proofs are finite objects, it seems plausible that only the barest, least doubtful, mathematical apparatus should be needed to prove interesting things about them. Proof theory, it seemed, might be the way to pass from simpler to more advanced and powerful mathematics without any danger of unsoundness. In computer jargon, Hilbert hoped to 'bootstrap' mathematics, starting with a weak system, acceptable even to a thoroughgoing sceptic and certainly to Brouwer, and justifying, at least in some sense, the rest of higher mathematics.[‡]

After a flurry of activity stimulated by Hilbert's ambitious programme, several positive results were achieved, but perhaps more strikingly, many

---

[†] It seems that Hilbert conceived of metamathematics much earlier (Hilbert 1905). However, it was only later that he started to see it as a possible answer to Brouwer's critique.

[‡] Tait (1981) has argued quite convincingly that the system of so-called *primitive recursive arithmetic* (PRA) provides a concrete formal system that accords well with Hilbert's own description of an acceptable starting point. This is often presented as a special quantifier-free logic (Goodstein 1957), but can also be formulated using a set of first-order axioms that have the same Π_1 consequences. Ironically, this is exactly the kind of reductionism that Hilbert's programme envisaged!

inherent limitations of formal proof systems were found. The first and best-known are doubtless Gödel's famous incompleteness theorems. However, there are numerous other related results, and in the following presentation we will distort the historical order somewhat, both for ease of exposition and to place emphasis on results directly showing the limitations of automated theorem proving.

7.2 Tarski's theorem on the undefinability of truth

We have seen that the theory of linear integer and natural number arithmetic is decidable (Cooper's algorithm, Section 5.7) and that over the reals, an analogous theory with addition *and* multiplication is decidable (Hörmander's algorithm, Section 5.9). By contrast, the theory of integers or natural numbers with addition and multiplication is, in a precise sense, very far from being decidable. In what follows we will prove this and some other key undecidability results, starting with a theorem on the 'undefinability of truth' due to Tarski (1936).[†]

Before describing this result, we will fix a first-order language to be used consistently for most of this chapter. We include a constant 0, a unary successor function written S, binary functions '+' and '·', and binary relations $=$, $<$ and $\leq$. There are no other constant symbols, though in discussions we often use $\overline{n}$ to abbreviate a zero-successor representation of the numeral n, for example $\overline{4}$ for $S(S(S(S(0))))$. The following OCaml function can be used to generate numerals in this form:

```
let rec numeral n =
  if n =/ Int 0 then Fn("0",[])
  else Fn("S",[numeral(n -/ Int 1)]);;
```

The intended interpretation of this language is over $\mathbb{N}$ with the usual assignments of functions and relations: '+' to addition and so on. When we say in what follows that a formula is *true* we mean that it is true in the ordinary sense: it holds in this 'intended interpretation' or 'standard model' over $\mathbb{N}$, not necessarily in *all* interpretations. For example, $\forall x.\ x + 0 = x$ is true because it holds in the standard model, even though we can find other interpretations in which it fails (just change the standard model to interpret 0 as the number 1, for example).

So now we know what 'truth' means in Tarski's theorem: the property of being a true formula (in the standard model). What about definability?

[†] Though Gödel (1931) had earlier arrived at something very similar on the way to his incompleteness theorems.

Definable relations, sets and functions

An n-ary relation R on a set D, which we can think of as a subset of D^n or a function $D^n \to$ bool, is said to be *definable* in a language L and interpretation M with domain D if there is a formula p based on the language L, with n free variables $x_1, \ldots, x_n$, such that

$$R = \{(a_1, \ldots, a_n) \in D^n \mid \texttt{holds } M \ (x_i \mapsto a_i) \ p\},$$

where $x_i \mapsto a_i$ denotes the valuation that maps each x_i to the corresponding a_i. We will in the following be interested in definability in the set $D = \mathbb{N}$ based on the language specified earlier – for brevity we will just say 'definable in arithmetic'. The above model-theoretic definition makes our usual fussy distinctions between variables and their interpretation, but a few simple examples should make the concept of definability in arithmetic clear: either of the formulas $\exists n. \ m = 2 \cdot n$ and $\forall n. \ \neg(m = 2 \cdot n + 1)$ defines the unary relation of evenness (divisibility by 2), and $n < m \lor m < n$ defines the binary relation of inequality '$\neq$'.

As we have noted, we will treat sets and relations interchangeably, so we can equally well say that $\exists n. \ m = 2 \cdot n$ defines the set of even numbers. We will also extend definability to *functions* by considering them as relations. An n-ary function $f : \mathbb{N}^n \to \mathbb{N}$ is said to be definable iff its graph $\{(a_1, \ldots, a_n, a_{n+1}) \mid f(a_1, \ldots, a_n) = a_{n+1}\}$ is definable as a relation. Note that this does *not* mean that there is a corresponding *term* defining it directly as a function – this is a much weaker notion. For example, it's easy to see that there is no term in our language directly representing the truncating halving function $n \mapsto \lfloor n/2 \rfloor$, yet its graph is defined by the formula $n = 2 \cdot q \lor n = 2 \cdot q + 1$. Even if we want to use a definable function in an intricately nested way inside term, we can always reduce it to the simple relational form by flattening, e.g. $x + f(y, z) + f(f(a, b), c) > k$ to the existential formula $\exists r \ s \ t. \ F(y, z, r) \land F(a, b, s) \land F(s, c, t) \land x + r + t > k$ or the universal formula $\forall r \ s \ t. \ F(y, z, r) \land F(a, b, s) \land F(s, c, t) \Rightarrow x + r + t > k$.

Arithmetization of syntax

As we have defined it, *truth* is a property of formulas, rather than numbers, so it doesn't immediately make sense to talk of its being definable in arithmetic. But we can fix this by choosing some appropriate mapping g from formulas to natural numbers, and consider definability of the image of a set of formulas under g. The numbering function g is known as a *Gödel numbering*, since the idea was first used by Gödel, and we often write $\ulcorner p \urcorner$ for $g(p)$. These corner quotes, due to Quine, are intended to reflect the similarity with quotation marks in ordinary language, indicating that we are referring to the sentence itself as a syntactic object rather than its underlying meaning.[†]

We will explicitly define our Gödel numbering in OCaml for concreteness, mapping into the type `num` of unlimited integers to avoid the danger of overflow. It is crucial in what follows that it should be injective, i.e. that $\ulcorner p \urcorner = \ulcorner q \urcorner$ only if p and q are the same formula. We will not, however, bother to make it bijective; there will be natural numbers that are not the Gödel number of any formula.

First we need to map strings to natural numbers. An OCaml string can be considered a finite (possibly empty) list of characters $c_0, \ldots, c_{n-1}$, each c_i having a value in the range 0–255. We will map such a string to the number $\sum_{i=0}^{n-1} 256^i (c_i + 1)$. Note that this value uniquely determines the length, since the code s of a string of length n lies in the range $1 + 256 + \cdots + 256^{n-1} \le s \le 256 \cdot (1 + 256 + \cdots + 256^{n-1}) < 1 + 256 + \cdots + 256^n$. Thus, if two strings have the same code, they have the same length, so the injectivity of the mapping follows from the usual uniqueness of a (base 256) positional representation. In fact, since the range identified above for n-element strings contains exactly 256^n numbers, it also follows that this mapping, at least, is surjective. So we won't have to worry later about whether a particular number could correspond to a string.

```
let number s =
   itlist (fun i g -> Int(1 + Char.code(String.get s i)) +/ Int 256 */ g)
          (0--(String.length s - 1)) (Int 0);;
```

Next we introduce a pairing function $\mathbb{N} \times \mathbb{N} \to \mathbb{N}$, which we abbreviate $\langle x, y \rangle$ and define as $(x + y)^2 + x + 1$:

```
let pair x y = (x +/ y) */ (x +/ y) +/ x +/ Int 1;;
```

We should prove that this function is injective. First note that if $\langle x', y' \rangle = \langle x, y \rangle$ we must also have $x' + y' = x + y$. For if, say $x' + y' > x + y$, then since the natural numbers are discrete we have $x' + y' \ge x + y + 1$ and therefore we can derive a contradiction:

$$
\begin{aligned}
\langle x', y' \rangle &= (x' + y')^2 + x' + 1 \\
&\ge (x' + y')^2 + 1 \\
&\ge (x + y + 1)^2 + 1 \\
&= (x + y)^2 + 2(x + y) + 2
\end{aligned}
$$

[†] Indeed, Quine introduced them as a formal version of quotation, not for Gödel numbers.

$$\geq \quad (x+y)^2 + x + 2$$
$$> \quad (x+y)^2 + x + 1 = \langle x, y \rangle.$$

So if $\langle x', y' \rangle = \langle x, y \rangle$ we must have $x' + y' = x + y$. But then we also have $x' = x$ by cancelling $(x+y)^2 + 1$ from both sides, and then $y' = y$ by subtraction.

The additional '$+1$' in the pairing function is not necessary for injectivity. However, it's convenient to be able to assume that $\langle x, y \rangle > 0$ for all $x, y \in \mathbb{N}$. Then we get a natural and unambiguous encoding of a finite list of numbers as a single number, using 0 as the empty list:

$$[x_1; x_2; x_2; \cdots; x_n] = \langle x_1, \langle x_2, \langle \cdots, \langle x_n, 0 \rangle \rangle \rangle \rangle.$$

Now we define Gödel numberings injecting into $\mathbb{N}$ the terms:

```
let rec gterm tm =
  match tm with
    Var x -> pair (Int 0) (number x)
  | Fn("0",[]) -> pair (Int 1) (Int 0)
  | Fn("S",[t]) -> pair (Int 2) (gterm t)
  | Fn("+",[s;t]) -> pair (Int 3) (pair (gterm s) (gterm t))
  | Fn("*",[s;t]) -> pair (Int 4) (pair (gterm s) (gterm t))
  | _ -> failwith "gterm: not in the language";;
```

and hence the formulas:

```
let rec gform fm =
  match fm with
    False -> pair (Int 0) (Int 0)
  | True -> pair (Int 0) (Int 1)
  | Atom(R("=",[s;t])) -> pair (Int 1) (pair (gterm s) (gterm t))
  | Atom(R("<",[s;t])) -> pair (Int 2) (pair (gterm s) (gterm t))
  | Atom(R("<=",[s;t])) -> pair (Int 3) (pair (gterm s) (gterm t))
  | Not(p) -> pair (Int 4) (gform p)
  | And(p,q) -> pair (Int 5) (pair (gform p) (gform q))
  | Or(p,q) -> pair (Int 6) (pair (gform p) (gform q))
  | Imp(p,q) -> pair (Int 7) (pair (gform p) (gform q))
  | Iff(p,q) -> pair (Int 8) (pair (gform p) (gform q))
  | Forall(x,p) -> pair (Int 9) (pair (number x) (gform p))
  | Exists(x,p) -> pair (Int 10) (pair (number x) (gform p))
  | _ -> failwith "gform: not in the language";;
```

(In discussions we use the same corner quotes for the Gödel numbering of both terms $\ulcorner t \urcorner$ and formulas $\ulcorner p \urcorner$.) Since the **number** and **pair** functions are injective, so are these mappings. Our Gödel numbering is designed for simplicity rather than compactness, and the numbers produced tend to be on the large side for interesting formulas.

```
# gform <<~(x = 0)>>;;
- : num = 2116574771128325487937994357299494
```

Outline of Tarski's theorem

Consider the set T of codes of true formulas in the language of arithmetic:[†]

$$T = \{\ulcorner p \urcorner \mid p \text{ is true in } \mathbb{N}\}.$$

For example, T contains the following number:

```
# gform <<x = x>>;;
- : num = 735421674029290002
```

because $x = x$ is true in $\mathbb{N}$ (and indeed in any interpretation) but it does not contain the number $\langle 11, 0 \rangle = 133$, which is not the Gödel number of *any* formula, and nor does it contain $\ulcorner 0 < 0 \urcorner = 1767$ since $0 < 0$ is false in $\mathbb{N}$ (though not all interpretations).

Tarski's theorem states that the set T is *not* definable in arithmetic. This might appear a mere technical curiosity. But it will emerge that many other sets of codes of 'provable' formulas P *are* definable. For example, in the next section we will show that the set of formulas provable from, or equivalently (by the completeness Theorem 6.3) logical consequences of, the first-order axioms PA for so-called *Peano arithmetic*:

$$P = \{\ulcorner p \urcorner \mid PA \vdash p\} = \{\ulcorner p \urcorner \mid PA \models p\}$$

is definable, and later we will sketch a proof that the set of codes of formulas enumerable (in a sense to be made precise) using *any* particular computer program is definable. Since the set of codes of provable formulas is definable but the set of codes of true formulas is not, it follows that the sets of true and provable formulas must themselves be different (assuming we used a fixed coding throughout). Thus at least one of the following must hold:

- some true formula is not provable ('semantical incompleteness'),
- some provable formula is not true ('unsoundness').

Later we will present much more refined forms of this basic observation, but it's useful to keep that motivation in mind through the technical details to follow.

[†] Later, we will find it useful to restrict ourselves to the set of true *sentences*, but that is not necessary for the argument presented here.

Many things are definable

We will establish Tarski's theorem by assuming the existence of a definition of truth and building from it another clearly impossible definition. To support that step we first need several positive results that various sets of natural numbers, and relations over natural numbers, *are* definable in arithmetic. The divisibility relation 'm divides n' is definable as follows:[†]

$$m|n =_{\text{def}} \exists x.\, x \leq n \wedge n = m \cdot x.$$

When we give such a 'definition', the claim is that the corresponding equivalence (replacing '$=_{\text{def}}$' by '$\Leftrightarrow$') holds in $\mathbb{N}$. This means that we can replace any instance of the left-hand side (here $s|t$) by an appropriate substitution instance of the right-hand side, without changing the interpretation of the formula in $\mathbb{N}$. Using divisibility, we can easily express primality:

$$\text{prime}(p) =_{\text{def}} 2 \leq p \wedge \forall n.\, n < p \Rightarrow n|p \Rightarrow n = 1.$$

We write $\text{primepow}(p, x)$ to indicate that p is a prime number and x is some power of it, possibly $x = p^0 = 1$. We don't have the exponential function in our language, so we can't make the natural definition $\text{prime}(p) \wedge \exists n.\, x = p^n$. However, a little thought shows that the following also works:[‡]

$$\text{primepow}(p, x) =_{\text{def}} \text{prime}(p) \wedge \neg(x = 0) \wedge \forall z.\, z \leq x \Rightarrow z|x \Rightarrow z = 1 \vee p|z.$$

Now we will show that whenever a binary relation R is definable, so is its reflexive transitive closure R^*.[§] Recall (See Appendix 1) that $R^*(x, y)$ iff there is a sequence $x = x_0, x_1, \ldots, x_n = y$ such that $R(x_i, x_{i+1})$ for each $0 \leq i \leq n - 1$. This is in its turn equivalent to the existence of a prime p greater than all the x_i and a number of the form

$$m = x_0 + x_1 p + x_2 p^2 + \cdots + x_n p^n$$

for some such sequence (x_i). But the various x_i can be extracted from such an m by division and remainder operations, all of which are straightforwardly definable. There must exist some $Q = p^n$ such that $x = x_0$ is the remainder of m modulo p, y is the truncated quotient of m by Q, and for all smaller q that are powers of p we have $R(a, b)$ whenever $m = r + q \cdot (a + p \cdot (b + p \cdot s))$ for some $r < q$, $a < p$ and $b < p$ (since a and b are then adjacent elements

---

[†] The '$x \leq n$' isn't necessary, but makes evident a technical property called Δ_0-definability, to be considered later. In what follows, simply observe that the formulas given *do* correctly define the concepts, even if not in the most immediately obvious or natural way.

[‡] The idea of defining powers of primes in this way is due to John Myhill.

[§] This is a further simplification of a clever encoding given by Smullyan (1992).

of the encoded sequence). Thus we can define

$$R^*(x, y) =_{\text{def}}$$
$$\exists m\, p\, Q.\ \text{primepow}(p, Q) \wedge x < p \wedge y < p \wedge$$
$$(\exists s.\ m = x + p \cdot s) \wedge$$
$$(\exists r.\ r < Q \wedge m = r + Q \cdot y) \wedge$$
$$\forall q.\ q < Q$$
$$\Rightarrow \text{primepow}(p, q)$$
$$\Rightarrow \exists r\, a\, b\, s.\ m = r + q \cdot (a + p \cdot (b + p \cdot s)) \wedge$$
$$r < q \wedge a < p \wedge b < p \wedge R(a, b).$$

This result opens the way to defining the graphs of *primitive recursive* functions. Roughly speaking, a primitive recursive function f is one where $f(n+1)$ can be defined in terms of just $f(n)$ and n using other functions that are very basic or themselves primitive recursive. For example, the factorial function is primitive recursive because $(n + 1)! = (n + 1) \cdot n!$, as is the exponential function because $x^{n+1} = x \cdot x^n$. On the other hand, the usual recurrence $f(n + 2) = f(n + 1) + f(n)$ for the Fibonacci numbers does not have this simple pattern of recursion, so some reformulation is needed to show that it can also be defined primitive recursively. And some functions with slightly more involved recursive definitions have *no* primitive recursive equivalent.[†]

We will now prove that if $f : \mathbb{N} \to \mathbb{N}$ is defined by the following primitive recursive schema for some constant a and definable $g : \mathbb{N} \times \mathbb{N} \to \mathbb{N}$, then f is itself definable:

$$f(0) = a,$$
$$f(S(n)) = g(n, f(n)).$$

Suppose g, that is the relation $g(x, y) = z$, is defined by a formula $G(x, y, z)$. Then the following defines the relation between $\langle n, z \rangle$ and the 'next' term $\langle S(n), g(n, z) \rangle$:

$$R(u, v) = \exists x\, y\, z.\ G(x, y, z) \wedge u = \langle x, y \rangle \wedge v = \langle S(x), z \rangle.$$

By the previous result, we know that since R is definable, so is its reflexive transitive closure R^*. Now if the term t defines the constant a, the following

---

[†] In 1928 Ackermann showed that the function defined by these clauses has no primitive recursive equivalent: $A(0, n, m) = n + m$, $A(1, n, m) = nm$, $A(2, n, m) = n^m$ and thereafter $A(k + 1, n, 0) = n$ and $A(k + 1, n, m + 1) = A(k, n, A(k + 1, n, m))$. Simplified 2-argument versions were later introduced by Rosza Peter and Raphael Robinson and are often called 'Ackermann's function' without discrimination (Calude, Marcus and Tevy 1979).

binary relation defines exactly the graph of the required primitive recursive function f:

$$S(n,p) =_{\text{def}} R^*(\langle 0, t \rangle, \langle n, p \rangle).$$

As instances of this general result, we can see that various common numerical functions such as the factorial $n!$ and exponential m^n are definable. But we won't need any of those in what follows, only a more obscure function we will call gnumeral, taking a natural number n to the Gödel number of the zero-successor numeral $\overline{n}$:

$$\text{gnumeral}(n) = \ulcorner \overbrace{S(S(\cdots S(0)\cdots))}^{n \text{ times}} \urcorner$$

and which we can implement in OCaml as:

```
let gnumeral n = gterm(numeral n);;
```

We have $\ulcorner 0 \urcorner = \langle 1, 0 \rangle = 3$ and $\ulcorner S(n) \urcorner = \langle 2, \ulcorner n \urcorner \rangle$. Plugging these into the general definition schema for primitive recursion, and simplifying a bit because the appropriate $g(n, y) = \langle 2, y \rangle$ is actually definable by a term, we get the following 1-step relation:

$$\text{GNUMERAL}_1(a, b) =_{\text{def}} \exists x \, y. \, a = \langle x, y \rangle \wedge b = \langle S(x), \langle 2, y \rangle \rangle.$$

We extend this to its reflexive transitive closure GNUMERAL_1^* using the general schema and so to a definition for GNUMERAL, the graph of the gnumeral function:

$$\text{GNUMERAL}(n, p) =_{\text{def}} \text{GNUMERAL}_1^*(\langle 0, 3 \rangle, \langle n, p \rangle).$$

Self-referential sentences

The proof of Tarski's theorem is a formalization of the classic *Liar paradox* 'this sentence is false'. However, there's no obvious way in logic for a sentence to refer back to *itself* as the English phrase 'this sentence' apparently does. The trick we will use to encode this self-reference is perhaps best appreciated by considering the analogous method in natural language. Define the *diagonalization* of a string to be the result of replacing all (unquoted) instances of the letter 'x' in that string by the entire string in quotes. Here's an OCaml implementation; to keep track of nested quotes, we will use distinct 'open' and 'close' quotation marks, but one can mentally identify them with ordinary string quotes.

```
let diag s =
  let rec replacex n l =
    match l with
       [] -> if n = 0 then "" else failwith "unmatched quotes"
     | "x"::t when n = 0 -> "‘"^s^"’"^replacex n t
     | "‘"::t -> "‘"^replacex (n + 1) t
     | "’"::t -> "’"^replacex (n - 1) t
     | h::t -> h^replacex n t in
  replacex 0 (explode s);;
```

For example:

```
# diag("p(x)");;
- : string = "p(‘p(x)’)"
# diag("This string is diag(x)");;
- : string = "This string is diag(‘This string is diag(x)’)"
```

The second example already shows a form of self-reference: the string *is* in a strong sense what it says it is: 'diag("This string is diag(x)")'. It's not syntactically identical – evidently *no* string can be the same as a proper segment of itself. But it's equivalent when the meaning of diag is understood; indeed it *is* identical to the OCaml invocation that produced it. We will use essentially the same technique to find, given any unary predicate P, a 'fixpoint' ϕ such that $P(\phi)$ means exactly the same thing as ϕ:

```
# let phi = diag("P(diag(x))");;
val phi : string = "P(diag(‘P(diag(x)’))"
```

We can express this in 'natural', though convoluted, language, by spelling out the intended meaning of diag explicitly (Franzén 2005):

```
# diag("The result of substituting the quotation of x for ‘x’ in x \
          has property P");;
- : string =
"The result of substituting the quotation of ‘The result of
substituting the quotation of x for ‘x’ in x has property P’ for ‘x’
in ‘The result of substituting the quotation of x for ‘x’ in x has
property P’ has property P"
```

This phrase 'the result of substituting ...' expresses substitution without actually doing it, just as the OCaml construct 'let x = 2 in x + x' does. We can use likewise use this 'quasi-substitution' to perform 'quasi-diagonalization'.

```
# let qdiag s = "let ‘x’ be ‘"^s^"’ in "^s;;
val qdiag : string -> string = <fun>
```

Because we don't have to substitute, the implementation is simpler, and we can get a fixpoint for a predicate in exactly the same way, albeit one that needs a little more unravelling:

```
# let phi = qdiag("P(qdiag(x))");;
val phi : string = "let 'x' be 'P(qdiag(x))' in P(qdiag(x))"
```

For a more detailed study of various logical aspects of self-reference, see Smullyan (1994).[†]

The fixpoint lemma

We will now render this construction in logical form and so prove the key fixed point theorem (Carnap 1937).[‡] Suppose $P[x]$ is any arithmetical formula with exactly one free variable x. We will show how to construct a sentence ϕ such that $\phi \Leftrightarrow P\lceil\overline{\phi}\rceil$ is true in arithmetic. The construction follows the plan in the previous subsection with numeral representations of Gödel numbers taking the place of string quotation. Diagonalization of a formula p with respect to a variable x can be defined by $\mathrm{diag}_x(p) = \mathsf{subst}\ (x \mapsto \lceil p \rceil)\ p$, and can be implemented as:

```
let diag x p = subst (x |=> numeral(gform p)) p;;
```

However, later work is easier using quasi-substitution $\mathrm{qsubst}(x, t, p) = \exists x.\ x = t \wedge p$, which is logically equivalent to $\mathsf{subst}\ (x \mapsto t)\ p$ whenever $x \notin \mathrm{FVT}(t)$. In particular, we can define quasi-diagonalization by $\mathrm{qdiag}_x(p) = \mathrm{qsubst}(x, \lceil p \rceil, p) = \exists x.\ x = \lceil p \rceil \wedge p$:

```
let qdiag x p = Exists(x,And(mk_eq (Var x) (numeral(gform p)),p));;
```

A natural counterpart of our fixpoint construction `diag("P(diag(x))")` would be something like the following:

$$\phi = \mathrm{qdiag}_x(P[\overline{\lceil \mathrm{qdiag}_x(\#x) \rceil}]),$$

where $\#$ is some left inverse of the Gödel numbering satisfying $\#\lceil p \rceil = p$ for all formulas p. (Since the Gödel numbering is injective, there must exist such an inverse.) We can't literally write down a formula containing the inverse $\#$, but note that:

[†] Similar tricks can be used to create programs, often called *quines*, that produce exactly their own text as output (Bratley and Millo 1972). See `martin.jambon.free.fr/quine.ml.html` for a short quine in OCaml.

[‡] Gödel had already applied it in a special case that we consider in the next section.

$\ulcorner \text{qdiag}_x(p) \urcorner$

$$
\begin{aligned}
&= \quad \ulcorner \exists x.\, x = \overline{\ulcorner p \urcorner} \wedge p \urcorner \\
&= \quad \langle 10, \langle \text{number}(x), \ulcorner x = \overline{\ulcorner p \urcorner} \wedge p \urcorner \rangle \rangle \\
&= \quad \langle 10, \langle \text{number}(x), \langle 5, \langle \ulcorner x = \overline{\ulcorner p \urcorner} \urcorner, \ulcorner p \urcorner \rangle \rangle \rangle \rangle \\
&= \quad \langle 10, \langle \text{number}(x), \langle 5, \langle \langle 1, \langle \ulcorner x \urcorner, \ulcorner \overline{\ulcorner p \urcorner} \urcorner \rangle \rangle, \ulcorner p \urcorner \rangle \rangle \rangle \rangle \\
&= \quad \langle 10, \langle \text{number}(x), \langle 5, \langle \langle 1, \langle \langle 0, \text{number}(x) \rangle \rangle, \text{gnumeral}(\ulcorner p \urcorner) \rangle \rangle, \ulcorner p \urcorner \rangle \rangle \rangle \rangle.
\end{aligned}
$$

This means that the following binary predicate:

$$
\text{QDIAG}_x(n, y) \Leftrightarrow \exists k.\ \text{GNUMERAL}(n, k)\ \wedge
$$
$$
\langle 10, \langle \text{number}(x), \langle 5, \langle \langle 1, \langle \langle 0, \text{number}(x) \rangle \rangle, k \rangle \rangle, n \rangle \rangle \rangle \rangle = y
$$

has the property that $\text{QDIAG}_x(\ulcorner p \urcorner, y)$ holds in $\mathbb{N}$ precisely if $y = \overline{\ulcorner \text{qdiag}_x(p) \urcorner}$ does. So we can deduce Carnap's fixpoint (or *diagonal*) lemma.

Lemma 7.3 *Let $P[x]$ be a formula in the language of arithmetic with just the free variable x, and define $\phi =_{\text{def}} qdiag_x(\exists y.\,\text{QDIAG}_x(x, y) \wedge P[y])$. Then $\phi \Leftrightarrow P[\overline{\ulcorner \phi \urcorner}]$ holds in $\mathbb{N}$.*

Proof Note the following chain of equivalences in $\mathbb{N}$:

$$
\begin{aligned}
\phi \quad &= \quad \text{qdiag}_x(\exists y.\,\text{QDIAG}_x(x, y) \wedge P[y]) \\
&\Leftrightarrow \quad \text{diag}_x(\exists y.\,\text{QDIAG}_x(x, y) \wedge P[y]) \\
&= \quad \exists y.\,\text{QDIAG}_x(\ulcorner \exists y.\,\text{QDIAG}_x(x, y) \wedge P[y] \urcorner, y) \wedge P[y] \\
&\Leftrightarrow \quad \exists y.\, y = \overline{\ulcorner \text{qdiag}_x(\exists y.\,\text{QDIAG}_x(x, y) \wedge P[y]) \urcorner} \wedge P[y] \\
&\Leftrightarrow \quad P[\overline{\ulcorner \text{qdiag}_x(\exists y.\,\text{QDIAG}_x(x, y) \wedge P[y]) \urcorner}] \\
&\Leftrightarrow \quad P[\overline{\ulcorner \phi \urcorner}]
\end{aligned}
$$

as required.

$\square$

Tarski's theorem

We now have all the ingredients we need to prove Tarski's theorem on the undefinability of truth.

Theorem 7.4 *There is no formula in the language of arithmetic that defines the set of Gödel numbers of true formulas, i.e. the set $\{\ulcorner p \urcorner \mid p \text{ is true in } \mathbb{N}\}$.*

Proof Suppose that $\text{Tr}[x]$ were such a formula, with free variable x. By the fixpoint Lemma 7.3 applied to the formula $\neg\text{Tr}[x]$, there is a sentence ϕ such that $\phi \Leftrightarrow \neg\text{Tr}[\ulcorner\phi\urcorner]$ is true in $\mathbb{N}$. But by hypothesis, $\text{Tr}[\ulcorner\phi\urcorner]$ holds in $\mathbb{N}$ iff ϕ is true in $\mathbb{N}$, and therefore $\neg\text{Tr}[\ulcorner\phi\urcorner]$ holds in $\mathbb{N}$ iff ϕ is *not* true in $\mathbb{N}$. Therefore $\phi \Leftrightarrow \neg\text{Tr}[\ulcorner\phi\urcorner]$ cannot hold in $\mathbb{N}$, and we have reached a contradiction. □

7.3 Incompleteness of axiom systems

Now we'll show that, by contrast with the set of true sentences, the set of *provable* sentences in the first-order proof system from Chapter 6 *is* definable. In fact we will prove more generally that whenever (the set of Gödel numbers of) A is definable, so is (the set of Gödel numbers of) $\text{Cn}(A) = \{p \mid A \vdash p\} = \{p \mid A \models p\}$; these sets are the same by Theorem 6.3.

For a start, it's convenient to be able to check that a certain Gödel number does indeed correspond to a term, or a formula. Consider the definable binary relation TERM_1:

$$
\begin{aligned}
\text{TERM}_1(x,y) =_{\text{def}} \quad & (\exists l\ u.\ x = l \wedge y = \langle\langle 0, u\rangle, l\rangle) \vee \\
& (\exists l.\ x = l \wedge y = \langle\langle 1, 0\rangle, l\rangle) \vee \\
& (\exists t\ l.\ x = \langle t, l\rangle \wedge y = \langle\langle 2, t\rangle, l\rangle) \vee \\
& (\exists n\ s\ t\ l.\ (n = 3 \vee n = 4) \wedge \\
& \qquad x = \langle s, \langle t, l\rangle\rangle \wedge y = \langle\langle n, \langle s, t\rangle\rangle, l\rangle).
\end{aligned}
$$

By design, this is true exactly for pairs of the following form. (Note that we use here the surjectivity of the **number** mapping from strings to numbers, ensuring that any number corresponds to a variable.)

$$
\begin{aligned}
l \quad &, \quad \langle\ulcorner x\urcorner, l\rangle \\
l \quad &, \quad \langle\ulcorner 0\urcorner, l\rangle \\
\langle\ulcorner t\urcorner, l\rangle \quad &, \quad \langle\ulcorner S(t)\urcorner, l\rangle \\
\langle\ulcorner s\urcorner, \langle\ulcorner t\urcorner, l\rangle\rangle \quad &, \quad \langle\ulcorner s + t\urcorner, l\rangle \\
\langle\ulcorner s\urcorner, \langle\ulcorner t\urcorner, l\rangle\rangle \quad &, \quad \langle\ulcorner s \cdot t\urcorner, l\rangle
\end{aligned}
$$

By earlier results, the reflexive-transitive closure TERM_1^* is also definable. The underlying idea is that if we think of both parameters as lists, encoded with repeated pairing, then $\text{TERM}_1(l_1, l_2)$ holds if l_1 results from one step of 'deconstruction' of the first element of l_2, either breaking a composite term into two subterms or removing it if it is a variable or constant; $\text{TERM}_1^*(l_1, l_2)$ then holds if we can pass from l_2 to l_1 by *repeated* 'destruction' steps.

To make this precise, note that if $m = \langle a_1, \ldots, \langle a_k, 0 \rangle \ldots \rangle$ is a list of Gödel numbers of terms and $\mathrm{TERM}_1(m, n)$, then n is also a list of Gödel numbers of terms, and by induction, the same applies when $\mathrm{TERM}_1^*(m, n)$. Since trivially all the elements of the list 0 (of which there are none) are Gödel numbers of terms, so is n whenever $\mathrm{TERM}_1^*(0, [n])$. Conversely, by induction on terms t, for any a we have $\mathrm{TERM}_1^*(a, \langle \ulcorner t \urcorner, a \rangle)$. Putting these together, we see that $\mathrm{TERM}_1^*(0, \langle n, 0 \rangle)$ iff n is the Gödel number of a term in the language, so we define

$$\mathrm{TERM}(n) =_{\mathrm{def}} \mathrm{TERM}_1^*(0, \langle n, 0 \rangle).$$

We will use the same technique four more times to define other syntactic properties and the notion of provability. First, we define the set of Gödel numbers of valid formulas of the language via

$$\begin{aligned}
\mathrm{FORM}_1(x, y) = \ & (\exists l. \ x = l \wedge y = \langle \langle 0, 0 \rangle, l \rangle) \vee \\
& (\exists l. \ x = l \wedge y = \langle \langle 0, 1 \rangle, l \rangle) \vee \\
& (\exists n \ s \ t \ l. \ (n = 1 \vee n = 2 \vee n = 3) \wedge \\
& \quad \mathrm{TERM}(s) \wedge \mathrm{TERM}(t) \wedge \\
& \quad x = l \wedge y = \langle \langle n, \langle s, t \rangle \rangle, l \rangle) \vee \\
& (\exists p \ l. \ x = \langle p, l \rangle \wedge y = \langle \langle 4, p \rangle, l \rangle) \vee \\
& (\exists n \ p \ q \ l. \ (n = 5 \vee n = 6 \vee n = 7 \vee n = 8) \wedge \\
& \quad x = \langle p, \langle q, l \rangle \rangle \wedge y = \langle \langle n, \langle p, q \rangle \rangle, l \rangle) \vee \\
& (\exists n \ u \ p \ l. \ (n = 9 \vee n = 10) \wedge \\
& \quad x = \langle p, l \rangle \wedge y = \langle \langle n, \langle u, p \rangle \rangle, l \rangle)
\end{aligned}$$

and

$$\mathrm{FORM}(n) =_{\mathrm{def}} \mathrm{FORM}_1^*(0, \langle n, 0 \rangle).$$

In order to state the two side-conditions that arise with axioms, $x \notin \mathrm{FVT}(t)$ and $x \notin \mathrm{FV}(p)$, we define corresponding binary relations. The formula $\mathrm{FREETERM}(m, n)$ means 'n is the Gödel number of a term t in which the variable x with $\mathrm{number}(x) = m$ does not appear'. We can simply modify the relation TERM_1 to have the extra parameter m indicating the variable number, disallowing terms built from it by using the additional condition $u \neq m$:

$$\begin{aligned}
\mathrm{FREETERM}_1(m, x, y) =_{\mathrm{def}} \ & \\
& (\exists l \ u. \ \neg(u = m) \wedge x = l \wedge y = \langle \langle 0, u \rangle, l \rangle) \vee \\
& (\exists l. \ x = l \wedge y = \langle \langle 1, 0 \rangle, l \rangle) \vee \\
& (\exists t \ l. \ x = \langle t, l \rangle \wedge y = \langle \langle 2, t \rangle, l \rangle) \vee \\
& (\exists n \ s \ t \ l. \ (n = 3 \vee n = 4) \wedge \\
& \quad x = \langle s, \langle t, l \rangle \rangle \wedge y = \langle \langle n, \langle s, t \rangle \rangle, l \rangle),
\end{aligned}$$

then produce FREETERM as its reflexive transitive closure, considering it as a binary relation between x and y, with the additional variable m simply carried through as an additional parameter:

$$\text{FREETERM}(m, n) =_{\text{def}} \text{FREETERM}_1^*(m, 0, \langle n, 0 \rangle).$$

Similarly we define $FREEFORM(m, n)$ meaning 'n is the Gödel number of a formula p in which the variable x with $\text{number}(x) = m$ does not appear free'. Again, we can introduce the additional parameter m and replace each TERM(t) by FREETERM(m, t). However, since x is not free in $\forall x.\, p$ or $\exists x.\, p$, we add a clause for that at the end:

$$
\begin{aligned}
\text{FREEFORM}_1&(m, x, y) =_{\text{def}} \\
&(\exists l.\, x = l \wedge y = \langle \langle 0, 0 \rangle, l \rangle) \vee \\
&(\exists l.\, x = l \wedge y = \langle \langle 0, 1 \rangle, l \rangle) \vee \\
&(\exists n\ s\ t\ l.\ (n = 1 \vee n = 2 \vee n = 3) \wedge \\
&\qquad\quad \text{FREETERM}(m, s) \wedge \text{FREETERM}(m, t) \wedge \\
&\qquad\quad x = l \wedge y = \langle \langle n, \langle p, q \rangle \rangle, l \rangle) \vee \\
&(\exists p\ l.\, x = \langle p, l \rangle \wedge y = \langle \langle 4, p \rangle, l \rangle) \vee \\
&(\exists n\ p\ q\ l.\ (n = 5 \vee n = 6 \vee n = 7 \vee n = 8) \wedge \\
&\qquad\quad x = \langle p, \langle q, l \rangle \rangle \wedge y = \langle \langle n, \langle p, q \rangle \rangle, l \rangle) \vee \\
&(\exists n\ u\ p\ l.\ (n = 9 \vee n = 10) \wedge \\
&\qquad\quad x = \langle p, l \rangle \wedge y = \langle \langle n, \langle u, p \rangle \rangle, l \rangle) \vee \\
&(\exists n\ p\ l.\ (n = 9 \vee n = 10) \wedge \\
&\qquad\quad x = l \wedge \text{FORM}(p) \wedge y = \langle \langle n, \langle m, p \rangle \rangle, l \rangle).
\end{aligned}
$$

As with FREETERM, we set FREEFORM to be the reflexive transitive closure of FREEFORM$_1$, regarded as a binary relation between x and y with the additional variable m as a parameter:

$$\text{FREEFORM}(m, n) =_{\text{def}} \text{FREEFORM}_1^*(m, 0, \langle n, 0 \rangle).$$

For reasons of modularity, we first produce a formula defining the set of axiom schemas (i.e. the inference rules other than modus ponens and generalization) and then incorporate it into an arithmetization of the whole inference system. These axiom schemas can be defined by a straightforward disjunction. The relation AXIOM(n) defined next means 'n is the Gödel number of a formula that is an axiom'. Note that we only include congruence axioms for functions and predicates in the language of arithmetic, i.e. S, '$+$', '$\cdot$', '$<$' and '$\leq$'.

AXIOM$(a) =_{\text{def}}$

$(\exists p\, q.\ \text{FORM}(p) \wedge \text{FORM}(q) \wedge a = \langle 7, \langle p, \langle 7, \langle q, p\rangle\rangle\rangle\rangle) \vee$

$(\exists p\, q\, r.\ \text{FORM}(p) \wedge \text{FORM}(q) \wedge \text{FORM}(r) \wedge$
$\qquad a = \langle 7, \langle\langle 7, \langle p, \langle 7, \langle q, r\rangle\rangle\rangle\rangle, \langle 7, \langle\langle 7, \langle p, q\rangle\rangle, \langle 7, \langle p, r\rangle\rangle\rangle\rangle\rangle\rangle) \vee$

$(\exists p.\ \text{FORM}(p) \wedge$
$\qquad a = \langle 7, \langle\langle 7, \langle\langle 7, \langle p, \langle 0, 0\rangle\rangle\rangle, \langle 0, 0\rangle\rangle\rangle, p\rangle\rangle) \vee$

$(\exists x\, p\, q.\ \text{FORM}(p) \wedge \text{FORM}(q) \wedge$
$\qquad a = \langle 7, \langle\langle 9, \langle x, \langle 7, \langle p, q\rangle\rangle\rangle\rangle, \langle 7, \langle\langle 9, \langle x, p\rangle\rangle, \langle 9, \langle x, q\rangle\rangle\rangle\rangle\rangle\rangle) \vee$

$(\exists x\, p.\ \text{FREEFORM}(x, p) \wedge a = \langle 7, \langle p, \langle 9, \langle x, p\rangle\rangle\rangle\rangle) \vee$

$(\exists x\, t.\ \text{FREETERM}(x, t) \wedge a = \langle 10, \langle x, \langle 1, \langle\langle 0, x\rangle, t\rangle\rangle\rangle\rangle) \vee$

$(\exists t.\ \text{TERM}(t) \wedge a = \langle 1, \langle t, t\rangle\rangle) \vee$

$(\exists s\, t.\ \text{TERM}(s) \wedge \text{TERM}(t) \wedge$
$\qquad a = \langle 7, \langle\langle 1, \langle s, t\rangle\rangle, \langle 1, \langle\langle 2, s\rangle, \langle 2, t\rangle\rangle\rangle\rangle\rangle) \vee$

$(\exists s\, t\, u\, v.\ \text{TERM}(s) \wedge \text{TERM}(t) \wedge \text{TERM}(u) \wedge \text{TERM}(v) \wedge$
$\qquad a = \langle 7, \langle\langle 1, \langle s, t\rangle\rangle, \langle 7, \langle\langle 1, \langle u, v\rangle\rangle, \langle 1, \langle\langle 3, \langle s, u\rangle\rangle, \langle 3, \langle t, v\rangle\rangle\rangle\rangle\rangle\rangle\rangle\rangle) \vee$

$(\exists s\, t\, u\, v.\ \text{TERM}(s) \wedge \text{TERM}(t) \wedge \text{TERM}(u) \wedge \text{TERM}(v) \wedge$
$\qquad a = \langle 7, \langle\langle 1, \langle s, t\rangle\rangle, \langle 7, \langle\langle 1, \langle u, v\rangle\rangle, \langle 1, \langle\langle 4, \langle s, u\rangle\rangle, \langle 4, \langle t, v\rangle\rangle\rangle\rangle\rangle\rangle\rangle\rangle) \vee$

$(\exists s\, t\, u\, v.\ \text{TERM}(s) \wedge \text{TERM}(t) \wedge \text{TERM}(u) \wedge \text{TERM}(v) \wedge$
$\qquad a = \langle 7, \langle\langle 1, \langle s, t\rangle\rangle, \langle 7, \langle\langle 1, \langle u, v\rangle\rangle, \langle 7, \langle\langle 1, \langle s, u\rangle\rangle, \langle 1, \langle t, v\rangle\rangle\rangle\rangle\rangle\rangle\rangle\rangle) \vee$

$(\exists s\, t\, u\, v.\ \text{TERM}(s) \wedge \text{TERM}(t) \wedge \text{TERM}(u) \wedge \text{TERM}(v) \wedge$
$\qquad a = \langle 7, \langle\langle 1, \langle s, t\rangle\rangle, \langle 7, \langle\langle 1, \langle u, v\rangle\rangle, \langle 7, \langle\langle 2, \langle s, u\rangle\rangle, \langle 2, \langle t, v\rangle\rangle\rangle\rangle\rangle\rangle\rangle\rangle) \vee$

$(\exists s\, t\, u\, v.\ \text{TERM}(s) \wedge \text{TERM}(t) \wedge \text{TERM}(u) \wedge \text{TERM}(v) \wedge$
$\qquad a = \langle 7, \langle\langle 1, \langle s, t\rangle\rangle, \langle 7, \langle\langle 1, \langle u, v\rangle\rangle, \langle 7, \langle\langle 3, \langle s, u\rangle\rangle, \langle 3, \langle t, v\rangle\rangle\rangle\rangle\rangle\rangle\rangle\rangle) \vee$

$(\exists p\, q.\ \text{FORM}(p) \wedge \text{FORM}(q) \wedge$
$\qquad a = \langle 7, \langle\langle 8, \langle p, q\rangle\rangle, \langle 7, \langle p, q\rangle\rangle\rangle\rangle) \vee$

$(\exists p\, q.\ \text{FORM}(p) \wedge \text{FORM}(q) \wedge$
$\qquad a = \langle 7, \langle\langle 8, \langle p, q\rangle\rangle, \langle 7, \langle q, p\rangle\rangle\rangle\rangle) \vee$

$(\exists p\, q.\ \text{FORM}(p) \wedge \text{FORM}(q) \wedge$
$\qquad a = \langle 7, \langle\langle 7, \langle p, q\rangle\rangle, \langle 7, \langle\langle 7, \langle q, p\rangle\rangle, \langle 8, \langle p, q\rangle\rangle\rangle\rangle\rangle\rangle) \vee$

$(a = \langle 8, \langle\langle 0, 1\rangle, \langle 7, \langle\langle 0, 0\rangle, \langle 0, 0\rangle\rangle\rangle\rangle\rangle) \vee$

$(\exists p.\ \text{FORM}(p) \wedge$
$\qquad a = \langle 8, \langle\langle 4, p\rangle, \langle 7, \langle p, \langle 0, 0\rangle\rangle\rangle\rangle\rangle) \vee$

$(\exists p\, q.\ \text{FORM}(p) \wedge \text{FORM}(q) \wedge$
$\qquad a = \langle 8, \langle\langle 5, \langle p, q\rangle\rangle, \langle 7, \langle\langle 7, \langle p, \langle 7, \langle q, \langle 0, 0\rangle\rangle\rangle\rangle\rangle, \langle 0, 0\rangle\rangle\rangle\rangle\rangle) \vee$

$(\exists p\, q.\ \text{FORM}(p) \wedge \text{FORM}(q) \wedge$
$\qquad a = \langle 8, \langle\langle 6, \langle p, q\rangle\rangle, \langle 4, \langle 5, \langle\langle 4, p\rangle, \langle 4, q\rangle\rangle\rangle\rangle\rangle\rangle) \vee$

$(\exists x\, p.\ \text{FORM}(p) \wedge$
$\qquad a = \langle 8, \langle\langle 10, \langle x, p\rangle\rangle, \langle 4, \langle 9, \langle x, \langle 4, p\rangle\rangle\rangle\rangle\rangle\rangle).$

To define the set of all provable formulas, we can repeat the same approach yet again using reflexive transitive closure, this time of the following relation:

$$\mathrm{Pr}_1(x,y) =_{def} \ (\exists a.\ \mathrm{AXIOM}(a) \wedge y = \langle a, x \rangle) \ \vee$$
$$(\exists p\,q\,l.\ x = \langle \langle 7, \langle p, q \rangle \rangle, \langle p, l \rangle \rangle \wedge y = \langle q, l \rangle) \ \vee$$
$$(\exists p\,u\,l.\ x = \langle p, l \rangle \wedge y = \langle \langle 9, \langle u, p \rangle \rangle, l \rangle)$$

Now we can define the set of Gödel numbers of provable formulas in the language by $\mathrm{Pr}(n) =_{def} \mathrm{Pr}_1^*(0, \langle n, 0 \rangle)$. More generally, given any definable set A of additional axioms, let $\mathrm{Ax}(a)$ be a formula defining it, and define $\mathrm{Pr}_A(n)$ replacing the formula $\mathrm{AXIOM}(a)$ by $\mathrm{AXIOM}(a) \vee \mathrm{Ax}(a)$ in the definition of Pr_1. Then $\mathrm{Pr}_A(n)$ represents exactly the set of Gödel numbers of $\mathrm{Cn}(A) = \{p \mid A \vdash p\}$. We are now ready to prove a weak form of Gödel's First Incompleteness Theorem:

Theorem 7.5 *Let A be any set of formulas such that the set $\{\ulcorner p \urcorner \mid p \in A\}$ is definable. Then $\mathrm{Cn}(A)$ does not coincide with the formulas true in $\mathbb{N}$; either some of the axioms A are false in $\mathbb{N}$ or there is a formula p that is true in $\mathbb{N}$ but not a logical consequence of A.*

Proof We have seen that $\mathrm{Cn}(A)$ is definable, whereas the set of true formulas is not, by Tarski's theorem. Thus, either there are truths of $\mathbb{N}$ that are not in $\mathrm{Cn}(A)$, or there are false assertions in $\mathrm{Cn}(A)$. Since all the logical inference rules preserve truth, the latter implies that there must have been false assertions in A. $\qquad\square$

Assuming that the axioms A are all true in $\mathbb{N}$, we have concluded what we might term *semantical incompleteness*: some true formula is unprovable. This sense of 'incompleteness' is analogous to incompleteness of a proof system as discussed in Section 4.3, but with the crucial difference that it involves truth in the standard model rather than logical validity in general. (Our first-order proof system *is* complete in that $A \models p$ iff $A \vdash p$, but for definable A neither of those equivalent notions is the same as truth of p in $\mathbb{N}$.) It immediately implies incompleteness in the sense of Section 5.6:

Corollary 7.6 *Let A be any set of formulas true in $\mathbb{N}$ such that the set $\{\ulcorner p \urcorner \mid p \in A\}$ is definable. Then there is a sentence p such that neither $A \vdash p$ nor $A \vdash \neg p$, i.e. the theory $\mathrm{Cn}(A)$ is incomplete.*

Proof By the previous theorem, there is a formula q that is true in $\mathbb{N}$ yet unprovable from A. Let p be its universal closure $\mathtt{generalize}(q)$. Since $\vdash p \Rightarrow q$, it follows that $A \not\vdash p$. On the other hand, all formulas in A, and hence all logical consequences of A, are true in $\mathbb{N}$, so since $\neg p$ is false we must have $A \not\vdash \neg p$. $\qquad\square$

Note carefully that the definability of A was assumed in these results – *some* restriction on A is certainly necessary, since the conclusion trivially fails if we choose for A the set of all true formulas. Contrast the Löwenheim–Skolem theorems (Section 3.16), which imply that *any* first-order axiom set with an infinite model has 'unintended' models. Yet it may still happen that all these models agree on their *first-order* consequences, as we can see from the existence of complete theories such as algebraically closed fields of characteristic zero (Section 5.8), or the theory of a specific model (i.e. the set all formulas that hold in that model). Gödel's theorem tells us something different, that sound and definable axiom systems for arithmetic are incomplete *even in their first-order consequences*.

The assumption of definability is met by all conventional mathematical axiom systems. In particular, any finite set of formulas $\{p_1, \ldots, p_n\}$ is trivially definable by $\mathrm{Ax}(n) = n = \ulcorner p_1 \urcorner \vee \cdots \vee n = \ulcorner p_n \urcorner$. The same applies to axioms defined by a finite set of schemas. For example, one popular axiom system, called PA (Peano arithmetic) consists of the basic axioms

$$\forall n.\, \neg(S(n) = 0),$$
$$\forall m\, n.\, S(m) = S(n) \Rightarrow m = n,$$
$$(\forall n.\, 0 + n = n) \wedge (\forall m\, n.\, S(m) + n = S(m + n)),$$
$$(\forall n.\, 0 \cdot n = 0) \wedge (\forall m\, n.\, S(m) \cdot n = m \cdot n + n),$$

together with the infinite set of instances of the induction principle, where $P[n]$ is any formula in the language with at least one free variable n:

$$P[0] \wedge (\forall n.\, P[n] \Rightarrow P[S(n)]) \Rightarrow \forall n.\, P[n].$$

It's easy to see that this axiom scheme is definable. As usual it's simpler to avoid arithmetizing substitution by considering all formulas of the form

$$(\exists x.\, x = 0 \wedge P) \wedge (\forall n.\, (\exists x.\, x = n \wedge P) \Rightarrow (\exists x.\, x = S(n) \wedge P)) \Rightarrow \forall x.\, P$$

for $n \notin \mathrm{FV}(P)$, which is easily seen to be equivalent.

7.4 Gödel's incompleteness theorem

Gödel indeed seems to have discovered his first incompleteness theorem by noting that provability is arithmetically definable whereas arithmetic truth is not. However, the final published form of the theorem (Gödel 1931) was sharper, and we turn to this now.

Having demonstrated that provability from a definable axiom set A is definable by a formula Pr_A we no longer need to talk about a putative definition of truth at all. Instead of considering a sentence that 'asserts its own falsity', we can consider one that 'asserts its own unprovability' from axioms A in the sense that the following holds in $\mathbb{N}$:

$$G \Leftrightarrow \neg\text{Pr}_A(\ulcorner G \urcorner),$$

or one that 'asserts the provability of its own negation', meaning that the following holds:

$$H \Leftrightarrow \text{Pr}_A(\ulcorner \neg H \urcorner),$$

The fixpoint Lemma 7.3 assures us that there are indeed sentences with such properties.[†] If fact, if we define a formula H such that $H \Leftrightarrow \text{Pr}_A(\ulcorner \neg H \urcorner)$ is true in $\mathbb{N}$ and define $G =_{\text{def}} \neg H$, then $G \Leftrightarrow \neg\text{Pr}_A(\ulcorner G \urcorner)$ holds in $\mathbb{N}$, and vice versa. What can we conclude about such sentences? Let us first assume that the axioms A are sound, so all formulas p with $A \vdash p$ are true in $\mathbb{N}$.

• Suppose $A \vdash G$. This means exactly that the corresponding arithmetization $\text{Pr}_A(\ulcorner G \urcorner)$ is true in $\mathbb{N}$. But since $G \Leftrightarrow \neg\text{Pr}_A(\ulcorner G \urcorner)$ in $\mathbb{N}$ we conclude that G is *false* in $\mathbb{N}$. Since the axioms are sound, this is impossible.

• Suppose $A \vdash \neg G$. Then by soundness, $\neg G$ is true in $\mathbb{N}$, and from $G \Leftrightarrow \neg\text{Pr}_A(\ulcorner G \urcorner)$ we conclude that $\text{Pr}_A(\ulcorner G \urcorner)$ is true and therefore $A \vdash G$. However, we then have both $A \vdash G$ and $A \vdash \neg G$, so $A \vdash \bot$, and since $\bot$ is certainly not true in $\mathbb{N}$ (or any other interpretation), this is impossible.

We conclude that $A \nvdash G$ and $A \nvdash \neg G$, i.e. once again that $\text{Cn}(A)$ is an incomplete theory. The basic conclusion matches Theorem 7.5 and its corollary, but the proof here is constructive: given a particular sound axiom system A we can, at least in principle, exhibit a specific sentence G that is neither provable nor refutable based on axioms A (see Exercise 7.4).

This proof is also interesting because it only appeals to soundness for three *specific* sentences: G (to prove $A \nvdash G$) and $\neg G$ and $\bot$ (to prove $A \nvdash \neg G$). At first sight, this might appear uninteresting, because G is a large and complicated formula featuring many more or less arbitrary encoding details, and moreover is dependent on A itself. However, we will see that G and $\neg G$ belong to some important general classes.

Δ_0 *formulas*

Definition 7.7 *A formula in the language of arithmetic is said to be Δ_0 if all its quantifiers are bounded, i.e. each quantified subformula is of the form*

[†] More precisely, for H we can apply the fixpoint lemma with $H \Leftrightarrow \text{Pr}_A(\langle 4, \ulcorner H \urcorner \rangle)$, which is equivalent in $\mathbb{N}$ to the fixpoint stated with the number expressed as a canonical numeral.

$\forall x.\ x \leq t \Rightarrow P[x]$, $\forall x.\ x < t \Rightarrow P[x]$, $\exists x.\ x \leq t \wedge P[x]$ or $\exists x.\ x < t \wedge P[x]$ with $x \notin FVT(t)$.

The special interest of this class is that there is a straightforward algorithm for deciding whether any given Δ_0-sentence, i.e. Δ_0 formula with no free variables, is true in $\mathbb{N}$. (One can think of Δ as the first letter of 'decidable' for this reason.) First of all, evaluation of a term `tm` in a valuation `v` can be considered just a special case of `termval`:

```
let rec dtermval v tm =
  match tm with
    Var x -> apply v x
  | Fn("0",[]) -> Int 0
  | Fn("S",[t]) -> dtermval v t +/ Int 1
  | Fn("+",[s;t]) -> dtermval v s +/ dtermval v t
  | Fn("*",[s;t]) -> dtermval v s */ dtermval v t
  | _ -> failwith "dtermval: not a ground term of the language";;
```

The key point of Δ_0 formulas arises when we consider whether a quantified formula holds. Generally, in order to decide this, we need to examine infinitely many possibilities, so our implementation of `holds` (Section 3.3) only considered the special case of finite interpretations. However, if all quantifiers are bounded, we can effectively determine truth or falsity. For propositional connectives, we proceed in the obvious way, but defer handling of quantifiers to a mutually recursive function `dhquant`:

```
let rec dholds v fm =
  match fm with
    False -> false
  | True -> true
  | Atom(R("=",[s;t])) -> dtermval v s = dtermval v t
  | Atom(R("<",[s;t])) -> dtermval v s </ dtermval v t
  | Atom(R("<=",[s;t])) -> dtermval v s <=/ dtermval v t
  | Not(p) -> not(dholds v p)
  | And(p,q) -> dholds v p & dholds v q
  | Or(p,q) -> dholds v p or dholds v q
  | Imp(p,q) -> not(dholds v p) or dholds v q
  | Iff(p,q) -> dholds v p = dholds v q
  | Forall(x,Imp(Atom(R(a,[Var y;t])),p)) -> dhquant forall v x y a t p
  | Exists(x,And(Atom(R(a,[Var y;t])),p)) -> dhquant exists v x y a t p
  | _ -> failwith "dholds: not an arithmetical delta-formula"
```

The `dhquant` function first checks that the quantifier is indeed bounded as required, and evaluates the bound. (The restriction that the quantified variable does not occur in the bound itself is important here, since it ensures that all variables in the bound have been assigned values by this stage of the recursion.) If the bound evaluates to n, we can decide the quantified formula by checking the body only for values $0, 1, \ldots, n - 1$ or $0, 1, \ldots, n$ depending on whether the bounding inequality is $<$ or $\leq$:

```
and dhquant pred v x y a t p =
  if x <> y or mem x (fvt t) then failwith "dholds: not delta" else
  let m = if a = "<" then dtermval v t -/ Int 1 else dtermval v t in
  pred (fun n -> dholds ((x |-> n) v) p) (Int 0 --- m);;
```

Many of the formulas from Section 7.2 defining arithmetical predicates are in fact Δ_0, often by design. For example, we expressed divisibility as $m|n =_{\text{def}} \exists x.\, x \leq n \land n = m \cdot x$ with a bounded quantifier precisely to make it Δ_0, even though the 'simpler' formula $m|n =_{\text{def}} \exists x.\, n = m \cdot x$ is equivalent. Likewise our formulas for 'prime' and 'primepow' are Δ_0. The following function generates a formula asserting that the integer p is prime using our arithmetic encoding:

```
let prime_form p = subst("p" |=> numeral(Int p))
  <<S(S(0)) <= p /\
    forall n. n < p ==> (exists x. x <= p /\ p = n * x) ==> n = S(0)>>;;
```

and we can indeed evaluate specific instances with the decider:

```
# dholds undefined (prime_form 100);;
- : bool = false
# dholds undefined (prime_form 101);;
- : bool = true
```

Of course, for non-trivial formulas, this is not really feasible in practice, but the decidability *in principle* of Δ_0-formulas is an important theme.

Σ_1 and Π_1 formulas

Our construction for reflexive transitive closure does not (indeed could not, as we shall see eventually) preserve the property of Δ_0-ness: even if $R(x, y)$ itself is Δ_0, $R^*(x, y)$ is not. However, at least the unbounded quantifiers are all existential, and this is highly significant.

Suppose $P[x]$ is such that the truth of $P[n]$ is decidable for any particular numeral n, e.g. if $P[x]$ is a Δ_0-formula. Then although there may be no algorithm to *decide* $\exists x.P[x]$, there is at least a naive algorithm that can verify that $\exists x.\, P[x]$ is true if indeed it is: try all possible $n = 0, 1, 2, \ldots$ in order until $P[n]$ is found to be true. (If the algorithm is applied to a false formula, it will run forever, so this is only a semi-decision procedure.) Conversely, there is a straightforward algorithm that can confirm that $\forall x.\, P[x]$ is false when it is: try all n in order until some $P[n]$ is found to be false.

Roughly speaking, we say that a formula in prenex form is Σ_1 if all unbounded quantifiers are existential, and Π_1 if all unbounded quantifiers are universal. (The choice of letters corresponds to 'sum' and 'product', a traditional terminology for existential and universal quantifiers respectively.) More generally, we say that it is Σ_n (respectively Π_n) if it contains n alternating blocks of like quantifiers with the outer one existential (resp. universal). However, we will define this notion more precisely to allow it to apply to non-prenex formulas and take into account logical signs. For example $(\forall x.\ P[x]) \Rightarrow (\exists y.\ Q[y])$ counts as Σ_1 because the universal quantifier is effectively negated and hence 'really' an existential one. To make our definition in OCaml, we start by setting up a type to denote three classes of formulas, Σ, Π and Δ:

```
type formulaclass = Sigma | Pi | Delta;;
```

and reflect symmetries between them by an 'opposite' map.

```
let opp = function Sigma -> Pi | Pi -> Sigma | Delta -> Delta;;
```

Now we define the classification function taking a formula class `c`, a non-negative integer `n` and a formula `fm`, and telling us whether the formula belongs to the corresponding class, which we call c_n. (Arguably we should also check that the formula is in the language of arithmetic, but we regard that as a separate question since the classification of formulas may be of interest for other languages.)

```
let rec classify c n fm =
  match fm with
    False | True | Atom(_) -> true
  | Not p -> classify (opp c) n p
  | And(p,q) | Or(p,q) -> classify c n p & classify c n q
  | Imp(p,q) -> classify (opp c) n p & classify c n q
  | Iff(p,q) -> classify Delta n p & classify Delta n q
  | Exists(x,p) when n <> 0 & c = Sigma -> classify c n p
  | Forall(x,p) when n <> 0 & c = Pi -> classify c n p
  | (Exists(x,And(Atom(R(("<"|"<="),[Var y;t])),p))|
     Forall(x,Imp(Atom(R(("<"|"<="),[Var y;t])),p)))
        when x = y & not(mem x (fvt t)) -> classify c n p
  | Exists(x,p) | Forall(x,p) -> n <> 0 & classify (opp c) (n - 1) fm;;
```

In what follows, we will be exclusively concerned with the cases Σ_1, Π_1 and $\Delta_0 = \Sigma_0 = \Pi_0$. Note that *bounded* quantifiers can still be intermixed arbitrarily in Σ_n and Π_n formulas without affecting their classification, and arbitrarily many quantifiers of the same kind can occur in blocks, e.g.

```
# classify Sigma 1
  <<forall x. x < 2
           ==> exists y z. forall w. w < x + 2
                            ==> w + x + y + z = 42>>;;
- : bool = true
```

This means that to verify a general Σ_1-formula, we can't just recursively 'try all n in order' when confronted with $\exists x.\, P[x]$. Consider for example $\exists m\; n.\, m = n + 1$. This is true, but if we first try to set $m = 0$ we get the false sentence $\exists n.\, 0 = n + 1$ and so the recursive attempt to verify this would loop indefinitely.

However, if a Σ_1-formula is true, there is some m that is an adequate bound for *all* the existential quantifiers. One can prove this inductively on the structure of the formula. For example, suppose $\exists x\; y.\, P[x, y]$ is true. Then there is some n such that $\exists y.\, P[n, y]$ is true. Now if k is a suitable bound for the existentials in $\exists y.\, P[n, y]$, then $m = \max(n, k)$ is a suitable bound for the formula as a whole. Similarly, if $\forall x.\, x \le n \Rightarrow P[x]$ is true, each $P[k]$ for $k = 0, \ldots, n$ is true, and for each there is a corresponding bound m_k, and then $\max(m_0, \ldots, m_n)$ is a suitable bound for $\forall x.\, x \le n \Rightarrow P[x]$ as a whole.

The following function can be used either to verify a true Σ_1-formula (if the argument `sign` is the identity mapping) or refute a false Π_1-formula (if the argument `sign` is Boolean negation), assuming in both cases that m is an adequate bound of this kind for all the unbounded quantifiers of the appropriate sign:

```
let rec veref sign m v fm =
  match fm with
    False -> sign false
  | True -> sign true
  | Atom(R("=",[s;t])) -> sign(dtermval v s = dtermval v t)
  | Atom(R("<",[s;t])) -> sign(dtermval v s </ dtermval v t)
  | Atom(R("<=",[s;t])) -> sign(dtermval v s <=/ dtermval v t)
  | Not(p) -> veref (not ** sign) m v p
  | And(p,q) -> sign(sign(veref sign m v p) & sign(veref sign m v q))
  | Or(p,q) -> sign(sign(veref sign m v p) or sign(veref sign m v q))
  | Imp(p,q) -> veref sign m v (Or(Not p,q))
  | Iff(p,q) -> veref sign m v (And(Imp(p,q),Imp(q,p)))
  | Exists(x,p) when sign true
       -> exists (fun n -> veref sign m ((x |-> n) v) p) (Int 0---m)
  | Forall(x,p) when sign false
       -> exists (fun n -> veref sign m ((x |-> n) v) p) (Int 0---m)
  | Forall(x,Imp(Atom(R(a,[Var y;t])),p)) when sign true
       -> verefboundquant m v x y a t sign p
  | Exists(x,And(Atom(R(a,[Var y;t])),p)) when sign false
       -> verefboundquant m v x y a t sign p
```

where the mutually recursive `verefboundquant` handles bounded quantifiers, first checking the appropriate syntactic conditions and then performing a case analysis:

```
and verefboundquant m v x y a t sign p =
  if x <> y or mem x (fvt t) then failwith "veref" else
  let m = if a = "<" then dtermval v t -/ Int 1 else dtermval v t in
  forall (fun n -> veref sign m ((x |-> n) v) p) (Int 0 --- m);;
```

We defined these dual functions purely to get a smooth recursion, and we will only be interested in verifying true Σ_1-formulas:

```
let sholds = veref (fun b -> b);;
```

Although this function depends on having a suitable bound m, we can, if the formula is indeed true, find the first m for which the formula is true:

```
let sigma_bound fm = first (Int 0) (fun n -> sholds n undefined fm);;
```

For example, here we verify that $\exists p\, x.\, p < x \wedge \mathrm{primepow}(p, x)$; a sufficient bound is $m = 4$, since we can set $p = 2$, $x = 4$:

```
# sigma_bound
  <<exists p x.
    p < x /\
    (S(S(0))) <= p /\
    forall n. n < p
              ==> (exists x. x <= p /\ p = n * x) ==> n = S(0)) /\
    ~(x = 0) /\
    forall z. z <= x
              ==> (exists w. w <= x /\ x = z * w)
                  ==> z = S(0) \/ exists x. x <= z /\ z = p * x>>;;
- : num = 4
```

Gödel's first incompleteness theorem

We now sharpen our earlier results by specializing various relevant concepts to the classes of Σ_1 and Π_1 formulas. First we establish some terminology:

- a relation R is Σ_1-definable [Π_1-definable] if it is definable by a Σ_1-formula [a Π_1-formula];
- a set of axioms A is Σ_1-sound [Π_1-sound] if whenever p is a Σ_1-sentence [Π_1-sentence] and $A \vdash p$, then p is true in $\mathbb{N}$;
- a set of axioms A is Σ_1-complete [Π_1-complete] if whenever p is a Σ_1-sentence [Π_1-sentence] that is true in $\mathbb{N}$ then $A \vdash p$.

Let us now look back systematically at our arithmetic definitions. As noted above, 'divides', 'prime' and 'primepow' are all Δ_0. Moreover, provided $R(x, y)$ is a Σ_1-formula, so is the reflexive-transitive closure construction $R^*(x, y)$, since 'primepow', which occurs both positively and negatively, is Δ_0 and all other unbounded quantifiers introduced are existential. All the formulas from Section 7.3 up to and including 'Pr' are Σ_1-formulas, since they *only* use positive existential quantifiers, with the proviso that the subsidiary relation 'Ax' defining the set of non-logical axioms A should itself be Σ_1.

In the fixpoint Lemma 7.3, provided $P[x]$ is a Σ_1-formula, so is the fixpoint ϕ such that $\phi \Leftrightarrow P[\ulcorner\phi\urcorner]$, since the pseudo-substitution concept just uses an existential quantifier. So, given the fixpoint with $H \Leftrightarrow \mathrm{Pr}_A(\ulcorner\neg H\urcorner)$, we find that H is a Σ_1-sentence, and therefore its negation G, which satisfies $G \Leftrightarrow \neg\mathrm{Pr}_A(\ulcorner G\urcorner)$, is a Π_1-sentence. Let us emphasize:

If the set of axioms A is Σ_1-definable then there is a Π_1-sentence G such that $G \Leftrightarrow \neg\mathrm{Pr}_A(\ulcorner G\urcorner)$ is true in $\mathbb{N}$, where $\mathrm{Pr}_A(\ulcorner p\urcorner)$ holds in $\mathbb{N}$ iff $A \vdash p$.

We can now obtain quite a sharp and pleasingly symmetric variant of Gödel's theorem; the proof is essentially as before, but taking care to observe the classes to which the formulas belong.

Theorem 7.8 *Let A be a Σ_1-definable set of axioms and G the corresponding Π_1-sentence such that $G \Leftrightarrow \neg\mathrm{Pr}_A(\ulcorner G\urcorner)$ holds in $\mathbb{N}$ (where $\mathrm{Pr}_A(\ulcorner p\urcorner)$ holds in $\mathbb{N}$ iff $A \vdash p$). If A is Π_1-sound, $A \nvdash G$ yet G is true; if A is Σ_1-sound, $A \nvdash \neg G$.*

Proof Suppose A is Π_1-sound. If $A \vdash G$, then its arithmetization $\mathrm{Pr}_A(\ulcorner G\urcorner)$ is true in $\mathbb{N}$. But since $G \Leftrightarrow \neg\mathrm{Pr}_A(\ulcorner G\urcorner)$ in $\mathbb{N}$ we conclude that G is *false* in $\mathbb{N}$. This is impossible by Π_1-soundness, so we have reached a contradiction and must conclude $A \nvdash G$. But then $\neg\mathrm{Pr}_A(\ulcorner G\urcorner)$ is true and therefore so is G.

Suppose A is Σ_1-sound. If $A \vdash \neg G$, then (remember that G is a Π_1-formula so $\neg G$ is a Σ_1-formula) $\neg G$ is true in $\mathbb{N}$, and from $G \Leftrightarrow \neg\mathrm{Pr}_A(\ulcorner G\urcorner)$ we conclude that $\mathrm{Pr}_A(\ulcorner G\urcorner)$ is true and therefore $A \vdash G$. Since both $A \vdash G$ and $A \vdash \neg G$, we have $A \vdash \bot$, and as $\bot$ is false and trivially a Σ_1-formula, this contradicts Σ_1-soundness. We therefore conclude $A \nvdash \neg G$. $\square$

We can conclude without reference to the particular sentence G.

Corollary 7.9 *If a Σ_1-definable set of axioms A is Π_1-sound, it is not Π_1-complete, and if it is both Π_1-sound and Σ_1-sound, it is incomplete.*

Proof If A is Π_1-sound, then $A \nvdash G$ yet G is true, so A is not Π_1-complete. If it is also Σ_1-sound, then $A \nvdash \neg G$, so neither G nor its negation is provable from A, i.e. A is incomplete. $\qquad\square$

If A is consistent ($A \nvdash \bot$) and Σ_1-complete, then it must be Π_1-sound. For if p is a Π_1-formula that is false in $\mathbb{N}$, its negation $\neg p$ is a true Σ_1-formula, so by Σ_1-completeness we have $A \vdash \neg p$. It is therefore impossible that $A \vdash p$ since then $A \vdash \bot$, contradicting consistency. The dual result can be obtained similarly, so:

- consistency and Σ_1-completeness imply Π_1-soundness,
- consistency and Π_1-completeness imply Σ_1-soundness.

We will later exhibit a specific axiom system Q and prove in detail that it is Σ_1-complete. But, for the present, let us just observe that any 'realistic' set of axioms for arithmetic is likely to be Σ_1-complete, because it just needs to be able to prove the various simple arithmetical facts implicitly underlying our algorithm `sholds` above. For this reason, it's usual to state Gödel's first incompleteness theorem assuming as a matter of course the hypothesis of Σ_1-completeness, so throwing into sharp relief the more interesting hypothesis of consistency.

Corollary 7.10 *Let A be a Σ_1-definable set of axioms A that is Σ_1-complete. If A is consistent, then it is not Π_1-complete; if it is both consistent and Σ_1-sound, it is incomplete.*

Note that this is a significantly stronger result than the one we reached at the beginning of this section, where we assumed that the axioms A were sound, i.e. all consequences were true in $\mathbb{N}$. Here, we only need consistency of the axioms to ensure that G is true yet unprovable, and even to show that $\neg G$ is unprovable we do not need full soundness, only Σ_1-soundness, also called *1-consistency*.[†]

This might be regarded as an insignificant technicality, since presumably we will use axioms we believe are sound. Nevertheless, Gödel's result itself shows that there is a real distinction between consistency and (even Σ_1) soundness. Given a consistent and Σ_1-complete axiom set A, there is a Π_1-sentence G that is true in $\mathbb{N}$ yet such that $A \nvdash G$. This means that the augmented set of axioms $A' = A \cup \{\neg G\}$ is still consistent, for if $A \cup \{\neg G\} \vdash \bot$

[†] Gödel's theorem is sometimes stated assuming not Σ_1-soundness but 'ω-consistency', meaning that if $A \vdash \neg P[\overline{n}]$ for all $n \in \mathbb{N}$, then $A \nvdash \exists x.\, P[x]$. These two concepts are closely related, but ω-consistency is a bit stronger than needed because it applies to an arbitrary $P[x]$. We can in fact assume that $P[x]$ is itself a Σ_1-formula, or even a Δ_0-formula.

we would also have $A \vdash G$. However, A' is not Σ_1-sound, because it proves the false Σ_1-formula $\neg G$.

7.5 Definability and decidability

Even before the articulation of his consistency programme, Hilbert was deeply interested in questions of decidability. For instance, his tenth problem asked whether there exists a general algorithm for deciding whether a Diophantine equation has a solution. Later, Hilbert posed the question of whether a systematic decision method for first-order validity exists – the *Entscheidungsproblem* (decision problem). After Hilbert himself and many others failed to find such a method, attention increasingly turned to the possibility of proving mathematically the *nonexistence* of such a method.

Mathematical impossibility results of this kind were not unknown at the time, e.g. the impossibility of trisecting an angle using ruler-and-compass constructions, or of solving all quintic equations by radicals. But here the class of methods considered is relatively easily formalized, whereas the general notion of 'decision method' had apparently never been analyzed when Hilbert presented his *Entscheidungsproblem*. The question of delimiting the effectively calculable (in modern terms, computable) functions caused much discussion in the 1930s. One difficulty is the possibility of 'diagonalizing out' of any set of functions. Presumably the computable functions must be capable of being enumerated, perhaps with duplications, e.g. by putting all possible descriptions ('programs') in alphabetical order. If the effectively calculable functions $\mathbb{N} \to \mathbb{N}$ are enumerated $\psi_0, \psi_1, \psi_2, \ldots$, then the 'diagonal' function $d(n) = \psi_n(n) + 1$ cannot occur as any ψ_k since then $\psi_k(k) = \psi_k(k) + 1$. Yet intuitively it should be considered effectively calculable, since there is an easily describable routine for calculating it: find the nth string in alphabetical order, execute that as a program on argument n and add 1.

However, diagonalizing out is no counterargument provided we allow *partial* computable functions that may be undefined for certain arguments, and this turned out to be the key to several successful definitions. Church (1936) proposed 'a definition of effective calculability which is thought to correspond satisfactorily to the somewhat vague intuitive notion'. The identification of 'effectively calculable' with Church's formal definition is usually known as *Church's thesis*. However, the independent yet mathematically equivalent definition by Turing (1936) was widely regarded as more satisfying, so the phrase *Church–Turing thesis* is often used. In what follows, we will present Turing's definition of computability in terms of what are now known as *Turing machines*.

From our present perspective and given the aims of this book, we can hardly resist the identification of 'property P is decidable' with 'there is a fixed computer program that given any n, tells us whether $P(n)$ holds'. However it's important to remember that in Hilbert's time electronic computers and modern programming languages had not been developed. The analysis undertaken by the pioneers such as Turing was of *human* computational activity: a person accurately following a definite procedure fixed in advance without individual creativity. In the words of Wittgenstein (1980) 'Turing's 'Machines' [...] are *humans* who calculate', and to emphasize the distinction, Gandy (1988) maintains a useful spelling distinction between a human 'computor' and a mechanical 'computer'. Turing's analysis was regarded as the most successful not because of the particular detail of Turing machines but because his model was based on entirely plausible finiteness limitations on human computation (Sieg 1994). It may indeed be that the same limits apply to all human mental activity and to all physical systems, but this is not obvious (Gandy 1980; Pour-El and Richards 1980).

Turing machines

We imagine a Turing machine as a discretely operating finite device, equipped with a *tape* that is unbounded in both directions and divided into discrete squares, each of which can hold one of a fixed finite number of characters. The machine is equipped with a 'head' that can move left and right along the tape (or equivalently, move the tape right or left past itself) and at any time is 'scanning' some particular square. Although we will work with a purely mathematical formalization of this conception, the following traditional picture will surely be helpful:

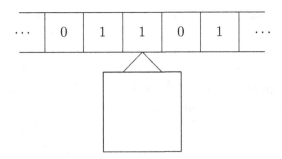

The machine is at any time in one of a finite number of 'states', and the action at each time step is entirely determined by the current state and the character scanned. This action may be to write a new symbol on the scanned square and/or move one square to the left or right. The finiteness of the set of states corresponds to the assumption that a human computor can only be in one of a finite number of 'states of mind'. One may indeed doubt that this restriction applies to human thought in general, but it seems clear that it must apply when calculating in discrete steps without error. For if one were to admit an infinite number of states of mind, there would be arbitrarily 'similar' states of mind for which different actions would be taken. It is hard to believe that accurate discrimination between infinitely many states of mind is possible.

Similarly, when performing a long calculation one cannot instantly refer to any point in a huge pile of paper containing previous results. Unless it was something in the last few pages, one would need to search through the pile, perhaps using numbers previously added to help one locate the data required. That is, looking beyond some range r must be decomposed into a sequence of more primitive operations and should not belong to the repertoire of basic operations. Turing's original paper allowed the machine to look at any square within a fixed range r, but the further restriction to a single square can be shown to make no difference.

People do not usually work by writing characters in discrete squares. However, in order to perform a computation without error, people *do* need somehow to organize their work in a way that helps them to refer to previously written material without ambiguity, and it seems entirely plausible that any such discipline could be adapted to a regime of discrete squares. Indeed, children learning arithmetic are often encouraged to work in exercise books ruled into squares, and one can show that the 2-dimensional nature of the paper is not essential.

The characters people write when doing calculations *are* usually drawn from a finite set of symbols. Although in principle the use of subscripts and superscripts etc. gives a potentially infinite variety of mathematical symbols, in practice people usually make do with a limited set. Besides, one can always analyze composite symbols down into combinations of a fixed finite set, even of two symbols. (Indeed, in order to make the symbol 'Π_1^0' appear in this book, the author enters the characters '\Pi^0_1' on his keyboard, and this is decomposed inside the computer to a sequence of binary digits.) Similar remarks apply to huge numbers written as strings of decimals. Indeed, as Turing noted, in general it is *necessary* to analyze long symbols down to simple components, since one cannot see at a glance whether two similar-looking strings of numbers are actually the same, but must decompose this recognition into a sequence of simpler tasks. Of course, there are infinite variations in how characters are actually drawn on paper, but to perform a calculation without error one must always be able to recognize a previously written symbol without ambiguity, and it seems hard to believe that any human is capable of distinguishing infinitely many symbols without error. Indeed, it's unexceptional to make mistakes in calculations precisely by misreading a symbol previously written without due care.

We will not further consider Turing's conceptual analysis of computation, but refer the reader to the original paper by Turing (1936) and various expositions (Kleene 1952; Minsky 1967; Gandy 1988; Sieg 1994). Instead, we turn to the precise mathematical formulation of the Turing machine concept and its realization in OCaml. The symbols on the tape could be drawn from any type, but we will set up a special enumerated type, whose members we think of as 0 and 1:

```
type symbol = Blank | One;;
```

The action of the machine at any time will be to (possibly) write a new symbol on the tape and possibly move one square left or right. In order to have a concrete representation of Turing machine 'programs', we also define an enumerated type of directions:

```
type direction = Left | Right | Stay;;
```

The Turing machine tape can be considered simply as a function from integers to symbols. At any point in a computation (even a nonterminating one), only finitely many squares will be explicitly read or written by the machine, so a finite partial function suffices, and having a concrete representation is often useful. As part of the 'tape' data we include the current position r of the head. (Of course we could adopt a view that the head is always at 0 and the tape moves rather than the machine.) Thus:

```
type tape = Tape of int * (int,symbol)func;;
```

By convention we will assume that the tape starts blank except for the input data – see later for more details about the input and output of data. We don't know a priori how many squares will be used, so we simply regard undefined squares as Blank (i.e. 0). The following looks at the current character, with this default in mind:

```
let look (Tape(r,f)) = tryapplyd f r Blank;;
```

Conversely, the following writes a character on the tape, by updating the value of the tape at r to hold symbol s:

```
let write s (Tape(r,f)) = Tape (r,(r |-> s) f);;
```

and the following moves the tape head in a specified direction:

```
let move dir (Tape(r,f)) =
  let d = if dir = Left then -1 else if dir = Right then 1 else 0 in
  Tape(r+d,f);;
```

According to the definition, the action of a machine is determined entirely by the current state and the scanned character; that action may be to write a new character and/or move left or right. Using numbers to denote states, the 'configuration' of the machine is the current state together with the contents of the tape:

```
type config = Config of int * tape;;
```

A *program* can simply be considered a mapping, taking a pair of a state and a symbol and giving a new character, a direction of movement, and a new state, hence allowing us to interpret a program step-by-step by the appropriate changes in configuration. The following function runs a program until a configuration is reached with no action defined, at which point it terminates. By convention, we will use only nonnegative integers for states, with state 1 being the starting state and state 0 the final state, but a run will treat any 'undefined' situation as entering state 0. This is reflected in the code below.

```
let rec run prog (Config(state,tape) as config) =
  let stt = (state,look tape) in
  if defined prog stt then
    let char,dir,state' = apply prog stt in
    run prog (Config(state',move dir (write char tape)))
  else config;;
```

We now define what it means for a Turing machine to compute a numerical function $f : \mathbb{N}^n \to \mathbb{N}$. All numbers will be expressed in unary, as a (possibly empty) sequence of 1s followed by a terminating 0. Of course, this is a grossly inefficient convention, making even trivial arithmetic operations barely feasible, but using a better encoding is slightly more complicated and we are not really interested in practical feasibility in this whole analysis. A Turing machine program expects its head to be at a position scanning a blank square, with the input arguments $a_1, \ldots, a_n$ laid out immediately to the right in order. If it terminates, it does so with the head scanning a blank square, immediately to the right of which is the output $f(a_1, \ldots, a_n)$, again in unary. We can set up the initial tape for a list of arguments $a_1, \ldots, a_n$ as follows:

```
let input_tape =
  let writen n =
    funpow n (move Left ** write One) ** move Left ** write Blank in
  fun args -> itlist writen args (Tape(0,undefined));;
```

and extract the final result thus:

```
let rec output_tape tape =
  let tape' = move Right tape in
  if look tape' = Blank then 0
  else 1 + output_tape tape';;
```

Overall program execution now consists of setting up the inputs, running the program, and returning the value on the output tape:

```
let exec prog args =
  let c = Config(1,input_tape args) in
  let Config(_,t) = run prog c in
  output_tape t;;
```

Definition 7.11 *A total function $f : \mathbb{N}^n \to \mathbb{N}$ is (Turing machine) computable if there is a fixed program p that computes it for all arguments, i.e. such that for all $a_1, \ldots, a_n \in \mathbb{N}$, program p terminates on inputs $a_1, \ldots, a_n$ and we have:*

$$\mathsf{exec}\ p\ [a_1; \cdots; a_n] = f(a_1, \ldots, a_n).$$

More generally, a partial *function $f : \mathbb{N}^n \to \mathbb{N}$ is computable if there is a fixed program p such that on each set of arguments $a_1, \ldots, a_n \in \mathbb{N}$, the program terminates if and only if $f(a_1, \ldots, a_n)$ is defined, and when it terminates satisfies the equation above.*

For example, here is a simple program to compute the successor function $S(a) = a + 1$. In state 1, the machine skips right over the expected 0 and enters state 2. In state 2, it keeps moving right over 1s, and when a zero is encountered, writes a 1 instead (to perform the successor operation), moves right and enters state 3. In state 3, regardless of the current character, it writes a terminating 0 and then moves left and enters state 4. In this state it keeps scanning left over 1s till the head returns to its starting position, at which point it enters state 0 to terminate.

```
let prog_suc = itlist (fun m -> m)
 [(1,Blank) |-> (Blank,Right,2);
  (2,One) |-> (One,Right,2);
  (2,Blank) |-> (One,Right,3);
  (3,Blank) |-> (Blank,Left,4);
  (3,One) |-> (Blank,Left,4);
  (4,One) |-> (One,Left,4);
  (4,Blank) |-> (Blank,Stay,0)]
 undefined;;
```

This program shows that the successor function is computable. We can try it out on some examples to reassure ourselves that we didn't make a mistake:

```
# exec prog_suc [0];;
- : int = 1
# exec prog_suc [1];;
- : int = 2
# exec prog_suc [19];;
- : int = 20
```

Of course, the successor function is somewhat trivial, and it may seem far from obvious that more interesting functions are computable according to our definition. However, with careful organization, it's quite easy to create Turing machine programs for complicated computable functions. One systematic approach is to consider writing programs in a simple structured imperative programming language. By sensibly organizing variables on the tape (perhaps using the left part of the tape as a 'stack' for local variables), one can quite easily 'compile' such programs down to Turing machine programs. We will not dwell further on this here, since the Turing machine model of computation is well-accepted and we are concerned with its limitations rather than its generality.

Σ_1 *formulas and computability*

Just as we arithmetized formulas and proofs, we can similarly arithmetize Turing machine configurations and the action of Turing machine programs. Note that, by definition, only finitely many squares of a Turing machine tape are ever non-blank, so we can code the contents of the tape up as a number. Perhaps the most convenient way is as a triple $\langle c, \langle l, r \rangle \rangle$ where:

- c is the contents of the currently scanned square (0 for `Blank` and 1 for `One`);
- l is the contents of the tape to the left, considered as a binary number with the least significant bit immediately to the left of the head;
- r is the contents of the tape to the right, considered as a 'backward' binary number with the least significant bit immediately to the right of the head.

For example, the tape shown in the earlier illustration, assuming that all other squares are blank, would have the code $\langle 1, \langle 1, 2 \rangle \rangle$. Now the basic actions of the Turing machine can be represented as simple transformations on such triples. If the currently scanned square is blank, the transformation arising from writing a `One` is

$$\langle 0, \langle l, r \rangle \rangle \mapsto \langle 1, \langle l, r \rangle \rangle,$$

while the appropriate transformation for moving left one square is

$$\langle c, \langle l, r \rangle \rangle \mapsto \langle l \bmod 2, \langle l \operatorname{div} 2, 2r + c \rangle \rangle.$$

It's not hard to express these as Σ_1-formulas; in fact since we always have $x < \langle x, y \rangle$ and $y < \langle x, y \rangle$, we can easily bound the variables and write them as Δ_0-formulas. If we add one more component s to our tuple to specify the state, we can represent the whole configuration of a Turing machine by $\langle s, \langle c, \langle l, r \rangle \rangle \rangle$ and so write each transition specified by the program as a Δ_0-formula defining a binary '1-step transition' relation on encoded configurations. Explicitly, the instruction

$$(s_0, c_0) \mapsto (c, d, s),$$

indicating that when in state s_0 scanning symbol c_0 one should write symbol c, move in direction d and enter state s, can be defined as a binary relation $R(m, n)$ as follows

- $(s_0, c_0) \mapsto (c, \mathtt{Stay}, s)$ gives the formula

$$\exists l\ r.\ l < m \wedge r < m \wedge$$
$$m = \langle s_0, \langle c_0, \langle l, r \rangle \rangle \rangle \wedge$$
$$n = \langle s, \langle c, \langle l, r \rangle \rangle \rangle;$$

- $(s_0, c_0) \mapsto (c, \mathtt{Left}, s)$ gives the formula

$$\exists l\ r\ c_1.\ c_1 < 2 \wedge l < n \wedge r < m \wedge$$
$$m = \langle s_0, \langle c_0, \langle 2 \cdot l + c_1, r \rangle \rangle \rangle \wedge$$
$$n = \langle s, \langle c_1, \langle l, 2 \cdot r + c \rangle \rangle \rangle;$$

- $(s_0, c_0) \mapsto (c, \mathtt{Right}, s)$ gives the formula

$$\exists l\ r\ c_1.\ \ c_1 < 2 \wedge l < m \wedge r < n \wedge$$
$$m = \langle s_0, \langle c_0, \langle l, 2 \cdot r + c_1 \rangle \rangle \rangle \wedge$$
$$n = \langle s, \langle c_1, \langle 2 \cdot l + c, r \rangle \rangle \rangle.$$

Thus, given any Turing machine program $\mathtt{prog}$, we can create a Δ_0-formula defining the corresponding 1-step transition relation simply by constructing a formula like the above for each instruction, and then creating a big disjunction of them all, say $TM_{\mathtt{prog}}$. Now suppose $\mathtt{prog}$ computes a function $f : \mathbb{N}^n \to \mathbb{N}$. Then the graph of f is defined by the following formula $F(a_1, \ldots, a_n, a)$:

$$\exists m\ n\ c_0\ c_1\ l_0\ l_1\ r_0\ r_1.$$
$$c_0 < 2 \wedge c_1 < 2 \wedge$$
$$TM^*_{\mathtt{prog}}(m, n) \wedge$$
$$m = \langle 1, \langle c_0, \langle l_0, r_0 \rangle \rangle \rangle \wedge$$
$$n = \langle 0, \langle c_1, \langle l_1, r_1 \rangle \rangle \rangle \wedge$$
$$c_0 + 2 \cdot r_0 = (2^{a_1} - 1) + 2^{a_1+1}((2^{a_2} - 1) + 2^{a_2+1}(\cdots + 2^{a_n+1} r_0')) \wedge$$
$$c_1 + 2 \cdot r_1 = (2^a - 1) + 2^{a+1} \cdot r_1'.$$

(The expressions of the form $2^a - 1$ simply represent a successive $\mathtt{One}$ characters on the tape, and those of the form $2^{a+1} \cdot r$ imply a following $\mathtt{Blank}$.) Since the exponential function, being primitive recursive, is definable by a Σ_1-formula (see Section 7.2), we can write this too as a Σ_1-formula. We thus conclude that the graph of a computable function is definable by a Σ_1-formula. In fact, we can go further than merely *computable* functions. Intuitively we think of a set S as *semicomputable* if there is a computable search procedure that for $x \in S$ will eventually confirm this fact by terminating, but will otherwise fail to terminate. More formally:

Definition 7.12 *A set $S \subseteq \mathbb{N}^n$ is said to be* recursively enumerable *(r.e.), or* semicomputable *or* semidecidable, *if it is the domain of a partial computable function, i.e. of the form $S = \{a \in \mathbb{N}^n \mid f(a) \text{ is defined}\}$ for a computable $f : \mathbb{N}^n \to \mathbb{N}$.*

If $R(\overline{x}, y)$ defines the graph of a partial recursive $f : \mathbb{N}^n \to \mathbb{N}$, then $\exists y. R(\overline{x}, y)$ defines its domain, so we conclude that any r.e. set is Σ_1-definable. Conversely, any Σ_1-definable set is r.e., since it is the domain of the computable function $\mathtt{sigma\_bound}$. (To be completely rigorous we should implement this function as a Turing machine program, but we will not delve into such detail here.) Thus we conclude:

A set is recursively enumerable if and only if it is Σ_1-definable.

This provides the critical link we want between computability and Σ_1-formulas. If we can prove some set is not definable by a Σ_1-formula, it will follow that not only is it not computable, but it is not even r.e., so there is no hope even of enumerating it using a computer program. For example, Tarski's theorem on the undefinability of truth shows that arithmetic truth is not definable at all, let alone Σ_1-definable. It follows that arithmetic truth is not even *semicomputable*. This contrasts with first-order consequence: given that we have complete proof procedures such as tableaux, this is at least semicomputable. Before we show in the next section that it is not computable, we note the following

Theorem 7.13 *The characteristic function* $\chi_S : \mathbb{N}^n \to \mathbb{N}$ *of a set* $S \subseteq \mathbb{N}^n$ *(defined as* $\chi_S(x) = 1$ *for* $x \in S$ *and* $\chi_S(x) = 0$ *for* $x \notin S$*) is computable if and only if both* S *and its complement* $\mathbb{N}^n - S$ *are recursively enumerable.*

Proof If f is computable, then one can easily define a function g that terminates on x precisely if $\chi_S(x) = 0$, or precisely if $\chi_S(x) = 1$. In OCaml one might define `let rec g(x) = if chi_S(x) = 0 then 1 else g(x)`, and the corresponding construction for Turing machines is similar. Thus both S and its complement are r.e. Conversely, if both S and its complement are r.e., we have search procedures for both and can run them interleaved in parallel and see which terminates first, returning 1 or 0 accordingly (see Theorem 5.2). Again, translating this into the Turing machine formalism is technical but not difficult. $\square$

This can be formulated in terms of definability: a set is decidable if it is definable by a Σ_1-formula *and* definable by a Π_1-formula, or as we will say, is Δ_1. (Note carefully that this is more general than being defined by a Δ_1 *formula*, i.e. one that is itself both Σ_1 and Π_1, which is actually the same as being Δ_0.) In much of the literature, one sees the overloaded word *recursive* used instead of *decidable* or *computable*. This historical accident helps to explain the expression 'recursively enumerable'.

7.6 Church's theorem

We will now show very explicitly that a particular set of axioms Q is Σ_1-complete. Because this set is finite, we will be able to deduce other important results including the undecidability of first-order validity.

Robinson arithmetic

We will use the following axioms, collected into a single conjunction. We call them `robinson` since similar axioms were first introduced by R. M. Robinson (1950); in discussions we use the traditional symbol Q:

```
let robinson =
 <<(forall m n. S(m) = S(n) ==> m = n) /\
   (forall n. ~(n = 0) <=> exists m. n = S(m)) /\
   (forall n. 0 + n = n) /\
   (forall m n. S(m) + n = S(m + n)) /\
   (forall n. 0 * n = 0) /\
   (forall m n. S(m) * n = n + m * n) /\
   (forall m n. m <= n <=> exists d. m + d = n) /\
   (forall m n. m < n <=> S(m) <= n)>>;;
```

A little reflection will show that these axioms are all true in the intended interpretation $\mathbb{N}$, and consequently, whenever $\vdash Q \Rightarrow p$, p is also true in $\mathbb{N}$. It bears emphasizing that this is an extremely weak system of axioms that cannot even prove, for example, $\forall n.\, n + 0 = n$; this means that minor differences in formulation can be highly significant (see Exercise 7.6). Although we collected the axioms into a conjunction, it's convenient to separate them into individual axioms, each one an implication with antecedent Q:

```
let [suc_inj; num_cases; add_0; add_suc; mul_0;
     mul_suc; le_def; lt_def] = conjths robinson;;
```

The derived inference rules we develop below will consistently return implicational theorems with an antecedent Q. For this reason, it's convenient to have some 'right' variants of inference rules to use a fixed antecedent A (this will normally be Q, but this is inessential). The following respectively perform specialization (from $\vdash A \Rightarrow \forall x.\, p[x]$ to $\vdash A \Rightarrow p[t]$), modus ponens (from $\vdash A \Rightarrow p \Rightarrow q$ and $\vdash A \Rightarrow p$ to $\vdash A \Rightarrow q$) and transitivity of implication (from $\vdash A \Rightarrow p \Rightarrow q$ and $\vdash A \Rightarrow q \Rightarrow r$ to $\vdash A \Rightarrow p \Rightarrow r$):

```
let right_spec t th = imp_trans th (ispec t (consequent(concl th)));;

let right_mp ith th =
  imp_unduplicate(imp_trans th (imp_swap ith));;

let right_imp_trans th1 th2 =
  imp_unduplicate(imp_front 2 (imp_trans2 th1 (imp_swap th2)));;
```

and the following perform symmetry of equality (from $\vdash A \Rightarrow s = t$ to $\vdash A \Rightarrow t = s$) and transitivity of equality ($\vdash A \Rightarrow s = t$ and $\vdash A \Rightarrow t = u$ to $\vdash A \Rightarrow s = u$):

```
let right_sym th =
  let s,t = dest_eq(consequent(concl th)) in imp_trans th (eq_sym s t);;

let right_trans th1 th2 =
  let s,t = dest_eq(consequent(concl th1))
  and t',u = dest_eq(consequent(concl th2)) in
  imp_trans_chain [th1; th2] (eq_trans s t u);;
```

Evaluation of terms

The first step towards Σ_1-completeness is evaluation of ground terms to numerals by proof, e.g. deriving $\vdash Q \Rightarrow S(S(0)*0+S(0)) = S(S(0))$. We do this using two mutually recursive functions. The first, robop, just unfolds a step of the 'recursive definition' of addition or multiplication, while robeval evaluates a ground term by evaluating subterms and then calling robop:

```
let rec robop tm =
  match tm with
    Fn(op,[Fn("0",[]);t]) ->
        if op = "*" then right_spec t mul_0
        else right_trans (right_spec t add_0) (robeval t)
  | Fn(op,[Fn("S",[u]);t]) ->
        let th1 = if op = "+" then add_suc else mul_suc in
        let th2 = itlist right_spec [t;u] th1 in
        right_trans th2 (robeval (rhs(consequent(concl th2))))

and robeval tm =
  match tm with
    Fn("S",[t]) ->
        let th = robeval t in
        let t' = rhs(consequent(concl th)) in
        imp_trans th (axiom_funcong "S" [t] [t'])
  | Fn(op,[s;t]) ->
        let th1 = robeval s in
        let s' = rhs(consequent(concl th1)) in
        let th2 = robop (Fn(op,[s';t])) in
        let th3 = axiom_funcong op [s;t] [s';t] in
        let th4 = modusponens (imp_swap th3) (axiom_eqrefl t) in
        right_trans (imp_trans th1 th4) th2
  | _ -> add_assum robinson (axiom_eqrefl tm);;
```

For example:

```
# robeval <<|S(0) + (S(S(0)) * ((S(0) + S(S(0)) + S(0))))|>>;;
- : thm =
|- ... ==> S(0) + S(S(0)) * (S(0) + S(S(0)) + S(0)) =
           S(S(S(S(S(S(S(S(S(0)))))))))
```

Additional consequences of the Robinson axioms

The algorithm to prove all true Σ_1-formulas from Q depends on various auxiliary properties. It makes the derived rule code more efficient and less cluttered if we prove the most directly applicable theorems once and for all, so they can merely be instantiated later. The following lists consequences we will need:

```
let robinson_consequences =
 <<(forall n. S(n) = 0 ==> false) /\
   (forall n. 0 = S(n) ==> false) /\
   (forall m n. (m = n ==> false) ==> (S(m) = S(n) ==> false)) /\
   (forall m n. (exists d. m + d = n) ==> m <= n) /\
   (forall m n. S(m) <= n ==> m < n) /\
   (forall m n. (forall d. d <= n ==> d = m ==> false)
              ==> m <= n ==> false) /\
   (forall m n. (forall d. d < n ==> d = m ==> false)
              ==> m < n ==> false) /\
   (forall n. n <= 0 \/ exists m. S(m) = n) /\
   (forall n. n <= 0 ==> n = 0) /\
   (forall m n. S(m) <= S(n) ==> m <= n) /\
   (forall m n. m < S(n) ==> m <= n) /\
   (forall n. n < 0 ==> false)>>;;
```

We we will see in due course how each of these is applied in the algorithm; let us turn to the proof, using our interactive prover from Chapter 6. We start by adding equality properties, since the LCF-style prover we have developed does not deal with equality automatically.

```
let robinson_thm =
  prove (Imp(robinson,robinson_consequences))
  [note("eq_refl",<<forall x. x = x>>) using [axiom_eqrefl (Var "x")];
   note("eq_trans",<<forall x y z. x = y ==> y = z ==> x = z>>)
      using [eq_trans (Var "x") (Var "y") (Var "z")];
   note("eq_sym",<<forall x y. x = y ==> y = x>>)
      using [eq_sym (Var "x") (Var "y")];
   note("suc_cong",<<forall a b. a = b ==> S(a) = S(b)>>)
      using [axiom_funcong "S" [Var "a"] [Var "b"]];
   note("add_cong",
        <<forall a b c d. a = b /\ c = d ==> a + c = b + d>>)
      using [axiom_funcong "+" [Var "a"; Var "c"] [Var "b"; Var "d"]];
   note("le_cong",
        <<forall a b c d. a = b /\ c = d ==> a <= c ==> b <= d>>)
      using [axiom_predcong "<=" [Var "a"; Var "c"] [Var "b"; Var "d"]];
   note("lt_cong",
        <<forall a b c d. a = b /\ c = d ==> a < c ==> b < d>>)
      using [axiom_predcong "<" [Var "a"; Var "c"] [Var "b"; Var "d"]];
```

Next, we assume the axioms and give each one a useful label for later reference:

```
assume ["suc_inj",<<forall m n. S(m) = S(n) ==> m = n>>;
        "num_nz",<<forall n. ~(n = 0) <=> exists m. n = S(m)>>;
        "add_0",<<forall n. 0 + n = n>>;
        "add_suc",<<forall m n. S(m) + n = S(m + n)>>;
        "mul_0",<<forall n. 0 * n = 0>>;
        "mul_suc",<<forall m n. S(m) * n = n + m * n>>;
        "le_def",<<forall m n. m <= n <=> exists d. m + d = n>>;
        "lt_def",<<forall m n. m < n <=> S(m) <= n>>];
```

We can deduce some natural consequences of the axioms, only one of which needs a non-trivial proof:

```
note("not_suc_0",<<forall n. ~(S(n) = 0)>>) by ["num_nz"; "eq_refl"];
so conclude <<forall n. S(n) = 0 ==> false>> at once;
so conclude <<forall n. 0 = S(n) ==> false>> by ["eq_sym"];
note("num_cases",<<forall n. (n = 0) \/ exists m. n = S(m)>>)
      by ["num_nz"];
note("suc_inj_eq",<<forall m n. S(m) = S(n) <=> m = n>>)
   by ["suc_inj"; "suc_cong"];
so conclude
   <<forall m n. (m = n ==> false) ==> (S(m) = S(n) ==> false)>>
   at once;
conclude <<forall m n. (exists d. m + d = n) ==> m <= n>>
   by ["le_def"];
conclude <<forall m n. S(m) <= n ==> m < n>> by ["lt_def"];
conclude <<forall m n. (forall d. d <= n ==> d = m ==> false)
                   ==> m <= n ==> false>>
   by ["eq_refl"; "le_cong"];
conclude <<forall m n. (forall d. d < n ==> d = m ==> false)
                   ==> m < n ==> false>>
   by ["eq_refl"; "lt_cong"];
have <<0 <= 0>> by ["le_def"; "add_0"];
so have <<forall x. x = 0 ==> x <= 0>>
   by ["le_cong"; "eq_refl"; "eq_sym"];
so conclude <<forall n. n <= 0 \/ (exists m. S(m) = n)>>
   by ["num_nz"; "eq_sym"];
note("add_eq_0",<<forall m n. m + n = 0 ==> m = 0 /\ n = 0>>) proof
 [fix "m"; fix "n";
  assume ["A",<<m + n = 0>>];
  cases <<m = 0 \/ exists p. m = S(p)>> by ["num_cases"];
    so conclude <<m = 0>> at once;
    so have <<m + n = 0 + n>> by ["add_cong"; "eq_refl"];
    so our thesis by ["A"; "add_0"; "eq_sym"; "eq_trans"];
  qed;
    so consider ("p",<<m = S(p)>>) at once;
    so have <<m + n = S(p) + n>> by ["add_cong"; "eq_refl"];
    so have <<m + n = S(p + n)>> by ["eq_trans"; "add_suc"];
    so have <<S(p + n) = 0>> by ["A"; "eq_sym"; "eq_trans"];
    so our thesis by ["not_suc_0"];
  qed];
so conclude <<forall n. n <= 0 ==> n = 0>> by ["le_def"];
```

Next come some monotonicity properties of '≤':

```
have <<forall m n. S(m) <= S(n) ==> m <= n>> proof
 [fix "m"; fix "n";
  assume ["lesuc",<<S(m) <= S(n)>>];
  so consider("d",<<S(m) + d = S(n)>>) by ["le_def"];
  so have <<S(m + d) = S(n)>> by ["add_suc"; "eq_sym"; "eq_trans"];
  so have <<m + d = n>> by ["suc_inj"];
  so conclude <<m <= n>> by ["le_def"];
  qed];
 so conclude <<forall m n. S(m) <= S(n) ==> m <= n>> at once;
```

and finally some relations between '<' and '≤':

```
 so conclude <<forall m n. m < S(n) ==> m <= n>> by ["lt_def"];
 fix "n";
 assume ["hyp",<<n < 0>>];
 so have <<S(n) <= 0>> by ["lt_def"];
 so consider("d",<<S(n) + d = 0>>) by ["le_def"];
 so have <<S(n + d) = 0>> by ["add_suc"; "eq_trans"; "eq_sym"];
 so our thesis by ["not_suc_0"];
 qed];;
```

We now bind the conjuncts of the consequences to mnemonic names:

```
let [suc_0_1; suc_0_r; suc_inj_false;
     expand_le; expand_lt; expand_nle; expand_nlt;
     num_lecases; le_0; le_suc; lt_suc; lt_0] =
  map (imp_trans robinson_thm) (conjths robinson_consequences);;
```

The Σ_1-prover

Our next requirements are to prove a true equation between ground terms,
i.e. return $\vdash Q \Rightarrow s = t$ when s and t are ground terms with the same value:

```
let rob_eq s t =
  let sth = robeval s and tth = robeval t in
  right_trans sth (right_sym tth);;
```

and refute false ones, i.e. return $\vdash Q \Rightarrow s = t \Rightarrow \bot$ when s and t are
ground terms with different values. First we define a corresponding function
on numerals, which refutes $S(s) = S(t)$ by recursively refuting $s = t$:

```
let rec rob_nen(s,t) =
  match (s,t) with
     (Fn("S",[s']),Fn("0",[])) -> right_spec s' suc_0_1
   | (Fn("0",[]),Fn("S",[t'])) -> right_spec t' suc_0_r
   | (Fn("S",[u]),Fn("S",[v])) ->
       right_mp (itlist right_spec [v;u] suc_inj_false) (rob_nen(u,v))
   | _ -> failwith "rob_ne: true equation or unexpected term";;
```

and then combine this with evaluation of the ground terms:

```
let rob_ne s t =
  let sth = robeval s and tth = robeval t in
  let s' = rhs(consequent(concl sth))
  and t' = rhs(consequent(concl tth)) in
  let th = rob_nen(s',t') in
  let xth = axiom_predcong "=" [s; t] [s'; t'] in
  right_imp_trans (right_mp (imp_trans sth xth) tth) th;;
  right_imp_trans (right_mp (imp_trans sth xth) tth) th;;
```

We're going to deal with many constructs by eliminating them in terms of others. This includes all logical connectives besides $\bot$, $\Rightarrow$ and $\forall$. In tableaux (Section 6.6) we were trying to refute a formula, and here we're trying to prove one, so we need to derive the implication in the other direction from `eliminate_connective`:

```
let introduce_connective fm =
  if not(negativef fm) then iff_imp2(expand_connective fm)
  else imp_add_concl False (iff_imp1(expand_connective(negatef fm)));;
```

In one case a little more refinement is needed. The following function, given a term $\neg(\exists x.\ x < t \land P[x])$, returns $\vdash (\forall x.\ x < t \Rightarrow P[x] \Rightarrow \bot) \Rightarrow \neg(\exists x.\ x < t \land P[x])$, to preserve the canonical forms for bounded quantifiers when passing from a negated existential quantifier to a universal one:

```
let elim_bex fm =
  match fm with
    Imp(Exists(x,And(p,q)),False) ->
        let pq = And(p,q) and pqf = Imp(p,Imp(q,False)) in
        let th1 = imp_swap(imp_refl(Imp(pqf,False))) in
        let th2 = imp_trans th1 (introduce_connective(Imp(pq,False))) in
        imp_trans (genimp x th2) (exists_left_th x pq False)
  | _ -> failwith "elim_bex";;
```

We'll even eliminate atomic formulas other than equations by replacing them with other Σ_1-formulas, e.g. $s \leq t$ by $\exists d.\ s + d = t$ and $s \not\leq t$ (really $s \leq t \Rightarrow \bot$) by $\forall d.\ d \leq t \Rightarrow d = s \Rightarrow \bot$. From an efficiency standpoint this is silly, but it means we don't need similar evaluation functions to `rob_eq` and `rob_ne` for the other atoms. Thus, our procedure to eliminate constructs is:

```
let sigma_elim fm =
  match fm with
    Atom(R("<=",[s;t])) -> itlist right_spec [t;s] expand_le
  | Atom(R("<",[s;t])) -> itlist right_spec [t;s] expand_lt
  | Imp(Atom(R("<=",[s;t])),False) -> itlist right_spec [t;s] expand_nle
  | Imp(Atom(R("<",[s;t])),False) -> itlist right_spec [t;s] expand_nlt
  | Imp(Exists(x,And(p,q)),False) -> add_assum robinson (elim_bex fm)
  | _ -> add_assum robinson (introduce_connective fm);;
```

The most substantial task in proving true Σ_1-formulas is verifying bounded universally quantified formulas $\forall x.\ x \leq t \Rightarrow P[x]$. After evaluating t to a numeral, perhaps the most natural approach would be to exploit the fact that $x \leq S(n) \Leftrightarrow x \leq n \vee x = S(n)$ to decompose the problem $\forall x.\ x \leq S(n) \Rightarrow P[x]$ into $P[S(n)]$ and $\forall x.\ x \leq n \Rightarrow P[x]$. Unfortunately, a peculiarity of the Robinson axioms in our form is that the equivalence $x \leq S(n) \Leftrightarrow x \leq n \vee x = S(n)$ is not provable (see Exercise 7.6). Instead we take a slightly different tack, reducing $\forall x.\ x \leq S(n) \Rightarrow P[x]$ to $P[0]$ and $\forall x.\ x \leq n \Rightarrow P[S(n)]$, which we can justify directly on the basis of the axioms.

The following function takes two theorems of the form $\vdash Q \Rightarrow \forall x.\ x \leq 0 \Rightarrow P[x]$ (it's technically simpler to use this instead of $\vdash Q \Rightarrow P[0]$) and $\vdash Q \Rightarrow \forall x.\ x \leq n \Rightarrow P[S(x)]$ and returns $\vdash Q \Rightarrow \forall x.\ x \leq S(n) \Rightarrow P[x]$. The inference process takes us from the second input theorem $\vdash Q \Rightarrow \forall x.\ x \leq n \Rightarrow P[S(x)]$, using the monotonicity theorem `le_suc`, to $\vdash Q \Rightarrow S(x) \leq S(n) \Rightarrow P[S(x)]$, and so to $\vdash y = S(x) \Rightarrow Q \Rightarrow y \leq S(n) \Rightarrow P[y]$ and finally to $\vdash (\exists x.\ y = S(x)) \Rightarrow Q \Rightarrow y \leq S(n) \Rightarrow P[y]$. We easily derive $\vdash y = 0 \Rightarrow Q \Rightarrow y \leq S(n) \Rightarrow P[y]$ from the other input theorem, and hence using the case-splitting property `num_lecases` we get simply $\vdash Q \Rightarrow y \leq S(n) \Rightarrow P[y]$. From this we get the required theorem $\vdash Q \Rightarrow \forall x.\ x \leq S(n) \Rightarrow P[x]$. Note that we need to take care over bound variable names: we pick a y that does not occur, even bound, in the formula of interest, so that replacing x by y does not cause variable renaming; then at the end (`tha`) we do a trivial equality substitution with $0 = 0$ to ensure that the bound variable name matches up with the arbitrary name m in the axiom `num_lecases`.

```
let boundquant_step th0 th1 =
  match concl th0,concl th1 with
    Imp(_,Forall(x,Imp(_,p))),
        Imp(_,Forall(_,Imp(Atom(R("<=",[_;t])),_))) ->
    let th2 = itlist right_spec [t;Var x] le_suc in
    let th3 = right_imp_trans th2 (right_spec (Var x) th1) in
    let y = variant "y" (var(concl th1)) in
    let q = Imp(Atom(R("<=",[Var x; Fn("S",[t])])),p) in
    let qx = consequent(concl th3) and qy = subst (x |=> Var y) q in
    let th4 = imp_swap(isubst (Fn("S",[Var x])) (Var y) qx qy) in
    let th5 = exists_left x (imp_swap (imp_trans th3 th4)) in
    let th6 = spec (Var x) (gen y th5) in
    let th7 = imp_insert (antecedent q) (right_spec (Var x) th0) in
    let th8 = ante_disj (imp_front 2 th7) th6 in
    let th9 = right_spec (Var x) num_lecases in
    let a1 = consequent(concl th9) and a2 = antecedent(concl th8) in
    let tha = modusponens (isubst zero zero a1 a2)
                          (axiom_eqrefl zero) in
    gen_right x (imp_unduplicate(imp_trans (imp_trans th9 tha) th8));;
```

We are now ready for the main function to prove true Σ_1 formulas:

```
let rec sigma_prove fm =
  match fm with
    False -> failwith "sigma_prove"
  | Atom(R("=",[s;t])) -> rob_eq s t
  | Imp(Atom(R("=",[s;t])),False) -> rob_ne s t
  | Imp(p,q) when p = q -> add_assum robinson (imp_refl p)
  | Imp(Imp(p,q),False) ->
        let pth = sigma_prove p and qth = sigma_prove (Imp(q,False)) in
        right_mp (imp_trans qth (imp_truefalse p q)) pth
  | Imp(p,q) when q <> False ->
        let m = sigma_bound fm in
        if sholds m undefined q then imp_insert p (sigma_prove q)
        else imp_trans2 (sigma_prove (Imp(p,False))) (ex_falso q)
  | Imp(Forall(x,p),False) ->
        let m = sigma_bound (Exists(x,Not p)) in
        let n = first (Int 0) (fun n ->
          sholds m undefined (subst (x |=> numeral n) (Not p))) in
        let ith = ispec (numeral n) (Forall(x,p)) in
        let th = sigma_prove (Imp(consequent(concl ith),False)) in
        imp_swap(imp_trans ith (imp_swap th))
  | Forall(x,Imp(Atom(R(("<="|"<" as a),[Var x';t])),q))
        when x' = x & not(occurs_in (Var x) t) -> bounded_prove(a,x,t,q)
  | _ -> let th = sigma_elim fm in
        right_mp th (sigma_prove (antecedent(consequent(concl th))))
```

This handles easy cases first such as $p \Rightarrow p$ and equational literals. Formulas of the form $(p \Rightarrow q) \Rightarrow \bot$, effectively conjunctions, are proved by recursively proving p and $q \Rightarrow \bot$ and composing the results with `imp_truefalse`. For those of the form $p \Rightarrow q$ we prove whichever of q and $p \Rightarrow \bot$ is provable with the smaller bound m on the existential quantifiers. For existential formulas $(\forall x.\ P[x]) \Rightarrow \bot$ we find the first n such that $\neg P[n]$ holds and then prove that recursively and deduce what we want. Universally quantified formulas pass to another mutually recursive function `bounded_prove` described next, and all other constructs are eliminated. For any bounded universal quantifier, the first order of business is to evaluate the bound to a numeral; the main work is done by another mutually recursive function `boundednum_prove`:

```
and bounded_prove(a,x,t,q) =
  let tth = robeval t in
  let u = rhs(consequent(concl tth)) in
  let th1 = boundednum_prove(a,x,u,q)
  and th2 = axiom_predcong a [Var x;t] [Var x;u] in
  let th3 = imp_trans tth (modusponens th2 (axiom_eqrefl (Var x))) in
  let a,b = dest_imp(consequent(concl th3)) in
  let th4 = imp_swap(imp_trans_th a b q) in
  gen_right x (right_mp (imp_trans th3 th4) (right_spec (Var x) th1))
```

That function deals with the case of strict bounds $\forall x.\, x < n \Rightarrow P[x]$ using the fact that $\vdash Q \Rightarrow x < 0 \Rightarrow \bot$ or exploiting the implication $\vdash Q \Rightarrow x < S(n) \Rightarrow x \leq n$ to reduce matters to the non-strict case. These are dealt with by a routine inference leading from $x \leq 0$ to $x = 0$ and by the main stepping function `boundquant_step`:

```
and boundednum_prove(a,x,t,q) =
  match a,t with
    "<",Fn("0",[]) ->
        gen_right x (imp_trans2 (right_spec (Var x) lt_0) (ex_falso q))
  | "<",Fn("S",[u]) ->
        let th1 = itlist right_spec [u;Var x] lt_suc in
        let th2 = boundednum_prove("<=",x,u,q) in
        let th3 = imp_trans2 th1 (imp_swap(right_spec (Var x) th2)) in
        gen_right x (imp_unduplicate(imp_front 2 th3))
  | "<=",Fn("0",[]) ->
        let q' = subst (x |=> zero) q in
        let th1 = imp_trans (eq_sym (Var x) zero)
                            (isubst zero (Var x) q' q) in
        let th2 = imp_trans2 (right_spec (Var x) le_0) th1 in
        let th3 = imp_swap(imp_front 2 th2) in
        gen_right x (right_mp th3 (sigma_prove q'))
  | "<=",Fn("S",[u]) ->
        let fm' = Forall(x,Imp(Atom(R("<=",[Var x;zero])),q))
        and fm'' = Forall(x,Imp(Atom(R("<=",[Var x;u])),
                            subst (x |=> Fn("S",[Var x])) q)) in
        boundquant_step (sigma_prove fm') (sigma_prove fm'');;
```

For example, here we prove just from the Robinson axioms that there exists a prime number:

```
|- sigma_prove
  <<exists p.
      S(S(0)) <= p /\
      forall n. n < p
                ==> (exists x. x <= p /\ p = n * x) ==> n = S(0)>>;;
- : thm =
|-
... ==>
(exists p.
   S(S(0)) <= p /\
   (forall n. n < p ==> (exists x. x <= p /\ p = n * x) ==> n = S(0)))
```

Church's theorem

Without any of the careful encoding of Pr_A as a Σ_1-formula, we can see quite directly using the fixpoint Lemma 7.3 that *unprovability* from Σ_1-sound and Σ_1-complete axioms A is not Σ_1-definable. Combined with the fact that all r.e. sets are Σ_1-definable (Section 7.5), we conclude that unprovability from such an A is not r.e., and therefore that provability from A is undecidable. For the proof, suppose there were a Σ_1-formula $U(n)$ representing the set $\{\ulcorner p \urcorner \mid A \nvdash p\}$ of formulas not provable from A. By the fixpoint lemma, we can find a ϕ such that

$$\phi \Leftrightarrow U(\ulcorner \phi \urcorner)$$

is true in $\mathbb{N}$. Moreover, $U(\ulcorner \phi \urcorner)$ is a Σ_1-sentence by hypothesis, and therefore, by the construction of the fixpoint in the proof of Lemma 7.3, so is ϕ itself. If axioms A are both Σ_1-sound and Σ_1-complete, then ϕ is provable iff it is true. On the other hand, because the fixpoint property holds in $\mathbb{N}$, ϕ is true iff $U(\ulcorner \phi \urcorner)$ is true, i.e. iff ϕ is *not* provable, a contradiction.

We next prove the simple but important observation that removing finitely many axioms from an undecidable theory yields another undecidable theory. Note that we are considering decidability of sentences in a fixed language, even if we remove all the axioms involving some symbols. (For example, Presburger arithmetic can be considered a subtheory of the highly undecidable theory of $\mathbb{Z}$, but it is not decidable if we retain multiplication in the language even without axioms for it. Indeed, it's fairly obvious that without any such axioms we can't expect to decide anything non-trivial about multiplication.)

Theorem 7.14 *If B is finite and $Cn(A)$ is undecidable, then $Cn(A-B)$ is undecidable (for formulas in the same language).*

Proof Let b be the conjunction of the universal closures of all the formulas in B. We have $A \vdash p$ iff $A - B \vdash b \Rightarrow p$. Thus, if we could decide $Cn(A-B)$ we could also decide $Cn(A)$. $\qquad\qquad\square$

We have shown in great detail that Q is Σ_1-complete, and we will take for granted that it is sound (in particular Σ_1-sound) since the axioms are 'obviously true' in $\mathbb{N}$. (One could insist on a rigorous *proof* of Σ_1-soundness, but if one doubts such an elementary observation, much else in this book would need to be re-examined first.) So we can deduce the undecidability of first-order validity, a theorem originally due to Church (1936):

Theorem 7.15 *The set of logical truths (even in the language of arithmetic) is not recursive.*

Proof Since Q is undecidable, Theorem 7.14 tells us that any theory axiomatized by a subset of Q arrived at by removing finitely many axioms is also undecidable. Since Q is finite, this applies to the smallest theory in the language, i.e. the logically valid formulas in that language. □

This finally allows us to conclude that a semi-decision procedure for first-order logic is the best we could hope for. We will sketch several sharper forms of this result in the next section.

7.7 Further limitative results

There are plenty of other interesting limitative results, which, however, are not quite so directly relevant to the theme of this book and/or require (even) more formidable technicalities. We content ourselves here with giving brief overviews of a few related topics.

Consistency and Hilbert's programme

Recall that Hilbert's clever idea was to establish in an elementary way, by analyzing proofs themselves, that concrete results proved using more controversial parts of abstract mathematics (e.g. infinite sets) were nevertheless true. More explicitly, suppose we identify 'concrete results' with 'results clearly expressible as Π_1-formulas', and assume that our axioms are at least Σ_1-complete. Then it would suffice to establish, in a suitably elementary way, just the *consistency* of the axioms, because we know (see Section 7.4) that Σ_1-completeness and consistency together imply Π_1-soundness.[†] This identification of 'concrete result' and 'Π_1 sentence' may seem questionable, but many important results of mathematics *are* expressible as Π_1-formulas. The still-unresolved Goldbach conjecture that every even number ≥ 4 is the sum of two primes can be written quite directly in that form:

$$\forall n.\, n \geq 2 \Rightarrow \exists p.\, p \leq 2 \cdot n \wedge \exists q.\, q \leq 2 \cdot n \wedge \mathrm{prime}(p) \wedge \mathrm{prime}(q) \wedge 2 \cdot n = p + q.$$

With a bit more work, Fermat's last theorem can be written as a Π_1-sentence (by expressing exponentiation as a Σ_1-formula in the antecedent of an implication), and so can even the Riemann hypothesis about the location of complex zeros of the ζ-function (Kreisel 1958b). Proving any of these results from a *consistent* Σ_1-complete axiom system would establish their truth even if not all the axioms are *true*. A similar observation is that if a Π_1 sentence p is *not refutable* from a Σ_1-complete axiom system, it must be

---

[†] It's not clear that Hilbert perceived this immediately. The emphasis he placed on consistency may have just been because it was at least a necessary condition, regardless of the search for stronger conservation results.

true. For instance, showing that the weak axioms Q are unable to refute the Goldbach conjecture would amount to proving it!

Gödel's second incompleteness theorem

Most of the technical difficulty of Gödel's first incompleteness theorem was concentrated in establishing the surprising 'this sentence is unprovable' fixpoint property. Once we have that, the essence of the proof is quite simple, so much so that if we set it up carefully, our automated procedures can handle it. The following formulation assumes the fixpoint property for G, the fact that G is a Π_1-formula, soundness and completeness for Σ_1 formulas and a couple of lemmas about truth and formula classifications. From this it follows that $\vdash G$ iff $\vdash \neg G$, and so we can see that if either of these holds, the system is inconsistent.

```
meson
 <<(True(G) <=> ~(|--(G))) /\ Pi(G) /\
   (forall p. Sigma(p) ==> (|--(p) <=> True(p))) /\
   (forall p. True(Not(p)) <=> ~True(p)) /\
   (forall p. Pi(p) ==> Sigma(Not(p)))
   ==> (|--(Not(G)) <=> |--(G))>>;;
 ...
- : int list = [5; 5]
```

This hints at another noteworthy aspect of Gödel's proof: it can itself be subjected to an additional level of formalization and proved inside the arithmetic theory being considered. Gödel argued on this basis that a sufficiently strong theory is unable to prove its own consistency – his second incompleteness theorem. More explicitly, assuming Pr_A defines provability from a set of axioms A (after Gödel numbering), it is clear that:

$$\mathrm{Con}(A) =_{\mathrm{def}} \neg\mathrm{Pr}_A(\ulcorner \bot \urcorner)$$

expresses the consistency of A. Now Gödel's second theorem asserts that for a wide class of axiom systems A, this is not itself provable in A, i.e. $A \nvdash \mathrm{Con}(A)$, unless A *is* in fact inconsistent, in which case it proves anything.

The technicalities arising from a further level of formalization are quite forbidding. The paper in which Gödel presented his first incompleteness theorem was explicitly numbered '*I*', the intention being that a sequel would provide a completely rigorous proof of the second incompleteness theorem. However, this paper never appeared, and Hilbert and Bernays (1939) may have been the first to give a rigorous demonstration. They tried to isolate the technical complexities in a number of key properties of provability that suffice for the second theorem. There were later greatly simplified by Löb (1955) to the following *derivability conditions*:

1 if $A \vdash p$ then $A \vdash \mathrm{Pr}_A(\ulcorner p \urcorner)$,
2 $A \vdash \mathrm{Pr}_A(\ulcorner p \Rightarrow q \urcorner) \Rightarrow \mathrm{Pr}_A(\ulcorner p \urcorner) \Rightarrow \mathrm{Pr}_A(\ulcorner q \urcorner)$,
3 $A \vdash \mathrm{Pr}_A(\ulcorner p \urcorner) \Rightarrow \mathrm{Pr}_A(\ulcorner \mathrm{Pr}_A(\ulcorner p \urcorner) \urcorner)$.

Condition (1) follows from the fact that Pr_A is a correct arithmetization together with Σ_1-completeness, and (2) just arithmetizes the closure of provability under *modus ponens*. Condition (3), which is essentially a further arithmetization of (1), is much harder to establish. Indeed, the axioms A need to be somewhat stronger than Q for (3) to be provable at all. Boolos (1995) gives a reasonably detailed sketch for Peano arithmetic of formalized Σ_1-completeness (if p is a Σ_1-formula then $PA \vdash p \Rightarrow \mathrm{Pr}_{PA}(\ulcorner p \urcorner)$), of which (3) is a special case.

Anyway, once we have the derivability conditions and a formalized version $A \vdash G \Leftrightarrow \neg \mathrm{Pr}_A(G)$ of the fixpoint property, the proof is quite easy, even to formalize assuming a few object-logic inference rules. We use F to denote $\bot$, writing $\neg p$ as $p \Rightarrow F$, and deduce that a system that can prove its own consistency $(A \vdash \mathrm{Pr}_A(F) \Rightarrow F)$ is in fact inconsistent $(A \vdash F)$:

```
let godel_2 = prove
<<(forall p. |--(p) ==> |--(Pr(p))) /\
  (forall p q. |--(imp(Pr(imp(p,q)),imp(Pr(p),Pr(q))))) /\
  (forall p. |--(imp(Pr(p),Pr(Pr(p)))))
  ==> (forall p q. |--(imp(p,q)) /\ |--(p) ==> |--(q)) /\
      (forall p q. |--(imp(q,imp(p,q)))) /\
      (forall p q r. |--(imp(imp(p,imp(q,r)),imp(imp(p,q),imp(p,r)))))
      ==> |--(imp(G,imp(Pr(G),F))) /\ |--(imp(imp(Pr(G),F),G))
          ==> |--(imp(Pr(F),F)) ==> |--(F)>>
[assume ["lob1",<<forall p. |--(p) ==> |--(Pr(p))>>;
        "lob2",<<forall p q. |--(imp(Pr(imp(p,q)),imp(Pr(p),Pr(q))))>>;
        "lob3",<<forall p. |--(imp(Pr(p),Pr(Pr(p))))>>];
 assume ["logic",<<(forall p q. |--(imp(p,q)) /\ |--(p) ==> |--(q)) /\
                   (forall p q. |--(imp(q,imp(p,q)))) /\
                   (forall p q r. |--(imp(imp(p,imp(q,r)),
                                    imp(imp(p,q),imp(p,r)))))>>];
 assume ["fix1",<<|--(imp(G,imp(Pr(G),F)))>>;
         "fix2",<<|--(imp(imp(Pr(G),F),G))>>];
 assume ["consistency",<<|--(imp(Pr(F),F))>>];
 have <<|--(Pr(imp(G,imp(Pr(G),F))))>> by ["lob1"; "fix1"];
 so have <<|--(imp(Pr(G),Pr(imp(Pr(G),F))))>> by ["lob2"; "logic"];
 so have <<|--(imp(Pr(G),imp(Pr(Pr(G)),Pr(F))))>> by ["lob2"; "logic"];
 so have <<|--(imp(Pr(G),Pr(F)))>> by ["lob3"; "logic"];
 so note("L",<<|--(imp(Pr(G),F))>>) by ["consistency"; "logic"];
 so have <<|--(G)>> by ["fix2"; "logic"];
 so have <<|--(Pr(G))>> by ["lob1"; "logic"];
 so conclude <<|--(F)>> by ["L"; "logic"];
 qed];;
```

Nothing in this proof actually depends on the fact that F denotes falsity; if we take some other sentence S and construct a fixpoint such that $A \vdash G \Leftrightarrow (\mathrm{Pr}_A(\ulcorner G \urcorner) \Rightarrow S)$, we can conclude from $A \vdash \mathrm{Pr}_A(\ulcorner S \urcorner) \Rightarrow S$ simply that $A \vdash S$ (Löb 1955). Since Gödel's theorem is derived from a fixpoint such that $G \Leftrightarrow \neg\mathrm{Pr}_A(\ulcorner G \urcorner)$, it's natural to wonder what properties a fixpoint $S \Leftrightarrow \mathrm{Pr}_A(\ulcorner S \urcorner)$ would have (Henkin 1952). Löb's theorem provides an answer: if $\vdash S \Leftrightarrow \mathrm{Pr}_A(\ulcorner S \urcorner)$ then in fact $\vdash S$, even if we just assume implication in one direction.

Gödel's second theorem was widely accepted as destroying Hilbert's programme as originally set out. For if one cannot prove $T \vdash \mathrm{Con}(T)$ for a reasonable system T, then a fortiori one cannot prove $S \vdash \mathrm{Con}(T)$ where S is a weaker system than T. However, note that it's *not* true that if $S \vdash \mathrm{Con}(T)$ then S must be stronger than T; it could be stronger in some ways and weaker in others.[†] For example, given that PA is sound and therefore consistent, Gödel's second theorem implies that $PA' = PA \cup \{\neg\mathrm{Con}(PA)\}$ is also consistent, i.e. that $\mathrm{Con}(PA')$ is true. And one can quite easily prove $PA \vdash \mathrm{Con}(PA') \Rightarrow \mathrm{Con}(PA)$ since $\vdash \mathrm{Ax}_{PA} \Rightarrow \mathrm{Ax}_{PA'}$ for the corresponding arithmetizations of the axiom sets. Now $PA'' = PA \cup \{\mathrm{Con}(PA')\}$ can trivially prove the consistency of PA'. Yet it is not properly stronger than PA' (indeed it is actually inconsistent with it) because $PA'' \nvdash \neg\mathrm{Con}(PA)$, since PA'' is true and $\neg\mathrm{Con}(PA)$ is false.

Gödel's second theorem does not rule out the possibility of a more limited Hilbert-style bootstrapping of mathematics. Even though one might not be able to prove in a suitably restricted way the consistency of *all* mathematics, one might be able to prove the consistency of a reasonable subset, enough for many applications. For example, 'WKL_0' (Friedmann 1976) a fragment of second order arithmetic including restricted induction and the 'weak König lemma' as axioms, is strong enough to prove, albeit via some coding, many of the traditional results in analysis. This raises the possibility of a quite significant *partial* realization of Hilbert's programme (Simpson 1988b), and motivates the exploration of still more powerful systems with similar conservation properties (Simpson 1998).

Another possibility is that one might be able to prove a *relative* consistency result $A \vdash \mathrm{Con}(S) \Rightarrow \mathrm{Con}(T)$ for some accepted system of axioms A. Again, there are several genuine examples, such as the proof by Gödel (1938) himself of the consistency of the Generalized Continuum Hypothesis (GCH) and Axiom of Choice relative to the axioms of Zermelo–Fraenkel (ZF) set theory. This result $A \vdash \mathrm{Con}(ZF) \Rightarrow \mathrm{Con}(ZFC + GCH)$ can be proved using a

---

[†] It is at least true that it must be properly stronger in its Π_1 consequences, assuming Σ_1-completeness.

weak set of axioms A, and so arguably does provide genuine reassurance that ZFC plus GCH is consistent provided ZF is. However, Gödel's second incompleteness theorem still reminds us of the limitations of this approach: if $T \vdash \mathrm{Con}(S)$ then it is impossible even that $T \vdash \mathrm{Con}(S) \Rightarrow \mathrm{Con}(T)$, let alone $A \vdash \mathrm{Con}(S) \Rightarrow \mathrm{Con}(T)$ for a reassuringly weak A, since that would immediately imply the impossible $T \vdash \mathrm{Con}(T)$. This means, for example, that there is no hope of an elementary relative consistency proof for ZF relative to Z (essentially ZF without the Axiom of Replacement), or Z relative to elementary number theory. This does allow us to draw interesting conclusions in the other direction, though, for example that the formula I asserting the existence of an inaccessible cardinal is not provable in ZF set theory, precisely because $ZF + I \vdash \mathrm{Con}(ZF)$.

Reflection principles

Gödel's first theorem essentially just asserts the unprovability of *some* true Π_1-formula: note that the statement of Corollary 7.10 doesn't mention the particular formula G used in our proof, and we could have proved it using other formulas or even completely nonconstructively. The second theorem, however, refers essentially to a *specific* unprovable sentence $\mathrm{Con}(A)$. This sentence depends not only on the axioms A themselves but on the particular formula $\mathrm{Ax}(p)$ used to define them. By choosing a suitable formula $\mathrm{Ax}'(p)$, still equivalent in $\mathbb{N}$ to $\mathrm{Ax}(p)$, one can sometimes arrive at a corresponding consistency statement $\mathrm{Con}'(A)$ such that $A \vdash \mathrm{Con}'(A)$. A trivial example would be $\mathrm{Ax}'(p) =_{\mathrm{def}} \mathrm{Ax}(p) \wedge \mathrm{Con}(A)$ for some reasonably strong A. Feferman (1960) shows that for certain axiomatic systems like PA there are more subtle and troubling instances of this phenomenon. So one needs to distinguish carefully between 'natural' and 'pathological' representations of the same axiom set; in the philosophical jargon, *intensional* aspects become important. Resnik (1974) discusses the philosophical significance of this fact.

Now, while Gödel's incompleteness theorems point to the weakness of formal systems, they also suggest systematic procedures for making a given system stronger. For example, given some axiom system S_0, a natural way of strengthening it is the addition of a new axiom amounting to a statement of S_0's consistency:

$$S_1 = S_0 \cup \{\mathrm{Con}(S_0)\}.$$

This gives a new system, and a corresponding new provability predicate and assertion of consistency. Now the procedure can be iterated, giving S_2, S_3 and so on, even infinitely; this idea was first investigated by Turing (1939) and further developed by Feferman (1962). Franzén (2002) gives a detailed treatment, emphasizing the important role 'nonstandard' characterizations of axioms mentioned above play in the apparent power of such iterated extensions.

Feferman coined the term 'reflection principle' for an assertion, like a statement of consistency, that amounts to an expression of trust in a system of axioms, which is not directly provable from those axioms but is believed to be true by 'reflecting upon' those axioms from outside (Kreisel and Lévy 1968). It is possible for a consistent theory to become inconsistent on the addition of a reflection principle, even a simple statement of consistency. For example, Gödel's theorems show that if S is consistent, so is $T = S \cup \{\neg\text{Con}(S)\}$, but $\text{Con}(T)$ implies $\text{Con}(S)$, so the further addition of $\text{Con}(T)$ to T yields an inconsistent system. However, it follows from Feferman's work that a Σ_1-sound system remains so even on transfinitely many additions of various strong reflection principles, such as a Löb schema $\vdash \text{Pr}_A(\ulcorner p \urcorner) \Rightarrow p$. A related but much 'safer' idea is to extend the logic with a reflection *rule*:

$$\frac{A \vdash \text{Pr}_A(\ulcorner \phi \urcorner)}{A \vdash \phi}.$$

The addition of this may be inconsistent (again, consider the system T above that is not Σ_1-sound). However Σ_1-soundness of A guarantees not only that the new system is Σ_1-sound, but actually has the *same theorems*, since every Σ_1-formula, such as an assertion of provability, is provable iff true. Nevertheless, by adding this as a new rule of inference, it may be possible to produce proofs of feasible length that would not have been feasible, even while possible in principle, without it (see Exercise 7.10). Such rules have often been suggested in connection with using reflection to verify derived inference rules (Knoblock and Constable 1986; Allen, Constable, Howe and Aitken 1990).

Hilbert's tenth problem

We showed earlier that a relation over $\mathbb{N}$ is recursively enumerable iff it is definable by a Σ_1-formula. In fact, a much sharper result holds: we need no inequalities, propositional connectives or quantifier alternations. A relation $R(a_1, \ldots, a_n)$ is r.e. iff it is *Diophantine*, i.e. definable over $\mathbb{N}$ by a formula that is simply an existentially quantified equation:

$$\exists x_1, \ldots, x_k.\, s = t,$$

where s and t are terms of the usual language of arithmetic whose variables are among $\{a_1, \ldots, a_n, x_1, \ldots, x_k\}$. And since the language consists of constants and the addition and multiplication operators, all terms are effectively polynomials (with positive coefficients), so we can think of these as being put in some standard form and regard the relation as

$$\exists x_1, \ldots, x_k.\, p(a_1, \ldots, a_n, x_1, \ldots, x_k) = q(a_1, \ldots, a_n, x_1, \ldots, x_k).$$

The same result holds if we consider definability over $\mathbb{Z}$, in which case we can consider the even simpler canonical form

$$\exists x_1, \ldots, x_k.\, p(a_1, \ldots, a_n, x_1, \ldots, x_k) = 0.$$

The fact that every r.e. relation is Diophantine settles Hilbert's tenth problem: there can be no algorithm to decide whether a polynomial has integer solutions. For any such algorithm could be used, via the Diophantine representation of r.e. sets, to solve some undecidable problem such as first-order validity or the halting problem.

Davis first conjectured that every r.e. set is Diophantine, perhaps based on the observation that Diophantine sets satisfy many of the same closure properties that r.e. sets do. For example, the intersection and union of Diophantine sets are Diophantine because $p = 0 \wedge q = 0 \Leftrightarrow p^2 + q^2 = 0$ and $p = 0 \vee q = 0 \Leftrightarrow pq = 0$. But it is far from easy to show that one can define r.e. sets without using bounded universal quantification, and Davis's conjecture resisted proof for some time. Building on a normal form result for Σ_1-formulas due to Davis (1950), an important step was taken by J. Robinson (1952), who proved that a sufficient condition that every r.e. set be Diophantine is that there should exist *some* Diophantine function of exponential growth. The first such function was exhibited by Matiyasevich (1970), who finally proved that all r.e. sets are Diophantine by finding a Diophantine representation for the predicate

$$\phi(u, v) =_{\mathrm{def}} v = \mathtt{fib}_{2u},$$

where $\mathtt{fib}_n$ is the nth Fibonacci number:

$$\begin{aligned}
\mathtt{fib}_0 &= 0, \\
\mathtt{fib}_1 &= 1, \\
\mathtt{fib}_{n+2} &= \mathtt{fib}_{n+1} + \mathtt{fib}_n.
\end{aligned}$$

Although fairly long and technical, the proof uses only elementary techniques, and an accessible treatment can be found in the textbook by Matijasevich (1993), while an alternative based on solutions to the Pell equation is presented in some other logic books such as Smoryński (1980). Rather than appeal to Robinson's early results, there is a striking way of using a Diophantine representation for binomial coefficients to simulate Turing machines or register machines directly (Jones and Matiyasevich 1984); see Exercise 7.20.

The theory of rationals

We have shown that the theory of reals with addition and multiplication is decidable (Section 5.9), whereas the theory of integers based on the same language is not even recursively enumerable (Section 7.2). Given this huge gulf, it's natural to wonder about the status of a corresponding theory of rationals, which in some sense lies 'in between'. In fact, this theory is as undecidable as the integer theory, because the set of integers is definable by a formula in the theory of rationals, as first shown by J. Robinson (1949). Using some results about quadratic forms, she proves that a rational number n is an integer iff it satisfies the following formula:

$$Z(n) =_{\text{def}} \forall a\, b.\, \phi(a, b, 0) \wedge (\forall m.\, \phi(a, b, m) \Rightarrow \phi(a, b, m+1)) \Rightarrow \phi(a, b, n),$$

where

$$\phi(a, b, k) =_{\text{def}} \exists x\, y\, z.\, 2 + abk^2 + bz^2 = x^2 + ay^2.$$

Consequently, any formula over $\mathbb{Z}$ can be mapped into a corresponding formula over $\mathbb{Q}$ by relativizing the quantifiers using $Z(n)$, and so undecidability follows from undecidability of the theory of integers. However, if we consider the special case of deciding formulas:

$$\exists x_1, \ldots, x_n.\, p(x_1, \ldots, x_n) = 0,$$

the rational analogue of Hilbert's tenth problem, the undecidability cannot similarly be read off from the result for the integers because $Z(n)$ is not a purely existential formula, while even the sharpest such definition known at present (Poonen 2007) contains one quantifier alternation. Of course, we can map every such formula into an equivalent assertion over $\mathbb{Z}$ just by clearing denominators, but the resulting polynomial is of a rather special character – the result of clearing denominators will always be homogeneous, i.e. all monomials will have the same multidegree; see. Exercise 7.15 below. The nonexistence of a general decision procedure does not exclude the possibility of one for this restricted class. In fact, the status of Hilbert's tenth problems for the rationals, and for homogeneous polynomials over the integers, are to the best of the author's knowledge at time of writing, still unsolved problems.

A related problem that definitely *is* decidable (Ax 1967) is whether, given an integer polynomial equation $q(x_1, \ldots, x_n) = 0$, for all primes p there is a solution modulo p, i.e. $\forall p. \exists x_1, \ldots, x_n. q(x_1, \ldots, x_n) \equiv 0 \pmod{p}$.

Sharper forms of Church's theorem

Full first-order validity may be undecidable, but we've seen that it is decidable for some classes of formulas, such as those with certain quantifier prefixes. In order to prove that validity for formulas in a certain class K is *not* decidable, a common technique is to prove that K represents a 'reduction class', i.e. that there is a computable function f mapping each formula p to some $f(p) \in K$ such that validity of p is equivalent to validity of $f(p)$. If K is indeed a reduction class, no algorithm can exist for validity in K, for then we could obtain one for all of first-order logic by just applying f and then the algorithm.

For example, the class K of formulas with a quantifier prefix of the form $\exists^n \forall^n$ is a reduction class (note that this is dual to the decidable AE fragment). This follows from Skolem normal form: given any first order formula, one can find an equisatisfiable one by performing the first order analogue of definition CNF, introducing new predicate symbols to stand for all subformulas – see Exercise 3.4. Let us assume we first transform the formula to NNF and therefore only need implications for the definitions. The resulting formula is a conjunction with each conjunct of the form

$$\forall x_1 \ldots x_n. R(x_1, \ldots, x_n) \Rightarrow P[x_1, \ldots, x_n].$$

These are all universally quantified at the outside, and the only ones with quantifiers inside are of the form

$$\forall x_1 \ldots x_n. R(x_1, \ldots, x_n) \Rightarrow \forall y. [x_1, \ldots, x_n, y]$$

and

$$\forall x_1 \ldots x_n. R(x_1, \ldots, x_n) \Rightarrow \exists y. [x_1, \ldots, x_n, y].$$

When prenexed, the most complicated quantifier structure is therefore $\forall^n \exists$. However, we have a conjunction of such clauses so when prenexed the result is of the form $\forall^n \exists^m$. Dually, for validity, the resulting formula is of the form $\exists^n \forall^m$. Consequently, there can be no decision procedure for such formulas.

The decidability of the monadic fragment of logic is also a sharp result in the sense that first-order validity in a language with no functions and just one binary predicate is undecidable (Kalmár 1936). This isn't entirely surprising: although we have proved Church's theorem using a language with several function and predicate symbols for arithmetic, it is known that arithmetic can be formalized in a set theory finitely axiomatized by a single binary membership relation. This result was further sharpened by Rabin (1965) to show that the theory of a single irreflexive and symmetric binary relation (a 'graph') is undecidable. By contrast, the theory of a binary total order relation is decidable; Rabin (1969) gives a relatively simple proof of an even stronger result.

Another somewhat different direction in which the unsolvability of first-order logic with equality can be sharpened is the following. Our proof methods were almost all justified via Herbrand's theorem, asserting that a formula $\forall x_1 \ldots x_n.\ P[x_1, \ldots, x_n]$ is unsatisfiable iff there is a finite set of m ground instances such that

$$P[t_1^1, \ldots, t_n^1] \wedge \cdots \wedge P[t_1^m, \ldots, t_n^m]$$

is propositionally unsatisfiable. We can imagine separating the semi-decision procedures based on Herbrand's theorem into two parts: first finding the minimum necessary multiplicity m, and *then*, given m, finding the appropriate instances – the latter is often referred to as the *Herbrand skeleton problem*. It's quite easy to see that, for pure first-order logic, we can always, given m, test whether there are any suitable instances giving an unsatisfiable formula, by a unification-based enumeration of possibilities as in the crude initial forms of tableaux. In some sense therefore, all the undecidability resides in finding m. However, one can deduce from the unsolvability of 'simultaneous rigid E-unification' (Degtyarev and Voronkov 1995) that the Herbrand skeleton problem for first-order logic *with equality* is unsolvable; Voda and Komara (1995) prove a strong form of this result.

The Rosser construction

In the proof of the usual form of Gödel's first incompleteness theorem for a Σ_1-complete set of axioms A, we required only simple consistency of A to ensure that the Gödel sentence G is unprovable, $A \nvdash G$. But to show that $A \nvdash \neg G$, we used the stronger hypothesis of Σ_1-soundness, aka 1-consistency. In fact, by considering the Gödel sentence for the axiom system $A' = A \cup \{\neg G\}$ we can see that some stronger assumption than simple consistency is definitely necessary – see Exercise 7.16. However, Rosser (1936) later strengthened Gödel's theorem by showing, given a suitable axiom system A, how to exhibit a different sentence R such that, assuming only that A is consistent, neither $A \vdash R$ nor $A \vdash \neg R$.

We have seen that provability (from a Σ_1-definable set of axioms A) is definable by a Σ_1-formula $\mathrm{Pr}_A(n)$. Using the trick of relativizing all but the outermost quantifier (Exercise 7.5) we can assume it to be of the form $\exists p.\,\mathrm{Proof}(p,n)$ for a Δ_0-formula $\mathrm{Proof}(p,n)$, which we think of as meaning 'p encodes a proof of the formula with Gödel number n'. Thinking of p as a 'proof' may be a little artificial given that our encoding of provability did not explicitly consider any distinct notion of 'proof', but it is technically inconsequential and seems to be a useful psychological crutch. Now consider the following variant:

$$\overline{\mathrm{Proof}}(p,\ulcorner\phi\urcorner) =_{\mathrm{def}} \mathrm{Proof}(p,\ulcorner\phi\urcorner) \wedge \forall q.\, q \le p \Rightarrow \neg\mathrm{Proof}(q,\ulcorner\neg\phi\urcorner).$$

In other words, we think of $\overline{\mathrm{Proof}}(p,\ulcorner\phi\urcorner)$ as 'p encodes a proof of ϕ and no smaller number encodes a proof of $\neg\phi$'. Now, assuming that the system is consistent, $\mathrm{Proof}(p,n)$ and $\overline{\mathrm{Proof}}(p,n)$ actually define the same relation over $\mathbb{N}$, because if $\mathrm{Proof}(p,\ulcorner\phi\urcorner)$ then for no q, and a fortiori for no $q \le p$, does $\mathrm{Proof}(q,\ulcorner\neg\phi\urcorner)$ hold. We proceed to diagonalize and obtain an analogue R of the Gödel sentence:

$$A \vdash R \Leftrightarrow \neg\overline{\mathrm{Pr}_A}(\ulcorner R\urcorner).$$

One can show from this that either $A \vdash R$ or $A \vdash \neg R$ leads to a contradiction, though one needs an additional property of A beyond Σ_1-completeness: that $A \vdash \forall x.\, x \le \overline{n} \vee \overline{n} \le x$ for any *particular* numeral $\overline{n}$. (This is the case for our axioms Q, and probably for any realistic set of arithmetic axioms.)

Essential undecidability

A theory is said to be *essentially undecidable* if every consistent extension of it is undecidable. (By an extension of a theory T we mean any T' such that $T' \vdash p$ for each $p \in T$.) In the proof of Church's theorem we argued that any theory T that is both sound and complete for Σ_1-sentences is undecidable. One can sharpen this to assume just Σ_1-completeness and *consistency*, not necessarily Σ_1-soundness, by showing that the equivalence in the fixpoint Lemma 7.3 is not just true in $\mathbb{N}$ but actually *provable*. Since Q is Σ_1-complete, so is any extension of it, and we can conclude that Q (more properly the theory $\mathrm{Cn}(Q)$) is essentially undecidable.

We say that two theories T and T' are *compatible* if $T \cup T'$ is consistent. A theory is said to be *strongly undecidable* if any other theory compatible with it is undecidable. Note that a finitely axiomatized essentially undecidable theory is also strongly undecidable by Theorem 7.14: if T is such a theory with finite axiomatization A, $\mathrm{Cn}(A \cup T')$ is undecidable, since $T \subseteq \mathrm{Cn}(A \cup T')$

and T is essentially undecidable, and hence so is T', using finiteness of A. In particular we conclude that *any theory compatible with Q is undecidable.* Since Q holds in $\mathbb{N}$, we also see that *every subtheory of $\mathbb{N}$ is undecidable.*

Besides being a strong result in itself, one can use this to deduce undecidability of various related theories via interpretation of one theory in another, an approach systematically worked out in Tarski, Mostowski and Robinson (1953). For example, because an integer is nonnegative iff it is a sum of four squares, Q can be interpreted inside a suitable theory of integers by relativizing quantifiers; by a similar argument involving strong undecidability, we can deduce that any subtheory of the ring of integers (in the same language) is undecidable. In particular, the theory of rings is undecidable, though as we saw in Section 5.10 the universal fragment *is* decidable. Using Julia Robinson's definition of $\mathbb{Z}$ in $\mathbb{Q}$, one can similarly show that the theory of fields is undecidable. In a surprising contrast, the theory of *finite* fields is decidable (Ax 1968), though the theory of finite rings is also undecidable (Rabin 1965).

7.8 Retrospective: the nature of logic

If we ask ourselves what makes the material in this book distinctively *logical* rather than traditionally *mathematical* we can answer in two different ways. In one sense our reasoning has been more general: the use of an expressive formal language with explicit quantifiers has led us to generalizations of classic decision problems in mathematics, e.g. Tarski's method as a generalization of Sturm's algorithm. Even though many results could have been reached without explicit use of logical language, in practice this was not done.[†] On the other hand, we may consider our reasoning more limited in that we've restricted ourselves to analyzing strictly *logical* truths. Admittedly, we sometimes considered deduction from powerful sets of axioms, but the notion of logical truth has always been central.

As noted in the introduction, however, we haven't defined the concept of logical consequence very precisely. We ended up identifying logical reasoning with reasoning valid in first-order logic. Is this a valid formal counterpart of any of the traditional (and arguably vague) distinctions such as necessary/contingent, analytic/synthetic, a priori/a posteriori? This is not so clear, though some have certainly made such claims (Carnap 1935). But perhaps even more fundamental than the detail of first-order logic is the

---

[†] There are some exceptions. For example, the logical investigation of the analytic hierarchy was paralleled in descriptive set theory, using projection of multidimensional sets instead of a syntactic notion of quantification. Indeed, it was only later that the deep interrelations with recursion theory were pointed out.

question of formal checkability of proofs. Intuitively, a chain of logical deductions should not leave one suspecting that hidden assumptions or knowledge have been smuggled in. Verifying the validity of a logical proof spelled out in enough detail should require from the reader no real intelligence or knowledge of the subject matter – this is exactly why it is so persuasive. In principle, a sufficiently detailed proof could be verified by a clerk, or even a machine. While this seems to understate the intellectual difficulty of proof, it accurately reflects the view many mathematicians have of the axiomatic method.

For first-order logic, there are indeed formal counterparts of the notion of a chain of logical inferences that can be decidably *checked* by machine, as we've seen. For first-order logic augmented with the arithmetic of positive integers, though, we've seen on the contrary that by Tarski's theorem no such methods can exist even in principle; this also applies to still more powerful formal systems such as higher-order logic or set theory. In all such systems, whatever specific way of exhibiting and checking proofs is chosen, there will always be truths that cannot be verified mechanically.

So we might regard checkability by machine as the fundamental property that makes a proof truly *logical*. Thus, one can argue that the possibility of automated theorem proving and proof checking has profound philosophical significance. But we hardly need to indulge in self-justification given that it's all just so much fun.

Further reading

There are many books about the foundations of mathematics and the philosophical background to Hilbert's programme, e.g. Kneebone (1963) and Wilder (1965). Van Stigt (1990) is an account of Brouwer's life and work, including an exegesis of his intuitionistic philosophy, while Edwards (1989) analyzes the philosophical views of Kronecker. For more on intuitionistic logic and constructive mathematics see Mints (2000), Troelstra and van Dalen (1988) and Beeson (1984). Kreisel (1958a) discusses Hilbert's programme; numerous papers in vol. 53 (1988) of the *Journal of Symbolic Logic* discuss this programme in a modern context. There are several books containing collections of papers on the foundations of mathematics, e.g. Benacerraf and Putnam (1983) and Hintikka (1969) as well as the predominantly technical collection of Van Heijenoort (1967).

Many logic texts such as Enderton (1972) and Mendelson (1987) discuss Gödel's incompleteness theorems. The monograph by Smullyan (1992) has strongly influenced our presentation here, e.g. in beginning with Tarski's theorem. Gödel's theorems have a fame that reaches beyond the confines of formal logic. The temptation to assimilate Gödel's results into some broader intellectual or cultural trends seems hard to resist. Franzén (2005) is not only a general overview of Gödel's theorems but a systematic debunking of various misapprehensions about them. For more on reflection principles and transfinite progressions of theories, see Feferman (1991), while Franzén (2002) discusses the whole incompleteness phenomenon with a particular focus on progressions of theories.

The reader may have noticed that the nested quotations like $\mathrm{Pr}(\ulcorner \mathrm{Pr}(\ulcorner p \urcorner) \urcorner)$ get messy and difficult to read. It's convenient to use $\Box p$ as an abbreviation for $\mathrm{Pr}(\ulcorner p \urcorner)$, with $\Box\Box p$ for $\mathrm{Pr}(\ulcorner \mathrm{Pr}(\ulcorner p \urcorner) \urcorner)$ etc. In fact, this can be more than a handy notion: one can consider a special kind of 'modal' logic where a provability predicate is added as a new formula constructor, and Solovay (1976) has shown that all modally expressible properties that Pr satisfies can be proved directly by modal reasoning. Accounts of this are given by Boolos (1995) and by Smoryński (1985). For more on modal logic in general, see Mints (1992) and Hughes and Cresswell (1996).

Many standard logic texts include some material on computability, e.g. Boolos and Jeffrey (1989), while there are numerous other texts designed for the computer scientist such as Minsky (1967). We have barely scratched the surface of the subject of computable functions and recursively enumerable sets; see Davis, Sigal and Weyuker (1994) for an introduction. One extension of the concept (Turing 1939) is to *relative* computability, where one considers whether a function f would be computable given an 'oracle' computing some other computable function g – see Odifreddi (1989) for an account of the resulting hierarchies, as well as much other material. One can also consider the field of computable real numbers and computable functions of a real variable (Aberth 1980) – Goodstein (1960) uses a even more limited primitive recursive arithmetic. Hodges (1983) gives an account of Turing's eventful life, discussing his theoretical work in mathematical logic as well as his practical role in code-breaking and the development of modern digital computers.

Gödel's results can be proved using formalizations of other informal paradoxes such as Berry's 'the smallest integer that cannot be named in fewer than thirteen words' (Chaitin 1970; Boolos 1989). Subsequently Chaitin (1974) proved a different incompleteness theorem based on his own notion of algorithmic complexity (aka Kolmogorov complexity), giving a perspective on the incompleteness phenomenon that has led to much philosophical discussion (Raatikainen 1998).

Exercises

7.1   We deliberately chose a pairing with $\langle x, y \rangle \neq 0$, to simplify encoding of lists. Show that the Cantor pairing function $\langle x, y \rangle = \frac{(x+y)^2 + 3x + y}{2}$ is actually bijective, i.e. for all $z \in \mathbb{N}$ there are unique x and y with $\langle x, y \rangle = z$. A much more difficult result, due to Fueter and Polya, is that the Cantor pairing and the variant obtained by swapping x and y are the *only* quadratic polynomials with real coefficients that induce a bijection $\mathbb{N}^2 \to \mathbb{N}$. Still more difficult is the conjecture that there are no other polynomials of *any* degree with real coefficients that induce a bijection $\mathbb{N}^2 \to \mathbb{N}$ – this and several related generalizations are still open problems at time of writing (Smoryński 1980).

7.2   We remarked that as an easy consequence of the closure of Σ_1 relations under reflexive–transitive closure, the (graph of the) exponential function is Σ_1. Prove that in fact it is Δ_0, i.e. definable by a formula with all quantifiers bounded (Bennet 1962). You may find it useful to observe that one can compute the exponential by binary recursion $x^{2y} = (x^y)^2$ and $x^{2y+1} = x \cdot (x^y)^2$, and the successive values in the recursion decrease geometrically, making it possible to bound a representation of the construction sequence in terms of the final value $x^y = z$. For a particularly clean and elegant realization of this idea for the special case $x = 2$, see Voda (2001). Can you generalize his construction to $x^y = z$ for arbitrary x?

7.3   We showed that if $R(x, y)$ is Σ_1, so is its reflexive transitive closure $R^*(x, y)$. Suppose $R(x, y)$ implies that $x \leq y$. Show that the *complement* of the reflexive transitive closure is also Σ_1. (Hint: consider bounds for the unbounded quantifiers in the existing expressions.)

7.4   Write a program to take a formula defining a set of axioms A, assumed sound, and explicitly produce a sentence p that is true in $\mathbb{N}$ but not first-order provable from A. Roughly, you just need to automate the constructions from the first sections of this chapter. However, you will need to make the encodings significantly more economical for this to be practical. In particular, Gödel numbers in our scheme tend to blow up too quickly, and the zero-successor numerals are not practical. Can you circumvent all these problems?

7.5   Show that every Σ_1-formula is equivalent in $\mathbb{N}$ to one of the special form $\exists m. D[m]$ where $D[m]$ is a Δ_0-formula. (This can be considered a form of the Kleene normal form theorem.) Is it always the case that this equivalence can be proved using only our weak axioms of arithmetic Q?

7.6   Suppose we modify the Robinson axioms Q by asserting $m \leq n \Leftrightarrow \exists d.\, d + m = n$ instead of $m \leq n \Leftrightarrow \exists d.\, m + d = n$. Show that, in the resulting system Q', we cannot derive $\forall x.\, 0 \leq x$ whereas we can in Q, but conversely $Q' \vdash \forall x.\, x \leq x$ whereas this cannot be derived in Q. (Show unprovability rigorously – i.e. exhibit a countermodel rather than observing that the obvious attempts to prove it don't seem to work.) Show however that Q' is still Σ_1-complete and implement an algorithm to prove true Σ_1-sentences from Q'. Observe that it is actually slightly simpler to use Q' because $Q' \vdash \forall x\, y.\, x \leq S(y) \Leftrightarrow x = S(y) \vee x \leq y$. However, show that it is impossible to use Q' to perform the Rosser construction.

7.7   Instead of generalizing the *proof* of Gödel's second theorem to give Löb's theorem, prove Löb's theorem directly from Gödel's second theorem using the following idea due to Kripke: suppose that we have $A \vdash \mathrm{Pr}_A(\ulcorner S \urcorner) \Rightarrow S$ and apply Gödel's second theorem to $A \cup \{\neg S\}$.

7.8   We prove Löb's theorem using a fixpoint L with $L \Leftrightarrow (\mathrm{Pr}_A(\ulcorner L \urcorner) \Rightarrow S)$. Instead, prove it using the fixpoint $L \Leftrightarrow \mathrm{Pr}_A(\ulcorner L \Rightarrow S \urcorner)$ (this is due to Kreisel). Use the same idea to obtain the *formalized* version of Löb's theorem, i.e. $A \vdash \mathrm{Pr}_A(\ulcorner \mathrm{Pr}_A(\ulcorner S \urcorner) \Rightarrow S \urcorner) \Rightarrow \mathrm{Pr}_A(\ulcorner S \urcorner)$.

7.9   Let S be a set of arithmetic axioms that is Σ_1-complete and satisfies the Löb derivability conditions, and T be an extension of S (meaning $T \vdash p$ for all $p \in S$). Show that for any Π_1-formula ϕ, if $T \vdash \phi$ then $S \cup \{\mathrm{Con}(T)\} \vdash \phi$. Hence prove that for any Π_1-formula ϕ, $T \cup \{\neg\mathrm{Con}(T)\} \vdash \phi$ if and only if $T \vdash \phi$. (This is attributed by Smoryński (1991) to Kreisel.)

7.10   Given any total recursive function f, use the (provable) fixpoint lemma to produce a formula ϕ that states 'all proofs of ϕ are longer than $f(\ulcorner \phi \urcorner)$'. (a) Deduce that ϕ is in fact provable, but not in $\leq f(\ulcorner \phi \urcorner)$ steps, and hence that a formula may require a proof that is arbitrarily long compared with its own size. (b) Take f to be a suitably large constant function and consider in detail how to *formalize* the reasoning in (a) within the system (assume an underlying axiom system like PA with provable Σ_1-completeness). Hence show that one can find formulas ϕ where any proof of ϕ is arbitrarily longer than some proof of $\mathrm{Pr}(\ulcorner \phi \urcorner)$, and hence a reflection rule would make a significant practical difference.

7.11   Show that if a theory has a r.e. axiomatization, then it has a recursive axiomatization, i.e. one where it's decidable whether a formula is an axiom (Craig 1952). Hint: $a \wedge a \wedge a \wedge a \Leftrightarrow a$.

7.12   We have already defined Σ_1-soundness (1-consistency) as soundness for Σ_1 sentences. More generally, define n-consistency as soundness for Σ_n sentences. Show that we can define n-consistency by a Π_{n+1} formula. Hence, or otherwise, show that a theory can be n-consistent without being $(n+1)$-consistent.

7.13   Show that the *univariate* case of Hilbert's tenth problem, over either $\mathbb{N}$ or $\mathbb{Q}$, is decidable. (Hint: if a polynomial with integer coefficients has a root s/t in its lowest terms, then t must divide the leading coefficient and s the constant coefficient.)

7.14   Show that for each of the structures $\mathbb{Z}$, $\mathbb{Q}$ and $\mathbb{R}$, the validity of any purely existentially quantified formula can be reduced to an equivalent problem asking whether a single equation has solutions. Thus, the decidability of the analogue of Hilbert's tenth problem is exactly equivalent in each case to the decidability of the entire existential/universal theory. (You might find it useful to use the fact that every nonnegative integer or rational is the sum of four squares, and keep in mind the Rabinowitsch trick.)

7.15   We observed that the statement $\exists x_1, \ldots, x_n. \, p(x_1, \ldots, x_n) = 0$ over the rationals is equivalent to $\exists a_1, \ldots, a_n, b_1, \ldots, b_n. \, b_1 \neq 0 \wedge \cdots \wedge n_n \neq 0 \wedge p(a_1/b_1, \ldots, a_n/b_n) = 0$ over the integers, and after clearing denominators, the equation $p(a_1/b_1, \ldots, a_n/b_n)$ is homogeneous. Show in fact that one can formulate the integer problem *and* the nontriviality conditions $b_i \neq 0$ as a homogeneous problem, and hence that the analogue of Hilbert's tenth problem for rationals is precisely equivalent to the problem for integers and homogeneous polynomials.

7.16   If A is consistent, we know from Gödel's theorem that $A \nvdash G$ and hence $A \cup \{\neg G\} \nvdash \bot$; that is, $A' = A \cup \{\neg G\}$ is also consistent. Now considering the corresponding Gödel sentence G' for the new axiom system A', show that nonetheless $A' \vdash \neg G'$, and hence that simple consistency does not ensure that the negation of the Gödel sentence is unprovable.

7.17   Show, assuming the Löb derivability conditions and the provable fixpoint $A \vdash G \Leftrightarrow \neg \mathrm{Pr}_A(\ulcorner G \urcorner)$, that in fact $A \vdash G \Leftrightarrow \mathrm{Con}(A)$, i.e. G is provably equivalent to the standard statement of consistency $\mathrm{Con}(A) = \neg \mathrm{Pr}_A(\ulcorner \bot \urcorner)$.

7.18   Just as Tarski's theorem can be considered a formalization of the liar paradox 'this sentence is false', observe that Löb's theorem can be considered as a formalization of a paradox: 'if this sentence is true, then Santa Claus exists'. (This point was made by one of the referees of Löb's original paper, probably Henkin.) Deduce (informally) from the truth of this sentence that Santa Claus exists.

7.19   Assume the existence of a recursively enumerable set S whose complement is *not* r.e. (From Church's theorem we know the set of Gödel numbers of formulas provable from Q is such a set, but we might choose to obtain it by other means, e.g. the undecidability of the halting problem.) Show how to deduce Gödel's first incompleteness theorem directly from this without any use of the fixpoint lemma.

7.20   Prove Lucas's theorem about binomial coefficients: for any a and b one has $\binom{2a}{2b+1} \equiv 0 \pmod 2$ while $\binom{2a}{2b} \equiv \binom{2a+1}{2b} \equiv \binom{2a+1}{2b+1} \equiv \binom{a}{b}$ $\pmod 2$. Hence show that the relation $\binom{n}{k} \equiv 1 \pmod 2$ defines the 'subset' relation, considering the numbers k and n as encodings of sets via their bits (e.g. $37 = 2^0 + 2^2 + 2^5$ representing the set $\{0, 2, 5\}$). Show also that with this encoding one has $(m \cap n = \emptyset) \Leftrightarrow n \subseteq m + n$. Hence, assuming a Diophantine representation for the binomial coefficient function, find one for set unions.

Appendix 1

Mathematical background

In this appendix we collect together some useful mathematical background. Readers may prefer to read the main text and refer to this appendix only if they get stuck. We do not give much in the way of proofs and the style is terse and rather dull, so this is not a substitute for standard texts. For example, Forster (2003) discusses in detail almost all the topics here, as well as much relevant material in logic and computability and some more advanced topics in set theory.

Mathematical notation and terminology

We use 'iff' as a shorthand for 'if and only if' and 'w.r.t.' for 'with respect to'. We write $x \mid y$, read 'x divides y', to mean that y is an integer multiple of x, e.g. $3 \mid 6$, $1 \mid x$ and $x \mid 0$. We use the usual arithmetic operations ('$+$' etc.) on numbers; we generally write xy for the product of x and y, but sometimes write $x \cdot y$ to emphasize that there is an operation involved and make the syntax more regular. An operation such as addition for which the order of the two arguments is irrelevant ($x + y = y + x$) is called *commutative*, and an operation where the association does not matter ($x + (y + z) = (x + y) + z$) is said to be *associative*. We also use the conventional equality and inequality relations ('$=$', '$\leq$' etc.) on numbers, and sometimes emphasize that an equation is the *definition* of a concept by decorating the equality sign with def, e.g. $\tan(x) =_{\text{def}} \sin(x)/\cos(x)$. We indicate that a relation does not hold by striking a diagonal line through its symbol, e.g. $x \neq y$ (x is not equal to y) or $3 \nmid 7$ (7 is not divisible by 3). We sometimes refer to $x \neq y$ as a *inequation*, to be distinguished from an *inequality* like $x \leq y$ and $x > y$. (In the literature, *disequation* is sometimes used instead of inequation.) The *greatest common divisor* (GCD) of two integers m and n is the largest integer d such that $d \mid m$ and $d \mid n$, while their lowest common multiple (LCM) is the smallest integer $e > 0$ such that $m \mid e$ and $n \mid e$. If $n \mid (x - y)$ we say that x and y are *congruent modulo n* and write $x \equiv y \pmod{n}$. Given an expression like $x + y \cdot x$, to *instantiate* the expression is to produce an 'instance' of it by setting the variables consistently to some expressions, e.g. $12 + x^2 \cdot 12$, and the process of doing so is called *instantiation*.

Sets

A set is a collection of objects viewed as a single entity. We write $x \in S$ to indicate that x is a member of a set S. Particular finite sets may be given by enumerating their elements within braces, e.g. $\{1, 2, 3\}$; the empty set may be written as $\{\}$ or with the special symbol $\emptyset$. The singleton set $\{a\}$ has exactly one element a, and is not the same as a itself. (For example, $\{\emptyset\}$ has one element while $\emptyset$ has none.) We use the following symbols for particular infinite sets: $\mathbb{N}$ for the set of natural numbers (nonnegative whole numbers $\{0, 1, 2, \ldots\}$), $\mathbb{Z}$ for the integers (whole numbers), $\mathbb{Q}$ for the rational numbers, $\mathbb{R}$ for the real numbers and $\mathbb{C}$ for the complex numbers. We will also use the notation $\{f[x] \mid P[x]\}$, where $E[x]$ symbolizes a generic expression using a variable x, to denote 'the set of all $f[x]$ such that $P[x]$', where $P[x]$ is some property. For example, $\{n^2 \mid n \in \mathbb{Z}\}$ is the set of squares of whole numbers, $\{0, 1, 4, 9, 16, \ldots\}$. Two sets are defined to be equal if and only if they have the same elements (the 'principle of extensionality'), i.e. $S = T$ iff for all x we have $x \in S$ iff $x \in T$. We write $S \subseteq T$ to indicate that S is a subset of T, i.e. that for all x such that $x \in S$ we also have $x \in T$. Note that $S = T$ iff both $S \subseteq T$ and $T \subseteq S$, while we always have $\emptyset \subseteq S$. When $S \subseteq T$ but not $T \subseteq S$, we say that S is a *proper* subset of T and write $S \subset T$. (Take care: some, mainly older, books use $\subset$ for the ordinary subset relation.)

We write $S \cap T$ for the *intersection* of S and T, i.e. the set of elements that are in *both* S and T. Similarly, $S \cup T$ denotes the *union* of S and T, the set of elements that are in either S or T *or both*. Finally, $S \setminus T$ or just $S - T$ is the set of elements that are in S but not T. Just as addition of two numbers is generalized to a summation over a finite range of numbers, e.g. $\Sigma_{k=0}^{n} k^2$, we sometimes take intersections or unions of a finite or infinite family of sets, e.g. $\bigcap_{i \in \mathbb{N}} T_i$. The Cartesian product $S \times T$ is the set of pairs whose first member is in S and whose second member is in T, i.e. $\{(x, y) \mid x \in S \text{ and } x \in T\}$. (We take 'pair' to be a basic construct, but the thoroughgoing set theory enthusiast can regard (x, y) as a shorthand for $\{\{x\}, \{x, y\}\}$; note that by extensionality this has the key properties that $(x, y) = (x', y')$ iff $x = x'$ and $y = y'$.) The n-fold Cartesian product $S \times \cdots \times S$ is written S^n.

Relations

An n-ary relation on a set S is regarded as a subset of S^n. The most important case is a binary relation, i.e. a subset of $S \times S$. If R is a binary relation, we often write $R(x, y)$ as a natural shorthand for $(x, y) \in R$. Some common relations are traditionally written infix, e.g. $x \leq y$ rather than $\leq (x, y)$ or $(x, y) \in \leq$. A binary relation R is said to be

- reflexive when for all $x \in S$ we have $R(x, x)$;
- irreflexive when for *no* $x \in S$ do we have $R(x, x)$;
- symmetric when for all $x, y \in S$ we have $R(x, y)$ iff $R(y, x)$;
- transitive when for all $x, y, z \in S$, if $R(x, y)$ and $R(y, z)$ then also $R(x, z)$;
- antisymmetric when for all $x, y \in S$, if $R(x, y)$ and $R(y, x)$ then $x = y$;
- connected when for all $x, y \in S$, either $R(x, y)$ or $R(y, x)$ (or both).

For example, the usual ordering $\leq$ on numbers is reflexive, transitive, antisymmetric and connected, but not symmetric nor irreflexive; the equality relation $=$ has all properties other than irreflexivity; the subset relation $\subseteq$ is reflexive, transitive and antisymmetric, but not irreflexive, symmetric nor connected. We use some special phrases to denote combinations of these basic properties, saying that a relation is:

- a preorder when it is reflexive and transitive;
- a (partial) order when it is reflexive, transitive and antisymmetric;
- a total order or linear order when it is reflexive, transitive, antisymmetric and connected;
- an equivalence relation when it is reflexive, symmetric and transitive.

For example, the divisibility relation $|$ on integers is a preorder (it is not antisymmetric since $1 \mid -1$ and $-1 \mid 1$), the subset relation $\subseteq$ is a partial order, $\leq$ on integers is a total order and $=$ is an equivalence relation.

Every equivalence relation $\equiv$ can be used to partition a set into *equivalence classes*, sets of elements that are mutually equivalent. We write $[a]$ for the equivalence class containing a, i.e. $\{b \mid b \equiv a\}$. Note that $[a] = [b]$ iff $a \equiv b$ while $[a] \cap [b] = \emptyset$ iff $a \not\equiv b$.

Functions

A function $f : A \to B$ is commonly regarded as a rule mapping elements of A to elements of B, such as the function $f : \mathbb{Z} \to \mathbb{Z}$ defined by $f(x) = x^2$, which we can write without giving it the name f simply as $x \mapsto x^2$. The crucial property of a function is not that it is defined via a rule, but just that the value of $f(x)$ is completely determined by the value of x: this justifies the usual practice of substitution in expressions, that is, reasoning that if $x = y$ then $f(x) = f(y)$. Otherwise a function is just a kind of relation between two sets, one that with each $x \in A$, associates *exactly one* element $y \in B$ (a *partial function* associates *at most* one, so a function is a special kind of partial function). This associated relation is known as the *graph* of the function. For a function $f : A \to B$ we describe A as the *domain* of the function and B as its *codomain*, written $\mathrm{dom}(f)$ and $\mathrm{cod}(f)$ respectively. The *range* of f, written $\mathrm{ran}(f)$, is the set of elements of B that are actually of the form $f(a)$ for some $a \in A$. For the squaring function $f(x) = x^2$, we have given the codomain as $\mathbb{Z}$ but the range is just the set of integer squares $\{0, 1, 4, 9, 16, \ldots\}$ and we could have chosen any set including these elements as the codomain. The *image* of a set S under a function f, sometimes written $f[S]$, is just $\{f(x) \mid x \in S\}$, so in particular we have have $\mathrm{ran}(f) = f[\mathrm{dom}(f)]$.

As well as using $x \mapsto e[x]$ as a general anonymous function definition defining the result in terms of an expression $e[x]$ involving the argument x, we will sometimes write $x \Mapsto y$ for the function that maps the *specific* argument value x to the result y and is otherwise undefined, or more generally $x_1 \Mapsto y_1, \ldots, x_n \Mapsto y_n$ for the function mapping each x_i to the corresponding y_i and otherwise undefined. Moreover, we sometimes write $(x \mapsto y)f$ to mean the modification of the function f to return value y on the specific argument value x, i.e. the function f' that maps $f'(x) = y$ and $f'(x') = f(x')$ for $x' \neq x$. These two usages have counterparts in our OCaml operations on finite partial functions (see Appendix 2).

We say that $f : A \to B$ is *injective* (or *one–one* or an *injection*) iff whenever $f(a) = f(a')$ then $a = a'$, i.e. at most one element of A is mapped to any element of B. For example, the squaring function on $\mathbb{Z}$ is not injective because $f(-1) = f(1)$ but $-1 \neq 1$, whereas the squaring function on $\mathbb{N}$ is injective. Dually, a function $f : A \to B$ is said to be *surjective* if each element of B is of the form $f(a)$ for some $a \in A$, i.e. at least one element of A is mapped to each element of B. If a function is both injective and surjective it is called *bijective* (or a *one-to-one correspondence* or a *bijection*). This means that for each $y \in B$ there is *exactly one* $x \in A$ such that $f(x) = y$. Note that if $f : A \to B$ is injective, then considered as a function into its range, $f : A \to f[A]$, it is bijective.

Given two functions $g : A \to B$ and $f : B \to C$, we can form their *composition* $f \circ g : A \to C$, which applies both functions in turn: $(f \circ g)(a) = f(g(a))$. If a function $f : A \to B$ is bijective, then there is a well-defined *inverse function* $f^{-1} : B \to A$, such that $f^{-1} \circ f = 1_A$, and $f \circ f^{-1} = 1_B$, where 1_A and 1_B are the *identity functions* on A and B respectively, i.e.

$1_A(x) = x$ for all $x \in A$. Indeed, considering f's graph, we simply replace each pair (x, y) by (y, x). Injectivity of f ensures that this yields a function, and surjectivity of f ensures that it is total on B. Even if f is not bijective, we will sometimes use the *inverse image* notation $f^{-1}[C] = \{x \in A \mid f(x) \in C\}$. This is not to assert the existence of an inverse to f, though the reader may readily confirm that if f is bijective the two readings coincide. Given $f : A \to B$ and $g : B \to C$, if $g \circ f$ is injective, so is f, and if $g \circ f$ is surjective, so is g. So if $f : A \to B$ and $g : B \to A$ are such that both $g \circ f$ and $f \circ g$ are bijective (in particular if $g \circ f = 1_A$ and $f \circ g = 1_B$), then f and g are both bijective.

A set $S \subseteq T$ may be identified with its *characteristic function* or *indicator function* $\chi_S : T \to \{0, 1\}$ defined by $f(x) = 1$ for $x \in S$ and $f(x) = 0$ for $x \notin S$. We can naturally generalize from sets to *multisets* or *bags* by allowing finitely many repetitions, i.e. considering a multiset of elements of T as a function $T \to \mathbb{N}$.

Cardinals

The *cardinality* $|S|$ of a set S is essentially its size (number of elements), e.g. $|\{1, 7, 9\}| = 3$. However, we will sometimes want to talk about the cardinality of *infinite* sets, which we can't directly measure using ordinary numbers. It is possible to set up a more general theory of infinite 'cardinal numbers', but this requires some set-theoretic machinery, and for the simple uses we will make of cardinality, another approach suffices. Arguably even more fundamental than measuring sets against numbers is just comparing the sizes of two sets by trying to pair up elements from each and seeing whether we end up with a bijection or run out of elements in one of the sets. (Just as, for example, one can determine which body is hotter by seeing which way heat flows, without the need for a specific scale of temperature.) This process naturally generalizes to infinite sets, so we define:

$|A| = |B|$, there is a bijection $f : A \to B$,
$|A| \leq |B|$, there is an injection $i : A \to B$,
$|A| < |B|$, there is an injection $i : A \to B$ but none $j : B \to A$.

Note that we are not ascribing any independent meaning to the notation $|A|$, but only interpreting it in equations or inequalities as a shorthand for a statement about the existence of functions. But this has all the properties we might expect, such as transitivity of the inequality relation: if $|A| \leq |B|$ and $|B| \leq |C|$ then $|A| \leq |C|$ (to prove this, consider function composition). The *Schröder–Bernstein* theorem asserts that it is also antisymmetric, i.e. if $|A| \leq |B|$ and $|B| \leq |A|$ then $|A| = |B|$. On the assumption of the Axiom of Choice (see Section 3.6) the relation is also connected, i.e. for any sets A and B, either $|A| \leq |B|$ or $|B| \leq |A|$.

Cardinality of infinite sets has some counterintuitive properties. It is easy to see that $|\mathbb{N}| \leq |\mathbb{N} \times \mathbb{N}|$, since $i(n) = (0, n)$ is injective. More surprising is that $p(m, n) = (m+n)^2 + m + 1$ is injective (see Section 7.2 for a proof), so $|\mathbb{N} \times \mathbb{N}| \leq |\mathbb{N}|$ and by the Schröder–Bernstein theorem $|\mathbb{N} \times \mathbb{N}| = |\mathbb{N}|$ (one can also exhibit a bijection explicitly, e.g. by enumerating pairs via diagonals). On the other hand, not all infinite sets have the same cardinality. Cantor, using a famous 'diagonal' argument, proved that $|\mathbb{N}| < |\mathbb{R}|$ and for any set A, $|A| < |\wp(A)|$, where $\wp(A)$, the *power set* of A, is the set of all subsets of A, e.g. $\wp(\{0, 1\}) = \{\emptyset, \{0\}, \{1\}, \{0, 1\}\}$. If $|A| \leq |\mathbb{N}|$ then A is said to be *countable* or *denumerable*, so $|\mathbb{N}| < |\mathbb{R}|$ implies that the real numbers are *uncountable*. We assume that the antonyms *finite* and *infinite* are already familiar, though we can define them rigorously in various ways, depending on the set-theoretic presuppositions we want to make. For example, the 'Dedekind' definition is that S is infinite if there is a function $f : S \to S$ that is injective but not surjective, and finite otherwise. We say that a set is *cofinite* if its complement in some larger set understood implicitly is finite. For instance, a set $S \subseteq \mathbb{N}$ may be said to be cofinite if $\mathbb{N} \setminus S$ is finite.

Inductive definitions

In mathematical logic, we often use *inductive definitions* to define syntactic notions, e.g. well-formed formulas or provable formulas. That is, we define a set S by means of a set of rules of the form 'if ... then ... $\in S$', where the 'if' part may itself involve membership of some object(s) in S. For example, a rule might say that if both $p \Rightarrow q$ and p are members of the set P of provable formulas, so is q (see Section 6.4). But in what sense does a set of such rules 'define' a set?

To take a down-to-earth example, we may define the set E of even numbers by saying '$0 \in E$' and 'if $n \in E$ then $(n + 2) \in E$'. Conventionally, such definitions are presented by writing all the rules as follows, the lines being used to separate assumptions (if any) and conclusion.

$$\overline{0 \in E}$$

$$\frac{n \in E}{(n + 2) \in E}$$

(Sometimes assumptions that do not assert membership of the set being defined are written to the right-hand side of the line instead, and called 'side conditions' – this is largely a matter of taste.) An inductive definition states that the set being defined is closed under the rules, and crucially that it is the *least* set closed under the rules, i.e. one that is a subset of any other set closed under the rules. (In general there may be many sets closed under the rules; for instance the rules above for E are satisfied by the set of *all* natural numbers as well as by the set of even numbers.)

But how do we know that there *is* a least set closed under the rules? A good try is to consider the set of *all* sets closed under the rules, and take their intersection. If only we knew this intersection to be closed under the rules, then it would certainly be the least such set. But in general we don't know that; for example there are no sets at all closed under the following rule:

$$\frac{n \notin E}{n \in E}.$$

Since we will be relying on inductive definitions a lot, we want to clarify exactly when they work. Crudely speaking, we need the hypotheses of the rules to make only 'positive' assertions about membership in the set being defined. We will now make this precise and put it in a slightly more general context (Andersen and Petersen 1991) using the notion of monotonicity of a function w.r.t. the subset relation. Observe that any inductive definition can be written in an equivalent form as a single rule with conclusion $x \in S$ where x is just a variable and S is the set being defined. The following paradigm for the 'even numbers' example should illustrate how:

$$\frac{n = 0 \text{ or there exists } m \text{ such that } n = m + 2 \text{ and } m \in E}{n \in E}.$$

Abstracting away from the details of this example, we have, for some property $P[S, n]$ the rule 'if $P[S, n]$ then $n \in S$', and if we abbreviate $f(S) = \{n \mid P[S, n]\}$, this is equivalent to simply $f(S) \subseteq S$. Our earlier plan in this context was to define:

$$T = \bigcap \{S \mid f(S) \subseteq S\}$$

and hope that $f(T) \subseteq T$. The Knaster–Tarski fixpoint theorem (Knaster 1928; Tarski 1955) asserts that in fact $f(T) = T$, provided that the function f is *monotone* (monotonically increasing), i.e. if $S \subseteq S'$ then $f(S) \subseteq f(S')$. It is easy to see that rules with hypotheses making only 'positive' instances of membership in the set being defined yield such a monotone set function. Thus when making an inductive definition in such cases we can immediately conclude:

- The inductively defined set *is* closed under the rules, i.e. $f(T) \subseteq T$. In the even number example, this means that indeed $0 \in E$ and whenever $n \in E$, also $(n + 2) \in E$.
- The inductively defined set is the *least* set closed under the rules, i.e. if $f(T') \subseteq T'$ then $T \subseteq T'$. For the even number example, given any set E' such that $0 \in E'$ and for all $n \in E'$ we have $(n+2) \in E'$, we can conclude that $E \subseteq E'$. If we apply this to the set of elements satisfying a property P, it is known as *rule induction*, because to show that all elements in the inductively defined set have property P we merely need to show that the rules 'preserve' P, e.g. for the even number example that $P(0)$ and whenever $P(n)$ we also have $P(n + 2)$.
- Since we actually have a fixpoint $f(T) = T$, we get a cases theorem showing that each element of T arises from others via the rules. For the even number example, we can conclude that each $n \in E$ is either 0 or of the form $m + 2$ for some $m \in E$.

The set of natural numbers itself can be regarded as inductively generated as a subset of some set T given an element $0 \in T$ and a 'successor' function $S : T \to T$ by the rules (i) $0 \in \mathbb{N}$ and (ii) whenever $n \in \mathbb{N}$ then also $S(n) \in \mathbb{N}$. Rule induction in this case is nothing but the usual principle of mathematical induction. Note that this induction principle is valid regardless of whether the elements 0, $S(0)$, $S(S(0))$ etc. are distinct, though we do need those properties for $\mathbb{N}$ to have other properties of the natural numbers (like being infinite).

Further examples we use extensively in this book are the various 'closures' of a binary relation R. The *transitive closure* of R, written $\mathrm{TC}(R)$ or R^+, is the smallest transitive relation extending R. Likewise we sometimes use the *reflexive transitive closure* $\mathrm{RTC}(R)$ or R^*, and the *reflexive symmetric transitive closure*. All of these can be regarded as inductively defined, for example the RTC by:

$$\overline{R^*(x, x)}$$

$$\frac{R(x, y)}{R^*(x, y)}$$

$$\frac{R^*(x, y) \quad R^*(y, z)}{R^*(x, z)}$$

We could instead have made an equivalent definition more explicitly, e.g. that $R^*(x, y)$ if either $x = y$ or there is a possibly-empty finite sequence of values $x_1, \ldots, x_n$ such that each two adjacent elements in the sequence

$x, x_1, \ldots, x_n, y$ are related by R. However, using the inductive formulation, we can often use rule induction to establish properties in a more elegant way.

Wellfoundedness

The usual principle of mathematical induction allows us to establish that $P(n)$ holds for all $n \in \mathbb{N}$ by showing (i) that $P(0)$ and (ii) that whenever $P(n)$ then also $P(n+1)$. We can strengthen this to the principle of *complete induction* where in part (ii) we may establish $P(n+1)$ assuming not merely $P(n)$ but $P(m)$ for *all* $m \leq n$, i.e. for all $m < n+1$. (To prove this, just apply the usual principle of induction to the stronger property $P'(n)$ that for all $m \leq n$ we have $P(m)$.) We can reformulate this to speak only of the ordering, not the arithmetic operations, and this hints at a broad generalization to an arbitrary set X and any binary relation on it. We symbolize this binary relation $\prec$, but we are not assuming transitivity, totality, or the fact that it is the irreflexive form of an ordering. Any of the following, as well as some other statements (Rudnicki and Trybulec 1999), are equivalent and may be taken as the definition of '$\prec$ is *wellfounded*':

- the principle of wellfounded induction: to show that $P(x)$ for all x, it suffices to establish $P(x)$ for all x such that $P(x')$ for each $x' \prec x$;
- the minimal element principle: every nonempty subset S of X contains a *minimal* element, i.e. an $m \in S$ such that there is no $x \in S$ with $x \prec m$;
- the absence of infinite descending chains: there is no infinite sequence $x_0, x_1, x_2, \ldots$ of elements (not necessarily distinct) in X such that for all $i \in \mathbb{N}$ we have $x_{i+1} \prec x_i$.

Complete induction states exactly that the natural numbers are well-founded, in the form of wellfounded induction. (Note that the case $P(0)$ is automatically included since there are no $m < 0$ and so the hypothesis holds trivially.) On the other hand, we can see that the set of integers is not, since for example there are subsets with no minimal element (e.g. all of $\mathbb{Z}$), and there are infinite descending chains such as $0, -1, -2, -3, \ldots$

Note that a wellfounded relation must be irreflexive, for if $x \prec x$ the set $\{x\}$ would have no minimal element, and indeed the relation must be strongly antisymmetric because if $x \prec y$ and $y \prec x$ the set $\{x, y\}$ would likewise have no minimal element. If $\preceq$ is a total order such that the corresponding irreflexive order $\prec$ (where $x \prec y$ means $x \preceq y$ and $y \npreceq x$) is wellfounded, then $\preceq$ is said to be a *wellorder* and the set X is said to be *wellordered* by $\preceq$. For a relation derived from a total order in this way, a *minimal* element m a set $S \subseteq X$ is the same thing as a *least* element, i.e. for all $x \in S$ we have $m \preceq x$.

If $\sqsubset$ is a subrelation of $\prec$ (i.e. whenever $x \sqsubset y$ we have $x \prec y$) and $\prec$ is wellfounded, then so is $\sqsubset$; this is almost immediate from the 'least element' form. Moreover, if $\prec$ is a wellfounded relation on X and we define another relation on a set A by $a \sqsubset a' =_{\text{def}} f(a) \prec f(a')$, then $\sqsubset$ is wellfounded regardless of the function f. In the case where $\prec$ is the usual order on $\mathbb{N}$, we refer to f as a *measure function*. If each $\prec_i$ is a binary relation on X_i, we define the *lexicographic* relation on the Cartesian product $X_1 \times \cdots \times X_n$ by $(x_1, \ldots, x_n) \sqsubset (x'_1, \ldots, x'_n)$ iff for some $1 \le i \le n$ we have $x_i \prec_i x'_i$ while for all $1 \le j < i$ we have $x_j = x'_j$. This is called lexicographic because it corresponds to the way words are sorted in a dictionary, first on the initial letter and if those are equal, the next letter, and so on. If each $\prec_i$ is wellfounded then so is the lexicographic relation $\sqsubset$. (To prove this, note that for any nonempty $S \subseteq X_1 \times \cdots \times X_n$ there must be a minimal m_1 such that there is an element $(m_1, x_2, \ldots, x_n)$ in S, and so on.) For example, the relation on pairs of natural numbers $(m, n) \sqsubset (m', n')$ that holds if either $m < m'$ or $m = m'$ and $n < n'$ is wellfounded. Thus, a relation may be wellfounded even if there is an element, like $(1, 0)$ here, with infinitely many predecessors, here all numbers $(0, n)$.

Some ways of building relations from others preserve wellfoundedness. In particular, if $\prec$ is wellfounded, so is its transitive closure $\prec^+$, as one can prove by induction. If $\prec$ is a relation on T, we define the *multiset order* on the multisets $T \to \mathbb{N}$ by setting $m \sqsubset m'$ iff m results from m' by removing at least one instance of some element x and perhaps changing arbitrarily the multiplicities of elements $y \prec x$, or more formally if there is an element $x \in T$ with $m(x) < m'(x)$ and $m(y) = m'(y)$ for $y \ne x$ unless $y \prec x$. (For example, if $\prec$ is the usual ordering on $\mathbb{N}$, removing a '7' but adding ninety '6's and a billion '1's.) If $\prec$ is wellfounded, then so is the corresponding multiset ordering $\sqsubset$ (Dershowitz and Manna 1979; Nipkow 1998).

Appendix 2

OCaml made light of

This appendix summarizes the main things a reader needs to know about the programming environment we use. I hope it will provide a useful quick overview, but this appendix is no substitute for a textbook on functional programming like Cousineau and Mauny (1998) or Paulson (1991).[†] There are numerous other texts on OCaml and CAML Light available online, e.g. a fairly comprehensive OCaml book[‡] and some old lecture notes on CAML Light by the present author.[§]

Functional programming

OCaml supports several styles of programming, but its roots lie in *functional programming*, and almost all of our code is written in a purely functional style. In brief, the idea of functional programming is that a program is simply an expression, and execution means evaluation of the expression. Although this point of view may seem outlandish to those with experience of more traditional *imperative* programming, supported by common languages like C and Java, an expression-centric view is already familiar from other contexts such as spreadsheet programming.

The centrepiece of imperative programming is the successive modification, via assignment statements `x = e` or `x := e`, of a number of program variables, known collectively as the *state*. These assignment statements are invoked in a particular order using sequential execution (sometimes indicated by ';') and built into more complex constructs using `if` tests, `while` loops and so on.

Functional programming represents a radical departure from this model.

[†] These books are based respectively on CAML Light (which is very close indeed to OCaml) and SML (which is fundamentally similar but looks rather different).

[‡] `caml.inria.fr/pub/docs/oreilly-book/`

[§] `www.cl.cam.ac.uk/teaching/Lectures/funprog-jrh-1996/index.html`

603

Functional programs do not use program variables, i.e. there is no explicit notion of state. Consequently, they do not use assignments, since there is nothing to assign to. Furthermore the idea of executing multiple commands in sequence is meaningless, since the first command can make no difference to the second, there being no state to mediate between them. However, on the positive side, functional programs can use functions in far more sophisticated ways. Functions can be treated in much the same way as simpler objects like integers: they can be passed to other functions as arguments and returned as results, and in general calculated with. Instead of sequencing and looping, functional programs make extensive use of *recursive* functions, i.e. functions that are defined in terms of themselves.

The OCaml toplevel

We will be using the OCaml *toplevel*, an *interpreter* for OCaml programs.[†] This is already installed by default on many Linux and Cygwin distributions, and in any case it is freely available and quite easy to install on almost any modern computing platform, either using your favourite software package manager (e.g. `apt-get`) or directly via the following URL:

<code>caml.inria.fr/ocaml/index.en.html</code>.

Once OCaml is installed, you can start the toplevel, either by selecting it from an appropriate menu or simply by typing `ocaml` into a shell (command prompt). You should see something like the following, where the first line shows the command prompt `$` followed by the user's `ocaml` command, and the rest is the response of the OCaml interpreter:

```
$ ocaml
        Objective Caml version 3.10.0

#
```

The interpreter prints an introductory banner, and then a hash symbol '#', which is OCaml's prompt for the user to enter something. To submit input for processing, the user should type it followed by *two* successive terminating semicolons *and* 'enter'. For example, here we evaluate the expression $2 + 2$:

```
# 2 + 2;;
- : int = 4
#
```

[†] OCaml can also be *compiled* using `ocamlopt` to object code, but the interpreter is much more convenient for experimentation. The code package for this book contains an example of how to compile the code; see the Makefile entry `compiled`.

OCaml replies, not only printing the result of the expression but also indicating its *type*, which is `int` ('integer'). It then prints its prompt once again ready for the user's next input. Until the user explicitly terminates the process, e.g. by typing `control/d`[†] into the toplevel, it will keep doing this indefinitely, accepting input, evaluating it, and printing the result. For this reason the toplevel is often called a *read-eval-print loop*.

Expressions and definitions

Roughly speaking, you can do three things in the OCaml toplevel: issue directives, evaluate expressions and make definitions. The most useful directive for now is probably the following:

```
# #use "filename";;
```

which reads OCaml source from a file called `filename` just as if it had been typed into the toplevel. For example, the packaged code for this book can be loaded in this way from a file called `"init.ml"`. And if you want to write non-trivial OCaml code of your own, you should save it in a file and then you can just load it instead of re-typing it.

We have already seen an example of evaluating an expression $2 + 2$ in the toplevel. If you simply type in the expression (followed by `;;` and enter) it will get evaluated and the result printed, but nothing else will change. However, you can instead give (or *bind*, in the customary jargon) a name to the result of evaluating an expression using a *definition* of the form '`let x = e`'. Thereafter the name `x` can be used to recall that result and make further use of it. For example:

```
# let x = 2 + 2;;
val x : int = 4
# 6 * x;;
- : int = 24
```

You can also make multiple bindings in the same definition using the syntax '`let` *binding* `and` $\cdots$ `and` *binding*', e.g.

```
# let x = 7 and y = 6;;
val x : int = 7
val y : int = 6
# x * y;;
- : int = 42
```

[†] That is, pressing and holding the `Ctrl` key and pressing `d`, which is a traditional Unix end-of-file indication corresponding to ASCII 'EOT' (end of text).

Any names bound in a definition will remain bound in perpetuity for the rest of that toplevel session, unless overridden by later definitions of the same name. However, you can also write an expression involving a purely local definition using '*definition* in *expression*', in which case any bindings made in the definition are used only in the body of the expression and do not persist outside its evaluation. For example, here the binding of z is used inside the expression but is then 'forgotten':

```
# let z = 11 in z * z;;
- : int = 121
# z;;
Unbound value z
```

Definitions and expressions can be nested in arbitrary ways, e.g.

```
# let x =
    let y = 6 and z = 7 in
    3 * y + z;;
val x : int = 25
```

Note that binding is *static*: variables are just an abbreviation for the results of earlier evaluations, and later re-binding does not affect the results of expressions that used them, e.g.

```
# let x = 2;;
val x : int = 2
# let y = x + 3;;
val y : int = 5
# let x = 3;;
val x : int = 3
# y;;
- : int = 5
```

All OCaml expressions have a *type*, which can be thought of as a set in which the values reside. So far we have just used expressions of type int (integer). OCaml has several other basic built-in types. For example bool is a type of truth-values with two values true and false and various built-in operators such as the logical 'and' written &:

```
# let x = true;;
val x : bool = true
# x & false;;
- : bool = false
```

while string is a type of sequences of ASCII characters with operators such as concatenation ^:

```
# let x = "some" and y = "body" in x^y;;
- : string = "somebody"
```

We have not worried much about the types so far, but behind the scenes OCaml has not only been figuring out the types for itself (we never wrote down a type), but also checking we do not violate the typing discipline by, for example, adding a boolean value and an integer:

```
# true + 2;;
This expression has type bool but is here used with type int
```

OCaml uses *static typing*, meaning that when given an expression it first checks conformance to the type discipline before it even tries to actually evaluate it.

Functions

Given any two types α and β, OCaml has a type of functions from α to β, written as α -> β based on the usual mathematical notation for functions from a set α to a set β. One way to write down an expression with a function type is by analogy with the mathematical notation $x \mapsto e[x]$ ('the function mapping x to $e[x]$') which is written in OCaml as 'fun x -> e[x]', e.g. the successor function:

```
# fun x -> x + 1;;
- : int -> int = <fun>
```

Perhaps the most fundamental operation in functional programming is the application of a function to an argument. To apply a function f to an argument x in OCaml, simply juxtapose them as f x. In typical mathematical notation, application of a function f to an argument x is written $f(x)$, but OCaml does not require brackets unless they are needed to enforce grouping, e.g.

```
# (fun x -> x + 1) 1 * 2;;
- : int = 4
# (fun x -> x + 1) (1 * 2);;
- : int = 3
```

One can bind a function value to a name just as with any other expression:

```
# let suc = fun x -> x + 1;;
val suc : int -> int = <fun>
# suc 9;;
- : int = 10
```

though OCaml allows an alternative that may be more readable and means the same thing:

```
# let suc x = x + 1;;
val suc : int -> int = <fun>
```

As with the built-in operators, OCaml will complain if we violate the expected types, e.g. trying to apply our newly defined successor operation to a string instead of an integer:

```
# suc "1";;
This expression has type string but is here used with type int
```

OCaml allows functions with multiple arguments, written one after the other both in the argument list and when the function is applied:

```
# (fun x y -> x + y) 1 2;;
- : int = 3
```

However, if we look at the type of such a function, keeping in mind that an iterated function type $\alpha \to \beta \to \gamma$ should be interpreted as $\alpha \to (\beta \to \gamma)$:

```
# let add x y = x + y;;
val add : int -> int -> int = <fun>
```

we may argue that it is *not* a function of two arguments as such. Rather it is a function of *one* argument that returns another function (which then accepts the second argument). We could indeed have written the following, with exactly the same meaning:

```
# let add = fun x -> (fun y -> x + y);;
val add : int -> int -> int = <fun>
```

Implementing functions of multiple arguments in this way is known as *currying* after the logician Haskell Curry, and to support it juxtaposition of multiple expressions like 'f x y' is treated as left-associated: '(f x) y'. The curried form affords some flexibility: we can choose only to apply the function to its first argument, e.g. giving another definition of the successor operator:

```
# let suc' = add 1;;
val suc' : int -> int = <fun>
# suc' 1;;
- : int = 2
```

This kind of *partial evaluation* is actually quite often used in functional programming. At least it hints at the very general ways in which functional languages allow one to use functions: they can be given as arguments to, and returned as values from, other functions. The only important thing we can't do with functions is test them for equality as we can with members of basic types like `int`. Desirable as such comparisons might be from the point of view of mathematical regularity, equality of (even computable) functions is not itself computable in general.

```
# 1 = 2;;
- : bool = false
# suc = suc';;
Exception: Invalid_argument "equal: functional value".
```

Recursive functions

The OCaml expression 'if e_0 `then` e_1 `else` e_2' first evaluates e_0, and then evaluates either e_1 or e_2 according to whether e_0 is true or false, respectively. Note that the expression not chosen isn't evaluated at all, e.g. the $1/0$ in the first expression here, which on its own fails when evaluated:

```
# if 1 = 0 then 1/0 else 0/1;;
- : int = 0
# 1/0;;
Exception: Division_by_zero.
# (if false then 1 else 2) + (if true then 1 else 2);;
- : int = 3
```

Although readers accustomed to imperative languages may feel relief to see a familiar-looking construct, we should emphasize that this is an *expression*, and that both 'then' and 'else' branches are compulsory.[†]

A *recursive* function is one that is 'defined in terms of itself', i.e. where at least one value $f(x)$ is defined in terms of some other values $f(y)$ of the *same* function. A well-known example is the *Fibonacci sequence* $1, 1, 2, 3, 5, 8, 13, \ldots$ in which each element is the sum of the two preceding elements, that is,

---

[†] It is like C's conditional expression '$e_0?e_1:e_2$', rather than its `if` construct. Actually, OCaml does allow the `else` clause to be omitted provided the expression e_1 has type `unit`, but we will not exploit this feature.

$F_n = F_{n-2} + F_{n-1}$. In order to make such a recursive function definition in OCaml, one introduces the definition with 'let rec' instead of plain 'let':

```
# let rec fib n = if n <= 1 then 1 else fib(n - 2) + fib(n - 1);;
val fib : int -> int = <fun>
# fib 5;;
- : int = 8
# fib 6;;
- : int = 13
```

Many functions can be defined recursively, even if doing so looks artificial and execution is inefficient:

```
# let rec mul x y = if x = 0 then 0 else y + mul (x - 1) y;;
val mul : int -> int -> int = <fun>
# mul 6 7;;
- : int = 42
```

One can also define, using **and**, several functions that are *mutually recursive*, i.e. are defined in terms of each other in some way. For example, here we define (inefficient) tests for whether a nonnegative integer is even or odd:

```
# let rec even n = if n = 0 then true else odd(n - 1)
  and       odd n = if n = 1 then true else even(n - 1);;
val even : int -> bool = <fun>
val odd : int -> bool = <fun>
# even 42;;
- : bool = true
```

To see the contrast and parallels between recursion and imperative implementations using **while** loops, consider a simple version of Euclid's algorithm for computing the greatest common divisor of m and n. We might implement it recursively as follows, based on the observation that the GCD of m and n is the same as that of m and $n - m$:

```
# let rec gcd m n =
    if m = 0 then n
    else if n = 0 then m
    else if m < n then gcd m (n - m)
    else gcd (m - n) n;;
val gcd : int -> int -> int = <fun>
# gcd 12 15;;
- : int = 3
```

In an imperative language we might go through a loop, using assignments to modify the two starting values m and n until one of them becomes zero. In the underlying implementation, the execution is similar in the two cases. But by making the definition as a recursive function, all the 'intermediate' values are explicitly referred to as values of `gcd` for other arguments, rather than being the anonymous and ephemeral intermediate values of a variable. In this way the same fundamental concepts are expressed in a more static way that is closer to mathematics. For this reason it is often more straightforward to reason analytically about functional programs, whereas imperative programs need special methods to reason about how properties of the state evolve (Floyd 1967; Hoare 1969; Dijkstra 1976a).

A recursive function definition where the result of each recursive call is used immediately to give the overall result, rather than being further modified, is called *tail recursive*. For example, the `gcd` definition above is tail recursive, because both `gcd m (n - m)` and `gcd (m - n) n` directly give the overall result `gcd m n` rather than being further modified. By contrast, the following definition of the factorial function

```
# let rec fact n = if n = 0 then 1 else n * fact(n - 1);;
```

is *not* tail recursive because the result of the recursive call is then multiplied by n. The OCaml interpreter specially optimizes the execution of tail recursive functions so that the recursion is replaced by a simple loop updating a fixed stock of variables. Since this can be more memory-efficient, functional programmers sometimes strive to make some key functions tail recursive. For example, the factorial function can be recoded in a tail-recursive style by adding an extra parameter called an *accumulator* to the main recursion:

```
# let fact =
    let rec fact2 n a = if n = 0 then a else fact2 (n - 1) (n * a) in
    fun n -> fact2 n 1;;
val fact : int -> int = <fun>
# fact 5;;
- : int = 120
```

Polymorphism and type inference

OCaml is *strongly typed*, meaning that in any expression the subcomponents need to have compatible types, and the interpreter will not even attempt to coerce them to make things work, as happens in some languages. On the other hand, it is possible for the same expression to have multiple possible types, in a controlled way. For example, the *identity function* just returns its argument:

```
# let identity x = x;;
val identity : 'a -> 'a = <fun>
```

Note that the type returned is (an ASCII symbolization of) $\alpha \rightarrow \alpha$ where α is a *type variable*. This indicates that the function is *polymorphic*, i.e. can be used with arguments of various types, even in the same expression:

```
# identity 1;;
- : int = 1
# identity "yes";;
- : string = "yes"
# (identity identity) (identity 1);;
- : int = 1
```

When the user enters a definition, OCaml automatically computes the types of all the components and assigns a *most general* type (Milner 1978). Note that a polymorphic function might not admit arguments of *any* type as `identity` did, but just only those with types of a certain form. The most general type uses type variables to indicate that form schematically. For example, let us define an 'iteration' function to evaluate the n-fold function application $f(f(\cdots f(x)\cdots))$:

```
# let rec funpow n f x = if n < 1 then x else funpow (n-1) f (f x);;
val funpow : int -> ('a -> 'a) -> 'a -> 'a = <fun>
# funpow 10 (fun x -> x + x) 1;;
- : int = 1024
```

Although `funpow` is polymorphic, the first argument needs to be an integer and the second a function with the *same* domain and range, i.e. a value with some type $\sigma \rightarrow \sigma$, and the third argument needs to have the same type σ.

This style of polymorphism is often known as *parametric polymorphism* (Strachey 2000).[†] The key idea of parametric polymorphism is that all the instances 'do the same thing' structurally, in contrast to *overloading* or *ad hoc polymorphism* (which OCaml does not have) where a function may behave completely differently on different types. We will not make the notion of 'doing the same thing' precise, but another typical example of a parametrically polymorphic function is a list reversal function that works regardless of the nature of the list's elements.

Recursive types and pattern-matching

While it already has a few built-in types, OCaml allows the user to define new ones via the **type** keyword. The simplest case is an *enumerated type* where the implicit set has a particular finite size and the user gives a name to each member. These names are called *constructors* since they construct

---

[†] In some languages like Java, parametrically polymorphic functions are said to be *generic*.

members of the new type, and OCaml requires that they start with an uppercase letter to distinguish them from ordinary values:

```
# type ternary = Zero | One | Unknown;;
type ternary = Zero | One | Unknown
```

You can then define functions over the new type as usual, e.g.

```
# let andgate a b =
    if a = Zero or b = Zero then Zero
    else if a = Unknown or b = Unknown then Unknown
    else One;;
val andgate : ternary -> ternary -> ternary = <fun>
# andgate Zero Unknown;;
- : ternary = Zero
```

Types can also be defined that contain a copy of one or more existing types, e.g. a 'sum' type where each element is a suitably tagged element either of type α or type β:

```
# type ('a,'b)sum = Inl of 'a | Inr of 'b;;
type ('a, 'b) sum = Inl of 'a | Inr of 'b
```

This is like a *disjoint union* of two sets in mathematics: it contains a 'copy' of each set, but in contrast to an ordinary set union, they are tagged or modified to make sure they are disjoint and that given an element of the union we can decide which set it comes from; one way of representing this mathematically is $\{(0, x)|x \in S\} \cup \{(1, y)|y \in T\}$. In the OCaml type definition, sum is not merely a *type* but rather a *type constructor* like the function arrow -> that builds a new type out of existing types. An even simpler such type constructor is the built-in OCaml product type. The Cartesian product of types σ and τ is written $\sigma * \tau$, and the constructor that maps two elements x and y into a member of this type is written as an infix comma, i.e. $x, y.$[†] These are close to the usual mathematical notation $\sigma \times \tau$ and (x, y), though, as with function application, the brackets round pairs are optional unless needed to establish precedence. There are two built-in functions **fst** and **snd** to return the first and second member of a pair, e.g.

```
# let p = 1,2;;
val p : int * int = (1, 2)
# fst p;;
- : int = 1
```

[†] Strictly speaking, and despite the misleadingly identical concrete syntax, constructors themselves do not take paired arguments, and one can consider the pair as just another recursive type with some syntactic sugar. Also, if tuples are written without brackets as x,y,z etc. they are treated as primitive tuples, not as iterated pairing.

Instead of currying, one can define a function of multiple arguments as a function with a single argument that is itself a Cartesian product. OCaml's built-in operators can be treated directly as functions by enclosing them in brackets, and they are then always considered curried. Thus, the first two definitions here are equivalent, and the third is an 'uncurried' variant using a paired argument:

```
# let f x y = x + y;;
val f : int -> int -> int = <fun>
# let f = (+);;
val f : int -> int -> int = <fun>
# let f(x,y) = x + y;;
val f : int * int -> int = <fun>
```

New types can also be defined in terms of *themselves*, giving so-called *recursive* types. For example, here we define a type where each member is either (i) a leaf node parametrized by a member of some existing type α or (ii) an internal node with two subnodes, each of which is itself a member of the type being defined. The net effect is that this is a type of finite but arbitrarily large binary trees with leaves labelled by members of type α:

```
# type ('a)btree =
    Leaf of 'a
  | Branch of ('a)btree * ('a)btree;;
type 'a btree = Leaf of 'a | Branch of 'a btree * 'a btree
```

To construct members of the new type, just apply the constructors to arguments, e.g.

```
# Branch(Leaf "a",Leaf "b");;
- : string btree = Branch (Leaf "a", Leaf "b")
# Branch(Branch(Leaf 1,Leaf 2),Leaf 3);;
- : int btree = Branch (Branch (Leaf 1, Leaf 2), Leaf 3)
```

In order to do the opposite, i.e. get the subcomponents out of an object of the new type, one can use the 'match *expression* with $p_1 | \cdots | p_n$' construct, where each p_i is of the form '*pattern->expression*' and each *pattern* indicates a schematic form of expression. The meaning is that the patterns are examined one at a time, the first one that the expression matches is selected and the variables in the pattern instantiated accordingly, e.g.

```
# match Leaf "a" with
    Leaf x -> "leaf_"^x
  | Branch(a,  b) -> "branch";;
- : string = "leaf_a"
```

It is common to combine pattern-matching and recursion, e.g. in the following function that adds up all the leaf values in a binary tree of integers:

```
# let rec leafsum t =
    match t with
      Leaf n -> n
    | Branch(t1,t2) -> leafsum t1 + leafsum t2;;
val leafsum : int btree -> int = <fun>
# leafsum(Branch(Branch(Leaf 1,Leaf 2),Leaf 3));;
- : int = 6
```

Pattern-matching isn't limited to members of recursive types, but it's most valuable there because one can always determine how each element of a type is constructed. For example, we might write a zero test this way:

```
# let iszero n = match n with 0 -> true | x -> false;;
val iszero : int -> bool = <fun>
```

but we can't use a term like 'm + n' as a pattern because a value doesn't have a unique decomposition in such a form. A useful generalization of patterns that OCaml supports is a **when** guard, which restricts matches to those satisfying a certain condition, e.g.

```
# match Leaf "a" with Leaf x when x <> "b" -> "a" | _ -> "b";;
- : string = "a"
```

One can consider recursive types as being defined inductively (see Appendix 1) as a subset of some suitably large starting set, in a way that all constructors are distinct and injective. And we will sometimes prove properties using a rule induction principle of the kind arising from inductive definitions, which in this context is usually known as *structural induction*. For example, to show that some property holds for all our binary trees, it suffices to show that (i) it holds for all leaves 'Leaf x', and (ii) if it holds for two subtrees s and t, then it holds for the composite term Branch(s,t). In such a case we are said to proceed by *induction on the structure of* our type of trees.

Exceptions

OCaml expressions, even well-typed ones, may fail, e.g. the example of 1/0. In such cases they are said to *raise* (or *throw*) an *exception*. By default, if any subexpression raises an exception, that exception propagates out and causes the whole expression to raise the same exception.

```
# (100 + 1 / 0) + 99;;
Exception: Division_by_zero.
```

However, it's possible to *catch* or *handle* an exception using the construct 'try *expression* with *epattern* -> *alternative*', where the *epattern* is a pattern-matching clause for a special type of exceptions. For example, we might define our own version of division where $n/0 = 0$ as follows:

```
# let mydiv m n = try m / n with Division_by_zero -> 0;;
val mydiv : int -> int -> int = <fun>
# mydiv 7 0;;
- : int = 0
```

All the code we develop later is designed to raise exceptions of the form `Failure s` where `s` is a string. We will sometimes catch all exceptions of that form without discrimination. Catching absolutely all exceptions by using just a variable as a pattern might be problematic since a keyboard interrupt (control/c or whatever) also generates an exception, one that we probably wouldn't want to catch for fear of making the entire program uninterruptible.

Lists

OCaml has a built-in recursive type of lists, which can be considered as finite sequences, or 'one-sided' binary trees. In effect, lists are defined as follows:

```
type ('a)list = Nil | Cons of 'a * 'a list;;
```

except that the infix notation `h::t` is used instead of `Cons(h,t)`, and the syntactic sugar `[a;b;c]` may be used in place of `a::(b::(c::Nil))` and so on, including the special case `[]` for what we called `Nil`. For example, the following recursive function appends (joins together) two lists:

```
# let rec append l l' =
    match l with
      [] -> l'
    | h::t -> h::(append t l');;
val append : 'a list -> 'a list -> 'a list = <fun>
# append [1;2;3] [4;5];;
- : int list = [1; 2; 3; 4; 5]
```

though the same function is built into OCaml and instead of `append l l'` can be written `l @ l'`. Note carefully the distinction between `[h;t]`, which is a 2-element list with elements `h` and `t`, and `h::t` which is a list with head `h` and tail `t` and so one element longer than the list `t`.

Our common OCaml functions

Our theorem-proving code is based on a number of common utility functions collected in the file lib.ml. In this section we will give a short summary, mostly describing what they do, but in a few cases actually discussing the implementation. First of all, we will very occasionally use printing expressions like the following:

```
# print_int (6 + 7);;
13- : unit = ()
# print_string "Hello\n";;
Hello
- : unit = ()
```

These are both just expressions returning the only member, written (), of a 1-element type **unit**. However, evaluating these expressions has the side-effect of printing something to the output device. When using such expressions with a side-effect, we sometimes want to execute them one after another, and we will use the traditional-looking sequencing operation '$e_1 ; e_2$'. However, this is used only when we are printing out information for the user, and we never use imperative code or sequencing in the innards of our theorem-proving programs. We also sometimes use **time f x**, which evaluates **f x** but also tells us how long that evaluation took in seconds, useful for testing the efficiency of various functions.

OCaml's built-in integer type **int** is sometimes inadequate because it has a limited size, so instead we will often use a different type **num** of arbitrary-precision rational numbers supported by a special library. In order to load this library, the following directive is sufficient on many platforms:

```
#load "nums.cma";;
```

However, on some platforms (including at the time of writing Cygwin under Windows), dynamic loading is not supported and it is necessary to first build a new OCaml toplevel with the **num** library preloaded.[†] Anyway, once the library is loaded it's easy enough to use: create a small integer of type **num** using the **Int** constructor or a larger one from a string using **int_of_string**, and use the usual arithmetic operators with an extra '/' character, even for equality and inequality tests (the built-in polymorphic comparisons are not useful) e.g.

[†] For example, do 'ocamlmktop -o ocamlnum nums.cma' to create the new toplevel ocamlnum and then invoke that instead of the usual one.

```
# Int 3 +/ Int 1 // Int 7;;
- : num = 22/7
# Int 3 // Int 4 </ num_of_string "12345";;
- : bool = true
```

We also define `gcd_num` and `lcm_num` to compute GCDs and LCMs of integers of type `num`. To create a list of integers from m to n, of type `int` or `num`, use `m--n` or `m---n` respectively.

The following rather general functions all have one-line definitions so we leave the reader to see what they do. The most important is the infix function composition `**`, corresponding to $(f \circ g)(x) = f(g(x))$. Note also the undefined function `undef` and the function modifier `valmod x y f`, the latter corresponding to the mathematical notation $(x \mapsto y)f$; the same things in the context of finite partial functions (see below) are `undefined` and `(x |-> y) f`.

```
let ( ** ) = fun f g x -> f(g x);;

let can f x = try f x; true with Failure _ -> false;;

let rec first n p = if p(n) then n else first (n +/ Int 1) p;;

let non p x = not(p x);;

let rec repeat f x = try repeat f (f x) with Failure _ -> x;;

let undef x = failwith "undefined function";;

let valmod a y f x = if x = a then y else f(x);;
```

We use numerous utility functions for list manipulations. Rather than exhaustively explain each one, we give a paradigmatic example and leave it to the reader who wants more detail to examine their (short) definitions. Note in particular the usefulness of the list iteration functions such as `itlist` for expressing various repeated operations over lists without requiring another recursive function. The distinction between `map` and `mapfilter` is that the latter removes elements of the list for which the function fails (i.e. raises a `Failure` exception) whereas `map` will propagate out any exception.

```
butlast [1;2;3;4] = [1;2;3]
chop_list 3 [1;2;3;4;5] = ([1;2;3],[4;5])
do_list f [1;2;3] = (f 1; f 2; f 3)
el 2 [0;1;2;3] = 2
end_itlist f [1;2;3;4] = f 1 (f 2 (f 3 4))
exists p [1;2;3] = (p 1) or (p 2) or (p 3)
explode "hello" = ["h";"e";"l";"l";"o"]
forall p [1;2;3] = (p 1) & (p 2) & (p 3)
forall2 p [1;2;3] [a;b;c] = (p 1 a) & (p 2 b) & (p 3 c)
hd [1;2;3] = 1
implode ["w";"x";"y";"z"] = "wxyz"
insertat 3 9 [0;1;2;3;4;5] = [0;1;2;9;3;4;5]
itlist f [1;2;3] x = f 1 (f 2 (f 3 x))
itlist2 f [a;b;c] [1;2;3] x = f a 1 (f b 2 (f c 3 x))
last [1;2;3;4] = 4
length [1;2;3] = 3
map f [1;2;3] = [f 1; f 2; f 3]
map2 f [a;b;c] [1;2;3] = [f a 1; f b 2; f c 3]
mapfilter f [1;2;3] = [f 1; f 2; f 3]
replicate 4 9 = [9;9;9;9]
rev [1;2;3;4] = [4;3;2;1]
tl [1;2;3;4] = [2;3;4]
unzip [(1,a);(2,b);(3,c)] = ([1;2;3],[a;b;c])
zip [1;2;3] [a;b;c] = [(1,a); (2,b); (3,c)]
```

The expression `filter p l` returns the sublist of elements of l for which
p holds, while `partition p l` separates l into a pair of sublists for which p
does and does not hold. The expression `find p l` finds the first element of l
that satisfies p, while `tryfind f l` applies f to the first element of l where
it does not fail, and `index x l` returns the position of the first instance of
x in the list l, the head of the list being zero. In similar style, `earlier l x
y` tests if the first instance of x occurs in l before the first instance of y.

To sort a list l w.r.t. a simple ordering relation `ord` use `sort ord l`, and
in order to remove *adjacent* duplicated elements from a list, use `uniq l`, e.g.

```
# sort (<) [3;1;4;1;5;9;2;6;5;3;5];;
- : int list = [1; 1; 2; 3; 3; 4; 5; 5; 5; 6; 9]
# uniq(sort (<) [3;1;4;1;5;9;2;6;5;3;5]);;
- : int list = [1; 2; 3; 4; 5; 6; 9]
```

You can create an ordering relation that applies a measure function and
compares the results over the integers using `increasing` and `decreasing`,
e.g.

```
# sort (increasing length) [[1]; [1;2;3]; []; [3; 4]];;
- : int list list = [[]; [1]; [3; 4]; [1; 2; 3]]
```

To find the element of a list l that maximizes or minimizes a function f, use `maximize f l` or `minimize f l` respectively.

In all our code, we represent (finite) sets simply as lists, in a standard order and with no duplicates. All the following 'set' operations work for arbitrary input lists, but always return the ordered duplicate-free kind and will be more efficient when their arguments are also in that standard form. The expression `setify l` converts a list to this form while `union s t`, `intersect s t` and `subtract s t` implement set union, intersection and difference of the sets s and t. The relations `subset s t` and `psubset s t` test, respectively, whether s is a subset of t, or a proper subset, and `set_eq s t` tests if the two lists are equal as sets. The call `insert x s` inserts one new element into a set s, while `mem x s` tests if x is in the set s. The expression `unions l` takes the iterated union of a set of sets, while `image f s` takes the image of a set under a function f, just like `map f s` but maintaining standard form, e.g.

```
# unions [[1;2;3]; [4; 8; 12]; [3;6;9;12]; [1]];;
- : int list = [1; 2; 3; 4; 6; 8; 9; 12]
# image (fun x -> x mod 2) [1;2;3;4;5];;
- : int list = [0; 1]
```

For enumerative algorithms we often want to create all sets satisfying some constraints: `allsets n l` produces all n-element subsets of l, `allsubsets l` produces all subsets of l and `allnonemptysubsets l` produces all nonempty subsets of l, e.g.

```
# allsubsets [1;2;3];;
- : int list list =
[[]; [1]; [1; 2]; [1; 2; 3]; [1; 3]; [2]; [2; 3]; [3]]
# allnonemptysubsets [1;2;3];;
- : int list list = [[1]; [1; 2]; [1; 2; 3]; [1; 3]; [2]; [2; 3]; [3]]
# allsets 2 [1;2;3];;
- : int list list = [[1; 2]; [1; 3]; [2; 3]]
```

The function `allpairs` applies a function of two arguments over all pairs from the input lists, and `alldistinctpairs` just produces all pairs of distinct elements from a single list, e.g.

```
# allpairs (fun x y -> x * y) [2;3;5] [7;11];;
- : int list = [14; 22; 21; 33; 35; 55]
# distinctpairs [1;2;3;4];;
- : (int * int) list = [(1, 2); (1, 3); (1, 4); (2, 3); (2, 4); (3, 4)]
```

Although OCaml lets us treat functions in many ways that other programming languages disallow, general functions can still be unsuitable for some applications. We often want to consider only functions with a finite domain that are undefined outside that domain, and may want to compare functions for equality or in general treat them as more concrete and less inscrutable objects. A traditional data structure in such cases is an *association list*, which is essentially the graph of a function as a list of pairs. Then the call `assoc x l` applies such a function, i.e. finds the first pair in the list `l` with first element `x` and returns the corresponding second element:

```
# assoc 3 [1,2; 2,4; 3,9; 4,16];;
- : int = 9
```

Although association lists are simple and convenient, they can be inefficient when the list becomes long. In most cases we use a somewhat more elaborate type of *finite partial functions* (FPFs); the OCaml type of finite partial functions from α to β is just (α, β)`func`. Conceptually these FPFs are much like association lists, but in general they are more efficient and they are also canonical, so one can test if two functions are equal (same domain and same values on that domain) just using the usual OCaml equality operator.

The empty, everywhere undefined FPF is `undefined`, while `is_undefined` tests whether a FPF is that empty one. To update the FPF `f` with a new mapping from `x` to `y`, use `(x |-> y) f`, and to create a function defined only for the value `x` and mapping it to `y`, use `(x |=> y)`. To test if an FPF `f` is defined for `x`, use `defined f x`, and to remove any definition for the value `x` use `undefine x f`. In order to apply the FPF `f` to an argument `x`, use `apply f x`, or the variants `tryapplyd f x z` and `tryapplyl f x` that return a default value of, respectively, `z` and the empty list if `f` is undefined at `x`. To compose an OCaml function `g` with an FPF `f`, i.c. replace each assignment $x \mapsto y$ in `f` with $x \mapsto g(y)$, use `mapf g f`. To get the graph, domain and range of a FPF, use `graph`, `dom` and `ran` respectively, while to create a FPF from two equally-sized lists of inputs and outputs, use `fpf`, e.g.

```
# let smallsqs = fpf [1;2;3] [1;4;9];;
val smallsqs : (int, int) func = <func>
# graph smallsqs;;
- : (int * int) list = [(1, 1); (2, 4); (3, 9)]
# graph (undefine 2 smallsqs);;
- : (int * int) list = [(1, 1); (3, 9)]
# graph ((3 |-> 0) smallsqs);;
- : (int * int) list = [(1, 1); (2, 4); (3, 0)]
# apply smallsqs 3;;
- : int = 9
```

We sometimes want to manipulate equivalence relations (partitions) on finite sets. For this purpose the following operations on a type (α)`partition` are useful. The value `unequal` is an empty partition, and `equated` p is the domain of the partition p. The expression `equivalent` p x y tests if x and y are equivalent w.r.t. p, while `canonize` p x produces a canonical representative of the p-equivalence class containing x, and `equate` (x,y) p produces a new partition that results from merging the x and y classes in p, i.e. the smallest equivalence relation containing p such that x and y are equivalent.

Appendix 3
Parsing and printing of formulas

Although parsing and printing support is vital to making the programs in this book usable for experimentation, we have deferred a detailed discussion of how parsing and printing are done to the present appendix. This is partly because the material is fairly unexciting and rather peripheral to the main concerns of the book, and partly because, while first used in the propositional logic chapter, it actually covers full first-order logic and so doesn't clearly fit at any point in the otherwise systematic sequence.

General parsing functions

We often need to parse infix operators of various kinds, e.g. the logical connectives like ==> and the arithmetic operators like +. For most of these we adopt a policy of right-association, i.e. interpreting $a \oplus b \oplus c$ as $a \oplus (b \oplus c)$. However, this is a bit unnatural for '$-$', since we want to read $x - y - z$ as $(x - y) - z$ not $x - (y - z)$. We therefore want to be able to insist on either left or right associativity. Both can be subsumed by the following generic parsing function that lets us associate the subitems however we want:

```
let rec parse_ginfix opsym opupdate sof subparser inp =
  let e1,inp1 = subparser inp in
  if inp1 <> [] & hd inp1 = opsym then
    parse_ginfix opsym opupdate (opupdate sof e1) subparser (tl inp1)
  else sof e1,inp1;;
```

This has two function arguments: **sof** takes the current input and combines it in some way with the items arrived at so far, while **opupdate** modifies the function appropriately when a new item is parsed. This may look obscure, but it should become clearer looking at the following examples, which show how using the same core function we can parse a list of items and combine them in either a left or right associated manner, or even just collect them all into a list. We will use the last of these to parse the list of arguments to a function $f(t_1, t_2, \ldots, t_3)$, treating the comma as another infix symbol.

```
let parse_left_infix opsym opcon =
  parse_ginfix opsym (fun f e1 e2 -> opcon(f e1,e2)) (fun x -> x);;

let parse_right_infix opsym opcon =
  parse_ginfix opsym (fun f e1 e2 -> f(opcon(e1,e2))) (fun x -> x);;

let parse_list opsym =
  parse_ginfix opsym (fun f e1 e2 -> (f e1)@[e2]) (fun x -> [x]);;
```

In the same spirit of generality, it's useful to define general 'parser combinators' to cover a few other common idioms and so avoid duplicating essentially the same piece of code (Burge 1975). The following function applies a function to the first element of a pair, the idea being to modify the returned abstract syntax tree while leaving the 'unparsed input' alone:

```
let papply f (ast,rest) = (f ast,rest);;
```

The next function checks if the head of a list (typically the list of unparsed input) is some particular item, but also first checks that the list is nonempty before looking at its head:

```
let nextin inp tok = inp <> [] & hd inp = tok;;
```

The last function deals with the common situation of syntactic items enclosed in brackets. It simply calls the subparser and then checks and eliminates the closing bracket. In principle, the terminating character can be anything, so this function could equally be used for other purposes, but we will always use ')' for the `cbra` ('closing bracket') argument.

```
let parse_bracketed subparser cbra inp =
  let ast,rest = subparser inp in
  if nextin rest cbra then ast,tl rest
  else failwith "Closing bracket expected";;
```

Parsing formulas

Lexical issues are unproblematical. The lexical analyzer developed in the introduction (Section 1.7) was already designed to understand composite symbolic characters like '==>', so it can be used unchanged.

Formulas are a little involved to parse, because of infix predicate symbols. For example, input '$k(x)$' could be a complete atomic formula with predicate symbol k, or it could be a term $k(x)$ to be followed by an infix relation symbol as in $k(x) < k(y)$. Similarly, an opening bracket '(' could introduce a bracketing of a formula, e.g. $(P(x) \Rightarrow Q(x)) \Rightarrow P(x)$, or of a term, e.g. $(x \cdot y) \cdot z = x \cdot (y \cdot z)$. In order to allow both possibilities, we first attempt to parse an atomic formula as a term followed by an infix predicate symbol, and only if that fails proceed to considering other kinds of formulas. For this to work we require both a restricted parser **ifn** for these infix atoms and a more general one **afn** for arbitrary atoms. (If we used **afn** everywhere then, for example, '$((x) = 1)$' would fail to parse.)

```
let rec parse_atomic_formula (ifn,afn) vs inp =
  match inp with
    [] -> failwith "formula expected"
  | "false"::rest -> False,rest
  | "true"::rest -> True,rest
  | "("::rest -> (try ifn vs inp with Failure _ ->
                  parse_bracketed (parse_formula (ifn,afn) vs) ")" rest)
  | "~"::rest -> papply (fun p -> Not p)
                  (parse_atomic_formula (ifn,afn) vs rest)
  | "forall"::x::rest ->
      parse_quant (ifn,afn) (x::vs) (fun (x,p) -> Forall(x,p)) x rest
  | "exists"::x::rest ->
      parse_quant (ifn,afn) (x::vs) (fun (x,p) -> Exists(x,p)) x rest
  | _ -> afn vs inp
```

The main function has several cases, and delegates quantifier parsing to another function **parse_quant** that absorbs the list of variables, allowing the convention of omitting repeated quantifiers, then recursively parses the body:

```
and parse_quant (ifn,afn) vs qcon x inp =
  match inp with
    [] -> failwith "Body of quantified term expected"
  | y::rest ->
      papply (fun fm -> qcon(x,fm))
             (if y = "." then parse_formula (ifn,afn) vs rest
              else parse_quant (ifn,afn) (y::vs) qcon y rest)
```

As usual the overall function is built up from an atomic formula parser by cascading instances of **parse_infix** in order of precedence, following the conventions established in chapter 2 with '/\\' coming highest and '<=>' lowest.

```
and parse_formula (ifn,afn) vs inp =
   parse_right_infix "<=>" (fun (p,q) -> Iff(p,q))
      (parse_right_infix "==>" (fun (p,q) -> Imp(p,q))
         (parse_right_infix "\\/" (fun (p,q) -> Or(p,q))
            (parse_right_infix "/\\" (fun (p,q) -> And(p,q))
               (parse_atomic_formula (ifn,afn) vs)))) inp;;
```

Printing formulas

Instead of mapping an expression to a string and then printing it, as in Section 1.8, we will just print it directly on the standard output, and instead of concatenating substrings inside the printer we just output the pieces sequentially. Moreover, we try to break output intelligently across lines to reflect its structure, and for this we rely on a special OCaml library called **Format**.

In the theorem proving code for this book there was a line 'open Format;;' early on, so this is already set up and certain functions like print_string are being taken from the **Format** library. We will not explain this in full detail, but the basic idea is that every time we reach a natural starting point, such as following an opening bracket, we issue an **open_box n** command, which ensures that if lines are subsequently broken, they will be aligned **n** places from the current character position. In each case, after dealing with the corresponding sub-tree we issue a corresponding **close_box** command. Moreover, rather than simply printing spaces after operators using **print_string** we use the special **print_space** function. This will *either* print a space as usual, or if it seems more appropriate, split the line and start again at the position defined by the current innermost box.

For example, the following modifies a basic printer **f x y** to have this kind of 'boxing' wrapped round it, and also bracketing it when the Boolean input **p** is 'true':

```
let bracket p n f x y =
  (if p then print_string "(" else ());
  open_box n; f x y; close_box();
  (if p then print_string ")" else ());;
```

In order to conform to the convention of omitting the quantifier symbol with repeated quantifiers, it's convenient to have a function that breaks up a quantified term into its quantified variables and body. This takes a flag **isforall** to specify whether the quantifier being stripped down is universal or existential.

```
let rec strip_quant fm =
  match fm with
    Forall(x,(Forall(y,p) as yp)) | Exists(x,(Exists(y,p) as yp)) ->
        let xs,q = strip_quant yp in x::xs,q
  | Forall(x,p) | Exists(x,p) -> [x],p
  | _ -> [],fm;;
```

Printing is parametrized by a function to print atoms, which is the parameter **pfn** of the main printing function. This contains mutually recursive functions **print_infix** to print instances of infix operators and **print_prefix** to print iterated prefix operations without multiple brackets. This is only actually used for negation, so that ¬(¬p) is printed as ¬¬p.

```
let print_formula pfn =
  let rec print_formula pr fm =
    match fm with
      False -> print_string "false"
    | True -> print_string "true"
    | Atom(pargs) -> pfn pr pargs
    | Not(p) -> bracket (pr > 10) 1 (print_prefix 10) "~" p
    | And(p,q) -> bracket (pr > 8) 0 (print_infix 8 "/\\") p q
    | Or(p,q) ->  bracket (pr > 6) 0 (print_infix  6 "\\/") p q
    | Imp(p,q) ->  bracket (pr > 4) 0 (print_infix 4 "==>") p q
    | Iff(p,q) ->  bracket (pr > 2) 0 (print_infix 2 "<=>") p q
    | Forall(x,p) -> bracket (pr > 0) 2 print_qnt "forall" (strip_quant fm)
    | Exists(x,p) -> bracket (pr > 0) 2 print_qnt "exists" (strip_quant fm)
  and print_qnt qname (bvs,bod) =
    print_string qname;
    do_list (fun v -> print_string " "; print_string v) bvs;
    print_string "."; print_space(); open_box 0;
    print_formula 0 bod;
    close_box()
  and print_prefix newpr sym p =
   print_string sym; print_formula (newpr+1) p
  and print_infix newpr sym p q =
    print_formula (newpr+1) p;
    print_string(" "^sym); print_space();
    print_formula newpr q in
  print_formula 0;;
```

The main toplevel printer just adds the guillemot-style quotations round the formula so that it looks like the quoted formulas we parse.

```
let print_qformula pfn fm =
  open_box 0; print_string "<<";
  open_box 0; print_formula pfn fm; close_box();
  print_string ">>"; close_box();;
```

Parsing first-order terms and formulas

As noted in the main text, we adopt the convention that only numerals and the empty list constant `nil` are considered as constants, so we define a corresponding function:

```
let is_const_name s = forall numeric (explode s) or s = "nil";;
```

In order to check whether a name is within the scope of a quantifier, all the parsing functions take an additional argument `vs` which is the set of bound variables in the current scope. Parsing is then straightforward: we have a function for the special 'atomic' terms:

```
let rec parse_atomic_term vs inp =
  match inp with
    [] -> failwith "term expected"
  | "("::rest -> parse_bracketed (parse_term vs) ")" rest
  | "-"::rest -> papply (fun t -> Fn("-",[t])) (parse_atomic_term vs rest)
  | f::"("::")"::rest -> Fn(f,[]),rest
  | f::"("::rest ->
      papply (fun args -> Fn(f,args))
             (parse_bracketed (parse_list "," (parse_term vs)) ")" rest)
  | a::rest ->
      (if is_const_name a & not(mem a vs) then Fn(a,[]) else Var a),rest
```

and build up parsing of general terms via parsing of the various infix operators, in precedence order.

```
and parse_term vs inp =
  parse_right_infix "::" (fun (e1,e2) -> Fn("::",[e1;e2]))
    (parse_right_infix "+" (fun (e1,e2) -> Fn("+",[e1;e2]))
      (parse_left_infix "-" (fun (e1,e2) -> Fn("-",[e1;e2]))
        (parse_right_infix "*" (fun (e1,e2) -> Fn("*",[e1;e2]))
          (parse_left_infix "/" (fun (e1,e2) -> Fn("/",[e1;e2]))
            (parse_left_infix "^" (fun (e1,e2) -> Fn("^",[e1;e2]))
              (parse_atomic_term vs)))))) inp;;
```

We can turn this into a convenient function for the user in the normal way:

```
let parset = make_parser (parse_term []);;
```

For formulas, recall that the generic formula parser requires a special recognizer for 'infix' atomic formulas like $s < t$, so we define that first:

```
let parse_infix_atom vs inp =
  let tm,rest = parse_term vs inp in
  if exists (nextin rest) ["="; "<"; "<="; ">"; ">="] then
        papply (fun tm' -> Atom(R(hd rest,[tm;tm'])))
               (parse_term vs (tl rest))
  else failwith "";;
```

We then use this is one of the options in parsing a general atomic formula. Note that we allow nullary predicates to be written without brackets, i.e. just '*P*', not necessarily '*P*()'.

```
let parse_atom vs inp =
  try parse_infix_atom vs inp with Failure _ ->
  match inp with
  | p::"("::")"::rest -> Atom(R(p,[])),rest
  | p::"("::rest ->
      papply (fun args -> Atom(R(p,args)))
             (parse_bracketed (parse_list "," (parse_term vs)) ")" rest)
  | p::rest when p <> "(" -> Atom(R(p,[])),rest
  | _ -> failwith "parse_atom";;
```

Now the overall function is defined as usual and we set up the default parsers for quotations. Note that we have things set up so that anything in quotations with bars <<|like this|>> gets passed to `secondary_parser`, while anthing else in quotations gets passed to `default_parser`.

```
let parse = make_parser
  (parse_formula (parse_infix_atom,parse_atom) []);;

let default_parser = parse;;

let secondary_parser = parset;;
```

Printing first-order terms and formulas

Now we consider printing, first of terms. Most of this is similar to what we have seen before for formulas except that we include a special function `print_fargs` for printing a function and argument list $f(t_1, \ldots, t_n)$. Note also that since some infix operators are now left associative, we need an additional flag `isleft` to the `print_infix_term` function so that brackets are included only on the necessary side of iterated applications. We then have three functions with some mutual recursion, for terms themselves:

```
let rec print_term prec fm =
  match fm with
    Var x -> print_string x
  | Fn("^",[tm1;tm2]) -> print_infix_term true prec 24 "^" tm1 tm2
  | Fn("/",[tm1;tm2]) -> print_infix_term true prec 22 " /" tm1 tm2
  | Fn("*",[tm1;tm2]) -> print_infix_term false prec 20 " *" tm1 tm2
  | Fn("-",[tm1;tm2]) -> print_infix_term true prec 18 " -" tm1 tm2
  | Fn("+",[tm1;tm2]) -> print_infix_term false prec 16 " +" tm1 tm2
  | Fn("::",[tm1;tm2]) -> print_infix_term false prec 14 "::" tm1 tm2
  | Fn(f,args) -> print_fargs f args
```

a function and its arguments:

```
and print_fargs f args =
  print_string f;
  if args = [] then () else
    (print_string "(";
     open_box 0;
     print_term 0 (hd args); print_break 0 0;
     do_list (fun t -> print_string ","; print_break 0 0; print_term 0 t)
             (tl args);
     close_box();
     print_string ")")
```

and an infix operation:

```
and print_infix_term isleft oldprec newprec sym p q =
  if oldprec > newprec then (print_string "("; open_box 0) else ();
  print_term (if isleft then newprec else newprec+1) p;
  print_string sym;
  print_break (if String.sub sym 0 1 = " " then 1 else 0) 0;
  print_term (if isleft then newprec+1 else newprec) q;
  if oldprec > newprec then (close_box(); print_string ")") else ();;
```

As usual, we set up the overall printer and install it.

```
let printert tm =
  open_box 0; print_string "<<|";
  open_box 0; print_term 0 tm; close_box();
  print_string "|>>"; close_box();;

#install_printer printert;;
```

Printing of formulas is straightforward via the atom printing function:

```
let print_atom prec (R(p,args)) =
  if mem p ["="; "<"; "<="; ">"; ">="] & length args = 2
  then print_infix_term false 12 12 (" "^p) (el 0 args) (el 1 args)
  else print_fargs p args;;
```

as follows:

```
let print_fol_formula = print_qformula print_atom;;

#install_printer print_fol_formula;;
```

References

Abdulla, P. A., Bjesse, P. and Eén, N. (2000) Symbolic reachability analysis based on SAT-solvers. In Graf, S. and Schwartzbach, M. (eds.), *Tools and Algorithms for the Construction and Analysis of Systems (TACAS'00)*, Volume 1785 of *Lecture Notes in Computer Science*. Springer-Verlag.

Aberth, O. (1980) *Computable Analysis*. McGraw-Hill.

Abian, A. (1976) *Boolean Rings*. Branden Press.

Abramsky, S., Gabbay, D. M. and Maibaum, T. S. E. (eds.) (1992) *Handbook of Logic in Computer Science, Volume 2. Background: Computational Structures*. Clarendon Press.

Ackermann, W. (1928) Über die Erfüllbarkeit gewisser Zählausdrücke. *Mathematische Annalen*, **100**, 638–649.

Ackermann, W. (1954) *Solvable Cases of the Decision Problem*. Studies in Logic and the Foundations of Mathematics. North-Holland.

Adams, W. W. and Loustaunau, P. (1994) *An Introduction to Gröbner Bases*, Volume 3 of *Graduate Studies in Mathematics*. American Mathematical Society.

Agrawal, M., Kayal, N. and Saxena, N. (2004) PRIMES is in P. *Annals of Mathematics*, **160**, 781–793.

Aho, A. V., Sethi, R. and Ullman, J. D. (1986) *Compilers: Principles, Techniques and Tools*. Addison-Wesley.

Aichinger, E. (1994) *Interpolation with Near-rings of Polynomial Functions*. Ph. D. thesis, Johannes Kepler Universität Linz. Author's Diplomarbeit.

Aigner, M. and Ziegler, G. M. (2001) *Proofs from The Book* (2nd edn.). Springer-Verlag.

Akers, S. B. (1978) Binary decision diagrams. *ACM Transactions on Computers*, **C-27**, 509–516.

Allen, S., Constable, R., Howe, D. and Aitken, W. (1990) The semantics of reflected proof. In *Proceedings of the Fifth Annual Symposium on Logic in Computer Science*, Los Alamitos, CA, USA, pp. 95–107. IEEE Computer Society Press.

Andersen, F. and Petersen, K. D. (1991) Recursive boolean functions in HOL. See Archer, Joyce, Levitt and Windley (1991), pp. 367–377.

Andrews, P. B. (1976) Theorem proving by matings. *IEEE Transactions on Computers*, **25**, 801–807.

Andrews, P. B. (1981) Theorem proving via general matings. *Journal of the ACM*, **28**, 193–214.

Andrews, P. B. (1986) *An Introduction to Mathematical Logic and Type Theory: To Truth Through Proof.* Academic Press.

Andrews, P. B. (2003) Herbrand award acceptance speech. *Journal of Automated Reasoning*, **31**, 169–187.

Appel, K. and Haken, W. (1976) Every planar map is four colorable. *Bulletin of the American Mathematical Society*, **82**, 711–712.

Archer, M., Joyce, J. J., Levitt, K. N. and Windley, P. J. (eds.) (1991) *Proceedings of the 1991 International Workshop on the HOL Theorem Proving System and its Applications*, University of California at Davis, Davis CA, USA. IEEE Computer Society Press.

Armando, A., Castellini, C. and Giunchiglia, E. (1999) SAT-based procedures for temporal reasoning. In *Proceedings of the 5th European conference on Planning*, Lecture Notes in Computer Science, pp. 97–108. Springer-Verlag.

Aschenbrenner, M. (2004) Ideal membership in polynomial rings over the integers. *Journal of the American Mathematical Society*, **17**, 407–441.

Astrachan, O. L. and Stickel, M. E. (1992) Caching and lemmaizing in model elimination theorem provers. In Kapur, D. (ed.), *11th International Conference on Automated Deduction*, Volume 607 of *Lecture Notes in Computer Science*, pp. 224–238. Springer-Verlag.

Aubrey, J. (1898) *Brief Lives.* Clarendon Press. Edited from the author's MSS by Andrew Clark.

Avigad, J. and Friedman, H. (2006) Combining decision procedures for the reals. *Logical Methods in Computer Science*, **2**(4), 1–42.

Ax, J. (1967) Solving diophantine problems modulo every prime. *Annals of Mathematics, 2nd series*, **85**, 161–183.

Ax, J. (1968) The elementary theory of finite fields. *Annals of Mathematics, 2nd series*, **88**, 239–271.

Baader, F. (ed.) (2003) *Automated Deduction – CADE-19*, Volume 2741 of *Lecture Notes in Computer Science*. Springer-Verlag.

Baader, F. and Nipkow, T. (1998) *Term Rewriting and All That.* Cambridge University Press.

Babić, D. and Musuvathi, M. (2005) *Modular Arithmetic Decision Procedure.* Technical Report TR-2005-114, Microsoft Research, Redmond.

Bachmair, L., Dershowitz, N. and Plaisted, D. A. (1989) Completion without failure. In Aït-Kaci, H. and Nivat, M. (eds.), *Resolution of Equations in Algebraic Structures. Volume 2: Rewriting Techniques*, pp. 1–30. Academic Press.

Bachmair, L. and Ganzinger, H. (1994) Rewrite-based equational theorem proving with selection and simplification. *Journal of Logic and Computation*, **3**, 217–247.

Bachmair, L. and Ganzinger, H. (2001) Resolution theorem proving. See Robinson and Voronkov (2001), pp. 19–99.

Bachmair, L., Ganzinger, H. and Voronkov, A. (1997) *Elimination of Equality via Transformations with Ordering Constraints.* Technical report MPI-I-97-2-012, Max-Planck-Institut für Informatik.

Back, R., Grundy, J. and Wright, J. v. (1996) *Structured Calculational Proof.* Technical Report 65, Turku Centre for Computer Science (TUCS), Lemminkäisenkatu 14 A, FIN-20520 Turku, Finland. Also available as Technical Report TR-CS-96-09 from the Australian National University.

Baker, T., Gill, J. and Solovay, R. M. (1975) Relativizations of the $P = NP$ question. *SIAM Journal on Computing*, **4**, 431–442.

Ball, T., Cook, B., Lahriri, S. K. and Rajamani, S. K. (2004) Zapato: automatic theorem proving for predicate abstraction refinement. In Alur, R. and Peled, D. A. (eds.), *Computer Aided Verification, 16th International Conference, CAV 2004*, Volume 3114 of *Lecture Notes in Computer Science*, pp. 457–461. Springer-Verlag.

Barendregt, H. P. (1984) *The Lambda Calculus: Its Syntax and Semantics*, Volume 103 of *Studies in Logic and the Foundations of Mathematics*. North-Holland.

Barrett, C. (2002) *Checking Validity of Quantifier-Free Formulas in Combinations of First-Order Theories*. Ph. D. thesis, Stanford University Computer Science Department.

Barrett, C., Dill, D. and Levitt, J. (1996) Validity checking for combinations of theories with equality. In Srivas, M. and Camilleri, A. (eds.), *Proceedings of the First International Conference on Formal Methods in Computer-Aided Design (FMCAD'96)*, Volume 1166 of *Lecture Notes in Computer Science*, pp. 187–201. Springer-Verlag.

Barrett, C., Sebastiani, R., Seshia, S. and Tinelli, C. (2008) Satisfiability modulo theories. In Biere, A., van Maaren, H. and Walsh, T. (eds.), *Handbook of Satisfiability, vol. 4*. IOS Press. To appear.

Barrett, C., Shikanian, I. and Tinelli, C. (2007) An abstract decision procedure for a theory of inductive data types. *Journal on Satisfiability, Boolean Modeling and Computation*, **3**, 21–46.

Barwise, J. and Etchemendy, J. (1991) *The Language of First-Order Logic* (2nd edn.). CSLI.

Barwise, J. and Keisler, H. (eds.) (1991) *Handbook of mathematical logic*, Volume 90 of *Studies in Logic and the Foundations of Mathematics*. North-Holland.

Basu, S., Pollack, R. and Roy, M.-F. (2006) *Algorithms in Real Algebraic Geometry*, Volume 10 of *Algorithms and Computation in Mathematics*. Springer-Verlag.

Baumgartner, P. and Furbach, U. (1993) *Model Elimination without Contrapositives and its Application to PTTP*. Research report 12-93, Institute for Computer Science, University of Koblenz, Koblenz, Germany.

Baumgartner, P. and Tinelli, C. (2003) The model evolution calculus. See Baader (2003), pp. 350–364.

Baumgartner, P. and Tinelli, C. (2005) The model evolution calculus with equality. See Nieuwenhuis (2005), pp. 392–408.

Bayardo, R. J. and Schrag, R. C. (1997) Using CSP look-back techniques to solve real-world SAT instances. In *Proceedings of the Fourteenth National Conference on Artificial Intelligence (AAAI'97)*, Menlo Park CA, pp. 203–208. AAAI Press.

Bayer, D. (1982) *The Division Algorithm and the Hilbert Scheme*. Ph. D. thesis, Harvard University.

Beckert, B. and Posegga, J. (1995) lean$T^A P$: Lean, tableau-based deduction. *Journal of Automated Reasoning*, **15**, 339–358.

Beeson, M. J. (1984) *Foundations of Constructive Mathematics: Metamathematical Studies*, Volume 3 of *Ergebnisse der Mathematik und ihrer Grenzgebiete*. Springer-Verlag.

Bell, E. T. (1934) Exponential numbers. *The American Mathematical Monthly*, **41**, 411–419.

Bell, J. L. and Slomson, T. S. (1969) *Models and Ultraproducts*. North-Holland.

Beltyokov, A. P. (1974) Decidability of the universal theory of natural numbers with addition and divisibility (Russian). *Sem. Leningrad Otd. Mat. Inst. Akad. Nauk*

SSSR, **40**, 127–130. English translation in *Journal of Mathematical Sciences*, **14**, 1436–1444, 1980.

Benacerraf, P. and Putnam, H. (1983) *Philosophy of Mathematics: Selected Readings* (2nd edn.). Cambridge University Press.

Benedetti, R. and Risler, J.-J. (1990) *Real Algebraic and Semi-algebraic Sets*. Hermann.

Bennet, J. H. (1962) *On Spectra*. Ph. D. thesis, Princeton University.

Berkeley, G. (1734) *The Analyst; or, a Discourse Addressed to an Infidel Mathematician*. J. Tonson, London.

Bernays, P. and Schönfinkel, M. (1928) Zum Entscheidungsproblem der mathematischen Logik. *Mathematische Annalen*, **99**, 401–419.

Bertot, Y., Dowek, G., Hirschowitz, A., Paulin, C. and Théry, L. (eds.) (1999) *Theorem Proving in Higher Order Logics: 12th International Conference, TPHOLs'99*, Volume 1690 of *Lecture Notes in Computer Science*. Springer-Verlag.

Beth, E. W. (1955) Semantic entailment and formal derivability. *Mededelingen der Koninklijke Nederlandse Akademie van Wetenschappen, new series*, **18**, 309–342.

Beth, E. W. (1958) On machines which prove theorems. *Simon Stevin Wissen-Natur-Kundig Tijdschrift*, **32**, 49–60.

Bibel, W. (1987) *Automated Theorem Proving* (2nd edn.). Vieweg Verlag.

Bibel, W. and Kowalski, R. (eds.) (1980) *5th Conference on Automated Deduction*, Volume 87 of *Lecture Notes in Computer Science*. Springer-Verlag.

Bibel, W. and Schreiber, J. (1975) Proof search in a Gentzen-like system of first order logic. In Gelenbe, E. and Potier, D. (eds.), *Proceedings of the International Computing Symposium*, pp. 205–212. North-Holland.

Biere, A., Cimatti, A., Clarke, E. M. and Zhu, Y. (1999) Symbolic model checking without BDDs. In *Proceedings of the 5th International Conference on Tools and Algorithms for Construction and Analysis of Systems*, Volume 1579 of *Lecture Notes in Computer Science*, pp. 193–207. Springer-Verlag.

Biggs, N. L., Lloyd, E. K. and Wilson, R. J. (1976) *Graph Theory 1736–1936*. Clarendon Press.

Birkhoff, G. (1935) On the structure of abstract algebras. *Proceedings of the Cambridge Philosophical Society*, **31**, 433–454.

Bjesse, P. (1999) *Symbolic Model Checking with Sets of States Represented as Formulas*. Technical Report SC-1999-100, Department of Computer Science, Chalmers University of Technology.

Björk, M. (2005) A first order extension of Stålmarck's method. In Sutcliffe, G. and Voronkov, A. (eds.), *Logic for Programming, Artificial Intelligence, and Reasoning, LPAR '05*, Volume 3835 of *Lecture Notes in Computer Science*, pp. 276–291. Springer-Verlag.

Bledsoe, W. W. (1984) Some automatic proofs in analysis. See Bledsoe and Loveland (1984), pp. 89–118.

Bledsoe, W. W. and Loveland, D. W. (eds.) (1984) *Automated Theorem Proving: After 25 Years*, Volume 29 of *Contemporary Mathematics*. American Mathematical Society.

Blum, M. (1993) Program result checking: a new approach to making programs more reliable. In Lingas, A., Karlsson, R. and Carlsson, S. (eds.), *Automata, Languages and Programming, 20th International Colloquium,*

ICALP93, Proceedings, Volume 700 of *Lecture Notes in Computer Science*, pp. 1–14. Springer-Verlag.

Bocheński, I. M. (1961) *A History of Formal Logic*. Notre Dame.

Bochnak, J., Coste, M. and Roy, M.-F. (1998) *Real Algebraic Geometry*, Volume 36 of *Ergebnisse der Mathematik und ihrer Grenzgebiete*. Springer-Verlag.

Bonet, M. L., Buss, S. R. and Pitassi, T. (1995) Are there hard examples for Frege systems? In Clote, P. and Remmel, J. B. (eds.), *Feasible Mathematics II*, Volume 13 of *Progress in Computer Science and Applied Logic*, pp. 30–56. Birkhäuser.

Boole, G. (1847) *The Mathematical Analysis of Logic*. Cambridge University Press.

Boolos, G. S. (1989) A new proof of the Gödel incompleteness theorem. *Notices of the American Mathematical Society*, **36**, 388–390.

Boolos, G. S. (1995) *The Logic of Provability*. Cambridge University Press.

Boolos, G. S. and Jeffrey, R. C. (1989) *Computability and Logic* (3rd edn.). Cambridge University Press. First edition 1974.

Boone, W. (1959) The word problem. *Annals of Mathematics*, **70**, 207–265.

Börger, E., Grädel, E. and Gurevich, Y. (2001) *The Classical Decision Problem*. Springer-Verlag.

Boulton, R. J. (1992) A lazy approach to fully-expansive theorem proving. In Claesen, L. J. M. and Gordon, M. J. C. (eds.), *Proceedings of the IFIP TC10/WG10.2 International Workshop on Higher Order Logic Theorem Proving and its Applications*, Volume A-20 of *IFIP Transactions A: Computer Science and Technology*, pp. 19–38. North-Holland.

Boulton, R. J. (1993) *Efficiency in a Fully-expansive Theorem Prover*. Technical Report 337, University of Cambridge Computer Laboratory. Author's PhD thesis.

Boy de la Tour, T. (1990) Minimizing the number of clauses by renaming. See Stickel (1990), pp. 558–572.

Boyer, R. S. and Moore, J. S. (1977) A lemma driven automatic theorem prover for recursive function theory. In *Proceedings of the 5th International Joint Conference on Artificial Intelligence*, MIT, pp. 511–519. Department of Computer Science, Carnegie-Mellon University.

Boyer, R. S. and Moore, J. S. (1979) *A Computational Logic*. ACM Monograph Series. Academic Press.

Bozzano, M., Bruttomesso, R., Cimatti, A. *et al.* (2005) Efficient satisfiability modulo theories via delayed theory combination. In Etessami, K. and Rajamani, S. K. (eds.), *Computer Aided Verification, 17th International Conference, CAV 2005*, Volume 3576 of *Lecture Notes in Computer Science*, pp. 335–349. Springer-Verlag.

Brace, K. S., Rudell, R. L. and Bryant, R. E. (1990) Efficient implementation of a BDD package. In *Proceedings of 27th ACM/IEEE Design Automation Conference*, pp. 40–45, IEEE Computer Soceity Press.

Bradley, A. R. and Manna, Z. (2007) *The Calculus of Computation: Decision Procedures with Applications to Verification*. Springer-Verlag.

Bradley, A. R., Manna, Z. and Sipma, H. B. (2006) What's decidable about arrays? In Emerson, E. A. and Namjoshi, K. S. (eds.), *Verification, Model Checking, and Abstract Interpretation, 7th International Conference, VMCAI 2006*, Volume 3855 of *Lecture Notes in Computer Science*, pp. 427–442. Springer-Verlag.

Brand, D. (1975) Proving theorems with the modification method. *SIAM Journal on Computing*, **4**, 412–430.

Bratley, P. and Millo, J. (1972) Computer recreations; self-reproducing automata. *Software – Practice and Experience*, **2**, 397–400.

Bryant, R. E. (1985) Symbolic verification of MOS circuits. In Fuchs, H. (ed.), *Proceedings of the 1985 Chapel Hill Conference on VLSI*, pp. 419–438. Computer Science Press.

Bryant, R. E. (1986) Graph-based algorithms for Boolean function manipulation. *IEEE Transactions on Computers*, **C-35**, 677–691.

Bryant, R. E. (1991) On the complexity of VLSI implementations and graph representations of Boolean functions with application to integer multiplication. *IEEE Transactions on Computers*, **C-40**, 205–213.

Bryant, R. E. (1992) Symbolic Boolean manipulation with ordered binary-decision diagrams. *ACM Computing Surveys*, **24**, 293–318.

Bryant, R. E., Lahiri, S. K. and Seshia, S. A. (2002) Modeling and verifying systems using a logic of counter arithmetic with lambda expressions and uninterpreted functions. In Brinksma, E. and Larsen, K. G. (eds.), *Computer Aided Verification, 14th International Conference, CAV 2002*, Volume 2404 of *Lecture Notes in Computer Science*, pp. 79–92. Springer-Verlag.

Buchberger, B. (1965) *Ein Algorithmus zum Auffinden der Basiselemente des Restklassenringes nach einem nulldimensionalen Polynomideal*. Ph.D. thesis, Mathematisches Institut der Universität Innsbruck. English translation in *Journal of Symbolic Computation* 41 (2006), 475–511.

Buchberger, B. (1970) Ein algorithmisches Kriterium fur die Lösbarkeit eines algebraischen Gleichungssystems. *Aequationes Mathematicae*, **4**, 374–383. English translation 'An algorithmical criterion for the solvability of algebraic systems of equations' in Buchberger and Winkler (1998), pp. 535–545.

Buchberger, B. (1998) An introduction to Gröbner bases. See Buchberger and Winkler (1998).

Buchberger, B. and Winkler, F. (eds.) (1998) *Gröbner Bases and Applications*, Number 251 in London Mathematical Society Lecture Note Series. Cambridge University Press.

Buchholz, W. (1995) Proof-theoretic analysis of termination proofs. *Annals of Pure and Applied Logic*, **75**, 57–65.

Bumcrot, R. (1965) On lattice complements. *Proceedings of the Glasgow Mathematical Association*, **7**, 22–23.

Bundy, A. (1983) *The Computer Modelling of Mathematical Reasoning*. Academic Press.

Bundy, A. (1991) A science of reasoning. See Lassez and Plotkin (1991), pp. 178–198.

Burch, J. R., Clarke, E. M., McMillan, K. L., Dill, D. L. and Hwang, L. J. (1992) Symbolic model checking: 10^{20} states and beyond. *Information and Computation*, **98**, 142–170.

Burch, J. R. and Dill, D. L. (1994) Automatic verification of pipelined microprocessor control. In Dill, D. L. (ed.), *Computer Aided Verification, 6th International Conference, CAV '94*, Volume 818 of *Lecture Notes in Computer Science*, pp. 68–80. Springer-Verlag.

Burge, W. H. (1975) *Recursive Programming Techniques*. Addison-Wesley.

Burkill, J. C. and Burkill, H. (1970) *A Second Course in Mathematical Analysis*. Cambridge University Press. New printing 1980.

Burris, S. and Sankappanavar, H. P. (1981) *A Course in Universal Algebra*. Springer-Verlag.

Calude, C., Marcus, S. and Tevy, I. (1979) The first example of a recursive function which is not primitive recursive. *Historia Mathematica*, **6**, 380–384.

Carnap, R. (1935) *Philosophy and Logical Syntax*. Thoemmes Press. Reprinted 1996.

Carnap, R. (1937) *The Logical Syntax of Language*. International library of psychology, philosophy and scientific method. Routledge & Kegan Paul. Translated from *Logische Syntax der Sprache* by Amethe Smeaton (Countess von Zeppelin), with some new sections not in the German original.

Caviness, B. F. and Johnson, J. R. (eds.) (1998) *Quantifier Elimination and Cylindrical Algebraic Decomposition*, Texts and monographs in symbolic computation. Springer-Verlag.

Cegielski, P. (1981) Théorie élémentaire de la multiplication des entiers naturels. In Berline, C., McAloon, K. and Ressayre, J.-P. (eds.), *Model Theory and Arithmetic*, Volume 890 of *Lecture Notes in Mathematics*, pp. 44–89. Springer-Verlag.

Ceruzzi, P. E. (1983) *Reckoners: the Prehistory of the Digital Computer, from Relays to the Stored Program Concept, 1933–1945*. Greenwood Press.

Chaieb, A. (2008) *Automated Methods for Formal Proofs in Simple Arithmetics and Algebra*. Ph.D. thesis, Institut für Informatik, Technische Universität München. Submitted.

Chaitin, G. J. (1970) Computational complexity and Gödel's incompleteness theorem (abstract). *Notices of the American Mathematical Society*, **17**, 672.

Chaitin, G. J. (1974) Information-theoretic limitations of formal systems. *Journal of the ACM*, **21**, 403–424.

Chang, C. C. and Keisler, H. J. (1992) *Model Theory* (3rd edn.), Volume 73 of *Studies in Logic and the Foundations of Mathematics*. North-Holland.

Chang, C.-L. (1970) The unit proof and the input proof in theorem proving. *Journal of the ACM*, **17**, 698–707.

Chang, C.-L. and Lee, R. C. (1973) *Symbolic Logic and Mechanical Theorem Proving*. Academic Press.

Cherlin, G. L. (1976) Model theoretic algebra. *Journal of Symbolic Logic*, **41**, 537–545.

Chou, S.-C. (1984) Proving elementary geometry theorems using Wu's algorithm. See Bledsoe and Loveland (1984), pp. 243–286.

Chou, S.-C. (1988) *Mechanical Geometry Theorem Proving*. Reidel.

Chou, S.-C. and Gao, X.-S. (2001) Automated reasoning in geometry. See Robinson and Voronkov (2001), pp. 707–748.

Church, A. (1936) An unsolvable problem of elementary number-theory. *American Journal of Mathematics*, **58**, 345–363.

Church, A. (1941) *The Calculi of Lambda-conversion*, Volume 6 of *Annals of Mathematics Studies*. Princeton University Press.

Church, A. (1956) *Introduction to Mathematical Logic*. Princeton University Press.

Church, A. and Rosser, J. B. (1936) Some properties of conversion. *Transactions of the American Mathematical Society*, **39**, 472–482.

Clarke, E. M. and Emerson, E. A. (1981) Design and synthesis of synchronization skeletons using branching-time temporal logic. In Kozen, D. (ed.), *Logics of Programs*, Volume 131 of *Lecture Notes in Computer Science*, pp. 52–71. Springer-Verlag.

Clarke, E. M., Grumberg, O. and Peled, D. (1999) *Model Checking*. MIT Press.

Clocksin, W. F. and Mellish, C. S. (1987) *Programming in Prolog* (3rd edn.). Springer-Verlag.

Coarfa, C., Demopoulos, D. D., Alfonso, S. M. A., Subramanian, D. and Vardi, M. (2000) Random 3-SAT: the plot thickens. In Dechter, R. (ed.), *Proceedings of the 6th International Conference on Principles and Practice of Constraint Programming*, Volume 1894 of *Lecture Notes in Computer Science*, pp. 243–261. Springer-Verlag.

Cohen, J., Trilling, L. and Wegner, P. (1974) A nucleus of a theorem-prover described in ALGOL-68. *International Journal of Computer and Information Sciences*, **3**, 1–31.

Cohen, P. J. (1969) Decision procedures for real and p-adic fields. *Communications in Pure and Applied Mathematics*, **22**, 131–151.

Cohn, A. G. (1985) On the solution of Schubert's steamroller in many sorted logic. In Joshi, A. K. (ed.), *Proceedings of the 9th International Joint Conference on Artificial Intelligence*, pp. 1169–1174, Morgan Kaufman.

Cohn, P. M. (1965) *Universal Algebra*. Harper's series in modern mathematics. Harper and Row.

Cohn, P. M. (1974) *Algebra*, Volume 1 (Second edn.). Wiley.

Collins, G. E. (1976) Quantifier elimination for real closed fields by cylindrical algebraic decomposition. In Brakhage, H. (ed.), *Second GI Conference on Automata Theory and Formal Languages*, Volume 33 of *Lecture Notes in Computer Science*, pp. 134–183. Springer-Verlag.

Colmerauer, A. (1990) An introduction to Prolog III. *Communications of the ACM*, **33**(7), 69–90.

Colmerauer, A., Kanoi, H., Roussel, P. and Pasero, R. (1973) *Un système de communication homme-machine en français*. Technical report, Artificial Intelligence Group, University of Aix-Marseilles, Luminay, France.

Comon, H., Narendran, P., Nieuwenhuis, R. and Rusinowitch, M. (1998) Decision problems in ordered rewriting. In *Proceedings of the Thirteenth Annual IEEE Symposium on Logic in Computer Science*, pp. 276–286. IEEE Computer Society Press.

Constable, R. (1986) *Implementing Mathematics with The Nuprl Proof Development System*. Prentice-Hall.

Conway, J. H. and Sloane, N. J. A. (1993) The kissing number problem. In Conway, J. H. and Sloaue, N. J. A. (eds.), *Sphere Packings, Lattices, and Groups* (2nd edn.)., pp. 21–24. Springer-Verlag.

Cook, B., Podelski, A. and Rybalchenko, A. (2006) Termination proofs for systems code. In Ball, T. (ed.), *Proceedings of Conference on Programming Language Design and Implementation, PLDI*, pp. 415–426. ACM Press.

Cook, S. A. (1971) The complexity of theorem-proving procedures. In *Proceedings of the 3rd ACM Symposium on the Theory of Computing*, pp. 151–158, ACM.

Cooper, D. C. (1972) Theorem proving in arithmetic without multiplication. See Melzer and Michie (1972), pp. 91–99.

Corbineau, P. (2008) A declarative language for the Coq proof assistant. In Miculan, M., Scagnetto, I. and Honsell, F. (eds.), *Types for Proofs and Programs: International Workshop TYPES 2007*, Volume 4941 of *Lecture Notes in Computer Science*, pp. 69–84. Springer-Verlag.

Corcoran, J. (1980) Categoricity. *History and Philosophy of Logic*, **1**, 187–207.

Coudert, O., Berthet, C. and Madre, J.-C. (1989) Verification of synchronous sequential machines based on symbolic execution. In Sifakis, J. (ed.),

Automatic Verification Methods for Finite State Systems, Volume 407 of *Lecture Notes in Computer Science*, pp. 365–373. Springer-Verlag.

Cousineau, G. and Mauny, M. (1998) *The Functional Approach to Programming*. Cambridge University Press.

Cox, D., Little, J. and O'Shea, D. (1992) *Ideals, Varieties, and Algorithms*. Springer-Verlag.

Craig, W. (1952) On axiomatizability within a system. *Journal of Symbolic Logic*, **18**, 30–32.

Craig, W. (1957) Three uses of the Herbrand–Genzen theorem in relating model theory and proof theory. *Journal of Symbolic Logic*, **22**, 269–285.

Crawford, J. and Auton, L. (1996) Experimental results on the crossover point in random 3SAT. *Artificial Intelligence*, **81**, 31–57.

Cutland, N. (ed.) (1988) *Nonstandard Analysis and its Applications*, Volume 10 of *London Mathematical Society student texts*. Cambridge University Press.

Cyrluk, D., Möller, M. O. and Reuß, H. (1997) An efficient decision procedure for the theory of fixed-size bit-vectors. In Grumberg, O. (ed.), *Computer-aided Verification, 9th International Conference CAV '97*, Volume 1254 of *Lecture Notes in Computer Science*, pp. 60–71. Springer-Verlag.

Dantzig, G. B. (1963) *Linear Programming and Extensions*. Princeton University Press.

Davenport, J. H. and Heintz, J. (1988) Real quantifier elimination is doubly exponential. *Journal of Symbolic Computation*, **5**, 29–35.

Davey, B. A. and Priestley, H. A. (1990) *Introduction to Lattices and Order*. Cambridge University Press.

Davis, M. (1950) Arithmetical problems and recursively enumerable predicates (abstract). *Journal of Symbolic Logic*, **15**, 77–78.

Davis, M. (1957) A computer program for Presburger's algorithm. In *Summaries of talks presented at the Summer Institute for Symbolic Logic, Cornell University*, pp. 215–233. Institute for Defense Analyses, Princeton, NJ. Reprinted in Siekmann and Wrightson (1983a), pp. 41–48.

Davis, M. (ed.) (1965) *The Undecidable: Basic Papers on Undecidable Propositions, Unsolvable Problems and Computable Functions*. Raven Press.

Davis, M. (1977) *Applied Nonstandard Analysis*. Academic Press.

Davis, M. (1981) Obvious logical inferences. In Haupes, P. J. (ed.), *Proceedings of the Seventh International Joint Conference on Artificial Intelligence*, pp. 530–531, William Kaufman.

Davis, M. (1983) The prehistory and early history of automated deduction. See Siekmann and Wrightson (1983a), pp. 1–28.

Davis, M. (2000) *The Universal Computer: the Road from Leibniz to Turing*. W. W. Norton and Company. Paperback edition (2001) entitled *Engines of Logic: Mathematicians and the Origin of the Computer*.

Davis, M., Logemann, G. and Loveland, D. (1962) A machine program for theorem proving. *Communications of the ACM*, **5**, 394–397.

Davis, M. and Putnam, H. (1960) A computing procedure for quantification theory. *Journal of the ACM*, **7**, 201–215.

Davis, M. and Schwartz, J. T. (1979) Metatheoretic extensibility for theorem verifiers and proof-checkers. *Computers and Mathematics with Applications*, **5**, 217–230.

Davis, M. D., Sigal, R. and Weyuker, E. J. (1994) *Computability, Complexity, and Languages: Fundamentals of Theoretical Computer Science* (2nd edn.). Academic Press.

Davis, P. J. and Cerutti, E. (1976) FORMAC meets Pappus: some observations on elementary analytic geometry by computer. *The American Mathematical Monthly*, **76**, 895–905.

de Bruijn, N. G. (1951) A colour problem for infinite graphs and a problem in the theory of relations. *Proceedings of the Koninklijke Nederlandse Akademie van Wetenschappen, series A*, **54**, 371–373.

de Bruijn, N. G. (1970) The mathematical language AUTOMATH its usage and some of its extensions. See Laudet, Lacombe, Nolin and Schützenberger (1970), pp. 29–61.

de Bruijn, N. G. (1972) Lambda calculus notation with nameless dummies, a tool for automatic formula manipulation, with application to the Church–Rosser theorem. *Indagationes Mathematicae*, **34**, 381–392.

de Bruijn, N. G. (1980) A survey of the project AUTOMATH. In Seldin, J. P. and Hindley, J. R. (eds.), *To H. B. Curry: Essays in Combinatory Logic, Lambda Calculus, and Formalism*, pp. 589–606. Academic Press.

de Nivelle, H. (1995) *Ordering Refinements of Resolution*. Ph.D. thesis, Technische Universiteit Delft.

Degtyarev, A. and Voronkov, A. (1995) *Simultaneous Rigid E-unification is Undecidable*. Technical report 105, Computing Science Department, Uppsala University. Also available on the Web as `ftp://ftp.csd.uu.se/pub/papers/reports/0105.ps.gz`.

Degtyarev, A. and Voronkov, A. (2001) Equality reasoning in sequent-based calculi. See Robinson and Voronkov (2001), pp. 611–706.

Dershowitz, N. (1979) A note on simplification orderings. *Information Processing Letters*, **9**, 212–215.

Dershowitz, N. and Manna, Z. (1979) Proving termination with multiset orderings. *Communications of the ACM*, **22**, 465–476.

Devlin, K. (1997) *Goodbye Descartes: the End of Logic and the Search for a New Cosmology of the Mind*. Wiley.

Di Cosmo, R. and Dufour, T. (2004) The equational theory of $< \mathbb{N}, 0, 1, +, \times, \uparrow >$ is decidable, but not finitely axiomatisable. In Baader, F. and Voronkov, A. (eds.), *Logic for Programming, Artificial Intelligence, and Reasoning, LPAR '04*, Volume 3452 of *Lecture Notes in Computer Science*, pp. 240–256. Springer-Verlag.

Dickson, L. E. (1913) Finiteness of the odd perfect and primitive abundant numbers with n distinct prime factors. *American Journal of Mathematics*, **35**, 413–422.

Dijkstra, E. W. (1976a) *A Discipline of Programming*. Prentice-Hall.

Dijkstra, E. W. (1976b) Formal techniques and sizeable programs (EWD563). See Dijkstra (1982a), pp. 205–214. Paper prepared for Symposium on the Mathematical Foundations of Computing Science, Gdansk 1976.

Dijkstra, E. W. (ed.) (1982a) *Selected Writings on Computing: a Personal Perspective*. Springer-Verlag.

Dijkstra, E. W. (1982b) On Webster, bugs and Aristotle. See Dijkstra (1982a), pp. 288–291.

Dijkstra, E. W. (1985) Invariance and non-determinacy. In Hoare, C. A. R. and Shepherdson, J. C. (eds.), *Mathematical Logic and Programming Languages*, Prentice-Hall International Series in Computer Science, pp. 157–165. Prentice-Hall. The papers in this volume were first published in the *Philosophical Transactions of the Royal Society*, Series A, **312**, 1984.

Dijkstra, E. W. (1989) On an exercise of Tony Hoare's. Available on the Web as `www.cs.utexas.edu/users/EWD/ewd12xx/EWD1062.PDF`.

Dijkstra, E. W. (1996) Three very little problems from Eindhoven (EWD 1230). Available on the Web as `www.cs.utexas.edu/users/EWD/ewd12xx/EWD1230.PDF`.

Dijkstra, E. W. (1997) Proving an implication via its converse (EWD 1266a). Date approximate. Available on the Web as `www.cs.utexas.edu/users/EWD/ewd12xx/EWD1266a.PDF`.

Dijkstra, E. W. and Scholten, C. S. (1990) *Predicate Calculus and Program Semantics*. Springer-Verlag.

Dines, L. L. (1919) Systems of linear inequalities. *Annals of Mathematics*, **20**, 191–199.

Doner, J. and Tarski, A. (1969) An extended arithmetic of ordinal numbers. *Fundamenta Mathematicae*, **65**, 95–127.

Downey, P. (1972) *Undecidability of Presburger Arithmetic with a Single Monadic Predicate Letter*. Technical Report 18-72, Center for Research in Computing Technology, Harvard University.

Downey, P. J., Sethi, R. and Tarjan, R. (1980) Variations on the common subexpression problem. *Journal of the ACM*, **27**, 758–771.

Dreben, B. and Goldfarb, W. D. (1979) *The Decision Problem: Solvable Cases of Quantificational Formulas*. Addison-Wesley.

Duffy, D. A. (1991) *Principles of Automated Theorem Proving*. Wiley.

Dumitriu, A. (1977) *History of Logic* (4 volumes). Abacus Press. Revised, updated and enlarged translation of the second edition of the Romanian *Istoria Logicii* (Editura Didactică, 1975) by Duiliu Zamfirescu, Dinu Giurcăneanu and Doina Doneaud.

Ebbinghaus, H.-D., Hermes, M., Hirzebruch, F. *et al.* (1990) *Numbers*, Volume 123 of *Graduate Texts in Mathematics*. Springer-Verlag. Translation of the 2nd edition of *Zahlen*, 1988.

Edwards, H. M. (1989) Kronecker's views on the foundations of mathematics. In Rowe, D. E. and McCleary, J. (eds.), *The History of Modern Mathematics; Volume 1: Ideas and Their Reception*, pp. 67–77. Academic Press.

Eén, N. and Sörensson, N. (2003) An extensible SAT-solver. In Giunchiglia, E. and Tacchella, A. (eds.), *Theory and Applications of Satisfiability Testing: 6th International Conference SAT 2003*, Volume 2919 of *Lecture Notes in Computer Science*, pp. 502–518. Springer-Verlag.

Eklof, P. (1973) Lefschetz's principle and local functors. *Proceedings of the AMS*, **37**, 333–339.

Elcock, E. W. (1991) Absys, the first logic-programming language: a view of the inevitability of logic programming. See Lassez and Plotkin (1991), pp. 701–721.

Enderton, H. B. (1972) *A Mathematical Introduction to Logic*. Academic Press.

Engel, P. (1991) *The Norm of Truth: an Introduction to the Philosophy of Logic*. Harvester Wheatsheaf. Translated from the French *La norme du vrai* by Miriam Kochan and Pascal Engel.

Engeler, E. (1993) *Foundations of Mathematics: Questions of Analysis, Geometry and Algorithmics*. Springer-Verlag. Original German edition *Metamathematik der Elementarmathematik* in the *Series Hochschultext*.

Engelking, R. (1989) *General Topology*, Volume 6 of *Sigma Series in Pure Mathematics*. Heldermann Verlag.

Ershov, Y. L., Lavrov, I. A., Taimanov, A. D. and Taitslin, M. A. (1965) Elementary theories. *Russian Mathematical Surveys*, **20**, 35–105.

Estermann, T. (1956) On the fundamental theorem of algebra. *Journal of the London Mathematical Society*, **31**, 238–240.

Evans, T. (1951) On multiplicative systems defined by generators and relations I: normal form theorems. *Proceedings of the Cambridge Philosophical Society*, **47**, 637–649.

Fages, F. (1984) Associative-commutative unification. See Shostak (1984a), pp. 194–208.

Fages, F. and Huet, G. (1986) Complete sets of unifiers and matchers in equational theories. *Theoretical Computer Science*, **43**, 189–200.

Faugère, J.-C. (2002) A new efficient algorithm for computing Gröbner bases without reduction to zero. In Mora, T. (ed.), *Proceedings of the 2002 International Symposium on Symbolic and Algebraic Computation (ISSAC)*, Lille, France, pp. 75–83, ACM.

Fay, M. (1979) First order unification in an equational theory. In *Proceedings of the 4th Workshop on Automated Deduction*, Austin, Texas, pp. 161–167. Academic Press.

Feferman, S. (1960) Arithmetization of metamathematics in a general setting. *Fundamenta Mathematicae*, **49**, 35–92.

Feferman, S. (1962) Transfinite recursive progressions of axiomatic theories. *Journal of Symbolic Logic*, **27**, 259–316.

Feferman, S. (1968) Lectures on proof theory. In Löb, M. H. (ed.), *Proceedings of the Summer School in Logic*, Volume 70 of *Lecture Notes in Mathematics*. Springer-Verlag.

Feferman, S. (1974) Applications of many-sorted interpolation theorems. In Henkin, L. (ed.), *Tarski Symposium: Proceedings of an International Symposium to Honor Alfred Tarski*, Volume XXV of *Proceedings of Symposia in Pure Mathematics*, pp. 205–223. American Mathematical Society.

Feferman, S. (1991) Reflecting on incompleteness. *Journal of Symbolic Logic*, **56**, 1–49.

Feferman, S. and Vaught, R. L. (1959) The first-order properties of algebraic systems. *Fundamenta Mathematicae*, **47**, 57–103.

Feigenbaum, E. A. and Feldman, J. (eds.) (1995) *Computers & Thought*. AAAI Press/MIT Press.

Fermueller, C., Leitsch, A., Tammet, T. and Zamov, N. (1993) *Resolution Methods for the Decision Problem*, Volume 679 of *Lecture Notes in Computer Science*. Springer-Verlag.

Ferrante, J. and Rackoff, C. (1975) A decision procedure for the first order theory of real arithmetic with order. *SIAM Journal on Computing*, **4**, 69–76.

Ferreira, M. C. F. and Zantema, H. (1995) Well-foundedness of term orderings. In Dershowitz, N. (ed.), *Conditional Term Rewriting Systems, Proceedings of the Fourth International Workshop CTRS-94*, Volume 968 of *Lecture Notes in Computer Science*, pp. 106–123. Springer-Verlag.

Fischer, M. J. and Rabin, M. O. (1974) Super-exponential complexity of Presburger arithmetic. In *SIAMAMS: Complexity of Computation: Proceedings of a Symposium in Applied Mathematics of the American Mathematical Society and the Society for Industrial and Applied Mathematics*, pp. 27–41. American Mathematical Society.

Fitch, F. B. (1952) *Symbolic Logic: an Introduction*. The Ronald Press Company.

Fitting, M. (1990) *First-Order Logic and Automated Theorem Proving*. Graduate Texts in Computer Science. Springer-Verlag. Second edition 1996.

Fitting, M. (1999) Introduction [to tableaux]. In D'Agostino, M., Gabbay, D. M., Hähnle, R. and Posegga, J. (eds.), *Handbook of Tableau Methods*, pp. 1–43. Kluwer Academic Publishers.

Flanagan, C., Joshi, R., Ou, X. and Saxe, J. B. (2003) Theorem proving using lazy proof explication. See Hunt and Somenzi (2003), pp. 355–367.

Fleuriot, J. (2001) *A Combination of Geometry Theorem Proving and Nonstandard Analysis with Application to Newton's Principia*. Distinguished dissertations. Springer-Verlag. Revised version of author's Ph.D. thesis.

Floyd, R. W. (1967) Assigning meanings to programs. In *Proceedings of AMS Symposia in Applied Mathematics, 19: Mathematical Aspects of Computer Science*, pp. 19–32. American Mathematical Society.

Fontaine, P. (2004) *Techniques for Verification of Concurrent Systems with Invariants*. Ph.D. thesis, Institut Montefiore, Université de Liège.

Ford, J. and Shankar, N. (2002) Formal verification of a combined decision procedure. See Voronkov (2002), pp. 347–362.

Forster, T. (2003) *Logic, Induction and Sets*, Volume 56 of *London Mathematical Society Student Texts*. Cambridge University Press.

Fourier, J.-B. J. (1826) Solution d'une question particulière du calcul des inégalités. In *Nouveau bulletin des sciences par la société philomatique de Paris*, pp. 99–100. Méquignon-Marvis.

Franzén, T. (2002) *Inexhaustibility*, Volume 16 of *ASL Lecture Notes in Logic*. Association for Symbolic Logic/A. K. Peters.

Franzén, T. (2005) *Gödel's Theorem. An Incomplete Guide to its Use and Abuse*. A. K. Peters.

Frege, G. (1879) *Begriffsschrift, eine der arithmetischen nachgebildete Formelsprache des reinen Denkens*. Louis Nebert, Halle. English translation, 'Begriffsschrift, a formula language, modeled upon that of arithmetic, for pure thought' in Van Heijenoort (1967), pp. 1–82.

Frege, G. (1893) *Grundgesetze der Arithmetik begriffsschrift abgeleitet*. Jena. Partial English translation by Montgomery Furth in *The Basic Laws of Arithmetic. Exposition of the System*, University of California Press, 1964.

Friedmann, H. (1976) Systems of second order arithmetic with restricted induction, I, II (abstracts). *Journal of Symbolic Logic*, **41**, 193–220.

Fuchs, D. (1988) *Cooperation Between Top-down and Bottom-up Theorem Provers by Subgoal Clause Transfer*. Technical Report SR-98-01, University of Kaiserslautern.

Furbach, U. and Shankar, N. (eds.) (2006) *Proceedings of the Third International Joint Conference, IJCAR 2006*, Volume 4130 of *Lecture Notes in Computer Science*. Springer-Verlag.

Gabbay, D. M., Hogger, C. J. and Robinson, J. A. (eds.) (1993) *Handbook of Logic in Artificial Intelligence and Logic Programming, volume 1 (logical foundations)*. Oxford University Press.

Gandy, R. (1980) Church's thesis and principles for mechanisms. In Barwise, J., Keistes, H. J. and Kuren, K. (eds.), *The Kleene Symposium*, Volume 101 of *Studies in Logic and the Foundations of Mathematics*, pp. 123–148. North-Holland.

Gandy, R. (1988) The confluence of ideas in 1936. In Herken, R. (ed.), *The Universal Turing Machine: a Half-Century Survey*, pp. 55–111. Oxford University Press.

Ganzinger, H. (2002) Shostak light. See Voronkov (2002), pp. 332–346.

Gårding, L. (1997) *Some Points of Analysis and Their History*, Volume 11 of *University Lecture Series*. American Mathematical Society/Higher Education Press.

Gardner, M. (1958) *Logic Machines and Diagrams*. McGraw-Hill.

Gardner, M. (1975) Mathematical games: six sensational discoveries that somehow or another have escaped public notice. *Scientific American*, **232**(4), 127–131.

Garey, M. R. and Johnson, D. S. (1979) *Computers and Intractibility: a Guide to the Theory of NP-Completeness*. Freeman and Company.

Garnier, R. and Taylor, J. (1996) *100% Mathematical Proof*. Wiley.

Gelerntner, H. (1959) Realization of a geometry-theorem proving machine. In *Proceedings of the International Conference on Information Processing, UNESCO House*, pp. 273–282. Also appears in Siekmann and Wrightson (1983a), pp. 99–117 and in Feigenbaum and Feldman (1995), pp. 134–152.

Gentzen, G. (1935) Untersuchungen über das logische Schliessen. *Mathematische Zeitschrift*, **39**, 176–210, 405–431. This was Gentzen's Inaugural Dissertation at Göttingen. English translation, 'Investigations into Logical Deduction', in Szabo (1969), p. 68–131.

Geser, A. (1990) *Relative Termination*. Ph.D. thesis, University of Passau.

Giese, M. (2001) Incremental closure of free variable tableaux. In Goré, R., Leitsch, A. and Nipkow, T. (eds.), *Proceedings of the International Joint Conference on Automated Reasoning*, Volume 2083 of *Lecture Notes in Computer Science*, pp. 545–560. Springer-Verlag.

Gilmore, P. C. (1960) A proof method for quantification theory: its justification and realization. *IBM Journal of Research and Development*, **4**, 28–35.

Girard, J.-Y. (1987) *Proof Theory and Logical Complexity, volume 1*. Studies in proof theory. Bibliopolis.

Girard, J.-Y., Lafont, Y. and Taylor, P. (1989) *Proofs and Types*, Volume 7 of *Cambridge Tracts in Theoretical Computer Science*. Cambridge University Press.

Gödel, K. (1930) Die Vollständigkeit der Axiome des logischen Funktionenkalküls. *Monatshefte für Mathematik und Physik*, **37**, 349–360. English translation 'The completeness of the axioms of the functional calculus of logic' in Van Heijenoort (1967), pp. 582–591.

Gödel, K. (1931) Über formal unentscheidbare Sätze der Principia Mathematica und verwandter Systeme, I. *Monatshefte für Mathematik und Physik*, **38**, 173–198. English translation, 'On formally undecidable propositions of Principia Mathematica and related systems, I', in Van Heijenoort (1967), pp. 592–618 and Davis (1965), pp. 4–38.

Gödel, K. (1932) Ein Spezialfall des Entscheidungsproblems der theoretischen Logic. *Ergebnisse eines mathematischen Kolloquiums*, **2**, 27–28.

Gödel, K. (1938) The consistency of the axiom of choice and the generalized continuum hypothesis. *Proceedings of the National Academy of Sciences*, **24**, 556–557.

Goel, A., Sajid, K., Zhou, H., Aziz, A. and Singhal, V. (1998) BDD based procedures for a theory of equality with uninterpreted functions. In Hu, A. and Vardi, M. (eds.), *Computer Aided Verification, 10th International Conference, CAV '98*, Volume 1427 of *Lecture Notes in Computer Science*, pp. 244–255. Springer-Verlag.

Goldberg, E. and Novikov, Y. (2002) BerkMin: a fast and robust Sat-solver. In Kloos, C. D. and Franca, J. D. (eds.), *Design, Automation and Test in Europe*

Conference and Exhibition (DATE 2002), Paris, France, pp. 142–149. IEEE Computer Society Press.

Goldfarb, W. D. (1984) The unsolvability of the Gödel class with identity. *Journal of Symbolic Logic*, **49**, 1237–1252.

Gonthier, G. (2005) A computer-checked proof of the four colour theorem. Available at `research.microsoft.com/~gonthier/4colproof.pdf`.

Goodstein, R. L. (1957) *Recursive Number Theory*. Studies in Logic and the Foundations of Mathematics. North-Holland.

Goodstein, R. L. (1960) *Recursive Analysis*. Studies in Logic and the Foundations of Mathematics. North-Holland.

Goodstein, R. L. (1971) *Development of Mathematical Logic*. Logos Press.

Gordon, M. J. C. (1982) Representing a logic in the LCF metalanguage. In Néel, D. (ed.), *Tools and Notions for Program Construction: an Advanced Course*, pp. 163–185. Cambridge University Press.

Gordon, M. J. C. (1988) *Programming Language Theory and its Implementation: Applicative and Imperative Paradigms*. Prentice-Hall International Series in Computer Science. Prentice-Hall.

Gordon, M. J. C. (2000) From LCF to HOL: a short history. In Plotkin, G., Stirling, C. and Tofte, M. (eds.), *Proof, Language, and Interaction: Essays in Honour of Robin Milner*. MIT Press.

Gordon, M. J. C., Hale, R., Herbert, J., Wright, J. v. and Wong, W. (1994) Proof checking for the HOL system. In Basin, D., Giunchiglia, F. and Kaufmann, M. (eds.), *12th International Conference on Automated Deduction, Workshop 1A: Correctness and Metatheoretic Extensibility of Automated Reasoning Systems*, INRIA Lorraine, pp. 49–50. Available as Technical Report number 9405-10 from IRST (Istituto per la Ricerca Scientifica e Tecnologia), Trento, Italy.

Gordon, M. J. C. and Melham, T. F. (1993) *Introduction to HOL: a Theorem Proving Environment for Higher Order Logic*. Cambridge University Press.

Gordon, M. J. C., Milner, R. and Wadsworth, C. P. (1979) *Edinburgh LCF: a Mechanised Logic of Computation*, Volume 78 of *Lecture Notes in Computer Science*. Springer-Verlag.

Goubault-Larrecq, J. and Mackie, I. (1997) *Proof Theory and Automated Deduction*, Volume 6 of *Applied Logic Series*. Kluwer.

Grädel, E., Kolaitis, P. G. and Vardi, M. Y. (1997) On the decision problem for two-variable first-order logic. *Bulletin of Symbolic Logic*, **3**(1), 53–69.

Graham, R. L., Rothschild, B. L. and Spencer, J. H. (1980) *Ramsey Theory*. Wiley.

Grayling, A. C. (1990) *An Introduction to Philosophical Logic*. Duckworth. First edition published by Harvester Press, 1982.

Green, C. (1969) Applications of theorem proving to problem solving. In *Proceedings of the International Joint Conference on Artificial Intelligence*, Washington DC, pp. 219–239. William Kaufman.

Grigor'ev, D. (1988) The complexity of deciding Tarski algebra. *Journal of Symbolic Computation*, **5**, 65–108.

Groote, J. F. (2000) The propositional formula checker Heerhugo. *Journal of Automated Reasoning*, **24**, 101–125.

Grothendieck, A. (1964) *Éléments de Géométrie Algébraique IV: Étude locale de schémas et des morphismes de schémas*, Volume 20 of *Publications Mathématiques*. IHES.

Grötschel, M., Lovász, L. and Schrijver, A. (1993) *Geometric algorithms and combinatorial optimization*. Springer-Verlag.

Guard, J. R., Oglesby, F. C., Bennett, J. H. and Settle, L. G. (1969) Semi-automated mathematics. *Journal of the ACM*, **16**, 49–62.

Gurevič, R. (1985) Equational theory of positive numbers with exponentiation. *Proceedings of the American Mathematical Society*, **94**, 135–141.

Gurevič, R. (1990) Equational theory of positive numbers with exponentiation is not finitely axiomatizable. *Annals of Pure and Applied Logic*, **49**, 1–30.

Haack, S. (1978) *Philosophy of Logics*. Cambridge University Press.

Hales, T. C. (2006) Introduction to the Flyspeck project. In Coquand, T., Lombardi, H. and Roy, M.-F. (eds.), *Mathematics, Algorithms, Proofs*, Volume 05021 of *Dagstuhl Seminar Proceedings*. Internationales Begegnungs- und Forschungszentrum füer Informatik (IBFI), Schloss Dagstuhl, Germany.

Halmos, P. R. (1963) *Lectures on Boolean algebras*, Volume 1 of *Van Nostrand Mathematical Studies*. Van Nostrand.

Halmos, P. R. and Givant, S. (1998) *Logic as Algebra*. Dolciani Mathematical Expositions. Mathematical Association of America.

Halpern, J. Y. (1991) Presburger arithmetic with unary predicates is Π_1^1-complete. *Journal of Symbolic Logic*, **56**, 637–642.

Harrison, J. (1995) *Metatheory and Reflection in Theorem Proving: a Survey and Critique*. Technical Report CRC-053, SRI Cambridge. Available on the Web as www.cl.cam.ac.uk/users/jrh/papers/reflect.ps.gz.

Harrison, J. (1996a) A Mizar mode for HOL. See Wright, Grundy and Harrison (1996), pp. 203–220.

Harrison, J. (1996b) Optimizing proof search in model elimination. In McRobbie, M. A. and Slaney, J. K. (eds.), *13th International Conference on Automated Deduction*, Volume 1104 of *Lecture Notes in Computer Science*, pp. 313–327. Springer-Verlag.

Harrison, J. (1996c) Proof style. In Giménez, E. and Paulin-Mohring, C. (eds.), *Types for Proofs and Programs: International Workshop TYPES'96*, Volume 1512 of *Lecture Notes in Computer Science*, pp. 154–172. Springer-Verlag.

Harrison, J. (1998) *Theorem Proving with the Real Numbers*. Springer-Verlag. Revised version of author's Ph.D. thesis.

Harrison, J. (2000) Formal verification of floating point trigonometric functions. In Hunt, W. A. and Johnson, S. D. (eds.), *Formal Methods in Computer-Aided Design: Third International Conference FMCAD 2000*, Volume 1954 of *Lecture Notes in Computer Science*, pp. 217–233. Springer-Verlag.

Harrison, J. and Théry, L. (1998) A sceptic's approach to combining HOL and Maple. *Journal of Automated Reasoning*, **21**, 279–294.

Harrop, R. (1958) On the existence of finite models and decision procedures for propositional calculi. *Proceedings of the Cambridge Philosophical Society*, **54**, 1–13.

Harvey, W. and Stuckey, P. (1997) A unit two variable per inequality integer constraint solver for constraint logic programming. *Australian Computer Science Communications*, **19**, 102–111.

Hayes, P. J. (1973) Computation and deduction. In *Proceedings of the 2nd Mathematical Foundations of Computer Science (MFCS) Symposium*, pp. 105–118. Czechoslovak Academy of Sciences.

Heawood, P. J. (1890) Map-colour theorem. *Quarterly Journal of Pure and Applied Mathematics*, **24**, 332–338. Reprinted in Biggs, Lloyd and Wilson (1976).

Henkin, L. (1949) The completeness of the first-order functional calculus. *Journal of Symbolic Logic*, **14**, 159–166.

Henkin, L. (1952) A problem concerning provability. *Journal of Symbolic Logic*, **17**, 160.

Henschen, L. and Wos, L. (1974) Unit refutations and Horn sets. *Journal of the ACM*, **21**, 590–605.

Herbrand, J. (1930) Recherches sur la théorie de la démonstration. *Traveaux de la Société des Sciences et de Lettres de Varsovie, Classe III*, **33**, 33–160. English translation 'Investigations in proof theory: the properties of true propositions' in Van Heijenoort (1967), pages 525–581.

Hermann, G. (1926) Die Frage der endlich vielen Schritte in der Theorie der Polynomialideale. *Mathematische Annalen*, **95**, 736–788.

Hertz, H. (1894) *Prinzipien der Mechanik*. Johann Ambrosius Barth.

Hilbert, D. (1899) *Grundlagen der Geometrie*. Teubner. English translation *Foundations of Geometry* published in 1902 by Open Court, Chicago.

Hilbert, D. (1905) Über die Grundlagen der Logik und der Arithmetik. In *Verhandlungen des dritten internationalen Mathematiker-Kongresses in Heidelberg*, pp. 174–185. Teubner. English translation 'On the foundations of logic and arithmetic' in Van Heijenoort (1967), pp. 129–138.

Hilbert, D. (1922) Die logischen Grundlagen der Mathematik. *Mathematische Annalen*, **88**, 151–165.

Hilbert, D. and Ackermann, W. (1950) *Principles of Mathematical Logic*. Chelsea. Translation of *Grundzüge der theoretischen Logik*, 2nd edition (1938; first edition 1928); translated by Lewis M. Hammond, George G. Leckie and F. Steinhardt; edited with notes by Robert E. Luce.

Hilbert, D. and Bernays, P. (1939) *Grundlagen der Mathematik, vol. 2*. Springer-Verlag.

Hill, P. M. and Lloyd, J. W. (1994) *The Gödel Programming Language*. MIT Press.

Hindley, J. R. (1964) *The Church–Rosser Property and a Result in Combinatory Logic*. Ph.D. thesis, University of Newcastle-upon-Tyne.

Hindley, J. R. and Seldin, J. P. (1986) *Introduction to Combinators and λ-Calculus*, Volume 1 of *London Mathematical Society Student Texts*. Cambridge University Press.

Hintikka, J. (1955) Form and content in quantification theory. *Acta Philosophica Fennica – Two Papers on Symbolic Logic*, **8**, 8–55.

Hintikka, J. (1969) *The Philosophy of Mathematics*. Oxford Readings in Philosophy. Oxford University Press.

Hintikka, J. (1996) *The Principles of Mathematics Revisited*. Cambridge University Press.

Hoare, C. A. R. (1969) An axiomatic basis for computer programming. *Communications of the ACM*, **12**, 576–580, 583.

Hodges, A. (1983) *Alan Turing: the Enigma*. Burnett Books/Hutchinson.

Hodges, W. (1977) *Logic*. Penguin.

Hodges, W. (1993a) Logical features of Horn clauses. See Gabbay, Hogger and Robinson (1993), pp. 449–503.

Hodges, W. (1993b) *Model Theory*, Volume 42 of *Encyclopedia of Mathematics and its Applications*. Cambridge University Press.

Hofbauer, D. and Lautemann, C. (1989) Termination proofs and the length of derivations. In Dershowitz, N. (ed.), *Proceedings of the 3rd International Conference on Rewriting Techniques and Applications*, Volume 355 of *Lecture Notes in Computer Science*, pp. 167–177. Springer-Verlag.

Hong, H. (1990) *Improvements in CAD-based Quantifier Elimination.* Ph.D. thesis, Ohio State University.

Hooker, J. N. (1988) A quantitative approach to logical inference. *Decision Support Systems*, **4**, 45–69.

Hörmander, L. (1983) *The Analysis of Linear Partial Differential Operators II*, Volume 257 of *Grundlehren der mathematischen Wissenschaften.* Springer-Verlag.

Hsiang, J. (1985) Refutational theorem proving using term-rewriting systems. *Artificial Intelligence*, **25**, 255–300.

Hubert, E. (2001) Notes on triangular sets and triangular-decomposition algorithms (I and II). In Langar, U. and Winkler, F. (eds.), *Symbolic and Numerical Scientific Computing*, Volume 2630 of *Lecture Notes in Computer Science*, pp. 1–87. Springer-Verlag.

Huet, G. (1980) Confluent reductions: abstract properties and applications to term rewriting systems. *Journal of the ACM*, **27**, 797–821.

Huet, G. (1981) A complete proof of correctness of the Knuth–Bendix completion procedure. *Journal of Computer and System Sciences*, **23**, 11–21.

Huet, G. (1986) Formal structures for computation and deduction. Course notes, Carnegie-Mellon University; available at `pauillac.inria.fr/~huet/PUBLIC/Formal_Structures.ps.gz`.

Huet, G. and Lévy, J.-J. (1991) Computations in orthogonal rewriting systems, I and II. See Lassez and Plotkin (1991), pp. 395–443.

Huet, G. and Oppen, D. C. (1980) Equations and rewrite rules: a survey. In Book, R. V. (ed.), *Formal Language Theory: Perspectives and Open Problems*, pp. 349–405. Academic Press.

Hughes, G. E. and Cresswell, M. J. (1996) *A New Introduction to Modal Logic.* Routledge & Kegan Paul.

Hughes, J. (1995) The design of a pretty-printing library. In Jeuring, J. and Meijer, E. (eds.), *Advanced Functional Programming*, Volume 925 of *Lecture Notes in Computer Science*, pp. 53–96. Springer-Verlag.

Hullot, J. M. (1980) Canonical forms and unification. See Bibel and Kowalski (1980), pp. 318–334.

Hunt, W. A. and Somenzi, F. (eds.) (2003) *Computer Aided Verification, 15th International Conference, CAV 2003*, Volume 2725 of *Lecture Notes in Computer Science.* Springer-Verlag.

Hurd, A. E. and Loeb, P. A. (1985) *An Introduction to Nonstandard Real Analysis.* Academic Press.

Hurd, J. (1999) Integrating Gandalf and HOL. See Bertot, Dowek, Hirschowitz, Paulin and Théry (1999), pp. 311–321.

Hurd, J. (2001) *Formal Verification of Probabilistic Algorithms.* Ph.D. thesis, University of Cambridge.

Huskey, V. R. and Huskey, H. D. (1980) Lady Lovelace and Charles Babbage. *Annals in the History of Computing*, **2**, 229–329.

Husserl, E. (1900) *Logische Untersuchungen.* Halle. English translation by J. N. Findlay: *Logical Investigations*, published by the Humanities Press, NY, 1970. Based on revised, 1913 Halle edition.

Huth, M. and Ryan, M. (1999) *Logic in Computer Science: Modelling and Reasoning about Systems.* Cambridge University Press.

Jacobs, S. and Waldmann, U. (2005) Comparing instance generation methods for automated reasoning. In Beckert, B. (ed.), *Automated Reasoning with Analytic*

Tableaux and Related Methods, TABLEAUX 2005, Volume 3702 of *Lecture Notes in Computer Science*, pp. 153–168. Springer-Verlag.

Jacobson, N. (1989) *Basic Algebra I* (2nd ed.). W. H. Freeman.

Jaffar, J., Maher, M. J., Stuckey, P. J. and Yap, R. H. C. (1994) Beyond finite domains. In Borning, A. (ed.), *Principles and Practice of Constraint Programming, Second International Workshop, PPCP'94*, Volume 874 of *Lecture Notes in Computer Science*, pp. 86–94. Springer-Verlag.

Jaskowski, S. (1934) On the rules of supposition in formal logic. *Studia Logica*, **1**, 5–32.

Jech, T. J. (1973) *The Axiom of Choice*, Volume 75 of *Studies in Logic and the Foundations of Mathematics*. North-Holland.

Jensen, K. and Wirth, N. (1974) *Pascal User Manual and Report*. Springer-Verlag.

Jereslow, R. G. (1988) Computation-oriented reductions of predicate to propositional logic. *Decision Support Systems*, **4**, 183–197.

Jevons, W. S. (1870) On the mechanical performance of logical inference. *Philosophical Transactions of the Royal Society*, **160**, 497–518.

Johnstone, P. T. (1987) *Notes on Logic and Set Theory*. Cambridge University Press.

Jones, J. P. and Matiyasevich, Y. (1984) Register machine proof of the theorem on exponential diophantine representation. *Journal of Symbolic Logic*, **49**, 818–829.

Kahr, A. S., Moore, E. F. and Wang, H. (1962) Entscheidungsproblem reduced to the $\forall\exists\forall$ case. *Proceedings of the National Academy of Sciences of the United States of America*, **48**, 365–377.

Kaivola, R. and Aagaard, M. D. (2000) Divider circuit verification with model checking and theorem proving. In Aagaard, M. and Harrison, J. (eds.), *Theorem Proving in Higher Order Logics: 13th International Conference, TPHOLs 2000*, Volume 1869 of *Lecture Notes in Computer Science*, pp. 338–355. Springer-Verlag.

Kaivola, R. and Kohatsu, K. (2001) Proof engineering in the large: formal verification of the Pentium (R) 4 floating-point divider. In Margaria, T. and Melham, T. (eds.), *11th IFIP WG 10.5 Advanced Research Working Conference, CHARME 2001*, Volume 2144 of *Lecture Notes in Computer Science*, pp. 196–211. Springer-Verlag.

Kalmár, L. (1935) Über die Axiomatisierbarkeit des Aussagenkalküls. *Acta Scientiarum Mathematicarum (Szeged)*, **7**, 222–243.

Kalmár, L. (1936) Zurückführung des Entscheidungsproblems auf den Fall von Formeln mit einer einzigen binären. *Compositio Mathematica*, **4**, 137–144.

Kandri-Rody, A. and Kapur, D. (1984) Algorithms for computing Gröbner bases of polynomial ideals over various Euclidean rings. In Fitch, J. (ed.), *EUROSAM 84: International Symposium on Symbolic and Algebraic Computation*, Volume 174 of *Lecture Notes in Computer Science*, pp. 195–206. Springer-Verlag.

Kandri-Rody, A., Kapur, D. and Narendran, P. (1985) An ideal-theoretic approach to word problems and unification problems over finitely presented commutative algebras. In Jouannaud, J.-P. (ed.), *Rewriting Techniques and Applications*, Volume 202 of *Lecture Notes in Computer Science*, France, pp. 345–364. Springer-Verlag.

Kapur, D. (1988) A refutational approach to geometry theorem proving. *Artificial Intelligence*, **37**, 61–93.

Kapur, D. (1998) Automated geometric reasoning: Dixon resultants, Gröbner bases, and characteristic sets. In Wang, D. (ed.), *Automated Deduction in Geometry*, Volume 1360 of *Lecture Notes in Computer Science*. Springer-Verlag.

Kapur, D. and Zhang, H. (1991) A case study of the completion procedure: proving ring commutativity problems. See Lassez and Plotkin (1991), pp. 360–394.

Karmarkar, N. (1984) A new polynomial-time algorithm for linear programming. *Combinatorica*, **4**, 373–395.

Kaufmann, M., Manolios, P. and Moore, J. S. (2000) *Computer-Aided Reasoning: an Approach*. Kluwer.

Keisler, H. J. (1996) *Mathematical Logic and Computability*. McGraw-Hill.

Kelley, J. L. (1975) *General Topology*, Volume 27 of *Graduate Texts in Mathematics*. Springer-Verlag. First published by D. van Nostrand in 1955.

Kempe, A. B. (1879) On the geographical problem of the four colours. *American Journal of Mathematics*, **2**, 193–200. Reprinted in Biggs, Lloyd and Wilson (1976).

Khachian, L. G. (1979) A polynomial algorithm in linear programming. *Soviet Mathematics Doklady*, **20**, 191–194.

Kirkpatrick, S. and Selman, B. (1994) Critical behavior in the satisfiability of random Boolean expressions. *Science*, **264**, 1297–1301.

Kirousis, L. M., Kranakis, E., Krizanc, D. and Stamatiou, Y. C. (1998) Approximating the unsatisfiability threshold of random formulas. *Random Structures and Algorithms*, **12**, 253–269.

Kleene, S. C. (1952) *Introduction to Metamathematics*. North-Holland.

Klop, J. W. (1992) Term rewriting systems. See Abramsky, Gabbay and Maibaum (1992), pp. 1–116.

Knaster, B. (1928) Un théorème sur les fonctions d'ensembles. *Annales de la Société Polonaise de Mathématique*, **6**, 133–134.

Kneale, W. and Kneale, M. (1962) *The Development of Logic*. Clarendon Press.

Kneebone, G. T. (1963) *Mathematical Logic and the Foundations of Mathematics: an Introductory Survey*. D. Van Nostrand.

Knoblock, T. and Constable, R. (1986) Formalized metareasoning in type theory. In *Proceedings of the First Annual Symposium on Logic in Computer Science, Cambridge, MA, USA*, pp. 237–248. IEEE Computer Society Press.

Knuth, D. E. (1969) *The Art of Computer Programming; Volume 2: Seminumerical Algorithms*. Addison-Wesley Series in Computer Science and Information processing. Addison-Wesley.

Knuth, D. E. (1974) Computer science and its relation to mathematics. *The American Mathematical Monthly*, **81**, 323–343. Reprinted in Knuth (1996), pp. 5–29.

Knuth, D. E. (1996) *Selected Papers on Computer Science*. CSLI Publications. Cambridge University Press.

Knuth, D. E. and Bendix, P. (1970) Simple word problems in universal algebras. In Leech, J. (ed.), *Computational Problems in Abstract Algebra*. Pergamon Press.

Koren, I. (1992) *Computer Arithmetic Algorithms*. Prentice-Hall.

Korf, R. E. (1985) Depth-first iterative-deepening: an optimal admissible tree search. *Artificial Intelligence*, **27**, 97–109.

Kowalski, R. A. (1970a) The case for using equality axioms in automatic demonstration. See Laudet, Lacombe, Nolin and Schützenberger (1970), pp. 112–127.

Kowalski, R. A. (1970b) *Studies in the Completeness and Efficiency of Theorem-proving by Resolution*. Ph.D. thesis, University of Edinburgh.

Kowalski, R. A. (1974) Predicate logic as a programming language. In Rosenfeld, J. L. (ed.), *Information Processing 74, Proceedings of IFIP Congress 74*, pp. 569–574. North-Holland.

Kowalski, R. A. (1975) A proof procedure using connection graphs. *Journal of the ACM*, **22**, 572–595.

Kowalski, R. A. and Kuehner, D. (1971) Linear resolution with selection function. *Artificial Intelligence*, **2**, 227–260.

Kreisel, G. (1956) Some uses of metamathematics. *British Journal for the Philosophy of Science*, **7**, 161–173.

Kreisel, G. (1958a) Hilbert's programme. *Dialectica*, **12**, 346–372. Revised version in Benacerraf and Putnam (1983).

Kreisel, G. (1958b) Mathematical significance of consistency proofs. *Journal of Symbolic Logic*, **23**, 155–182.

Kreisel, G. and Krivine, J.-L. (1971) *Elements of Mathematical Logic: Model Theory* (Revised second edn.). *Studies in Logic and the Foundations of Mathematics*. North-Holland. First edition 1967. Translation of the French *Eléments de logique mathématique, théorie des modeles* published by Dunod, Paris in 1964.

Kreisel, G. and Lévy, A. (1968) Reflection principles and their use for establishing the complexity of axiomatic systems. *Zeitschrift für mathematische Logik und Grundlagen der Mathematik*, **14**, 97–142.

Kroening, D. and Strichman, O. (2008) *Decision Procedures: an Algorithmic Point of View*. Springer-Verlag.

Kropf, T. (1999) *Introduction to Formal Hardware Verification*. Springer-Verlag.

Krstić, S. and Conchon, S. (2003) Canonization for disjoint unions of theories. See Baader (2003), pp. 197–211.

Krstić, S. and Goel, A. (2007) Architecting solvers for SAT modulo theories: Nelson–Oppen with DPLL. In Konev, B. and Wolter, F. (eds.), *Frontiers of Combining Systems, 6th International Symposium, FroCoS 2007*, Volume 4720 of *Lecture Notes in Computer Science*, pp. 1–27. Springer-Verlag.

Krstić, S., Goel, A., Grundy, J. and Tinelli, C. (2007) Combined satisfiability modulo parametric theories. In Grumberg, O. and Huth, M. (eds.), *Proceedings of the 13th International Conference on Tools and Algorithms for the Construction and Analysis of Systems, TACAS 2007*, Volume 4424 of *Lecture Notes in Computer Science*, pp. 618–631. Springer-Verlag.

Kruskal, J. B. (1960) Well-quasi-ordering, the tree theorem, and Vazsonyi's conjecture. *Transactions of the American Mathematical Society*, **95**, 210–225.

Kuncak, V., Nguyen, H. H. and Rinard, M. C. (2005) An algorithm for deciding BAPA: Boolean algebra with Presburger arithmetic. See Nieuwenhuis (2005), pp. 260–277.

Kunz, W. and Pradhan, D. K. (1994) Recursive learning: a new implication technique for efficient solutions to CAD problems – test, verification, and optimization. *IEEE Transactions on Computer-Aided Design of Integrated Circuits and Systems*, **13**, 1143–1157.

Lagarias, J. (1985) The $3x + 1$ problem and its generalizations. *The American Mathematical Monthly*, **92**, 3–23. Available on the Web as www.cecm.sfu.ca/organics/papers/lagarias/index.html.

Lahiri, S. K., Bryant, R. E., Goel, A. and Talupur, M. (2004) Revisiting positive equality. In Jensen, K. and Podelski, A. (eds.), *Tools and Algorithms for the Construction and Analysis of Systems (TACAS'04)*, Volume 2988 of *Lecture Notes in Computer Science*, pp. 1–15. Springer-Verlag.

Lahiri, S. K. and Musuvathi, M. (2005) *An Efficient Decision Procedure for UTVPI constraints*. Technical Report MSR-TR-2005-67, Microsoft Research.

Lakatos, I. (1976) *Proofs and Refutations: the Logic of Mathematical Discovery*. Cambridge University Press. Edited by John Worrall and Elie Zahar. Derived from Lakatos's Cambridge Ph.D. thesis; an earlier version was published in the *British Journal for the Philosophy of Science*, **14**.

Lakatos, I. (1980) Cauchy and the continuum: the significance of non-standard analysis for the history and philosophy of mathematics. In Worrall, J. and Currie, G. (eds.), *Mathematics, Science and Epistemology. Imre Lakatos: Philosophical Papers vol. 2*, pp. 43–60. Cambridge University Press.

Lam, C. W. H. (1990) How reliable is a computer-based proof? *The Mathematical Intelligencer*, **12**, 8–12.

Lang, S. (1994) *Algebra* (3rd edn.). Addison-Wesley.

Langford, C. H. (1927) Some theorems on deducibility. *Annals of Mathematics (2nd series)*, **28**, 16–40.

Lassez, J.-L. and Plotkin, G. (eds.) (1991) *Computational Logic: Essays in Honor of Alan Robinson*. MIT Press.

Laudet, M., Lacombe, D., Nolin, L. and Schützenberger, M. (eds.) (1970) *Symposium on Automatic Demonstration*, Volume 125 of *Lecture Notes in Mathematics*. Springer-Verlag.

Lazard, D. (1988) Quantifier elimination: optimal solution for two classical examples. *Journal of Symbolic Computation*, **5**, 261–266.

Lee, C. Y. (1959) Representation of switching circuits by binary-decision programs. *Bell System Technical Journal*, **38**, 985–999.

Leitsch, A. (1997) *The Resolution Calculus*. Springer-Verlag.

Lescanne, P. (1984) Term rewriting systems and algebra. See Shostak (1984a), pp. 166–174.

Leśniewski, S. (1929) Grunzüge eines neuen Systems der Grundlagen der Mathematik. *Fundamenta Mathematicae*, **14**, 1–81. English translation, 'Fundamentals of a new system of the foundations of mathematics' in Surma, Srzednicki, Barnett and Rickey (1992), vol. II, pp. 410–605.

Letz, R., Mayr, K. and Goller, C. (1994) Controlled integrations of the cut rule into connection tableau calculi. *Journal of Automated Reasoning*, **4**, 297–338.

Letz, R., Schumann, J., Bayerl, S. and Bibel, W. (1992) SETHEO: a high-performance theorem prover. *Journal of Automated Reasoning*, **8**, 183–212.

Letz, R. and Stenz, G. (2001) Model elimination and connection tableau procedures. In Robinson, A. and Voronkov, A. (eds.), *Handbook of Automated Reasoning, volume II*, pp. 2015–2114. MIT Press.

Levitt, J. R. (1999) *Formal Verification Techniques for Digital Systems*. Ph.D. thesis, Stanford University.

Lewis, H. R. (1978) Renaming a set of clauses as a Horn set. *Journal of the ACM*, **25**, 134–135.

Liberatore, P. (2000) On the complexity of choosing the branching literal in DPLL. *Artificial Intelligence*, **116**, 315–326.

Lifschitz, V. (1980) Semantical completeness theorems in logic and algebra. *Proceedings of the American Mathematical Society*, **79**, 89–96.

Lifschitz, V. (1986) *Mechanical Theorem Proving in the USSR: the Leningrad School*. Monograph Series on Soviet Union. Delphic Associates. See also 'What is the inverse method?', *Journal of Automated Reasoning*, **5**, 1–23, 1989.

Lindemann, F. (1882) Über die Zahl π. *Mathematische Annalen*, **120**, 213–225.

Lipshitz, L. (1978) The Diophantine problem for addition and divisibility. *Transactions of the American Mathematical Society*, **235**, 271–283.

Littlewood, J. E. (1941) Mathematical notes (14): every polynomial has a root. *Journal of the London Mathematical Society*, **16**, 95–98.

Lloyd, J. W. (1984) *Foundations of Logic Programming*. Springer-Verlag.

Löb, M. H. (1955) Solution of a problem of Leon Henkin. *Journal of Symbolic Logic*, **20**, 115–118.

Löchner, B. (2006) Things to know when implementing LPO. *International Journal on Artificial Intelligence Tools*, **15**, 53–80.

Locke, J. (1689) *An Essay concerning Human Understanding*. William Tegg, London.

Łojasiewicz, S. (1964) Triangulations of semi-analytic sets. *Annali della Scuola Normale Superiore di Pisa, ser. 3*, **18**, 449–474.

Loos, R. and Weispfenning, V. (1993) Applying linear quantifier elimination. *The Computer Journal*, **36**, 450–462.

Loveland, D. W. (1968) Mechanical theorem-proving by model elimination. *Journal of the ACM*, **15**, 236–251.

Loveland, D. W. (1970) A linear format for resolution. See Laudet, Lacombe, Nolin and Schützenberger (1970), pp. 147–162.

Loveland, D. W. (1978) *Automated Theorem Proving: a Logical Basis*. North-Holland.

Luckham, D. (1970) Refinements in resolution theory. See Laudet, Lacombe, Nolin and Schützenberger (1970), pp. 163–190.

Łukasiewicz, J. (1951) *Aristotle's Syllogistic from the Standpoint of Modern Formal Logic*. Clarendon Press.

Lyndon, R. C. (1959) An interpolation theorem in the predicate calculus. *Pacific Journal of Mathematics*, **9**, 192–142.

Mac Lane, S. (1936) Some interpretations of abstract linear dependence in terms of projective geometry. *American Journal of Mathematics*, **58**, 236–240.

Macintyre, A. (1981) The laws of exponentiation. In Berline, C., McAloon, K. and Ressayre, J.-P. (eds.), *Model Theory and Arithmetic*, Volume 890 of *Lecture Notes in Mathematics*, pp. 185–197. Springer-Verlag.

Macintyre, A. (1991) Model completeness. See Barwise and Keisler (1991), pp. 139–180.

Macintyre, A. and Wilkie, A. J. (1996) On the decidability of the real exponential field. In Odifreddi, P. (ed.), *Kreiseliana: About and Around Georg Kreisel*, pp. 441–467. A. K. Peters.

MacKenzie, D. (2001) *Mechanizing Proof: Computing, Risk and Trust*. MIT Press.

Madre, J. C. and Billon, J. P. (1988) Proving circuit correctness using formal comparison between expected and extracted behavior. In *Proceedings of the 25th ACM/IEEE Design Automation Conference (DAC '88)*, Los Alamitos, CA, pp. 205–210. IEEE Computer Society Press.

Mahboubi, A. and Pottier, L. (2002) Elimination des quantificateurs sur les réels en Coq. In *Journées Francophones des Langages Applicatifs (JFLA)*, available on the Web from `www.lix.polytechnique.fr/~assia/Publi/jfla02.ps`.

Maher, D. and Makowski, J. (2001) Literary evidence for Roman arithmetic with fractions. *Classical Philology*, **96**, 376–399.

Malik, S., Wang, A., Brayton, R. K. and Sangiovanni-Vincentelli, A. (1988) Logic verification using binary decision diagrams in a logic synthesis environment.

In *Proceedings of the International Conference on Computer-Aided Design*, pp. 6–9. IEEE.

Maltsev, A. (1936) Untersuchungen aus dem Gebiete der mathematischen Logik. *Matematicheskii Sbornik*, **43**, 323–336. English translation, 'Investigations in the Realm of Mathematical Logic', in Wells (1971), pp. 1–14.

Manzano, M. (1993) Introduction to many-sorted logic. In Meinke, K. and Tucker, J. V. (eds.), *Many-sorted Logic and its Applications*, pp. 3–86. John Wiley and Sons.

Marciszewski, W. and Murawski, R. (1995) *Mechanization of Reasoning in a Historical Perspective*, Volume 43 of *Poznań Studies in the Philosophy of the Sciences and the Humanities*. Rodopi.

Marcja, A. and Toffalori, C. (2003) *A Guide To Classical and Modern Model Theory*. Kluwer.

Marques-Silva, J. P. and Sakallah, K. A. (1996) GRASP – a new search algorithm for satisfiability. In *Proceedings of IEEE/ACM International Conference on Computer-Aided Design*, pp. 220–227, IEEE Computer Society Press.

Martelli, A. and Montanari, U. (1982) An efficient unification algorithm. *ACM Transactions on Programming Languages and Systems*, **4**, 258–282.

Martin, U. and Nipkow, T. (1990) Ordered rewriting and confluence. See Stickel (1990), pp. 366–380.

Maslov, S. J. (1964) An inverse method of establishing deducibility in classical predicate calculus. *Doklady Akademii Nauk*, **159**, 17–20.

Mates, B. (1972) *Elementary Logic* (2nd ed.). Oxford University Press.

Matijasevich, Y. V. (1993) *Hilbert's Tenth Problem*. MIT Press.

Matiyasevich, Y. V. (1970) Enumerable sets are Diophantine. *Soviet Mathematics Doklady*, **11**, 354–358.

Matiyasevich, Y. V. (1975) On metamathematical approach to proving theorems of discrete mathematics. *Seminars in Mathematics, Steklov Institute*, **49**, 31–50. In Russian. English translation in *Journal of Mathematical Sciences*, **10** (1978), 517–533.

Mauthner, F. (1901) *Beiträge zu einer Kritik der Sprache (3 vols)*. Berlin.

McCarthy, J. (1962) *LISP 1.5 Programmer's Manual*. MIT Press.

McCarthy, J. (1963) A basis for a mathematical theory of computation. In Braffort, P. and Hirshberg, D. (eds.), *Computer Programming and Formal Systems*, Studies in Logic and the Foundations of Mathematics, pp. 33–70. North-Holland.

McCune, W. (1997) Solution of the Robbins problem. *Journal of Automated Reasoning*, **19**, 263–276.

McCune, W. and Padmanabhan, R. (1996) *Automated Deduction in Equational Logic and Cubic Curves*, Volume 1095 of *Lecture Notes in Computer Science*. Springer-Verlag.

McKenzie, R. (1975) On spectra, and the negative solution of the decision problem for identities having a finite non-trivial model. *Journal of Symbolic Logic*, **40**, 186–196.

McKinsey, J. C. C. (1943) The decision problem for some classes of sentences without quantifiers. *Journal of Symbolic Logic*, **8**, 61–76.

McLaughlin, S. (2006) An interpretation of Isabelle/HOL in HOL Light. See Furbach and Shankar (2006), pp. 192–204.

McLaughlin, S. and Harrison, J. (2005) A proof-producing decision procedure for real arithmetic. See Nieuwenhuis (2005), pp. 295–314.

McMillan, K. L. (2003) Interpolation and SAT-based model checking. See Hunt and Somenzi (2003), pp. 1–13.

Mehlhorn, K. Nher, S., seel, M. *et al.* (1996) Checking geometric programs or verification of geometric structures. In *Proceedings of the 12th Annual Symposium on Computational Geometry (FCRC'96)*, Philadelphia, pp. 159–165. Association for Computing Machinery.

Mekler, A. H., Nelson, E. and Shelah, S. (1993) A variety with solvable, but not uniformly solvable, word problem. *Proceedings of the London Mathematical Society*, **66**, 223–256.

Melham, T. F. (1989) Automating recursive type definitions in higher order logic. In Birtwistle, G. and Subrahmanyam, P. A. (eds.), *Current Trends in Hardware Verification and Automated Theorem Proving*, pp. 341–386. Springer-Verlag.

Melham, T. F. (1991) A package for inductive relation definitions in HOL. See Archer, Joyce, Levitt and Windley (1991), pp. 350–357.

Melzer, B. and Michie, D. (eds.) (1972) *Machine Intelligence 7*. Elsevier.

Mendelson, E. (1987) *Introduction to Mathematical Logic* (3rd edn.). *Mathematics Series*. Wadsworth and Brooks Cole.

Métivier, Y. (1983) About the rewriting systems produced by the Knuth–Bendix completion algorithm. *Information Processing Letters*, **16**, 31–34.

Michaux, C. and Ozturk, A. (2002) Quantifier elimination following Muchnik. Université de Mons-Hainaut, Institute de Mathématique, Preprint 10, `w3.umh.ac.be/math/preprints/src/Ozturk020411.pdf`.

Mignotte, M. (1991) *Mathematics for Computer Algebra*. Springer-Verlag.

Mill, J. S. (1865) *An Examination of Sir William Hamilton's Philosophy, and of the Principal Philosophical Questions Discussed in his Writings*. Longmans Green.

Milner, R. (1978) A theory of type polymorphism in programming. *Journal of Computer and Systems Sciences*, **17**, 348–375.

Minsky, M. L. (1967) *Computation: Finite and Infinite Machines. Prentice-Hall Series in Automatic Computation*. Prentice-Hall.

Mints, G. (1992) *A Short Introduction to Modal Logic*, Volume 30 of *CSLI Lecture Notes*. Cambridge University Press.

Mints, G. (2000) *A Short Introduction to Intuitionistic Logic*. Kluwer.

Mishra, B. (1993) *Algorithmic Algebra*. Springer-Verlag.

Monk, J. D. (1976) *Mathematical Logic*, Volume 37 of *Graduate Texts in Mathematics*. Springer-Verlag.

Monk, L. (1975) *Elementary-recursive Decision Procedures*. Ph.D. thesis, University of California at Berkeley.

Moore, G. H. (1982) *Zermelo's Axiom of Choice: its Origins, Development, and Influence*, Volume 8 of *Studies in the History of Mathematics and Physical Sciences*. Springer-Verlag.

Moore, J. S., Lynch, T. and Kaufmann, M. (1998) A mechanically checked proof of the correctness of the kernel of the $AMD5_K86$ floating-point division program. *IEEE Transactions on Computers*, **47**, 913–926.

Mortimer, M. (1975) On language with two variables. *Zeitschrift für mathematische Logik und Grundlagen der Mathematik*, **21**, 135–140.

Moschovakis, Y. N. (1980) *Descriptive Set Theory*, Volume 100 of *Studies in Logic and the Foundations of Mathematics*. North-Holland.

Moser, M., Lynch, C. and Steinbach, J. (1995) *Model Elimination with Basic Ordered Paramodulation*. Technical Report AR-95-11, Institut für Informatik, Technische Universität München.

Moser, M. and Steinbach, J. (1997) *STE-modification Revisited.* Technical Report AR-97-03, Institut für Informatik, Technische Universität München.

Moskewicz, M. W., Madigan, C. F., Zhao, Y., Zhang, L. and Malik, S. (2001) Chaff: Engineering an efficient SAT solver. In *Proceedings of the 38th Design Automation Conference (DAC 2001)*, pp. 530–535. ACM Press.

Mostowski, A. (1952) On direct products of theories. *Journal of Symbolic Logic*, **17**, 1–31.

Motzkin, T. S. (1936) *Beiträge zur Theorie der linearen Ungleichungen.* Ph.D. thesis, Universität Zurich.

Narboux, J. (2007) A graphical user interface for formal proofs in geometry. *Journal of Automated Reasoning*, **39**, 161–180.

Nash-Williams, C. S. J. A. (1963) On well-quasi-ordering finite trees. *Proceedings of the Cambridge Philosophical Society*, **59**, 833–835.

Nathanson, M. B. (1996) *Additive Number Theory: the Classical Bases*, Volume 164 of *Graduate Texts in Mathematics*. Springer-Verlag.

Nederpelt, R. P., Geuvers, J. H. and Vrijer, R. C. d. (eds.) (1994) *Selected Papers on Automath*, Volume 133 of *Studies in Logic and the Foundations of Mathematics*. North-Holland.

Nelson, G. and Oppen, D. (1980) Fast decision procedures based on congruence closure. *Journal of the ACM*, **27**, 356–364.

Nelson, G. and Oppen, D. (1979) Simplification by cooperating decision procedures. *ACM Transactions on Programming Languages and Systems*, **1**, 245–257.

Nemhauser, G. L. and Wolsey, L. A. (1999) *Integer and Combinatorial Optimization. Wiley-Interscience Series in Discrete Mathematics and Optimization.* Wiley.

Newborn, M. (2001) *Automated Theorem Proving: Theory and Practice.* Springer-Verlag.

Newell, A. and Simon, H. A. (1956) The logic theory machine. *IRE Transactions on Information Theory*, **2**, 61–79.

Newman, M. H. A. (1942) On theories with a combinatorial definition of "equivalence". *Annals of Mathematics*, **43**, 223–243.

Nicod, J. G. (1917) A reduction in the number of primitive propositions of logic. *Proceedings of the Cambridge Philosophical Society*, **19**, 32–41.

Nieuwenhuis, R. (ed.) (2005) *CADE-20: 20th International Conference on Automated Deduction, proceedings*, Volume 3632 of *Lecture Notes in Computer Science*. Springer-Verlag.

Nieuwenhuis, R., Oliveras, A. and Tinelli, C. (2006) Solving SAT and SAT modulo theories: from an abstract Davis–Putnam–Logemann–Loveland procedure to DPLL(T). *Journal of the ACM*, **53**, 937–977.

Nipkow, T. (1998) An inductive proof of the wellfoundedness of the multiset order. Available from www4.informatik.tu-muenchen.de/~nipkow/misc/multiset.ps.

Noll, H. (1980) A note on resolution: how to get rid of factoring without losing completeness. See Bibel and Kowalski (1980), pp. 250–263.

Nonnengart, A. and Weidenbach, C. (2001) Computing small clause normal forms. See Robinson and Voronkov (2001), pp. 335–367.

Novikov, P. S. (1955) The algorithmic insolubility of the word problem in group theory. *Trudy Mat. Inst. Steklov*, **44**, 1–143.

Obua, S. and Skalberg, S. (2006) Importing HOL into Isabelle/HOL. See Furbach and Shankar (2006), pp. 298–302.

Odifreddi, P. (1989) *Classical Recursion Theory: the Theory of Functions and Sets of Natural Numbers*, Volume 125 of *Studies in Logic and the Foundations of Mathematics*. North-Holland.

Ohlbach, H.-J., Gabbay, D. and Plaisted, D. (1994) *Killer Transformations*. Technical report MPI-I-94-226, Max-Planck-Institut für Informatik.

O'Leary, D. J. (1991) Principia Mathematica and the development of automated theorem proving. In Drucker, T. (ed.), *Perspectives on the History of Mathematical Logic*, pp. 48–53. Birkhäuser.

O'Leary, J., Zhao, X., Gerth, R. and Seger, C.-J. H. (1999) Formally verifying IEEE compliance of floating-point hardware. *Intel Technology Journal*, **1999-Q1**, 1–14. Available on the Web as `download.intel.com/technology/itj/q11999/pdf/floating_point.pdf`.

Oppen, D. (1980a) Complexity, convexity and combinations of theories. *Theoretical Computer Science*, **12**, 291–302.

Oppen, D. (1980b) Prettyprinting. *ACM Transactions on Programming Languages and Systems*, **2**, 465–483.

Osgood, W. F. (1916) On functions of several complex variables. *Transactions of the American Mathematical Society*, **17**, 1–8.

Papadimitriou, C. H. (1981) On the complexity of integer programming. *Journal of the ACM*, **28**, 765–768.

Paris, J. and Harrington, L. (1991) A mathematical incompleteness in Peano Arithmetic. See Barwise and Keisler (1991), pp. 1133–1142.

Parrilo, P. A. (2003) Semidefinite programming relaxations for semialgebraic problems. *Mathematical Programming*, **96**, 293–320.

Paulson, L. C. (1987) *Logic and Computation: Interactive Proof with Cambridge LCF*, Volume 2 of *Cambridge Tracts in Theoretical Computer Science*. Cambridge University Press.

Paulson, L. C. (1991) *ML for the Working Programmer*. Cambridge University Press.

Paulson, L. C. (1992) Designing a theorem prover. See Abramsky, Gabbay and Maibaum (1992), pp. 415–475.

Paulson, L. C. (1994) *Isabelle: a Generic Theorem Prover*, Volume 828 of *Lecture Notes in Computer Science*. Springer-Verlag. With contributions by Tobias Nipkow.

Pelletier, F. J. (1986) Seventy-five problems for testing automatic theorem provers. *Journal of Automated Reasoning*, **2**, 191–216. Errata, *JAR* **4** (1988), 235–236.

Petkovšek, M., Wilf, H. S. and Zeilberger, D. (1996) $A = B$. A. K. Peters.

Pixley, C. (1990) A computational theory and implementation of sequential hardware equivalence. In *Proceedings of the DIMACS Workshop on Computer Aided Verification*, pp. 293–320. DIMACS (technical report 90-31).

Plaisted, D. A. (1990) A sequent-style model elimination strategy and a positive refinement. *Journal of Automated Reasoning*, **6**, 389–402.

Plaisted, D. A. (1993) Equational reasoning and term rewriting systems. See Gabbay, Hogger and Robinson (1993), pp. 273–364.

Plaisted, D. A. and Greenbaum, S. (1986) A structure-preserving clause form transformation. *Journal of Symbolic Computation*, **2**, 293–304.

Plaisted, D. A. and Zhu, Y. (1997) Ordered semantic hyper linking. In *Proceedings of the Fourteenth National Conference on Articifial Intelligence (AAAI-97)*, pp. 472–477, MIT Press, distributed for AIII Press.

Plotkin, G. (1972) Building-in equational theories. See Melzer and Michie (1972), pp. 73–90.

Pnueli, A., Ruah, S. and Zuck, L. (2001) Automatic deductive verification with invisible invariants. In Margaria, T. and Yi, W. (eds.), *Proceedings of TACAS01: Tools and Algorithms for the Construction and Analysis of Systems*, Volume 2031 of *Lecture Notes in Computer Science*. Springer-Verlag.

Poizat, B. (2000) *A Course in Model Theory: an Introduction to Contemporary Mathematical Logic*. Springer-Verlag.

Polya, G. (1954) *Induction and Analogy in Mathematics*. Princeton University Press.

Poonen, B. (2007) Characterizing integers among rational numbers with a universal-existential formula. Available at `math.berkeley.edu/~poonen/papers/ae.pdf`.

Post, E. L. (1921) Introduction to a general theory of elementary propositions. *American Journal of Mathematics*, **43**, 163–185. Reprinted in Van Heijenoort (1967), pp. 264–283.

Post, E. L. (1941) *The Two-valued Iterative Systems of Mathematical Logic*. Princeton University Press.

Pour-El, M. B. and Richards, J. I. (1980) *Computability in Analysis and Physics. Perspectives in Mathematical Logic*. Springer-Verlag.

Pratt, V. R. (1977) Two easy theories whose combination is hard. Technical note, MIT. Available at `boole.stanford.edu/pub/sefnp.pdf`.

Prawitz, D. (1965) *Natural Deduction; a Proof-theoretical Study*, Volume 3 of *Stockholm Studies in Philosophy*. Almqvist and Wiksells.

Prawitz, D. (1971) Ideas and results in proof theory. In Fenstad, J. E. (ed.), *Proceedings of the Second Scandinavian Logic Symposium*, pp. 237–309. North-Holland.

Prawitz, D., Prawitz, H. and Voghera, N. (1960) A mechanical proof procedure and its realization in an electronic computer. *Journal of the ACM*, **7**, 102–128.

Presburger, M. (1930) Über die Vollständigkeit eines gewissen Systems der Arithmetik ganzer Zahlen, in welchem die Addition als einzige Operation hervortritt. In *Sprawozdanie z I Kongresu metematyków słowiańskich, Warszawa 1929*, pp. 92–101, 395. Warsaw. Annotated English version by Stansifer (1984).

Pugh, W. (1992) The Omega test: a fast and practical integer programming algorithm for dependence analysis. *Communications of the ACM*, **8**, 102–114.

Queille, J. P. and Sifakis, J. (1982) Specification and verification of concurrent programs in CESAR. In *Proceedings of the 5th International Symposium on Programming*, Volume 137 of *Lecture Notes in Computer Science*, pp. 195–220. Springer-Verlag.

Quine, W. V. (1950) *Methods of Logic*. Harvard University Press.

Raatikainen, P. (1998) On interpreting Chaitin's incompleteness theorem. *Journal of Philosophical Logic*, **27**, 569–586.

Rabin, M. O. (1965) A simple method for undecidability proofs and some applications. In Bar-Hillel, Y. (ed.), *Logic and Methodology of Sciences*, pp. 58–68. North-Holland.

Rabin, M. O. (1969) Decidability of second order theories and automata on infinite trees. *Transactions of the American Mathematical Society*, **141**, 1–35.

Rabin, M. O. (1991) Decidable theories. See Barwise and Keisler (1991), pp. 595–629.

Ramsey, F. P. (1930) On a problem of formal logic. *Proceedings of the London Mathematical Society (2)*, **30**, 361–376.

Ranise, S., Ringeissen, C. and Zarba, C. G. (2005) Combining data structures with nonstably infinite theories using many-sorted logic. In Gramlich, B. (ed.), *Proceedings of the Workshop on Frontiers of Combining Systems*, Volume 3717 of *Lecture Notes in Computer Science*, pp. 48–64. Springer-Verlag.

Rasiowa, H. and Sikorski, R. (1970) *The Mathematics of Metamathematics* (3rd edn.), Volume 41 of *Monografie Matematyczne, Instytut Matematyczny Polskiej Akademii Nauk*. Polish Scientific Publishers.

Reckhow, R. A. (1976) *On the Lengths of Proofs in Propositional Calculus*. Ph.D. thesis, University of Toronto.

Reddy, C. R. and Loveland, D. W. (1978) Presburger arithmetic with bounded quantifier alternation. In *Proceedings of the Tenth Annual ACM Symposium on Theory of Computing*, pp. 320–325. ACM Press.

Reeves, S. and Clarke, M. (1990) *Logic for Computer Science*. Addison-Wesley.

Resnik, M. D. (1974) On the philosophical significance of consistency proofs. *Journal of Philosophical Logic*, **3**, 133–147. Reprinted in Shanker (1988), pp. 115–130.

Reuß, H. and Shankar, N. (2001) Deconstructing Shostak. In *Proceedings of the Sixteenth Annual IEEE Symposium on Logic in Computer Science*, pp. 19–28. IEEE Computer Society Press.

Revesz, P. (2004) Quantifier-elimination for the first-order theory of boolean algebras with linear cardinality constraints. In Gottlob, G., Benczúr, A. A. and Demetrovics, J. (eds.), *Advances in Databases and Information Systems, 8th East European Conference, ADBIS 2004*, Volume 3255 of *Lecture Notes in Computer Science*, pp. 1–21. Springer-Verlag.

Reynolds, J. C. (1993) The discoveries of continuations. *Lisp and Symbolic Computation*, **6**, 233–247.

Reynolds, J. C. (2002) Separation logic: a logic for shared mutable data structures. In *Proceedings of the Seventeenth Annual IEEE Symposium on Logic in Computer Science*, pp. 55–74. IEEE Computer Society Press.

Reznick, B. (2000) Some concrete aspects of Hilbert's 17th problem. In Delzell, C. N. and Madden, J. J. (eds.), *Real Algebraic Geometry and Ordered Structures*, Volume 253 of *Contemporary Mathematics*, pp. 251–272. American Mathematical Society.

Richardson, D. (1968) Some unsolvable problems involving elementary functions of a real variable. *Journal of Symbolic Logic*, **33**, 514–520.

Ritt, R. F. (1938) *Differential Equations from Algebraic Standpoint*, Volume 14 of *AMS Colloquium Publications*. American Mathematical Society.

Ritt, R. F. (1950) *Differential Algebra*. AMS Colloquium Publications. American Mathematical Society. Republished in 1966 by Dover.

Robertson, N., Sanders, D. P., Seymour, P. and Thomas, R. (1996) A new proof of the four-colour theorem. *Electronic Research Announcements of the American Mathematical Society*, **2**, 17–25.

Robinson, A. (1956) A result on consistency and its application to the theory of definition. *Indagationes Mathematicae*, **18**, 47–58.

Robinson, A. (1957) Proving a theorem (as done by man, logician, or machine). In *Summaries of Talks Presented at the Summer Institute for Symbolic Logic*. Second edition published by the Institute for Defense Analysis, 1960. Reprinted in Siekmann and Wrightson (1983a), pp. 74–76.

Robinson, A. (1959) Solution of a problem of Tarski. *Fundamenta Mathematicae*, **47**, 179–204.

Robinson, A. (1963) *Introduction to Model Theory and to the Metamathematics of Algebra.* *Studies in Logic and the Foundations of Mathematics.* North-Holland.

Robinson, A. (1966) *Non-standard Analysis. Studies in Logic and the Foundations of Mathematics.* North-Holland.

Robinson, G. and Wos, L. (1969) Paramodulation and theorem-proving in first-order theories with equality. In Melzer, B. and Michie, D. (eds.), *Machine Intelligence 4*, pp. 135–150. Elsevier.

Robinson, J. (1949) Definability and decision problems in arithmetic. *Journal of Symbolic Logic*, **14**, 98–114. Author's Ph.D. thesis.

Robinson, J. (1952) Existential definability in arithmetic. *Transactions of the American Mathematical Society*, **72**, 437–449.

Robinson, J. A. (1965a) Automatic deduction with hyper-resolution. *International Journal of Computer Mathematics*, **1**, 227–234.

Robinson, J. A. (1965b) A machine-oriented logic based on the resolution principle. *Journal of the ACM*, **12**, 23–41.

Robinson, J. A. and Voronkov, A. (eds.) (2001) *Handbook of Automated Reasoning, volume I.* MIT Press.

Robinson, R. M. (1950) An essentially undecidable axiom system. In *Proceedings of the International Congress of Mathematicians, vol. 1*, pp. 729–730.

Robu, J. (2002) *Geometry Theorem Proving in the Frame of Theorema Project.* Ph. D. thesis, RISC-Linz.

Rosser, J. B. (1936) Extensions of some theorems of Gödel and Church. *Journal of Symbolic Logic*, **1**, 87–91.

Roy, M.-F. (2000) The role of Hilbert problems in real algebraic geometry. In Camina, R. and Fajstrup, L. (eds.), *Proceedings of the 9th general meeting on European Women in Mathematics*, pp. 189–200. Hindawi.

Rudnicki, P. (1987) Obvious inferences. *Journal of Automated Reasoning*, **3**, 383–393.

Rudnicki, P. (1992) An overview of the MIZAR project. Available on the Web as `web.cs.ualberta.ca/~piotr/Mizar/Doc/MizarOverview.ps`.

Rudnicki, P. and Trybulec, A. (1999) On equivalents of well-foundedness. *Journal of Automated Reasoning*, **23**, 197–234.

Russell, B. (1968) *The Autobiography of Bertrand Russell.* Allen & Unwin.

Russinoff, D. (1998) A mechanically checked proof of IEEE compliance of a register-transfer-level specification of the AMD-K7 floating-point multiplication, division, and square root instructions. *LMS Journal of Computation and Mathematics*, **1**, 148–200. Available on the Web at `www.russinoff.com/papers/k7-div-sqrt.html`.

Rydeheard, D. and Burstall, R. (1988) *Computational Category Theory.* Prentice-Hall.

Sarges, H. (1976) Ein Beweis des Hilbertischen Basissatzes. *Journal für die reine und angewandte Mathematik*, **283–284**, 436–437.

Scarpellini, B. (1969) On the metamathematics of rings and integral domains. *Transactions of the American Mathematical Society*, **138**, 71–96.

Schenk, H. (2003) *Computational Algebraic Geometry.* Cambridge University Press.

Schilpp, P. A. (ed.) (1944) *The Philosophy of Bertrand Russell,* Volume 5 of *The Library of Living Philosophers.* Northwestern University.

Schmidt-Schauss, M. (1988) Implication of clauses is undecidable. *Theoretical Computer Science*, **59**, 287–296.

Schoenfeld, A. (1985) *Mathematical Problem Solving*. Academic Press.

Schönfinkel, M. (1924) Über die Bausteine der mathematischen Logik. *Mathematische Annalen*, **92**, 305–316. English translation, 'On the building blocks of mathematical logic' in Van Heijenoort (1967), pp. 357–366.

Schoutens, H. (2001) Muchnik's proof of Tarski–Seidenberg. Notes available from `www.math.ohio-state.edu/~schoutens/PDF/Muchnik.pdf`.

Schulz, S. (1999) System abstract: E 0.3. In Ganzinger, H. (ed.), *Automated Deduction – CADE-16*, Volume 1632 of *Lecture Notes in Computer Science*, pp. 297–301. Springer-Verlag.

Schumann, J. (1994) DELTA – a bottom-up preprocessor for top-down theorem provers. In Bundy, A. (ed.), *12th International Conference on Automated Deduction*, Volume 814 of *Lecture Notes in Computer Science*, pp. 774–777. Springer-Verlag.

Schwabhäuser, H., Szmielev, W. and Tarski, A. (1983) *Metamathematische Methoden in der Geometrie*. Springer-Verlag.

Scott, D. (1962) A decision method for validity of sentences in two variables. *Journal of Symbolic Logic*, **27**, 377.

Scott, D. (1993) A type-theoretical alternative to ISWIM, CUCH, OWHY. *Theoretical Computer Science*, **121**, 411–440. Annotated version of a 1969 manuscript.

Seger, C.-J. H. and Bryant, R. E. (1995) Formal verification by symbolic evaluation of partially-ordered trajectories. *Formal Methods in System Design*, **6**, 147–189.

Seidenberg, A. (1954) A new decision method for elementary algebra. *Annals of Mathematics*, **60**, 365–374.

Semënov, A. L. (1984) Logical theories of one-place functions on the set of natural numbers. *Mathematics of the USSR Izvestiya*, **22**, 587–618.

Shankar, N. (1994) *Metamathematics, Machines and Gödel's Proof*, Volume 38 of *Cambridge Tracts in Theoretical Computer Science*. Cambridge University Press.

Shanker, S. G. (ed.) (1988) *Gödel's Theorem in Focus*, Philosophers in Focus series. Croom Helm.

Sheeran, M. and Stålmarck, G. (2000) A tutorial on Stålmarck's proof procedure for propositional logic. *Formal Methods in System Design*, **16**, 23–58.

Sheffer, H. M. (1913) A set of five independent postulates for Boolean algebras. *Transactions of the American Mathematical Society*, **14**, 481–488.

Shostak, R. (1978) An algorithm for reasoning about equality. *Communications of the ACM*, **21**, 356–364.

Shostak, R. (1979) A practical decision procedure for arithmetic with function symbols. *Journal of the ACM*, **26**, 351–360.

Shostak, R. (ed.) (1984a) *7th International Conference on Automated Deduction*, Volume 170 of *Lecture Notes in Computer Science*, Napa, CA. Springer-Verlag.

Shostak, R. (1984b) Deciding combinations of theories. *Journal of the ACM*, **31**, 1–12.

Sieg, W. (1994) Mechanical procedures and mathematical experience. In George, A. (ed.), *Mathematics and Mind: Papers from the Conference on the Philosophy of Mathematics held at Amherst College, 5–7 April 1991*, pp. 71–117. Oxford University Press.

Siekmann, J. and Wrightson, G. (eds.) (1983a) *Automation of Reasoning – Classical Papers on Computational Logic, Vol. I (1957-1966).* Springer-Verlag.

Siekmann, J. and Wrightson, G. (eds.) (1983b) *Automation of Reasoning – Classical Papers on Computational Logic, Vol. II, (1967-1970).* Springer-Verlag.

Simmons, H. (1970) The solution of a decision problem for several classes of rings. *Pacific Journal of Mathematics*, **34**, 547–557.

Simpson, S. (1988a) Ordinal numbers and the Hilbert basis theorem. *Journal of Symbolic Logic*, **53**, 961–974.

Simpson, S. (1988b) Partial realizations of Hilbert's program. *Journal of Symbolic Logic*, **53**, 349–363.

Simpson, S. G. (1998) *Subsystems of Second Order Arithmetic.* Springer-Verlag.

Skolem, T. (1920) Logisch-kombinatorische Untersuchungen über die Erfüllbarkeit und Beweisbarkeit mathematischen Sätze nebst einem Theoreme über dichte Mengen. *Skritfer utgit av Videnskabsselskapet i Kristiania, I; Matematisk-naturvidenskabelig klasse*, **4**, 1–36. English translation 'Logico-combinatorial investigations in the satisfiability or provability of mathematical propositions: A simplified proof of a theorem by L. Löwenheim and generalizations of the theorem' in Van Heijenoort (1967), pp. 252–263.

Skolem, T. (1922) Einige Bemerkungen zur axiomatischen Begründung der Mengenlehre. In *Matematikerkongress i Helsingfors den 4-7 Juli 1922, Den femte skandinaviska matematikerkongressen, Redogörelse.* Akademiska Bokhandeln, Helsinki. English translation 'Some remarks on axiomatized set theory' in Van Heijenoort (1967), pp. 290–301.

Skolem, T. (1928) Über die mathematische Logik. *Norsk Matematisk Tidsskrift*, **10**, 125–142. English translation 'On mathematical logic' in Van Heijenoort (1967), pp. 508–524.

Skolem, T. (1931) Über einige Satzfunktionen in der Arithmetik. *Skrifter Vitenskapsakadetiet i Oslo, I*, **7**, 1–28.

Slagle, J. R. (1967) Automatic theorem proving with renamable and semantic resolution. *Journal of the ACM*, **14**, 687–697.

Slind, K. (1991) *An Implementation of Higher Order Logic.* Technical Report 91-419-03, University of Calgary Computer Science Department. Author's Master's thesis.

Slind, K. (1996) Function definition in higher order logic. See Wright, Grundy and Harrison (1996), pp. 381–398.

Slobodová, A. (2007) Challenges for formal verification in industrial setting. In Brim, L., Haverkort, B. R., Leucker, M. and van de Pol, J. (eds.), *Proceedings of 11th FMICS and 5th PDMC*, Volume 4346 of *Lecture Notes in Computer Science*, pp. 1–22. Springer-Verlag.

Smoryński, C. (1980) *Logic Number Theory I: An Introduction.* Springer-Verlag.

Smoryński, C. (1981) Skolem's solution to a problem of Frobenius. *The Mathematical Intelligencer*, **3**, 123–132.

Smoryński, C. (1985) *Self-Reference and Modal Logic.* Springer-Verlag.

Smoryński, C. (1991) The incompleteness theorems. See Barwise and Keisler (1991), pp. 821–865.

Smullyan, R. M. (1992) *Gödel's Incompleteness Theorems*, Volume 19 of *Oxford Logic Guides*. Oxford University Press.

Smullyan, R. M. (1994) *Diagonalization and Self-Reference*, Volume 27 of *Oxford Logic Guides*. Oxford University Press.

Sokołowski, S. (1983) *A Note on Tactics in LCF*. Technical Report CSR-140-83, University of Edinburgh, Department of Computer Science.

Solovay, R. M. (1976) Provability interpretations of modal logic. *Israel Journal of Mathematics*, **25**, 287–304.

Somogyi, Z., Henderson, F. and Conway, T. (1994) The implementation of Mercury: an efficient purely declarative logic programming language. In *Proceedings of the ILPS'94 Postconference Workshop on Implementation Techniques for Logic Programming Languages*.

Stålmarck, G. (1994a) A proof theoretic concept of tautological hardness. Unpublished manuscript.

Stålmarck, G. (1994b) System for determining propositional logic theorems by applying values and rules to triplets that are generated from Boolean formula. United States Patent number 5,276,897; see also Swedish Patent 467 076.

Stålmarck, G. and Säflund, M. (1990) Modeling and verifying systems and software in propositional logic. In Daniels, B. K. (ed.), *Safety of Computer Control Systems, 1990 (SAFECOMP '90)*, pp. 31–36. Pergamon Press.

Stansifer, R. (1984) *Presburger's Article on Integer Arithmetic: Remarks and Translation*. Technical Report CORNELLCS:TR84-639, Cornell University Computer Science Department.

Steinitz, E. (1910) Algebraische Theorie der Körper. *Journal für die reine und angewandte Mathematik*, **137**, 167–309.

Stickel, M. E. (1981) A unification algorithm for associative-commutative functions. *Journal of the ACM*, **28**, 423–434.

Stickel, M. E. (1986) Schubert's steamroller problem: formulations and solutions. *Journal of Automated Reasoning*, **2**, 89–101.

Stickel, M. E. (1988) A Prolog technology theorem prover: implementation by an extended Prolog compiler. *Journal of Automated Reasoning*, **4**, 353–380.

Stickel, M. E. (ed.) (1990) *10th International Conference on Automated Deduction*, Volume 449 of *Lecture Notes in Computer Science*. Springer-Verlag.

Strachey, C. (2000) Fundamental concepts in programming languages. *Higher-Order and Symbolic Computation*, **13**, 11–49. First print of an unpublished manuscript written in 1967.

Strawson, P. (1952) *Introduction to Logical Theory*. Methuen.

Stump, A., Dill, D. L., Barrett, C. W. and Levitt, J. (2001) A decision procedure for an extensional theory of arrays. In *Proceedings of the Sixteenth Annual IEEE Symposium on Logic in Computer Science*, pp. 29–37. IEEE Computer Society Press.

Sturm, C. (1835) Mémoire sue la résolution des équations numériques. *Mémoire des Savants Etrangers*, **6**, 271–318.

Surányi, J. (1950) Contributions to the reduction theory of the decision problem, second paper. *Acta Mathematica Academiae Scientiarum Hungaricae*, **1**, 261–270.

Surma, S. J., Srzednicki, J. T., Barnett, D. I. and Rickey, V. F. (eds.) (1992) *Stanisław Leśniewski: Collected Works*. Kluwer Academic Publishers.

Sutcliffe, G. and Suttner, C. B. (1998) The TPTP problem library: CNF release v1.2.1. *Journal of Automated Reasoning*, **21**, 177–203.

Syme, D. (1997) *DECLARE: a Prototype Declarative Proof System for Higher Order Logic*. Technical Report 416, University of Cambridge Computer Laboratory.

Szabo, M. E. (ed.) (1969) *The Collected Papers of Gerhard Gentzen, Studies in Logic and the Foundations of Mathematics*. North-Holland.

Szmielew, W. (1955) Elementary properties of Abelian groups. *Fundamenta Mathematicae*, **41**, 203–271.

Tait, W. W. (1981) Finitism. *Journal of Philosophy*, **78**, 524–546.

Tarski, A. (1936) Der Wahrheitsbegriff in den formalisierten Sprachen. *Studia Philosophica*, **1**, 261–405. English translation, 'The Concept of Truth in Formalized Languages', in Tarski (1956), pp. 152–278.

Tarski, A. (1941) *Introduction to Logic, and to the Methodology of Deductive Sciences*. Oxford University Press. Reprinted by Dover, 1995. Revised edition of the original Polish text *O logice matematycznej i metodzie dedukcyjnej*, published in 1936.

Tarski, A. (1949) Arithmetical classes and types of Boolean algebras, preliminary report. *Bulletin of the American Mathematical Society*, **55**, 64, 1192.

Tarski, A. (1951) *A Decision Method for Elementary Algebra and Geometry*. University of California Press. Previous version published as a technical report by the RAND Corporation, 1948; prepared for publication by J. C. C. McKinsey. Reprinted in Caviness and Johnson (1998), pp. 24–84.

Tarski, A. (1955) A lattice-theoretical fixpoint theorem and its applications. *Pacific Journal of Mathematics*, **5**, 285–309.

Tarski, A. (ed.) (1956) *Logic, Semantics and Metamathematics*. Clarendon Press.

Tarski, A. (1959) What is elementary geometry? In Henkin, L., Suppes, P. and Tarski, A. (eds.), *The Axiomatic Method (With Special Reference to Geometry and Physics)*, pp. 16–29. North-Holland. Reprinted in Hintikka (1969).

Tarski, A. (1965) A simplified formalization of predicate logic with identity. *Arkhiv für mathematische Logik und Grundlagenforschung*, **7**, 61–79.

Tarski, A., Mostowski, A. and Robinson, R. M. (1953) *Undecidable Theories. Studies in Logic and the Foundations of Mathematics*. North-Holland. Three papers: 'A general method in proofs of undecidability', 'Undecidability and essential undecidability in arithmetic' and 'Undecidability of the elementary theory of groups'; all but the second are by Tarski alone.

Tinelli, C. and Harandi, M. (1996) A new correctness proof of the Nelson–Oppen combination procedure. In Baader, F. and Schulz, K. U. (eds.), *Frontiers of Combining Systems, First International Workshop FroCoS'96*, Volume 3 of *Applied Logic Series*, pp. 103–120. Kluwer Academic Publishers.

Tinelli, C. and Zarba, C. (2005) Combining nonstably infinite theories. *Journal of Automated Reasoning*, **33**, 209–238.

Toyama, Y. (1987a) Counterexamples to termination for the direct sum of term rewriting systems. *Information Processing Letters*, **25**, 141–143.

Toyama, Y. (1987b) On the Church–Rosser property for the direct sum of term rewriting systems. *Journal of the ACM*, **34**, 128–143.

Troelstra, A. S. and Schwichtenberg, H. (1996) *Basic Proof Theory*, Volume 43 of *Cambridge Tracts in Theoretical Computer Science*. Cambridge University Press.

Troelstra, A. S. and van Dalen, D. (1988) *Constructivism in Mathematics, vol. 1*, Volume 121 of *Studies in Logic and the Foundations of Mathematics*. North-Holland.

Trybulec, A. (1978) The Mizar-QC/6000 logic information language. *ALLC Bulletin (Association for Literary and Linguistic Computing)*, **6**, 136–140.

Trybulec, A. and Blair, H. A. (1985) Computer aided reasoning. In Parikh, R. (ed.), *Logics of Programs*, Volume 193 of *Lecture Notes in Computer Science*, pp. 406–412. Springer-Verlag.

Tseitin, G. S. (1968) On the complexity of derivations in the propositional calculus. In Slisenko, A. O. (ed.), *Studies in Constructive Mathematics and Mathematical Logic, Part II*, pp. 115–125. Zap. Nauchn. Sem. Leningrad Otdel. Mat. Inst. Steklov. Translated from original Russian.

Turing, A. M. (1936) On computable numbers, with an application to the Entscheidungsproblem. *Proceedings of the London Mathematical Society (2)*, **42**, 230–265.

Turing, A. M. (1939) Systems of logic based on ordinals. *Proceedings of the London Mathematical Society (2)*, **45**, 161–228. Reprinted in Davis (1965), pp. 154–222.

van Dalen, D. (1994) *Logic and Structure* (3rd edn.). Springer-Verlag.

van den Dries, L. (1988) Alfred Tarski's elimination theory for real closed fields. *Journal of Symbolic Logic*, **53**, 7–19.

van der Waerden, B. L. (1991) *Algebra, volume 1*. Springer-Verlag.

Van Heijenoort, J. (ed.) (1967) *From Frege to Gödel: a Source Book in Mathematical Logic 1879–1931*. Harvard University Press.

van Stigt, W. P. (1990) *Brouwer's Intuitionism*, Volume 2 of *Studies in the History and Philosophy of Mathematics*. North-Holland.

Velev, M. N. and Bryant, R. E. (1999) Superscalar processor verification using efficient reduction of the logic of equality with uninterpreted functions to propositional logic. In Pierre, L. and Kropf, T. (eds.), *Correct Hardware Design and Verification Methods, 10th IFIP WG 10.5 Advanced Research Working Conference, CHARME '99*, Volume 1703 of *Lecture Notes in Computer Science*, pp. 37–53. Springer-Verlag.

Voda, P. J. (2001) *A Note on the Exponential Relation in Peano Arithmetic II*. Technical Report TR609, Institute of Informatics, Comenius University, Bratislava, Slovakia. Available on the Web via `www.fmph.uniba.sk/~voda/exp1.ps`.

Voda, P. J. and Komara, J. (1995) *On Herbrand Skeletons*. Technical Report TR102, Institute of Informatics, Comenius University, Bratislava, Slovakia. Available on the Web via `www.fmph.uniba.sk/~voda/herbrand.ps.gz`.

Voronkov, A. (ed.) (2002) *Automated Deduction – CADE-18*, Volume 2392 of *Lecture Notes in Computer Science*. Springer-Verlag.

Walther, C. (1985) A mechanical solution of Schubert's steamroller by many-sorted resolution. *Artificial Intelligence*, **26**, 217–224.

Wang, H. (1960) Toward mechanical mathematics. *IBM Journal of research and development*, **4**, 2–22.

Warren, H. S. (2002) *Hacker's Delight*. Addison-Wesley.

Watterson, B. (1988) *Something under the Bed is Drooling*. Andrews McMeel.

Waugh, A. (1991) *Will this do? The First Fifty Years of Auberon Waugh: an Autobiography*. Arrow Books.

Weil, A. (1946) *Foundations of Algebraic Geometry*, Volume 29 of *AMS Colloquium Publications*. American Mathematical Society. Revised edition 1962.

Weispfenning, V. (1997) Quantifier elimination for real algebra – the quadratic case and beyond. *Applicable Algebra in Engineering Communications and Computing*, **8**, 85–101.

Weispfenning, V. (1999) Mixed real–integer linear quantifier elimination. In *Proceedings of the ISSAC (ACM SIGSAM International Symposium on Symbolic and Algebraic Computation)*, pp. 129–136. ACM Press.

Weispfenning, V. (2000) Deciding linear-transcendental problems. *SIGSAM Bulletin*, **34**(1), 1–3. Full paper available as report MIP-0005, Universität Passau.

Weispfenning, V. and Becker, T. (1993) *Groebner Bases: a Computational Approach to Commutative Algebra. Graduate Texts in Mathematics.* Springer-Verlag.

Weiss, W. and D'Mello, C. (1997) *Fundamentals of Model Theory.* Available from `www.math.toronto.edu/~weiss/model_theory.html`.

Wells, B. F. (ed.) (1971) *The Metamathematics of Algebraic Systems: Anatolii Maltsev's Collected Papers 1936–67, Studies in Logic and the Foundations of Mathematics.* North-Holland.

Wenzel, M. (1999) Isar – a generic interpretive approach to readable formal proof documents. See Bertot, Dowek, Hirschowitz, Paulin and Théry (1999), pp. 167–183.

Weyhrauch, R. W. (1980) Prolegomena to a theory of mechanized formal reasoning. *Artificial Intelligence*, **13**, 133–170.

Whitehead, A. N. (1919) *An Introduction to Mathematics.* Williams and Norgate.

Whitehead, A. N. and Russell, B. (1910) *Principia Mathematica (3 vols).* Cambridge University Press.

Wiedijk, F. (2001) Mizar light for HOL Light. In Boulton, R. J. and Jackson, P. B. (eds.), *14th International Conference on Theorem Proving in Higher Order Logics: TPHOLs 2001*, Volume 2152 of *Lecture Notes in Computer Science*, pp. 378–394. Springer-Verlag.

Wiedijk, F. (2006) *The Seventeen Provers of the World*, Volume 3600 of *Lecture Notes in Computer Science*. Springer-Verlag.

Wildberger, N. J. (2005) *Divine Proportions: Rational Trigonometry to Universal Geometry.* Wild Egg Books, Sydney.

Wilder, R. L. (1965) *Introduction to the Foundations of Mathematics.* Wiley.

Wilkie, A. J. (1996) Model completeness results for expansions of the ordered field of reals by restricted Pfaffian functions and the exponential function. *Journal of the American Mathematical Society*, **9**, 1051–1094.

Wilkie, A. J. (2000) On exponentiation – a solution to Tarski's high school algebra problem. In Macintyre, A. (ed.), *Connections between Model Theory and Algebraic and Analytic Theory*, Volume 6 of *Quaderni di Matematica*. Dipartimento di Matematica, Napoli. Publication of 1981 preprint.

Williams, H. P. (1976) Fourier–Motzkin elimination extended to integer programming problems. *Journal of Combinatorial Theory*, **21**, 118–123.

Wilson, J. N. (1990) Compact normal forms in propositional logic and integer programming formulations. *Computers and Operations Research*, **17**, 309–314.

Wittgenstein, L. (1922) *Tractatus Logico-Philosophicus.* Routledge & Kegan Paul.

Wittgenstein, L. (1956) *Remarks on the Foundations of Mathematics.* Blackwell. Edited by G. H. von Wright, R. Rhees and G. E. M. Anscombe; translated by G. E. M. Anscombe.

Wittgenstein, L. (1980) *Remarks on the Philosophy of Psychology, vol. 1.* Blackwell.

Wong, W. (1993) *Recording HOL Proofs.* Technical Report 306, University of Cambridge Computer Laboratory.

Wos, L. (1994) The power of combining resonance with heat. *Journal of Automated Reasoning*, **17**, 23–81.

Wos, L. (1998) Programs that offer fast, flawless, logical reasoning. *Communications of the ACM*, **41**(6), 87–102.

Wos, L., Overbeek, R., Lusk, E. and Boyle, J. (1992) *Automated Reasoning: Introduction and Applications.* McGraw Hill.

Wos, L. and Pieper, G. W. (1999) *A Fascinating Country in the World of Computing: Your Guide to Automated Reasoning.* World Scientific.

Wos, L. and Pieper, G. W. (2003) *Automated Reasoning and the Discovery of Missing and Elegant Proofs*. Ave Maria Press.

Wos, L., Robinson, G. and Carson, D. (1965) Efficiency and completeness of the set of support strategy in theorem proving. *Journal of the ACM*, **12**, 536–541.

Wos, L., Robinson, G., Carson, D. and Shalla, L. (1967) The concept of demodulation in theorem proving. *Journal of the ACM*, **14**, 698–709.

Wright, J. v., Grundy, J. and Harrison, J. (eds.) (1996) *Theorem Proving in Higher Order Logics: 9th International Conference, TPHOLs'96*, Volume 1125 of *Lecture Notes in Computer Science*. Springer-Verlag.

Wu, W.-t. (1978) On the decision problem and the mechanization of theorem proving in elementary geometry. *Scientia Sinica*, **21**, 157–179.

Yap, C. K. (2000) *Fundamental Problems of Algorithmic Algebra*. Oxford University Press.

Zammit, V. (1999a) On the implementation of an extensible declarative proof language. See Bertot, Dowek, Hirschowitz, Paulin and Théry (1999), pp. 185–202.

Zammit, V. (1999b) *On the Readability of Machine Checkable Formal Proofs*. Ph. D. thesis, University of Kent at Canterbury.

Zamov, N. K. and Sharanov, V. I. (1969) On a class of strategies which can be used to establish decidability by the resolution principle. *Issled, po konstruktivnoye matematikye i matematicheskoie logikye, III*, **16**, 54–64. English translation by the UK National Lending Library Russian Translating Programme 5857, Boston Spa, Yorkshire.

Zermelo, E. (1908) Neuer Beweis für die Möglichkeit einer Wohlordnung. *Mathematische Annalen*, **65**, 107–128. English translation, 'A new proof of the possibility of a wellordering' in Van Heijenoort (1967), pp. 183–198.

Zhang, H. (1997) SATO: an efficient propositional prover. In McCune, W. (ed.), *Automated Deduction – CADE-14*, Volume 1249 of *Lecture Notes in Computer Science*, pp. 272–275. Springer-Verlag.

Index

Printed in the United States
By Bookmasters